# The Guru's Guide to SQL Server™ Stored Procedures, XML, and HTML

# The Guru's Guide to SQL Server™ Stored Procedures, XML, and HTML

*Ken Henderson*

✦ Addison-Wesley

**Boston    San Francisco    New York**
**London    Toronto    Sydney    Tokyo    Singapore    Madrid**
**Mexico City    Munich    Paris    Cape Town    Hong Kong    Montreal**

The publisher offers discounts on this book when ordered in quantity for special sales. For more information, please contact:

Pearson Education Corporate Sales Division
201 W. 103rd Street
Indianapolis, IN 46290
(800) 428-5331
corpsales@pearsoned.com

Visit Addison-Wesley on the Web: www.aw.com/cseng/

*Library of Congress Cataloging-in-Publication Data*
Henderson, Ken.
    The Guru's guide to SQL server™ stored procedures, XML, and HTML / Ken Henderson.
        p. cm.
    Includes bibliographical references and index.
    ISBN 0-201-70046-8
    1. Client/server computing.    2. SQL server.    I. Title.
    QA76.9.C55 H45 2002
    005.75'85—dc21

Part One photograph by Ken Henderson
Part Two photograph (from the Grand Canyon) by Anna M. Dillon
Part Three photograph (from the Henderson Wildlife Refuge) by Kenneth D. Henderson
Part Four photograph (from the Grand Canyon) by Anna M. Dillon
Part Five photograph (from the Henderson Wildlife Refuge) by Kenneth D. Henderson

For information on obtaining permission for use of material from this work, please submit a written request to:

Pearson Education, Inc.
Rights and Contracts Department
75 Arlington Street, Suite 300
Boston, MA 02116
Fax: (617) 848-7047

ISBN 1-201-70046-8
Text printed on recycled paper
1 2 3 4 5 6 7 8 9 10—CRS—0504030201
First printing, December 2001

*For T*

# Contents

Foreword . . . . . . . . . . . . . . . . . . . . . . . . . . . . . . . . . . . . . . . . . . . xv
Preface . . . . . . . . . . . . . . . . . . . . . . . . . . . . . . . . . . . . . . . . . . . . xvii
Introduction . . . . . . . . . . . . . . . . . . . . . . . . . . . . . . . . . . . . . . . . . xxiii


**PART I—THE BASICS** . . . . . . . . . . . . . . . . . . . . . . . . . . . . . . . **1**

**Chapter 1**  **Stored Procedure Primer** . . . . . . . . . . . . . . . . . . . . **3**

What Is a Stored Procedure? . . . . . . . . . . . . . . . . . . . . . . . . . . . . 3
Stored Procedure Advantages . . . . . . . . . . . . . . . . . . . . . . . . . . . 4
Creating a Stored Procedure . . . . . . . . . . . . . . . . . . . . . . . . . . . . 5
Altering Stored Procedures . . . . . . . . . . . . . . . . . . . . . . . . . . . . 17
Executing Stored Procedures . . . . . . . . . . . . . . . . . . . . . . . . . . . 18
Extended Stored Procedures . . . . . . . . . . . . . . . . . . . . . . . . . . . 32
Environmental Issues . . . . . . . . . . . . . . . . . . . . . . . . . . . . . . . . 34
Parameters . . . . . . . . . . . . . . . . . . . . . . . . . . . . . . . . . . . . . . . 37
Flow Control Language . . . . . . . . . . . . . . . . . . . . . . . . . . . . . . . 42
Errors . . . . . . . . . . . . . . . . . . . . . . . . . . . . . . . . . . . . . . . . . . . 44
Nesting . . . . . . . . . . . . . . . . . . . . . . . . . . . . . . . . . . . . . . . . . . 46
Recursion . . . . . . . . . . . . . . . . . . . . . . . . . . . . . . . . . . . . . . . . 46
Summary . . . . . . . . . . . . . . . . . . . . . . . . . . . . . . . . . . . . . . . . . 47

**Chapter 2**  **Suggested Conventions** . . . . . . . . . . . . . . . . . . . . . **49**

Source Formatting . . . . . . . . . . . . . . . . . . . . . . . . . . . . . . . . . . 50
Coding Conventions . . . . . . . . . . . . . . . . . . . . . . . . . . . . . . . . . 64
Summary . . . . . . . . . . . . . . . . . . . . . . . . . . . . . . . . . . . . . . . . . 72

**Chapter 3**  **Common Design Patterns** . . . . . . . . . . . . . . . . . . . . **73**

The Law of Parsimony . . . . . . . . . . . . . . . . . . . . . . . . . . . . . . . . 74
Idioms . . . . . . . . . . . . . . . . . . . . . . . . . . . . . . . . . . . . . . . . . . . 75

Design Patterns . . . . . . . . . . . . . . . . . . . . . . . . . . . . . 84
Summary. . . . . . . . . . . . . . . . . . . . . . . . . . . . . . . . . 102

**Chapter 4    Source Code Management . . . . . . . . . . . . . . . 103**
The Benefits of Source Code Management. . . . . . . . . . . . . . . . 104
The dt Procedures . . . . . . . . . . . . . . . . . . . . . . . . . . . 105
Best Practices . . . . . . . . . . . . . . . . . . . . . . . . . . . . . 106
Version Control from Query Analyzer . . . . . . . . . . . . . . . . . . 113
Automating Script Generation with Version Control . . . . . . . . . . . 115
Summary. . . . . . . . . . . . . . . . . . . . . . . . . . . . . . . . . 119

**Chapter 5    Database Design . . . . . . . . . . . . . . . . . . . 121**
General Approach. . . . . . . . . . . . . . . . . . . . . . . . . . . . 121
Modeling Tools. . . . . . . . . . . . . . . . . . . . . . . . . . . . . 122
The Sample Project . . . . . . . . . . . . . . . . . . . . . . . . . . . 123
The Five Processes . . . . . . . . . . . . . . . . . . . . . . . . . . . 123
The Five Phases Examined . . . . . . . . . . . . . . . . . . . . . . . 124
Defining the Functions of the Application . . . . . . . . . . . . . . . . 127
Modeling Business Processes. . . . . . . . . . . . . . . . . . . . . . . 131
Entity-Relationship Modeling . . . . . . . . . . . . . . . . . . . . . . 143
Relational Data Modeling . . . . . . . . . . . . . . . . . . . . . . . . 162
Summary. . . . . . . . . . . . . . . . . . . . . . . . . . . . . . . . . 181

**Chapter 6    Data Volumes . . . . . . . . . . . . . . . . . . . . 183**
Approaches to Generating Data. . . . . . . . . . . . . . . . . . . . . . 183
Speed . . . . . . . . . . . . . . . . . . . . . . . . . . . . . . . . . 197
Summary. . . . . . . . . . . . . . . . . . . . . . . . . . . . . . . . . 197

**PART II—OBJECTS . . . . . . . . . . . . . . . . . . . . . . . . . . . 199**

**Chapter 7    Error Handling . . . . . . . . . . . . . . . . . . . . 201**
Error Reporting. . . . . . . . . . . . . . . . . . . . . . . . . . . . . 201
Handling Errors . . . . . . . . . . . . . . . . . . . . . . . . . . . . 203
Summary. . . . . . . . . . . . . . . . . . . . . . . . . . . . . . . . . 214

**Chapter 8    Triggers . . . . . . . . . . . . . . . . . . . . . . . . . . . . . . . 215**

Determining What Has Changed . . . . . . . . . . . . . . . . . . . . . . . . . 216
Managing Sequential Values . . . . . . . . . . . . . . . . . . . . . . . . . . . . 222
Trigger Restrictions . . . . . . . . . . . . . . . . . . . . . . . . . . . . . . . . . 224
INSTEAD OF Triggers. . . . . . . . . . . . . . . . . . . . . . . . . . . . . . . . . 226
Triggers and Auditing . . . . . . . . . . . . . . . . . . . . . . . . . . . . . . . . 229
Transactions . . . . . . . . . . . . . . . . . . . . . . . . . . . . . . . . . . . . . . 234
Execution. . . . . . . . . . . . . . . . . . . . . . . . . . . . . . . . . . . . . . . . 234
Calling Stored Procedures . . . . . . . . . . . . . . . . . . . . . . . . . . . . . 235
Nested Triggers . . . . . . . . . . . . . . . . . . . . . . . . . . . . . . . . . . . . 239
Disabling Triggers . . . . . . . . . . . . . . . . . . . . . . . . . . . . . . . . . . . 239
Best Practices . . . . . . . . . . . . . . . . . . . . . . . . . . . . . . . . . . . . . 240
Summary . . . . . . . . . . . . . . . . . . . . . . . . . . . . . . . . . . . . . . . . 243

**Chapter 9    Views. . . . . . . . . . . . . . . . . . . . . . . . . . . . . . . . . . 245**

Meta-data . . . . . . . . . . . . . . . . . . . . . . . . . . . . . . . . . . . . . . . . 245
Restrictions . . . . . . . . . . . . . . . . . . . . . . . . . . . . . . . . . . . . . . . 247
ANSI SQL Schema Views . . . . . . . . . . . . . . . . . . . . . . . . . . . . . . 249
Updatable Views . . . . . . . . . . . . . . . . . . . . . . . . . . . . . . . . . . . 265
The WITH CHECK OPTION Clause. . . . . . . . . . . . . . . . . . . . . . . . 266
Derived Tables . . . . . . . . . . . . . . . . . . . . . . . . . . . . . . . . . . . . . 267
Parameterized Views . . . . . . . . . . . . . . . . . . . . . . . . . . . . . . . . . 268
Dynamic Views . . . . . . . . . . . . . . . . . . . . . . . . . . . . . . . . . . . . . 269
Partitioned Views . . . . . . . . . . . . . . . . . . . . . . . . . . . . . . . . . . . 271
Indexed Views . . . . . . . . . . . . . . . . . . . . . . . . . . . . . . . . . . . . . 286
Designing Modular Indexed Views . . . . . . . . . . . . . . . . . . . . . . . . 288
Summary . . . . . . . . . . . . . . . . . . . . . . . . . . . . . . . . . . . . . . . . 289

**Chapter 10   User-Defined Functions . . . . . . . . . . . . . . . . . . . . . 291**

Scalar Functions . . . . . . . . . . . . . . . . . . . . . . . . . . . . . . . . . . . . 291
Table-Value Functions . . . . . . . . . . . . . . . . . . . . . . . . . . . . . . . . 292
Inline Functions . . . . . . . . . . . . . . . . . . . . . . . . . . . . . . . . . . . . 295
Limitations . . . . . . . . . . . . . . . . . . . . . . . . . . . . . . . . . . . . . . . 296
Meta-data . . . . . . . . . . . . . . . . . . . . . . . . . . . . . . . . . . . . . . . . 300
Creating Your Own System Functions . . . . . . . . . . . . . . . . . . . . . . 304
UDF Cookbook . . . . . . . . . . . . . . . . . . . . . . . . . . . . . . . . . . . . . 307
Summary . . . . . . . . . . . . . . . . . . . . . . . . . . . . . . . . . . . . . . . . 335

## PART III—HTML, XML, AND .NET . . . . . . . . . . . . . . . . . . . . . . . . 337

### Chapter 11  HTML . . . . . . . . . . . . . . . . . . . . . . . . . . . . . . . . . 339

Origins . . . . . . . . . . . . . . . . . . . . . . . . . . . . . . . . . . . . . . . . . . . . . 339
Producing HTML from Transact-SQL . . . . . . . . . . . . . . . . . . . . . 340
Producing HTML from sp_makewebtask . . . . . . . . . . . . . . . . . . . 344
Summary . . . . . . . . . . . . . . . . . . . . . . . . . . . . . . . . . . . . . . . . . . . 351

### Chapter 12  Introduction to XML . . . . . . . . . . . . . . . . . . . . . . . . 353

Wooden Nickels . . . . . . . . . . . . . . . . . . . . . . . . . . . . . . . . . . . . . 353
XML: An Overview . . . . . . . . . . . . . . . . . . . . . . . . . . . . . . . . . . . 356
HTML: Simplicity Comes at a Price . . . . . . . . . . . . . . . . . . . . . . 357
XML: A Brief History . . . . . . . . . . . . . . . . . . . . . . . . . . . . . . . . . 358
XML versus HTML: An Example . . . . . . . . . . . . . . . . . . . . . . . . . 358
Document Type Definitions . . . . . . . . . . . . . . . . . . . . . . . . . . . . 364
XML Schemas . . . . . . . . . . . . . . . . . . . . . . . . . . . . . . . . . . . . . . 367
Extensible Stylesheet Language Transformation (XSLT) . . . . . . . 370
Document Object Model . . . . . . . . . . . . . . . . . . . . . . . . . . . . . . . 378
Further Reading . . . . . . . . . . . . . . . . . . . . . . . . . . . . . . . . . . . . . 379
Tools . . . . . . . . . . . . . . . . . . . . . . . . . . . . . . . . . . . . . . . . . . . . . . 379
Summary . . . . . . . . . . . . . . . . . . . . . . . . . . . . . . . . . . . . . . . . . . . 380

### Chapter 13  XML and SQL Server: HTTP Queries . . . . . . . . . . . . . 381

Accessing SQL Server over HTTP . . . . . . . . . . . . . . . . . . . . . . . 382
URL Queries . . . . . . . . . . . . . . . . . . . . . . . . . . . . . . . . . . . . . . . . 385
Template Queries . . . . . . . . . . . . . . . . . . . . . . . . . . . . . . . . . . . . 393
Summary . . . . . . . . . . . . . . . . . . . . . . . . . . . . . . . . . . . . . . . . . . . 400

### Chapter 14  XML and SQL Server: Retrieving Data . . . . . . . . . . . . 401

SELECT...FOR XML . . . . . . . . . . . . . . . . . . . . . . . . . . . . . . . . . . 401
RAW Mode . . . . . . . . . . . . . . . . . . . . . . . . . . . . . . . . . . . . . . . . . 402
AUTO Mode . . . . . . . . . . . . . . . . . . . . . . . . . . . . . . . . . . . . . . . . 403
ELEMENTS . . . . . . . . . . . . . . . . . . . . . . . . . . . . . . . . . . . . . . . . . 404
EXPLICIT Mode . . . . . . . . . . . . . . . . . . . . . . . . . . . . . . . . . . . . . 406
Mapping Schemas . . . . . . . . . . . . . . . . . . . . . . . . . . . . . . . . . . . 415
Summary . . . . . . . . . . . . . . . . . . . . . . . . . . . . . . . . . . . . . . . . . . . 420

**Chapter 15   XML and SQL Server: OPENXML** . . . . . . . . . . . . . . . . **421**

The Flags Parameter . . . . . . . . . . . . . . . . . . . . . . . . . . . . . . . 425
Edge Table Format . . . . . . . . . . . . . . . . . . . . . . . . . . . . . . . . . 426
Inserting Data with OPENXML() . . . . . . . . . . . . . . . . . . . . . . . 427
Web Release 1 . . . . . . . . . . . . . . . . . . . . . . . . . . . . . . . . . . . . 431
Limitations . . . . . . . . . . . . . . . . . . . . . . . . . . . . . . . . . . . . . . 448
Summary . . . . . . . . . . . . . . . . . . . . . . . . . . . . . . . . . . . . . . . . 458


**Chapter 16   .NET and the Coming Revolution** . . . . . . . . . . . . . . **459**

.NET: The Future of Applications Development . . . . . . . . . . . . . . 465
What Is .NET? . . . . . . . . . . . . . . . . . . . . . . . . . . . . . . . . . . . . 466
On Microsoft Bashing . . . . . . . . . . . . . . . . . . . . . . . . . . . . . . . 474
Microsoft Bigotry? . . . . . . . . . . . . . . . . . . . . . . . . . . . . . . . . . 475
Summary . . . . . . . . . . . . . . . . . . . . . . . . . . . . . . . . . . . . . . . . 476


**PART IV—ADVANCED TOPICS** . . . . . . . . . . . . . . . . . . . . . . . . . **477**

**Chapter 17   Performance Considerations** . . . . . . . . . . . . . . . . . **479**

Indexing . . . . . . . . . . . . . . . . . . . . . . . . . . . . . . . . . . . . . . . . . 480
Statistics . . . . . . . . . . . . . . . . . . . . . . . . . . . . . . . . . . . . . . . . . 492
Query Optimization . . . . . . . . . . . . . . . . . . . . . . . . . . . . . . . . . 498
Summary . . . . . . . . . . . . . . . . . . . . . . . . . . . . . . . . . . . . . . . . 511


**Chapter 18   Debugging and Profiling** . . . . . . . . . . . . . . . . . . . . **513**

Debugging . . . . . . . . . . . . . . . . . . . . . . . . . . . . . . . . . . . . . . . 513
Profiling . . . . . . . . . . . . . . . . . . . . . . . . . . . . . . . . . . . . . . . . . 516
Stress Testing . . . . . . . . . . . . . . . . . . . . . . . . . . . . . . . . . . . . . 524
Summary . . . . . . . . . . . . . . . . . . . . . . . . . . . . . . . . . . . . . . . . 528


**Chapter 19   Automation** . . . . . . . . . . . . . . . . . . . . . . . . . . . . . . **529**

A Brief Overview of COM . . . . . . . . . . . . . . . . . . . . . . . . . . . . . 529
SQL Server and COM Automation . . . . . . . . . . . . . . . . . . . . . . . 536
Summary . . . . . . . . . . . . . . . . . . . . . . . . . . . . . . . . . . . . . . . . 554

**Chapter 20    Extended Stored Procedures** . . . . . . . . . . . . . . . . . . **555**

Open Data Services . . . . . . . . . . . . . . . . . . . . . . . . . . . . . . . . . . . 556
A Simple Example . . . . . . . . . . . . . . . . . . . . . . . . . . . . . . . . . . . . 562
A Better Example . . . . . . . . . . . . . . . . . . . . . . . . . . . . . . . . . . . . . 567
Making Extended Procedures Easier to Use . . . . . . . . . . . . . . . . . . 575
Debugging Extended Procedures . . . . . . . . . . . . . . . . . . . . . . . . . . 576
Isolating Extended Procedures . . . . . . . . . . . . . . . . . . . . . . . . . . . 577
xp_setpriority . . . . . . . . . . . . . . . . . . . . . . . . . . . . . . . . . . . . . . . 578
Summary . . . . . . . . . . . . . . . . . . . . . . . . . . . . . . . . . . . . . . . . . . . 584


**Chapter 21    Administrative Stored Procedures** . . . . . . . . . . . . . . **585**

sp_readtextfile . . . . . . . . . . . . . . . . . . . . . . . . . . . . . . . . . . . . . . . 585
sp_diff . . . . . . . . . . . . . . . . . . . . . . . . . . . . . . . . . . . . . . . . . . . . . 588
sp_generate_script . . . . . . . . . . . . . . . . . . . . . . . . . . . . . . . . . . . 590
sp_start_trace . . . . . . . . . . . . . . . . . . . . . . . . . . . . . . . . . . . . . . . 602
sp_stop_trace . . . . . . . . . . . . . . . . . . . . . . . . . . . . . . . . . . . . . . . 607
sp_list_trace . . . . . . . . . . . . . . . . . . . . . . . . . . . . . . . . . . . . . . . . 609
sp_proc_runner . . . . . . . . . . . . . . . . . . . . . . . . . . . . . . . . . . . . . . 612
sp_create_backup_job . . . . . . . . . . . . . . . . . . . . . . . . . . . . . . . . . 617
sp_diffdb . . . . . . . . . . . . . . . . . . . . . . . . . . . . . . . . . . . . . . . . . . . 622
Summary . . . . . . . . . . . . . . . . . . . . . . . . . . . . . . . . . . . . . . . . . . . 625


**Chapter 22    Undocumented Transact-SQL** . . . . . . . . . . . . . . . . . . **627**

What Defines Undocumented? . . . . . . . . . . . . . . . . . . . . . . . . . . . . 628
Undocumented Procedures . . . . . . . . . . . . . . . . . . . . . . . . . . . . . . 628
Creating INFORMATION_SCHEMA Views . . . . . . . . . . . . . . . . . . . . . 655
Creating System Functions . . . . . . . . . . . . . . . . . . . . . . . . . . . . . . 656
Undocumented DBCC Commands . . . . . . . . . . . . . . . . . . . . . . . . . 658
Undocumented Functions . . . . . . . . . . . . . . . . . . . . . . . . . . . . . . . 667
Undocumented Trace Flags . . . . . . . . . . . . . . . . . . . . . . . . . . . . . . 671
Summary . . . . . . . . . . . . . . . . . . . . . . . . . . . . . . . . . . . . . . . . . . . 672


**Chapter 23    Arrays** . . . . . . . . . . . . . . . . . . . . . . . . . . . . . . . . . . . **675**

xp_array.dll . . . . . . . . . . . . . . . . . . . . . . . . . . . . . . . . . . . . . . . . . 676
Array System Functions . . . . . . . . . . . . . . . . . . . . . . . . . . . . . . . . 689

The Pièce de Rèsistance. . . . . . . . . . . . . . . . . . . . . . . . . . . . . 692

Multidimensional Arrays . . . . . . . . . . . . . . . . . . . . . . . . . . . . 694

Summary. . . . . . . . . . . . . . . . . . . . . . . . . . . . . . . . . . . . . . 698

## PART V—ESSAYS ON SOFTWARE ENGINEERING . . . . . . . . . . . . . . . 701

## Chapter 24   Creating a Workable Environment . . . . . . . . . . . . . 703

Get Rid of Distractions . . . . . . . . . . . . . . . . . . . . . . . . . . . . . 705

Close the Door. . . . . . . . . . . . . . . . . . . . . . . . . . . . . . . . . . . 706

Internal Distractions. . . . . . . . . . . . . . . . . . . . . . . . . . . . . . . 706

Form Over Function. . . . . . . . . . . . . . . . . . . . . . . . . . . . . . . . 707

Silence Is Golden; Communication Divine. . . . . . . . . . . . . . . . . 708

Conclusion. . . . . . . . . . . . . . . . . . . . . . . . . . . . . . . . . . . . . . 708

Epilogue . . . . . . . . . . . . . . . . . . . . . . . . . . . . . . . . . . . . . . . 708

## Chapter 25   Evolutionary Development . . . . . . . . . . . . . . . . . . 711

*Kaizen* . . . . . . . . . . . . . . . . . . . . . . . . . . . . . . . . . . . . . . . . 713

The Benefits of Small Changes . . . . . . . . . . . . . . . . . . . . . . . . 713

*Soft*ware. . . . . . . . . . . . . . . . . . . . . . . . . . . . . . . . . . . . . . . 714

*Soft*ware Eutropy. . . . . . . . . . . . . . . . . . . . . . . . . . . . . . . . . 715

Refactoring . . . . . . . . . . . . . . . . . . . . . . . . . . . . . . . . . . . . . 716

Selling Management (or Yourself) on Refactoring . . . . . . . . . . . . 718

When Not to Refactor . . . . . . . . . . . . . . . . . . . . . . . . . . . . . . 721

Databases. . . . . . . . . . . . . . . . . . . . . . . . . . . . . . . . . . . . . . 722

Can You Refactor Instead of Design?. . . . . . . . . . . . . . . . . . . . 724

A House Built Upon the Sand . . . . . . . . . . . . . . . . . . . . . . . . . 724

Extreme Programming. . . . . . . . . . . . . . . . . . . . . . . . . . . . . . 725

Conclusion. . . . . . . . . . . . . . . . . . . . . . . . . . . . . . . . . . . . . . 732

Epilogue . . . . . . . . . . . . . . . . . . . . . . . . . . . . . . . . . . . . . . . 732

## Chapter 26   The Gestalt of Testing. . . . . . . . . . . . . . . . . . . . . . 733

Where to Begin . . . . . . . . . . . . . . . . . . . . . . . . . . . . . . . . . . 735

The Futility of Testing . . . . . . . . . . . . . . . . . . . . . . . . . . . . . . 737

Types of Tests . . . . . . . . . . . . . . . . . . . . . . . . . . . . . . . . . . . 738

When to Test. . . . . . . . . . . . . . . . . . . . . . . . . . . . . . . . . . . . 739

Testing Can Save Time . . . . . . . . . . . . . . . . . . . . . . . . . . . . . 739

Testing in the Extreme . . . . . . . . . . . . . . . . . . . . . . . . . . . . . . . . . . . 740
Other Types of Testing . . . . . . . . . . . . . . . . . . . . . . . . . . . . . . . . . . . 741
Conclusion. . . . . . . . . . . . . . . . . . . . . . . . . . . . . . . . . . . . . . . . . . . . . 745
Epilogue . . . . . . . . . . . . . . . . . . . . . . . . . . . . . . . . . . . . . . . . . . . . . . 745

**References** . . . . . . . . . . . . . . . . . . . . . . . . . . . . . . . . . . **747**
**Index** . . . . . . . . . . . . . . . . . . . . . . . . . . . . . . . . . . . . . . **749**

# Foreword

This is a book that deserves a prominent place by anyone who aspires to be a professional developer of SQL Server applications.

I had the honor and pleasure to be the first development manager for Microsoft SQL Server. During my 11-plus years in the group, I hired many of the key developers of the product, and worked alongside them. I came to learn a lot about characteristics that are common to great developers: Passion. That genius in software development (to paraphrase Einstein) really is 1% inspiration and 99% perspiration. There exists a near fanaticism that "good enough" isn't. One must strive for perfection. The professional writes efficient, industrial-strength, well-documented code that can be maintained, understood, and enhanced for years to come by not just himself, but by others too. Many a truly brilliant newly graduated computer science major takes several years to mature from being a hot and clever coder to being a true professional developer. (A few never could make the transition, and had short careers—at least in my group.) They are familiar with the prominent algorithms in their area of specialty. Mastery of their development languages and tools is a given. And shortcuts don't cut it for a real professional. Every boundary condition must be considered, provided for, and tested before the code is checked in. Assertions in code are a must. Return codes are always checked. Extensive comments are imperative. Reuse of code is essential. Code inspections and walkthroughs are welcomed and routine. When you make that check-in of code, it's like signing your name to a work of art. It meets your own high standards. And you never stop learning. Professionals are students of their craft throughout their careers. In our industry, if you are not moving your skills forward, you are going backward.

I loved reading the advance manuscript of this work. All the traits I mention earlier fly off the pages as you read this book. During my Microsoft tenure, I often would meet with SQL Server customers. All too often, it was in the context of an application that wasn't working as smoothly or performing as well as the developers had hoped. I earned a reputation as a sort of "Mr. Fix-It" for such troubled applications, and helped turn some prominent near failures into great success stories. I loved that part of my job. I enjoyed the customer interaction, even though it often started out as very testy meetings. SQL Server itself is often the whipping boy for poorly developed applications. Certainly there were times when SQL Server itself had some bug or shortcoming that contributed to the problem, and the product itself became orders of magnitude more refined, robust, and fast with each new version over the years, as it will continue to do. But, even in the rough early days of version 1.x, enormous improvements in performance or simplicity could be made largely from better use of SQL Server stored procedures. It was not uncommon to see 100-fold and more performance increases because of smarter stored procedure usage. Once we got the shrill managers out of the room in one of these troubled application reviews, great progress could be made. Although I managed a large group myself, and even hold an MBA from a top university, I never considered myself a manager. I always considered myself a developer—and developers know how to talk to other developers and respect strong ideas and superior techniques. This is what you will find in this book: an experienced developer talking to other developers. Ken writes in a clear, first-person style that is unfortunately not common in technical books. He is not afraid to state opinions, and all real developers know that opinions and beliefs in software development are essential because there are few truths that can be held to be self-evident. All too often, in my past experience, the crux of the issue in a troubled app came down to the simple truth that the developers didn't take the SQL code as serious as they should have or place as much importance on it as they placed on the C, C++, or other programming language code that comprised the remainder of their application. In many cases, they had only a cursory understanding of SQL and database usage at all. And these were usually very smart people, but they hadn't yet made the commitment to excellence in an unfamiliar area or to be real professionals, at least by my definition. The reality is that many of those situations and meetings would have never taken place had the developers read, studied, and taken this book to heart before they plunged into writing their first SQL Server application. Take the time to read and study this book. It's one step in your commitment to excellence as a professional developer of SQL Server applications.

Congratulations, Ken, and thank you for writing this book. Like your earlier work, *The Guru's Guide to Transact-SQL*, I wish it had existed 10 years ago.

—Ron Soukup
*September 2001*

# Preface

The message of this book is that building stored procedures in Transact-SQL is like building programs in any other language. It requires the same type of skill, planning, attention to detail, and overall grasp of technology that successful development in other programming languages requires. To master Transact-SQL, one must first master the fundamentals of software development itself, then build on this foundation by embracing Transact-SQL as a programming language in its own right. This book teaches you how to do that.

If you are new to SQL Server, there are probably better books than this one to introduce you to Transact-SQL stored procedure programming. This book is really geared toward the intermediate-to-advanced developer. It assumes you already know how to write Transact-SQL queries and how to build stored procedures. Other than some introductory remarks to prime the discussion, this book offers little in the way of beginner-level instruction. It is aimed at developers with moderate to advanced skills who want to become better stored procedure programmers—developers who want to go to the next level of software craftsmanship as it relates to Transact-SQL, stored procedure programming, and XML.

The opening epigraph of my previous book, *The Guru's Guide to Transact-SQL*, is a quote by my friend, the renowned author and lecturer Joe Celko, regarding the importance of unlearning procedural programming in order to master nonprocedural languages such as SQL. At the time, I agreed with Joe that writing Transact-SQL code in a procedural manner was the single biggest impediment to writing good Transact-SQL code. When I penned the first *Guru's Guide* book, I firmly believed that attempting to code in Transact-SQL in the same way that, say, C++ is written was the main reason that people who are competent developers in other languages often run into difficulties when they try to code in Transact-SQL. Their whole approach was wrong, I reasoned, and that's why they had problems. I believed that they weren't *thinking* like database programmers; that instead, they were thinking like traditional programmers, which just won't work in the world of database programming. So I thought.

Since then, I've had a change of heart. I once read an interview in which Edward Van Halen said that a band's music albums are snapshots of where the

**xvii**

band is at a particular point in time (musically and otherwise). This is true of books too. *The Guru's Guide to Transact-SQL* is where I was circa 1998 and 1999, when I wrote it. Since then, my thinking on the relationship between procedural programming and Transact-SQL has evolved a bit (or so I'd like to think). Why? Well, let me tell you a little story . . .

Sometime during the two years I spent writing the first *Guru's Guide*, one of the book's technical reviewers wrote to ask me about an article I'd written several years before for my column in *Sybase Developer's Journal* that demonstrated some tricks with bitmasks in Transact-SQL. He wanted to know if I could send a copy of the article because he was doing some work with bitmasks and wanted to use one of the techniques about which I'd written. I searched high and low for the article, but couldn't find it anywhere on the various computers I use. The machine on which I'd written the column had long since been retired, as had any backup tapes I might have had of it—had they ever existed in the first place.

Finally, a search on the Internet turned up the ancient piece, and I forwarded it to the fellow who'd asked for it. With some amusement, I sat at my desk and read through the article for a few minutes (most writers *really* like to read what they write, no matter how old it is and no matter what they tell you). I wondered to myself: *What ever possessed me to try these bit-twiddling techniques in Transact-SQL of all things? Why do I think of things like this in the first place?* I wondered what drove me to make discoveries like the techniques about which I'd written the article. I reasoned that if I could figure out how or why I went about making discoveries like this, perhaps I could unlock the secret of innovation itself, or, at least, how I occasionally stumble upon it. Perhaps I could move to the next level as a Transact-SQL coder myself.

I thought about it for a few days and finally realized why I came up with ideas like the bit-twiddling technique. The conclusion I came to was that, as much as I would have liked to have believed that I thought of them all on my own, many of my "discoveries" in Transact-SQL were the result of what those in academia refer to as *cross-pollination*. It was *because of,* not in spite of, my experiences with other languages that I'd come up with a number of the innovative coding techniques I'd discovered over the years. Most of the discoveries I'd made in Transact-SQL had grown from seeds planted in my brain by my work in traditional programming languages such as Pascal, C/C++, assembly language, and various others. It occurred to me that there were likely scant few true *innovations* originating in the relatively pubescent world of Transact-SQL programming. After all, languages like C and Pascal had predated Transact-SQL by many years—and languages like COBOL and BASIC by even longer. We don't see many *new* problems in the world of computing. What we see are *new* solutions to the same *old* problems. People were solving these problems long before Transact-SQL or SQL Server even existed. Surely most of the discoveries to be made in the field of software engineering have already been made. Surely those of us innovating in Transact-SQL are merely standing on the shoulders of the giants who came before us.

In their book, *The Pragmatic Programmer*, Andrew Hunt and Dave Thomas make the bold recommendation that people who aspire to be better programmers should learn at least one new programming language per year. I'll make the same recommendation here. If you want to master Transact-SQL stored procedure programming, you should master programming itself first. Programming, coding, software engineering—whatever you want to call it— requires many years *and many languages* to master. Like the martial arts apprentice who must first master a number of separate martial arts before he can attain an advanced belt, a programmer who would master Transact-SQL should master the various aspects of programming in general before he can hope to master Transact-SQL.

The big-picture perspective and the cross-pollination that interdisciplinary work affords is the chief reason universities require schooling in fields outside one's major focus of study. By studying the way that other fields do things, you see the many similarities and differences between your field and theirs, you gain deeper insight into those similarities and differences, and you learn to apply what you've discovered about topics completely outside your field to your own work in ways that have perhaps not been tried before. In other words, you learn to innovate. By embracing the broad view of the world the university espouses, you begin to understand your field more holistically: You begin to understand its *philosophy* more intimately, and you begin to grasp where it fits in the grand scheme of things.

I think the same kinds of insight can be gained through studying languages and techniques outside the realm of SQL Server. Were it not for my work in assembly language and my study of the works of masters like Steve Gibson, I might never have stumbled upon the bit-twiddling techniques about which I wrote that ancient column. If not for my work in Pascal and Delphi and my study of code by gurus such as Anders Hejlsberg and Kim Kokkonen, I wouldn't have come up with a good number of the techniques I've developed in Transact-SQL over the years, including many of the data manipulation routines you'll see in this book. My research into common design patterns in Transact-SQL was inspired by the book *Design Patterns* by Erich Gamma and company, which I keep close at hand for my work in languages such as C++ and Object Pascal. The book *The Practice of Programming*, by Brian Kernighan and Rob Pike, has largely influenced my insistence on idiomatic programming. I'm a stickler for testing because of books like *After the Gold Rush* by Steve McConnell and *Extreme Programming Explained* by Kent Beck, and I'm a big proponent of the value of refactoring because of works like *Refactoring: Improving the Design of Existing Code* by Martin Fowler. Many of the algorithms discussed in this book were inspired by those in Donald Knuth's three-volume work, *The Art of Computer Programming,* and by Jon Bentley's book, *Programming Pearls,* as well as by many others.

None of these books are about Transact-SQL per se, or even about SQL Server. None of them demonstrate techniques that can be easily translated to a set-oriented language like SQL. They are, however, about programming, and my work in other languages is responsible for my knowledge of them. I have benefited—immensely—from interdisciplinary work, from the cross-pollination between my work in Transact-SQL and my work in other languages, and from the perspective such work affords a programmer. And I think you will too.

So, rather than preaching that you must give up your sinful procedural programming ways in order to reach the nirvana that is Transact-SQL mastery, I will instead encourage you to explore other languages and other tools. Pick one per year—it can be any language or tool in which you're not already an expert—anything from Visual Basic to Delphi to Ruby to C#, C++, or Java. Come up with a few projects to undertake with your new language, ideally (but not necessarily) things that tie it back to SQL Server in some way, and then dive in. Buy the books you need, read the newsgroups, do the research, build your software. You will be surprised at how much you learn about programming, and how much you grow as a developer through the experience.

Then, sometime throughout these research projects, think about how you might apply what you're learning to your work as a Transact-SQL developer. How does SQL Server employ this or that language element that is featured by the tool you're studying? How does it implement functionality that you've found particularly helpful in your new language? How do they differ? How does, say, OLE Automation differ between Transact-SQL and Delphi? Given that Transact-SQL, like all of SQL Server, is written in C and C++, what language nuances can you trace to its origins?

After a few years of this, and after you've gained the perspective that forays into the world outside of SQL Server can afford, you will be well on your way to having the tools necessary to truly master Transact-SQL and stored procedure programming. You will appreciate software engineering as a discipline; you will love programming for its own sake. This is the key to mastering any programming language, including Transact-SQL.

So, my apologies to Joe Celko notwithstanding, I no longer believe that procedural programming is the single biggest impediment to good Transact-SQL coding. It is quite the opposite. Not truly grasping a language's strengths and weaknesses—the things that make it unique—is the single biggest impediment to building good software with it. And you can only gain the perspective necessary to accurately assess those strengths and weaknesses through interdisciplinary work and cross-pollination. In Transact-SQL's case, its strength is set-oriented development, its chief weakness is top-down programming. This doesn't mean that you can only write set-oriented programs with Transact-SQL or that writing procedural Transact-SQL code is only for the foolhardy. After all, they call them stored *procedures* for a reason. It just means that your style of coding will be different with Transact-SQL than it would be with, say, Visual Basic. This is not just true of Transact-SQL; it's true of many languages. Many languages have nuances and idioms that make them unique. You wouldn't code in C++ the way you code in Visual Basic, either. Use the right tool for the job. Play to your tool's strengths and stay away from its weaknesses. Become intimate with those strengths and weaknesses by mastering not only the tool, but also software development in general. The purpose is to become a master programmer, not just a stored procedure expert.

And about that conversation we had over dinner in San Francisco, Joe: I still think C# is the best thing to happen to programming in a good long while.

*Ken Henderson*
*January 2001*

# Introduction

Rather than merely providing a catalog of coding tricks and syntax subtleties, this book teaches the *philosophy* of Transact-SQL programming and shows you how to apply this philosophy to develop *your own* coding techniques and solutions to real-world problems. This book takes the position that the "why" is at least as important as the "how" and that a balanced approach to learning Transact-SQL—one that stresses the theoretical as much as it stresses the practical—is preferable to an unbalanced approach.

You'll notice that this book delves into a number of subjects not traditionally associated directly with stored procedure programming. We cover XML, HTML, .NET, and a number of other seemingly ancillary subjects. The reason for this is simple: When you build real-world software, you tend to work with a number of different technologies. Rarely do you build stored procedures in a vacuum. This book acknowledges that fact by covering many of these related technologies from the perspective of the SQL Server stored procedure developer.

XML is relevant because you typically access SQL Server's XML features via stored procedures and T-SQL queries. The same is true for HTML. We discuss .NET because Microsoft has announced that the next version of SQL Server will permit stored procedures to be developed using the new .NET languages, C#, and VB.NET. I felt a book about SQL Server development—even one focused on stored procedure development—should at least mention .NET and talk about some of the many exciting features it has in store for SQL Server developers. There may be some resistance among Transact-SQL programmers to moving their code to .NET and the Common Language Runtime. I felt a book like this should help lead the way by providing a broad overview of the technology and by giving developers some tips on what they can expect from it.

This book discusses Transact-SQL development in the larger context of software development. It delves into a number of foundational software engineering concepts: best practices, code management strategies, design patterns and idioms, software testing, and many others. These are all fundamental to sound development in any programming language, including Transact-SQL.

This book seeks to elevate the status of Transact-SQL to that of traditional languages such as Visual Basic and C++. It teaches you how to master Transact-SQL as a programming language rather than merely as a query language or a scripting facility for SQL Server.

As with its predecessor, this book stays away from excessive screenshots and other filler devices typically found in computer books. I have expressly avoided fattening the book through unnecessary figures, sidebars, diagrams, and the like. Instead, I've included figures where they're helpful, but have omitted them elsewhere. I've trimmed query results fairly frequently throughout the book (you'll see "Results abridged" when this happens), while still including complete code listings whenever possible. Bloated technical books are one of my pet peeves, so I do my best to avoid creating them myself.

When I began writing this book, I had the following design goals in mind:

- Pick up where my last book, *The Guru's Guide to Transact-SQL*, left off. Provide an evolutionary path for those that have mastered that book.
- Teach the *philosophy* of Transact-SQL programming, not just its syntax, techniques, or hidden tricks.
- Speak to the similarities and differences between Transact-SQL programming and software development in other computer languages.
- Avoid rehashing the SQL Server Books Online as much as possible.
- Thoroughly cover topics related to Transact-SQL stored procedure programming (such as extended procedures, database design, and XML) that are commonly omitted or covered only in a cursory fashion in books such as this.
- Proceed from the basic to the advanced within each chapter and throughout the book.
- Produce a balanced book, one that treats the theoretical and practical aspects of Transact-SQL stored procedure programming evenhandedly.
- Construct each chapter so that it's self-contained—so that it relies on objects created in other chapters as little as possible.
- Avoid excessive screenshots and other types of padding devices often seen in computer books.
- Innovate. Show techniques, approaches, and ways of thinking about Transact-SQL programming that have not been explored before. Advance the current state-of-the-art in terms of Transact-SQL programming in particular and software engineering in general.
- Err on the side of generosity with code samples. Don't just tell readers how to do something. Show them.
- Include complete code samples within the chapter texts so that the book can be read through without requiring a computer or CD-ROM.

- Abridge code listings within chapter texts when formatting concerns necessitate and when doing so does not detract from the discussion at hand materially (include the entirety of all listing on the book's CD).
- Provide real-world code samples that have intrinsic value apart from the book. Provide example code that a reader could drop into place on her production server if she wanted to.
- Demonstrate that computer books can be well written and understandable, while still laden with useful technical information. Show that good writing and good technology are not mutually exclusive.
- Use modern coding techniques, with specific emphases on ANSI compliance and current version features and enhancements.
- Provide an easy-going, relaxed commentary with a lack of emphasis on formality. Be the reader's loyal companion as he works through the text. Communicate in writing the way that people typically speak.

These and others make up the goals I had when I sat down to write this book. Being a writer has its ups and downs. Everyday, I have goals I try to achieve. Sometimes I meet them; sometimes I don't. The thing is to keep trying when you fail—to figure out where you went wrong and how you can do better next time. The challenge is to shrug off the faint pale of discouragement and the other obstacles that keep you from reaching your full potential. The reward comes in seeing what great things you can accomplish when you overcome these obstacles and take your talents to the next level.

## About the Sample Databases

To make things easier on the reader, this book uses SQL Server's Northwind and pubs sample databases extensively. By using the sample databases that come with the product, I'm helping you avoid having to create lots of custom objects just to understand concepts that can easily be taught using what comes in the box. You'll nearly always be able to determine which database a particular example uses from the surrounding commentary or from the code itself. The Northwind database is used more often than pubs, so when it's not otherwise specified, or when in doubt, use Northwind.

Usually, modifications to these databases are made within transactions so that they can be reversed; however, for safety's sake, you should probably drop and recreate them after each chapter in which they're changed. The scripts to rebuild them (instnwnd.sql and instpubs.sql) can be found in the \Install subdirectory under the root SQL Server folder.

## Acknowledgments

This is the part of the book where I get to break into a kind of Oscar acceptance speech and thank all the "little people" who made the big night possible. It's where I get to talk about how hard writing books is and how many people made this particular one possible. Well, I'm not going to do that. Those of you who helped with the book know who you are, and you know how much I appreciate your efforts. The book wouldn't have happened without you—plain and simple. As always, my wife has arranged our family life around my hectic schedule so that we could give birth, once more, to one of my dreams. For that, I am ever in her debt, and she is ever in my heart.

## About the Author

Ken Henderson is a husband and father who lives in Dallas. When not writing books or software, he enjoys spending time reading, playing music, and watching his kids grow up. Henderson may be reached via email at khen@khen.com.

# PART I

# The Basics

# CHAPTER 1

# Stored Procedure Primer

*Today, average software development practices are becalmed in a windless sea of code-and-fix programming—a kind of flat-earth approach to software development that was proven ineffective 20 years ago.*

*—Steve McConnell[1]*

Working from the assumption that the human brain learns by associating new data with what it already knows, we'll spend this chapter building a base framework onto which we can assemble the knowledge conveyed by the remainder of the book. We'll touch on the topics covered in the book's other chapters, but we'll save the details for the chapters themselves. I'm assuming that you know some basic Transact-SQL with which we can associate these high-level concepts. We'll spend the remainder of the book filling in the details and expanding on what we cover here.

This chapter serves to prime the discussion on SQL Server stored procedure programming. It will tell you what a stored procedure is, how stored procedures are often used, and why and how you should use them. It will also jumpstart the treatment of Transact-SQL as a full-fledged programming language. If I could have you take one thing away from reading this book, it would be that Transact-SQL programming is very much like any other type of programming: It requires the same attention to detail, the same craftsmanship, and the same software engineering skill to do well.

## What Is a Stored Procedure?

A Transact-SQL stored procedure is a set of T-SQL code that is stored in a SQL Server database and compiled when used. You create this set of code

---

1. McConnell, Steve. *After the Gold Rush*. Redmond, WA: Microsoft Press, 1998. Page 91.

using the CREATE PROCEDURE command. You can use most Transact-SQL commands in a stored procedure; however, some commands (such as CREATE PROCEDURE, CREATE VIEW, SET SHOWPLAN_TEXT, SET SHOWPLAN_ALL, and so forth) must be the first (or only) statement in a command batch, and therefore aren't allowed in stored procedures. Most Transact-SQL commands behave the same in a stored procedure as they do in a command batch, but some have special capabilities or exhibit different behavior when executed within the context of a stored procedure. Listing 1–1 shows a simple stored procedure (only the code from the CREATE PROCEDURE line down to the ensuing GO actually constitutes the stored procedure):

**Listing 1–1** A simple stored procedure.

```
Use Northwind
GO
IF OBJECT_ID('dbo.ListCustomersByCity') IS NOT NULL
  DROP PROC dbo.ListCustomersByCity
GO
CREATE PROCEDURE dbo.ListCustomersByCity @Country nvarchar(30)='%'
AS
SELECT City, COUNT(*) AS NumberOfCustomers
FROM Customers
WHERE Country LIKE @Country
GROUP BY City
GO
EXEC dbo.ListCustomersByCity
```

# Stored Procedure Advantages

Although you can do most of the things a stored procedure can do with simple ad hoc Transact-SQL code, stored procedures have a number of advantages over ad hoc queries, including

- Execution plan retention and reuse
- Query autoparameterization
- Encapsulation of business rules and policies
- Application modularization
- Sharing of application logic between applications
- Access to database objects that is both secure and uniform
- Consistent, safe data modification

- Network bandwidth conservation
- Support for automatic execution at system start-up

I'll touch on each of these as we go along.

## Creating a Stored Procedure

As I've said, you use the Transact-SQL CREATE PROCEDURE command to create stored procedures. All that really happens when you create a procedure is that its syntax is checked and its source code is inserted into the syscomments system table. Generally, object names referenced by a procedure aren't resolved until it's executed. In SQL Server parlance, this is known as *deferred name resolution*.

"Syscomments" is a misnomer. The table doesn't store comments per se; it stores source code. The name is a vestige from the pre-7.0 days and was so named because it stored the optional source code to stored procedures (and other objects), whereas sysprocedures stored a pseudo-compiled version (a kind of normalized query tree) of the procedures themselves. This is no longer true, and the sysprocedures table no longer exists. Syscomments is now the sole repository for stored procedures, views, triggers, user-defined functions (UDFs), rules, and defaults. If you remove an object's source code from syscomments, you can no longer use that object.

### Deferred Name Resolution and an Interesting Exception

Before we go further, it's worth mentioning that there's an interesting exception to SQL Server's default deferred name resolution behavior. Run the code in Listing 1–2 in Query Analyzer:

**Listing 1–2** SQL Server doesn't allow you to include more than one CREATE TABLE statement for a given temporary table in the same stored procedure.

```
CREATE PROC testp @var int
AS
IF @var=1
  CREATE TABLE #temp (k1 int identity, c1 int)
ELSE
  CREATE TABLE #temp (k1 int identity, c1 varchar(2))
INSERT #temp DEFAULT VALUES
SELECT c1 FROM #temp
GO
```

The syntax contained in the stored procedure is seemingly valid, yet we get this message when we run it:

```
Server: Msg 2714, Level 16, State 1, Procedure testp, Line 6
There is already an object named '#temp' in the database.
```

Why? Obviously @var can't be both equal to one and not equal to one, right? To get a little closer to the answer, change the temporary table reference to a permanent table, like the one shown in Listing 1–3.

**Listing 1–3** Changing the table to a permanent table works around the temporary table limitation.

```
CREATE PROC testp @var int
AS
IF @var=1
  CREATE TABLE tempdb..temp (k1 int identity, c1 int)
ELSE
  CREATE TABLE tempdb..temp (k1 int identity, c1 varchar(2))
INSERT #temp DEFAULT VALUES
SELECT c1 FROM #temp
GO
```

This procedure is created without error. What's happening here? Why does SQL Server care whether the table created is a temporary or a permanent table? And why does it matter *now*—before the procedure is even executed and before the value of @var can be known?

What appears to be happening is that SQL Server resolves CREATE TABLE references to temporary tables *before* inserting the procedure into syscomments—an apparent vestige from the pre-7.0 days when object references were resolved when a procedure was first created. The same limitation applies to variable declarations and, therefore, to the **table** data type. You can't declare a variable more than once in a single stored procedure, even if the declarations reside in mutually exclusive units of code. This differs from how permanent tables are handled, and is the reason the code in Listing 1–3 runs without error. It appears that, beginning with SQL Server 7.0, deferred name resolution was enabled for permanent tables, but not for temporary ones. Whatever the case, you can't execute code like that shown in Listing 1–2, so here's a workaround (Listing 1–4):

**Listing 1–4** Including one CREATE TABLE statement, but two sets of ALTER TABLE statements, works around the problem.

```
CREATE PROC testp @var int
AS
CREATE TABLE #temp (k1 int identity)
IF @var=1
  ALTER TABLE #temp ADD c1 int
ELSE
  ALTER TABLE #temp ADD c1 varchar(2)
INSERT #temp DEFAULT VALUES
EXEC('SELECT c1 FROM #temp')
GO
```

This technique creates the table just once, then alters it to match the Data Definition Language (DDL) specification (spec) we want to end up with. Note the use of EXEC() to select the column we added with ALTER TABLE. The use of dynamic SQL is necessary because the newly added column isn't immediately visible to the procedure that added it. We're forced to create and execute an ad hoc query string to access it by name. (Note that you *can* reference the column indirectly—for example, through SELECT * or via an ordinal value in an ORDER BY clause, just not by name).

Another disadvantage of this approach is that it mixes DDL (the CREATE and ALTER statements) and Data Modification Language (DML; the INSERT and SELECT). Because of this, the procedure's execution plan must be recompiled when the INSERT is encountered (the temporary table's schema information (info) has changed since the original execution plan was formulated). Any stored procedure that creates a temporary table, then processes it further, will cause a plan recompile because the table's schema info did not exist when the execution plan was first created; however, the procedure in Listing 1–4 causes an *additional* recompile to occur because it alters this schema, then processes the table further. Particularly with large procedures in high-throughput environments, this can cause performance problems as well as blocking and concurrency issues because a compile lock is taken out on the stored procedure while the execution plan is being recompiled. Listing 1–5 presents a workaround that doesn't require the use of dynamic T-SQL:

**Listing 1–5** A workaround for the temporary table creation problem.

```
CREATE PROCEDURE testp4
AS
```

```
INSERT #temp DEFAULT VALUES
SELECT c1 FROM #temp
GO

CREATE PROC testp3
AS
CREATE TABLE #temp (k1 int identity, c1 varchar(2))
EXEC dbo.testp4
GO

CREATE PROC testp2
AS
CREATE TABLE #temp (k1 int identity, c1 int)
EXEC dbo.testp4
GO

CREATE PROC testp @var int
AS
IF @var=1
EXEC dbo.testp2
ELSE
EXEC dbo.testp3
GO
```

Although this technique alleviates the need for EXEC(), it also forces us to completely reorganize the stored procedure. In fact, we're forced to break the original procedure into four separate routines and call the fourth one redundantly from the second and third routines. Why? First, instead of having two CREATE TABLE statements for the same temporary table in one procedure—which, as we've discovered, isn't supported—we moved each CREATE TABLE to its own procedure. Second, because a temporary table is automatically dropped as soon as it goes out of scope, we can't simply create it, then return to the top-level routine and add rows to it or SELECT from it. We have to do that either in one of the procedures that created it or in a common routine that they call. We chose the latter, so procedures two and three call a fourth routine that takes care of inserting the row into the temporary table and selecting the **c1** column from it. (Because objects created in a procedure are visible to the procedures it calls, the fourth routine can "see" the table created by its caller.) This approach works, but is far from optimal. Think about how complex this would get for a really large procedure. Breaking it into multiple, distinct pieces may not be practical. Still, it avoids the necessity of having to create and execute an ad hoc T-SQL string and should generally perform better than that approach.

## Listing a Stored Procedure

Assuming the object is not encrypted, you can list the source code to a procedure, view, trigger, UDF, rule, or default object using the sp_helptext system procedure. An example is included in Listing 1–6:

**Listing 1–6** sp_helptext lists the source for a stored procedure.

```
EXEC dbo.sp_helptext 'ListCustomersByCity'
Text
--------------------------------------------------------------------------
CREATE PROCEDURE dbo.ListCustomersByCity @Country nvarchar(30)='%'
AS
SELECT City, COUNT(*) AS NumberOfCustomers
FROM Customers
WHERE Country LIKE @Country
GROUP BY City
```

## Permissions and Limitations

Only members of the sysadmin, db_owner, or db_ddladmin role (or those explicitly granted CREATE PROC permission by a member of the appropriate role) can execute CREATE PROCEDURE.

The maximum stored procedure size is 128MB. The maximum number of parameters a procedure may receive is 1,024.

## Creation Tips

Include a comment header with each procedure that identifies its author, purpose, creation date and revision history, the parameters it receives, and so forth. A common technique is to place this comment block either immediately before or just after the CREATE PROC statement itself (but before the rest of the procedure) to ensure that it's stored in syscomments and can be viewed from tools like Enterprise Manager and Query Analyzer's Object Browser. The system stored procedure that follows, sp_object_script_comments, generates comment headers for stored procedures, views, and similar objects (Listing 1–7):

**Listing 1–7** You can use sp_object_script_comments to generate stored procedure comment headers.

```
USE master
GO
IF OBJECT_ID('dbo.sp_object_script_comments') IS NOT NULL
```

```
  DROP PROC dbo.sp_object_script_comments
GO
CREATE PROCEDURE dbo.sp_object_script_comments
                    -- Required parameters
                    @objectname sysname=NULL,
                    @desc sysname=NULL,

                    -- Optional parameters
                    @parameters varchar(8000)=NULL,
                    @example varchar(8000)=NULL,
                    @author sysname=NULL,
                    @workfile sysname='', -- Force workfile to be generated
                    @email sysname='(none)',
                    @version sysname=NULL,
                    @revision sysname='0',
                    @datecreated smalldatetime=NULL,
                    @datelastchanged smalldatetime=NULL
/*

Object: sp_object_script_comments
Description: Generates comment headers for SQL scripts

Usage: sp_object_script_comments @objectname='ObjectName',
@desc='Description of object",@parameters='param1[,param2...]'

Returns: (None)

$Workfile: sp_object_script_comments.sql $

$Author: Khen $. Email: khen@khen.com

$Revision: 1 $

Example: sp_object_script_comments @objectname='sp_who', @desc='Returns a
list of currently running jobs', @parameters=[@loginname]

Created: 1992-04-03. $Modtime: 1/4/01 8:35p $.

*/
AS

IF (@objectname+@desc) IS NULL GOTO Help

PRINT '/*'
```

```
PRINT CHAR(13)
EXEC sp_usage @objectname=@objectname,
              @desc=@desc,
              @parameters=@parameters,
              @example=@example,
              @author=@author,
              @workfile=@workfile,
              @email=@email,
              @version=@version, @revision=@revision,
              @datecreated=@datecreated, @datelastchanged=@datelastchanged
PRINT CHAR(13)+'*/'

RETURN 0

Help:
EXEC dbo.sp_usage @objectname='sp_object_script_comments',
        @desc='Generates comment headers for SQL scripts',
        @parameters='@objectname=''ObjectName'',
        @desc=''Description of object",@parameters=''param1[,param2...]''''',
        @example='sp_object_script_comments @objectname=''sp_who'',
        @desc=''Returns a list of currently running jobs'',
        @parameters=[@loginname]',
        @author='Ken Henderson',
        @workfile='sp_object_script_comments.sql',
        @email='khen@khen.com',
        @version='3', @revision='1',
        @datecreated='19920403', @datelastchanged='19990701'
RETURN -1
GO
EXEC dbo.sp_object_script_comments
```

This procedure generates stored procedure comment headers by calling the sp_usage procedure included later in the chapter. It can be executed from any database by any procedure. To use sp_object_script_comments, simply pass it the required parameters, and it will create a fully usable comment block that identifies a procedure or other type of object and spells out its usage and key background info. You can copy this block of text and paste it into the header of the routine itself and—*voila!*—you've got a nicely formatted, informative comment block for your code.

In shops with lots of stored procedure code, it's common to locate each stored procedure in its own script and to store each script in a version control or source code management system. Many of these systems support special tags (these are known as *keywords* in Visual SourceSafe [VSS], the source code management system that I use) that you can embed in T-SQL comments. Through these tags, you allow the source code management system to automatically insert revision information, the name of the person who last changed the file, the date and time of the last change, and so on. Because the tags are embedded in comments, there's no danger that these changes will break your code. Basically, you're just allowing the system to take care of some of the housekeeping normally associated with managing source code. Many of the stored procedures listed in this book include tags recognized by VSS in their headers (these tags begin and end with $). See Chapter 4 for more information.

Allow the passing of a single help parameter such as '/?'—or no parameters—to return an informational message telling the caller how to use the procedure. Place the section that generates this usage information at the end of the procedure to keep it out of the way and to locate it consistently from procedure to procedure. An ideal way to do this is to set up and call a separate procedure that accepts parameters indicating usage information and returns it in a uniform format. Here's a stored procedure that does just that (Listing 1–8):

**Listing 1–8** You can use sp_usage to generate stored procedure usage info.

```
USE master
GO
IF OBJECT_ID('dbo.sp_usage') IS NOT NULL
  DROP PROC dbo.sp_usage
GO
CREATE PROCEDURE dbo.sp_usage
                -- Required parameters
                @objectname sysname=NULL,
                @desc sysname=NULL,
                -- Optional parameters
                @parameters varchar(8000)=NULL,
                @returns varchar(8000)='(None)',
                @example varchar(8000)=NULL,
                @workfile sysname=NULL,
                @author sysname=NULL,
                @email sysname='(none)',
                @version sysname=NULL,
                @revision sysname='0',
                @datecreated smalldatetime=NULL,
                @datelastchanged smalldatetime=NULL
/*

Object: sp_usage
```

Description: Provides usage information for stored procedures and
descriptions of other types of objects

Usage: sp_usage @objectname='ObjectName', @desc='Description of object'
              [, @parameters='param1,param2...']
              [, @example='Example of usage']
              [, @workfile='File name of script']
              [, @author='Object author']
              [, @email='Author email']
              [, @version='Version number or info']
              [, @revision='Revision number or info']
              [, @datecreated='Date created']
              [, @datelastchanged='Date last changed']

Returns: (None)

$Workfile: sp_usage.sql $

$Author: Khen $. Email: khen@khen.com

$Revision: 7 $

Example: sp_usage @objectname='sp_who', @desc='Returns a list of currently
running jobs', @parameters=[@loginname]

Created: 1992-04-03. $Modtime: 1/04/01 8:38p $.

```
*/
AS
SET NOCOUNT ON
IF (@objectname+@desc IS NULL) GOTO Help

PRINT 'Object: '+@objectname
PRINT 'Description: '+@desc

IF (OBJECTPROPERTY(OBJECT_ID(@objectname),'IsProcedure')=1)
OR (OBJECTPROPERTY(OBJECT_ID(@objectname),'IsExtendedProc')=1)
OR (OBJECTPROPERTY(OBJECT_ID(@objectname),'IsReplProc')=1)
OR (LOWER(LEFT(@objectname,3))='sp_') BEGIN -- Special handling for system
procedures
  PRINT CHAR(13)+'Usage: '+@objectname+' '+@parameters
  PRINT CHAR(13)+'Returns: '+@returns
END
-- $NoKeywords: $ -- Prevents the keywords below from being expanded in VSS
```

```
IF (@workfile IS NOT NULL)
  PRINT CHAR(13)+'$Workfile: '+@workfile+' $'
IF (@author IS NOT NULL)
  PRINT CHAR(13)+'$Author: '+@author+' $. Email: '+@email
IF (@version IS NOT NULL)
  PRINT CHAR(13)+'$Revision: '+@version+'.'+@revision+' $'
IF (@example IS NOT NULL)
  PRINT CHAR(13)+'Example: '+@example
IF (@datecreated IS NOT NULL) BEGIN -- Crop time if it's midnight
  DECLARE @datefmt varchar(8000), @dc varchar(30), @lc varchar(30)
  SET @dc=CONVERT(varchar(30), @datecreated, 120)
  SET @lc=CONVERT(varchar(30), @datelastchanged, 120)
  PRINT CHAR(13)+'Created: '+CASE
DATEDIFF(ss,CONVERT(char(8),@datecreated,108),'00:00:00') WHEN 0 THEN
LEFT(@dc,10) ELSE @dc END
+'. $Modtime: '+CASE
DATEDIFF(ss,CONVERT(char(8),@datelastchanged,108),'00:00:00') WHEN 0 THEN
LEFT(@lc,10) ELSE @lc END+' $.'
END


RETURN 0


Help:
EXEC dbo.sp_usage @objectname='sp_usage',              -- Recursive call
        @desc='Provides usage information for stored procedures and
descriptions of other types of objects',
        @parameters='@objectname=''ObjectName'', @desc=''Description of
object''
                [, @parameters=''param1,param2...'']
                [, @example=''Example of usage'']
                [, @workfile=''File name of script'']
                [, @author=''Object author'']
                [, @email=''Author email'']
                [, @version=''Version number or info'']
                [, @revision=''Revision number or info'']
                [, @datecreated=''Date created'']
                [, @datelastchanged=''Date last changed'']',
        @example='sp_usage @objectname=''sp_who''',
        @desc=''Returns a list of currently running jobs'',
        @parameters=[@loginname]',
        @author='Ken Henderson',
        @workfile='sp_usage.sql',
        @email='khen@khen.com',
        @version='3', @revision='1',
```

```
                @datecreated='4/3/92', @datelastchanged='7/1/99'
RETURN -1

GO
EXEC dbo.sp_usage
```

By passing in the appropriate parameters, you can use sp_usage to report usage info for any procedure. Sp_usage even calls itself for that very purpose (that's why we receive the warning message: "Cannot add rows to sysdepends for the current stored procedure because it depends on the missing object 'sp_usage.' The stored procedure will still be created."). Because Transact-SQL doesn't support subroutines, sp_usage uses a GOTO label to place the help message at the end of the procedure. This approach allows code at the start of the procedure to check for invalid parameter values and to jump quickly to the usage routine if necessary.

Set the QUOTED_IDENTIFIER and ANSI_NULLS options before you execute CREATE PROCEDURE (in its own command batch) because they're reset to the values they had at the time the procedure was created when it's executed (their values are stored in the **status** column of the procedure's row in sysobjects). This change lasts only for the duration of the procedure; afterward, they're restored to whatever they were before you executed the procedure. Setting QUOTED_IDENTIFIER or ANSI_NULLS *inside* a stored procedure has no effect on the execution of the stored procedure. To see how this works, run the code in Listing 1–9 in Query Analyzer:

**Listing 1–9** SET ANSI_NULLS has no effect inside a stored procedure.

```
USE tempdb
GO
SET ANSI_NULLS ON
GO
CREATE PROC testn
AS
SET ANSI_NULLS OFF
DECLARE @var int
SET @var=NULL
SELECT * FROM Northwind..Customers WHERE @var=NULL
GO
EXEC testn
```

(Results abridged)

```
CustomerID CompanyName                                        ContactName
---------- -------------------------------------------- ----------------
(0 row(s) affected)
```

If ANSI_NULLS is actually off at the time of the SELECT, as the SET command inside the procedure specifies, the SELECT should return all the rows in the Northwind Customers table. As you can see, this is not what happens. Now change the SET ANSI_NULLS command that precedes the CREATE PROCEDURE to turn ANSI null handling OFF, and rerun the procedure. You should see all the rows in the Customers table listed.

Set environmental options (e.g., NOCOUNT, LOCK_TIMEOUT, and so on) that materially affect the procedure early on. It's a good practice to set them at the very start of the procedure so that they stand out to other developers.

Avoid broken ownership chains when dealing with stored procedures and the objects they reference. Try to ensure that the owner of a stored procedure and the owner of the objects it references are the same. The best way to do this is by specifying the dbo user as the owner of every object you create. Having multiple objects with the same name but different owners adds an unnecessary layer of indirection to the database that's almost always more trouble than it's worth. While perhaps useful during the development phase of a project, it's definitely something you should avoid on production servers.

When used within a stored procedure, certain commands require the objects they reference to be owner qualified (an object reference is said to be owner qualified when the object name is prefixed with the name of the owner and a period) if the procedure is to be executed by users other than the owner. These commands are

- CREATE TABLE
- ALTER TABLE
- DROP TABLE
- TRUNCATE TABLE
- CREATE INDEX
- DROP INDEX
- UPDATE STATISTICS
- All DBCC commands

Don't use the **sp_** prefix for anything but system procedures. Because of the confusion it can cause, avoid creating procedures in user databases with the **sp_** prefix. Also, don't create nonsystem procedures in the master database. If a procedure is not a system procedure, it's likely that you don't need to put it in the master database in the first place.

Include USE *dbname* at the top of creation scripts for procedures that must reside in a specific database. This ensures that they end up where they belong and alleviates having to remember to set the current database context before executing the script.

Keep each stored procedure as simple and modular as possible. Ideally, a stored procedure will accomplish a single task or a small group of closely related tasks.

As a rule, SET NOCOUNT ON should be the first statement in every stored procedure you create because it minimizes network traffic between SQL Server and client applications. Setting NOCOUNT on disables DONE_IN_ PROC messages—the messages SQL Server normally sends to the client indicating the number of rows affected by a T-SQL statement. Because these messages are very rarely used, eliminating them conserves network bandwidth without really giving up any functionality and can speed up applications considerably. Note that you can disable DONE_IN_PROC messages for the entire server via a trace flag (3640) and for a particular user session via the **sp_ configure 'user options'** command. (In rare circumstances, disabling DONE_IN_PROC messages can cause problems with some applications—for example, some older versions of Microsoft Access and certain ill-behaved OLEDB providers).

Create a procedure using the WITH ENCRYPTION option if you want to keep its source code from being viewable by users. Don't delete it from syscomments. Doing so will render the procedure inaccessible and you'll have to drop and recreate it.

## Altering Stored Procedures

Just as you create stored procedures using the CREATE PROCEDURE command, you alter them with ALTER PROCEDURE. The advantage of using ALTER PROCEDURE to change a stored procedure is that it preserves access permissions, whereas CREATE PROCEDURE doesn't. A key difference between them is that ALTER PROCEDURE requires the use of the same encryption and recompile options as the original CREATE PROCEDURE statement. If you omit or change them when you execute ALTER PROCE-DURE, they'll be omitted or changed permanently in the actual procedure definition.

A procedure can contain any valid Transact-SQL command except these: CREATE DEFAULT, CREATE FUNCTION, CREATE PROC, CREATE RULE, CREATE SCHEMA, CREATE TRIGGER, CREATE VIEW, SET SHOWPLAN_TEXT, and SET SHOWPLAN_ALL. These commands must reside in their own command batches, and, therefore, can't be part of a stored procedure. Procedures *can* create databases, tables, and indexes, but not other procedures, defaults, functions, rules, schemas, triggers, or views.

---

**TIP:** You can work around this limitation—the inability to construct most other kinds of objects from within a stored procedure—by constructing a T-SQL string and executing it via sp_executesql or the EXEC() function, as shown in Listing 1–10:

**Listing 1–10** You can create procedures, views, UDFs, and other objects from within stored procedures by using sp_executesql and EXEC().

---

```
CREATE PROC test AS
DECLARE @sql nvarchar(100)
SET @sql=N'create proc dbo.test2 as select ''1'''
EXEC dbo.sp_executesql @sql
EXEC dbo.test2
GO
EXEC dbo.test
```

(Results)

```
Cannot add rows to sysdepends for the current stored procedure because it
depends on the missing object 'dbo.test2'. The stored procedure will still
be created.

----
1
```

---

The warning message is due to the fact that the test2 procedure doesn't exist when the test procedure is first created. You can safely ignore it.

## Executing Stored Procedures

Although executing a stored procedure can be as easy as listing it on a line by itself in a T-SQL command batch, you should make a habit of prefixing all stored procedure calls with the EXEC keyword, like this:

```
EXEC dbo.sp_who
```

Stored procedure calls without EXEC must be the first command in a command batch. Even if this were the case initially, inserting additional lines before the procedure call at some point in the future would break your code.

You should also be sure to owner-qualify procedure calls ("dbo" in the previous example). Omitting the owner from a procedure call causes SQL Server to momentarily place a compile lock on the procedure because it cannot locate it immediately in the procedure cache. This lock is released once the procedure-sans-owner is located in the cache, but can still cause problems in high-throughput environments. Owner-qualifying objects is simply a good habit to get into. It's one of those things you can do to save yourself problems down the road.

## INSERT and EXEC

The INSERT command supports calling a stored procedure to supply rows for insertion into a table. Listing 1–11 shows how:

**Listing 1–11** You can use INSERT...EXEC to save a stored procedure's output in a table.

```
CREATE TABLE #locks (spid int, dbid int, objid int, objectname sysname
NULL, indid int, type char(4), resource char(15), mode char(10), status
char(6))
INSERT #locks (spid, dbid, objid, indid, type, resource, mode, status)
EXEC dbo.sp_lock
SELECT * FROM #locks
DROP TABLE #locks
```

This is a handy way of trapping the output of a stored procedure in a table so that you can manipulate it or retain it for later use. Prior to the advent of cursor OUTPUT parameters, this was the only way to perform further work on a stored procedure's result set within Transact-SQL.

Note that INSERT...EXEC works with extended procedures that return result sets as well. A simple example is shown in Listing 1–12:

**Listing 1–12** INSERT...EXEC works with extended procedures as well.

```
CREATE TABLE #cmd_result (output varchar(8000))
INSERT #cmd_result
EXEC master.dbo.xp_cmdshell 'TYPE C:\BOOT.INI'
SELECT * FROM #cmd_result
DROP TABLE #cmd_result
```

## Execution Plan Compilation and Execution

When you execute a stored procedure for the first time, it's compiled into an execution plan. This plan is not compiled into machine code or even byte codes, but is pseudo-compiled in order to speed execution. By "pseudo-compiled" I mean that object references are resolved, join strategies and indexing selections are made, and an efficient plan for executing the work that the procedure is to carry out is rendered by the SQL Server query optimizer. The optimizer compares a number of potential plans for performing the procedure's work and selects the one it thinks will cost the least in terms of total execution time. It bases this decision on a number of factors, including the estimated I/O cost associated with each plan, the CPU cost, the memory requirements, and so on.

Once an execution plan has been created, it's stored in the procedure cache for future execution. This cache grows and contracts as necessary to store execution plans for the stored procedures and ad hoc queries executed by the server. SQL Server balances the need to supply adequate memory to the procedure cache with the server's other memory requirements, such as providing adequate resources for the data cache. Obviously, memory taken up by cached execution plans can't be used to cache data, so the server manages this carefully. Caching execution plans in memory saves the optimizer from having to construct a new plan each time a procedure is executed, and can improve performance dramatically.

## Monitoring Execution

You can inspect the manner in which SQL Server compiles, stores, and runs execution plans using SQL Server's Profiler utility. To observe what happens when you create and run a procedure, follow these steps:

1. Start the Query Analyzer utility, connect to your server, and load the stored procedure script from Listing 1–1 (you can find the complete script on the CD accompanying this book).
2. Start the Profiler utility. You should find it in your Microsoft SQL Server **Start|Programs** folder.
3. Click the New Trace button and connect to your server.
4. On the Events page, remove every event class from the list on the right except the SQL:BatchStarting event class in the TSQL group.
5. Add every event class in the Stored Procedures group on the left except the SP:StmtStarting and SP:StmtComplete events. (A trace template file that includes these events, BasicTrace.TDF, is on the CD accompanying this book).

6. Click the Run button at the bottom of the Trace Properties dialog.
7. Return to Query Analyzer and run the script.
8. Return to Profiler and click the Stop Selected Trace button. You should see something like the following in the events window:

(Results abridged)

```
EventClass            TextData
--------------------  -----------------------------------
SQL:BatchStarting     Use Northwind
SQL:BatchStarting     IF OBJECT_ID('dbo.ListCustomersByCi
SQL:BatchStarting     CREATE PROCEDURE dbo.ListCustomersB
SQL:BatchStarting     EXEC dbo.ListCustomersByCity
SP:CacheMiss
SP:CacheMiss
SP:CacheInsert
SP:Starting           EXEC dbo.ListCustomersByCity
SP:Completed          EXEC dbo.ListCustomersByCity
```

The trace output begins with four separate T-SQL command batches. Because the commands are separated by the GO batch terminator, each executes as a separate T-SQL batch. The last batch is the call to the stored procedure via the EXEC command. This call is responsible for the events that follow.

Note the SP:CacheInsert event immediately before the SP:Starting event. In conjunction with the SP:CacheMiss events, this tells us that ListCustomersByCity wasn't in the procedure cache when it was called, so an execution plan was compiled for it and inserted into the cache. The final two events in the trace, the SP:Starting and SP:Completed events, indicate that once the execution plan for the stored procedure was inserted into the cache, it was executed.

To see what happens when a procedure is executed directly from the cache, follow these steps:

1. Click the Start Selected Trace button to restart the trace.
2. Return to Query Analyzer, highlight the EXEC line in the query, and run it by itself.
3. Return to Profiler and stop the trace. You should see something like this:

(Results abridged)

```
EventClass            TextData
--------------------  ----------------------------
SQL:BatchStarting     EXEC dbo.ListCustomersByCity
SP:ExecContextHit
```

```
SP:Starting          EXEC dbo.ListCustomersByCity
SP:Completed         EXEC dbo.ListCustomersByCity
```

The ExecContextHit event tells us that an executable version of the stored procedure was found in the cache. Note the absence of the SP:CacheMiss and CacheInsert events. This tells us that the execution plan that was created and inserted into the cache when we ran the stored procedure the first time is reused when we run it a second time.

### Execution Plans

When SQL Server runs an execution plan, each step of the plan is processed and dispatched to an appropriate internal manager process (e.g., the T-SQL manager, the DDL and DML managers, the transaction manager, the stored procedure manager, the utility manager, the ODSOLE manager, and so on). SQL Server calls these managers repeatedly until it has processed all the steps in the execution plan.

Execution plans are never stored permanently. The only portion of a stored procedure that is stored on disk is its source code (in syscomments). Because they're cached in memory, cycling the server disposes of all current execution plans (as does the DBCC FREEPROCCACHE() command).

SQL Server automatically recreates a stored procedure's execution plan when

- The procedure's execution environment differs significantly from its creation environment (see Environmental Issues discussed later in the chapter for more information)
- The sysobjects **schema_ver** column changes for any of the objects the procedure references. The **schema_ver** and **base_schema_ver** columns are updated any time the schema information for a table changes. This includes column additions and deletions, data type changes, constraint additions and deletions, as well as rule and default bindings.
- The statistics have changed for any of the objects the procedure references. This means that the auto-update statistics and auto-create statistics events can cause stored procedure recompilation.
- An index is dropped that was referenced by the procedure's execution plan
- A copy of the procedure's execution plan is not available in the cache. Execution plans are removed from the cache to make room for new plans using a Least Recently Used (LRU) algorithm.

■ Certain other specialized circumstances occur, such as when a temporary table is modified a fixed number of times, when DDL and DML statements are interleaved, and when the sp_configure system procedure is called (sp_configure calls DBCC FREEPROCCACHE)

During the earlier discussion on creating procedures and SQL Server's limitation regarding having multiple CREATE TABLE statements for a temporary table in a single procedure, I mentioned that the ad hoc code approach (Listing 1–4) forces the procedure's execution plan to be recompiled while it's running. To see this for yourself, restart the trace we've been using and rerun the stored procedure from that query. You should see something like the following in Profiler:

```
EventClass              TextData
--------------------    -------------------------------------
SQL:BatchStarting       exec testp 2
SQL:StmtStarting        exec testp 2
SP:ExecContextHit
SP:Starting             exec testp 2
SQL:StmtStarting        -- testp CREATE TABLE #temp (k1 int identity)
SQL:StmtStarting        -- testp IF @var=1
SQL:StmtStarting        -- testp ALTER TABLE #temp ADD c1 varchar(2)
SP:Recompile
SP:CacheMiss
SP:CacheMiss
SP:CacheInsert
SQL:StmtStarting        -- testp ALTER TABLE #temp ADD c1 varchar(2)
SQL:StmtStarting        -- testp INSERT #temp DEFAULT VALUES
SP:Recompile
SP:CacheMiss
SP:CacheMiss
SP:CacheInsert
SQL:StmtStarting        -- testp INSERT #temp DEFAULT VALUES
SQL:StmtStarting        -- testp EXEC('SELECT c1 FROM #temp')
SQL:StmtStarting        -- Dynamic SQL SELECT c1 FROM #temp
SP:Completed            exec testp 2
```

Notice that not one, but two SP:Recompile events occur during the execution of the procedure: one when the ALTER TABLE is encountered (this statement refers to the temporary table created by the procedure, forcing a recompile) and another when the INSERT is encountered (this statement accesses the newly modified temporary table schema, again forcing a recompile). Assuming you've captured the SQL:StmtStarting or SP:StmtStarting event class in the trace, you'll typically see an SP:Recompile event enveloped in two identical StmtStarting events: The first one indicates that the statement began to be executed, but was put on hold so that the recompile could happen; the second indicates that the statement is actually executing now that the recompile has completed. This starting/stopping activity can have a serious impact on the time it takes the procedure to complete. It's worth pointing out again: Creating a temporary table within a procedure that you then process in other ways will cause the procedure's execution plan to be recompiled (one way to avoid temporary tables is to use local **table** variables instead). Moreover, interleaving DDL and DML within a procedure can also cause the plan to be recompiled. Because it can cause performance and concurrency problems, you want to avoid causing execution plan recompilation when you can.

Another interesting fact that's revealed by the trace is that the execution plan for the dynamic T-SQL string the procedure creates and executes is not cached. Note that there's no CacheMiss, CacheInsert, CacheHit, or ExecContextHit event corresponding to the dynamic SQL query near the end of the trace log. Let's see what happens when we change the EXEC() call to use sp_executesql instead (Listing 1–13):

**Listing 1–13** You can use sp_executesql rather than EXEC() to execute dynamic T-SQL.

```
USE tempdb
GO
drop proc testp
GO
CREATE PROC testp @var int
AS
CREATE TABLE #temp (k1 int identity)
IF @var=1
  ALTER TABLE #temp ADD c1 int
ELSE
  ALTER TABLE #temp ADD c1 varchar(2)
INSERT #temp DEFAULT VALUES
EXEC dbo.sp_executesql N'SELECT c1 FROM #temp'
GO
exec testp 2
```

When you execute the procedure, you should see trace output like this:

```
EventClass         TextData
-----------------  ------------------------------------------------------------
SQL:BatchStarting  exec testp 2

SQL:StmtStarting   exec testp 2

SP:CacheMiss
SP:CacheMiss
SP:CacheInsert
SP:Starting        exec testp 2

SQL:StmtStarting   -- testp CREATE TABLE #temp (k1 int identity)

SQL:StmtStarting   -- testp IF @var=1

SQL:StmtStarting   -- testp ALTER TABLE #temp ADD c1 varchar(2)

SP:Recompile
SP:CacheMiss
SP:CacheMiss
SP:CacheInsert

SQL:StmtStarting   -- testp ALTER TABLE #temp ADD c1 varchar(2)

SQL:StmtStarting   -- testp INSERT #temp DEFAULT VALUES

SP:Recompile
SP:CacheMiss
SP:CacheMiss
SP:CacheInsert
SQL:StmtStarting   -- testp INSERT #temp DEFAULT VALUES
SQL:StmtStarting   -- testp EXEC dbo.sp_executesql N'SELECT c1 FROM #temp'
SP:CacheMiss
SP:CacheMiss
SP:CacheInsert      SELECT c1 FROM #temp
SQL:StmtStarting   SELECT c1 FROM #temp
SP:Completed       exec testp 2
```

Note the SP:CacheInsert event that occurs for the dynamic SELECT statement now that we are calling it via sp_executesql. This indicates that the execution plan for the SELECT statement has been inserted into the cache so that it can be reused later. Whether it actually *will* be reused is another matter, but at least the possibility exists that it can be. If you run the procedure a second time, you'll see that the call to sp_executesql itself generates an ExecContextHit event rather than the CacheMiss event it causes the first time around. By using sp_executesql, we've been able to use the procedure cache to make the procedure run more efficiently. The moral of the story is this: sp_executesql is generally a more efficient (and therefore faster) method of executing dynamic SQL than EXEC().

### Forcing Plan Recompilation

You can also force a procedure's execution plan to be recompiled by

- Creating the procedure using the WITH RECOMPILE option
- Executing the procedure using the WITH RECOMPILE option
- Using the sp_recompile system procedure to "touch" any of the tables the procedure references (sp_recompile merely updates sysobjects' schema_ver column)

Once an execution plan is in the cache, subsequent calls to the procedure can reuse the plan without having to rebuild it. This eliminates the query tree construction and plan creation that normally occur when you execute a stored procedure for the first time, and is the chief performance advantage stored procedures have over ad hoc T-SQL batches.

### Automatically Loading Execution Plans

A clever way of loading execution plans into the cache at system start-up is to execute them via an autostart procedure. Autostart procedures must reside in the master database, but they can call procedures that reside in other databases, forcing those procedures' plans into memory as well. If you're going to take this approach, creating a single autostart procedure that calls the procedures you want to load into the cache rather than autostarting each procedure individually will conserve execution threads (each autostart routine gets its own thread).

---

**TIP:** To prevent autostart procedures from running when SQL Server first loads, start SQL Server with the 4022 trace flag. Adding –T4022 to the SQL Server command line tells the server not to run autostart procedures, but does not change their autostart status. The next time you start the server without the 4022 trace flag, they will again execute.

---

## Executing a Stored Procedure via Remote Procedure Calls (RPC)

As an aside, one thing I should mention here is that the call to a stored procedure need not be a T-SQL batch. The ADO/OLEDB, ODBC, and DB-Library APIs all support executing stored procedures via RPC. Because it bypasses much of the usual statement and parameter processing, calling stored procedures via the RPC interface is more efficient than calling them via T-SQL batches. In particular, the RPC API facilitates the repetitive invocation of a routine with different sets of parameters. You can check this out in Query Analyzer (which uses the ODBC API) by changing the EXEC line in the script to the line in Listing 1–14:

**Listing 1–14** Calling ListCustomersByCity via RPC

```
{CALL dbo.ListCustomersByCity}
```

This line uses the ODBC "call escape sequence" to invoke the routine using an RPC call. Restart the trace in Profiler, then execute the CALL command in Query Analyzer. You should see something like the following in the Profiler events window:
(Results abridged)

```
EventClass          TextData
------------------  --------------------------------
RPC:Starting        exec dbo.ListCustomersByCity
SP:ExecContextHit
SP:Starting         exec dbo.ListCustomersByCity
SP:Completed        exec dbo.ListCustomersByCity
RPC:Completed       exec dbo.ListCustomersByCity
```

Note the absence of the BatchStarting event. Instead, we have an RPC: Starting event followed, ultimately, by an RPC:Completed event. This tells us that the RPC API is being used to invoke the procedure. The procedure cache is unaffected by the switch to the RPC API; we still execute the procedure using the plan in the procedure cache.

## Temporary Procedures

You create temporary procedures the same way you create temporary tables— a prefix of a single pound sign (#) creates a local temporary procedure that is visible only to the current connection, whereas a double pound sign prefix (**##**) creates a global temporary procedure all connections can access.

Temporary procedures are useful when you want to combine the advantages of using stored procedures such as execution plan reuse and improved error handling with the advantages of ad hoc code. Because you can build and execute a temporary stored procedure at run-time, you get the best of both worlds. For the most part, sp_executesql can alleviate the necessity for temporary procedures, but they're still nice to have around when your needs exceed the capabilities of sp_executesql.

## System Procedures

System procedures reside in the master database and are prefixed with **sp_**. You can execute a system procedure from any database. When executed from a database other than the master, a system procedure runs within the context of that database. So, for example, if the procedure references the sysobjects table (which exists in every database) it will access the one in the database that was current when it was executed, not the one in the master database, even though the procedure actually resides in the master. Listing 1–15 is a simple system procedure that lists the names and creation dates of the objects that match a mask:

**Listing 1–15** A user-created system procedure that lists objects and their creation dates.

```
USE master
IF OBJECT_ID('dbo.sp_created') IS NOT NULL
  DROP PROC dbo.sp_created
GO
CREATE PROC dbo.sp_created @objname sysname=NULL
/*
Object: sp_created
Description: Lists the creation date(s) for the specified object(s)

Usage: sp_created @objname="Object name or mask you want to display"

Returns: (None)

$Author: Khen $. Email: khen@khen.com

$Revision: 2 $

Example: sp_created @objname="myprocs%"
```

```
Created: 1999-08-01. $Modtime: 1/04/01 12:16a $.
*/
AS
IF (@objname IS NULL) or (@objname='/?') GOTO Help
SELECT name, crdate FROM sysobjects
WHERE name like @objname
RETURN 0

Help:
EXEC dbo.sp_usage @objectname='sp_created',
        @desc='Lists the creation date(s) for the specified object(s)',
        @parameters='@objname="Object name or mask you want to display"',
        @example='sp_created @objname="myprocs%"',
        @author='Ken Henderson',
        @email='khen@khen.com',
        @version='1', @revision='0',
        @datecreated='19990801', @datelastchanged='19990815'
RETURN -1
GO
USE Northwind
EXEC dbo.sp_created 'Order%'
```

(Results)

```
name                          crdate
----------------------        ------------------------
Order Details                 2000-08-06 01:34:08.470
Order Details Extended        2000-08-06 01:34:10.873
Order Subtotals               2000-08-06 01:34:11.093
Orders                        2000-08-06 01:34:06.610
Orders Qry                    2000-08-06 01:34:09.780
```

As I've said, any system procedure, whether it's one you've created or one that ships with SQL Server, will use the current database context when executed. Listing 1–16 presents an example that uses one of SQL Server's own system stored procedures. It can be executed from any database to retrieve info on that database:

**Listing 1–16** System procedures assume the current database context when executed.

```
USE Northwind
EXEC dbo.sp_spaceused
```

```
database_name                         database_size       unallocated space
----------------------------------    -----------------   -----------------
Northwind                             163.63 MB           25.92 MB

reserved             data             index_size          unused
-----------------    -------------    -----------------   -----------------
4944 KB              2592 KB          1808 KB             544 KB
```

Sp_spaceused queries several of SQL Server's system tables to create the report it returns. Because it's a system procedure, it automatically reflects the context of the current database even though it resides in the master database.

Note that, regardless of the current database, you can force a system procedure to run in the context of a given database by qualifying its name with the database name (as though it resided in that database) when you invoke it. Listing 1–17 illustrates:

**Listing 1–17** You can force a system procedure to assume a specific database context.

```
USE pubs
EXEC Northwind..sp_spaceused
database_name                         database_size       unallocated space
----------------------------------    -----------------   -----------------
Northwind                             163.63 MB           25.92 MB

reserved             data             index_size          unused
-----------------    -------------    -----------------   -----------------
4944 KB              2592 KB          1808 KB             544 KB
```

In this example, even though sp_spaceused resides in the master and the current database is pubs, sp_spaceused reports space utilization info for the Northwind database because we qualified its name with Northwind when we invoked it. SQL Server correctly locates sp_spaceused in the master and executes it within the context of the Northwind database.

## System Objects versus System Procedures

User-created system procedures are listed as user objects rather than system objects in Enterprise Manager. Why? Because the system bit of a procedure's status column in sysobjects (0xC0000000) isn't set by default. You can call the undocumented procedure sp_MS_marksystemobject to set this bit. The lone parameter taken by the procedure is the name of the object with the system bit you wish to set. Many undocumented functions and DBCC command verbs do not work properly unless called from a system object (See Chapter 22 for more information). Check the IsMSShipped property of the OBJECTPROPERTY() function to determine whether an object's system bit has been set. Listing 1–18 is a code fragment that demonstrates this function:

**Listing 1–18** System procedures and system objects are two different things.

```
USE master
GO
IF OBJECT_ID('dbo.sp_test') IS NOT NULL
  DROP PROC dbo.sp_test
GO
CREATE PROC dbo.sp_test AS
select 1
GO
SELECT OBJECTPROPERTY(OBJECT_ID('dbo.sp_test'),'IsMSShipped') AS 'System
Object?', status, status & 0xC0000000
FROM sysobjects WHERE NAME = 'sp_test'
GO
EXEC sp_MS_marksystemobject 'sp_test'
GO
SELECT OBJECTPROPERTY(OBJECT_ID('dbo.sp_test'),'IsMSShipped') AS 'System
Object?', status, status & 0xC0000000
FROM sysobjects WHERE NAME = 'sp_test'
```

(Results)

```
System Object? status
-------------- ----------- -----------
0              1610612737  1073741824

(1 row(s) affected)

System Object? status
-------------- ----------- -----------
1              -536870911  -1073741824
(1 row(s) affected)
```

As I've said, there are a variety of useful features that do not work correctly outside system procedures. For example, a stored procedure can't manipulate full text indexes via DBCC CALLFULLTEXT() unless its system bit is set. Regardless of whether you actually end up using this functionality, it's instructive to at least know how it works.

# Extended Stored Procedures

Extended procedures are routines residing in DLLs that function similarly to regular stored procedures. They receive parameters and return results via SQL Server's Open Data Services API and are usually written in C or C++. They must reside in the master database and run within the SQL Server process space.

Although the two are similar, calls to extended procedures work a bit differently than calls to system procedures. Extended procedures aren't automatically located in the master database and they don't assume the context of the current database when executed. To execute an extended procedure from a database other than the master, you have to fully qualify the reference (e.g., EXEC master.dbo.xp_cmdshell 'dir').

A technique for working around these differences is to "wrap" an extended procedure in a system stored procedure. This allows it to be called from any database without requiring the **master** prefix. This technique is used with a number of SQL Server's own extended procedures. Many of them are wrapped in system stored procedures that have no purpose other than to make the extended procedures they call a bit handier. Listing 1–19 is an example of a system procedure wrapping a call to an extended procedure:

**Listing 1–19** System procedures are commonly used to "wrap" extended procedures.

```
USE master
IF (OBJECT_ID('dbo.sp_hexstring') IS NOT NULL)
  DROP PROC dbo.sp_hexstring
GO
CREATE PROC dbo.sp_hexstring @int varchar(10)=NULL, @hexstring
varchar(30)=NULL OUT
/*
Object: sp_hexstring
Description: Return an integer as a hexadecimal string
```

```
Usage: sp_hexstring @int=Integer to convert, @hexstring=OUTPUT parm to
receive hex string

Returns: (None)

$Author: Khen $. Email: khen@khen.com

$Revision: 1 $

Example: sp_hexstring "23", @myhex OUT
Created: 1999-08-02. $Modtime: 1/4/01 8:23p $.
*/
AS
IF (@int IS NULL) OR (@int = '/?') GOTO Help
DECLARE @i int, @vb varbinary(30)
SELECT @i=CAST(@int as int), @vb=CAST(@i as varbinary)
EXEC master.dbo.xp_varbintohexstr @vb, @hexstring OUT
RETURN 0
Help:
EXEC sp_usage @objectname='sp_hexstring',
        @desc='Return an integer as a hexadecimal string',
        @parameters='@int=Integer to convert, @hexstring=OUTPUT parm to
receive hex string',
        @example='sp_hexstring "23", @myhex OUT',
        @author='Ken Henderson',
        @email='khen@khen.com',
        @version='1', @revision='0',
        @datecreated='19990802', @datelastchanged='19990815'
RETURN -1

GO
DECLARE @hex varchar(30)
EXEC sp_hexstring 10, @hex OUT
SELECT @hex
```

(Results)
```
-----------------------------
0x0000000A
```

The whole purpose of sp_hexstring is to clean up the parameters to be passed to the extended procedure xp_varbintohexstr before calling it. Because sp_hexstring is a system procedure, it can be called from any database without requiring the caller to reference xp_varbintohexstr directly.

### Internal Procedures

A number of system-supplied stored procedures are neither true system procedures nor extended procedures—they're implemented internally by SQL Server. Examples of these include sp_executesql, sp_xml_preparedocument, most of the sp_cursor routines, sp_reset_connection, and so forth. These routines have stubs in master..sysobjects, and are listed as extended procedures, but they are actually implemented internally by the server, not within an external ODS-based DLL. This is important to know because you cannot drop these or replace them with updated DLLs. They can be replaced only by patching SQL Server itself, which normally only happens when you apply a service pack.

## Environmental Issues

A number of SQL Server environmental settings affect the behavior of stored procedures. You specify most of these via SET commands. They control the way that stored procedures handle nulls, quotes, cursors, BLOB fields, and so forth. Two of these—QUOTED_IDENTIFIER and ANSI_NULLS—are stored permanently in each procedure's status field in sysobjects, as I mentioned earlier in the chapter. That is, when you create a stored procedure, the status of these two settings is stored along with it. QUOTED_IDENTIFIER controls whether strings within double quotes are interpreted as object identifiers (e.g., table or column references), and ANSI_NULLS controls whether non-ANSI equality comparisons with NULLs are allowed.

SET QUOTED_IDENTIFIER is normally used with a stored procedure to allow the procedure to reference objects with names that contain reserved words, spaces, or other illegal characters. An example is provided in Listing 1–20.

**Listing 1–20** SET QUOTED_IDENTIFIER allows references to objects with names with embedded spaces.

```
USE Northwind
SET QUOTED_IDENTIFIER ON
GO
```

```
IF OBJECT_ID('dbo.listorders') IS NOT NULL
  DROP PROC dbo.listorders
GO
CREATE PROC dbo.listorders
AS
SELECT * FROM "Order Details"
GO
SET QUOTED_IDENTIFIER OFF
GO
EXEC dbo.listorders
```

(Results abridged)

| OrderID | ProductID | UnitPrice | Quantity | Discount |
|---------|-----------|-----------|----------|----------|
| 10248   | 11        | 14.0000   | 12       | 0.0      |
| 10248   | 42        | 9.8000    | 10       | 0.0      |
| 10248   | 72        | 34.8000   | 5        | 0.0      |
| 10249   | 14        | 18.6000   | 9        | 0.0      |
| 10249   | 51        | 42.4000   | 40       | 0.0      |
| 10250   | 41        | 7.7000    | 10       | 0.0      |

"Order Details" contains both a reserved word and a space, so it can't be referenced without special handling. In this case, we turned on quoted identifier support and enclosed the table name in double quotes, but a better way would be to use SQL Server's square brackets ( [ ] ) to enclose the name (e.g., [Order Details]) because this alleviates the need to change any settings. Note that bracketed object names are not supported by the ANSI/ISO SQL standard.

The ANSI_NULLS setting is even more useful to stored procedures. It controls whether non-ANSI equality comparisons with NULLs work properly. This is particularly important with stored procedure parameters that can receive NULL values. See Listing 1–21 for an example:

**Listing 1–21** SET ANSI_NULLS allows comparisons between variables or columns and NULL values to work as you would expect.

```
USE Northwind
IF (OBJECT_ID('dbo.ListRegionalEmployees') IS NOT NULL)
  DROP PROC dbo.ListRegionalEmployees
GO
SET ANSI_NULLS OFF
GO
CREATE PROC dbo.ListRegionalEmployees @region nvarchar(30)
```

```
AS
SELECT EmployeeID, LastName, FirstName, Region FROM employees
WHERE Region=@region

GO
SET ANSI_NULLS ON
GO

EXEC dbo.ListRegionalEmployees NULL
```

(Results)

| EmployeeID | LastName  | FirstName | Region |
|------------|-----------|-----------|--------|
| 5          | Buchanan  | Steven    | NULL   |
| 6          | Suyama    | Michael   | NULL   |
| 7          | King      | Robert    | NULL   |
| 9          | Dodsworth | Anne      | NULL   |

Thanks to SET ANSI_NULLS, the procedure can successfully compare a NULL @region with the **region** column in the Northwind Employees table. The query returns the rows that have NULL region values because, contrary to the ANSI SQL specification, SQL Server checks the NULL variable against the column for equality. The handiness of this becomes more evident when a procedure defines a large number of "NULL-able" parameters. Without the ability to test NULL values for equality in a manner identical to non-NULL values, each NULL-able parameter would require special handling (perhaps using the IS NULL predicate), very likely multiplying the amount of code necessary to process query parameters.

Because SQL Server stores the QUOTED_IDENTIFIER and ANSI_NULLS settings with each stored procedure, you can trust them to have the values you require when a procedure runs. The server restores them to the values they had when the procedure was created each time the procedure runs, then resets them afterward. Here's an example:

```
SET ANSI_NULLS ON
EXEC dbo.ListRegionalEmployees NULL
```

The stored procedure still executes as though ANSI_NULLS is set to OFF. Note that you can check the saved status of a procedure's QUOTED_IDENTIFIER and ANSI_NULLS settings via the OBJECTPROPERTY() function. An example is provided in Listing 1–22:

**Listing 1–22** You can check the ANSI_NULLS and QUOTED_IDENTIFIER status for a procedure using the OBJECTPROPERTY function.

```
USE Northwind
SELECT OBJECTPROPERTY(OBJECT_ID('dbo.ListRegionalEmployees'),
'ExecIsAnsiNullsOn') AS 'AnsiNulls'
```

(Results)

```
AnsiNulls
-----------
0
```

A number of other environmental commands affect how stored procedures execute. SET XACT_ABORT, SET CURSOR_CLOSE_ON_COMMIT, SET TEXTSIZE, SET IMPLICIT_TRANSACTIONS, and numerous others help determine how a stored procedure behaves when executed. If you have a stored procedure that requires a SET command to have a particular value to run properly, set it to that value as early as possible in the procedure and document why it's necessary via comments.

# Parameters

Parameters can be passed to stored procedures by name or by position. An example of each method is presented in Listing 1–23:

**Listing 1–23** You can pass procedure parameters by position or by name.

```
EXEC dbo.sp_who 'sa'
EXEC dbo.sp_who @loginame='sa'
```

Obviously, the advantage of referencing parameters by name is that you can specify them out of order.

You can force a parameter for which a default value has been defined to use that default by omitting it altogether or by passing it the DEFAULT keyword, as in Listing 1–24:

**Listing 1–24** Passing DEFAULT for a parameter causes it to assume its default value.

```
EXEC dbo.sp_who @loginame=DEFAULT
```

You can specify NULL to supply individual parameters with NULL values. This is sometimes handy for procedures that expose special features when parameters are omitted or set to NULL. An example is presented in Listing 1–25:

**Listing 1–25** You can pass NULL to a parameter.

```
EXEC dbo.sp_who @loginame=NULL
```

(Results abridged)

| spid | ecid | status | loginame |
| --- | --- | --- | --- |
| 1 | 0 | background | sa |
| 2 | 0 | background | sa |
| 3 | 0 | sleeping | sa |
| 4 | 0 | background | sa |
| 5 | 0 | background | sa |
| 6 | 0 | sleeping | sa |
| 7 | 0 | background | sa |
| 8 | 0 | background | sa |
| 9 | 0 | background | sa |
| 10 | 0 | background | sa |
| 11 | 0 | background | sa |
| 12 | 0 | background | sa |
| 13 | 0 | background | sa |
| 51 | 0 | sleeping | SKREWYTHIN\khen |
| 52 | 0 | sleeping | SKREWYTHIN\khen |
| 53 | 0 | sleeping | SKREWYTHIN\khen |

Here, sp_who returns a list of all active connections because its @loginame parameter is passed NULL. When a valid login name is specified, sp_who returns only those connections established by the specified login name. You'd see the same result if @loginame had not been supplied at all—all connections would be listed.

## Return Status Codes

Procedures return status codes via the RETURN command. For an example, see Listing 1–26:

**Listing 1–26** Use RETURN to render stored procedure status codes.

```
RETURN(-100)
-- and
RETURN -100
```

These return a status code of –100 to the caller of the procedure (the parameters are optional). A return code of 0 indicates success, values –1 through –14 indicate different types of failures (see the Books Online for descriptions of these), and values –15 through –99 are reserved for future use.

You can access a procedure's return code by assigning it to an integer variable, as in Listing 1–27:

**Listing 1–27** You can save a procedure's return status code to an integer variable.

```
DECLARE @res int
EXEC @res=dbo.sp_who
SELECT @res
```

## Output Parameters

In addition to the return status code that every stored procedure supports, you can use output parameters to return other types of values from a procedure. These parameters can be integers, character strings, dates, and even cursors. An example is provided in Listing 1–28:

**Listing 1–28** Cursor output parameters are handy for returning result sets.

```
USE pubs
IF OBJECT_ID('dbo.listsales') IS NOT NULL
  DROP PROC dbo.listsales
GO
CREATE PROC dbo.listsales @bestseller tid OUT, @topsales int OUT,
                    @salescursor cursor varying OUT
AS
SELECT @bestseller=bestseller, @topsales=totalsales
FROM (
      SELECT TOP 1 title_id AS bestseller, SUM(qty) AS totalsales
      FROM sales
      GROUP BY title_id
```

```
        ORDER BY 2 DESC) bestsellers

DECLARE s CURSOR
LOCAL
FOR SELECT * FROM sales

OPEN s

SET @salescursor=s
RETURN(0)
GO

DECLARE @topsales int, @bestseller tid, @salescursor cursor
EXEC dbo.listsales @bestseller OUT, @topsales OUT, @salescursor OUT
SELECT @bestseller, @topsales
FETCH @salescursor
CLOSE @salescursor
DEALLOCATE @salescursor
```

(Results abridged)

```
------ -----------
PS2091 108

stor_id ord_num   ord_date   qty  payterms  title_id
------- --------- ---------- ---- --------- --------
6380    6871      1994-09-14 5    Net 60    BU1032
```

Using a cursor output parameter is a good alternative for returning a result set to a caller. By using a cursor output parameter rather than a traditional result set, you give the caller control over how and when to process the result set. The caller can also determine various details about the cursor through system function calls before actually processing the result.

Output parameters are identified with the OUTPUT keyword (you can abbreviate this as "OUT"). Note the use of the OUT keyword in the procedure definition as well as in the EXEC parameter list. Output parameters must be identified in a procedure's parameter list as well as when the procedure is called.

The VARYING keyword is required for cursor parameters and indicates that the return value is nonscalar—that is, it can return more than one value. Cursor parameters can be output parameters only, so the OUT keyword is also required.

## Listing Procedure Parameters

You can list a procedure's parameters (which include its return status code, considered parameter 0) by querying the INFORMATION_SCHEMA.PARAMETERS view (Listing 1–29).

**Listing 1–29** INFORMATION_SCHEMA.PARAMETERS returns stored procedure parameter info.

```
USE Northwind
SELECT PARAMETER_MODE, PARAMETER_NAME, DATA_TYPE
FROM INFORMATION_SCHEMA.PARAMETERS
WHERE SPECIFIC_NAME='Employee Sales by Country'
```

(Results abridged)

```
PARAMETER_MODE  PARAMETER_NAME    DATA_TYPE
--------------  ----------------  ----------
IN              @Beginning_Date   datetime
IN              @Ending_Date      datetime
```

## General Parameter Notes

In addition to what I've already said about parameters, here are a few more tips:

- Check stored procedure parameters for invalid values early on.
- Human-friendly names allow parameters to be passed by name more easily.
- It's a good idea to provide default values for parameters when you can. This makes a procedure easier to use. A parameter default can consist of a constant or the NULL value.
- Because parameter names are local to stored procedures, you can use the same name in multiple procedures. If you have ten procedures that each take a user name parameter, name the parameter @UserName in all ten of them—for simplicity's sake and for general consistency in your code.
- Procedure parameter information is stored in the syscolumns system table.
- A stored procedure can receive as many as 1,024 parameters. If you have a procedure that you think needs more parameters than 1,024, you should probably consider redesigning it.
- The number and size of stored procedure local variables is limited only by the amount of memory available to SQL Server.

**Table 1–1** Stored Procedure-Related Functions

| Function | Returns |
|----------|---------|
| @@FETCH_STATUS | The status of the last FETCH operation |
| @@NESTLEVEL | The current procedure nesting level |
| @@OPTIONS | A bitmap of the currently specified user options |
| @@PROCID | The object ID of the current procedure |
| @@SPID | The process ID of the current process |
| @@TRANCOUNT | The current transaction nesting level |

## Automatic Variables, a.k.a. System Functions

By their very nature, automatic variables, also known as *system functions*, are usually the province of stored procedures. This makes most of them germane in some way to a discussion about stored procedures. Several, in fact, are used almost exclusively in stored procedures. Table 1–1 summarizes them.

# Flow Control Language

Certain Transact-SQL commands affect the order in which statements are executed in a stored procedure or command batch. These are referred to as *flow control* or *control-of-flow statements* because they control the flow of Transact-SQL code execution. Transact-SQL flow control language statements include IF...ELSE, WHILE, GOTO, RETURN, WAITFOR, BREAK, CONTINUE, and BEGIN...END. We'll discuss the various flow control commands further in the book, but for now here's a simple procedure that illustrates all of them (Listing 1–30):

**Listing 1–30** Flow control statements as they behave in the wild.

```
USE pubs
IF OBJECT_ID('dbo.listsales') IS NOT NULL
  DROP PROC dbo.listsales
GO
CREATE PROC dbo.listsales @title_id tid=NULL
AS

IF (@title_id='/?') GOTO Help      -- Here's a basic IF
```

```
-- Here's one with a BEGIN..END block
IF NOT EXISTS(SELECT * FROM titles WHERE title_id=@title_id) BEGIN
  PRINT 'Invalid title_id'
  WAITFOR DELAY '00:00:03' -- Delay 3 secs to view message
  RETURN -1
END

IF NOT EXISTS(SELECT * FROM sales WHERE title_id=@title_id) BEGIN
  PRINT 'No sales for this title'
  WAITFOR DELAY '00:00:03' -- Delay 3 secs to view message
  RETURN -2
END

DECLARE @qty int, @totalsales int
SET @totalsales=0

DECLARE c CURSOR
FOR SELECT qty FROM sales WHERE title_id=@title_id
OPEN c

FETCH c INTO @qty

WHILE (@@FETCH_STATUS=0) BEGIN       -- Here's a WHILE loop
  IF (@qty<0) BEGIN
    Print 'Bad quantity encountered'
    BREAK     -- Exit the loop immediately
  END ELSE IF (@qty IS NULL) BEGIN
    Print 'NULL quantity encountered -- skipping'
    FETCH c INTO @qty
    CONTINUE -- Continue with the next iteration of the loop
  END
  SET @totalsales=@totalsales+@qty
  FETCH c INTO @qty
END

CLOSE c
DEALLOCATE c

SELECT @title_id AS 'TitleID', @totalsales AS 'TotalSales'
RETURN 0     -- Return from the procedure indicating success

Help:
EXEC sp_usage @objectname='listsales',
      @desc='Lists the total sales for a title',
```

```
          @parameters='@title_id="ID of the title you want to check"',
          @example='EXEC listsales "PS2091"',
          @author='Ken Henderson',
          @email='khen@khen.com',
          @version='1', @revision='0',
          @datecreated='19990803', @datelastchanged='19990818'
WAITFOR DELAY '00:00:03' -- Delay 3 secs to view message
RETURN -1
GO

EXEC dbo.listsales 'PS2091'
EXEC dbo.listsales 'badone'
EXEC dbo.listsales 'PC9999'

TitleID TotalSales
------- -----------
PS2091  191
Invalid title_id
No sales for this title
```

# Errors

The @@ERROR automatic variable returns the error code of the last Transact-SQL statement. If there was no error, @@ERROR returns zero. Because @@ERROR is reset after each Transact-SQL statement, you must save it to a variable if you wish to process it further after checking it.

If you want to write robust code that runs for years without having to be reengineered, make a habit of checking @@ERROR often in your stored procedures, especially after data modification statements. A good indicator of resilient code is consistent error checking, and until Transact-SQL supports structured exception handling, checking @@ERROR frequently is the best way to protect your code against unforeseen circumstances.

## Error Messages

The system procedure sp_addmessage adds custom messages to the sysmessages table that can then be raised (returned to the client) by the RAISERROR command. User messages should have error numbers of 50,000 or higher. The chief advantage of using SQL Server's system messages facility is internationalization. Because you specify a language ID when you add a message via sp_addmessage, you can add a separate version of your application's messages for each language it supports. When your stored procedures then reference a message by number, the appropriate message will be returned to your application using SQL Server's current language setting.

## RAISERROR

Stored procedures report errors to client applications via the RAISERROR command. RAISERROR doesn't change the flow of a procedure; it merely displays an error message, sets the @@ERROR automatic variable, and optionally writes the message to the SQL Server error log and the NT application event log. RAISERROR can reference an error message added to the sysmessages table via the sp_addmessage system procedure, or you can supply it a message string of your own. If you pass a custom message string to RAISERROR, the error number is set to 50,000; if you raise an error by number using a message ID in the sysmessages table, @@ERROR is assigned the message number you raise. RAISERROR can format messages similarly to the C PRINTF() function, allowing you to supply your own arguments for the error messages it returns.

Both a severity and a state can be specified when raising an error message with RAISERROR. Severity values less than 16 produce informational messages in the application event log (when logged). A severity of 16 produces a warning message in the event log. Severity values greater than 16 produce error messages in the event log. Severity values up through 18 can be raised by any user; severity values 19 through 25 are reserved for members of the sysadmin role and require the use of the WITH LOG option. Severity values of 20 and higher are considered fatal and cause the client connection to be terminated.

State has no predefined meaning to SQL Server; it's an informational value that you can use to return state information to an application. Raising an error with a state of 127 will cause the ISQL and OSQL utilities to set the operating system ERRORLEVEL variable to the error number returned by RAISERROR.

The WITH LOG option copies the error message to the NT event log (if SQL Server is running on Windows NT, Windows 2000, or Windows XP) and the SQL Server error log regardless of whether the message was defined using the WITH_LOG option of sp_addmessage. The WITH NOWAIT option causes the message to be returned immediately to the client. The WITH SETERROR option forces @@ERROR to return the last error number raised, regardless of the severity of the error message. See Chapter 7 for detailed examples of how to use RAISERROR(), @@ERROR, and SQL Server's other error-handling mechanisms.

# Nesting

You can nest stored procedure calls up to 32 levels deep. Use the @@NESTLEVEL automatic variable to check the nesting level from within a stored procedure or trigger. From a command batch, @@NESTLEVEL returns 0. From a stored procedure called from a command batch and from first-level triggers, @@NESTLEVEL returns 1. From a procedure or trigger called from nesting level 1, @@NESTLEVEL returns 2; procedures called from level 2 procedures return level 3, and so on. Objects (including temporary tables) and cursors created within a stored procedure are visible to all objects it calls. Objects and cursors created in a command batch are visible to all the objects referenced in the command batch.

# Recursion

Because Transact-SQL supports recursion, you can write stored procedures that call themselves. Recursion can be defined as a method of problem solving wherein the solution is arrived at by repetitively applying it to subsets of the problem. A common application of recursive logic is to perform numeric computations that lend themselves to repetitive evaluation by the same processing steps. Listing 1–31 presents an example that features a stored procedure that calculates the factorial of a number:

**Listing 1–31** Stored procedures can call themselves recursively.

```
SET NOCOUNT ON
USE master
IF OBJECT_ID('dbo.sp_calcfactorial') IS NOT NULL
  DROP PROC dbo.sp_calcfactorial
GO
CREATE PROC dbo.sp_calcfactorial @base_number decimal(38,0), @factorial
decimal(38,0) OUT
AS
SET NOCOUNT ON
DECLARE @previous_number decimal(38,0)

IF ((@base_number>26) and (@@MAX_PRECISION<38)) OR (@base_number>32) BEGIN
  RAISERROR('Computing this factorial would exceed the server''s max.
numeric precision of %d or the max. procedure nesting level of
32',16,10,@@MAX_PRECISION)
```

```
      RETURN(-1)
END

IF (@base_number<0) BEGIN
   RAISERROR('Can''t calculate negative factorials',16,10)
   RETURN(-1)
END

IF (@base_number<2) SET @factorial=1 -- Factorial of 0 or 1=1
ELSE BEGIN
   SET @previous_number=@base_number-1
   EXEC dbo.sp_calcfactorial @previous_number, @factorial OUT -- Recursive
call
   IF (@factorial=-1) RETURN(-1) -- Got an error, return
   SET @factorial=@factorial*@base_number
   IF (@@ERROR<>0) RETURN(-1) -- Got an error, return
END
RETURN(0)
GO

DECLARE @factorial decimal(38,0)
EXEC dbo.sp_calcfactorial 32, @factorial OUT
SELECT @factorial
```

The procedure begins by checking to make sure it has been passed a valid number for which to compute a factorial. It then recursively calls itself to perform the computation. With the default maximum numeric precision of 38, SQL Server can handle numbers in excess of 263 decillion. (*Decillion* is the U.S. term for 1 followed by 33 zeros. In Great Britain, France, and Germany, 1 followed by 33 zeros is referred to as 1,000 quintillion.) As you'll see in Chapter 11, UDFs functions are ideal for computations like factorials.

## Summary

In this chapter you learned the basics of writing stored procedures. We discussed how to monitor stored procedure activity using the Profiler utility, and we dealt with several real-world stored procedure programming issues. You learned about the procedure cache, how SQL Server uses it, and how you can watch it for signs of inefficiencies in your code. You learned about many of the nuances and quirks in SQL Server's stored procedure programming language,

Transact-SQL, and you learned how to use them to your advantage and/or how to work around them as appropriate. You learned how to pass parameters to stored procedures, how to return stored procedure status codes, and how to return data via output parameters. We talked about how to nest stored procedures, as well as how to call them recursively. Hopefully, through all this, you've begun to glimpse a bit of the power available to you in Transact-SQL and SQL Server stored procedures. We'll build on this throughout the remainder of the book.

# CHAPTER 2

# Suggested Conventions

*Programming is like playing golf: it can be tedious and can frustrate you to your wit's end, but it's that one good shot out of a hundred— the one that zips down the fairway, around the trees, and up on to the green two feet from the cup—that keeps you coming back for more.*

*—H. W. Kenton*

I must admit a certain amount of trepidation about recommending what coding and formatting conventions you should use. Formatting and stylistic concerns are so personal and vary so much from programmer to programmer that I'm really not comfortable telling you what conventions *you* should use. Instead, I'll tell you what conventions I use and why.

Before I get into this, let me say that I don't think that using a particular system of coding conventions or formatting styles makes one a better programmer in and of itself. I think you should choose what works best for you. It's unlikely that following a rigid set of conventions will make you a vastly superior stored procedure developer. That said, *not* consistently following reasonable conventions *can* hamper you as a developer. Just ask anyone who's had to look at code that's formatted so strangely that it's difficult even to read, let alone figure out from a process standpoint. It's kind of hard to debug or extend code that you first have to decipher.

Also, I think the entire subject matter of stylistic conventions registers at the lower end of the spectrum in terms of importance. How you format your code isn't nearly as important as, say, what that code does and how it does it. That said, I get asked about coding conventions and source code formatting a lot, so it seemed reasonable that I should include my thoughts on the subject in this book.

# Source Formatting

I'll begin by dealing with source code formatting. Remember: It's not important that you format code the way that I do. What's most important is that you (and your team) format code consistently and logically. Find a system that works for you; then follow it.

## Capitalization

I uppercase Transact-SQL keywords, pretty much across the board. To me, this helps keywords stand out and lets me easily identify reserved words when I'm looking at a code listing, regardless of where that listing is. You might think this unnecessary given Query Analyzer's ability to highlight reserved words; however, I often need to view T-SQL code outside of Query Analyzer (for example, in the SQL Server error log, in a trace file, or in a text editor that doesn't highlight T-SQL-reserved words).

The exception to this would be data types: I lowercase data types. Why? Because I often create user-defined data types, and I don't uppercase user object names. By not uppercasing system-defined data types, I can keep all data types in the same case, which, to me, makes code more readable. The guiding principle I usually follow when deciding how to format code is that if a piece of code is formatted differently than other similar code, there should be a very good reason for it. Given that I already know which data types are system-defined, and can therefore distinguish them from user-defined types, upper-casing them serves no real purpose, and actually seems distracting when I view code formatted this way.

I use mixed case when referring to variables, parameters, column names, and object names such as tables, procedures, and views. To me, this helps set them apart from reserved words and supports the easy use of multiword names without requiring spaces or underbars.

I make an exception to this when I deal with system-defined objects or other objects that I did not create. With these objects, I usually match the original case of the object. So I type sysobjects, not SysObjects, and crdate, not CrDate. I do this so that my code will work on systems in which case sensitivity has been enabled, and because I often code in languages such as C++ and XML that are case sensitive. Almost unconsciously, I find myself matching the original case of the objects I reference in my code.

Naturally, this makes naming these objects sensibly in the first place all the more important. This is why I recommend you name the objects you create consistently *and* logically. Being consistent alone is not enough. It's possible to be consistently wrong. As Emerson said, "a foolish consistency is the hobgoblin of little minds, adored by little statesmen and philosophers and divines."[1]

## Indentation and White Space

I try to be flexible as well as economical with the way that I indent code. I think a good formatting style should balance the need to make code easily readable while minimizing script length, because longer scripts tend to be more difficult to wade through. In other words, you can get carried away with spreading out code and actually make it more difficult to read because you've made it substantially longer. Someone trying to read it will have to scroll through a much larger number of script lines than he otherwise would have to.

### Select

To me, there's no reason to break a short SELECT statement into multiple lines just so that it can be indented consistently with a much larger one. This is especially true of subqueries and derived columns. For example, I do this (Listing 2–1):

**Listing 2–1** I use simple formatting for simple queries.

```
IF EXISTS(SELECT * FROM Northwind.dbo.Customers)
```

I find this more readable and more sensible than the code shown in Listing 2–2.

**Listing 2–2** A style that I don't care much for.

```
IF EXISTS
   (
   SELECT
   *
   FROM
   Northwind.dbo.Customers
   )
```

1. Emerson, Ralph Waldo. "Self Reliance." *Self Reliance and Other Essays*. Mineola, NY: Dover Publications, 1993.

As long as vertical space is at a premium (and it always will be as long as code tends to flow vertically rather than horizontally), I do what I can to balance readability with economy of space. To me, there's no need to break a simple SELECT statement like the one in Listing 2–2 into multiple lines: It doesn't make the code more readable (in fact, it makes it *less* readable, in my opinion), and it belies the fact that what's really happening in the code is a very simple operation. In other words, the code looks more complicated than it is. It distracts from the fact that all we're doing in the IF statement is checking the table for the existence of rows. In my opinion, conveying the relative significance of a block of code is just as important as formatting code consistently. You have to balance standardization with common sense. If a piece of code is relatively trivial, you shouldn't have to scan the page just to locate its logical boundaries (for example, its parentheses or its BEGIN...END).

And even though formatting code using a style like the one in Listing 2–2 would certainly make this book longer and seemingly more substantial, I couldn't, with good conscience, do it. Substituting a single character or a single word (for example, "*" in Listing 2–2) for an entire line of text would obviously lengthen this book, but it wouldn't make the code any more readable. I try to conserve vertical space in this book just as you likely will in the code you write.

With more elaborate SELECT statements, I generally place each major clause on a separate line and left-align them. I usually place columns immediately to the right of the SELECT reserved word, and delimit them with commas as necessary. If there are too many columns to fit on the line, I merely continue the list on the next line, often indenting those on the second and following lines so that they line up with those on the first. Here's an example (Listing 2–3):

**Listing 2–3**  I align the columns in T-SQL statements when I can.

```
SELECT CustomerID, CompanyName, ContactName, ContactTitle, Address, City,
       Region, PostalCode, Country, Phone, Fax
FROM Northwind.dbo.Customers
WHERE City IN('London', 'Madrid')
```

Here's another example featuring a bigger SELECT (Listing 2–4):

**Listing 2–4**  I usually left-align the major clauses in T-SQL commands.

```
SELECT Region, COUNT(*) AS NumberOfCustomers
FROM Northwind.dbo.Customers
```

```
WHERE Region IS NOT NULL
GROUP BY Region
HAVING COUNT(*) > 1
ORDER BY Region
```

### Clauses and Predicates

As with the columns in a SELECT statement, I usually align the subclauses and predicates that make up the major clauses in a T-SQL command. For example, I usually left-align the various clauses in a multitable join and the predicates in a compound WHERE or HAVING clause. To me, this all seems logical. If we're only going to left-align the major clauses, the minor ones that make them up obviously can't be left-aligned. If they can't be left-aligned, we could either not worry about aligning them at all, or align them with one another. I chose the latter because I think it makes code easier to read. So, I often do something like this (Listing 2–5) when I have a compound clause:

**Listing 2–5** I often align the phrases in a compound clause.

```
SELECT CustomerID, CompanyName, ContactName, ContactTitle, Address, City,
       Region, PostalCode, Country, Phone, Fax
FROM Northwind.dbo.Customers
WHERE City='London'
   OR City='Madrid'
   OR City='Paris'
```

If I place the parts of a compound clause on the same line, I'll often delimit them with parentheses. See the section entitled "Parentheses" for more information.

### Expressions

If a CASE expression is relatively simple, I'll often embed it within a single line of code. If it's more complex, I'll break it into multiple lines. Listings 2–6 and 2–7 provide an example of each:

**Listing 2–6** Simple CASE expressions usually reside on a single line.

```
SELECT CustomerID, CompanyName, ContactName, ContactTitle,
       Phone, CASE WHEN Fax IS NULL THEN 'N' ELSE 'Y' END AS [Fax?]
```

```
FROM Northwind.dbo.Customers
WHERE City = 'London'
```

**Listing 2–7** More complex CASE expressions often span several lines.

```
SELECT CASE Region
        WHEN 'WA' THEN 'Phil'
        WHEN 'SP' THEN 'Xavier'
        WHEN 'BC' THEN 'Jean-Marc'

        ELSE 'Unknown'
        END AS Salesman,
        CustomerID, CompanyName, ContactName
FROM Northwind.dbo.Customers
ORDER BY Salesman
```

I basically take the same approach with functions and other types of expressions. If the expression is simple, I use simple formatting for it. If it's more complex, I allow it to span multiple lines and format it accordingly.

I regularly nest functions horizontally on a line, and I don't shy away from complex expressions if the need arises. For example, I often format code like this (Listing 2–8):

**Listing 2–8** Relatively simple expressions are usually formatted as a single line.

```
SELECT ContactName+'''s title is '+REPLACE(UPPER(ContactTitle),'SALES','MARKETING')
FROM Northwind.dbo.Customers
```

Certainly, I could break the nested REPLACE expression into multiple lines, but a competent developer should be able to glance at the code and know intuitively that it merely changes the word SALES to MARKETING in the **ContactTitle** column before concatenating it with ContactName. If this is the case, spreading the expression across multiple lines would serve no purpose other than to lengthen the script.

### BEGIN/END

I don't enclose stored procedures within an outer BEGIN/END pair. Doing so is unnecessary and just adds lines to a script. I also place BEGIN on the same line as the flow-control command with which it corresponds, and I align END with that same command. In other words, if BEGIN is being used by the Transact-SQL IF command to delimit a block of code, I place it on the same line as the IF and align END with the IF, not BEGIN. This differs from the way most people format Transact-SQL, but I have some pretty good reasons for this deviation from common practice. As I've said, I like to conserve vertical space in the scripts I write. If a piece of code doesn't deserve its own line of code from a significance standpoint, I often don't give it one. Because BEGIN and END do not actually correspond to executable code (you can't set a breakpoint in the Transact-SQL debugger on BEGIN or END, for example), they have less significance to me than the flow-control command to which they correspond. Visually pairing up END with BEGIN doesn't help me much, but matching it with its corresponding IF or WHILE might. For example, consider the stored procedure presented in Listing 2–9:

**Listing 2–9** You can format BEGIN/END pairs in a variety of ways.

```
CREATE PROC testd @var int AS
BEGIN
        IF @var=1
        BEGIN
          PRINT '1'
        END
        ELSE
        BEGIN
          PRINT 'not 1'
        END
END
```

There are only three lines of executable code in the entire procedure: the IF and the two PRINT statements. If you ran this procedure under the debugger in Query Analyzer, you could only set breakpoints on these three lines. By spreading the procedure out this way, your brain is forced to check through lots of "noise" lines—lines of code that don't really do much. Sure, the BEGIN/END lines indicate flow-control, so they're certainly more significant than, say, a comment, but they only have meaning within the context of other commands. So, for the same reason and in a manner very similar to the way I format curly braces in C++, I demote these noise lines to the dependent commands they are and format them accordingly (Listing 2–10):

**Listing 2–10** The previous procedure with fewer "noise" lines.

```
CREATE PROC testd @var int AS
IF @var=1 BEGIN
  PRINT '1'
```

```
END ELSE BEGIN
  PRINT 'not 1'
END
```

Note the placement of ELSE on the same line as the IF command's END. ELSE is another noise command in that it doesn't actually indicate executable code—you can't place a debugger breakpoint on ELSE. It delimits executable code and indicates the flow of execution through the procedure, but it does not execute itself.

In cases when the code corresponding to an IF or ELSE condition requires a single line only, I usually drop the BEGIN/END pair and put that code on the same line as the IF or ELSE, like this (Listing 2–11):

**Listing 2–11** The test procedure with no noise lines.

```
CREATE PROC testd @var int AS
IF @var=1 PRINT '1'
ELSE PRINT 'not 1'
```

An argument against this convention is that the IF line combines two executable lines into one script line—the IF and the PRINT—making the code difficult to trace in a debugger. However, the Query Analyzer debugger correctly indicates this by remaining on a line until all executable pieces have completed. In the case of the IF line, this means that stepping from the line with F10 will cause the debugger to remain on the line for an extra cycle so that the execution of the PRINT command can be shown (if 1 is passed into the procedure). In the case of the ELSE line, you simply won't reach the ELSE line unless the second PRINT executes. In other words, you don't need to place the code corresponding to the ELSE on its own line (to determine when it, rather than the ELSE, is being executed) because the ELSE will not otherwise be reached. Unlike the IF line, it does not itself correspond to executable code.

As you can see, reducing the number of noise lines in a script can have a significant impact on the total number of lines in the procedure. In this case, we reduced the procedure from eleven lines to just three.

## Parentheses

I have a habit of using parentheses more often than necessary, particularly with logical expressions. For example, I often use parentheses to delimit the predicate phrases in a compound WHERE or HAVING clause, especially when I place them on the same line. I also usually enclose the terms of a JOIN clause's

ON in parentheses, and I tend to wrap the logical conditions of the IF and WHILE commands in parentheses, as well. For me, this makes the code a bit more readable, although I'm sure the ultimate source of my tendency to do this is my work in languages such as C and C++, which require parentheses around logical expressions. Listing 2–12 presents an example:

**Listing 2–12** I often enclose logical expressions in parentheses.

```
CREATE PROC testd @var int AS
IF (@var=1)
  SELECT C.CompanyName, SUM(O.Freight) AS Freight
  FROM Customers C JOIN Orders O ON (C.CustomerID=O.CustomerID)
  WHERE (C.City='London') OR (C.City='Portland')
  GROUP BY C.CompanyName
  ORDER BY C.CompanyName
ELSE
  SELECT C.CompanyName, SUM(O.Freight) AS Freight
  FROM Customers C JOIN Orders O ON (C.CustomerID=O.CustomerID)
  WHERE (C.City='Paris') OR (C.City='Barcelona')
  GROUP BY C.CompanyName
  ORDER BY C.CompanyName
GO
```

The most important thing to remember regarding parentheses is that they help ensure order of precedence. They control the order in which clauses within an expression are evaluated. So, beyond the merely aesthetic, parentheses actually affect how your code executes.

## Horizontal Spacing

In the spirit of eliminating noise from T-SQL scripts, I'm often rather parsimonious when it comes to horizontal spacing. I don't place extra spaces around operators (e.g., "+," "=," "<>," and so on) or between parentheses and expressions. There's usually just one space between the SELECT keyword and its column list, and between the other major T-SQL command clauses and their subclauses.

## Column and Table Aliases

For column and table aliases, I take an approach that combines ANSI and non-ANSI elements. For column aliases, I take the ANSI approach. Despite my personal preference for the **Label=ColumnName** format, I usually use **Column-Name AS Label**. Although the former is more compact and seems more straightforward to me, the ANSI method has grown enough in popularity that I normally use it. Table aliases, however, are a different matter. With table aliases, I omit the AS and simply follow the table or view name with its alias. To me, this helps distinguish table aliases from column aliases, and satisfies my predilection for avoiding noise words in the code I write. Note that I don't always use aliases of either type in my code. It depends on the situation. For short queries over a single table, I'll often omit table aliases altogether.

When a query involves at least two tables, views, or table-valued functions, it's a good idea to prefix column references with their respective table aliases, even when a given column appears only once in the objects referenced by a query. The reason for this is twofold: First, it makes the code more readable. No guesswork is required to determine where a column originates. Second, it makes the code more robust. If you later add a table to the query that happens to contain a column with the same name as one of the unqualified columns, you'll get the dreaded "ambiguous column name" error message, and nobody likes those. Do yourself a favor: Disambiguate the column names in your queries before SQL Server forces you to.

To keep from confusing myself, my normal habit is to use one- or two-character abbreviations for table aliases. If I have more than one instance of a table within a query, I'll often append a number to the alias to indicate its nesting level. This encourages me to always qualify column references with table aliases (because the aliases are so short) and helps me follow my own code when nested queries, subqueries, and derived tables enter the picture.

## DDL

I follow the same sorts of formatting conventions with DDL statements as I do with other types of T-SQL. You've probably noticed that I put the parameter list and the AS for a stored procedure on the same line as the CREATE PROCEDURE. Again, this is in keeping with my philosophy of avoiding unnecessary noise in my code. AS doesn't represent executable code in a stored procedure, therefore it's relegated to share a line with its benefactor.

As for CREATE TABLE, I left-align the column names and sometimes the data types, but I'm not persnickety about it. As long as the formatting of a CREATE TABLE statement doesn't obscure the table layout, I don't think it's something worth spending a lot of time thinking about. Typically, you'll create far fewer tables than procedures and other types of objects. So, a basic CREATE TABLE statement looks like this in my code (Listing 2–13):

**Listing 2–13** I keep DDL pretty simple.

```
CREATE TABLE dbo.Customer
(CustomerID int identity PRIMARY KEY,
CustomerName varchar(40) NOT NULL,
Address varchar(60) NULL,
City varchar(20) NULL,
State char(2) NULL,
Zip varchar(10) NULL DEFAULT 'TX',
Country varchar(20) NULL,
Phone varchar(24) NULL,
Fax varchar(24) NULL
)
```

## Owner Qualification

Because qualifying an object name with its owner can actually improve performance, I try to remember to owner-qualify all object references. Not only does this avoid ambiguity in object name references, it can actually speed up access to a stored procedure because not owner-qualifying a stored procedure reference results in a momentary compile lock being taken out on the procedure, then released when the procedure is finally located in the cache. The lock duration may be quite short; however, if the stored procedure name is owner-qualified in the first place, the lock won't occur at all unless the procedure actually needs to be recompiled. This means that

```
EXEC dbo.sp_who
```

is preferable to

```
EXEC sp_who
```

even though both will work. Likewise,

```
CREATE PROCEDURE dbo.MyProc
```

is preferable to

```
CREATE PROCEDURE MyProc
```

because it alleviates any ambiguity there may be in the object reference.

Owner-qualifying names is simply a good habit to get into, regardless of whether it materially affects the performance of your system. (Note that scalar UDF references *must* be owner-qualified. Unlike other kinds of objects, the owner prefix isn't optional.)

## Abbreviations and Optional Keywords

I often abbreviate the keyword PROCEDURE in commands like CREATE PROCEDURE and DROP PROCEDURE. It's a minor point, but one worth mentioning: If syntax is optional and doesn't really make code any clearer, I see little reason to include it.

### Keywords

This is also true with optional keywords. I often omit them from my code. Examples include the INTO keyword with the INSERT command and the FROM keyword with DELETE. ANSI compatibility concerns aside, I often omit unnecessary syntax from the code I write. The most reliable, most robust code around is the code that isn't there in the first place. It never produces a syntax error, never breaks, is never made obsolete by changes in the tool, and it takes no precious screen real estate.

### Abbreviations for Common Words

When you abbreviate common words in the object names you create, try to be consistent. If you abbreviate number as "Num" in one name, abbreviate it similarly for all objects. Don't make it "No" in one table (e.g., CustNo) and "Number" in another (e.g., InvoiceNumber). Be consistent. It's a good idea to establish a standard set of these types of abbreviations before you even begin constructing objects.

## Passing Parameters

I usually pass stored procedure parameter values by position rather than name unless the procedure has a large number of parameters and I only want to pass a few of them, or the meaning of the values I'm passing isn't obvious from their positions. I suppose this mostly goes back to laziness: I don't like typing what I don't have to, and omitting parameter names certainly requires less typing than including them.

## Choosing Names

When I name an object, I'm careful to avoid naming conflicts between tables, views, UDFs, procedures, triggers, default and rule objects because their names must be unique. You can't, for example, have a stored procedure and a table with the same name. As I've mentioned before, I try to be descriptive without getting carried away.

One factor that's often overlooked when choosing names is what I call "speakability"—how easy a name is to speak in common conversation. If a name is rooted too deeply in computerese and technobabble, you may sound foolish when saying it and have difficulty talking about it with other people. Consider the following two names: SWCustomers and CUSTOMERS_IN_ THE_SOUTHWEST_REGION.

The second name is a real mouthful. It's simply too long and unwieldy to use in common conversation. People attempting to use it in conversation will instinctively shorten it. Why not start with a handier name in the first place? What real purpose does having such a long name serve? To follow a standard? Why not change the standard to follow common sense?

### Tables

I often use plural one-word entity-type names for tables and views (e.g., Customers). For a table that links two other tables in a many-to-many relationship, I'll often name the linking table after the tables it joins, as in CustomerSuppliers.

### Indexes

I name indexes after their keys. So, if an index has been built over the Customers table on the **CompanyName** and **ContactName** columns, I'll likely name it CompanyNameContactName, or something similar. Because index names do not have to be unique across a database, this strategy works well and lets me see, at a moment's glance, what the index's keys are. Occasionally, I also include a prefix indicating whether the index is clustered or nonclustered.

### Triggers

For triggers, I use a name that indicates the actions that fire the trigger, as well as the name of the table with which the trigger is associated (e.g., DeleteCustomer or InsertUpdateOrder). If the trigger has special characteristics (e.g., it's an INSTEAD OF trigger), I usually indicate this via a prefix to the name (e.g., InsteadOfDeleteCustomer).

### Variables

I never use more than a single at sign (@) when naming a local variable, and I frequently name variables after the columns to which they correspond (if applicable). If a variable represents a counter of some type, I'll often name it with a single character, just as you might name a loop control variable "i" or "x" in C++ or Java.

### Procedures

I often give procedures a verb-based name, as in PostPurchases or BuildHistory. Sometimes I give procedures and views a special prefix (e.g., **sp** or **V_**), depending on the number of procedures and views I have and the similarity of their names to other object names.

### UDFs

I name UDFs similarly to stored procedures. Sometimes I find myself prefixing UDF names with **Get...** because they return a value of some sort, but not often, because the fact that a UDF returns a value is implicit.

### Constraints

With constraints, I often allow the system to name my constraints because I usually use GUI tools to manipulate them. When I name them myself, I usually prefix primary key constraints with **PK_**, foreign key constraints with **FK_**, unique key constraints with **UK_**, and check constraints with **CK_**.

Occasionally, I get a little crazy and give a constraint an extremely long name that indicates exactly what it does. This provides the nifty side benefit of causing a useful "message" to display in client applications when the constraint is violated. For example, sometimes I do something like this (Listing 2–14):

**Listing 2–14** You can use long constraint names to implement rudimentary messages.

```
CREATE TABLE Samples
(SampleDate datetime NULL DEFAULT getdate(),
EmployeeID int NULL,
SampleAmount int NULL
CONSTRAINT [Sample Amount must not equal 0] CHECK (SampleAmount<>0),
CONSTRAINT [Invalid Employee ID] FOREIGN KEY (EmployeeID) REFERENCES
Employees (EmployeeID)
)
```

```
GO
INSERT Samples (SampleAmount) VALUES (0)
INSERT Samples (EmployeeID) VALUES (0)
```

(Results)

```
Server: Msg 547, Level 16, State 1, Line 1
INSERT statement conflicted with COLUMN CHECK constraint 'Sample Amount
must not equal 0'. The conflict occurred in database 'Northwind', table
'Samples', column 'SampleAmount'.
The statement has been terminated.
Server: Msg 547, Level 16, State 1, Line 1
INSERT statement conflicted with COLUMN FOREIGN KEY constraint 'Invalid
Employee ID'. The conflict occurred in database 'Northwind', table
'Employees', column 'EmployeeID'.
The statement has been terminated.
```

Because a constraint's name is included in the error message generated when it's violated, you get some idea of what the problem is from the constraint name itself, even if you don't process the message further. Because object names can be up to 128 characters long, this is a poor man's method of "attaching" a user-defined message to a constraint violation (a feature Sybase has had for years). Note that you can embed carriage returns in these ad hoc messages simply by embedding them in the constraint name, like this (Listing 2–15):

**Listing 2–15** You can include carriage returns in long object names.

```
CREATE TABLE Samples
(SampleDate datetime NULL DEFAULT getdate(),
EmployeeID int NULL,
SampleAmount int NULL
CONSTRAINT [
Sample Amount must not equal 0
] CHECK (SampleAmount<>0),
CONSTRAINT [
Invalid Employee ID
] FOREIGN KEY (EmployeeID) REFERENCES Employees (EmployeeID)
)
GO
INSERT Samples (SampleAmount) VALUES (0)
INSERT Samples (EmployeeID) VALUES (0)
```

(Results)

```
Server: Msg 547, Level 16, State 1, Line 1
INSERT statement conflicted with COLUMN CHECK constraint '
```

```
Sample Amount must not equal 0
'. The conflict occurred in database 'Northwind', table 'Samples', column
'SampleAmount'.
The statement has been terminated.
Server: Msg 547, Level 16, State 1, Line 1
INSERT statement conflicted with COLUMN FOREIGN KEY constraint '
Invalid Employee ID
'. The conflict occurred in database 'Northwind', table 'Employees', column
'EmployeeID'.
The statement has been terminated.
```

Of course, it's preferable to trap errors like this in your applications and display meaningful messages instead, but a human-readable constraint name is certainly better than one that reveals very little about a problem.

# Coding Conventions

I'll cover common coding and design patterns in more detail in Chapter 3, but discussing a few basic coding conventions is certainly worthwhile here. You'll see these conventions applied throughout this book, so it makes sense to talk about a few of them in advance.

As I've said, I'm uncomfortable telling you exactly what conventions you should use. I think you should find a system that works for you. Nevertheless, I've structured the following recommendations as a series as dos and don'ts because you may want to adopt some of them as guidelines for your own work. You may not agree with or even use all of these. My advice would be to read through them and adopt the ones that you feel make the most sense.

## Script Recommendations

The following recommendations apply to T-SQL scripts in general. Whether a script creates an object or constitutes a T-SQL command batch that you run on occasion, there are a number of conventions you can follow to make your life easier. Naturally, most of these are good practices regardless of whether you're authoring a script, a stored procedure, or some other type of SQL Server object.

### Dropping Objects

I usually check for the existence of an object before I attempt to drop it. Not doing so needlessly generates error messages, even when the DROP command is segmented in its own T-SQL batch. An error message should be something that grabs your attention, not something you regularly ignore. I try to avoid generating unnecessary error messages to keep from becoming desensitized to them.

### Comments

I decide what to "comment" in my code by balancing the need to clarify vague or ambiguous coding elements against the need to keep the code free of noise and needless clutter. Overcommenting is just as bad as undercommenting. I strive to write code that is self-documenting. Overcommenting a script can create substantially more work for you without really improving the readability of the code. The screen quickly fills with gobbledygook that anyone attempting to read the code later will have to wade through, not to mention the additional overhead of having to maintain these loquacious remarks every time you modify the code.

People working on overcommented code may be a bit confused by the sheer volume of comments because they won't know what's significant and what isn't. They won't know which comments to pay close attention to and which ones they can safely ignore. Comments that merely restate what is already abundantly clear from the code itself merely lengthen the script. And chances are, if code *needs* to be commented profusely in order to be readable, the code probably needs to be rewritten.

That said, when I'm forced to do something from a coding standpoint that isn't obvious and is something I feel those who work on the code down the road should know about, I comment it. I think every stored procedure of any significance should have a code block at the top of it that describes the procedure and what it does. As with any source code, tracking things like who changed the code last, when they changed it, and so forth, can also be quite handy. See Chapter 4 for more info.

And lest I forget to weigh in on the single biggest issue facing Transact-SQL developers in the 21st century: I don't have a problem with so-called "old-style" comments. I think slash-star (/*) comments are appropriate, even preferable, when a comment spans many lines. Whether this is the header at the top of a procedure or function (where you might occasionally reformat the text and, hence, find single-line comments a real pain), or deep within a procedure or script to prevent a block of code from executing, slash-star comments are certainly handier than double-hyphen comments in certain circumstances. As with all things programming: Use the right tool for the job. There's nothing wrong with slash-star comments when used properly.

### Extended Properties

In the same way that logical names help make a database self-documenting, extended properties allow you to make your objects more descriptive. Extended properties are name/value pairs that you can associate with a database object—a user, a column, a table, and so forth. These are handy for adding descriptive text to the objects you create. You add extended properties using the sp_addextendedproperty stored procedure, or using the Enterprise Manager or Query Analyzer Object Browser tools. The system function fn_listextendedproperty() lists the extended properties for an object. The sp_dropextendedproperty procedure drops an extended property. Here's some code that demonstrates extended properties.

```
USE Northwind
GO
CREATE TABLE CustomerList (c1 int identity, name varchar(30))
GO
EXEC sp_addextendedproperty 'Label', 'Customer Number (NN-XX-NNNN)',
'user', dbo, 'table', CustomerList, 'column', c1
GO
SELECT value
FROM ::fn_listextendedproperty (NULL, 'user', 'dbo', 'table',
'CustomerList', 'column', default)
GO
DROP TABLE CustomerList
```

(Results)

```
value
-----------------------------------------------------------------
Customer Number (NN-XX-NNNN)
```

### Script Files

There are certainly exceptions, but generally I store the source code for each database object I create in a separate script file. This provides maximum flexibility in terms of re-creating or modifying the object. It ensures that I don't accidentally drop or re-create objects I don't intend to, and that I don't apply procedure-specific settings such as QUOTED_IDENTIFIER to the wrong procedures. This also allows me to more easily manage the source code to the objects I create using a version control system—a big plus with lots of objects.

### Script Segments

If a script has multiple distinct segments that do not share local variables, I usually terminate each of them with GO in order to modularize the work the script is to perform. In this way, if there's an error in one of the segments, I can prevent it from causing the ones that follow it to fail. Conversely, if I *want* a script segment to execute *only* if its preceding segment doesn't generate an error, I leave out the GO and code the two batches as a single batch. If a serious enough error occurs early in the batch, the commands later in the batch will never be reached.

### USE

If a script must be run from a given database, I include the appropriate USE command as early in the script as possible. As I said earlier in the book, this helps ensure that any objects the script creates end up where they're supposed to, and alleviates having to remember to change the database context manually each time the script is executed.

When I include a single USE in a script, I almost always put it at the top of the script. This makes it easy to find and sets the stage for the code that follows. Another developer looking at the script should have no problem determining where the objects it references reside.

## Stored Procedures and Functions

The following recommendations relate specifically to stored procedures and functions. They're not unlike the recommendations you might encounter for any language: central variable declaration, modular routines, error checking, and so forth. For some reason, Transact-SQL developers often neglect these very basic practices. Following them can save you hours of bug chasing and can help you write code that is both maintainable and extendible.

### Variable Declaration

If possible, I declare the variables a stored procedure or function will use centrally—in one location—preferably at the start of the procedure or function. Although it's syntactically permissible to declare variables almost anywhere, having to search a routine to find a variable's declaration wastes time and makes code more difficult to follow.

### Stored Procedure Return Values

If a stored procedure can return a value other than zero (many do), it's often worth the trouble to check this value and react appropriately. Accordingly, I try to remember to return values from the stored procedures I write. Generally, a value of 0 indicates success; nonzero values indicate that an error has occurred.

### Parameters

I check the values passed into a stored procedure or UDF early, and return an error (or display a help message) when bad values are supplied. This makes the routine easier to use and prevents invalid values and/or operations from affecting my data.

### Default Parameter Values

I think it's a good practice to provide default values for stored procedure and UDF parameters. It makes them easier to use, more flexible, and less error prone.

### Errors

We'll cover this in more detail later in the book, but the mark of robust code is comprehensive error checking. I try to check for errors after key operations and respond accordingly. I usually check @@ERROR immediately after statements that may cause an error condition, and I check @@ROWCOUNT when the fact that a statement fails to affect any rows constitutes an error.

### Modularity

A series of smaller, logically simple routines is easier to deal with and easier to understand than a single, extremely long behemoth of a stored procedure. When I can, I break complex routines into smaller ones. This increased granularity can help performance by allowing part of a routine to get kicked out of the cache without disposing of all of it, and it makes my code generally easier to work on.

## Tables and Views

These recommendations relate to tables and views; specifically, how you use them in the code you write. Whether it's a script, a stored procedure, or a function, how you handle tables—the data containers of your database—is sometimes as important as what you do with them.

### Temporary Tables

I try not to overuse temporary tables. There are two reasons for this: One, they can cause throughput problems because of resource contention in tempdb. Two, SQL Server is more aggressive with keeping statistics updated on temporary tables than it is with permanent tables. This also can cause performance problems as well as unexpected stored procedure recompilation. One strategy for avoiding temporary tables is to use **table** variables. You can do most of the things with them that you can do with temporary tables, and they cause fewer resource contention problems in tempdb. Like all variables, they're automatically dropped when they go out of scope.

### Resource Cleanup

When I do use temporary tables, I try to remember to drop them when they're no longer needed. Leaving them lying around until a stored procedure returns or you log out of the server wastes system resources and may prevent future code from running in certain circumstances. The same is true for cursors: It's a good idea to close and deallocate them when you're finished with them. Your mother was right: Cleanliness is next to godliness. Clean up after yourself.

### System Tables

Unless there's just no other way, I try to avoid querying system tables directly. Beginning with SQL Server 7.0, Transact-SQL sports a rich set of property functions (e.g., DATABASEPROPERTY(), COLUMNPROPERTY(), OBJECTPROPERTY(), etc.) that greatly reduce the need to access system tables for meta-data and system-level information. Querying system tables directly is bad for two reasons: One, system tables can change between releases. Code you write today may not run tomorrow if you depend on a particular system table layout. Two, referencing system tables directly to get system-level info is usually less readable than the equivalent property or meta-data functions. For example, assume we've created these column statistics on the Northwind Customers table:

```
CREATE STATISTICS ContactTitle ON Customers(ContactTitle)
```

At some point in the future, we notice ContactTitle in an sp_helpindex listing and want to know whether it's a true index or merely a placeholder for statistics. Here are two queries that can tell us (Listings 2–16 and 2–17). One queries system tables directly; the other doesn't:

**Listing 2–16** A meta-data query that references system tables directly.

```
SELECT CASE WHEN i.status & 64 = 64 THEN 1 ELSE 0 END
FROM sysindexes i JOIN sysobjects o ON (i.id=o.id)
WHERE o.name='Customers'
AND i.name='ContactTitle'
```

**Listing 2–17** A meta-data query that's not only safer but also shorter.

```
SELECT INDEXPROPERTY(OBJECT_ID('Customers'),'ContactTitle','IsStatistics')
```

Both queries return 1 if ContactTitle is a statistics index. Which one's more readable? Not only is the INDEXPROPERTY() query more readable, it's also considerably shorter. And it has the added advantage of being immune to changes in the system tables.

In addition to the property functions, SQL Server includes a number of views and system stored procedures to help you access meta-data info. For example, you can query INFORMATION_SCHEMA.VIEWS to retrieve a list of the views defined in a database (Listing 2–18):

**Listing 2–18** You can use the INFORMATION_SCHEMA views to retrieve system-level info.

```
SELECT TABLE_NAME AS VIEW_NAME, CHECK_OPTION, IS_UPDATABLE
FROM INFORMATION_SCHEMA.VIEWS
ORDER BY VIEW_NAME
```

(Results abridged)

| VIEW_NAME | CHECK_OPTION | IS_UPDATABLE |
|---|---|---|
| Alphabetical list of products | NONE | NO |
| Category Sales for 1997 | NONE | NO |
| Current Product List | NONE | NO |
| Customer and Suppliers by City | NONE | NO |
| Invoices | NONE | NO |
| Order Details Extended | NONE | NO |
| Order Subtotals | NONE | NO |
| Orders Qry | NONE | NO |
| Product Sales for 1997 | NONE | NO |
| Products Above Average Price | NONE | NO |
| Products by Category | NONE | NO |
| Quarterly Orders | NONE | NO |
| Sales by Category | NONE | NO |
| Sales Totals by Amount | NONE | NO |
| Summary of Sales by Quarter | NONE | NO |
| Summary of Sales by Year | NONE | NO |

And as I've said, a number of system stored procedures exist that return catalog and meta-data info. Using them is preferable and more convenient than querying the system tables directly. For example, sp_tables lists the tables in a database, and sp_stored_procedures lists stored procedure info. There are numerous others. See the topic "Catalog Stored Procedures" in the Books Online, and the script instcat.sql (located in the SQL Server install folder) for more info.

## Transact-SQL

These last recommendations apply to Transact-SQL in general. Whether you're coding a stored procedure or just executing a T-SQL command batch from an application, following these practices can help you write better code.

### Ad hoc T-SQL

When I can, I avoid executing ad hoc T-SQL via the EXEC() function. There are two reasons for this. One, the execution plans generated by ad hoc queries aren't as likely to be reused as those of stored procedures. Two, ad hoc T-SQL is notoriously difficult to debug. When I use it, I find myself executing lots of PRINT commands just to see what my T-SQL command variable contains at different points in the procedure. Because it all but defeats Query Analyzer's ability to locate coding errors automatically, you're pretty much on your own in terms of finding errors when you build and execute T-SQL dynamically.

So, if possible, I place my code in regular stored procedures, functions, etc., and call those objects. This is nearly always preferable to any of the dynamic T-SQL approaches. If I must execute T-SQL that's generated at runtime, I try to use the sp_executesql extended procedure. It's often considerably faster than EXEC(), and execution plans created to service sp_executesql are inserted into the procedure cache and can be reused.

### COMPUTE and PRINT

COMPUTE is bad news because it actually causes multiple result sets to be created. You have to iterate through all of them to get all the rows returned by a COMPUTE query. The ROLLUP and CUBE operators are preferable because they do all that COMPUTE does and more, and they do it without requiring additional result sets.

PRINT is less than ideal because, as of this writing, ADO doesn't correctly return informational messages unless a message with a severity greater than 10 also happens to have been generated. In other words, when executing a query using ADO, you'll never see PRINT messages unless a real error message has also been generated for the same query.

# Summary

In this chapter, you learned about a number of formatting and coding conventions that can help you churn out better Transact-SQL. Many of these apply regardless of whether you're creating a stored procedure or some other type of SQL Server-related object. You shouldn't assume that the list presented here is comprehensive or even applicable to every development team in every situation. The point is this: Adopting and consistently following sound formatting and coding conventions can help you produce better code with less effort.

# CHAPTER 3

# Common Design Patterns

*The harder it is to see the design in the code, the harder it is to preserve it.*

*—Martin Fowler*[1]

In their book, *Design Patterns*, Erich Gamma and company (commonly known as the "Gang of Four" or GoF) propose that there are certain patterns in software design that expert developers regularly use and recognize in code written by others. *Design Patterns* seeks to formally catalog these patterns so that developers may benefit from them without spending years learning them the hard way—through experience alone. The idea is to promote the discussion of and research into software design patterns as a distinct area of computer science so that, having been formalized, software design patterns can continue to evolve and proliferate as software engineering itself does.

The book *The Practice of Programming* espouses a similar philosophy. In it, author Brian Kernighan proposes that programming languages have *idioms*—conventions that experienced developers use to build common coding elements.[2] These are similar to design patterns, but are finer in granularity. I like to think of them as *mini patterns* or *pattern fragments*. Idioms are more generic than design patterns. They have more to do with the language than with solving a particular type of problem.

Although both of these books discuss software design from the standpoint of object-oriented programming (OOP) languages, I have long believed that common design patterns and idioms also exist in query languages such as Transact-SQL. Expert developers regularly use certain common techniques to build the code they write. The purpose of this chapter is to catalog a few of these and to help jumpstart a discussion of Transact-SQL design patterns and idioms. For succinctness, idioms and design patterns are discussed together. Just keep in mind that, although closely related, they're really two different things.

---

1. Fowler, Martin. *Refactoring: Improving the Design of Existing Code*. Reading, MA: Addison-Wesley, 1999. Page 55.
2. Kernighan, Brian. *The Practice of Programming*. Reading, MA: Addison-Wesley, 1999. Page 11.

# The Law of Parsimony

In philosophy, *the law of parsimony* (a.k.a., Ockham's razor) states that the simplest of two or more competing theories is preferred to more complex ones. To the software designer, this means that the simplest approach to providing the required functionality is usually the best. Creating unnecessary complexities and obfuscation does not make one a better coder. In fact, it's exactly the opposite. From my experience, the best programmers, regardless of language, are those with a gift for being able to create solutions to intricate problems from simple inventions and techniques. The best code has a sense of elegance to it that derives from its simplicity. It is *better* code because it is *simpler* code.

In his book *Refactoring: Improving the Design of Existing Code*, Martin Fowler had this to say on the subject: "You build the simplest thing that can possibly work."[3] I agree with this statement to a point. A concern I have is that one man's simple is another man's complex. Sizing up the complexity of a proposed solution can be a completely subjective task. What's obvious and intuitive to you may confuse me to no end. Another concern I have is that oversimplifying a problem or failing to consider the long-term ramifications of the design decisions you make can cause problems down the road. The law of parsimony should never be used as an excuse to abandon forethought and the grasp of the overall picture.

You'll see the law of parsimony in evidence in many of the idioms and design patterns covered in this chapter. One of the most productive things you can do to write better code and to clean up existing code is to remove unnecessary complexity. Doing so helps you not just now, but six months from now when you or someone else must work on the code again. It is an investment in the future health of your code. If a loop to execute a block of code a given number of times runs forward in some places and backward in others—for no apparent reason—the code contains needless complexity. People reading through it are forced to note that, even though the code looks different, it actually performs the same function as another, more straightforward code block. A prime tenet of good software design is the elimination of differences that make no difference—variations *without* a purpose—so that what remains are those worth noting.

And, although there may be many ways to do something, generally the simplest, most straightforward approach is best. We have enough complex software engineering problems to solve without creating them for ourselves through poor coding practices.

---

3. Fowler, Martin. *Refactoring: Improving the Design of Existing Code*. Reading, MA: Addison-Wesley, 1999. Page 68.

# Idioms

As I've said, I believe every programming language is characterized by its idioms—the techniques experienced developers use to solve common problems—and Transact-SQL is no exception. In this section, I'll discuss a few common Transact-SQL idioms. The list is by no means exhaustive, but there should be enough here to get you started thinking about the idioms that make up the language. Once you begin thinking this way, you'll begin to see idioms everywhere you look. A programming language's idioms are like the basic tools one might find in a toolbox. Every toolbox should have a certain basic set of them, although some toolboxes have more variety than others. Experienced developers tend to have lots of tools, just like the experienced craftsman or the veteran machinist.

## Querying Meta-data

Although there are numerous ways to return meta-data about an object, experienced developers usually take this approach:

1. Use meta-data functions (e.g., OBJECTPROPERTY()) if possible.
2. If no function exists that returns the info you need, query the INFORMATION_SCHEMA views (e.g., INFORMATION_SCHEMA. PARAMETERS).
3. If no INFORMATION_SCHEMA view meets your needs, check the system catalog procedures (e.g., sp_tables).
4. If all else fails, query the system tables directly (e.g., sysobjects, syscolumns, and so on).

Obviously, there are numerous ways to retrieve meta-data. For example, the two queries in Listing 3–1 are functionally identical:

**Listing 3–1** Two ways of retrieving a database name using its identifier.

```
SELECT dbid FROM master..sysdatabases where name='pubs'
SELECT DB_ID('pubs')
```

The idiomatic, or conventional, technique among experienced Transact-SQL coders is the second one. It's not only shorter than the first technique, it's also impervious to changes in the sysdatabases table. This holds for most meta-data queries: As a rule, avoid querying the system tables directly. Instead, follow the four-step progression listed earlier.

## Creating an Object

Experienced T-SQL coders check for the existence of an object before attempting to create it. There are three reasons for this. One, if the object already exists, but shouldn't, you may want to provide special handling (for example, you may want to exit the script or stop the procedure immediately). Two, if an object already exists but is not unexpected, you may want to drop it. Three, attempting to create an object that already exists will result in an error message being raised, but may go undetected by your script. For example, your T-SQL script may attempt to create a table that already exists within its own batch. When this fails, the batch will terminate, but processing will continue with the first statement in the next batch. If the remainder of the script expects columns or data to be present in the table that aren't, the result could be disastrous.

As with querying other types of meta-data, there are numerous ways to check for the existence of an object. Let's look a few of them. Listing 3–2 presents Method 1:

**Listing 3–2** A method of checking for the existence of an object.

```
IF EXISTS(SELECT * FROM sysobjects WHERE name = 'authors')
  DROP TABLE dbo.authors
GO
CREATE TABLE dbo.authors
...
```

You see techniques like this mostly in code migrated from releases of SQL Server prior to 7.0. The code works, but has some fundamental flaws. The first flaw is that the code queries the sysobjects system table directly. If the layout of that table were to change, the code would break.

The second flaw is that the code doesn't check the owner of the object. So if a user other than dbo has created an object named authors, the DROP TABLE statement will be reached, regardless of whether dbo.authors exists. Let's look at another method (Listing 3–3):

Method 2:

**Listing 3–3** Another method of checking for the existence of an object.

```
IF EXISTS(SELECT * FROM INFORMATION_SCHEMA.TABLES WHERE TABLE_NAME =
'authors'
```

```
AND TABLE_SCHEMA='dbo')
  DROP TABLE dbo.authors
GO
CREATE TABLE dbo.authors
...
```

This method is much improved over the previous one because it does not query the system tables directly. Instead, it takes an ANSI-compliant approach: It uses the INFORMATION_SCHEMA.TABLES view to determine whether user dbo has a table named authors. Although this works, it's a little verbose and requires the use of a subquery and a view to check for the existence of an object. There's a much more common technique, as shown in Method 3 (Listing 3–4):

**Listing 3–4** An idiomatic technique for checking object existence.

```
IF OBJECT_ID('dbo.authors') IS NOT NULL
  DROP TABLE dbo.authors
GO
CREATE TABLE dbo.authors
...
```

This technique is probably the most prevalent and is the one I use myself. It's not dependent on the layout of the sysobjects table; it's short and concise—as it should be—and is efficient from an execution standpoint.

The only real problem with this technique is that it does not check the object type, an advantage Method 2 has because it implicitly eliminates all object types except tables and views by scanning INFORMATION_SCHEMA. TABLES.

A slight variation on this method solves the problem. Method 4 (Listing 3–5) uses the OBJECTPROPERTY() meta-data function to check the type of the object:

**Listing 3–5** A refinement that also checks object type.

```
IF (OBJECT_ID('dbo.authors') IS NOT NULL) AND
(OBJECTPROPERTY(OBJECT_ID('dbo.authors'),'IsTable')=1)
  DROP TABLE dbo.authors
GO
CREATE TABLE dbo.authors
...
```

Personally, I use Method 3 more than Method 4 because it's shorter and object names must be unique across types anyway. The bottom line is: Experienced T-SQL developers use either Method 3 or Method 4 almost exclusively. The idiomatic way of checking for the existence of an object is to use one of these two techniques.

## Setting the Database Context

For scripts that depend on a specific database context, the conventional technique is to include USE as early as possible in the script to set the database context. Although you could change the current database using the combo box in Query Analyzer or via the -d OSQL command-line option, the idiomatic approach—the usual convention among capable developers—is to include a USE statement.

That said, how do we check to see whether the USE statement worked? Not checking could have disastrous results. You may end up dropping objects in the master database, for example. The normal convention is to do something like that shown in Listing 3–6.

**Listing 3–6** Changing the database context and checking it afterward.

```
USE pubs2
GO
IF DB_NAME()<>'pubs2' BEGIN
  RAISERROR('Wrong database.',16,10)
  RETURN
END
GO
```

Here, we use the DB_NAME() meta-data function to check the current database context. It may seem that we could just check the @@ERROR automatic variable after the USE to see whether it succeeded, but that's not the case. USE errors terminate the current command batch, so no error checking is possible. This means that code like this (Listing 3–7) doesn't work as we might like:

**Listing 3–7** USE errors terminate the current batch, making error checking impossible.

```
-- Bad TSQL - doesn't work
USE pubs2
IF @@ERROR<>0 BEGIN
  RAISERROR('Wrong DB.',16,10)
```

```
    RETURN
END
GO
```

## Emptying a Table

There are a couple of methods for completely emptying a table. The one you choose depends on your needs. The most obvious method of deleting all the rows in the table is to execute the DELETE statement with no filter (no WHERE clause), like this:

```
DELETE Customers
```

This works, but every row deletion is recorded in the transaction log, making it impractical for large tables.

A faster and more conventional method of quickly deleting all the rows in a table is to use the TRUNCATE TABLE command, like this:

```
TRUNCATE TABLE Customers
```

Normally, TRUNCATE TABLE will complete almost immediately, even for extremely large tables. TRUNCATE TABLE is faster than DELETE because it's a minimally logged operation—only its extent operations are recorded in the transaction log. Keep in mind that this means that using it impacts database recovery, so it's not without cost. Also keep in mind that you can't use TRUNCATE TABLE with a table with foreign key references.

So, the idiomatic or conventional method of quickly emptying a table is to use TRUNCATE TABLE unless its impact on database recovery is unacceptable or foreign keys reference the table.

## Copying a Table

Copying the structure (and, optionally, the data) of an existing table to a new table is something we do fairly often in database applications. We start with a template of some type, then replicate it to a work table into which we can then insert new rows, add columns and indexes, define new constraints, and so forth.

There are several ways of copying a table, but only one of them is really conventional. The first method involves issuing a CREATE TABLE statement that happens to contain the same DDL as the original source table. There's no easy way to ensure that it actually does match the original table, and even if it does for now, changing the structure of the underlying table in the future will break the de facto link between the two.

Still another way is to use the sp_OA Automation stored procedures to instantiate a SQL-DMO Table object corresponding to the source table and call the object's Script method. This will generate a CREATE TABLE script for the table that can then be executed from T-SQL (either via SQL-DMO or by using xp_cmdshell to call OSQL.EXE). Although this would work (Chapter 21 includes an example procedure, sp_generate_script, that takes this approach), it's unnecessarily circuitous if all you want to do is copy a table. There's an easier way—and one that's more idiomatic too.

SELECT...INTO is a wonderful T-SQL extension for easily creating a copy of a table (without its constraints) or a permanent copy of a query result, for that matter. Anything you can get to via SELECT, you can save to a permanent table. So, creating a copy of a table is as simple as Listing 3–8:

**Listing 3–8** SELECT...INTO is a quick way to copy a table.

```
SELECT * INTO newtable FROM oldtable
```

To create an empty copy of the table, supply a false WHERE condition (Listing 3–9), like this:

**Listing 3–9** SELECT...INTO can also create an empty copy of an existing table.

```
SELECT * INTO newtable FROM oldtable
WHERE 0=1
```

Zero never equals one, so no data will be copied, but the table will be created, nonetheless. Like TRUNCATE TABLE, SELECT...INTO is a minimally logged operation, so using it affects database recovery. That said, it's commonly used, especially to create temporary tables, and you should be able to recognize this idiom on sight. As used here, SELECT...INTO is really an implementation of the GoF Prototype pattern, as I'll discuss later in the chapter.

## Variable Assignment

Although SELECT can be used to assign variables, the SET command is increasingly becoming the preferred method of doing so. Even though they basically work the same way, SET is a tad briefer and can assign cursor variables as well as scalar variables. SELECT, on the other hand, can assign multiple variables at once and can assign values from a table or view without requiring a subquery, so it's still appropriate in certain situations, particularly for multivariable assignments.

Although the difference between the two may seem minor, and my discussion of it a bit fastidious, the acts of setting a variable versus that of returning a result set *are* fundamentally different actions, so it makes sense to use two different commands for them. When you see SET used in a block of T-SQL code, you know exactly what it's doing—assigning a value to a variable. If you consistently follow a convention of assigning variables exclusively with SET and performing data selection with SELECT, you make your code easier to read—both for you and for those that follow you.

## Looping

Although using the WHILE construct is easily the most straightforward way of looping in a T-SQL code block, there are other ways of repeatedly executing code. See Listing 3–10:

**Listing 3–10** There are several ways to loop in Transact-SQL.

```
DECLARE @var int
SET @var=0
mytag:
SET @var=@var+1
IF (@var<10) GOTO mytag
```

This works, but it's not idiomatic. Why not? Because it doesn't mesh with the approach capable developers would take to solve the same problem. It's not natural. It unnecessarily involves a nonstructured concept like GOTO with no real benefit. Listing 3–11 presents one that's a bit better, but that's also not idiomatic:

**Listing 3–11** Using the WHILE construct isn't necessarily idiomatic.

```
DECLARE @var int
SET @var=10
WHILE (@var>0) BEGIN
  SET @var=@var-1
END
```

Why isn't it idiomatic? Because it iterates backward through the loop for no good reason. Remember: A language's idioms are its set of natural approaches to common problems. Iterating backward through a loop without reason is not the most natural means of cycling through the loop; looping forward is. Here's the idiomatic form (Listing 3–12):

**Listing 3–12** The idiomatic form of a loop in T-SQL.

```
DECLARE @var int
SET @var=0
WHILE (@var<10) BEGIN
  SET @var=@var+1
END
```

Not only is the code shorter, it's more obvious. A capable developer can take one look at it and know intuitively that it performs the code between the BEGIN/END pair ten times. This is an example of what I mean when I say that T-SQL has idioms like any other language. Although you can "loop" using a variety of techniques, the forward WHILE technique is the most natural—and therefore the most idiomatic—of the lot.

## Nullability

The proper handling of NULL values has vexed database programmers for decades. The fact that the recommended methods of dealing with them have changed over the years and that they differ from vendor to vendor hasn't helped anything either. Still, there's a Transact-SQL idiom for dealing with NULL values in databases (Listing 3–13). It looks like this:

**Listing 3–13** The nullability idiom.

```
SELECT *
FROM Customers
WHERE Region IS NOT NULL
```

Notice that the WHERE clause isn't

```
WHERE Region<>NULL
```

or

```
WHERE ISNULL(Region,'')=''
```

Even though each of these might work (given the proper ANSI_NULLS setting), neither is the most straightforward or natural approach. The < > approach requires that ANSI_NULLS be set to FALSE because the ANSI/ISO SQL standard stipulates that comparisons with NULL always yield NULL. Failing to set ANSI_NULLS properly before the comparison (or, in the case of a stored procedure, before the procedure is compiled) results in no rows being returned. The ISNULL() approach needlessly converts NULL values to empty strings and fails to take into account the possibility that some Region values may indeed be empty strings. So, neither of the alternative approaches works as well or is as natural as the first one.

### Retrieving the Topmost Rows

It's common to need to return the first *n* rows of a result set or table. There are several ways of doing this, but only one idiomatic way. The idiomatic form is shown in Listing 3–14:

**Listing 3–14** The topmost idiom.

```
SELECT TOP 10 *
FROM Customers
ORDER BY CompanyName
```

Because Transact-SQL provides a special extension just for returning the top *n* rows from a query, the most natural approach to the top *n* problem is to use that extension. As I've mentioned, there are other ways. Here's one of them (Listing 3–15):

**Listing 3–15** A nonidiomatic topmost query.

```
SET ROWCOUNT 10
SELECT *
FROM Customers
ORDER BY CompanyName
SET ROWCOUNT 0
```

This technique needlessly involves SET ROWCOUNT even though the TOP extension is available. It's more code and doesn't perform as well in certain circumstances. Here's another alternative (Listing 3–16):

**Listing 3–16** Another topmost approach.

```
DECLARE c CURSOR FOR
SELECT *
FROM Customers
ORDER BY CompanyName
FOR READ ONLY
```

```
OPEN c

DECLARE @i int
SET @i=0

FETCH c
WHILE (@@FETCH_STATUS=0) AND (@i<9) BEGIN
  SET @i=@i+1
  FETCH c
END

CLOSE c
DEALLOCATE c
```

Obviously, this approach is the worst of all. It's a horrendous mess. It involves a cursor, a variable, and a loop—needlessly and illogically. It returns each row as its own result set (by virtual of the separate calls to FETCH) and requires several times the code of the idiomatic form. It's also slower and more memory intensive. It's unfortunately the kind of approach inexperienced Transact-SQL coders sometimes take.

## Design Patterns

As I said at the top of the chapter, recognizing and using design patterns is just as beneficial in Transact-SQL as it is in other languages. Although most published design patterns are geared toward OOP languages, there are many that are equally useful in Transact-SQL. Recognizing OOP design patterns in a non-OOP language such as Transact-SQL requires a keen eye and the ability to think abstractly.

There are a number of parallels between OOP design patterns and the patterns one may find in Transact-SQL. There are also numerous patterns that only apply to set-oriented languages such as Transact-SQL. I'll discuss a few of each in this section, but the list is by no means complete. When you review someone else's Transact-SQL, try to identify the design patterns at work in it. Recognizing design pattern applications helps make code more readable and more modular.

### Iterator

It's common to need to perform a complex operation (one not easily accomplished with a single T-SQL statement) on every member in a series of like objects. We may want to call a stored procedure, perform a calculation, or execute some dynamic T-SQL on each element in a collection of similar elements. The Iterator pattern provides a template for addressing this situation.

*Design Patterns* defines an Iterator pattern as one whose stated intent is: "Provides a way to access the elements of an aggregate object sequentially without exposing its underlying representation."[4] Not coincidentally, a synonym for Iterator is Cursor. Providing a sequential access path to the rows in a table without exposing the details of how it retrieves those rows is exactly what a cursor does. It allows the T-SQL developer to focus on the rows she seeks, not on how to find them. Listing 3–17 presents an example:

**Listing 3–17**  An example of the Iterator pattern.

```
DECLARE customerlist CURSOR
FOR SELECT CompanyName FROM Customers
FOR READ ONLY

DECLARE @CompanyName varchar(40)

OPEN customerlist

FETCH customerlist INTO @CompanyName
WHILE (@@FETCH_STATUS=0) BEGIN
  EXEC CalcCompanyTaxes @CompanyName
  FETCH customerlist INTO @CompanyName
END

CLOSE customerlist
DEALLOCATE customerlist
```

By definition, a design pattern is also an idiomatic form. The Iterator pattern is no exception: The previous example code is the idiomatic form of cursor use in Transact-SQL. Although there are other ways to structure the loop or to dispose of the cursor, this is the most natural and straightforward form.

Beyond being an idiom, though, Iterator is a design pattern that experienced Transact-SQL developers recognize immediately, and one they use often. It provides a standardized method of iterating through the objects in a list of similar objects, regardless of what they are.

Once a cursor is defined, the Transact-SQL code and the database operations necessary to furnish it with data are unimportant to the code that uses it.

---

4. Gamma, Erich, et al. *Design Patterns*. Reading, MA: Addison-Wesley, 1995. Page 257.

The FETCH command doesn't care about the details behind the cursor—its only concern is the cursor itself. It requests data and the cursor delivers it.

To see how generally applicable this pattern is, consider the example in Listing 3–18:

**Listing 3–18** Executing a command against every object in a database.

```
DECLARE tables CURSOR
FOR SELECT TABLE_NAME FROM INFORMATION_SCHEMA.TABLES
FOR READ ONLY

DECLARE @table sysname

OPEN tables

FETCH tables INTO @table
WHILE (@@FETCH_STATUS=0) BEGIN
  EXEC sp_help @table
  FETCH tables INTO @table
END

CLOSE tables
DEALLOCATE tables
```

This code lists detailed info for the tables in a database. Note how similar in form it is to the earlier example. This form is the design pattern. Even though the specifics change from one application of the pattern to the next, the form is the same. Experienced T-SQL developers can take one look at this code and know exactly what it does. They immediately begin looking for the variable parts of the pattern—the sections that change from application to application— to see what it is the pattern is being applied to do.

---

**NOTE:** Because a cursor can be returned as an output parameter from a stored procedure, it's possible to completely insulate the code that uses it from the code that defines it. This further abstracts the notion of an Iterator facility in Transact-SQL and resembles the GoF Iterator pattern even more closely.

---

In addition to being an idiomatic form, the Transact-SQL Iterator pattern also contains some idiomatic forms of its own—three to be exact. First, notice the declaration of the cursor. There are numerous ways to declare a cursor. For example, you could declare a local cursor variable, then assign a cursor definition to it. This would work, but would be a needless deviation. Remember: When we deviate from established conventions, we want to do so for good reason so that developers reading our code in the future will know what to take note of and what not to—so that they won't be needlessly distracted by inconsequential differences.

Second, notice the loop. We discussed the idiomatic form of a T-SQL WHILE loop earlier. Certainly, the looping behavior could be accomplished through other means—through the use of a GOTO, for example—but again this would be a deviation from what's most natural for no apparent reason. So the loop itself is an idiomatic form. Lastly, notice the cleanup code for the cursor. The call to CLOSE is immediately followed by a call to DEALLOCATE. Why? Couldn't you just deallocate the cursor? Wouldn't it be automatically closed? Well, yes, in fact, it would. However, this is neither the most natural approach nor the most common among experienced developers. Experienced developers clean up after themselves, and they close things they open. CLOSE counteracts OPEN and DEALLOCATE reverses DECLARE, so including both keeps the code symmetrical as well as logical.

## Intersector

As a set-oriented language, set operations are something that Transact-SQL is particularly good at. The most common of these is set intersection. In SQL, set intersection happens through joins. The members in one set (a table or view) are compared with those in another, and the elements that exist in both are returned as the intersection.

The Intersector pattern represents a template for Transact-SQL set intersection. It features an ANSI-style inner join to determine the values two tables have in common. Listing 3–19 presents an example:

**Listing 3–19** The Intersector pattern at work.

```
SELECT c.CompanyName, o.OrderID
FROM Customers c INNER JOIN Orders o ON (c.CustomerID=o.CustomerID)
```

(Results abridged)

```
CompanyName                                OrderID
------------------------------------------ -----------
Alfreds Futterkiste                        10643
Alfreds Futterkiste                        10692
Alfreds Futterkiste                        10702
Alfreds Futterkiste                        10835
```

| | |
|---|---|
| Alfreds Futterkiste | 10952 |
| Alfreds Futterkiste | 11011 |
| Ana Trujillo Emparedados y helados | 10308 |
| Ana Trujillo Emparedados y helados | 10625 |
| Ana Trujillo Emparedados y helados | 10759 |
| Ana Trujillo Emparedados y helados | 10926 |
| Antonio Moreno Taquería | 10365 |
| Antonio Moreno Taquería | 10507 |
| Antonio Moreno Taquería | 10535 |
| Antonio Moreno Taquería | 10573 |

Pretty straightforward, isn't it? Although this code is definitely of the elementary variety, it's important to be able to recognize the pattern on sight. When you see it in code, you should immediately think: *Okay, we're looking for the rows in the first table with matching values in the second one.* Pattern recognition—that's the secret to interpreting complex code.

Of course, numerous variations of the Intersector pattern exist. Using outer joins and theta joins, we can get well beyond simple set intersections. That said, they all follow the same pattern. The join condition may be different, but the question we're answering with each type of join is the same: Which rows in one table relate (or don't relate) to those in the other?

Note that there are other ways to implement set intersection and its variants. However, there's just one that's idiomatic—the one demonstrated in Listing 3–19. Although you can join tables using WHERE clause conditions, it's inadvisable because certain types of joins (outer joins) can actually return incorrect results when expressed in the WHERE clause (this has to do with associative clauses and join order; see *The Guru's Guide to Transact-SQL* for more info). The most natural approach to constructing a join is the one taken in Listing 3–19.

## Qualifier

Beyond returning data, qualifying (or filtering) data is probably the most common thing Transact-SQL coders do. Qualifying data amounts to filtering the rows returned by a query based on the values in a column or columns. In SQL, data is usually qualified using the WHERE clause of the SELECT statement (Listing 3–20):

**Listing 3–20** The Qualifier pattern.

```
SELECT *
FROM Customers
WHERE Country='Mexico'
```

This is a very basic example, but the pattern is still in evidence. Whether the WHERE clause is a simple one like the one in Listing 3–20 or a more complex expression featuring compound clauses and subqueries, the pattern is the same: This is the way you qualify the rows in a result set using Transact-SQL.

Note that there are other ways of filtering a result set. For example, you could put your filter criteria in the HAVING clause instead of the WHERE clause, like this (Listing 3–21):

**Listing 3–21** An unnatural filter.

```
SELECT City, COUNT(*) AS NumberInCity
FROM Customers
GROUP BY City
HAVING City LIKE 'A%'
```

The problem with the code in Listing 3–21 is that it needlessly makes use of a HAVING clause when a WHERE clause would do. The WHERE approach is the more idiomatic, or natural, of the two. Other developers looking at the code may attach some significance to the fact that HAVING is used here instead of WHERE, when in fact there's no good reason for it. Here's the query restated to use WHERE (Listing 3–22):

**Listing 3–22** The idiomatic form of the Qualifier pattern.

```
SELECT City, COUNT(*) AS NumberInCity
FROM Customers
WHERE City Like 'A%'
GROUP BY City
```

The purpose of a HAVING clause is to filter the query *after* the result set has been gathered (for example, based on the value of an aggregate function). It's unnecessary in Listing 3–21, and, in fact, SQL Server translates the HAVING clause to a WHERE clause internally. If you compare the execution plan for the query in Listing 3–21 with the one in Listing 3–22, you'll see that they're the same. If SQL Server didn't perform this optimization and the table contained a large number of rows, performance would likely suffer markedly because all rows would be gathered from the table before the filter was applied.

## Executor

For all the power of Transact-SQL, it's fairly common to need to construct dynamic T-SQL and execute it from a stored procedure or batch. Particularly when you need to parameterize the name of an object or a column—something Transact-SQL itself doesn't normally allow—sometimes you simply have no alternative. The Executor pattern provides a template for creating and executing dynamic T-SQL strings (Listing 3–23):

**Listing 3–23** The Executor pattern.

```
DECLARE @s int, @sql nvarchar(128)

DECLARE spids CURSOR FOR

SELECT spid
FROM master..sysprocesses
WHERE spid<>@@SPID AND net_address<>''
FOR READ ONLY

OPEN spids

FETCH spids INTO @s
WHILE (@@FETCH_STATUS=0) BEGIN
  SET @sql='KILL '+CAST(@s AS varchar)
  EXEC sp_executesql @sql
  FETCH spids INTO @s
END

CLOSE spids
DEALLOCATE spids
```

This example opens a cursor against the sysprocesses pseudo-table and creates dynamic T-SQL statements that terminate every user connection except the current one. Notice that I say *user* connection. We distinguish between user connections and system connections by examining the **net_address** column in sysprocesses. A system connection has an empty **net_address** column. We keep from attempting to terminate the current connection (this isn't allowed, anyway) by checking the automatic variable @@SPID.

You could put any valid T-SQL code you wanted in the **@sql** variable. The sp_executesql procedure would attempt to execute it regardless. You could also loop on other conditions and across other data sources. For example, you could loop through the objects in the current database and construct a dynamic T-SQL command to do something with them.

Note the use of sp_executesql. You could use EXEC() here instead. I encourage the use of sp_executesql because it's more flexible and will perform well in a larger number of scenarios than EXEC(). For one thing, sp_executesql supports parameterized queries. This encourages plan reuse and will lead to generally better performance. The example in Listing 3–23 doesn't happen to have any parameters (only valid search parameters are allowed; you can't substitute object names or connection IDs, for example), but if it did, sp_executesql would be a better choice than EXEC(). sp_executesql can also return a result code from the dynamic T-SQL call. If the dynamic code raises an error with a severity of 11 or more, sp_executesql will return the error number in its result code.

So, even though EXEC() would work equally well in this particular instance, sp_executesql is the approach most often taken by experienced T-SQL developers for the reasons I've listed. This makes it more idiomatic than the EXEC() approach and is the reason I've used it to build the pattern example.

## Conveyor

The Conveyor pattern provides a mechanism for returning a code or result up through a call stack. Say, for example, that you have three procedures: ProcA, ProcB, and ProcC. ProcA calls ProcB, and ProcB calls ProcC. When ProcC runs, an unexpected problem occurs, and you want to convey that info back up the chain to ProcA. How do you do this? The Conveyor pattern shows how (Listing 3–24):

**Listing 3–24** The Conveyor pattern.

```
CREATE PROC ProcC AS
IF OBJECT_ID('no_exist') IS NOT NULL
  SELECT * FROM no_exist
ELSE
  RETURN(-1)
GO


CREATE PROC ProcB AS
DECLARE @res int
EXEC @res=ProcC
RETURN(@res)
GO


CREATE PROCEDURE ProcA AS
DECLARE @res int
EXEC @res=ProcB
SELECT @res
```

```
GO

EXEC ProcA
```

(Results)

```
-----------
-1
```

Note the way that we use stored procedure result codes to pass the original return code from procedure to procedure. This works great for integers, but what if you want to return an error *message* instead of a code? The pattern still holds (Listing 3–25):

**Listing 3–25**  The Conveyor pattern can convey data of any type.

```
USE tempdb
GO
DROP PROC ProcA, ProcB, ProcC
GO
CREATE PROC ProcC @Msg varchar(128) OUT AS
IF OBJECT_ID('no_exist') IS NOT NULL
  SELECT * FROM no_exist
ELSE
  SET @Msg='Table doesn''t exist'
GO

CREATE PROC ProcB @Msg varchar(128) OUT AS
EXEC ProcC @Msg OUT
GO

CREATE PROCEDURE ProcA AS
DECLARE @Msg varchar(128)
EXEC ProcB @Msg OUT
SELECT @Msg
GO

EXEC ProcA
```

(Results)

```
----------------------------------------------------------------
Table doesn't exist
```

In this application of the pattern, we simply use output parameters to convey the message up the call stack to the topmost procedure. Because we can use virtually any data type here (including a cursor), we have the flexibility to return any information we want.

A final application of the pattern would be to transmit a real error code up through the chain to the original calling routine. Listing 3–26 presents an example:

**Listing 3–26** The Conveyor pattern can convey errors as well as messages.

```
CREATE PROC ProcC AS
  DECLARE @err int
  IF @@TRANCOUNT=0
    ROLLBACK TRAN -- Error, we're not in a tran
  SET @err=@@ERROR
  RETURN(@err)
GO

CREATE PROC ProcB AS
DECLARE @res int
EXEC @res=ProcC
RETURN(@res)
GO

CREATE PROCEDURE ProcA AS
DECLARE @res int
EXEC @res=ProcB
SELECT @res
GO
EXEC ProcA
```

(Results)

```
Server: Msg 3903, Level 16, State 1, Procedure ProcC, Line 4
The ROLLBACK TRANSACTION request has no corresponding BEGIN TRANSACTION.

-----------
3903
```

Regardless of the specific application, the Conveyor pattern provides a mechanism for conveying information along a chain of stored procedures. In this sense, Conveyor is similar to GoF's Chain of Responsibility pattern.

## Restorer

The Restorer pattern provides a mechanism for cleaning up resource utilization when an error condition occurs. Restoring the operating environment is particularly important in the middle of a transaction. In order to avoid orphaning a transaction, it's crucial that you properly handle error conditions when a transaction is active. Orphaned transactions can hold locks and block other connections from working. Here's an implementation of the Restorer pattern (Listing 3–27):

**Listing 3–27** The Restorer pattern cleans up the environment when trouble strikes.

```
CREATE PROC ProcR AS
DECLARE @err int

BEGIN TRAN

Update Customers SET City = 'Dallas'

SELECT 1/0 -- Force an error
SET @err=@@ERROR

IF @err<>0 BEGIN
  ROLLBACK TRAN
  RETURN(@err)
END

COMMIT TRAN
GO

DECLARE @res int
EXEC @res=ProcR
SELECT @res
```

(Results)

```
Server: Msg 8134, Level 16, State 1, Procedure ProcR, Line 8
Divide by zero error encountered.
-----------
8134
```

The key pieces of this pattern are the caching of the error code, and the IF block that reacts to nonzero errors. We cache @@ERROR because it's reset by the next successful statement execution. Once we've cached it, we check the saved value and roll back the active transaction if an error has occurred. We could just as easily have cleaned up other types of resources (Listing 3–28):

**Listing 3–28** The Restorer pattern cleans up the environment when trouble strikes.

```
CREATE PROC ProcR AS
DECLARE @err int

CREATE TABLE ##myglobal
(c1 int)

INSERT ##myglobal DEFAULT VALUES

SELECT 1/0 -- Force an error
SET @err=@@ERROR

IF @err<>0 BEGIN
  DROP TABLE ##myglobal
  RETURN(@err)
END

DROP TABLE ##myglobal

GO

DECLARE @res int
EXEC @res=ProcR
SELECT @res
```

(Results)

```
Server: Msg 8134, Level 16, State 1, Procedure ProcR, Line 9
Divide by zero error encountered.
-----------
8134
```

Here we drop a global temporary table when an error occurs. There are a number of different types of cleanup we could perform here, the most important of which is transactional cleanup. Apply the Restorer pattern to avoid orphaned transactions and unnecessary blocking.

A variation of Restorer applies the pattern proactively to clean up problems that may have been inherited by a block of code, but were not caused by it. An example is presented in Listing 3–29:

**Listing 3–29** You can apply the Restorer pattern proactively.

```
CREATE PROC ProcR AS

IF @@TRANCOUNT<>0  -- Rollback old transactions before starting another
  ROLLBACK TRAN

DECLARE @err int

BEGIN TRAN

Update Customers SET City = 'Dallas'

SELECT 1/0 -- Force an error
SET @err=@@ERROR

IF @err<>0 BEGIN
  ROLLBACK TRAN
  RETURN(@err)
END

COMMIT TRAN
GO

DECLARE @res int
EXEC @res=ProcR
SELECT @res
```

(Results)

```
Server: Msg 8134, Level 16, State 1, Procedure ProcR, Line 12
Divide by zero error encountered.
-----------
8134
```

Notice the first ROLLBACK in the procedure. This ROLLBACK occurs when the procedure detects an active transaction (@@TRANCOUNT<>0) when it first starts. Because this is considered an error, the procedure rolls back the open transaction (a single call to ROLLBACK rolls back all active transactions for a connection, regardless of nesting) before starting another. In this sense, it's implementing the Restorer pattern proactively—to clean up after others who may have left the environment in a transitive state. Coding this sort of logic into your applications is especially important when connection pooling is being used with SQL Server (very common with Web servers). Because one virtual connection can leave an open transaction that can affect later users of the same physical connection, it's important that your code knows how to protect itself from rogue transactions and other undesirable remnants.

---

**TIP:** Transact-SQL's error-handling constructs are far from airtight. They don't always work the way you might expect them to or the way that they should work. For example, there are plenty of errors that are severe enough to terminate the current command batch. When they occur, they prevent any error-handling code that might follow them (even in a stored procedure) from being reached. So, even if your code checks @@ERROR and calls ROLLBACK when a problem occurs, there are errors that will prevent it from ever being executed. This is probably the most common cause of orphaned transactions and is the reason the code you write should check for an orphaned transaction before beginning another.

---

## Prototype

According to *Design Patterns*, the intent of the Prototype pattern is to "specify the kinds of objects to create using a prototypical instance, and create new objects by copying the prototype."[5] In other words, you start with a template or prototypical instance of an object, and use an implementation of the Prototype pattern to replicate it in cookie-cutter fashion.

The most obvious Transact-SQL implementation of the Prototype pattern is the SELECT…INTO construct. Because it places the result set of a SELECT statement into a table of its own, SELECT…INTO can be used to easily replicate the contents of a table or view, as shown in Listing 3–30:

**Listing 3–30** A Transact-SQL implementation of the Prototype pattern.

```
SELECT *
INTO NewCustomers
FROM Customers
```

---

5. Ibid. Page 117.

Because SELECT...INTO has all the power of a plain SELECT statement, you can change the prototype in transit by specifying a column list, WHERE clause criteria, or even a GROUP BY or HAVING clause. This gives the Transact-SQL implementation of the pattern much more flexibility than most OOP implementations and leverages the power of SQL as a set-oriented language. For example, you can supply a false WHERE clause to create an empty copy of the table (Listing 3–31):

**Listing 3–31** An implementation of Prototype that creates an empty copy.

```
SELECT *
INTO NewCustomers
FROM Customers
WHERE 0=1
```

Here we clone the table's structure, but omit its data. Using a false WHERE clause with SELECT...INTO is an easy way to replicate the structure of a table without incurring the expense or log activity of copying its data. Another variation of the pattern allows you to specify new data when cloning the table, like this (Listing 3–32):

**Listing 3–32** This T-SQL Prototype pattern implementation supplies new data during the copy.

```
SELECT IDENTITY(int, 1,1) AS CustNo, *
INTO NewCustomers
FROM Customers
```

You could also specify new columns, columns from other tables or views (via a join), constants, or functions. The possibilities are endless. The bottom line here is that you should be able to recognize the Prototype pattern on sight and know that SELECT...INTO is the most common implementation of it in Transact-SQL.

## Singleton

The purpose of the Singleton pattern is to ensure that only one instance of a class exists at any given time and to provide an access path into that instance. In relational database terms, this could have a couple of different implementations. Strictly speaking, the equivalent to an object-oriented class, in an

RDBMS, is a table. An instance of the class would be a row in the table, so an obvious implementation of Singleton would be to ensure that the table has just one row, like this (Listing 3–33):

**Listing 3–33** A Transact-SQL implementation of the Singleton design pattern.

```
USE tempdb
GO
DROP TABLE LastCustNo
GO
CREATE TABLE LastCustNo
(LastCustNo int)
GO
INSERT LastCustNo VALUES (1)
GO
CREATE TRIGGER LastCustNoInsert ON LastCustNo FOR INSERT AS
IF (SELECT COUNT(*) FROM LastCustNo)>1 BEGIN
    RAISERROR('You may not insert more than one row into this table',16,10)
    ROLLBACK TRAN
END
GO
INSERT LastCustNo VALUES (2) -- Fails because of trigger
GO
SELECT * FROM LastCustNo
```

Thanks to the trigger, only one row is allowed to exist in the table at any one time. If you attempt to insert a row, and the table already contains at least one row, an error is raised and the transaction is rolled back. Of course, BULK INSERT (with trigger execution disabled) can skirt this, but, short of intentionally circumventing it, our trigger-based Singleton implementation is pretty foolproof.

Note the use of IF (SELECT COUNT(*) FROM LastCustNo)>1 to determine whether the table already has a row. Why do we test >1 instead of =1? Very simple. With the exception of INSTEAD OF triggers, Transact-SQL triggers run *after* an operation has completed, but before that operation has been committed to the database. This means that, from the perspective of the trigger, the LastCustNo table appears to have two rows in it until we roll back the transaction. This also prevents us from using the EXISTS() predicate to test the table for rows, as in IF EXISTS(SELECT * FROM LastCustNo). Because newly inserted rows appear to the trigger to be in the table until we roll back the transaction, testing EXISTS() would prevent a row from being inserted into the table, even if the table was empty prior to the insertion attempt.

Another application of Singleton in relational database terms is in the use of primary and unique key constraints to prevent multiple instances of the same row. In other words, if we equate a table to a class and rows to instances (objects) of that class, applying Singleton to prevent multiple instances of a row amounts to adding a primary key or a unique key constraint to the table.

From a SQL Server application standpoint, a possible use of the Singleton pattern is in keeping multiple instances of an application from connecting to the server. For example, if you already have one instance of the Check Writer program connected to the database, you may not want to allow another to connect until the first one disconnects.

There are a couple of SQL Server facilities that come in handy in situations like this. The first one is the application locks facility. SQL Server allows you to use its lock manager to manage resources outside the server. In this case, you could take out an application lock when your app started, then release it when the app closed. By taking out the lock in Exclusive mode, you'd prevent another instance of the app from running until you released it. Here's some code:

```
DECLARE @res int
BEGIN TRAN
EXEC @res = sp_getapplock @Resource = 'Check Writer',
            @LockMode = 'Exclusive'
-- Return to your app

-- Then execute this when the app exits
EXEC @res = sp_releaseapplock @Resource = 'Check Writer'
ROLLBACK TRAN
```

The problem with this approach is the potential for it to keep a transaction open for an extended period of time. Generally speaking, you should not leave a transaction open for long periods of time or when a user is being prompted for input. Because sp_getapplock requires an open user transaction in order for it to take out the lock we've requested, it may not be the best tool to use in this situation. Let's look at a better one:

```
IF EXISTS(SELECT * FROM master..sysprocesses WHERE context_info=0x123456)
   RAISERROR('You can run only one copy of this application at a time',20,1)
    WITH LOG
ELSE
   SET CONTEXT_INFO 0x123456
```

This code uses the SET CONTEXT_INFO command to plug a user-defined value into sysprocesses on start-up. Then, each time the app starts, it checks for this value. If the value is there, a connection already exists with the special token, so the app raises an error that terminates its own connection. If the value is not there, the routine puts it there and proceeds to load the application.

This technique is one way of ensuring that only one instance of an application connects to SQL Server at a time, but there are others. For example, an application could set the host name session variable and query sysprocesses for it when it loaded. There are a number of different ways of implementing Singleton in Transact-SQL.

## Other Patterns

A number of other object-oriented design patterns have correspondents or loose equivalents in the realm of Transact-SQL. For example, a SQL Server view object approximates the GoF's Composite pattern, and a view with an INSTEAD OF trigger implements something resembling the Façade pattern: It provides a unified interface to a set of interfaces in a subsystem. In this analogy, the "set of interfaces" is the set of tables referenced by the view and the Transact-SQL code needed to update them. This code is implemented by the INSTEAD OF trigger. The user updates the data returned by the view as though it came from a single table, hence the view is the unified interface. The INSTEAD OF trigger takes the updates made to the view and dispatches them to the appropriate underlying tables. The whole of the implementation—the view, the trigger, and the underlying tables—represents an approximation of the Façade pattern. When you see a view with an INSTEAD OF trigger attached to it, it should be obvious that its designer intended to provide a unified interface to something more complex—that he or she intended to insulate you from the details associated with updating the view's underlying tables.

Another example of an object-oriented design pattern approximation in Transact-SQL is the Chain of Responsibility pattern. I mentioned the Chain of Responsibility pattern earlier in the discussion of the Conveyor pattern. Here we'll get into a little more detail. *Design Patterns* describes Chain of Responsibility as a pattern that avoids "coupling the sender of a request to its receiver by giving more than one object a chance to handle the request."[6] It goes on to say that to implement the pattern, you must "Chain the receiving objects and pass the request along the chain until an object handles it."[7] Think about this. What construct in Transact-SQL most closely implements the described behavior? Triggers. More specifically, nested triggers and multiple triggers per table. Triggers that perform operations that cause other triggers to fire implement the

6. Ibid. Page 223.

7. Ibid.

chaining behavior. The same could be said for multiple triggers on the same table. Let's say that you defined multiple INSERT triggers on a particular table and that each of these triggers was responsible for validating a different column in a newly inserted row. The insert "request," as it were, would, from a functional standpoint, be passed from trigger to trigger, with the triggers firing in no particular order. In either case, with multiple triggers on one table or with nested triggers, if any one of the triggers decides to reject the insert and roll back the transaction, all bets are off—the entire operation is aborted then and there. This implements the part of the pattern that calls for passing the request "along the chain until an object handles it." Although the analogy is not exact, the pattern is indeed there if you look for it.

Command is another GoF pattern with a correspondent in the world of Transact-SQL. Its *Design Patterns* definition is: "Encapsulates a request as an object, thereby letting you parameterize clients with different requests, queue or log requests, and support undoable operations."[8] See if you can figure this one out. What SQL Server element does this most sound like? Think about the "queue or log requests" capability and the "undoable operations." Right! The Transact-SQL implementation of the GoF Command pattern is the transaction! SQL Server's transaction log is the facility in which "requests" (changes to data) are logged. The change itself is the request, and operations are undoable by virtue of the fact that you can roll back the transaction.

There are other parallels between the GoF patterns and techniques commonly used to build Transact-SQL applications. Knowing, using, and recognizing common design patterns is just as important in Transact-SQL as it is in any other language. Pattern recognition helps make the overall layout of an application simpler and easier to understand, and pattern use helps keep a program modular and easier to extend.

## Summary

In this chapter we discussed common design elements—idioms and patterns—in Transact-SQL code. You learned about the importance of taking idiomatic, or natural, approaches to building software. Hopefully, you came to understand that deviating from established conventions and straightforward approaches comes at a cost—increased program complexity—and that you should avoid it when you can. You learned about some of the idioms and design patterns commonly used in Transact-SQL and the differences between idioms and patterns.

---

8. Ibid. Page 233.

# CHAPTER 4

# Source Code Management

*I'm not a great programmer, I'm just a good programmer with great habits.*

*—Kent Beck*[1]

I've placed this chapter as early as I have in the book because I think it's crucial to adopt good source code management habits if you're going to develop robust code for complex projects. Successfully building a sophisticated system with faulty code management practices in place is about as likely as building a space ship in a junkyard: Although it's theoretically possible, it's not very likely (Andy Griffith's *Salvage I* notwithstanding).

There's a tendency among Transact-SQL developers, especially inexperienced ones, to treat Transact-SQL code as though it's not "real" source code. They don't edit it with a decent editor. They're content to work eight hours a day in a tool that's more suited to editing batch files than program code. They don't comment their code or follow any of the standard conventions you might see with other types of programming languages. And they don't "version control" their code. They don't use source code management tools such as VSS, PVCS, or Source Integrity (Vertical Sky Software Manager) to manage their Transact-SQL source code.

Instead, stored procedure code is viewed as more of a database resource than program code, and is therefore managed in the atomic, transactional manner that other types of database objects normally are. From this perspective, Transact-SQL procedural code is just data. After all, it resides in the database in a table named syscomments, and it is protected from corruption via backups just like other data. So the thinking goes.

The purpose of this chapter is to refute the myth that Transact-SQL code is not "real" source code and to establish the value of source code management (a.k.a. version control) software in working with it. Although you could use vir-

---

1. Fowler, Martin. *Refactoring: Improving the Design of Existing Code*. Reading, MA: Addison-Wesley, 1999. Page 57.

**103**

tually any text file-based version control or source code management system to control your code, this chapter covers VSS because it's the one I use.

## The Benefits of Source Code Management

I suppose I should begin this discussion by talking about the benefits of storing your Transact-SQL code in a version control or source code management system. Some of these benefits aren't immediately obvious, so it's instructive to go through a few of them.

First and foremost, version controlling your code allows you to roll back to a previous version should you discover a bug or decide to scrap a code branch you've started. Because every version you've checked into the system is readily available, accessing a previous one is easy.

Second, version control systems usually provide difference-checking facilities. These are invaluable. When you've discovered a newly introduced coding problem and want to know what's causing it, you can check the differences between the broken version and the last one that worked, and usually find your problem. VSS has a visual difference-checking tool that places the two files side by side on the screen and highlights their differences.

Third, version control systems ensure version consistency. As you develop software and release products, your software will naturally begin to be categorized by version. Say that you discover six months after the release of a given product version that you need to compile that specific version again. Your version control system's ability to label versions and to retrieve a complete version in one step makes this a snap. You simply find the version with the label you want and instruct the system to retrieve it for you. Think about how complex this process would be without the assistance of a version control system. Once you located what you believed were the old version's source files, you'd have to check each one—perhaps hundreds or even thousands of them—and attempt to ensure that not only were they from the *right* version of the application, but also from the *same* version. And this assumes that you retained the old version's source code in the first place. In essence, you'd be forced to become a human version control system. Rather than creating software, you'd spend a fair amount of your time doing things better left to computers.

Fourth, source code management systems help protect source code from accidental loss or destruction. Because the source code is typically stored in a central repository (a database of some type), it's easy to back up and much easier to manage than hundreds or thousands of files scattered across the desktop machines of a development team.

Fifth, version control systems make change management much easier. Because those who change code must check it out before changing it and must check it back in before those changes take effect, it's easy to track who's changing what in the source code. If a change was ill advised or detrimental to the application, it can be easily rolled back. If a change necessitates an explanation or comments that further detail its purpose and scope, these can be included when the file is checked back into the system. Because changes to a given source code element can only be made by one developer at a time, version control systems prevent developers from accidentally overwriting one another's changes. In short, good source code management systems help manage source code. They elevate source code management from the equivalent of a messy desk to a well-organized filing cabinet that can support the development of complex projects.

---

**NOTE:** As I write this, a new generation of version control systems is on the horizon that changes the dynamics of source code management in important ways. These new systems handle change management and other source code management duties in ways that are more conducive to large programming teams. For example, one feature that's increasingly being touted is the support for simultaneous changes to a single source code file by multiple developers. In this scenario, the version control system performs a three-way (or *n*-way) difference check and resolves conflicts between different versions of the same member. Obviously, this could be a real boon to large teams with large source code files. With traditional version control systems, changes to a given source code file—even independent and unrelated changes—are precluded as long as someone else has the file checked out. It's not uncommon for a developer on a large team to spend a measurable amount of time asking people to check in a code member so that he can proceed with his work. As I've said, this chapter covers source code management from the perspective of more traditional tools such as VSS, but this new generation of tools is worth keeping an eye on.

---

# The dt Procedures

If you've installed Visual Studio Enterprise and snooped around the system tables on your server much, you may have noticed a set of Microsoft-supplied stored procedures with names that start with "dt." Visual Studio uses these procedures to provide source code management for Transact-SQL stored procedures.

A cursory check of these routines reveals that they use a COM object called SQLVersionControl.VCS_SQL. This object is used by Visual InterDev to manage stored procedure source code directly from the IDE. If you've installed the Visual InterDev Server Components, you already have this object installed on your system and could conceivably use the dt_% procedures even without using InterDev itself.

That said, not everyone will have Visual Studio Enterprise, so this chapter will show you how to manage Transact-SQL scripts using VSS Explorer and the COM interfaces provided by VSS itself.

# Best Practices

With something as management oriented as version control, it makes sense to begin with a discussion of what are commonly known in management circles as *best practices*. Best practices are techniques and approaches to accomplishing tasks that are better than others. Ostensibly, they are the best ways of doing things. All disciplines—especially engineering disciplines—have best practices. Most types of skilled work have techniques that work better than others. I'll talk about a few that I think you should follow regarding source code management.

## Store Objects in Scripts

Although you could conceivably store the Transact-SQL source code for the objects you create exclusively in the SQL Server databases in which they reside, this isn't a very good idea. Why? Because without tools like the dt_% procedures, you have no way of version controlling them. That is, you have no way of managing changes to them, of rolling back to a former version (without restoring an entire database backup), and no way of checking differences between versions. So, first and foremost, store the source to your objects in script files.

## Maintain Separate Scripts

Store each object in its own script file. This keeps the granularity of the system high, and helps you avoid blocking other developers from making changes to unrelated code. You can edit a procedure or other type of script without worrying about keeping other people from working.

## Don't Use Unicode

Save each script file in ANSI (non-Unicode) format. Not all version control systems can read Unicode (the current version of VSS can't), and even though this is the default format of the scripting facility in Enterprise Manager, you should not use it if you want to remain compatible with the majority of text file-based tools out there. For example, even though you can check a Unicode file into VSS, it is treated as a binary file because VSS doesn't recognize the Unicode text format. This means that you can't check for differences between versions of the file—a severe limitation.

## Use Labels to Denote Versions

Most version control systems have a facility that allows you to label or tag a version of your source code so that you can later reference it as a coherent group. Use these facilities to denote software or application versions. It'll save you trouble down the road. Obviously, the various source members in an application change at different rates. Their internal version numbers will differ. However, if you assign a versionwide label to the files that make up a given release of the software, you can retrieve and compile that release as often as you need to without having to synchronize the various internal revision numbers manually.

## Use Keywords to Sign Your Files

A common feature of version control systems is a facility that allows you to embed special keywords or tags in your source files that can be expanded into version-related info when you check in the files. In VSS, these are known as *keywords*, and they allow you to record such useful info as the person who last changed a file, the date and time of the last modification, the internal version number of the file, and many other useful tidbits, in the source files themselves.

VSS keywords are enclosed in a pair of $ symbols. For example, to embed the author of a given source member in that file, include the **$Author $** keyword. When the file is checked in, **$Author $** will be translated into the VSS user name of the last person to change the file.

Typically, you embed these keyword tags in comments so that they don't disturb your code. A good place to put these comments is at the top of your script files. Here's an example of a Transact-SQL comment block that I often use (Listing 4–1):

**Listing 4–1**  An example comment block.

```
/*

Object: sp_usage
Description: Provides usage information for stored procedures and
descriptions of other types of objects
```

```
Usage: sp_usage @objectname='ObjectName', @desc='Description of object'
            [, @parameters='param1,param2...']
            [, @example='Example of usage']
            [, @workfile='File name of script']
            [, @author='Object author']
            [, @email='Author email']
            [, @version='Version number or info']
            [, @revision='Revision number or info']
            [, @datecreated='Date created']
            [, @datelastchanged='Date last changed']

Returns: (None)

$Workfile: sp_usage.sql $

$Author: Khen $. Email: khen@khen.com

$Revision: 7 $

Example: sp_usage @objectname='sp_who', @desc='Returns a list of currently
running jobs', @parameters=[@loginname]

Created: 1992-04-03. $Modtime: 4/07/00 8:38p $.


*/
```

Note the text that VSS has inserted into each keyword tag. In the case of **$Workfile $**, VSS has inserted "sp_usage.sql" into the tag. In the case of **$Author $**, "khen" has been inserted.

---

**CAVEAT:** VSS keywords are case sensitive. If you use VSS and decide to embed these keywords in your Transact-SQL source files, be sure to enter them in the correct case. If you've enabled keyword expansion, but notice that some of the keywords you've entered aren't being expanded properly, check the case of the errant keywords.

---

You enable VSS keyword expansion by file extension using the VSS Administrator program. To turn on keyword expansion for a particular type of file, go to the General tab in the Tools|Options dialog in the VSS Administrator program. In the **Expand keywords in files of type** entry box, enter the file masks of the files in which you want keyword expansion to occur (e.g., *.SQL).

Table 4–1 lists the supported VSS keywords and what they signify.

**Table 4–1** VSS Keywords and Their Translations

| Keyword tag | Expanded to |
| --- | --- |
| **$Author: $** | Name of user who last changed file |
| **$Modtime: $** | Last modification date/time |
| **$Revision: $** | Internal VSS revision number |
| **$Workfile: $** | Name of file |
| **$Archive: $** | Name of VSS archive |
| **$Date: $** | Last check in date/time |
| **$Header: $** | A combination of **$Logfile: $, $Revision: $, $Date: $,** and **$Author: $** |
| **$History: $** | File history in VSS format |
| **$JustDate: $** | Last check-in date |
| **$Log: $** | File history in RCS format |
| **$Logfile: $** | Duplicate of **$Archive: $** |
| **$NoKeywords: $** | Turn off keyword expansion |

## Don't Encrypt Unless Absolutely Necessary

When you distribute SQL Server-based applications to customers and other third parties, you may be tempted to encrypt the source to your stored procedures, functions, and similar objects. Obviously this protects your code from prying eyes and keeps people from making changes to your code without your knowledge.

That said, unless you have real concerns about confidential or proprietary information being stolen, I recommend against encrypting your SQL Server objects. To me, encrypting SQL Server objects is usually more trouble than it's worth. There are a number of disadvantages to encrypting the source code to SQL Server objects. Let's discuss a few of them.

One, encrypted objects cannot be scripted, even by Enterprise Manager. That is, once a procedure or function is encrypted, you cannot retrieve its source from SQL Server. The well-known but undocumented methods of decoding encrypted source in earlier versions of SQL Server no longer work, and other methods one might discover are not supported by Microsoft. To make matters worse, if you attempt to script an encrypted object via Enterprise Manager using the default options, your new script will have a DROP statement for the object, but not a CREATE. Instead, all you'll see is a helpful comment informing you that scripting encrypted objects isn't supported (whereas, obviously, dropping them is). If you run this script, your object will be lost. It will be dropped, but not recreated.

Two, encrypted objects cannot be published as part of a SQL Server replication. If your customers set up replication operations to keep multiple servers
in synch, they'll run into problems if you encrypt your code.

Three, you can't check encrypted source code for version info (such as that
inserted by a source code management system). Because customers can load
backups that may reinstall an older version of your code over a newer one, it's
extremely handy to be able to check the code for version info *on the customer's
server.* If your code is encrypted, you can't easily do this. If it's not, and if you've
included version information in the source code, you should be able to easily
determine the exact version of an object the customer is using.

Listing 4–2 shows a procedure that you can use to list the version information in your SQL Server objects. Basically, it scans a database's syscomments
table for the keyword tags supported by VSS and produces a columnar report
of the objects with these embedded keywords. Running this procedure can give
you a quick bird's-eye view of the version info for all the Transact-SQL source
code in a database.

**Listing 4–2** A procedure to list VSS version information in stored procedures.

```
USE master
GO
IF OBJECT_ID('dbo.sp_GGShowVersion') IS NOT NULL
  DROP PROC dbo.sp_GGShowVersion
GO
CREATE PROC dbo.sp_GGShowVersion @Mask varchar(30)='%', @ObjType
varchar(2)='%'
/*

GGVersion: 2.0.1
Object: sp_GGShowVersion
Description: Shows version, revision and other info for procedures, views,
triggers, and functions

Usage: sp_GGShowVersion @Mask, @ObjType -- @Mask is an object name mask
(supports wildcards)
                                        indicating which objects to list
                                        @ObjType is an object type mask
                                        (supports wildcards)
                                        indicating which object types to list

                                        Supported object types include:
                                        P   Procedures
                                        V   Views
                                        TR  Triggers
                                        FN  Functions
```

```
Returns: (none)
$Workfile: sp_ggshowversion.SQL $

$Author: Khen $. Email: khen@khen.com

$Revision: 1 $

Example: sp_GGShowVersion

Created: 2000-04-03. $Modtime: 4/29/00 2:49p $.

*/
AS
DECLARE @GGVersion varchar(30), @Revision varchar(30), @author varchar(30),
@Date varchar(30), @Modtime varchar(30)
SELECT @GGVersion='GGVersion: ',@Revision='$'+'Revision: ',@Date='$'+'Date:
',@Modtime='$'+'Modtime: ',@Author='$'+'Author: '

SELECT DISTINCT Object=SUBSTRING(o.name,1,30),
        Type=CASE o.Type
        WHEN 'P' THEN 'Procedure'
        WHEN 'V' THEN 'View'
        WHEN 'TR' THEN 'Trigger'
        WHEN 'FN' THEN 'Function'
        ELSE o.Type
        END,
        Version=CASE
                WHEN CHARINDEX(@GGVersion,c.text)<>0 THEN
SUBSTRING(LTRIM(SUBSTRING(c.text,CHARINDEX(@GGVersion,c.text)+LEN(@GGVersio
n),10)),1,ISNULL(NULLIF(CHARINDEX(CHAR(13),LTRIM(SUBSTRING(c.text,CHARINDEX
(@GGVersion,c.text)+LEN(@GGVersion),10)))-1,-1),1))
        ELSE NULL
        END,
        Revision=CONVERT(int,
        CASE
        WHEN CHARINDEX(@Revision,c.text)<>0 THEN
SUBSTRING(LTRIM(SUBSTRING(c.text,CHARINDEX(@Revision,c.text)+LEN(@Revision)
,10))
,1,ISNULL(NULLIF(CHARINDEX('
',LTRIM(SUBSTRING(c.text,CHARINDEX(@Revision,c.text)+LEN(@Revision),10)))-
1,-1),1))
        ELSE '0'
        END),
        Created=o.crdate,
        Owner=SUBSTRING(USER_NAME(uid),1,10),
        'Last Modified By'=
```

```
SUBSTRING(LTRIM(SUBSTRING(c.text,CHARINDEX(@Author,c.text)+LEN(@Author),10)
),1,ISNULL(NULLIF(CHARINDEX('
$',LTRIM(SUBSTRING(c.text,CHARINDEX(@Author,c.text)+LEN(@Author),10)))-1,-
1),1)),
        'Last Checked In'=CASE WHEN CHARINDEX(@Date,c.text)<>0 THEN
SUBSTRING(LTRIM(SUBSTRING(c.text,CHARINDEX(@Date,c.text)+LEN(@Date),15)),1,
ISNULL(NULLIF(CHARINDEX('
$',LTRIM(SUBSTRING(c.text,CHARINDEX(@Date,c.text)+LEN(@Date),20)))-1,-
1),1)) ELSE NULL END,
        'Last
Modified'=SUBSTRING(LTRIM(SUBSTRING(c.text,CHARINDEX(@Modtime,c.text)+LEN(@
Modtime),20)),1,ISNULL(NULLIF(CHARINDEX('
$',LTRIM(SUBSTRING(c.text,CHARINDEX(@Modtime,c.text)+LEN(@Modtime),20)))-
1,-1),1))
FROM dbo.syscomments c RIGHT OUTER JOIN dbo.sysobjects o ON c.id=o.id
WHERE o.name LIKE @Mask
AND (o.type LIKE @ObjType AND o.TYPE in ('P','V','FN','TR'))
AND (c.text LIKE '%'+@Revision+'%' OR c.text IS NULL)
AND (c.colid=(SELECT MIN(c1.colid) FROM syscomments c1 WHERE c1.id=c.id) OR
c.text IS NULL)
ORDER BY Object
GO
GRANT ALL ON dbo.sp_GGShowversion TO public
GO
EXEC dbo.sp_GGShowVersion
```

(Results abridged)

```
Object                       Type       Version  Revision Created
------------------------     ---------  -------- -------- --------------------
sp_created                   Procedure  NULL     2        2000-04-08 00:19:51.680
sp_GGShowVersion             Procedure  2.0.1    1        2000-04-29 15:30:56.197
sp_hexstring                 Procedure  NULL     1        2000-04-08 15:12:21.610
sp_object_script_comments    Procedure  NULL     1        2000-04-29 12:59:08.250
sp_usage                     Procedure  NULL     6        2000-04-07 20:37:54.930
```

This procedure lists info for the VSS tags I use most, but could be modified to list any tag. Note the inclusion of the custom tag "GGVersion." You can use this tag to link Transact-SQL source with a particular version of your application. I've formatted GGVersion using the traditional layout of the Windows four-part VERSIONINFO ProductInfo field—the fourth part being supplied by VSS's **$Revision $** keyword.

# Version Control from Query Analyzer

Even though Query Analyzer itself has no built-in support for version control, you can use command-line utilities in conjunction with Query Analyzer's ability to run custom tools to add version control facilities to the environment. If your source code management system includes a command-line utility for performing code management tasks (most do), you can hook that utility into Query Analyzer's Tools menu. Moreover, because Query Analyzer provides special runtime tokens that allow you to pass the name of the current file (and many other key elements) to an outside tool, you can wire your version control tool almost seamlessly into the development environment.

As I've said, I use VSS, so the steps that follow show how to use the VSS command-line utility, SS.EXE, from within Query Analyzer. This is not to say that you couldn't use a different version control system with Query Analyzer. On the contrary, because most version control systems work similarly, the steps necessary to access a version control utility from Query Analyzer are likely to be comparable regardless of the actual package used.

To add an external tool to the Query Analyzer Tools menu, click the Tools|Customize menu option and select the Tools tab in the Customize dialog. The **Menu contents:** entry box in the center of the page is the list of currently installed tools. Double-click a blank entry to add a new one. Table 4–2 shows the VSS-related entries in my list:

**Table 4–2** VSS-Related Tool Menu Entries

| Name | Command | Arguments | Initial directory |
|------|---------|-----------|-------------------|
| Set Project Path | ss.exe | cp $/ggspxml/ch04/code | |
| Set Working folder | ss.exe | workfold $(FileDir) | |
| Add Current File | ss.exe | add $(FilePath) | $(FileDir) |
| Check Out Current File | ss.exe | checkout $(FileName)$(FileExt) -C- | $(FileDir) |
| Check In Current File | ss.exe | checkin $(FileName)$(FileExt) | $(FileDir) |
| Undo Check Out of Current File | ss.exe | undocheckout $(FileName)$(FileExt) | $(FileDir) |
| Diff Current File | Diff.bat | $(FileName)$(FileExt) | $(FileDir) |

If you set up Query Analyzer to call VSS using the information in Table 4–2, there are a few caveats of which you should be aware. First, be sure to assign your own project path and working folder using the Set Project Path and Set Working Folder options, respectively. Those listed in Table 4–2 are the ones I happen to be using at the moment. Second, keep in mind that most VSS commands prompt you for comments when invoked. I've disabled comment prompting on the Check Out Current File option, but not on the others. Add -C- to any command for which you want to disable comment prompting. Third, set the SSDIR environmental variable to point to the folder containing the SRCSAFE.INI file you wish to use if this differs from the default VSS search path.

Notice my use of the DIFF.BAT FILE for checking a file for version differences. Diff.bat contains just two lines:

```
ss diff %1
pause
```

The first line lists the differences between the local version of the current file and the one stored in the VSS database. The **pause** command allows you to view the difference output before returning to Query Analyzer. We call DIFF.BAT instead of **ss diff** directly because we want to see the output of the command before returning.

## Special Tokens

As you can see, Query Analyzer supports several special tokens (denoted with a $ symbol) that you can use to send runtime information to outside tools. Click the arrow buttons to the right of the **Arguments:** and **Initial directory:** entry boxes to list those available to you. Table 4–3 lists the ones that I use.

**Table 4–3** Query Analyzer Runtime Environment Tokens

| Token | Meaning |
|-------|---------|
| $(FilePath) | The full path to the current file |
| $(FileName) | The filename portion (without extension) of the current file |
| $(FileExt) | The file extension (including the leading period) of the current file |
| $(FileDir) | The directory path (no filename or extension) of the current file |

**CAUTION:** You may have noticed that Query Analyzer appends an asterisk to the current file's window caption when you modify the file. Because it apparently retrieves the name of the current file from the window caption, it makes the mistake of including the asterisk indicator when it passes the $(FileExt) or $(FilePath) tokens to an external tool. So, if you've modified the file, an invalid filename will be passed to your external tool. To get around this, simply save the file before invoking the tool. This is likely what you'd want to do anyway to ensure that the tool operates on the latest version of the file.

You can find a .REG file containing the registry entries necessary to add these tokens to your Query Analyzer setup on the CD accompanying this book. Run the file to add the settings in Table 4–3 to your Query Analyzer setup.

# Automating Script Generation with Version Control

Another nice feature of version control systems is their ability to automate file-based tasks using console applications and APIs. In conjunction with command-line compilers and scripting tools, these facilities allow you to easily do things like extract the latest version of a project from your code database and compile or run it from an automated process. Because the code is stored in a central database, and because the source code management system knows which version is most current, a simple API can provide all you need to construct automated processes to handle things like nightly test runs and weekly builds.

In VSS, this API is actually a COM interface that you can access from any Automation-capable programming environment such as Visual Basic or Delphi. Using the VSS Automation interface, you can do basically anything the VSS Explorer can do because it uses this interface itself. Via fairly trivial program code, you can navigate VSS project versions programmatically, check files in or out, extract specific project versions, and so forth.

## GGSQLBuilder

As an example of how powerful and easy this is, I've included a Delphi-based utility that can scan a VSS project tree for SQL scripts and extract them to a pair of T-SQL script files that you can then run. GGSQLBuilder finds each SQL script in a VSS project hierarchy, then scans backward through the various versions of the file and finds the last one to have a label assigned to it (this assumes that you label software versions before shipping them—a common practice) or the first version of the file if no version labels are found. Once it finds the correct version of each file, it appends that script to the script file it is building for the entire database.

GGSQLBuilder can be used interactively as well as from the command line. When run interactively, it takes the form of a wizard: It prompts you for the data it needs to locate your scripts, you choose some output filenames, and it finds and extracts your scripts. Using GGSQLBuilder's command-line interface, you can completely automate regular script generations.

## How GGSQLBuilder Works

I mentioned that GGSQLBuilder will extract your SQL scripts to a pair of T-SQL script files. Why two? Because GGSQLBuilder is designed to generate scripts for an end-user application that's built around SQL Server. It's specifically designed to help with generating the scripts necessary to publish an update to such an application.

Typically, end-user applications based on SQL Server make use of two types of databases: one or more user databases and the master database. As you might expect, user databases usually store end-user data and application-specific T-SQL code objects such as stored procedures and views. The master database, on the other hand, is typically used to store custom system procedures and functions that are either system-oriented routines or that contain code that needs to be shared by all databases. As a rule, you shouldn't store anything in the master database that doesn't meet these criteria. GGSQLBuilder is designed to make extracting these two types of script files painless. Once it has generated the two files, you can run the end-user script against as many user databases as necessary. For example, if you planned to use the end-user script as part of a software update, your update program could call OSQL and use its -d parameter to specify the database to run the script against. You could easily automate applying the script to multiple end-user databases by calling OSQL repetitively from a command file.

As for the master script file, you'd typically run it just once during the installation or update of your software. It would install or update new system objects in the master database that would then be usable across the system.

## The Advantages of Script Generation Tools

Why would you want to use a tool like GGSQLBuilder in the first place? Why not just ship the individual scripts themselves or use something like Enterprise Manager to create single script files? First, deploying hundreds or even thousands of individual script files to end users can be problematic. Every file you deploy increases the likelihood that an installation or update will fail. Second, unless you rebuild your customers' data every time you ship a software update, the scripts generated by Enterprise Manager are not suitable for updates. You probably wouldn't want DROP/CREATE TABLE statements in scripts meant to update an existing database.

## How GGSQLBuilder Selects and Orders SQL Scripts

How does GGSQLBuilder know what to consider a SQL script and to which file to extract it? It makes some basic assumptions about the organization of your VSS projects:

1. It assumes that the scripts for a given project reside in subproject folders with the names listed in Table 4–4.
2. It assumes that any scripts that need to be run against the master database will be located under a subproject named MasterDB.
3. It identifies SQL scripts in your VSS project tree by examining their extensions. By default, files with extensions matching those in Table 4–5 are considered T-SQL scripts.

Notice that the folders in Table 4–4 are listed in order of object dependence. Objects in the master database may need to exist before the creation of user objects, default objects will need to be created before tables that reference them can be created, tables need to be created before scripts that alter them can be executed, and so forth. GGSQLBuilder will write the scripts it finds in your VSS database to the output scripts using the folder order from Table 4–4.

**Table 4–4** VSS Project Folders that GGSQLBuilder Recognizes

| Folder name | Type |
| --- | --- |
| MasterDB | Scripts to be applied against the master database |
| Defaults | Default objects (e.g., CREATE DEFAULT) |
| Rules | Rule objects (e.g., CREATE RULE) |
| Tables | Tables (e.g., CREATE TABLE) |
| TableAlters | Table alterations (e.g., ALTER TABLE) |
| Triggers | Triggers (e.g., CREATE TRIGGER) |
| UDFs | UDFs (e.g., CREATE FUNCTION) |
| Views | View objects (e.g., CREATE VIEW) |
| StoredProcs | Stored procedures (e.g., CREATE PROC or ALTER PROC) |

**Table 4–5**  File Extensions that GGSQLBuilder Recognizes by Default

| Extension | File type |
|-----------|-----------|
| SQL | General SQL scripts |
| PRC | Stored procedures |
| TRG | Triggers |
| UDF | UDFs |
| TAB | Tables |
| VIW | Views |
| DEF | Defaults |
| RUL | Rules |
| UDT | User-defined data types |
| FTX | Full-text index |

This helps ensure that your scripts are executed in the right order and should preserve object dependencies.

The best way to learn about GGSQLBuilder is to run it interactively. If you have a VSS database with some SQL scripts checked into it, feel free to run GGSQLBuilder and allow it to attempt to locate those SQL scripts. If the project hierarchy is deep, you'll notice a delay while GGSQLBuilder examines every version of every file in the project tree. If you've grouped your script project folders (from Table 4–4) together under a single parent project folder (a good practice), you can instruct GGSQLBuilder to start its search with this project. Once GGSQLBuilder has found your scripts, allow it to build the two output script files to see how it works.

---

**CAUTION:**  Because GGSQLBuilder identifies SQL scripts based on file extension alone, it's possible that the output scripts it generates will contain object creation/destruction that you may not want. In other words, if you have a **create table** script checked into VSS and GGSQLBuilder finds it, you may end up with not only an unwanted CREATE TABLE statement, but also a DROP TABLE statement if the original script happened to contain one. The moral of the story is this: Use GGSQLBuilder's project tree to examine closely the SQL scripts that it identifies, and uncheck those that you do not want to appear in the output scripts.

---

Experiment with GGSQLBuilder and see whether it might help in developing updates to SQL Server-based applications and in automating script generation and testing. Keep one thing in mind, though: Tools like GGSQLBuilder won't be of any use to you unless your T-SQL code is stored in a source code management system.

## Summary

In this chapter you learned about version control software and the virtues of using it to manage Transact-SQL source code. Hopefully, you've come to the realization that T-SQL is "real" code and needs to be managed just like any other type of source code. We discussed several techniques for maximizing the usefulness of source code management software with Transact-SQL, and you were introduced to a couple new utilities that aid with using SQL Server and VSS together. Good programmers have good habits. Now is a good time to get into the habit of managing your source code—regardless of the originating tool or the programming language—with a version control system.

# CHAPTER 5

# Database Design

*There is a difference between knowledge and skills. Knowledge comes
and goes. Skills stay with you. They're what you have left when your
knowledge has succumbed to the frailties of human recollection and
the passage of time.*

—*H. W. Kenton*

This chapter covers database design from a pragmatist's point of view. It introduces you to various database design theory concepts and shows you how to apply these concepts in your work. It's aimed mainly at those with limited database design experience. If you're already familiar with basic relational database design, you may want to skip this chapter.

## General Approach

My approach to database application design may differ from what you've seen in other books. Rather than go into a long discourse on the intricacies of modern database theory, I'd prefer to be more pragmatic—more practical. I don't think discussing the fine details of Dr. Codd's historic paper, "A Relational Model of Data for Large Shared Data Banks," or the mathematics behind database normalization would be terribly beneficial or even appropriate in a book like this. There are plenty of books out there already that cover those subjects in depth. Instead, I'll focus my attention on helping you design and build real databases. We'll begin with a solid theoretical foundation, then move on to exploring how to apply theoretical concepts in real applications.

One of the most difficult things about writing technical books is the need to balance theory with how-to information. If a book leans too much to the pragmatic side of things, it becomes a glorified manual. It attempts to answer the How without addressing the Why. On the other hand, if a book is bent too much on abstract concepts, it can fail to be useful from a practical standpoint. People usually buy computer books to learn how to do something. Books that fail to teach anything of practical value are of limited use to the average practitioner.

The ideal place to be, then, is somewhere between the two. This is a goal I've attempted to achieve in this book in general and in this chapter in particular. Although I discuss how to use specific types of tools in designing databases and the like, I also try to give you a solid theoretical foundation on which to base the practical information you're learning. Hopefully, you'll find both Why and How addressed adequately.

## Modeling Tools

I've intentionally avoided writing this chapter from the perspective of using a particular tool to build the models we'll be exploring. There is no best modeling tool. What will work best for you depends on your needs. Visio is a nice modeler, particularly if you're a Microsoft Office user. You may find that CAST Software's AppViewer is a good fit for you. Or maybe Sybase's PowerDesigner is your favorite. Perhaps you like ERwin or ER/Studio; both are excellent products. Or maybe you need a modeler that runs on a variety of operating systems, so you use magna solutions' Silverun. Whatever the case, provided you've chosen a full-featured modeling tool, you should be able to work through the examples in this chapter just fine. The tool isn't nearly as important as the concepts, and most high-end data-modeling tools support the same basic core functionality set.

One tool that's not appropriate for high-end data modeling is SQL Server's Enterprise Manager. It's Database Diagram facility is a very basic tool that provides only rudimentary physical data-modeling facilities. As you'll soon see, database design does not begin with physical data modeling; it ends there. Database design begins with understanding the business requirements driving the design, then modeling the business processes necessary to address those requirements. Once the business process modeling phase is complete, entities can be derived and relationships can be established between them. And once the entity-relationship (E-R) phase is done, logical data modeling can ensue. Once you've completed these phases, *then* you're ready for physical modeling. Not before. If I could have you learn just one thing from reading this chapter, it would be that database design is not a physical process; it's a mental one. Business processes, entity relationships, and logical design all drive physical database design. They control what form a database ends up taking. Database designers who neglect these foundational aspects do so at their own peril, often ending up with databases that do not adequately address business needs or that are difficult to extend or maintain. Get the basics right, and the rest will begin to fall into place.

## The Sample Project

In this chapter we'll construct a preliminary database for a fictitious rental property management system called RENTMAN. I've always found that I learn more by building things, so I've created a sample project for us to work through together. As I said earlier, if you have a recent version of a full-featured data modeling tool, you should have no problem working through the examples in this chapter. The portion of RENTMAN that we'll construct here is very basic indeed, and any decent modeling tool should be able to handle it easily.

## The Five Processes

Database application development can be broken into five steps or general processes. These processes outline the normal procedure one follows when building database applications. Think of them as the tenets of database programming. You'll likely follow them in every database application you build.

The five general processes for building database applications are as follows:

1. Define the purpose and functions of the application.
2. Design the database foundation and application processes needed to implement those functions.
3. Transform the design into an application by creating the requisite database and program objects.
4. Test the application for compliance with the predefined purpose and functions.
5. Install the application for production use.

To put things a little more succinctly, these five processes can be reduced to the following five phases:

1. Analysis
2. Design

3. Construction
4. Testing
5. Deployment

---

**NOTE:** Historically, the construction phase has been referred to as the *coding phase*. However, in this age of visual development, coding doesn't seem to be as applicable as it once was, so I've changed it to construction. This term works regardless of whether coding, visual development, or application generation is involved in constructing the project.

---

I'll make a habit in this chapter of referring to the five processes using these easier-to-digest terms. They are not only more concise than the formal definitions of the five processes, they're also terms with which most software developers are already familiar. They make obvious the point that developing database software is just like developing any other kind of software: There is a methodical approach you usually take to produce desirable results.

## The Five Phases Examined

When you build anything—whether it's a software product, a house, a statue, anything—you go through a series of phases or steps that hopefully results in a finished product. The procedure is no different when you build applications. This series of steps isn't something you have to commit to memory and hope you don't forget. On the contrary, it's completely intuitive and is borne of simple logic. Rather than some rigid code that you must always be careful to follow, the five general processes I outlined earlier will likely occur to you naturally as you design databases and build applications.

As far as the actual work of constructing a database application is concerned, you can focus on just the first three of the five general processes. It's during the first three phases that the application is actually developed. Most of the challenges of building database apps lie in these three phases. This isn't to say that testing and deployment can be relegated to the end of the development process. On the contrary, they should occur *throughout* the process. However, the formal testing phase of a project (e.g., prerelease or beta testing) usually occurs once the software is pretty far along, and, obviously, deployment (release to manufacturing, or RTM) occurs after the software is thought to be complete.

## Analysis

The first application development phase is the analysis phase. Here you analyze what your application needs to do. You begin with a general statement of purpose, then qualify the statement with specific functions that the app must perform or allow the user to perform to serve its intended purpose. It is during the analysis phase that process modeling occurs. Process modeling amounts to describing the underlying business processes, resources, and data flows necessary for the application to fulfill its purpose.

## Design

The second phase is the design phase. Here you turn the analysis you performed in the first phase into a logical design. You translate the business processes modeled during your analysis into logical application and database design elements. This logical design describes what you're building in specific terms. The focus shifts from *what* the application will do to *how* it will do it. Here, you determine the application and database components necessary to implement the business process models defined in the analysis phase. One of the ways you do this is through logical data modeling and E-R diagrams. The end result is that you'll develop a separate design for each layer of your application.

## Construction

The third database application development phase is the construction phase. Here you turn the logical design you developed during the design phase into physical objects. This means that the logical database design you created will be translated into real database objects. Likewise, the application design you produced during the design phase will materialize as forms, code, services, components, and other program objects.

The last two of the five phases—testing and deployment—are mostly post-development concerns, so I won't get into them much here. As I said, each can and should be ongoing in nature, but they are still distinct phases of the overall process. Often, they result in a return to the first three phases anyway (through bugs being detected or requests for enhancements from users), so I'll only touch on them in our discussion of database design.

## On the Complexities of Database Development

The process of developing database applications is straightforward and intuitive. It's not unlike the approach one takes to building any other type of application, regardless of whether the app accesses databases. This may seem a bit simplistic, but it's from this perspective that I approach the task of developing database applications.

The difficulty that arises when applying this basic methodology to SQL Server application development is that there are at least two distinct pieces to even the simplest SQL Server application: the server portion and the client portion. Moreover, the objects that end up being created on the server are foundational to the application. That is, it's advantageous, if not mandatory, that they exist before the application itself is constructed. Also, the app won't work correctly if the database has problems. This duality doubles the work necessary to construct robust applications. Not only must the application be analyzed, designed, and constructed, the database must also go through the same process. In addition to this client- and server-side work, there is also the issue of getting the client and server to communicate with one another. Sometimes this is a task in and of itself. And adding middleware to the mix makes things even more interesting.

There's no easy way to completely remove the complexities surrounding database applications. CASE tools help, but applications must still be developed by developers. Modern database apps are complex, multilayer pieces of software. It's understandable that creating them requires some amount of expertise.

This chapter takes you through the analysis, design, and construction phases as they relate to databases. Getting the database design right is every bit as important as getting the application design right. If either one is faulty, your app isn't going to work very well.

## Database Theory Applied

Something you'll notice about this chapter is that I consider database design and database application design to be intrinsically linked. This seems obvious enough to me, although there are those who feel the two are completely different disciplines. From the pragmatist's point of view, the process of designing a database is foundational to the process of designing applications that use it. One certainly affects the other. I've never designed a database that wasn't intended to be accessed in some way by an application.

You have to remember that the database is just a means to an end—it's your way of meeting a customer's needs. Similarly, the client application functions as the conduit between the user and the database server. It, too, is just a tool for servicing your customer. Both the client app and the database server must work together to produce solutions that your users find acceptable.

In this chapter I'll take you through the process I use when designing database applications. I'll base the discussion on a solid grounding in database theory, with the emphasis on the task of constructing real applications.

## Defining the Purpose of the Application

The first step in designing any application—database or nondatabase—is to define the purpose of the application. What is the application to do? An application's statement of purpose should consist of a single sentence that includes the subject, the verb, and the verb's object. The subject is always the application, such as "This system . . ." or "The RENTMAN System . . .". The verb describes what the application is supposed to do, for example, "The system will manage . . ." or "The RENTMAN System will facilitate . . .". The object denotes the recipient of the application's actions. For example, "The system will manage summer camp registration" or "The RENTMAN System will facilitate rental property management."

The statement of purpose needs to be as simple and concise as you can make it. Don't waste time with flowery language or needless details. For example, avoid "for the organization" and "for the client" at the end of the statement because they're implicit. Also, try to avoid compound statements and conjunctions. Reducing the sentence to its simplest possible form will help keep you on course as you further describe what the app is supposed to do. You can expound more on your app's purpose when you later define the functions required to accomplish it.

Once you've developed a statement of purpose for the application, show it to the potential users of the new application and see if they agree. Don't be surprised if they don't understand your brevity, but try to get them to sanction your statement as accurate and complete. Although the statement will not enumerate the specifics of the application, it still needs to be broad enough to encompass the overall purpose of the application. Assure your users that the precise functions of the application will be addressed in a separate step. Get their thoughts on what they think those functions should be.

## Defining the Functions of the Application

Once the statement of purpose is in place, it's time to determine the application's prerequisite functions. What does the application need to do to accomplish its statement of purpose? Try to keep this to no more than a handful of major tasks, if possible. It's a great idea to develop these items using an outline. These functions should further define the application's statement of purpose, not go beyond it. Follow the same three-part format you used with the statement of purpose. For example, "The RENTMAN System will facilitate rental property management":

- It will log and maintain property leases.
- It will track ongoing property maintenance work.

- It will generate tenant billing information.
- It will provide historical information on individual properties.

Make sure you cover all the major functions of the application, but don't overdo it with excessive detail. Also, be sure that the tasks you list don't overlap. Don't list a task that's already covered by another item on the list.

## Designing the Database Foundation and Application Processes

One of the first things you discover about database design is that there's a lot more to it than merely designing databases. Business process modeling, E-R diagrams, and logical data modeling all play a part in the design process. You can think of the steps from business process modeling to constructing database objects as a continuum. Beginning with a 30,000-foot view of the business processes that will compose your app and zooming all the way down to individual database column definitions, you progress from the general to the specific. You progressively refine your understanding of the app's purpose until you're ready to translate that understanding into the app itself. This progression of refinement provides a systematic method of transforming the conceptual notions of what it is your app is supposed to do into real-life program elements.

The actual work of designing a database is not as arduous as it may seem. It begins with process modeling and ends with designing the physical objects that will make up the database. In this chapter we'll reduce database design to these three steps:

1. Document the business processes necessary to accomplish the app's required functions.
2. Diagram the entity relationships necessary to service these processes.
3. Create the logical database design necessary to implement these entity relationships and business processes.

See Figure 5–1 for an illustration of the correlation between the five application development processes and these three steps. Once you've developed your application's statement of purpose and derived its critical functions, the remaining analysis and design work boils down to just these three steps. You begin by modeling business processes that correspond to the functions you defined, then you diagram the entity relationships necessary to support those processes. You finish up by translating the E-R diagrams and business processes

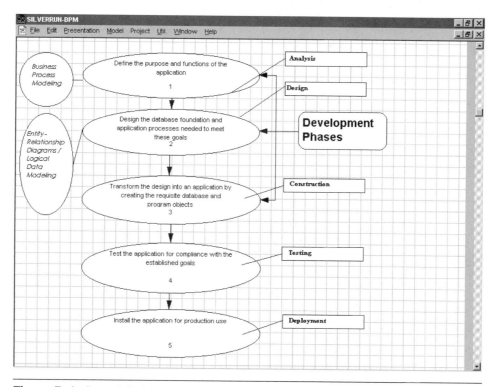

**Figure 5–1** A model showing the various elements of the five application development processes.

you developed into a logical model of your data. It's this logical schema that will be used to build your database during the construction phase.

The progression from process modeling to logical data modeling needn't be done manually. CASE tools are extremely capable at these sorts of things. As you'll soon see, they can help simplify the development process even further.

### CASE Tools

I suppose I should begin the discussion of CASE tools by saying that I don't believe that CASE tools are appropriate for every development project or that they will ever replace adequate planning or software craftsmanship. On the contrary, because they're computer-based, CASE tools have the same weaknesses that any other kind of software has—they do what you *tell* them to do, not necessarily what you *want* them to do.

I also happen to believe that CASE tools that attempt to automate every aspect of the development process get in the way of proficient application construction. Rather than aid in the process, they hinder it by attempting to automate things that cannot or should not be automated. Like George Jetson and his computerized treadmill, developers and modelers spend more time recovering from this overautomation than they would have spent had they not automated things so much in the first place.

As with anything designed to save time, you can reach a point of diminishing returns. When this happens, it's time to get back to the basics and focus on automation that is a help rather than a hindrance.

The role that CASE software should play in database development is that of a tool in the modeler's toolbox. Tools require skill to use. They also do not think for you or plan how you should approach solving problems. They merely help you more readily perform tasks that you could probably perform through other means. This is the ideal role for CASE tools in application modeling. No matter what tools you use, you still need to have a basic understanding of database design concepts and the workings of your back-end DBMS to develop optimal database applications.

Because much of the exploratory work that must be done to eventually arrive at a database design amounts to modeling real-world objects, it only makes sense that CASE tools should somehow figure into the mix. Today's CASE tools have come a long way from the pioneers of yesteryear. Without a doubt, it's now safer *and* faster to utilize CASE tools to assist in the design process than to do everything by hand.

By allowing us to model objects before they actually exist, CASE tools allow us to perform "what if" analysis on design elements before they become reality. Also, CASE tools can assist with the design process itself, and can even warn of potential problems with the design decisions we make. By constructing a model of what we want to do, we give the CASE tool the information it needs to help us do it. Some types of modeling to which CASE tools are particularly well-suited are:

**Business process modeling**—Applications consist of interrelated processes that perform functions essential to the app. Business process modeling involves formally diagramming those processes and how they interrelate. There are CASE tools with specific support for process modeling. Computer Associates' BPwin is one example; Microsoft's Visio is another.

**E-R modeling**—E-R diagrams are considered indispensable by most data modelers and designers. They provide a method of separating the logical representation of data from its physical implementation. E-R diagrams facilitate thinking of data elements in terms of the real-world objects they represent. There are many CASE tools dedicated to E-R modeling.

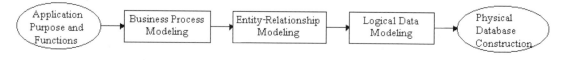

**Figure 5–2** CASE tools help transform ideas into physical database and application objects.

Computer Associates' ERwin is one such tool; Embarcadero's ER/Studio is another.

**Relational data modeling**—Despite the popularity of E-R modeling, it represents only part of the relational data modeling process. E-R diagrams are one way of expressing database relationships, but there are many others. There are a number of CASE tools that go beyond simple E-R diagramming and address the larger task of designing entire logical database schemas. Sybase's PowerDesigner is one such tool; CAST Software's AppBuilder is another.

In this chapter I'll show you how to use CASE tools to model real-world applications and how to transform these models into database and application objects. As Figure 5–2 illustrates, physical database objects evolve from logical data models. Logical data models are in turn borne of E-R diagrams, and E-R diagrams are derived from business process models. Business process models, for their part, embody the application's purpose and key functions. The progression from defining an application's purpose and essential functions to constructing it physically represents a gradual evolution in our understanding of what the application is supposed to do.

## Modeling Business Processes

Getting back to the subject of modeling itself, once you've defined your application's purpose and functions, you're ready to begin modeling the business processes that will define the application. I'll take you step by step through modeling the business processes for database applications. Once the process modeling is complete, you'll continue with E-R diagramming, then proceed to logical data modeling. Once you're analysis and design phases are complete, you'll implement your database design by creating the objects of which it's composed. At this point, you're finished with the database foundation and ready to move on to developing the application and/or middleware elements.

Business process models chart the relationships between four basic modeling elements: processes, external entities, stores, and data flows. Additionally, qualifiers, resources, and data structures further define the relationships between these elements. Table 5–1 outlines each model element and how it relates to the other elements.

Now that you have a few basic modeling terms under your belt, let's get started.

**Table 5–1** Business Process Modeling Elements

| Modeling element | Definition |
| --- | --- |
| Process | A task or decision to be carried out by an application or organization. Processes are expressed in terms of actions that are accomplished using resources. Examples of processes include hiring new employees, billing, tracking customer complaints, and so forth. |
| External entity | A person, organizational entity, or other object that is outside the business unit or application being described but interacts with it. External entities are either a source or destination of information in the system being modeled. Examples of external entities include customers, tenants, Congress, marketing, and so on. |
| Store | Data that is created, utilized, or changed by the system being modeled. Examples of stores include customer records, charts of accounts, account masters, property files, and so forth. |
| Flow | Goods or data moving between external entities, processes, and stores. Examples of flows include customer information, order shipment, express mail delivery, service request, and so forth. |
| Resource | An element of the system being modeled that is utilized in some way by a process. Examples of resources include a database server, a tape drive, a personnel manager, office supplies, and so on. |
| Qualifier | Further defines an external entity, flow, process, or store. For example, a qualifier may indicate that service requests are usually taken by phone or that employee hire information is sent to the home office via e-mail. |
| Data structure | Detailed information about the data contained in a store. Data structures enumerate the attributes of a store's contents. |

---

**TIP:** Naturally, you should settle on a notation style before you begin modeling. The obvious choice is UML (Unified Modeling Language), but there are many others. For business process modeling, other popular choices include Gane-Sarson, Merise, Yourdon-DeMarco, and Ward-Mellor. Some CASE tools support multiple modeling notations; some do not. Some even let you create your own or synthesize new ones from existing notions. Whatever the case, you'll want to settle on a notation and stick with it throughout the modeling process. Personally, I prefer Ward-Mellor notation.

---

Now that you at least have an idea of what you'll be modeling, let's proceed with translating the application functions you defined earlier into business process models.

## Getting Started Modeling Your Business Processes

To see how the functions-to-processes transition works, let's return to the sample application I mentioned earlier. Recall that I mentioned an app whose statement of purpose was the following: "The RENTMAN System will facilitate rental property management."

Some sample application functions for RENTMAN were:

- It will log and maintain property leases.
- It will track ongoing property maintenance work.
- It will generate tenant billing information.
- It will provide historical information on individual properties.

Modeling is like swimming: The best way to learn is simply to jump in. To see how you model the business processes that correspond to application functions, let's model the processes required to accomplish the first function—logging and maintaining property leases.

The task of modeling any business process goes like this:

1. Determine the external entities, processes, flows, and stores that are needed.
2. Decide how these elements relate to one another.
3. Diagram these elements and their relationships in the process model.

Because you know you'll be modeling rental property lease management, the following questions need answers:

- What external entities are needed to log and maintain property leases?
- What processes are involved?

- What resources will these processes require?
- What data stores will be needed?
- How does data flow from one element to another?

In this case, you can already deduce the following:

- You'll need at least one external entity—that of the prospective tenant.
- Separate processes will be required to handle lease processing and lease execution.
- Assuming the rental management company wants to track calls from prospective tenants, and wants to store tenant, lease, and property information separately, you'll need four data stores. These stores will stockpile calls, tenants, properties, and leases.
- As far as data flow between these elements, you can assume the following:
  - Prospective tenants contact the lease clerk at the property management office to inquire about available properties or enter into a lease contract.
  - The lease clerk logs each call as it is received, regardless of whether it results in a lease.
  - The lease clerk checks available properties before forwarding a lease to the lease manager.
  - Once a lease has been verified by the lease clerk, it is forwarded to the lease manager for execution.
  - Tenant information that is received during the lease is kept on file by the lease clerk.
  - The lease manager keeps a record of executed leases.

With these facts in mind, let's begin building the business process model for managing lease information.

## Adding External Entities

Begin by starting your modeling tool of choice and creating a new business process model. Next, find your tool's external entity object and drop it on to the upper left corner of your blank model. Set its name to Prospective Tenant. This object will represent the prospective tenant who will either inquire about available properties or who will call to enter into a lease on a particular property. Figure 5–3 illustrates what your model might look like so far.

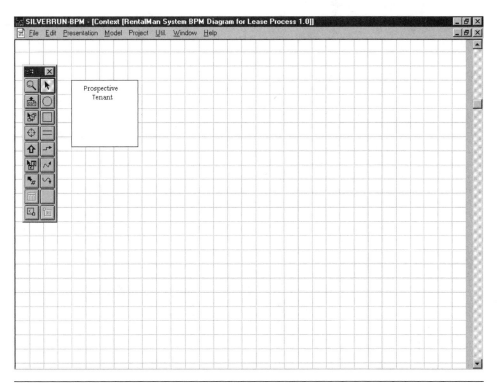

**Figure 5–3** Your new model with its first external entity in place.

## Adding Processes

Drop two process objects onto your model: one onto the upper middle and one onto the upper right. Set the name of the first process to Lease Processing and the second to Lease Execution. The Lease Processing object represents the receipt and verification of lease information. It's the focal point of the whole leasing process. The Lease Execution process represents actual leasing of the property. It entails turning over the keys and other items to the new tenant and making a record of the new lease. Figure 5–4 illustrates what your model might look like with these two processes in place.

## Adding Stores

Now drop four data store objects onto the bottom of the model. These will represent the data stores with which the other model elements will interact. Name the first one CALL, the second PROPERTY, the third TENANT, and the

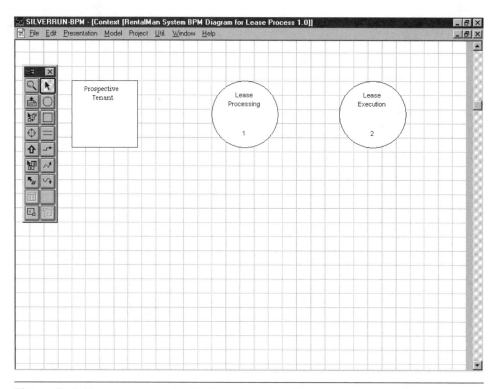

**Figure 5–4** Your new model with its external entity and process objects in place.

fourth one LEASE. Your process objects will send and receive data from these stores. Figure 5–5 shows what your model might look like at this point.

## Adding Flow Objects

Now that all your objects are in place, you're ready to define how they interrelate. You'll do this using flow objects.

Connect the Prospective Tenant and Lease Processing objects using a flow object that runs from left to right. Set the text label of the flow to Applies for Lease. This represents the application by the prospective tenant for a new property lease.

Now connect the Lease Processing and Prospective Tenant objects using a flow object that runs from right to left. Set its text to Notifies of Acceptance. This object represents the interaction between the leasing office and the prospective tenant.

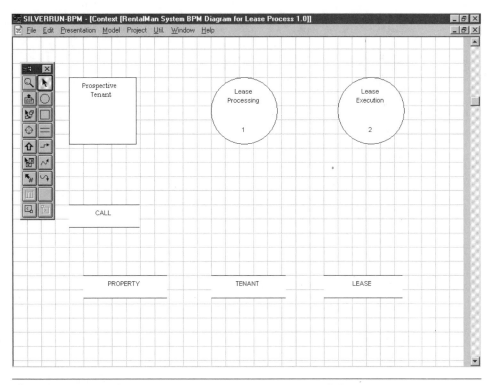

**Figure 5–5** Drop four store objects onto your new model.

Connect the Lease Processing and Lease Execution objects using a left-to-right flow object. Set its text to Verifies Lease. This represents the fact that a lease is forwarded to the manager for execution after it has been verified.

Now connect the Lease Execution and Prospective Tenant objects with a flow object that runs right to left. Set its text to Leases Property. Figure 5–6 illustrates what your model might look like with these objects in place.

The remaining connections all have to do with interacting with your data stores. Study Figure 5–7 carefully, then add the flow objects necessary to make your model match it.

## Adding Data Structures

You've now successfully modeled the process of leasing a property to a new tenant. You could further enhance the model, but the one you have so far is quite functional.

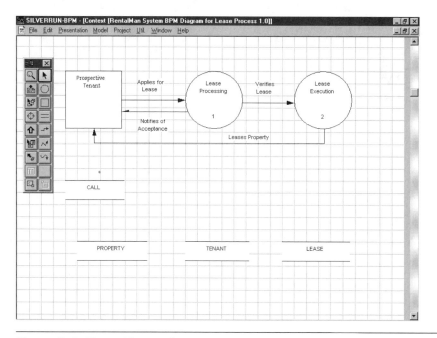

**Figure 5–6** Flow objects allow you to establish relationships between elements in your model.

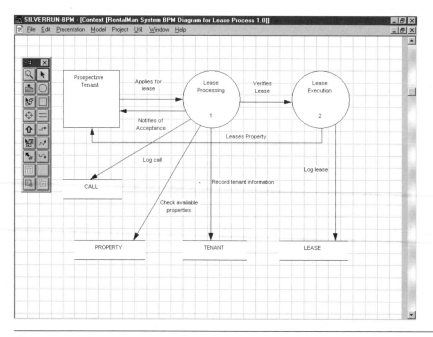

**Figure 5–7** This model diagrams the process of leasing a property to a new tenant.

A useful (but optional) thing to do at this point is to define the structures representing the data your store objects will contain. Most modeling tools allow you to specify attributes for your store data that can be used later during the E-R modeling process. These are often termed *data structures* or something similar, and correspond roughly to entities in E-R diagrams and tables in a relational database design.

Often, you can determine attribute-level information from source documents and forms provided by your client or through user interviews. What you want to do is find out as much about the information the system will store, as early as possible. Enumerating your database attributes early on will save you time later.

The task of adding data structure definitions to a business process model usually has two parts: First, define the data structures; second, associate data structures with store objects.

Begin by adding three data structures—CALL, LEASE, and TENANT—to your existing model (Figure 5–8).

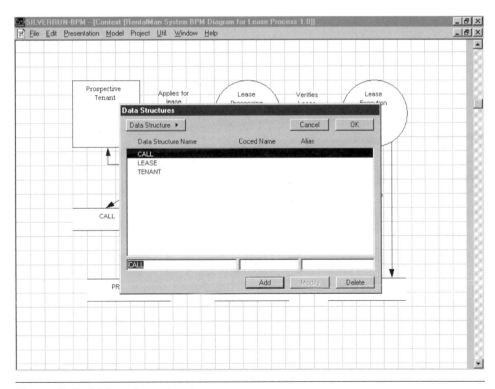

**Figure 5–8** Adding data structures.

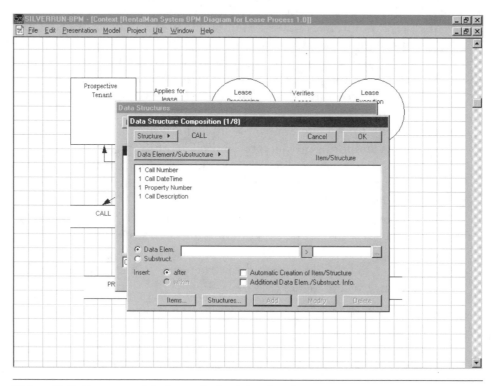

**Figure 5–9** You can add elements to data structures.

Once you've added all three data structures, the next step is to define their attributes. In some tools, this can be done in one step; in others, it takes multiple steps. Figure 5–9 illustrates the process of adding data structure attributes.

Let's now set up the attributes for each of the data structures you defined earlier. Add these elements to the CALL data structure:

- Call Number
- Call DateTime
- Property Number
- Call Description

Add these attribute elements to the LEASE data structure:

- Lease Number
- Tenant Number

- Property Address
- Property City
- Property State
- Property Zip
- Property Addition
- Property Bedrooms
- Property LivingAreas
- Property Bathrooms
- Property GarageType
- Property SchoolDistrict
- Property Deposit
- Property Rent
- Property Range
- Property Refrigerator
- Property Dishwasher
- Property CentralHeat
- Property CentralAir
- Property GasHeat
- Property PrivacyFence
- Property LastSprayDate
- Property LastLawnDate
- Lease BeginDate
- Lease EndDate
- Lease MovedInDate
- Lease MovedOutDate
- Lease Rent
- Lease PetDeposit
- Lease RentDueDay
- Lease LawnService

Add these elements to the TENANT data structure:

- Tenant Number
- Tenant Name
- Tenant Employer
- Tenant EmployerAddress
- Tenant EmployerCity
- Tenant EmployerState
- Tenant EmployerZip
- Tenant HomePhone
- Tenant WorkPhone

- Tenant ICEPhone
- Tenant Comments

Information such as this may come directly from lease applications, tenant records, and the like. Note that you're not attempting to normalize your data at this point. That comes later. For now, you just want to model, as closely as possible, the real-world objects with which your system will interact.

Notice that each attribute we add is prefixed with a store name. This is a good convention because these stores will later evolve into tables in the physical database. Doing things this way will likely help us during the E-R modeling stage.

Once you've set up your data structures, you're ready to link them to your store objects (Figure 5–10).

Now let's link your data structures with their corresponding store objects. Link the CALL data structure to the CALL store object, the TENANT data structure to the Tenant store and the LEASE data structure to the LEASE store object.

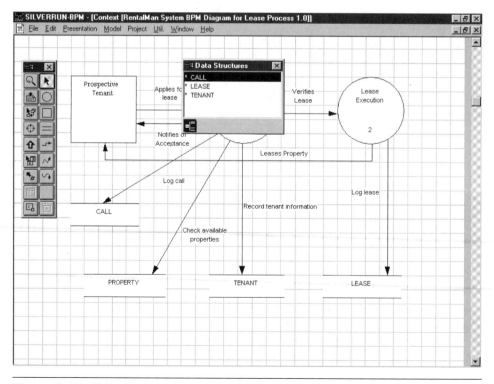

**Figure 5–10** You can associate data structures with stores.

Once your data structures are linked to their corresponding stores, you're finished with modeling the business processes associated with leasing rental properties. The next step is modeling the entity relationships necessary to service the business process model you just built.

Before you're ready to begin, though, you need to save the business process model you just defined to disk. If your tool has the option of adding your model to a repository for reuse in other models, save it to the repository as well. This will likely make creating E-R and logical data models easier down the road.

# Entity-Relationship Modeling

In 1976, Peter Chen published the first specification for viewing relational data as a collection of relationships between entities in "The Entity Relationship Model—Toward a Unified View of Data." Chen's work (along with that of other theorists such as Hammer and McLeod, proponents of the Semantic Data Model) gave rise to E-R diagrams—pictorial depictions of entity relationships—now a mainstay of logical data modeling.

One of the first things you'll discover about E-R modeling is that there's no sequential path from business processes to fully defined logical data models. Constructing entity relationships requires a lot of thought. It's a process you'll probably go through repeatedly before you feel comfortable with a given model.

## Types of E-R Diagrams

E-R diagrams usually come in one of two flavors. First, there's the standard Chen notation. Chen-style E-R diagrams approach modeling very granularly: Each diagram typically represents just one relationship between two entities. Figure 5–11 illustrates a simple Chen-style E-R model:

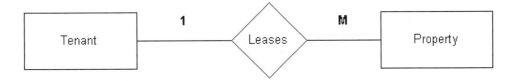

**Figure 5–11** An E-R diagram that follows the original Chen methodology.

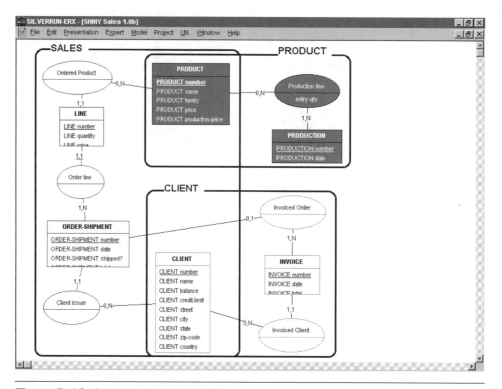

**Figure 5–12**  A more detailed E-R diagram that deviates from the classic Chen style.

The second type of E-R model is the detailed E-R diagram. Detailed E-R models have come about because the piecemeal approach taken by Chen-style notation results in hundreds (or even thousands) of individual diagrams for complex database designs. This isn't usually the case with detailed E-R models because all the relationships for a given entity are depicted in a single diagram. The diagram is entity-centric rather than relationship-centric. Detailed E-R diagrams usually contain attribute-level information and deviate from simple Chen-style notation in significant ways. Figure 5–12 shows what a detailed E-R diagram might look like.

Generally speaking, entities you define in E-R diagrams will correspond to tables in your relational model and later in your physical database implementation. This is why many popular E-R tools blend in elements of the relational model and physical design with E-R modeling. It's more economical to show the correlation between entities and tables than to force users to keep them separate.

## E-R Modeling Terms

Before we get very far into E-R modeling, we need to cover some basic modeling terms. Knowing these is essential to understanding the discussions that follow. The list in Table 5–2 isn't meant to be exhaustive, but it should give you a good sampling of the terms you'll encounter in this and other technical literature that broaches the subject of E-R and logical data modeling. Some of these terms apply only to E-R modeling; some relate to logical data modeling in general.

**Table 5–2**  Glossary of Essential E-R Data Modeling Terms

| Term | Definition |
| --- | --- |
| Entity | A real object—a person, place, event, or thing—about which you want to store data. Entities are also known as *entity classes*. |
| Entity instance | A specific item represented by an entity class. For example, customer John Doe would be an entity instance of the CUSTOMER entity class. Entity instances are sometimes referred to as *entity occurrences*. |
| E-R modeling | A type of logical data modeling that assumes all business elements can be generalized into archetypal ideals—abstract concepts. These conceptual entities are described in terms of their characteristics or *attributes*. They are related to one another through the actions they perform on each other. These actions establish *relationships* between the entities. E-R modeling visually depicts these relationships. |
| Subtype | An entity class that is a subset of a larger, more inclusive type of entity is known as a *supertype*. For example, the entity class FIREMAN may be a subtype of the supertype CITYWORKER. Subtypes typically inherit the supertype's attributes and relationships, and reserve the right to define their own. Groups of subtypes (e.g., FIREMAN, POLICEMAN, GARBAGEMAN) are known as subtype clusters. |
| Supertype | An entity class that is a superset of smaller, less inclusive entity classes, known as *subtypes*. For example, entity class AUTOMOBILE may be an entity supertype of the FORDAUTO, GMAUTO, and CHRYSLERAUTO entity subtypes. You'll often hear subtypes and supertypes referred to collectively as *s-types*. |

**Table 5–2** *(Continued)*

| Term | Definition |
|---|---|
| Attribute | A characteristic of an entity or entity relationship. Attributes describe entities in detail. For example, SocialSecurityNo would likely be an attribute of the EMPLOYEE entity class. |
| Domain | A particular type of data or range of values that an attribute allows. For example, applying the TDate domain to the HireDate attribute might require that all HireDate entries be valid dates. Likewise, applying the TNonZeroCost domain to the Price attribute might require that all Price values be nonzero. |
| Domain integrity | The rules that control the types of data a domain allows. Ensuring domain integrity, for example, makes certain that values contained in the Date domain are indeed valid dates and that values stored in Numeric attributes are indeed numbers. |
| Relationship | A link between two entities that establishes the behavior of one entity when something happens to the other. There are five basic types of entity relationships: one-to-many, many-to-many, one-to-one, mutually exclusive, and recursive. |
| Relational integrity | The rules that ensure relationships between entities are respected. For example, relational integrity would prevent the deletion of CUSTOMER entity instances that still have associated INVOICE entity instances. |
| Connectivity | Defines the mapping of associated entity instances in a relationship. For example, defining the connectivity between the INVOICE and CUSTOMER entities might specify that for every instance of the CUSTOMER entity, there can be many corresponding instances of the INVOICE class, because each customer can place multiple orders. |
| Cardinality | The actual number of related instances between the entities in entity relationships. It quantifies abstract relationships by elaborating on connectivity. For example, the cardinality between the INVOICE and CUSTOMER entities might ensure that for every INVOICE instance, there is at least one corresponding CUSTOMER instance. |
| Modality | Specifies whether the existence of an entity instance is optional or required in a relationship. Modality (also referred to as *optionality* or *existence*) refers to the minimum cardinality of relationships between entities. |

**Table 5–2**  *(Continued)*

| Term | Definition |
|------|-----------|
| Normalization | The removal of a data model's redundant, inconsistent, and convoluted elements. The idea behind normalization is to ensure that each entity instance represents no more than one real-world object. |
| Entity Identifier | The combination of attributes necessary to distinguish one entity instance from another |

There is a direct correlation between E-R modeling terms and relational modeling terms. Table 5–3 cross-references some of the E-R terms you just learned with their relational counterparts.

The best modeling tools treat E-R modeling as a subset of relational data modeling. Not only does E-R modeling not constitute the entirety of logical data modeling, it's also independent of physical design.

Now that you have an understanding of some basic modeling concepts, let's proceed with modeling the entity relationships necessary to support the processes you defined earlier.

## Building Your E-R Model

Thanks to having defined a complete business process model before beginning the E-R modeling process, you'll spend a lot less time developing a working E-R model than you otherwise would have. In this chapter, the main thing you'll accomplish by constructing an E-R model is normalizing your data.

**Table 5–3**  Cross-reference of E-R Terms with Relational Modeling Terms

| E-R term | Relational or logical design term |
|----------|-----------------------------------|
| Entity | Table |
| Entity occurrence/instance | Row |
| Entity identifier | Primary key |
| Unique identifier | Candidate key |
| Relationship | Foreign key |
| Attribute | Column |
| Domain | Data type |

**NOTE:** As a rule, normalization is a function of the relational data modeling or database design process. In this book, we're treating E-R modeling as the first step of this process. Some people completely separate the two types of modeling. Some go straight from E-R modeling to constructing database objects; others build relational models without bothering with E-R diagrams. In this book you'll learn to do both types of modeling. Once you finish modeling your entity relationships, you'll complete your logical database design. Although it may seem intuitive to hold off normalizing your data until the logical data modeling stage, most E-R tools provide normalization facilities of some sort, so we'll cover it here.

Let's get started building an E-R model for the lease business process model we designed earlier. Create a new E-R model, and, if your tool supports it, import your business process model from earlier (reference it in your tool's repository if necessary).

Insert each store from the business process model into your new E-R diagram. Depending on your tool, this should create entity objects that correspond to the store objects you defined in your process model. Your tool may prevent you from inserting the PROPERTY store because it does not have an associated data structure. Figure 5–13 shows what your model might look like so far.

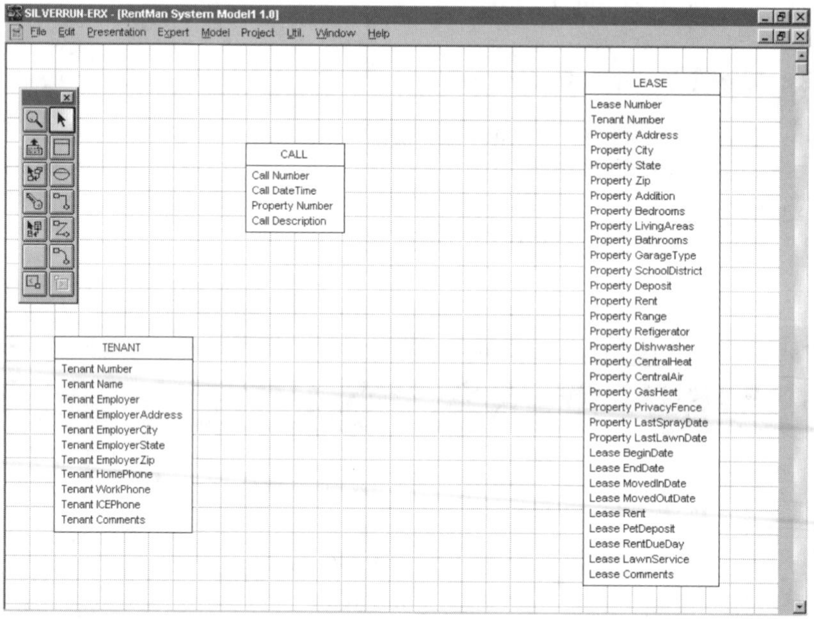

**Figure 5–13** Your model with the entity objects derived from your repository in place.

If your E-R tool has a normalization expert, you can avoid the tedium of having to normalize the model yourself. Without a normalization wizard or facility, the next step may be to decompose your entities into normalized entity classes, then link them to one another via entity relationships. This is generally the way things are done with E-R modeling.

If your tool sports a normalization wizard, you'll get to skip some of the real work of data modeling. In many cases, these types of facilities can completely normalize a model just by asking a few simple questions.

---

**NOTE:** I should point out here that some normalization wizards do an incomplete job of normalizing a database. You should always check the work of a normalization program before assuming it's right (which is another good reason to have an in-depth understanding of normalization yourself).

---

Assuming your E-R diagramming tool supports a normalization wizard or facility, invoke it now to normalize the model. Figure 5–14 illustrates what the model should look like once normalized. Arrange your entities and their associated relationships so that they do not overlap one another in the diagram.

After you've normalized your model, you should see a new entity, the PROPERTY entity. This entity should have been added by the normalization

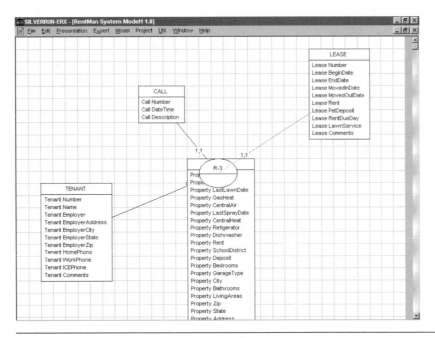

**Figure 5–14** Your model as it should appear after normalization.

expert due to redundancy in the LEASE entity. Set its name to PROPERTY. Figure 5–15 shows what the model should look like this far.

When you designed the data structure objects for the process model you defined earlier, you may have wondered why I didn't ask you to create a data structure for the PROPERTY store. Now you know the reason. The attributes needed by the PROPERTY store were already embedded in the LEASE data structure. I left them there to illustrate the power of using a CASE tool to assist in modeling data. Your E-R tool should have pulled those attributes relating to property from the LEASE entity and placed them in the new PROPERTY entity. The Property Number attribute should also have been copied from the CALL entity.

## Normalization

Because you likely just watched it happen before your very eyes, I suppose I should outline exactly what normalization is. Beyond the earlier glossary definition, normalization seeks to save work and reduce the potential for errors when

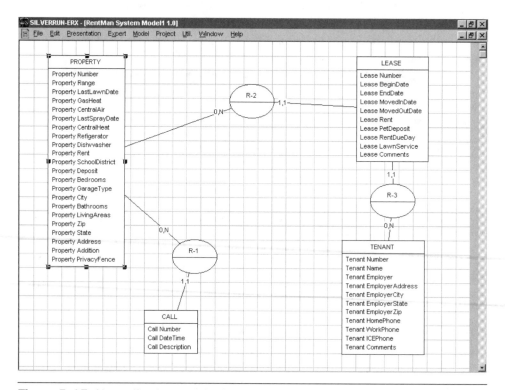

**Figure 5–15** Normalization results in a new entity being added to your design.

updating database table rows. For example, if you store a customer's address in every Invoice record, changing the customer's address means changing every occurrence of it in the Invoice table. If, on the other hand, that address information is stored separately in a Customer table, it only has to be changed in one place, greatly reducing the time it takes to change a customer's address as well as eliminating the possibility of a row in the Invoice table being missed.

Normalization is formally divided into five *forms* or stages, *first normal form* through *fifth normal form*. These obscure terms really just refer to the five sets of relational criteria that an entity either does or does not meet. Each successive stage builds on the previous one. Although there are technically five basic forms, in practice you'll probably use just the first three. The last two are generally regarded as too specialized for commonplace database design.

---

**NOTE:** Although we haven't yet discussed relational design in depth, I'm going to use relational terms like *table, row,* and *column* interchangeably with E-R terms like *entity, entity occurrence,* and *attribute* in the normalization discussion that follows. This is because I think the examples I give for each normal form will be easier to follow if expressed in terms of relational and physical database objects rather than abstract concepts.

---

### First Normal Form

In order for a table to be considered normalized to first normal form (1NF), each of its columns must be completely *atomic* and it must contain no *repeating groups*. A column is atomic when it contains only one element of data. For example, an **Address** column that contains not only a street address but also a city, state, and zip code is not completely atomic. Columns designed this way should be split into multiple columns to be fully compliant with first normal form. Keep in mind that the degree to which you should break down a column depends on its intended use—as with all things: be sensible.

A repeating group is a column that is repeated within a row definition for the sole purpose of storing multiple values for that attribute. For example, we could have taken the approach in designing our Tenant table of storing the property the tenant was renting within the Tenant table rather than separately in the Property table. This fails to allow for the possibility that a single tenant (for example, a corporation leasing a number of corporate apartments) may rent more than one property. To address this exclusively within the Tenant table, we would have to decide on the maximum number of properties a tenant may rent, then add the requisite supporting columns to the table. These repetitive columns would constitute a repeating group.

Some database tools and languages provide direct support for repeating groups, and, thereby encourage nonrelational design. Obviously, a design cannot be relational if it violates first normal form. An example of such a tool is Advanced Revelation. Its multivalue columns are actually repeating groups. Using them, which is a popular practice in AREV applications, violates first normal form. A similar nonrelational construct is Perl's associative array. Associative arrays are collections of name/value pairs that are stored as single variables. Although powerful in practice and certainly handy, they encourage coding and, thereby, database design, which violates first normal form. Another fine example of nonrelational language support is COBOL's <u>group-name occurs several times</u> syntax. COBOL's support for nonrelational elements isn't as surprising as it may seem because it predates relational databases. These types of constructs are to be avoided if you want to build well-designed relational database applications.

Whether you're building a database or a database application, repeating groups are a very poor design practice. I mention applications here because application design inevitably affects database design. After all, the information that's being shuffled around inside an app will most likely need to be stored at some point. As a practical matter, repeating groups present a number of design difficulties. First, returning to the Tenant table example, if we were to store all the properties rented by a tenant within the Tenant table, every tenant row would include the repeating property columns regardless of whether they were used. This would no doubt waste space in the database. Second, repeating groups present a challenge when it comes to processing the data they represent. In particular, properly formatting them on printed reports can be difficult. Not only do you have to deal with sets of rows, but you also have to deal with sets of columns, turning a one-dimensional task into a two-dimensional one. Third, if the maximum number of properties that a tenant may rent needs to be increased, the structure of the Tenant table must be changed, along with any applications that access it.

### Second Normal Form

In order for a table to be normalized in second normal form (2NF), each of its columns must be fully dependent on its primary key and on each attribute in the primary key when the key consists of multiple columns. This means that each nonkey column in a table must be uniquely identified by the table's primary key. Tables with a single-column primary key that are 1NF compliant are already 2NF compliant.

Let's take the example of the Invoice table again. If the table's primary key consists of the **LocationNo** and **InvoiceNo** columns, storing the name of the location in each row would violate second normal form. This is because the

**LocationName** column wouldn't be uniquely identified by the entirety of the primary key. It would depend only on the **LocationNo** column; the **InvoiceNo** column would have no effect on it. Instead, the **LocationName** column should be retrieved from the Location table through a join whenever it's needed, not permanently stored in the Invoice table. For a table to be 2NF compliant, all nonkey columns must be fully functionally dependent on the primary key. Transitive dependencies, however, are still allowed.

### Third Normal Form

In order for a table to be normalized in third normal form (3NF), each of its columns must be fully dependent on its primary key and independent of each other. So, along with meeting the qualifications of second normal form, each nonkey column in a table must be independent of the other nonkey columns. This means that, unlike 2NF, 3NF does not allow transitive dependencies.

Let's return to our Invoice table example. Let's say that the primary key of the table is again both LocationNo and InvoiceNo. One of the nonkey columns in the table would probably be the **CustomerNo** column. If, along with the **CustomerNo** column, the **CustomerName** column was also stored in the Invoice table, the table would fail the criteria for third normal form because the **CustomerNo** and **CustomerName** columns would be dependent on one another. If the **CustomerNo** column was changed, the **CustomerName** column would likely need to change with it, and vice versa. Instead, the **CustomerName** column should be located in a separate table (e.g., the Customer table) and accessed through a join when needed.

---

**NOTE:** An elaboration of third normal form, called *Boyce-Codd Normal Form* (BCNF), requires that each column on which another column depends must itself be a unique key. The column sets that can uniquely identify rows are known as *candidate keys*. A table's primary key is selected from these candidates. BCNF requires that any columns that depend on other columns must only depend on one of these candidates. This means that all determinates must be candidate keys. So, BCNF refines third normal form by allowing for intercolumn dependencies between candidate keys and nonkey columns. However, this doesn't violate third normal form, as it may appear, because the key on which the dependent columns rely is also a candidate key. It uniquely identifies the row, just as the table's primary key does. So, the dependency of a column on a candidate key other than the table's primary key is a purely academic distinction, because both the primary key and the nonprimary candidate key uniquely identify each row.

If this seems confusing, don't worry about it. Compliance through third normal form is the generally accepted criterion by which a table or entity is said to be normalized. A difference that makes no difference is no difference.

---

### Fourth Normal Form

Fourth normal form prohibits multivalue dependencies from existing between columns. If a column, rather than uniquely identifying another column, limits it to a set of predefined values, a multivalue dependency exists between them. Let's look at the Tenant table that we've been discussing. Let's assume for the moment that the only employer-related information you want to store for a Tenant is his employer's name, so you include the Employer attribute in the TENANT entity. In order for a tenant to have more than one employer (let's say he's a workaholic and writes books at night), you'd have to have a separate row in the Tenant table for each of his employers. All the attributes in each row would be identical, with the exception of the Employer attribute. It would differ between rows for a given tenant.

The relationship between the other columns in Tenant and the **Employer** column would amount to a multivalued dependency. For each **TenantNo** column, you might have multiple Employer values. As a matter of practice, you may want to allow for the possibility that a tenant could have more than one employer. Also, although unlikely, knowing which tenants work for a given employer may be of interest to you as well. In order to be fourth normal form compliant, then, you would have to create a separate table whose whole purpose is to cross-reference tenants with employers. Ideally, this new table would have just two columns—**TenantNo** and **Employer**—with both of them serving as parts of a compound primary key. Then, when you needed to list all the information for a given tenant, you would join the Tenant table with the new cross-reference table using their common **TenantNo** column.

In the real world, finding tables that are not fourth normal form compliant is not uncommon. Decomposing entities beyond third normal form sometimes results in more entities than people care to deal with. What is theoretically sound is not always practically sensible.

### Fifth Normal Form

Fifth normal form stipulates that if a table has three or more candidate keys and can be decomposed without losing data, it should be broken into separate tables for each candidate key. Fifth normal form comes into play very rarely for a couple of reasons. First, it's unusual to find a table with three or more separate column sets that uniquely identify rows. Second, excessive decomposition can result in inaccurate joins, such as those that produce new rows. For the most part, you don't see fifth normal form applied (or even discussed) in the real world. I include it here only for reference.

### Normalize, But Don't Overdo It

When you begin normalizing your data, it's important not to get too carried away. Overnormalization can have a devastating effect on performance. It can also needlessly complicate your database design. For instance, consider the example I mention in the discussion on fourth normal form. You may be tempted to set up a separate table for the employer information currently stored in the Tenant table. After all, **Employer** and **EmpAddress** are clearly dependent on one another, in violation of third normal form. But what real benefit would you realize from doing this? Probably very little. Employer information is probably only of interest to you as it relates to a given tenant. For example, you probably wouldn't care to list all tenants working for a given employer. And let's assume that you don't care to store more than one employer per tenant and that you'd never want to change all employer-related information *en masse*. If this is the case, setting up a separate table for tenant employers would likely add needless complexity to your model and generally be a waste of time.

There are also times when *limited denormalization* is the only way to get the performance you need. This is especially possible when working with large amounts of data. For example, suppose that you've built an application that processes millions of credit card receipts each day. Among other things, each receipt lists the card number, the amount of the transaction, and the card's expiration date. At the end of each day's work, your system needs to be able to print a report of all the credit cards used, the net amount of the day's transactions for each card, and each card's expiration date. Because you can easily join to the base credit card table to retrieve the expiration date of each card, you wisely normalize the credit card transaction table by not storing the expiration date from the receipts in it. This saves space in the database and avoids redundancy in the design. This is a better relational design, but has the unfortunate side effect of making your report run twice as long. It runs so long, in fact, that your client finds the application's performance unacceptable.

Speaking only in terms of database design, the resolution to this may be to store and use the expiration date as it is received in each transaction. Although this introduces redundancy into the database, it is *controlled* redundancy, and it is done by design for a specific purpose. Often, this is an acceptable deviation from strict relational policy.

The rule to follow when introducing controlled redundancy into a database design is this: *First* fully normalize the database, *then* introduce redundancy only when absolutely necessary. Resist the temptation to denormalize on a whim or to pass off poor relational design as performance tuning. Unless you work with very large sets of data, denormalizing is rarely necessary.

## Completing Your Model

Technically speaking, your model is now normalized, but there still remains work to be done. For one thing, no entity identifiers (primary keys) have been defined yet for the model. For another, we haven't checked the connections between the entities for correctness.

### Verifying Connectivity

Let's begin by verifying that the decisions made by the tool regarding entity connectivity are correct. There's a minor problem with your E-R diagram as it's currently defined. Look over Figure 5–15 and see if you can spot it. If you discover it, go ahead and correct it in the model. Figure 5–16 shows the model as it should appear. Compare it with Figure 5–15 and notice the change that occurred in the relationship between the CALL entity and the PROPERTY entity.

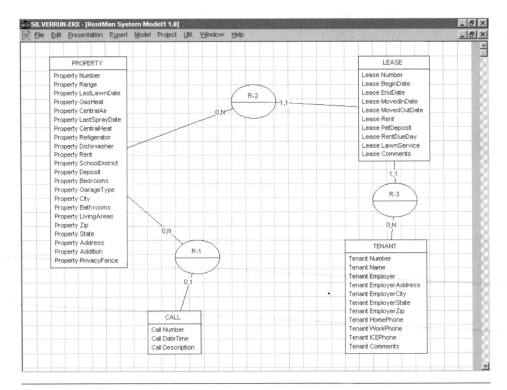

**Figure 5–16** Your model after its connections have been verified.

### Specifying Cardinality

Notice that the connectivity between the CALL and PROPERTY entity was changed from 1,1 to 0,1. What does this mean? The numbers you see on the diagram in Figure 5–16 represent the minimum and maximum cardinality, respectively, for the entities in the relationship. That is, a cardinality of 1,1 between the CALL and PROPERTY entities indicates that, at a minimum, at least one corresponding instance must exist in the PROPERTY entity for each instance in the CALL entity. In terms of the database itself, this means that each row stored in the Call table will require a valid PropertyNo from the Property table. PropertyNo cannot be left blank. As a manner of normal course, though, a PROPERTY instance need not exist in order for a CALL to exist (a person might call who doesn't yet lease a property), so Figure 5–16 reduced the minimum cardinality to 0. A zero cardinality is necessary if the leasing company wants to be able to record calls that don't reference a particular property, such as prospective tenant inquiries. This will allow the Call table's **PropertyNo** column to be left blank. You can't require the existence of a property reference in every call if you intend to record calls that don't reference properties.

Similarly, the maximum cardinality of 1 stipulates that, at a maximum, there can be just one corresponding PROPERTY instance for each CALL instance. This means that a given row in the Call table will be able to reference just one property. It may not reference multiple properties. Again, this is a good decision given that calls would normally either reference no specific property (such as during an inquiry by a prospective tenant) or a particular one (such as a repair request by a tenant).

Cardinality relationships are depicted from the perspective of the nearest entity. That is, you can construct a sentence like the following to make entity cardinality easier to comprehend:

For each NEAR ENTITY row, I need a minimum of MINIMUM CARDINALITY corresponding rows and a maximum of MAXIMUM CARDINALTY corresponding rows in the Far Entity table.

So, in this case, you'd construct the following sentence to express the cardinality of the CALL-PROPERTY relationship:

For each CALL row, I need a minimum of 0 corresponding rows and a maximum of 1 corresponding row in the Property table.

Note that a separate sentence is needed to express the relationship from the perspective of the PROPERTY entity. One sentence is usually not enough. For example, although a PROPERTY instance may not require the existence of a LEASE instance, a LEASE instance certainly requires a corresponding PROPERTY instance.

Entity relationships are frequently expressed in terms like these, and many CASE tools support annotating E-R diagrams with these types of sentences. Another way of expressing entity relationships as sentences follows this format:

`PARENT ENTITY has at least number CHILD ENTITY.`

So, returning to the CALL-PROPERTY example, you'd write

`CALL has at least zero PROPERTY`

to express minimum cardinality.

Likewise, the form

`PARENT ENTITY has at most number CHILD ENTITY`

can be used to express maximum cardinality. You'd write

`CALL has at most one PROPERTY`

to express the maximum cardinality between the Call and Property entities. There are a number of variations on this theme, but the idea is basically the same. You should use whatever works best for you.

## Choosing Entity Identifiers

The next step in completing your E-R model is to select an identifier for each entity. An entity identifier will translate into a primary key definition in your relational model.

Entity identifiers come in two flavors: natural identifiers and artificial or surrogate identifiers. A natural entity identifier is an entity attribute (or set of attributes) already present in the entity that uniquely identifies each entity instance. For example, the SocialSecurityNo attribute would be a natural identifier of the EMPLOYEE entity. An artificial identifier is an attribute that's added to an entity for the express purpose of giving the entity a unique identifier.

Adding an artificial identifier may be necessary for a couple of reasons. One, although another unique identifier exists, it may be too large or too unwieldy to work with practically. For example, a user may feel that typing an employee's social security number regularly is too much work and may request a shorter, less cumbersome employee number attribute. A second reason that you may have to add an artificial identifier is that an entity may not initially have a natural identifier. For example, without a CustomerNo attribute, a CUS-TOMER entity may not possess an attribute or group of attributes that can uniquely identify each entity instance.

In the case of the entities covered here, each entity has an artificial identifier. Despite the fact that you may be able to combine attributes in some of the entities to produce unique identifiers, for simplicity's sake I had you include surrogate identifiers to begin with. This saves time and helps ensure that you won't have problems later. Using your tool's method for doing so, identify the surrogate key in each of your entities. Table 5–4 lists the entities and their keys:

**Table 5–4**  The Surrogate Keys for Your Entities

| Entity | Key |
|--------|-----|
| CALL | Call Number |
| LEASE | Lease Number |
| PROPERTY | Property Number |
| TENANT | Tenant Number |

Figure 5–17 illustrates what your model might now look like.

## Finishing Touches

There are a number of additional things we could do to polish the model a bit more, but only a couple of them are really worthwhile. Before we move on to logical data modeling, let's set up cleaner names for the items in your model. By cleaner, I mean abbreviating or condensing your entity, attribute, or other object names to make them more implementation safe. Names that work fine in a diagram may be difficult or impossible to implement as database objects because they contain spaces or other illegal characters. Because the entities you've defined in your model will eventually become tables in your new database, it's important to use names that the target DBMS will accept. Although SQL Server's square brackets allow us to work with names containing otherwise illegal characters, it's smarter and easier just to use good names in the first place. Many E-R tools can clean up the names you've used in a diagram by converting them from human-readable monikers to DBMS-friendly ones. Sometimes no changes are needed; sometimes radical changes are necessary.

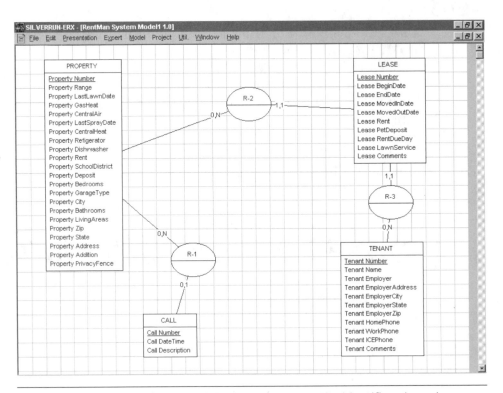

**Figure 5–17** Your model as it might appear once entity identifiers have been defined (keys are underlined).

If your E-R tool includes a name correction feature, invoke it now to condense the names in your model. Most tools will replace the names displayed in the diagram itself with these abbreviated names; some won't. Some tools store the new names internally; some allow you to choose which names to display on the diagram (the more human-readable versions or their abbreviated counterparts).

Figures 5–18 and 5–19 illustrate the name refinement process.

The last thing we'll do before moving on to relational modeling is name and save your model. Most modeling tools allow you to assign a textual name for the models you create that's independent of the filename. A good one for this model is E-R Diagram for Lease Process. Once you've named your model, save it to disk. You're now ready to move on to relational data modeling. Figure 5–20 illustrates what your completed E-R model might look like.

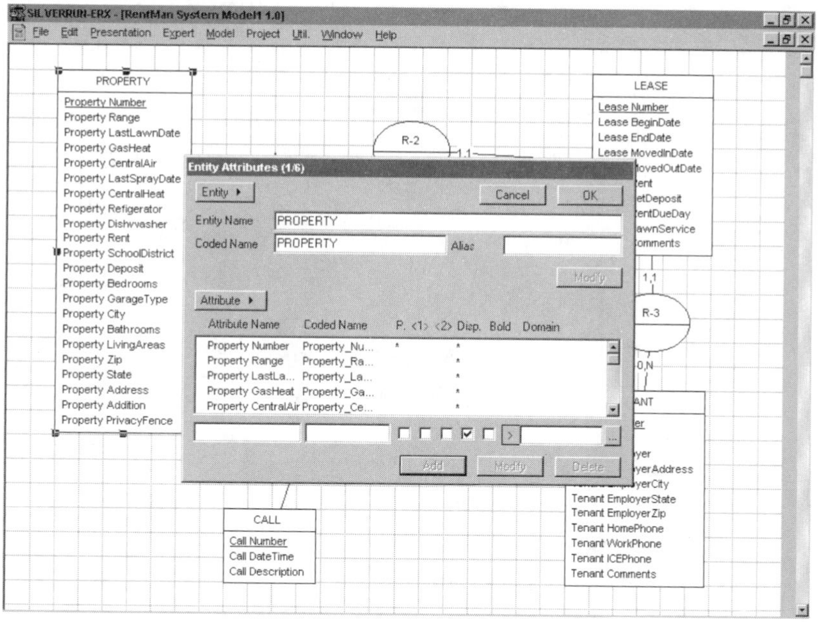

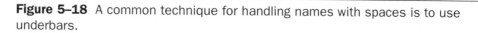

**Figure 5–18** A common technique for handling names with spaces is to use underbars.

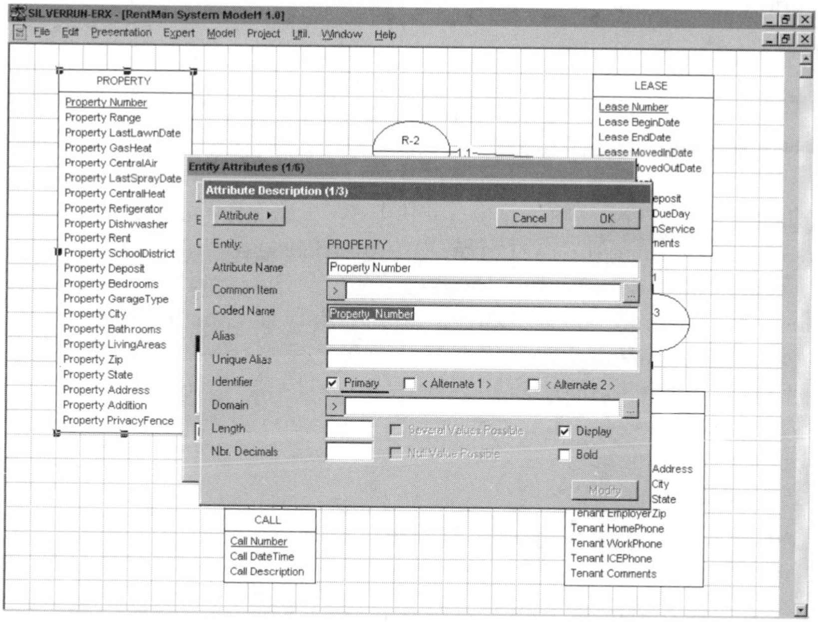

**Figure 5–19** It's better to use simpler names than to have to resort to SQL Server's square brackets.

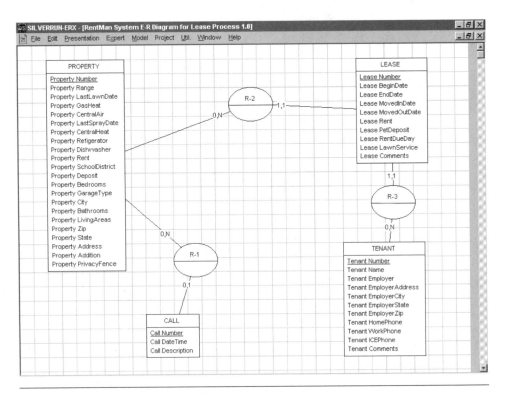

**Figure 5–20** Your completed E-R model.

# Relational Data Modeling

Now that you've successfully modeled the relationships between the entities needed to service the property leasing process, you're ready to move on to relational data modeling. Relational (or logical) data modeling is one step closer to the physical implementation of your database than E-R diagramming. Here you'll define primary keys, referential integrity constraints, and the like. Again, a CASE tool is indispensable here. A good CASE tool will not only make the task of modeling much easier, it will also generate the SQL necessary to implement your model.

## Logical Data Modeling Terms

Before we get started, let me cover some basic relational database and logical data modeling jargon. Table 5–5 lists what I consider essential relational modeling terms. I'm sure you're familiar with most of these already, but a little refresher is still probably worthwhile. Knowing these will help you better understand the discussions that follow. I don't intend for this glossary to be exhaustive, but hopefully you'll find it complete enough to be useful.

Now that you have a few more terms under your belt, let's proceed with the discussion on database design. In this section, you'll take the E-R diagram you built earlier and translate it into a full relational model. The end result of your work will be a Transact-SQL script that you could actually use to create your database objects.

**Table 5–5** Important Relational Modeling Terms and Concepts

| Term | Definition |
| --- | --- |
| Database | A collection of data organized into tables. A good metaphor for databases is the file cabinet. Databases contain tables that contain other data, just as file cabinets contain files that contain items of their own. |
| Table | The fundamental data container in a database. You can think of a relational table as a two-dimensional surface divided into rows and columns. To further the file cabinet metaphor, you can equate each table to a file in the filing cabinet. Tables house all the rows of a particular type. Just as a folder in a filing cabinet might contain all the items of a given type (for example, the entirety of a given vendor's invoices), so does a table in a database contain all the rows of a given type. |
| Row | Corresponds to a single real-world data object. It might be an invoice, a withdrawal from a savings account, or a listing in the phone book. Rows are the "meat and potatoes" of the database. You'll often hear rows referred to as *records*, although SQL purists prefer the use of *row*. This book uses the two terms interchangeably. In their simplest form, databases and tables are really just mechanisms for organizing rows. In our file cabinet analogy, a row is an item within a file folder in the file cabinet. If the file folder was titled Invoices, we would expect each element therein to be an invoice of some type. Likewise, each row in the Invoice table should contain an invoice of some type. |
| Column | An element within a row. A column represents a characteristic of the object represented by a table row. Columns are often referred to as *fields*, although SQL purists prefer *column*. This book uses both terms interchangeably. An example of a column would be the **Address** column in a Customer table. In and of itself, the address is ambiguous. In the context of its table, though, the column describes a customer's address. |

**Table 5–5** *(Continued)*

| Term | Definition |
|------|------------|
| Primary key | The column or set of columns in a table that uniquely identifies each row. An example of a primary key would be the **InvoiceNo** column in an Invoice table. The invoice number in each row of the table is unique to that one record; it is found in no other rows. If you save the value of the **InvoiceNo** column for a particular row and go elsewhere in the table, you can always return to the original row using only the invoice number as the key. The columns that make up a primary key are normally used to build an index on the table for fast access to its rows. |
| Foreign key | A column or set of columns that is inherited from another table. Usually, the inherited key is the primary key of the related table. A foreign key may or may not also be part of the primary key of its host table. Usually it isn't. For example, returning to the Invoice table mentioned earlier, the **CustomerNo** column in an Invoice table might be a foreign key that's inherited from the Customer table. The CustomerNo field couldn't be the Invoice table's primary key because it doesn't uniquely identify individual invoice rows—you might have several invoices for a single customer. However, because customer numbers stored in the Invoice table must be valid, the values stored in the **CustomerNo** column must be checked against the Customer table. Thus, the **CustomerNo** column in the Invoice table is a foreign key that is linked relationally to the Customer table's primary key. |
| Candidate key | A column or set of columns within a table that uniquely identifies its rows. Candidate keys are also referred to as *unique* keys. A table's primary key is selected from its candidate keys. |
| Constraint | A mechanism for ensuring that invalid data is prevented from getting into the database. There are two general types of constraints: referential integrity constraints and domain integrity constraints. Referential integrity constraints ensure that relationships between tables are respected. Domain constraints ensure that values that have incompatible data types, are out of bounds, or are otherwise invalid are prevented from getting into the database. |
| View | A logical representation of a subset of a table's data. Views themselves contain no data. They are SQL queries that can themselves be queried as though they were tables. A view usually provides access to a subset of a table's columns, its rows, or both. A view can implement constraints on the types of data modifications that are permissible on its underlying tables. |
| Trigger | A special type of stored procedure that executes when a given SQL statement is executed against a table. Triggers can be used to ensure referential or domain integrity. |

## Moving from E-R Diagram to Relational Model

To get started, load your E-R diagram into your relational data modeling tool (often, they're the same tool or part of the same suite). One of the first things you should specify for your new model is the target DBMS platform. Assuming your tool supports it, select SQL Server and the version of it that you'll be working with—for example, SQL Server 7.0 or SQL Server 2000 (some tools refer to SQL Server 2000 as version 8.0). Figure 5–21 illustrates what the model might look like once it's loaded.

## Constructing a Data Dictionary

The first thing you need to do with your new model is construct a data dictionary. Many relational modeling tools support data dictionary creation of some type through domains. A domain, you may recall, defines the type of data a column can contain. It's the rough equivalent of a user-defined data type in SQL Server. Regardless of whether you're using a CASE tool, the process of con-

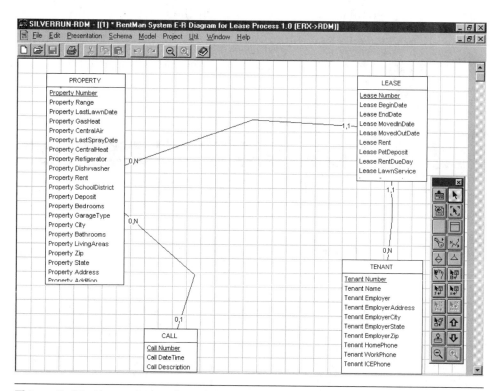

**Figure 5–21** Your relational model as it might initially appear.

structing a data dictionary (also known as an *attribute* or *field repository*) is quite straightforward. To build a data dictionary, follow these steps:

1. Create a master list of all the columns contained in the tables in your model. This doesn't need to be done in any particular tool—you just need to derive a master column list before proceeding.
2. Create domain definitions for those columns contained in more than one table or likely to be (such as through a foreign key reference).
3. Define business rules for each domain in your data dictionary. Column-level business rules control the data values that columns will accept. You might, for example, specify that the **Rent** column must always be nonzero or that the **EndDate** column in the Lease table must always be greater than the **BeginDate** column.
4. Apply the domains you've devised to the columns in your tables. Rather than being based on the stock data types supported by SQL Server, some of your columns will be based on domains instead. These domains will bring with them certain special characteristics, such as limiting the values a column will allow. We'll use your modeling tool to take the domains you define and apply them to the columns in your model.

Table 5–6 lists the domains needed by your model as it now stands. Add each one to your tool's concept of a data dictionary or field/column repository.

**Table 5–6** Domains Needed for Your Data Dictionary

| Name | Base Type | Length | Decimals | Default |
|------|-----------|--------|----------|---------|
| TAddition | varchar | 20 | N/A | 'Firewheel' |
| TAddress | varchar | 30 | N/A | None |
| TCity | varchar | 30 | N/A | 'Garland' |
| TComments | varchar | 80 | N/A | None |
| TPhone | varchar | 13 | N/A | None |
| TPropertyNo | integer | N/A | N/A | None |
| TRent | smallmoney | N/A | N/A | 750 |
| TRooms | tinyint | N/A | N/A | None |
| TSchoolDistrict | varchar | 20 | N/A | 'East Garland' |
| TState | char | 2 | N/A | 'TX' |
| TTenantNo | integer | N/A | N/A | None |
| TYesNo | bit | N/A | N/A | None |
| TZip | char | 10 | N/A | '75080' |

---

**NOTE:** If your tool supports the concept of optionality or nullability, make the TComments domain optional. As a rule, comments-type columns should not be required.

---

Notice that I've prefixed each domain name with a **T**. Here, **T** signifies type. It's a personal preference of mine. Use what works best for you. Of the various traditional programming language elements, domains most closely resemble typedefs (user-defined data type definitions in languages such as C and C++), so I treat domains and typedefs similarly. Figure 5–22 illustrates domain definition.

## Using Your Data Dictionary

Now that you've finished setting up your domain repository, you're ready to apply it to the columns in your tables. You'll also associate those columns that aren't based on domains directly with base types.

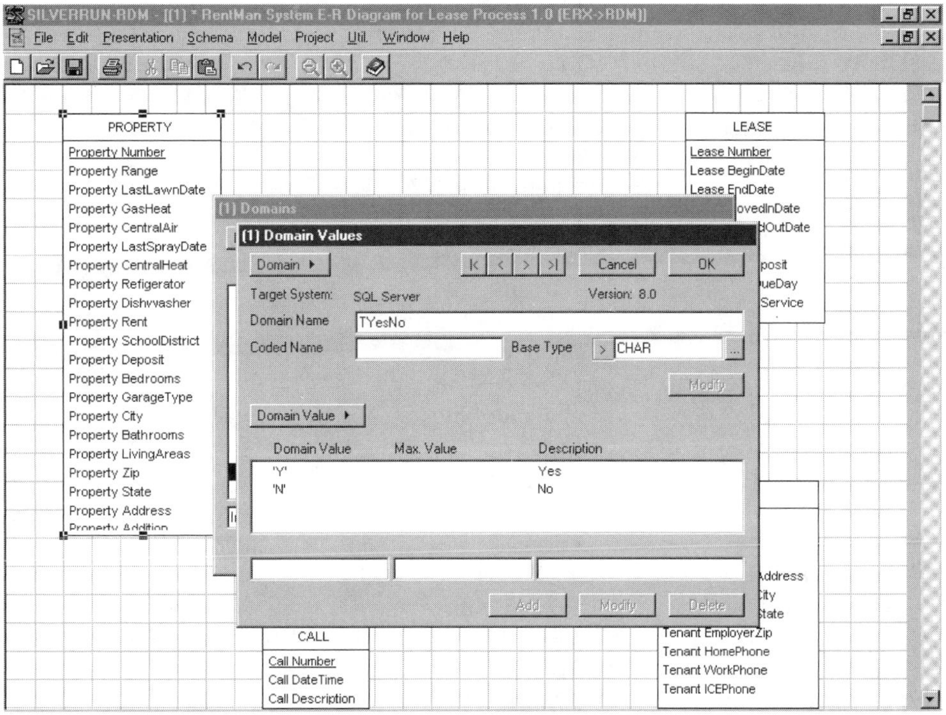

**Figure 5–22** You can define permissible values for domains you create.

Using your tool's facility for doing so, edit each column in the model so that its domain matches that listed in Table 5–7. Repeat this process for all the tables in your model.

**Table 5–7** The Column Definitions for the Tables in Your Relational Model

| Column | Domain | Length | Decimals |
|---|---|---|---|
| Addition | TAddition | | |
| Address | TAddress | | |
| Bathrooms | TRooms | | |
| Bedrooms | TRooms | | |
| BeginDate | smalldatetime | | |
| Call_DateTime | smalldatetime | | |
| Call_Number | integer | | |
| CentralAir | TYesNo | | |
| CentralHeat | TYesNo | | |
| City | TCity | | |
| Comments | TComments | | |
| Deposit | TRent | | |
| Description | varchar | 30 | |
| DishWasher | TYesNo | | |
| Employer | varchar | 30 | |
| EmployerAddress | TAddress | | |
| EmployerCity | TCity | | |
| EmployerState | TState | | |
| EmployerZip | TZip | | |
| EndDate | smalldatetime | | |
| GarageType | TRooms | | |
| GasHeat | TYesNo | | |
| HomePhone | TPhone | | |
| ICEPhone | TPhone | | |
| LastLawnDate | smalldatetime | | |
| LastSprayDate | TYesNo | | |
| LawnService | TYesNo | | |
| Lease_Number | integer | | |
| LivingAreas | TRooms | | |
| MovedInDate | smalldatetime | | |
| MovedOutDate | smalldatetime | | |
| Name | varchar | 30 | |
| PrivacyFence | TYesNo | | |
| Property_Number | TPropertyNo | | |
| Range | TYesNo | | |

**Table 5–7** *(Continued)*

| Column | Domain | Length | Decimals |
|---|---|---|---|
| Refrigerator | TYesNo | | |
| Rent | TRent | | |
| RentDueDay | tinyint | | |
| SchoolDistrict | TSchoolDistrict | | |
| State | TState | | |
| Tenant_Number | TTenantNo | | |
| WorkPhone | TPhone | | |
| Zip | TZip | | |

## Sizing Columns

As you define your columns, think about efficiency. Ask yourself, What's the smallest data type I can use for this column and still store the largest value it might ever have? Here are some general tips for efficiently sizing columns:

- If a field will never need to store a value greater than 255, store it as a tinyint. If a column may need to store a value greater than 255 but less than 32,767, use smallint. In general, use the smallest integer type you can for storing integer data.
- Use integers instead of floating-point types when you define numeric columns that will not need to store digits to the right of the decimal point.
- Use variable character types instead of fixed character types when the length of a character column may vary from row to row.
- Use the "small" versions of the datetime and money types (smalldatetime and smallmoney, respectively) when you can live with their loss of precision.
- Use the bit type to define Boolean columns instead of using integer or single-character data types.

## Describing Your Design

Describing your model elements via comments is a useful and worthwhile habit. In some shops, commenting in data models isn't even optional. The better modeling tools allow you to attach comments to any modeling element you wish. Oftentimes, these object comments are included in the SQL that the tool generates for you if your target platform supports them. Add comments to your model now to describe the objects it contains. Figure 5–23 illustrates.

Note that most tools allow you to add comments to individual columns, as well. Figure 5–24 illustrates.

Describing your model this way helps clarify your understanding of what you're building. In multiprogrammer projects, it also helps others understand what you were thinking when you designed a given object.

## Generating Foreign Keys

One of the final things you need to do is generate foreign key specifications for your model. Foreign keys are the physical implementation of the entity relationships constructed during the E-R modeling phase. Generating foreign keys causes the required columns to be propagated between tables. The way it usually works is that one table inherits the primary key of another. The inherited column or set of columns becomes a foreign key in the inheritor.

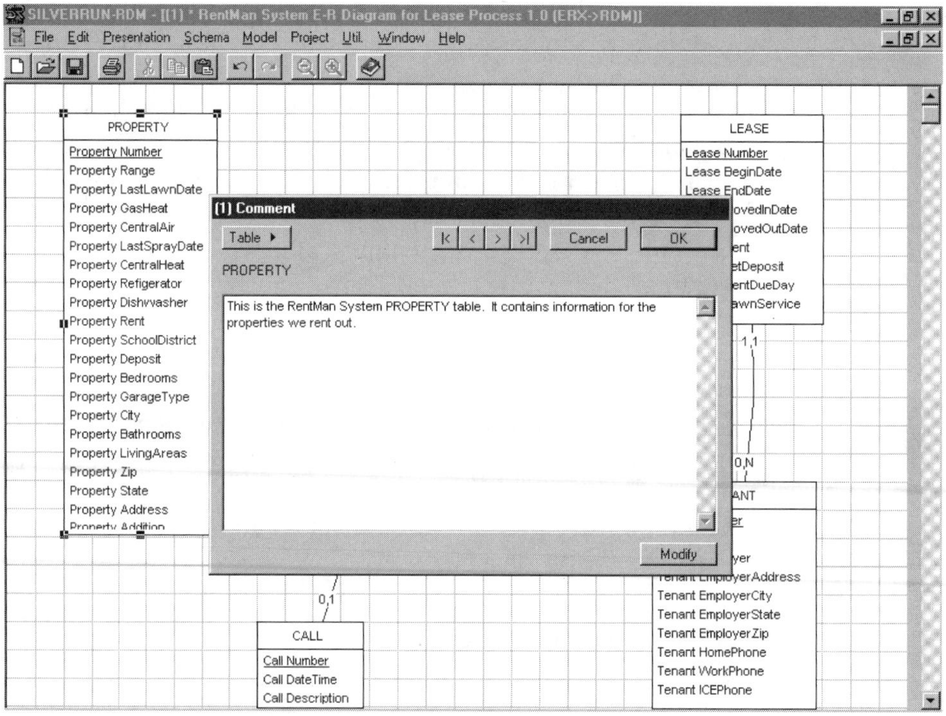

**Figure 5–23** Describe the tables in your model using comments.

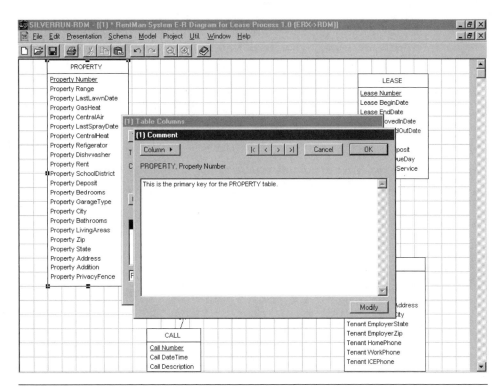

**Figure 5–24** Annotate the columns in your model using comments.

Using your tool's method of doing so, generate foreign keys for the tables in your model. You should then see a number of new columns added to your table objects. It's common for modeling tools to prefix these new columns with **FK**, signifying that they are foreign keys. Figure 5–25 illustrates what you might see.

Your model is now basically complete. You're just about ready to generate the Transact-SQL necessary to create the objects defined by the model.

## Verifying Model Integrity

Before you generate Transact-SQL to create your database objects, you should verify the integrity of your model. Most modeling tools include a facility of some type to assist with this. If your tool supports such a facility, invoke it now to check the integrity of the model.

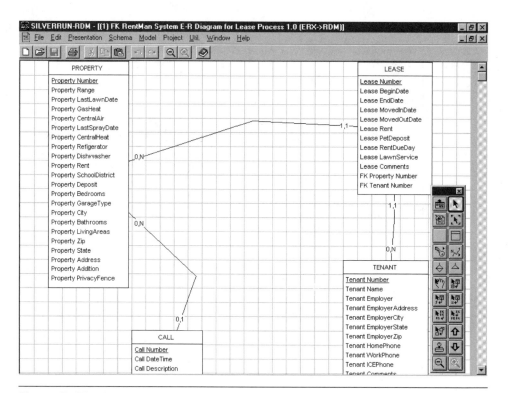

**Figure 5–25** Your logical data model with foreign keys in place.

Checking model integrity before generating T-SQL can save you from having to drop and recreate database objects because they were defined incorrectly. Good modeling tools check a number of aspects of your model and provide a fair measure of whether you're ready to proceed with DDL generation.

## Generating DDL

You've finished your model and now you're ready to generate the DDL necessary to physically implement it. Assuming your tool supports generating DDL scripts to create the objects contained in a model, use it to generate a T-SQL script that builds your database objects.

Listing 5–1 lists a SQL script that should resemble the one produced by your tool. Because you selected SQL Server as your target platform early on, the DDL generated consists of Transact-SQL.

**Listing 5–1** An example of the Transact-SQL that should be generated from your model.

```
USE master
GO
IF DB_ID('rentman') IS NOT NULL
  DROP DATABASE rentman
GO
CREATE DATABASE rentman
GO
USE rentman
GO
IF (DB_NAME()<>'rentman') BEGIN
  RAISERROR('Database create failed - aborting script', 20,1) WITH LOG
  RETURN
END
GO
CREATE RULE RAddition AS @value IN ('Deerfield', 'Firewheel', 'Legacy
Hills', 'Switzerland Estates', 'Sherwood', 'Rockknoll')
GO
CREATE DEFAULT DAddition AS 'Firewheel'
GO
EXEC sp_addtype TAddition , 'varchar(20) ', 'NOT NULL'
EXEC sp_bindrule RAddition, TAddition
EXEC sp_bindefault DAddition, TAddition
GO
EXEC sp_addtype TAddress , 'varchar(30)', 'NOT NULL'
GO
CREATE RULE RCity AS @value IN ('Oklahoma City', 'Norman', 'Edmond',
'Dallas', 'Garland', 'Plano')
GO
CREATE DEFAULT DCity AS 'Garland'
GO
EXEC sp_addtype TCity , 'varchar(30) ', 'NOT NULL'
EXEC sp_bindrule RCity, TCity
EXEC sp_bindefault DCity, TCity
GO
EXEC sp_addtype TComments , 'varchar(80)', 'NULL'
EXEC sp_addtype TPhone , 'varchar(12)', 'NOT NULL'
EXEC sp_addtype TPropertyNo , 'int', 'NOT NULL'
GO
CREATE DEFAULT DRent AS 750
GO
EXEC sp_addtype TRent , 'smallmoney', 'NOT NULL'
EXEC sp_bindefault DRent, TRent
```

```
GO
CREATE RULE RRooms AS @value IN (0, 1, 2, 3, 4, 5)
GO
EXEC sp_addtype TRooms , 'tinyint', 'NOT NULL'
EXEC sp_bindrule RRooms, TRooms
GO
CREATE RULE RSchoolDistrict AS @value IN ('Putnam City', 'Oklahoma City',
'Richardson', 'Edmond', 'East Garland', 'Dallas', 'Plano')
GO
CREATE DEFAULT DSchoolDistrict AS 'East Garland'
GO
EXEC sp_addtype TSchoolDistrict , 'varchar(20) ', 'NOT NULL'
EXEC sp_bindrule RSchoolDistrict, TSchoolDistrict
EXEC sp_bindefault DSchoolDistrict, TSchoolDistrict
GO
CREATE RULE RState AS @value IN ('OK', 'TX')
GO
CREATE DEFAULT DState AS 'TX'
GO
EXEC sp_addtype TState , 'char(2)', 'NOT NULL'
EXEC sp_bindrule RState, TState
EXEC sp_bindefault DState, TState
GO
EXEC sp_addtype TTenantNo , 'int', 'NOT NULL'
EXEC sp_addtype TYesNo , 'bit', 'NOT NULL'
GO
CREATE DEFAULT DZip AS '75080'
GO
EXEC sp_addtype TZip , 'varchar(10)', 'NOT NULL'
EXEC sp_bindefault DZip, TZip
GO


CREATE TABLE PROPERTY
(       Property_Number     TPropertyNo NOT NULL,
        Address             TAddress NOT NULL,
        City                TCity NOT NULL,
        State               TState NOT NULL,
        Zip                 TZip NOT NULL,
        Addition            TAddition NOT NULL,
        SchoolDistrict      TSchoolDistrict NOT NULL,
        Rent                TRent NOT NULL,
        Deposit             smallmoney NOT NULL,
        LivingAreas         TRooms NOT NULL,
```

```
        BedRooms           TRooms NOT NULL,
        BathRooms          TRooms NOT NULL,
        GarageType         TRooms NOT NULL,
        CentralAir         TYesNo NOT NULL,
        CentralHeat        TYesNo NOT NULL,
        GasHeat            TYesNo NOT NULL,
        Refigerator        TYesNo NOT NULL,
        Range              TYesNo NOT NULL,
        DishWasher         TYesNo NOT NULL,
        PrivacyFence       TYesNo NOT NULL,
        LastLawnDate       smalldatetime NOT NULL,
        LastSprayDate      TYesNo NOT NULL,
    PRIMARY KEY (Property_Number)
)
GO


CREATE TABLE TENANT
(   Tenant_Number      TTenantNo NOT NULL,
    Name               varchar(30) NOT NULL,
    Employer           varchar(30) NOT NULL,
    EmployerAddress    TAddress NOT NULL,
    EmployerCity       TCity NOT NULL,
    EmployerState      TState NOT NULL,
    EmployerZip        TZip NOT NULL,
    HomePhone          TPhone NOT NULL,
    WorkPhone          TPhone NOT NULL,
    ICEPhone           TPhone NOT NULL,
    Comments           TComments NULL,
    PRIMARY KEY (Tenant_Number)
)
GO


CREATE TABLE CALL
(   Call_Number        int NOT NULL,
    Call_DateTime      smalldatetime NOT NULL,
    Description        varchar(30) NOT NULL,
    Property_Number    TPropertyNo NULL,
    PRIMARY KEY (Call_Number),
    CONSTRAINT FK_PROPERTY1
     FOREIGN KEY (Property_Number)
        REFERENCES PROPERTY
)
GO
```

```
CREATE TABLE LEASE
(   Lease_Number        int NOT NULL,
    BeginDate           smalldatetime NOT NULL,
    EndDate             smalldatetime NOT NULL,
    MovedInDate         smalldatetime NOT NULL,
    MovedOutDate        smalldatetime NOT NULL,
    Rent                TRent NOT NULL,
    PetDeposit          smallmoney NOT NULL,
    RentDueDay          tinyint NOT NULL,
    LawnService         TYesNo NOT NULL,
    Comments            TComments NULL,
    Property_Number     TPropertyNo NOT NULL,
    Tenant_Number       TTenantNo NOT NULL,
    PRIMARY KEY (Lease_Number),
    CONSTRAINT FK_PROPERTY2
      FOREIGN KEY (Property_Number)
        REFERENCES PROPERTY,
    CONSTRAINT FK_TENANT3
      FOREIGN KEY (Tenant_Number)
        REFERENCES TENANT
)
GO
```

Notice that the script begins by creating the logical domains you defined as SQL Server user-defined data types. It then uses these data types to define your database tables. This is a good technique because it encapsulates your business rules as much as possible in reusable data types. You can use these types to build new columns as necessary. For example, if you needed to add another column that permits only 1 or 0, you can reuse the **TYesNo** type. This is the advantage of embedding your business rules in data types rather that directly in columns.

The one flaw with this approach is that it uses somewhat antiquated constructs for ensuring domain integrity—namely RULE and DEFAULT objects. The more modern—and certainly more portable method—is to use CHECK and DEFAULT table/column constraints. Good modeling tools allow you to generate Transact-SQL DDL either way: either using RULE and DEFAULT objects or using standard ANSI constraints. The constraints approach is actually more flexible because you can set up CHECK constraints that involve multiple columns (for example, EndDate must be equal to or later than BeginDate). You can't do this with RULE objects. Listing 5–2 shows the script generated using constraints to ensure domain integrity:

**Listing 5–2** The script regenerated using constraints instead of DEFAULT/RULE objects.

```
USE master
GO
IF DB_ID('rentman') IS NOT NULL
  DROP DATABASE rentman
GO
CREATE DATABASE rentman
GO
USE rentman
GO
IF (DB_NAME()<>'rentman') BEGIN
  RAISERROR('Database create failed - aborting script', 20,1) WITH LOG
  RETURN
END
GO
EXEC sp_addtype TAddition , 'varchar(20)', 'NOT NULL'
EXEC sp_addtype TAddress , 'varchar(30)', 'NOT NULL'
EXEC sp_addtype TCity , 'varchar(30)', 'NOT NULL'
EXEC sp_addtype TComments , 'varchar(80)', 'NULL'
EXEC sp_addtype TPhone , 'varchar(12)', 'NOT NULL'
EXEC sp_addtype TPropertyNo , 'int', 'NOT NULL'
EXEC sp_addtype TRent , 'smallmoney', 'NOT NULL'
EXEC sp_addtype TRooms , 'tinyint', 'NOT NULL'
EXEC sp_addtype TSchoolDistrict , 'varchar(20) ', 'NOT NULL'
EXEC sp_addtype TState , 'char(2)', 'NOT NULL'
EXEC sp_addtype TTenantNo , 'int', 'NOT NULL'
EXEC sp_addtype TYesNo , 'bit', 'NOT NULL'
EXEC sp_addtype TZip , 'varchar(10)', 'NOT NULL'
GO


CREATE TABLE PROPERTY
(       Property_Number    TPropertyNo NOT NULL,
        Address            TAddress NOT NULL,
        City               TCity NOT NULL,
        State              TState NOT NULL DEFAULT 'TX' CHECK (State IN ('OK',
'TX')),
        Zip                TZip NOT NULL DEFAULT '75080',
        Addition           TAddition NOT NULL DEFAULT 'Firewheel' CHECK (Addition IN
('Deerfield', 'Firewheel', 'Legacy Hills', 'Switzerland Estates', 'Sherwood',
'Rockknoll')),
        SchoolDistrict     TSchoolDistrict NOT NULL DEFAULT 'East Garland' CHECK
(SchoolDistrict IN ('Putnam City', 'Oklahoma City', 'Richardson', 'Edmond', 'East
Garland', 'Dallas', 'Plano')),
```

```
        Rent                TRent NOT NULL DEFAULT 750,
        Deposit             TRent NOT NULL DEFAULT 750,
        LivingAreas         TRooms NOT NULL CHECK (LivingAreas BETWEEN 0 AND 5),
        BedRooms            TRooms NOT NULL CHECK (BedRooms BETWEEN 0 AND 5),
        BathRooms           TRooms NOT NULL CHECK (BathRooms BETWEEN 0 AND 5),
        GarageType          TRooms NOT NULL CHECK (GarageType BETWEEN 0 AND 5),
        CentralAir          TYesNo NOT NULL,
        CentralHeat         TYesNo NOT NULL,
        GasHeat             TYesNo NOT NULL,
        Refigerator         TYesNo NOT NULL,
        Range               TYesNo NOT NULL,
        DishWasher          TYesNo NOT NULL,
        PrivacyFence        TYesNo NOT NULL,
        LastLawnDate        smalldatetime NOT NULL,
        LastSprayDate       TYesNo NOT NULL,
    PRIMARY KEY (Property_Number)
)
GO


CREATE TABLE TENANT
(   Tenant_Number       TTenantNo NOT NULL,
    Name                varchar(30) NOT NULL,
    Employer            varchar(30) NOT NULL,
    EmployerAddress     TAddress NOT NULL,
    EmployerCity        TCity NOT NULL DEFAULT 'Garland',
    EmployerState       TState NOT NULL DEFAULT 'TX',
    EmployerZip         TZip NOT NULL DEFAULT '75080',
    HomePhone           TPhone NOT NULL,
    WorkPhone           TPhone NOT NULL,
    ICEPhone            TPhone NOT NULL,
    Comments            TComments NULL,
    PRIMARY KEY (Tenant_Number)
)
GO


CREATE TABLE CALL
(   Call_Number         int NOT NULL,
    Call_DateTime       smalldatetime NOT NULL,
    Description         varchar(30) NOT NULL,
    Property_Number     TPropertyNo NULL,
    PRIMARY KEY (Call_Number),
    CONSTRAINT FK_PROPERTY1
    FOREIGN KEY (Property_Number)
        REFERENCES PROPERTY
```

```
)
GO

CREATE TABLE LEASE
(   Lease_Number       int NOT NULL,
    BeginDate          smalldatetime NOT NULL,
    EndDate            smalldatetime NOT NULL,
    MovedInDate        smalldatetime NOT NULL,
    MovedOutDate       smalldatetime NOT NULL,
    Rent               TRent NOT NULL DEFAULT 750,
    Deposit            TRent NOT NULL DEFAULT 750,
    RentDueDay         tinyint NOT NULL CHECK (RentDueDay BETWEEN 1 AND 15),
    LawnService        TYesNo NOT NULL,
    Comments           TComments NULL,
    Property_Number    TPropertyNo NOT NULL,
    Tenant_Number      TTenantNo NOT NULL,
    PRIMARY KEY (Lease_Number),
    CONSTRAINT FK_PROPERTY2
     FOREIGN KEY (Property_Number)
        REFERENCES PROPERTY,
    CONSTRAINT FK_TENANT3
     FOREIGN KEY (Tenant_Number)
        REFERENCES TENANT,
    CONSTRAINT CK_ENDDATE4
       CHECK (EndDate >= BeginDate),
    CONSTRAINT CK_MOVEOUTDATE5
       CHECK (MovedOutDate >= MovedInDate)
)
GO
```

Your model is basically complete. If your tool supports it, enter a description for your database schema before saving it. Figure 5–26 illustrates.

## Database Diagrams in Enterprise Manager

Even though Enterprise Manager's Database Diagram facility isn't suitable as a general-purpose modeling tool, it does offer some basic physical database modeling facilities. Using the Create New Database Diagram wizard, you can import an existing physical model into a diagram and manipulate it using the Database Diagram facility. It's rudimentary, but it comes free in the box, so it makes sense to use it when you need to do physical modeling and the facility's very basic capabilities meet your needs. Figure 5–27 shows the RENTMAN database loaded into an Enterprise Manager Database Diagram.

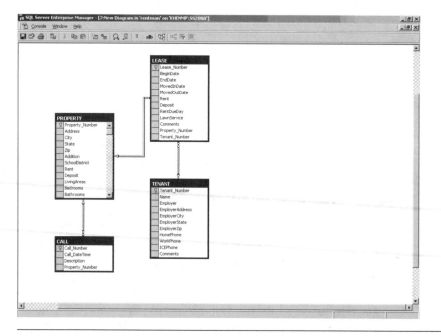

**Figure 5–26** Use the Schema Description dialog to specify your model's name.

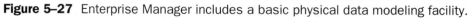

**Figure 5–27** Enterprise Manager includes a basic physical data modeling facility.

# Summary

Your relational data model is now complete. Hopefully you've gained some insight regarding how business process modeling, E-R modeling, and relational data modeling all interrelate. You began the hands-on work of this chapter with nothing but an idea as to what a hypothetical lease management application might need to do to be functional. You've ended the chapter having constructed three different models representing three different aspects of the app and its database requirements. This soup-to-nuts approach should get you well on your way to designing and building your own databases. It's an approach you can take regardless of the development tools you use.

# CHAPTER 6

# Data Volumes

*With design, I can think very fast, but my thinking is full of holes.*

*—Alistair Cockburn*[1]

As you work through the examples in this book and as you tune your own code for performance, you will occasionally need to create large volumes of test data. People have different techniques for doing this. Some keep test data in external files that they can BCP into the server, some keep test databases or test tables around for the express purpose of coming up with lots of data quickly. Others generate new test data each time they need it.

In this chapter we'll talk about some techniques for generating large volumes of data. There are third-party programs with elaborate facilities for generating test data for SQL Server, but you can generate basic test data of almost any quantity with some very simple queries.

## Approaches to Generating Data

The two most important ingredients in making test data are the uniqueness/randomness of the data and the time it takes to produce. Random data is usually better, and shorter creation times are better. What we want to do is produce data that is as random or unique as possible in as short a time as possible. These two variables are usually inversely proportional to one another. That is, you increase one at the expense of the other. Increasing data randomness also increases the time it takes to produce. Similarly, improving the time it takes to generate test data usually lessens its uniqueness.

Although the examples we'll cover typically only generate 100 rows of data, you can extend them to generate practically any number of rows. I've purposely avoided showing you the obvious technique of looping on a variable and inserting a single row with each iteration because that approach is slow and resource-

---

1. Fowler, Martin. *Refactoring: Improving the Design of Existing Code*. Reading, MA: Addison-Wesley, 1999. Page 67.

intensive. Each row inserted creates another entry in the transaction log. The technique is impractical for generating extremely large numbers of rows because it's too slow and because of its negative effect on the transaction log.

## Cross Join

The first approach I'll show you is the cross-join approach. It involves synthesizing data by leveraging SQL's ability to return a Cartesian product (the result of multiplying one table by another). Here's an example:

```
CREATE TABLE #list
(id int identity)
INSERT #list DEFAULT VALUES
INSERT #list DEFAULT VALUES
INSERT #list DEFAULT VALUES
INSERT #list DEFAULT VALUES
INSERT #list DEFAULT VALUES
INSERT #list DEFAULT VALUES
INSERT #list DEFAULT VALUES
INSERT #list DEFAULT VALUES
INSERT #list DEFAULT VALUES
INSERT #list DEFAULT VALUES

SELECT * FROM #list L1 CROSS JOIN #list L2
GO
DROP TABLE #list
```

(Results abridged)

```
id          id
----------  ----------
1           1
2           1
3           1
4           1
5           1
6           1
...
6           10
7           10
8           10
9           10
10          10
(100 row(s) affected)
```

The key line is the SELECT itself (in bold type). It's assumed that the table from which we're selecting would normally already exist.

You can increase the number of CROSS JOINs to multiply the number of rows generated. For example, to generate 1,000 rows instead of 100 in the previous example, we'd need only to set up another CROSS JOIN to the #List table. Through the power of exponential multiplication, you can quickly generate large volumes of data this way.

This technique works great for returning the data in a particular table, but what if we want to generate something besides what's already in a table? Here's a variation on the cross-join technique that returns completely new data:

```
CREATE TABLE #list
(id int identity)
INSERT #list DEFAULT VALUES
INSERT #list DEFAULT VALUES
INSERT #list DEFAULT VALUES
INSERT #list DEFAULT VALUES
INSERT #list DEFAULT VALUES
INSERT #list DEFAULT VALUES
INSERT #list DEFAULT VALUES
INSERT #list DEFAULT VALUES
INSERT #list DEFAULT VALUES
INSERT #list DEFAULT VALUES

SELECT IDENTITY(int, 1,1) AS Id, RAND(L1.id) AS RNum
INTO #list2
FROM #list L1 CROSS JOIN #list L2

SELECT * FROM #list2

GO
DROP TABLE #list,#list2
```

(Results abridged)

```
Id          RNum
----------- -------------------------------------------------------
1           0.71359199321292355
2           0.71359199321292355
3           0.71359199321292355
4           0.71359199321292355
5           0.71359199321292355
6           0.71359199321292355
```

```
...
96          0.71375968995424732
97          0.71375968995424732
98          0.71375968995424732
99          0.71375968995424732
100         0.71375968995424732

(100 row(s) affected)
```

Here, we use the IDENTITY() function to generate a sequential integer for the first column. Note the semirandomness of the **RNum** column. Obviously, it's not quite random, but we get a good mix of values by using the RAND() function and passing it a column from the CROSS JOIN as a seed. Can we do better? Absolutely. Here's a variation that mixes the data a bit better:

```
CREATE TABLE #list
(id int identity)
INSERT #list DEFAULT VALUES
INSERT #list DEFAULT VALUES
INSERT #list DEFAULT VALUES
INSERT #list DEFAULT VALUES
INSERT #list DEFAULT VALUES
INSERT #list DEFAULT VALUES
INSERT #list DEFAULT VALUES
INSERT #list DEFAULT VALUES
INSERT #list DEFAULT VALUES
INSERT #list DEFAULT VALUES

SELECT IDENTITY(int, 1,1) AS Id, RAND(CASE WHEN L1.id % 2 = 0 THEN L1.id
ELSE L2.id END) AS RNum
INTO #list2
FROM #list L1 CROSS JOIN #list L2

SELECT * FROM #list2

GO
DROP TABLE #list,#list2
```

(Results abridged)

```
Id          RNum
----------- -----------------------------------------------------
1           0.71359199321292355
2           0.7136106261841817
```

```
3          0.71359199321292355
4          0.7136478921266981
5          0.71359199321292355
6          0.71368515806921451
...
96         0.71368515806921451
97         0.71375968995424732
98         0.71372242401173092
99         0.71375968995424732
100        0.71375968995424732
```

```
(100 row(s) affected)
```

As you can see, the data still isn't really random, but it's at least mixed up a little more randomly. Can we do better? Can we generate data that's much more random in a timely fashion? Certainly. Have a look at this variation:

```
CREATE TABLE #list
(id int identity)
INSERT #list DEFAULT VALUES
INSERT #list DEFAULT VALUES
INSERT #list DEFAULT VALUES
INSERT #list DEFAULT VALUES
INSERT #list DEFAULT VALUES
INSERT #list DEFAULT VALUES
INSERT #list DEFAULT VALUES
INSERT #list DEFAULT VALUES
INSERT #list DEFAULT VALUES
INSERT #list DEFAULT VALUES

SELECT IDENTITY(int, 1,1) AS Id
INTO #list2
FROM #list L1 CROSS JOIN #list L2

SELECT Id, RAND(Id)*10000000000000 RNum FROM #list2
GO
DROP TABLE #list,#list2
```

(Results)

```
Id          RNum
----------  -------------------------------------------------------
1           7135919932129.2354
2           7136106261841.8174
```

```
3              7136292591554.3994
4              7136478921266.9814
5              7136665250979.5635
6              7136851580692.1455
...
96             7153621254824.5244
97             7153807584537.1074
98             7153993914249.6885
99             7154180243962.2715
100            7154366573674.8525
```

```
(100 row(s) affected)
```

Here we use the sequential number we generated using IDENTITY() as a seed to the RAND() function. This, of course, provides a unique seed for each invocation of the function and results in a random number for each row in the temporary table. Additionally, we multiply this random number by 10 trillion to return a positive real number between 1 and 10 trillion.

The only problem with this approach is that the random numbers generated are in order. For example, you could change the query to sort on the **RNum** column, like this:

```
SELECT Id, RAND(Id)*10000000000000 RNum FROM #list2 ORDER BY RNum
```

However, the order of the rows in the result set wouldn't change. That's a typical weakness of random number generators. Because they use a formula to generate numbers, they're susceptible to generating detectable patterns when supplied identical inputs or inputs that have a similar relationship to one another. In this case, the inputs have the same relationship to one another: Each Id value is one greater than the value before it in the table. One potential way around this is to create your own random number generator. We'll explore that possibility in the next section.

## Random()

In addition to SQL Server's built-in functions, you can use UDFs to assist with generating random data. Here's a variation of the previous example that does just that:

```
USE tempdb
GO
SET NOCOUNT ON
GO
```

```
DROP FUNCTION dbo.Random
GO
CREATE FUNCTION dbo.Random(@Seed int)
RETURNS int
AS
/*
Based on an algorithm from The Art of Computer Programming,
Volume 2, Seminumerical Algorithms, by Donald Knuth, pp. 185-6.
*/
BEGIN
  DECLARE @MM int, @AA int, @QQ int, @RR int, @MMM int, @AAA int,
  @QQQ int, @RRR int, @Result int, @X decimal(38,0), @Y decimal(38,0)
  SELECT @MM=2147483647, @AA=48271, @QQ=44488,
     @RR=3399, @MMM=2147483399, @AAA=40692, @QQQ=52774, @RRR=3791
  SET @X=@AA*(@Seed%@QQ)-@RR*CAST((@Seed/@QQ) AS int)
  IF (@X<0) SET @X=@X+@MM
  SET @Y=@AAA*(@Seed%@QQQ)-@RRR*CAST((@Seed/@QQQ) AS int)
  IF (@Y<0) SET @Y=@Y+@MMM
  SET @Result=@X-@Y
  IF (@Result<=0) SET @Result=@Result+@MM
  RETURN(@Result)
END
GO
DROP FUNCTION dbo.ScrambleFloat
GO
CREATE FUNCTION dbo.ScrambleFloat(@Float float, @Seed float)
RETURNS float
AS
BEGIN
  DECLARE @VFloat as varbinary(8), @VFSFloat int, @Return float
  SET @VFloat=CAST(@Float as varbinary(8))
  SET @Return=dbo.Random(@Seed) *
        ((CAST(CAST(SUBSTRING(@VFloat,5,1) AS int) AS float) *
        (CAST(SUBSTRING(@VFloat,7,1) AS int)) /
        ISNULL(NULLIF(CAST(SUBSTRING(@VFloat,6,1) AS int),0),1)) +
        CAST(SUBSTRING(@VFloat,8,1) AS int) -
        (CAST(SUBSTRING(@VFloat,3,1) AS int) %
        ISNULL(NULLIF(CAST(SUBSTRING(@VFloat,1,1) AS int),0),1))+
        (CAST(SUBSTRING(@VFloat,2,1) AS int) *
        CASE WHEN
           CAST(SUBSTRING(@VFloat,4,1) AS int) % 2 = 0 THEN 1 ELSE -1 END))
  RETURN(@Return)
END
GO
```

```
CREATE TABLE #list
(id int identity)
INSERT #list DEFAULT VALUES
INSERT #list DEFAULT VALUES
INSERT #list DEFAULT VALUES
INSERT #list DEFAULT VALUES
INSERT #list DEFAULT VALUES
INSERT #list DEFAULT VALUES
INSERT #list DEFAULT VALUES
INSERT #list DEFAULT VALUES
INSERT #list DEFAULT VALUES
INSERT #list DEFAULT VALUES

SELECT IDENTITY(int, 1,1) AS Id
INTO #list2
FROM #list L1 CROSS JOIN #list L2
SELECT Id, dbo.Random(Id) As Random,
dbo.ScrambleFloat(Id, DATEPART(ms, GETDATE())) AS Scrambled
FROM #list2
ORDER BY Scrambled

GO
DROP TABLE #list,#list2
```

(Results)

```
Id          Random      Scrambled
----------- ----------- --------------------------------------------------
--
29          219791      -722564027.05882347
44          333476      -673420171.23333335
13          98527       -574568537.4000001
28          212212      -544849779.53631282
74          560846      -523678459.07142854
98          742742      -507777842.00000006
96          727584      -477779538.77049184
...
79          598741      3028523768.1111112
41          310739      3259160366.647059
25          189475      3645254956.2000003
81          613899      3701346966.7777781
53          401687      4101890347.4999995
27          204633      4471710800.7000008
55          416845      4934363189.25
```

This code has several interesting features. First, note that we appear to get a random ordering of rows (it's not actually random, but at least it doesn't match the original order of the **Id** column). Second, note the use of the Random() UDF. We use it both in the SCRAMBLEFLOAT() function as well as to return a column in the result set. It uses an algorithm from Donald Knuth's three-volume work, *The Art of Computer Programming*,[2] to generate a random integer. We use it in SCRAMBLEFLOAT() because UDFs cannot use nondeterministic functions such as Transact-SQL's built-in RAND().

The SCRAMBLEFLOAT() function is also worth discussing. It literally takes a floating-point value apart and synthesizes a new value from it, using a seed value to help further randomize the process. It first casts the input value to a varbinary(8), then uses SUBSTRING() to disassemble it and turn it into a completely different floating-point value. It also randomizes the sign of the number so that the sign will vary somewhat from input value to input value. Although the values it returns should vary from run to run, their relationship to the input value and to the seed will not vary because a deterministic computation is used to transform the input value into the function result.

Run this code multiple times. What you should see is that the actual ordering of the rows does not change between runs, although the values returned by the SCRAMBLEFLOAT() function do. Even though the ordering doesn't change, it at least differs from the default ordering of the **Id** column, which is probably good enough for test data. That the ordering doesn't change is a result of the fact that the column on which we're ordering, although it appears to consist of random values, actually doesn't. SCRAMBLEFLOAT(), for all its machinations, returns predictable values. In other words, given a specific input value, SCRAMBLEFLOAT() will always return a value with a predictable relationship to the input value.

## Doubling

*Doubling*—inserting a table into itself until a desired size is reached—bears some similarities to the cross-tab techniques we've been examining. You'll find that this technique can produce fairly random data in a reasonable amount of time. Here's an example:

```
SET NOCOUNT ON
CREATE TABLE #list
(id int identity, PlaceHolder int NULL)
INSERT #list DEFAULT VALUES
INSERT #list DEFAULT VALUES
```

---

2. Knuth, Donald. *The Art of Computer Programming*, Volume 2, *Seminumerical Algorithms*. Reading, MA: Addison-Wesley, 1998. pp. 185–186.

```
INSERT #list DEFAULT VALUES
INSERT #list DEFAULT VALUES
INSERT #list DEFAULT VALUES
INSERT #list DEFAULT VALUES
INSERT #list DEFAULT VALUES
INSERT #list DEFAULT VALUES
INSERT #list DEFAULT VALUES
INSERT #list DEFAULT VALUES

SET NOCOUNT OFF
DECLARE @cnt int, @rcnt int, @targ int
SELECT @targ=100, @cnt=COUNT(*), @rcnt=@targ-COUNT(*) FROM #list
WHILE @rcnt>0 BEGIN
  SET ROWCOUNT @rcnt
  INSERT #list (PlaceHolder) SELECT PlaceHolder FROM #list
  SET @cnt=@cnt+@@ROWCOUNT
  SET @rcnt=@targ-@cnt
END
SET ROWCOUNT 0
SELECT Id, RAND(Id)*10000000000000 FROM #list

GO
DROP TABLE #list
```

## (Results abridged)

```
(10 row(s) affected)

(20 row(s) affected)

(40 row(s) affected)

(20 row(s) affected)

Id
----------- -----------------------------------------------------
1           7135919932129.2354
2           7136106261841.8174
3           7136292591554.3994
4           7136478921266.9814
5           7136665250979.5635
6           7136851580692.1455
...
96          7153621254824.5244
97          7153807584537.1074
98          7153993914249.6885
99          7154180243962.2715
```

```
100          7154366573674.8525
```

```
(100 row(s) affected)
```

Here we begin by setting @targ to the target number of rows, and @cnt and @rcnt to the number of rows in the table and the number of rows remaining to insert respectively. We then loop, inserting the table into itself, until we've reached the target number of rows.

Note the use of SET ROWCOUNT to govern the number of rows inserted into the table. This keeps us from going beyond the target row count. We have to use SET ROWCOUNT here instead of SELECT TOP because SELECT TOP does not allow a variable to be used for the number of rows to return.

## INSERT...EXEC

Another technique for generating lots of data relatively quickly is to use INSERT...EXEC to call a stored procedure that returns a large number of rows (even containing data that we don't care about using). Here's a query that first calls the SQLDIAG utility to create a report of your vital SQL Server statistics, then calls xp_cmdshell via INSERT...EXEC to generate a series of sequential integers:

```
SET NOCOUNT ON
SET ANSI_WARNINGS OFF
CREATE TABLE #list
(id int identity, PlaceHolder char(1) NULL)
EXEC master..xp_cmdshell 'sqldiag.exe -Oc:\temp\sqldiag.rpt',no_output

SET ROWCOUNT 100
INSERT #list (PlaceHolder)
EXEC master..xp_cmdshell 'TYPE c:\temp\sqldiag.rpt'
SET ROWCOUNT 0

SELECT Id FROM #list
GO
DROP TABLE #list
```

(Results abridged)

```
Id
-----------
1
2
3
```

```
4
5
6
...
96
97
98
99
100
```

Here we use xp_cmdshell to list a text file using TYPE (we also create the file in advance using the SQLDIAG utility, but, normally, you wouldn't regenerate the file each time). We disable ANSI_WARNINGS because we're intentionally truncating the rows we're returning from the text file. It's a generation mechanism only, and we don't care about its contents. The **PlaceHolder** column is exactly what its name implies—a placeholder. It exists in the table so that we can insert a single character into it for each row returned by the stored procedure. Simultaneous with **PlaceHolder** getting populated, the table's **Identity** column will be generated, which is actually what we're interested in. We're using the call to xp_cmdshell to generate a series of rows very quickly.

Note the use of SET ROWCOUNT to limit the number of rows returned. SET ROWCOUNT affects INSERT...EXEC just as it affects INSERT... SELECT.

Naturally, calling the command shell via xp_cmdshell has performance overhead associated with it. The actual procedure called isn't important, though, as you'll see in just a moment. What's important is that you can quickly generate large amounts of data by calling a stored procedure via INSERT...EXEC. Because you can't pass a table name into a procedure and insert data into it (without generating dynamic T-SQL, of course), the INSERT...EXEC technique is a handy way to synthesize large data volumes quickly.

## sp_generate_test_data

Sp_generate_test_data, listed in the example code that follows, allows us to insert any number of rows we want without needing a text file or other external data source. It takes a single parameter specifying the number of rows to generate, then returns them as a result set. These rows can then be inserted using INSERT...EXEC. Here's the code:

```
SET NOCOUNT ON
USE master
```

```
GO
IF OBJECT_ID('dbo.sp_generate_test_data') IS NOT NULL
  DROP PROC dbo.sp_generate_test_data
GO
CREATE PROC dbo.sp_generate_test_data @rowcount int
AS
DECLARE @var int
DECLARE @table TABLE (Id int identity)
SET @var=0
WHILE @var<@rowcount BEGIN
  INSERT @table DEFAULT VALUES
  SET @var=@var+1
END
SELECT * FROM @table
GO

CREATE TABLE #list
(id int)

INSERT #list (Id)
EXEC sp_generate_test_data 10

SELECT Id FROM #list
GO
DROP TABLE #list
```

(Results)

```
Id
-----------
1
2
3
4
5
6
7
8
9
10
```

Here we use a stored procedure, sp_generate_test_data, to generate a series of integers, then insert those integers into a table. We specify the number of rows to generate as a parameter to the procedure. The procedure merely inserts the number of rows specified into a table variable, then returns the rows in the table variable.

This technique works great if you want to insert a sequential list of integers into a table, but what if you don't? What if you want to insert data that's fairly randomized and you don't need a sequential set of integers? Do you have to write a new sp_generate_test_data procedure for each type of data you want to return? You can probably avoid that with this technique:

```
CREATE TABLE #list
(PlaceHolder int,
Random float DEFAULT (RAND()),
Today datetime DEFAULT (GETDATE())
)

INSERT #list (PlaceHolder)
EXEC sp_generate_test_data 10

SELECT Random, Today FROM #list
```

(Results)

| Random | Today |
| --- | --- |
| 0.0629477210736374 | 2001-08-05 18:07:03.607 |
| 0.0629477210736374 | 2001-08-05 18:07:03.607 |
| 0.0629477210736374 | 2001-08-05 18:07:03.607 |
| 0.0629477210736374 | 2001-08-05 18:07:03.607 |
| 0.0629477210736374 | 2001-08-05 18:07:03.607 |
| 0.0629477210736374 | 2001-08-05 18:07:03.607 |
| 0.0629477210736374 | 2001-08-05 18:07:03.607 |
| 0.0629477210736374 | 2001-08-05 18:07:03.607 |
| 0.0629477210736374 | 2001-08-05 18:07:03.607 |
| 0.0629477210736374 | 2001-08-05 18:07:03.607 |

As you can see, we generated a set of test data that doesn't actually use the integer returned by sp_generate_test_data. The rows generated aren't random, but at least we didn't have to set up a special query or stored procedure to create it.

Although most of the other techniques I've presented thus far will outperform the INSERT…EXEC technique, it's more convenient than most of them. Using it can be as simple as constructing a basic INSERT statement and supplying the number of rows you want to generate via a parameter to sp_generate_test_data.

**Table 6–1** Data Generation Timings (in milliseconds)

| Rows | WHILE loop | CROSS JOIN | CROSS JOIN RAND() | RANDOM()/ SCRAMBLEFLOAT() | Doubling | INSERT... EXEC |
|------|-----------|-----------|-------------------|---------------------------|----------|----------------|
| **100** | 140 | 170 | 203 | 576 | 106 | 170 |
| **10,000** | 1393 | 173 | 213 | 4970 | 533 | 1670 |
| **100,000** | 13780 | 783 | 1313 | 48873 | 4716 | 16330 |

## Speed

The various techniques for generating test data have varying performance characteristics. As I've said, there is usually a tradeoff between randomness and speed when creating large data volumes. Table 6–1 below summarizes my informal testing of the techniques demonstrated in this chapter. I've included timings for using a simple WHILE loop to insert data in order to provide a frame of reference (timings are in milliseconds):

As you can see, the simplest techniques are the fastest, whereas the ones that produce data which tends to be more random take longer than the others. Note that all the techniques except for the Random()/ScrambleFloat() and INSERT...EXEC techniques outperform the WHILE loop technique. In my opinion, the best technique for producing reasonably random test data as quickly as possible is the doubling technique. It's ten times as fast as the Random() technique and nearly three times as fast as a plain WHILE loop. It's the technique I use most often myself when I need to create test data.

## Summary

In this chapter you learned several techniques for generating large volumes of test data. Creating test data is something database developers and administrators frequently need to do, so it's helpful to know several techniques for doing so and what the tradeoffs between them are. As we've seen, the technique you choose is a matter of quality versus performance. Generating better quality (more random) test data takes longer than simply generating duplicate rows.

# PART II

# Objects

# CHAPTER 7

# Error Handling

*Great designers aren't afraid of complexity, and some of the best are drawn to it. But their goal is to make the seemingly complex simple.*

*—Steve McConnell* [1]

In this chapter we'll talk about the conventional ways of raising and handling errors in stored procedures, as well as some of the quirks you may run into with Transact-SQL error management. Transact-SQL's error-handling facilities work reasonably well, but they don't always work in the most logical fashion or as consistently as we might like. Even if you're careful to add error-handling code to every stored procedure on your server, you can't rely on it to work 100% of the time, even for low-severity errors. You must implement robust error handling in your client applications to complement the error handling in your Transact-SQL code. Microsoft has publicly announced that in the next version of SQL Server (code named Yukon), Transact-SQL will have structured exception-handling syntax built in. When this happens, you'll have better control over errors and unexpected conditions in your code. Until then, you may have to jump through a few hoops to get the error handling in your applications just right. That's what this chapter is about—showing you where the pitfalls are and giving you advice on how to avoid them.

## Error Reporting

We'll start off with a quick overview of the tools at your disposal for reporting errors to Transact-SQL code and to client applications. Transact-SQL's error reporting tools are neither elegant nor full featured, but they can usually be made to do what you want.

---

1. McConnell, Steve. *After the Gold Rush*. Redmond, WA: Microsoft Press, 1999. Page 26.

## RAISERROR

You report errors from stored procedures via return codes and the RAISER-ROR command. RAISERROR doesn't exit from the procedure, it simply returns the specified error message and sets the @@ERROR automatic variable. You can pass your own error message to RAISERROR to return, or you can reference a predefined error number/message combo in the sysmessages table. An error number is always returned by RAISERROR, regardless of whether you actually specify one. If you supply a custom message to RAISER-ROR, the error number is set to 50000, the maximum system-defined error number (user error numbers start at 50001).

You can format RAISERROR messages similarly to printf(). The message itself is the format string (complete with format specifiers such as %d and %s), and you can specify as many arguments as necessary to plug values into it. You can also add your own messages to the sysmessages table via sp_addmessage. These messages can contain format specifiers as well.

You specify both a severity and a state when using RAISERROR to return an error message. Errors with a severity less than 16 produce informational messages in the system event log (when logged), errors with a severity of 16 produce warning messages in the event log, and errors with severity values greater than 16 produce error messages in the event log. Any user can specify severity values up through 18; severity values 19 through 25 can only be raised by members of the sysadmin role and require the use of the WITH LOG option. Errors with severity values more than 20 are considered fatal and cause the client connection to terminate.

State is an informational value that you can return from RAISERROR to indicate state information to your front-end application. Specify a state value of 127 to cause the ISQL and OSQL utilities to set the operating system ERRORLEVEL environmental variable to the error number returned by RAISERROR. In releases of SQL Server prior to 7.0, ISQL exited immediately when a state of 127 was used. This is no longer true. Now it merely sets ERRORLEVEL. OSQL, however, still exits immediately.

RAISERROR supports several parameters that control how it works. The WITH LOG option copies the error message you raise to the application event log (assuming there is one) and the SQL Server error log regardless of whether the message was added to sysmessages using sp_addmessage's **with_log** option. WITH NOWAIT causes the message to be returned immediately to the client. Raising an error with NOWAIT also flushes the connection's output buffer, so it's a nice way to force PRINT and other pending messages to be sent immediately to the client. For example, to flush the output buffer without actually raising an error, you could do this:

```
RAISERROR ('', 0, 1) WITH NOWAIT
```

Any pending messages will be sent immediately to the client.

The WITH SETERROR option forces the automatic @@ERROR variable to return the last error number, regardless of its severity. This is handy for reporting user-defined informational messages using @@ERROR.

Use the system procedure sp_addmessage to add messages to the sysmessages table. Once added, these messages can be raised by RAISERROR. User messages must have error numbers of 50001 or higher. A big advantage of using SQL Server's messages facility is that it's language independent. Because you can specify a language with each message you add, you can have several messages with the same error number, but different language settings. You then raise errors using their codes, and the message that's returned depends on the language setting the user chose when installing SQL Server.

### xp_logevent

Use the xp_logevent extended procedure to add a message to the SQL Server error log or the NT event log without alerting the user. Messages logged by xp_logevent are not sent to the client. The message number or string you pass to xp_logevent is silently logged without client notification.

## Handling Errors

Of all the things that frustrate and bewilder Transact-SQL developers, error handling is probably at the top of the list. There are several reasons for this. Chief among them is that Transact-SQL's error handling simply doesn't work properly in some circumstances. It either doesn't work as documented or the way it works doesn't make any sense. Let's begin by talking about how error handling is supposed to work in Transact-SQL.

### @@ERROR

When an error occurs, @@ERROR normally contains its error number. Your code should check @@ERROR after significant operations. Listing 7–1 is an example of an error and the type of T-SQL code that's needed to handle it:

**Listing 7–1** Sample error handling code.

```
USE Northwind
DECLARE @c int
SELECT @c=COUNT(*) FROM ORDERS WHERE OrderDate = '20001201'
```

```
SELECT 1/@c
IF @@ERROR<>0 -- Check for an error
  PRINT 'Zero orders on file for the specified date'
```

(Results)

```
Server: Msg 8134, Level 16, State 1, Line 4
Divide by zero error encountered.
Zero orders on file for the specified date
```

Put aside for the moment that the error could be avoided altogether. Instead, look at the pattern being used here: We perform an operation, check a global error status variable, then react accordingly. This is the way that errors are usually handled in Transact-SQL because the language has no structured exception handling or ON ERROR GOTO-like syntax. You might call this Transact-SQL's basic Error Handler pattern.

## User Errors

According to the Books Online, errors with a severity of 11 through 16 are user errors and can be corrected by the user. Let's purposely cause one of these and see whether we can recover from it (Listing 7–2):

**Listing 7–2** Some errors terminate the current command batch.

```
USE Northwind
GO
SELECT * FROM MyTable
IF @@ERROR<>0 BEGIN
  PRINT 'Creating table...'
  CREATE TABLE MyTable
  (c1 int)
  INSERT MyTable DEFAULT VALUES
  SELECT * FROM MyTable
END
```

This code attempts to list a table, and if it gets an error, attempts to create the table and fill it with data because it assumes the error was caused by the table not existing. Here's the output from the query:

```
Server: Msg 208, Level 16, State 1, Line 1
Invalid object name 'MyTable'.
```

Notice the code that checks @@ERROR is never reached. Why? Because error 208 (Invalid object name) terminates the current command batch. The error-handling code is never reached, so it's impossible for our code to handle the error.

You might think that this is because the error has a severity of 16, but consider the code in Listing 7–3:

**Listing 7–3** Not all severity-16 errors terminate the command batch.

```
RAISERROR('Table not found',16,1)
IF @@ERROR<>0 BEGIN
  PRINT 'Creating table...'
  CREATE TABLE MyTable
  (c1 int)
  INSERT MyTable DEFAULT VALUES
  SELECT * FROM MyTable
  DROP TABLE MyTable
END
```

(Results)

```
Server: Msg 50000, Level 16, State 1, Line 1
Table not found
Creating table...
c1
-----------
NULL
```

Here, even though we raise an error with a severity level of 16, the batch isn't interrupted. Our error-handling code is reached and the table is created.

Perhaps you'd speculate that the code following the RAISERROR in Listing 7–3 is reached because the error wasn't the result of a true error—we forced it via RAISERROR. Have a look back at Listing 7–1. What we see there is a real error. We've divided by zero, and its severity is 16, yet we're able to handle the error. Some severity-16 errors terminate the current batch; some don't. There seems to be little rhyme or reason as to which ones do and which ones do not.

So there you have it: A bona fide quirk in Transact-SQL error handling. What can you do about it? Here's a workaround for handling errors that terminate the current command batch (Listing 7–4):

**Listing 7–4** A workaround for errors that terminate the command batch.

```
USE Northwind
GO
DECLARE @res int
EXEC @res=sp_executesql N'SELECT * FROM MyTable'
IF @res<>0 BEGIN
  PRINT 'Creating table...'
  CREATE TABLE MyTable
  (c1 int)
  INSERT MyTable DEFAULT VALUES
  SELECT * FROM MyTable
  DROP TABLE MyTable
END
```

(Results)

```
Server: Msg 208, Level 16, State 1, Line 1
Invalid object name 'MyTable'.
Creating table...
c1
-----------
NULL
```

By executing the suspect SQL using sp_executesql, we isolate it from the calling routine and prevent the error from terminating the procedure. The sp_executesql procedure can also come in quite handy for dealing with linked server errors. Linked server errors almost always terminate the current command batch. If a linked server with which you're communicating is a SQL Server, you can query it via sp_executesql to isolate the call from the rest of your code and prevent it from terminating the batch should an error occur. Here's an example:

```
EXEC MyOtherServer.master.dbo.sp_executesql N'SELECT * FROM sysdatabases'
```

Calling sp_executesql in this manner forces the query to run on the other server. This should generally help performance, especially when you're traversing lots of data on the remote server.

Even when you're not connecting to another SQL Server, sp_executesql can still be of help:

```
EXEC sp_executesql N'SELECT * FROM MyOtherServer.Northwind.dbo.MyTable'
```

The benefit of using sp_executesql here is the isolation it affords. Even if the query does not run completely on the other server, at least any errors produced won't terminate the current batch.

In this scenario, sp_executesql's return value will be the error code, if there is one. @@ERROR should also contain the error code. So, for example, you could easily convey the error code back up through the call stack like this (Listing 7–5):

**Listing 7–5** It's easy enough to convey the error message back up the chain.

```
CREATE PROC ListTable
AS
DECLARE @res int
EXEC @res=sp_executesql N'SELECT * FROM MyTable'
IF @res<>0 BEGIN
  PRINT 'Error listing table.'
  RETURN(@res)
END
GO
DECLARE @r int
EXEC @r=ListTable
SELECT @r
```

(Results)

```
Server: Msg 208, Level 16, State 1, Line 1
Invalid object name 'MyTable'.
Error listing table.
-----------
208
```

As you can see, we get the error message and handle it, then convey the error code back to the caller.

Note that you need not call sp_executesql to use this technique. A plain subroutine will do as well (Listing 7–6):

**Listing 7–6** When an error causes a procedure to exit, @@ERROR contains the error code.

```
CREATE PROC ListTable
AS
SELECT * FROM MyTable
```

```
GO
EXEC ListTable
IF @@ERROR<>0 BEGIN
  PRINT 'Creating table...'
  CREATE TABLE MyTable
  (c1 int)
  INSERT MyTable DEFAULT VALUES
  SELECT * FROM MyTable
  DROP TABLE MyTable
END

Server: Msg 208, Level 16, State 1, Procedure ListTable, Line 3
Invalid object name 'MyTable'.
Creating table...
c1
-----------
NULL
```

Here, rather than check the subprocedure's result code, we simply check @@ERROR immediately after returning from the routine. If an error caused the routine to exit, @@ERROR will be nonzero.

Note that we couldn't return the error from ListTable as a result code even if we wanted to. Again, once the error occurs, all bets are off. The procedure exits immediately and returns to the caller.

## Fatal Errors

As I've mentioned, errors with a severity of 20 or more are considered fatal and terminate the connection. What can you do about them? One workaround would be to use the xp_exec routine included in Chapter 20 to run the problematic code on a separate connection that shares the current connection's transaction space. Another would be to use xp_cmdshell to fire up OSQL.EXE and run the query on a separate connection (and in a separate process). Where there's a will, there's a kludge. The best strategy of all, though, is to find out what's causing such a serious error and remedy it.

## Problems That Seem Like Quirks but Aren't

Because @@ERROR is reset each time a statement executes successfully, processing it after an error can be tricky. For example, consider the code in Listing 7–7:

**Listing 7–7** @@ERROR is easily reset.

```
CREATE PROC ListTable
AS
SELECT * FROM MyTable
GO
EXEC ListTable
IF @@ERROR<>0 BEGIN
  PRINT @@ERROR
  PRINT 'An error occurred, attempting to create the table'
  CREATE TABLE MyTable
  (c1 int)
  INSERT MyTable DEFAULT VALUES
  SELECT * FROM MyTable
  DROP TABLE MyTable
END

Server: Msg 208, Level 16, State 1, Procedure ListTable, Line 3
Invalid object name 'MyTable'.
0
An error occurred, attempting to create the table
c1
-----------
NULL
```

As you can see from the output, @@ERROR is reset by the IF test. Obviously, this isn't what we intended. What you have to do instead is save off the value of @@ERROR immediately after the operation that you wanted to watch for errors. This way, exactly *when* @@ERROR gets reset is of no importance. We don't care; we've already cached its value. Here's the code rewritten to properly handle @@ERROR (Listing 7–8):

**Listing 7–8** Cache @@ERROR to avoid resetting it.

```
CREATE PROC ListTable
AS
SELECT * FROM MyTable
GO
DECLARE @res int
EXEC ListTable
SET @res=@@ERROR
IF @res<>0 BEGIN
  PRINT @res
```

```
      PRINT 'An error occurred, attempting to create the table'
      CREATE TABLE MyTable
      (c1 int)
      INSERT MyTable DEFAULT VALUES
      SELECT * FROM MyTable
      DROP TABLE MyTable
END
```

Make a habit of caching and checking @@ERROR after significant code executes, especially after DML operations. The chief characteristic of robust code is thorough error checking, and until Transact-SQL supports structured exception handling, @@ERROR is here to stay.

## @@ROWCOUNT

There are times when an error condition does not actually result in an error message or set an error code. One of these is when a data modification against a table unexpectedly fails to change any rows. You can determine the number of rows affected by the last DML statement (SELECT, INSERT, UPDATE, or DELETE) by checking @@ROWCOUNT. When @@ROWCOUNT indicates that no rows were affected, you can treat the condition just like any other error. Here's an example (Listing 7–9):

**Listing 7–9** Check @@ROWCOUNT to detect subtle errors.

```
CREATE PROC ListTable
AS
SELECT * FROM Northwind..Customers WHERE 1=0 -- Get no rows
GO
DECLARE @res int
EXEC ListTable
SET @res=@@ROWCOUNT
IF @res=0 BEGIN
  PRINT 'ListTable returned no rows'
END
```

Notice that I saved @@ROWCOUNT to a variable immediately after the EXEC. Like @@ERROR, @@ROWCOUNT can be easily reset, so it's important to cache it immediately after the operation you're tracking.

## Errors and Transaction Management

Probably the biggest problem with the lack of airtight error-handling facilities in Transact-SQL is the possibility that an aborted batch may orphan a transaction. If a batch with an open transaction is forced to abort due to an error, the transaction will be orphaned, and any locks that it holds will block other users. For example, consider the code in Listing 7–10:

**Listing 7–10** SQL Server detects orphaned transactions.

```
CREATE PROC TestTran AS
DECLARE @ERR int
BEGIN TRAN
SELECT * FROM MyTable
SET @ERR=@@ERROR
IF @ERR<>0 BEGIN
  RAISERROR('Encountered an error, rolling back',16,10)
  IF @@TRANCOUNT<>0 ROLLBACK
  RETURN(@ERR)
END
COMMIT TRAN
GO
EXEC TestTran
```

(Results)

```
Server: Msg 208, Level 16, State 1, Procedure TestTran, Line 4
Invalid object name 'MyTable'.
Server: Msg 266, Level 16, State 1, Procedure TestTran, Line 11
Transaction count after EXECUTE indicates that a COMMIT or ROLLBACK TRANSACTION
statement is missing. Previous count = 0, current count = 1.
```

As we discovered earlier, error 208 aborts the current batch, so the error-handling code that rolls back the transaction is never reached (notice SQL Server's warning about this immediately after the error message). What can you do about this? One method of dealing with it is to use the techniques from earlier in the chapter that isolate the problematic code into a subroutine so that it doesn't interrupt the execution flow of the caller. The problem is: Sometimes you don't know exactly what the "problematic" code is—it could be anything. A more foolproof method is to check the open transaction count on entrance to every routine that begins a transaction and issue a ROLLBACK if any transactions are open. Here's the procedure from Listing 7–10 modified to do this (Listing 7–11):

**Listing 7–11** A technique for dealing with orphaned transactions.

```
CREATE PROC TestTran AS
IF @@TRANCOUNT<>0 ROLLBACK -- Check for orphaned trans and rollback
DECLARE @ERR int
BEGIN TRAN
SELECT * FROM MyTable
SET @ERR=@@ERROR
IF @ERR<>0 BEGIN
  RAISERROR('Encountered an error, rolling back',16,10)
  IF @@TRANCOUNT<>0 ROLLBACK
  RETURN(@ERR)
END
COMMIT TRAN
GO
EXEC TestTran
```

As you can see, one line of code is all that it takes to deal with what could be a very serious problem. Of course, this approach relies on a procedure being called in order to roll back the orphaned transaction. Until it is, the transaction will remain active.

The ultimate solution is for your application to detect that an error has occurred and that it needs to roll back an open transaction. Barring that, the techniques presented here should help you work around some of the short-comings in Transact-SQL's error-handling facilities.

## SET XACT_ABORT

SET XACT_ABORT toggles whether a transaction is aborted when certain types of runtime errors occur. It's supposed to abort when any runtime error occurs; however, it's been my experience that this isn't always so. There are errors that it can't deal with, and hence, it's still possible to orphan a transaction with the option enabled.

The error that triggers the automatic rollback can be a system-generated error or a user error. It's very much like checking @@ERROR after every statement and rolling back the transaction if an error is detected. Here's an example of SET XACT_ABORT at work (Listing 7–12):

**Listing 7–12** SET XACT_ABORT can help avoid orphaned transactions.

```
CREATE PROC TestTran AS
DECLARE @ERR int
SET XACT_ABORT ON
BEGIN TRAN
DELETE Customers
SET @ERR=@@ERROR
IF @ERR<>0 BEGIN
  RAISERROR('Encountered an error, rolling back',16,10)
  IF @@TRANCOUNT<>0 ROLLBACK
  RETURN(@ERR)
END
COMMIT TRAN
GO
EXEC TestTran
GO
SELECT @@TRANCOUNT
```

(Results)

```
Server: Msg 547, Level 16, State 1, Procedure TestTran, Line 5
DELETE statement conflicted with COLUMN REFERENCE constraint
'FK_Orders_Customers'. The conflict occurred in database 'Northwind', table
'Orders', column 'CustomerID'.
-----------
0
```

The constraint violation causes the transaction to be aborted because SET XACT_ABORT is enabled. This is an easy way to roll back in response to a wide variety of different types of errors. However, not all errors can be trapped by SET XACT_ABORT. Some types of errors do not trigger a transaction rollback—even though you may need and expect them to. Here's an example (Listing 7–13):

**Listing 7–13** Some errors do not trigger XACT_ABORT's rollback.

```
CREATE PROC TestTran AS
DECLARE @ERR int
SET XACT_ABORT ON
BEGIN TRAN
SELECT * FROM NoTable
```

```
SET @ERR=@@ERROR
IF @ERR<>0 BEGIN
  RAISERROR('Encountered an error, rolling back',16,10)
  IF @@TRANCOUNT<>0 ROLLBACK
  RETURN(@ERR)
END
COMMIT TRAN
GO
EXEC TestTran
GO
SELECT @@TRANCOUNT
```

(Results)

```
Server: Msg 208, Level 16, State 1, Procedure TestTran, Line 5
Invalid object name 'NoTable'.
Server: Msg 266, Level 16, State 1, Procedure TestTran, Line 12
Transaction count after EXECUTE indicates that a COMMIT or ROLLBACK
TRANSACTION statement is missing. Previous count = 0, current count = 1.
-----------
1
```

Once again, error 208 proves fatal to the batch and orphans the transaction. Even though, logically, we'd expect XACT_ABORT to kick in and clear out the orphaned transaction, this is not what happens. Generally, SET XACT_ABORT cannot "catch" compile-time errors. This is probably a good place to make use of the workaround shown in Listing 7–11. If each stored procedure proactively rolls back orphaned transactions, hopefully the overall effect of the orphaned transactions on concurrency will be minimal. Until Transact-SQL has support for structured language exceptions, you'll have to make use of some of the workarounds demonstrated in this chapter to properly handle errors and avoid wasting or orphaning resources.

## Summary

In this chapter you learned how basic error handling works in Transact-SQL. You learned how to handle different types of errors in your own code and how to work around some of the quirks in Transact-SQL's error management. You learned about the importance of correctly managing transactions, and you were introduced to some ways of dealing with serious errors while transactions are active.

# CHAPTER 8

# Triggers

*I'd rather be a "Has Been" than a "Never Was" any day of the week.*

—*H. W. Kenton*

A trigger is a special type of stored procedure that executes when a specified DML operation (an INSERT, DELETE, or UPDATE, or any combination thereof) occurs. They're typically used to ensure that business rules are followed or to do other work when a data modification occurs. A trigger is the SQL equivalent of a 3GL callback function or a hooked interrupt vector.

You construct and attach triggers to tables using the CREATE TRIGGER command. When a table is dropped, so are its triggers.

Most of the details of stored procedure programming apply equally well to triggers. In fact, because you can call a stored procedure from a trigger, you can effectively do anything in a trigger that a stored procedure can do. One thing that triggers don't normally do is return result sets. Most front ends have no way of handling trigger-generated result sets, so you don't see this done very often. SQL Server doesn't permit triggers to return result codes.

Triggers fire once per statement, not per row, regardless of the number of rows changed by a given DML statement. You can set up triggers that fire *after* a DML operation (known as AFTER triggers, the default and most common type), and you can set up triggers that fire *instead of* a DML operation (INSTEAD OF triggers). We'll discuss each of these separately.

You can set up as many AFTER triggers as you want for a given table. Using sp_settriggerorder, you can designate a first and a last AFTER trigger on each table; the rest fire in no particular order. You're allowed just one INSTEAD OF trigger per DML operation on each table or view, although you can easily circumvent this by creating multiple views over the table or view in question and attaching INSTEAD OF triggers to each of them.

Declarative referential integrity (DRI) constraints have precedence over triggers. This means that a violation of a DRI constraint by a DML command will prevent triggers from executing.

# Determining What Has Changed

Inside a trigger, you can check which columns are being updated by a DML operation using the UPDATE() and COLUMNS_UPDATE() functions. The UPDATE() function returns TRUE or FALSE based on whether the value of a specified column is being set (regardless of whether it's actually changing). COLUMNS_UPDATED() returns a bitmap representing all the columns being set. Here's an example (Listing 8–1):

**Listing 8–1** A trigger example that demonstrates UPDATE().

```
USE tempdb
GO
CREATE TABLE ToyInventory
(Toy int identity,
 Type int,
 Onhand int
)
GO
CREATE TABLE ToyTypes
(Type int identity,
 MinOnhand int
)
GO
INSERT ToyTypes (MinOnhand) VALUES (10)
INSERT ToyTypes (MinOnhand) VALUES (20)
INSERT ToyTypes (MinOnhand) VALUES (15)
INSERT ToyTypes (MinOnhand) VALUES (50)

INSERT ToyInventory (Type, Onhand) VALUES (1, 50)
INSERT ToyInventory (Type, Onhand) VALUES (2, 50)
INSERT ToyInventory (Type, Onhand) VALUES (3, 50)
INSERT ToyInventory (Type, Onhand) VALUES (4, 50)

GO

CREATE TRIGGER ToyInventory_UPDATE ON ToyInventory AFTER UPDATE
AS
DECLARE @rcnt int
SET @rcnt=@@ROWCOUNT
```

```
IF @rcnt=0 RETURN
IF @rcnt > 1 BEGIN
  RAISERROR('You may only change one item at a time',16,10)
  ROLLBACK
  RETURN
END
IF (UPDATE(Onhand)) BEGIN
  IF EXISTS (SELECT * FROM ToyTypes t JOIN inserted i ON t.Type=i.Type
     WHERE t.MinOnhand>i.Onhand) BEGIN
       RAISERROR('You may not lower an item''s Onhand quantity below its
Minimum Onhand quantity',16,10)
    ROLLBACK
    RETURN
  END
END
GO
UPDATE ToyInventory SET Onhand=49 WHERE Toy=4  -- Fails because of trigger
GO
DROP TABLE ToyInventory, ToyTypes
GO
```

This example not only shows how to use the UPDATE() function, it also shows how to code triggers so that they don't break when presented with multiple rows. In this case, we simply don't allow multiple row changes. We begin by checking @@ROWCOUNT to see if any rows have been changed at all. If none have, we return immediately.

Next, we check to see whether more than one row has been changed. If so, we display an error message, roll back the transaction, and exit. Notice that we store @@ROWCOUNT in a variable so that we can check it multiple times: once to see if any rows have been changed and once to see if too many have been changed.

If we get past both of these tests, we've got just one row to deal with. We begin validating the data modifications by seeing whether the **Onhand** column of the table has been changed. If it has, we check the **MinOnhand** column in the ToyTypes table to see whether the inventory is about to be reduced too far. If the current on-hand amount (as reported by the inserted table) is too low, we display an error message, roll back the transaction, and return. If not, we allow it to proceed.

We could just as easily have used the COLUMNS_UPDATED() function instead of UPDATE(). It has the advantage of being able to test for the modification of multiple columns at once. COLUMNS_UPDATED() returns a varbinary bitmap that indicates which columns have changed. Bits are ordered from left to right, with lower number columns being represented by the left-most bits. Listing 8–2 presents the trigger rewritten to use COLUMNS_ UPDATED():

**Listing 8–2** A trigger example that demonstrates COLUMNS_UPDATED().

```
CREATE TRIGGER ToyInventory_UPDATE ON ToyInventory AFTER UPDATE
AS
DECLARE @rcnt int
SET @rcnt=@@ROWCOUNT
IF @rcnt=0 RETURN
IF @rcnt > 1 BEGIN
  RAISERROR('You may only change one item at a time',16,10)
  ROLLBACK
  RETURN
END
IF ((COLUMNS_UPDATED() & 4)<>0) BEGIN
  IF EXISTS (SELECT * FROM ToyTypes t JOIN inserted i ON t.Type=i.Type
      WHERE t.MinOnhand>i.Onhand) BEGIN
      RAISERROR('You may not lower an item''s Onhand quantity below its
Mininum Onhand quantity',16,10)
    ROLLBACK
    RETURN
  END
END
```

Notice the binary AND operation (signified by the & operator) that's used to determine whether the **Onhand** column is being modified. **Onhand** is the third column in the table, so we use a value of 4 (bits are numbered starting with 0, so the third bit corresponds to 2 raised to the power of 2, or 4; i.e., $2^0 = 1$, $2^1 = 2$, and $2^2 = 4$). If we wanted to test for multiple columns, we could easily do that. For example, we could test whether the first and second columns were being changed by testing COLUMNS_UPDATED() against the value of 3 because 3 has its 0 and 1 bits turned on ($2^0 = 1$, $2^1 = 2$, $1 + 2 = 3$). Here's a version of the trigger that checks for changes to multiple columns (Listing 8–3):

**Listing 8–3** You can check multiple columns with COLUMNS_UPDATED().

```
CREATE TRIGGER ToyInventory_UPDATE ON ToyInventory AFTER UPDATE
AS
```

```
DECLARE @rcnt int
SET @rcnt=@@ROWCOUNT
IF @rcnt=0 RETURN
IF @rcnt > 1 BEGIN
  RAISERROR('You may only change one item at a time',16,10)
  ROLLBACK
  RETURN
END


-- Test for changes to columns 2 and 3
IF ((COLUMNS_UPDATED() & 6)<>0) BEGIN  -- Test for changes to columns 2 and 3
  IF NOT EXISTS(SELECT * FROM ToyTypes t JOIN inserted i ON t.Type=i.Type) BEGIN
    RAISERROR('Invalid Toy Type',16,10)
    ROLLBACK
    RETURN
END
  IF EXISTS (SELECT * FROM ToyTypes t JOIN inserted i ON t.Type=i.Type
      WHERE t.MinOnhand>i.Onhand) BEGIN
      RAISERROR('You may not lower an item''s Onhand quantity below its Mininum
Onhand quantity',16,10)
    ROLLBACK
    RETURN
  END
END
```

Here we test against a value of 6 because we want to know whether the second and third columns (the **Type** and **Onhand** columns respectively) have been changed. Because $2^1 = 2$ and $2^2 = 4$, we OR these values together to return an integer with its second and third bits (bit numbers 1 and 2) enabled.

In INSERT triggers, COLUMNS_UPDATED() indicates that all columns are being set because all columns either receive explicit values or implicit ones via default constraints and nullability. An example is presented in Listing 8–4:

**Listing 8–4** INSERT operations enable all bits in COLUMNS_UPDATED().

```
USE tempdb
GO
CREATE TABLE ToyInventory
(Toy int identity,
 Type int NULL,
 Onhand int DEFAULT 10
)
GO
```

```
CREATE TRIGGER ToyInventory_INSERT ON ToyInventory AFTER INSERT
AS
IF @@ROWCOUNT=0 RETURN

DECLARE @ChangedColumns varbinary(8000), @Size int, @i int
SET @ChangedColumns=COLUMNS_UPDATED()
SET @Size=DATALENGTH(@ChangedColumns)*8
SET @i=0

WHILE @i<@Size BEGIN
  IF ((@ChangedColumns & POWER(2,@i))<>0)
    PRINT 'Column '+CAST(@i AS varchar)+' changed'
  SET @i=@i+1
END

GO

INSERT ToyInventory DEFAULT VALUES
GO
DROP TABLE ToyInventory
GO
```

(Results)

```
Column 0 changed
Column 1 changed
Column 2 changed
```

As you can see, even inserting DEFAULT VALUES into the table turns on the changed bit for all of its columns. Each of the three columns in ToyInventory has a different type of default value: **Toy** is an identity column, **Type** allows NULL values, and **Onhand** has a default constraint. As I said earlier, because each column in the table is required to receive a value of some type during an INSERT operation, COLUMNS_UPDATED() indicates that they've all been changed from within an INSERT trigger.

Note the loop we use to iterate through the changed column switches. It's worth discussing further. Here's the loop again:

```
WHILE @i<@Size BEGIN
  IF ((@ChangedColumns & POWER(2,@i))<>0)
    PRINT 'Column '+CAST(@i AS varchar)+' changed'
  SET @i=@i+1
END
```

Because we previously saved the value of COLUMNS_UPDATED() in the **@ChangedColumns** variable, we can now loop through it, bit by bit, and determine which columns have changed. This technique would work in any trigger, not just INSERT triggers.

Note the use of POWER() to synthesize a binary value to check **@ChangedColumns** against. Because we're dealing with binary data and bit manipulation, we're obviously working with powers of 2. We begin by setting **@Size** to the actual number of bits returned by COLUMNS_UPDATED() (rounded up to the nearest byte), then we loop through these bits and check each one to see whether it has been set. For the ones that are enabled, we print a simple message.

What if we wanted to list the column names rather than just generic "Column *n* changed" messages? This wouldn't be terribly difficult. Here's the trigger modified to do just that (Listing 8–5):

**Listing 8–5** It's easy to determine the names of the columns being changed.

```
USE tempdb
GO
CREATE TABLE ToyInventory
(Toy int identity,
 Type int NULL,
 Onhand int DEFAULT 10
)
GO
CREATE TRIGGER ToyInventory_INSERT ON ToyInventory AFTER INSERT
AS
IF @@ROWCOUNT=0 RETURN

DECLARE @ChangedColumns varbinary(8000), @Size int, @i int, @colname sysname
SET @ChangedColumns=COLUMNS_UPDATED()
SET @Size=DATALENGTH(@ChangedColumns)*8
SET @i=0
WHILE @i<@Size BEGIN
  IF ((@ChangedColumns & POWER(2,@i))<>0) BEGIN
      SELECT @ColName=COLUMN_NAME FROM INFORMATION_SCHEMA.COLUMNS
      WHERE TABLE_NAME='ToyInventory' AND ORDINAL_POSITION-1=@i
    PRINT 'Column '+@ColName+' changed'
  END
  SET @i=@i+1
END
GO
INSERT ToyInventory DEFAULT VALUES
```

(Results)

```
Column Toy changed
Column Type changed
Column Onhand changed
```

Note the use of the INFORMATION_SCHEMA.COLUMNS view to retrieve each column name using its ordinal index. This is preferable to querying the syscolumns table directly, although you could retrieve the same information from it.

# Managing Sequential Values

There was a time when dealing with identity columns in triggers was a black art. You had to jump through numerous hoops to get identity columns to work properly, and even then there were situations when it wasn't airtight. Thanks to the addition of SCOPE_IDENTITY() and IDENT_CURRENT() to Transact-SQL, this is no longer the case. As its name suggests, SCOPE_IDENTITY() retrieves the current value for an identity column within the current scope. IDENT_CURRENT(), on the other hand, doesn't care about the current scope. It just returns the latest identity value inserted into a table. These are both better tools than the venerable @@IDENTITY function. @@IDENTITY returns the last identity value inserted for the current connection, regardless of scope and regardless of the table in which the insert occurred. So if you insert a row into a table that has an **Identity** column, and that table has a trigger on it that inserts into another table that also has an **Identity** column, @@IDENTITY will return the value inserted into the second table immediately after the row insertion. This is not good. We probably don't care about the nested insert. Typically we want the value that was generated by our explicit insertion. This is what SCOPE_IDENTITY() is for. It is unaffected by identity value inserts in other scopes (e.g., within insert triggers). IDENT_CURRENT() is also useful in this situation because we can specify what table to retrieve the last identity for. Because a different table is being inserted into via the trigger in our scenario, IDENT_CURRENT() will return the identity value generated by our explicit insert.

This is best understood by way of example. Listing 8–6 is a sample script that illustrates a few of the nuances of dealing with identity values in triggers:

**Listing 8–6** The nuances of identity values and triggers.

```
USE tempdb
GO
CREATE TABLE ToyInventory
(Toy int identity,
 Type int,
 Onhand int
)
CREATE TABLE ToyAudit
(ToyAudit int identity,
 Operation varchar(10),
 Toy int,
 Type int,
 Change int
)
GO
-- Seed the tables
INSERT ToyInventory DEFAULT VALUES
INSERT ToyInventory DEFAULT VALUES
INSERT ToyInventory DEFAULT VALUES
GO
INSERT ToyAudit DEFAULT VALUES
GO
CREATE TRIGGER ToyInventory_INSERT ON ToyInventory AFTER INSERT
AS
IF @@ROWCOUNT=0 RETURN
INSERT ToyAudit
SELECT 'INSERT', * FROM inserted
PRINT 'From within the trigger:'
PRINT '@@IDENTITY='+CAST(@@IDENTITY AS varchar)+
    ' SCOPE_IDENTITY()='+CAST(SCOPE_IDENTITY() AS varchar)+

' IDENT_CURRENT(''ToyAudit'')='+CAST(IDENT_CURRENT('ToyAudit') AS varchar)
GO

INSERT ToyInventory DEFAULT VALUES
PRINT 'After the insert:'
PRINT '@@IDENTITY='+CAST(@@IDENTITY AS varchar)+
    ' SCOPE_IDENTITY()='+CAST(SCOPE_IDENTITY() AS varchar)
    +' IDENT_CURRENT(''ToyInventory'')='+
    CAST(IDENT_CURRENT('ToyInventory') AS varchar)
```

(Results)

```
From within the trigger:
@@IDENTITY=2 SCOPE_IDENTITY()=2 IDENT_CURRENT('ToyAudit')=2
After the insert:
@@IDENTITY=2 SCOPE_IDENTITY()=4 IDENT_CURRENT('ToyInventory')=4
```

Here we insert a row into a table on which an INSERT trigger has been defined that, in turn, inserts a row into another table. We display the values of @@IDENTITY, SCOPE_IDENTITY(), and IDENT_CURRENT() during the trigger execution as well as after the insert. Notice that the value of @@IDENTITY is the same in both cases. This is because it reflects the last identity value inserted for the current connection, regardless of the table or scope. In this case, the last identity value went into the ToyAudit table. What we're likely more interested in is the identity value generated by our insert into the ToyInventory table. This is where SCOPE_IDENTITY() and IDENT_CURRENT() come into play. After the insert, they both reflect the value we've just inserted into the table; however, SCOPE_IDENTITY() is a better choice in this case because IDENT_CURRENT() spans sessions—that is, another user could insert a row into ToyInventory just after we did, and we'd see their identity value in IDENT_CURRENT(). This is not true of SCOPE_IDENTITY(), so I think you'll find it generally more airtight and therefore more useful.

# Trigger Restrictions

There are a handful of restrictions that apply to triggers. First and foremost, there are a number of commands that are invalid within triggers because triggers run within (at least) implicit transactions, and these commands are not allowed within transactions:

- ALTER DATABASE
- CREATE DATABASE
- DISK INIT
- DISK RESIZE
- DROP DATABASE
- LOAD DATABASE
- LOAD LOG
- RECONFIGURE
- RESTORE DATABASE
- RESTORE LOG
- UPDATE STATISTICS

Because a number of commands require that they be the first statement in the current batch, running them from within a stored procedure or trigger requires special treatment. Examples of statements that must be the first statement in a batch include CREATE VIEW, CREATE PROCEDURE, and many others. Here's a trigger that creates a view and then inserts a row using that view (Listing 8–7):

**Listing 8–7** Like stored procedures, triggers can execute commands you might otherwise think were not allowed.

```
USE tempdb
GO
CREATE TABLE ToyInventory
(Toy int identity,
 Type int,
 Onhand int
)
CREATE TABLE ToyAudit
(ToyAudit int identity,
 Operation varchar(10),
 Toy int,
 Type int,
 Change int
)
GO
CREATE TRIGGER ToyInventory_INSERT ON ToyInventory AFTER INSERT
AS
IF @@ROWCOUNT=0 RETURN
EXEC('IF OBJECT_ID(''TA'') IS NOT NULL DROP VIEW TA')
EXEC('CREATE VIEW TA AS SELECT * FROM ToyAudit')
INSERT TA
SELECT 'INSERT', * FROM inserted
GO

INSERT ToyInventory DEFAULT VALUES
```

Because CREATE VIEW must be the first statement in a batch, we use EXEC to run it. This places it in its own batch. We also execute its DROP separately so that, again, the CREATE remains the first statement in its batch.

With the exception of CREATE TABLE, most object creation commands must be handled this way within a trigger. The upside is that you can use information from the current execution environment to build the CREATE dynamically.

There are also restrictions regarding INSTEAD OF triggers and cascading referential integrity. An INSTEAD OF trigger cannot be defined for an UPDATE operation on a table that has a cascading UPDATE constraint defined. The same is true for INSTEAD OF DELETE triggers—you can't create one on a table with a cascading DELETE constraint defined.

# INSTEAD OF Triggers

As its name suggests, an INSTEAD OF trigger executes *instead of* a DML operation. This is in contrast to AFTER triggers, which run after an operation has completed, but before the transaction has been committed. INSTEAD OF triggers are handy for updates against views and tables that would otherwise be too complex to handle with anything but a stored procedure.

Here's a simple INSTEAD OF trigger example (Listing 8–8):

**Listing 8–8** A simple INSTEAD OF trigger at work.

```
USE tempdb
GO
CREATE TABLE AussieArtists
(ArtistId int Identity,
 LastName varchar(30),
 FirstName varchar(30)
)
GO
INSERT AussieArtists VALUES ('Gibb', 'Barry')
INSERT AussieArtists VALUES ('Gibb', 'Maurice')
INSERT AussieArtists VALUES ('Gibb', 'Robin')
INSERT AussieArtists VALUES ('Gibb', 'Andy')
INSERT AussieArtists VALUES ('Newton-John', 'Olivia')
INSERT AussieArtists VALUES ('Crowe', 'Russell')
INSERT AussieArtists VALUES ('Hogan', 'Paul')
INSERT AussieArtists VALUES ('Kidman', 'Nicole')
INSERT AussieArtists VALUES ('Bozinov', 'Zarko')
INSERT AussieArtists VALUES ('Hay', 'Colin')

GO

CREATE VIEW VAussieArtists AS
```

```
SELECT FirstName+' '+LastName AS Name FROM AussieArtists
GO
CREATE TRIGGER VAussieArtists_INSERT ON VAussieArtists INSTEAD OF INSERT
AS
INSERT AussieArtists (FirstName, LastName)
SELECT LEFT(Name,ISNULL(NULLIF(CHARINDEX(' ',Name),0),255)-1),
SUBSTRING(Name,NULLIF(CHARINDEX(' ',Name),0)+1,255)
FROM inserted
GO
INSERT VAussieArtists (Name) VALUES ('Greg Ham')
GO
SELECT * FROM AussieArtists
GO
DROP TABLE AussieArtists
DROP VIEW VAussieArtists
GO
```

(Results)

| ArtistId | LastName | FirstName |
| --- | --- | --- |
| 1 | Gibb | Barry |
| 2 | Gibb | Maurice |
| 3 | Gibb | Robin |
| 4 | Gibb | Andy |
| 5 | Newton-John | Olivia |
| 6 | Crowe | Russell |
| 7 | Hogan | Paul |
| 8 | Kidman | Nicole |
| 9 | Bozinov | Zarko |
| 10 | Hay | Colin |
| 11 | Ham | Greg |

As you can see, the simple insert against the view is translated into a slightly more complex insert against the underlying table. Because we want to process the data before it goes into the underlying table, we use an INSTEAD OF trigger that parses the input and performs the insert itself.

Although you can have only one INSTEAD OF trigger for each DML operation (INSERT, UPDATE, or DELETE) on a table, you can work around this limitation by creating additional views on top of the table or view in question, each with their own INSTEAD OF triggers. Listing 8–9 presents an example:

**Listing 8–9** You can set up multiple INSTEAD OF triggers using views as placeholders.

```
USE tempdb
GO
CREATE TABLE AussieArtists
(ArtistId int Identity,
 LastName varchar(30),
 FirstName varchar(30)
)
GO
INSERT AussieArtists VALUES ('Gibb', 'Barry')
INSERT AussieArtists VALUES ('Gibb', 'Maurice')
INSERT AussieArtists VALUES ('Gibb', 'Robin')
INSERT AussieArtists VALUES ('Gibb', 'Andy')
INSERT AussieArtists VALUES ('Newton-John', 'Olivia')
INSERT AussieArtists VALUES ('Crowe', 'Russell')
INSERT AussieArtists VALUES ('Hogan', 'Paul')
INSERT AussieArtists VALUES ('Kidman', 'Nicole')
INSERT AussieArtists VALUES ('Bozinov', 'Zarko')
INSERT AussieArtists VALUES ('Hay', 'Colin')

GO

CREATE VIEW VAussieArtists AS
SELECT FirstName+' '+LastName AS Name FROM AussieArtists
GO
CREATE TRIGGER VAussieArtists_INSERT ON VAussieArtists INSTEAD OF INSERT
AS
INSERT AussieArtists (FirstName, LastName)
SELECT LEFT(Name,ISNULL(NULLIF(CHARINDEX(' ',Name),0),255)-1),
SUBSTRING(Name,NULLIF(CHARINDEX(' ',Name),0)+1,255)
FROM inserted

GO

CREATE VIEW VAussies AS
SELECT Name FROM VAussieArtists
GO
CREATE TRIGGER VAussies_INSERT ON VAussies INSTEAD OF INSERT
AS
INSERT VAussieArtists (Name)
SELECT UPPER(Name)
FROM inserted
GO
```

```
INSERT VAussies (Name) VALUES ('Greg Ham')
GO
SELECT * FROM AussieArtists
```

| ArtistId | LastName | FirstName |
| --- | --- | --- |
| 1 | Gibb | Barry |
| 2 | Gibb | Maurice |
| 3 | Gibb | Robin |
| 4 | Gibb | Andy |
| 5 | Newton-John | Olivia |
| 6 | Crowe | Russell |
| 7 | Hogan | Paul |
| 8 | Kidman | Nicole |
| 9 | Bozinov | Zarko |
| 10 | Hay | Colin |
| 11 | HAM | GREG |

As you can see, the first INSTEAD OF trigger splits the name into two fields, as it did in the last example. The second INSTEAD OF trigger uppercases the name before inserting it into the first view. Note that it doesn't insert directly into the table—only the first view does that. Instead, it inserts into the first view so that we can be sure that the name splitting occurs. You can use this technique—that of layering INSTEAD OF views on top of one another—to set up some fairly sophisticated processing without needing to resort to stored procedures.

## Triggers and Auditing

I've already touched on this a bit in a few of the examples, but this is a popular enough use of triggers that it bears further discussion. AFTER triggers are frequently used to create an audit trail of modifications to a table. You can simply record the modification act itself, or you can store the actual changes that were made. Here's a simple example of auditing implemented through triggers (Listing 8–10):

**Listing 8–10** A simple auditing trigger.

```
USE tempdb
GO
```

```
CREATE TABLE ToyInventory
(Toy int identity,
 Type int,
 Onhand int
)
CREATE TABLE ToyAudit
(ToyAudit int identity,
 Operation varchar(10),
 Toy int,
 Type int,
 Change int
)
GO
CREATE TRIGGER ToyInventory_INSERT ON ToyInventory AFTER INSERT
AS
IF @@ROWCOUNT=0 RETURN
INSERT ToyAudit
SELECT 'INSERT', * FROM inserted
GO

INSERT ToyInventory DEFAULT VALUES
GO
```

Here we simply record any inserts into the ToyInventory table in a second table named ToyAudit. ToyAudit includes a column that indicates the operation that produced the log record. The insert trigger on ToyInventory supplies the string 'INSERT' for it.

What if we wanted to do something a little more sophisticated? For example, what if we wanted to track the before and after image when a row is updated? Using an AFTER UPDATE trigger, this is pretty easy. Listing 8–11 shows how:

**Listing 8–11** An audit trigger can capture the before and after images of a row.

```
CREATE TABLE ToyInventory
(Toy int identity,
 Type int,
 Onhand int
)
GO
CREATE TABLE ToyAudit
(ToyAudit int identity,
 Operation varchar(20),
```

```
  Toy int,
  Type int,
  Onhand int
)
GO
INSERT ToyInventory (Type, Onhand) VALUES (1, 50)
INSERT ToyInventory (Type, Onhand) VALUES (2, 50)
INSERT ToyInventory (Type, Onhand) VALUES (3, 50)
INSERT ToyInventory (Type, Onhand) VALUES (4, 50)
GO

CREATE TRIGGER ToyInventory_UPDATE ON ToyInventory AFTER UPDATE
AS
IF @@ROWCOUNT=0 RETURN
INSERT ToyAudit (Operation, Toy, Type, Onhand)
SELECT 'UPDATE--BEFORE', * FROM deleted ORDER BY Toy
INSERT ToyAudit (Operation, Toy, Type, Onhand)
SELECT 'UPDATE-AFTER', * FROM inserted ORDER BY Toy
GO
UPDATE ToyInventory SET Onhand = 49
GO
SELECT * FROM ToyAudit ORDER BY Toy, Operation, ToyAudit
```

(Results)

| ToyAudit | Operation | Toy | Type | Onhand |
| --- | --- | --- | --- | --- |
| 1 | UPDATE--BEFORE | 1 | 1 | 50 |
| 5 | UPDATE-AFTER | 1 | 1 | 49 |
| 2 | UPDATE--BEFORE | 2 | 2 | 50 |
| 6 | UPDATE-AFTER | 2 | 2 | 49 |
| 3 | UPDATE--BEFORE | 3 | 3 | 50 |
| 7 | UPDATE-AFTER | 3 | 3 | 49 |
| 4 | UPDATE--BEFORE | 4 | 4 | 50 |
| 8 | UPDATE-AFTER | 4 | 4 | 49 |

This code demonstrates several techniques worth discussing further. First, it uses the logical table containing the before image of the updated rows—the **deleted** table—to insert them into the audit table. It then does the same for the after-image table, **inserted**, and inserts the after-image rows into the audit table. When it selects from each of the logical tables, it orders the insertion using the Toy column so that the identity values in the ToyAudit table will be generated in Toy sequence. This allows us to later select the rows in the Toy-

Audit table using Toy as the high-order key and ToyAudit as the low-order key. This produces the result set you see in the listing where a row's after image immediately follows its before image, even though they originally came from two different logical tables.

Note the use of a double hyphen to force the before-image audit records to sort before the after ones. Because we're sorting alphabetically on the **Operation** column, we need a way of sorting the word BEFORE ahead of AFTER. Inserting the second hyphen is a cheap and easy way to do this.

What if we wanted to audit which columns were changed? What if we wanted to include the list of modified columns when we added log records to the audit table? This is pretty easy to do using our earlier technique of cross-referencing the bitmap returned by COLUMNS_UPDATED() with the ORDINAL_POSITION column in INFORMATION_SCHEMA.COLUMNS. Here's the code (Listing 8–12):

**Listing 8–12** Using COLUMNS_UPDATED(), an audit trigger can record the names of modified columns.

```
USE tempdb
GO
CREATE TABLE ToyInventory
(Toy int identity,
 Type int,
 Onhand int
)
GO
CREATE TABLE ToyAudit
(ToyAudit int identity,
 Operation varchar(20),
 Toy int,
 Type int,
 Onhand int,
 ColumnsModified varchar(7000)
)
GO
INSERT ToyInventory (Type, Onhand) VALUES (1, 50)
INSERT ToyInventory (Type, Onhand) VALUES (2, 50)
INSERT ToyInventory (Type, Onhand) VALUES (3, 50)
INSERT ToyInventory (Type, Onhand) VALUES (4, 50)
GO

CREATE TRIGGER ToyInventory_UPDATE ON ToyInventory AFTER UPDATE
AS
```

```
IF @@ROWCOUNT=0 RETURN

DECLARE @ChangedColumns varbinary(8000)
SET @ChangedColumns=COLUMNS_UPDATED()

INSERT ToyAudit (Operation, Toy, Type, Onhand, ColumnsModified)
SELECT 'UPDATE--BEFORE', d.*, c.COLUMN_NAME
FROM deleted d JOIN INFORMATION_SCHEMA.COLUMNS c
ON ((c.TABLE_NAME='ToyInventory') AND ((@ChangedColumns &
POWER(2,c.ORDINAL_POSITION-1))<>0))
ORDER BY d.Toy

INSERT ToyAudit (Operation, Toy, Type, Onhand, ColumnsModified)
SELECT 'UPDATE-AFTER', i.*, c.COLUMN_NAME
FROM inserted i JOIN INFORMATION_SCHEMA.COLUMNS c
ON ((c.TABLE_NAME='ToyInventory') AND ((@ChangedColumns &
POWER(2,c.ORDINAL_POSITION-1))<>0))
ORDER BY i.Toy

GO

UPDATE ToyInventory SET Onhand = 49, Type=3
GO
SELECT * FROM ToyAudit ORDER BY Toy, Operation, ToyAudit, ColumnsModified
```

(Results)

| ToyAudit | Operation | Toy | Type | Onhand | ColumnsModified |
|----------|-----------|-----|------|--------|-----------------|
| 1  | UPDATE--BEFORE | 1 | 1 | 50 | Type |
| 2  | UPDATE--BEFORE | 1 | 1 | 50 | Onhand |
| 9  | UPDATE-AFTER | 1 | 3 | 49 | Type |
| 10 | UPDATE-AFTER | 1 | 3 | 49 | Onhand |
| 3  | UPDATE--BEFORE | 2 | 2 | 50 | Onhand |
| 4  | UPDATE--BEFORE | 2 | 2 | 50 | Type |
| 11 | UPDATE-AFTER | 2 | 3 | 49 | Onhand |
| 12 | UPDATE-AFTER | 2 | 3 | 49 | Type |
| 5  | UPDATE--BEFORE | 3 | 3 | 50 | Type |
| 6  | UPDATE--BEFORE | 3 | 3 | 50 | Onhand |
| 13 | UPDATE-AFTER | 3 | 3 | 49 | Type |
| 14 | UPDATE-AFTER | 3 | 3 | 49 | Onhand |
| 7  | UPDATE--BEFORE | 4 | 4 | 50 | Onhand |
| 8  | UPDATE--BEFORE | 4 | 4 | 50 | Type |
| 15 | UPDATE-AFTER | 4 | 3 | 49 | Onhand |
| 16 | UPDATE-AFTER | 4 | 3 | 49 | Type |

# Transactions

When a user transaction is not active, a trigger and the DML operation that fired it are considered a single transaction. This holds for any stored procedures or UDFs the trigger calls—everything runs from within the same transaction.

When a trigger generates a fatal error or executes ROLLBACK TRANSACTION, the currently active transaction is rolled back and the current command batch is terminated. If this transaction is a user transaction, all changes made in that transaction are discarded. If it is the default transaction that's created anytime a data modification occurs, only the changes made by that one operation are lost.

For INSERT operations, the inserted logical table lists the rows being appended to the table. For DELETE operations, the deleted table lists the rows about to be removed from the table. For UPDATE operations, the deleted table lists the old version of the rows about to be updated, and the inserted table lists the new version. You can query these tables to allow or prevent database modifications based on the columns or data the operations are attempting to modify. Rolling back the current transaction is normally the way a trigger aborts because SQL Server's Transact-SQL doesn't support a ROLLBACK TRIGGER command (à la Sybase). Note that you can't modify these logical tables; they're for inspection only. If you need to use a trigger to alter the data changes about to be applied to a table before they're actually applied, use an INSTEAD OF trigger.

Minimally logged operations (operations that do not generate row modification log records) do not fire triggers. So, for example, even though TRUNCATE TABLE deletes all the rows in a table, these row deletions aren't logged individually and therefore do not fire any delete triggers that may have been defined for the table.

# Execution

Triggers fire just after the work has been completed by the DML statement, but before it has been committed to the database. From the perspective of the trigger, the data changes that fired it appear to have already taken place. For example, within an INSERT trigger, the rows being inserted appear to the trigger to already be in the table.

A DML statement's execution plan branches to any triggers it fires just before returning. If the trigger permits the operation to proceed, and if no user transaction is present, any changes made by the DML statement are then committed to the database.

## Calling Stored Procedures

A good way of modularizing your trigger code and cutting down on redundancy is to place the code shared in common by multiple triggers into a stored procedure and call the stored procedure from the triggers. The problem with this is that the inserted and deleted logical tables aren't available from a stored procedure. However, remember that from the perspective of an AFTER trigger, the modifications that fired it appear to have already taken place. This is also true of any code the trigger calls, including stored procedures. So, stored procedures called by the trigger do indeed have access to the data in the inserted and deleted tables by way of the table itself. The trigger can pass them the information they need to locate the rows contained in the inserted or deleted tables using the underlying table. Here's some code to illustrate (Listing 8–13):

**Listing 8–13** Moving trigger code to stored procedures makes it more modular.

```
USE tempdb
GO
CREATE TABLE ToyInventory
(Toy int identity,
 Type int,
 Onhand int
)
GO
CREATE TABLE ToyTypes
(Type int identity,
 MinOnhand int
)
GO
INSERT ToyTypes (MinOnhand) VALUES (10)
INSERT ToyTypes (MinOnhand) VALUES (20)
INSERT ToyTypes (MinOnhand) VALUES (15)
INSERT ToyTypes (MinOnhand) VALUES (50)

INSERT ToyInventory (Type, Onhand) VALUES (1, 50)
INSERT ToyInventory (Type, Onhand) VALUES (2, 50)
INSERT ToyInventory (Type, Onhand) VALUES (3, 50)
```

```
INSERT ToyInventory (Type, Onhand) VALUES (4, 50)

GO

DROP PROC CheckRowcount
GO

CREATE PROC CheckRowcount @rcnt int
AS
        IF @rcnt > 1 BEGIN
          RAISERROR('You may only change one item at a time. You are
          attempting to change %d rows in a single operation.',16,10,@rcnt)
          ROLLBACK
          RETURN
        END
GO

DROP PROC CheckOnhand
GO

CREATE PROC CheckOnhand @Type int, @Onhand int
AS
IF EXISTS (SELECT * FROM ToyTypes WHERE Type=@Type AND MinOnhand>@OnHand)
BEGIN
  RAISERROR('You may not lower an item''s Onhand quantity below its Mininum
Onhand quantity',16,10)
  ROLLBACK
  RETURN
END
GO

CREATE TRIGGER ToyInventory_UPDATE ON ToyInventory AFTER UPDATE
AS
DECLARE @rcnt int
SET @rcnt=@@ROWCOUNT
IF @rcnt=0 RETURN
EXEC CheckRowcount @rcnt
IF (UPDATE(Onhand)) BEGIN
  DECLARE @Type int, @Onhand int
  SELECT @Type=Type, @Onhand=Onhand FROM inserted
  EXEC CheckOnhand @Type, @Onhand
END
GO
UPDATE ToyInventory SET Onhand=49 WHERE Toy=4 -- Fails because of trigger
```

(Results)

```
Server: Msg 50000, Level 16, State 10, Procedure CheckOnhand, Line 5
You may not lower an item's Onhand quantity below its Mininum Onhand
quantity
```

In this example we call two stored procedures from the trigger: one to check the number of rows being affected to be sure that we don't allow more than one row to be changed at a time, and one to ensure that the **Onhand** column has a valid value. Because we restrict the trigger to single-row updates, all we have to do to let CheckOnhand know what rows are being changed and what changes are being made to them is to cache the critical info in variables and pass them to CheckOnhand as parameters. CheckOnhand then takes these parameters and looks up the minimum on-hand value for the specified type in the ToyTypes table. If the on-hand value being inserted into ToyInventory is less than the minimum allowed, CheckOnhand raises an error message and rolls back the transaction.

Because both of these routines are now stored procedures, we can call them from other triggers. Moreover, updating our business rules is easier when these business rules are centralized in a small number of stored procedures rather than scattered across a collection of triggers. For example, when we moved the row count-checking code to its own procedure, we enhanced it to report the number of modifications being attempted when there are too many. If an operation attempts to change more than one row at a time, we display an error message and report the number of attempted changes. If this code was not ensconced in a stored procedure, we might have had to change every trigger on the system to ensure consistency between them.

What if we wanted to allow multirow operations, yet still be able to modularize our code in stored procedures? It's not much more difficult. Here's the code (Listing 8–14):

**Listing 8–14** You can access modified data from within stored procedures called by triggers.

```
USE tempdb
GO
CREATE TABLE ToyInventory
(Toy int identity PRIMARY KEY,
 Type int,
 Onhand int
)
GO
```

```
CREATE TABLE ToyTypes
(Type int identity PRIMARY KEY,
 MinOnhand int
)
GO
INSERT ToyTypes (MinOnhand) VALUES (10)
INSERT ToyTypes (MinOnhand) VALUES (20)
INSERT ToyTypes (MinOnhand) VALUES (15)
INSERT ToyTypes (MinOnhand) VALUES (50)

INSERT ToyInventory (Type, Onhand) VALUES (1, 50)
INSERT ToyInventory (Type, Onhand) VALUES (2, 50)
INSERT ToyInventory (Type, Onhand) VALUES (3, 50)
INSERT ToyInventory (Type, Onhand) VALUES (4, 50)

GO

DROP PROC CheckOnhand

GO

CREATE PROC CheckOnhand @MinToy int, @MaxToy int
AS
IF EXISTS (SELECT * FROM ToyTypes t JOIN ToyInventory i ON (t.Type=i.Type)
WHERE i.Toy BETWEEN @MinToy AND @MaxToy
AND MinOnhand>i.Onhand) BEGIN
  RAISERROR('You may not lower an item''s Onhand quantity below its Mininum
Onhand quantity',16,10)
  ROLLBACK
  RETURN
END
GO

CREATE TRIGGER ToyInventory_UPDATE ON ToyInventory AFTER UPDATE
AS
IF @@ROWCOUNT=0 RETURN
IF (UPDATE(Onhand)) BEGIN
      DECLARE @MinToy int, @MaxToy int
      SELECT @MinToy=MIN(Toy), @MaxToy=MAX(Toy)
      FROM inserted
  EXEC CheckOnhand @MinToy, @MaxToy
END
GO
UPDATE ToyInventory SET Onhand=Onhand-1
```

(Results)

```
Server: Msg 50000, Level 16, State 10, Procedure CheckOnhand, Line 7
You may not lower an item's Onhand quantity below its Mininum Onhand
quantity
```

Here we save the minimum and maximum values for the **Toy** column from the inserted logical table. All we need to establish is the range of values in Toy-Inventory that CheckOnhand should examine. Once we've done this, we pass this range into CheckOnhand via parameters.

CheckOnhand takes the parameters we've passed it and joins the ToyTypes and ToyInventory tables using an equi-join on the **Type** column and using a theta join on the **Onhand** column. If it finds rows in ToyInventory within the specified range of key values that have a lower on-hand quantity than they should, it raises an error message and rolls back the transaction. Thus, we have effectively moved the on-hand validation code from the trigger to a stored procedure it calls, and have given the procedure full access to the data currently being modified.

## Nested Triggers

Triggers can cause other triggers to fire if the nested triggers option has been enabled with sp_configure. Triggers can fire themselves recursively if the recursive triggers database option has been enabled. The @@NESTLEVEL automatic variable returns 1 within a first-level trigger, 2 within one it causes to fire, 3 for any it causes to fire, and so forth.

## Disabling Triggers

You can disable a trigger via the ALTER TABLE...DISABLE TRIGGER command. Disabled triggers can be reenabled using ALTER TABLE...ENABLE TRIGGER. Here are a few examples (Listing 8–15):

**Listing 8–15** Triggers can be disabled/enabled at will.

```
ALTER TABLE sales
DISABLE TRIGGER SalesQty_INSERT_UPDATE

ALTER TABLE sales
ENABLE TRIGGER SalesQty_INSERT_UPDATE
```

```
ALTER TABLE sales
DISABLE TRIGGER ALL

ALTER TABLE sales
ENABLE TRIGGER ALL
```

## Best Practices

Triggers are really just stored procedures in disguise. They have a few additional capabilities and nuances, but generally speaking, you take the same approach to writing a trigger as you would to build a stored procedure. A few additional thoughts:

- Make sure your triggers allow for the possibility that more than one row could be altered at once. Triggers that work fine with single-row operations often break when multirow operations come their way. Not allowing for multirow updates is the single most common error that trigger neophytes make.
- Begin each trigger by checking @@ROWCOUNT to see whether any rows have changed. If none have, exit immediately because there's nothing for the trigger to do.
- Use the UPDATE() and COLUMNS_UPDATED() functions to ensure the values you're wanting to verify have actually changed.
- Never wait for user input or any other user event within a trigger.
- Check for errors after significant operations within your triggers, especially DML operations. Commands within triggers should check for errors just as stored procedures should.
- Keep operations within a trigger to a minimum. Triggers should execute as quickly as possible to keep from adversely impacting system performance.
- Provide descriptive error messages without going overboard. Return user messages rather than obscure system error codes when possible.
- Modularize your triggers by locating code that's executed by multiple triggers or that's lengthy or complex in separate stored procedures.
- Check triggers that enforce referential integrity for robustness. Try every combination of columnar updates to be sure all scenarios are covered.
- Write a test script for every trigger you build. Make sure it tests every situation the trigger is supposed to handle.

Listing 8–16 presents a few more trigger examples:

**Listing 8–16** General trigger examples.

```
SET NOCOUNT ON
USE pubs
DROP TRIGGER SalesQty_INSERT_UPDATE
GO
CREATE TRIGGER SalesQty_INSERT_UPDATE ON sales AFTER INSERT, UPDATE AS

IF @@ROWCOUNT=0 RETURN -- No rows affected, exit immediately

IF (UPDATE(qty)) AND (SELECT MIN(qty) FROM inserted)<10 BEGIN
  RAISERROR('Minimum order is 10 units',16,10)
  ROLLBACK TRAN
  RETURN
END
GO


-- Test a single-row INSERT
BEGIN TRAN
  INSERT sales VALUES (6380,'ORD9997',GETDATE(),5,'Net 60','BU1032')
IF @@TRANCOUNT>0 ROLLBACK TRAN
GO


-- Test a multirow INSERT
BEGIN TRAN
  INSERT sales
  SELECT stor_id, ord_num+'A', ord_date, 5, payterms, title_id FROM sales
IF @@TRANCOUNT>0 ROLLBACK TRAN
GO


DROP TRIGGER Sales_DELETE
GO
CREATE TRIGGER Sales_DELETE ON sales AFTER DELETE AS

IF @@ROWCOUNT=0 RETURN -- No rows affected, exit immediately

IF (@@ROWCOUNT>1) BEGIN
  RAISERROR('Deletions of more than one row at a time are not permitted',16,10)
  ROLLBACK TRAN
  RETURN
END
GO
BEGIN TRAN
  DELETE sales
```

```
IF @@TRANCOUNT>0 ROLLBACK TRAN
GO


DROP TRIGGER Salesord_date_qty_UPDATE
GO
CREATE TRIGGER Salesord_date_qty_UPDATE ON sales AFTER INSERT, UPDATE AS

IF @@ROWCOUNT=0 RETURN -- No rows affected, exit immediately

-- Check to see whether the 3rd and 4th columns are being updated simultaneously
IF (COLUMNS_UPDATED() & (POWER(2,3-1) | POWER(2,4-1)))=12 BEGIN

  UPDATE s SET payterms='Cash'
  FROM sales s JOIN inserted i ON (s.stor_id=i.stor_id AND s.ord_num=i.ord_num)

  IF (@@ERROR<>0) -- UPDATE generated an error, rollback transaction
    ROLLBACK TRANSACTION
  RETURN

END
GO


-- Test with a single-row UPDATE
BEGIN TRAN
  UPDATE sales SET ord_date=GETDATE(), qty=15
  WHERE stor_id=7066 and ord_num='A2976'

  SELECT * FROM sales
  WHERE stor_id=7066 and ord_num='A2976'
IF @@TRANCOUNT>0 ROLLBACK TRAN
GO


-- Test with a multirow UPDATE
BEGIN TRAN
  UPDATE sales SET ord_date=GETDATE(), qty=15
  WHERE stor_id=7066

  SELECT * FROM sales
  WHERE stor_id=7066
IF @@TRANCOUNT>0 ROLLBACK TRAN
Server: Msg 50000, Level 16, State 10, Procedure CheckSalesQty, Line 3
Minimum order is 10 units
Server: Msg 50000, Level 16, State 10, Procedure CheckSalesQty, Line 3
Minimum order is 10 units
```

```
Server: Msg 50000, Level 16, State 10, Procedure CheckSalesDelete, Line 3
Deletions of more than one row at a time are not permitted
stor_id ord_num             ord_date                    qty    payterms      title_id
------- -------------------- --------------------------- ------ ------------- --------
7066    A2976                1999-06-13 01:10:16.193     15     Cash          PC8888
stor_id ord_num             ord_date                    qty    payterms      title_id
------- -------------------- --------------------------- ------ ------------- --------
7066    A2976                1999-06-13 01:10:16.243     15     Cash          PC8888
7066    QA7442.3             1999-06-13 01:10:16.243     15     Cash          PS2091
```

## Summary

In this chapter you learned how to use triggers to accomplish a variety of practical tasks. You learned how triggers are sometimes used to ensure referential integrity within a database, and how triggers can be set up on views as well as tables. You learned some techniques for writing efficient and low-maintenance trigger code, and you learned a bit about how triggers are processed internally by the server.

# CHAPTER 9

# Views

*I want to personally thank all those who have doubted me in the past. All those who gave up on me, who thought little of me, who underestimated me—you have been a source of inspiration. You have caused me to work faster and try harder than I otherwise would have, and, for that, I owe you a debt of gratitude.*

*—H. W. Kenton*

An SQL Server view object is a static query that you can use as a kind of virtual table in a SELECT, INSERT, UPDATE, or DELETE. A view consists of a SELECT statement stored permanently as a separate object using SQL's CREATE VIEW command. A view is typically used to encapsulate a complicated join or query so that it can be accessed like a table.

View columns can consist of columns from tables or other views, aggregates, constants, and expressions (computed columns). Some views can be updated; some can't. Whether a view can be updated depends largely on whether SQL Server can resolve an update to one of its rows to a single row in an underlying base table. All views must eventually reference a base table or nontabular expression (an expression that doesn't require a table—GETDATE(), for example), although views can be "nested," meaning that a view can reference other views as long as the dependence tree eventually resolves to base tables or nontabular expressions.

## Meta-data

The OBJECTPROPERTY() meta-data function supports a number of properties that relate to views. Table 9–1 summarizes them.

**Table 9–1** View-Related OBJECTPROPERTY() Values

| Property | Function |
|---|---|
| ExecIsAnsiNullsOn | Indicates whether ANSI_NULLS was on when the view was created or altered |
| ExecIsQuotedIdentOn | Indicates whether QUOTED_IDENTIFIER was on when the view was created or altered |
| HasAfterTrigger | Indicates whether the view has an AFTER trigger |
| HasInsertTrigger | Indicates whether the view has an INSERT trigger |
| HasInsteadOfTrigger | Indicates whether the view has an INSTEAD OF trigger |
| HasUpdateTrigger | Indicates whether the view has an UPDATE trigger |
| IsAnsiNullsOn | Indicates whether ANSI_NULLS was on when the view was created or altered (same as ExecIsAnsiNullsOn) |
| IsDeterministic | Indicates whether the view consistently returns the same results given the same criteria |
| IsExecuted | Returns 1 for views and other executable objects: triggers, stored procedures, UDFs, and tables with computed columns |
| IsIndexable | Indicates that an index can be created over the view |
| IsIndexed | Indicates that the view is indexed |
| IsQuotedIdentOn | Indicates whether QUOTED_IDENTIFIER was on when the view was created or altered (same as ExecIsQuotedIdentOn) |
| IsSchemaBound | Indicates whether the view is schema bound |
| IsView | Returns 1 for views |

## Listing the Source Code for a View

Unless a view was created using the WITH ENCRYPTION option, you can use sp_helptext to retrieve its source code. You can also inspect and modify view source code in Enterprise Manager, as well as many SQL-DMO-enabled administration tools. Here's some sample code that returns the source of the syslogins system view (Listing 9–1):

**Listing 9–1**  sp_helptext can list a view's source code.

```
USE master
EXEC sp_helptext syslogins

Text
---------------------------------------------------------------------------
CREATE VIEW syslogins AS SELECT
    sid = convert(varbinary(85), sid),
    status = convert(smallint, 8 +
            CASE WHEN (xstatus & 2)=0 THEN 1 ELSE 2 END),
    createdate = convert(datetime, xdate1),
    updatedate = convert(datetime, xdate2),
    accdate = convert(datetime, xdate1),
    totcpu = convert(int, 0),
    totio = convert(int, 0),
    spacelimit = convert(int, 0),
    timelimit = convert(int, 0),
    resultlimit = convert(int, 0),
    name = convert(sysname, name),
    dbname = convert(sysname, db_name(dbid)),
    password = convert(sysname, password),
    language = convert(sysname, language),
    denylogin = convert(int, CASE WHEN (xstatus&1)=1 THEN 1 ELSE 0 END),
    hasaccess = convert(int, CASE WHEN (xstatus&2)=2 THEN 1 ELSE 0 END),
    isntname = convert(int, CASE WHEN (xstatus&4)=4 THEN 1 ELSE 0 END),
    isntgroup = convert(int, CASE WHEN (xstatus&12)=4 THEN 1 ELSE 0 END),
    isntuser = convert(int, CASE WHEN (xstatus&12)=12 THEN 1 ELSE 0 END),
    sysadmin = convert(int, CASE WHEN (xstatus&16)=16 THEN 1 ELSE 0 END),
    securityadmin = convert(int, CASE WHEN (xstatus&32)=32 THEN 1 ELSE 0 END),
    serveradmin = convert(int, CASE WHEN (xstatus&64)=64 THEN 1 ELSE 0 END),
    setupadmin = convert(int, CASE WHEN (xstatus&128)=128 THEN 1 ELSE 0 END),
    processadmin = convert(int, CASE WHEN (xstatus&256)=256 THEN 1 ELSE 0 END),
    diskadmin = convert(int, CASE WHEN (xstatus&512)=512 THEN 1 ELSE 0 END),
    dbcreator = convert(int, CASE WHEN (xstatus&1024)=1024 THEN 1 ELSE 0 END),
    bulkadmin = convert(int, CASE WHEN (xstatus&4096)=4096 THEN 1 ELSE 0 END),
    loginname = convert(sysname, name)
FROM sysxlogins WHERE srvid IS NULL
```

# Restrictions

Transact-SQL doesn't support temporary views, although you can create static views in tempdb and achieve a similar effect. A derived table is also an approximation of a temporary view, as is a table variable with the results of a SELECT statement stored in it.

Views aren't allowed to reference temporary tables—only references to other views or permanent base tables are allowed.

As a rule, ORDER BY is not allowed in views, so the following syntax is not valid:

```
- _Not_ valid Transact-SQL syntax
CREATE VIEW myauthors AS
SELECT * FROM authors
ORDER BY au_lname
```

There is, however, a workaround. You can use Transact-SQL's TOP extension to allow ORDER BY in views, like this (Listing 9–2):

**Listing 9–2** SELECT TOP can work around the ORDER BY restriction.

```
CREATE VIEW myauthors AS
SELECT TOP 100 PERCENT *
FROM authors
ORDER BY au_lname
```

The query in Listing 9–3 shows that ORDER BY is in effect when we issue a simple query against the view:

**Listing 9–3** Including ORDER BY in the view orders the result set.

```
SELECT au_id, au_lname, au_fname
FROM myauthors
```

| au_id | au_lname | au_fname |
|-------|----------|----------|
| 409-56-7008 | Bennet | Abraham |
| 648-92-1872 | Blotchet-Halls | Reginald |
| 238-95-7766 | Carson | Cheryl |
| 722-51-5454 | DeFrance | Michel |
| 712-45-1867 | del Castillo | Innes |
| 427-17-2319 | Dull | Ann |
| 213-46-8915 | Green | Marjorie |
| 527-72-3246 | Greene | Morningstar |
| 472-27-2349 | Gringlesby | Burt |
| 846-92-7186 | Hunter | Sheryl |
| 756-30-7391 | Karsen | Livia |

| | | |
|---|---|---|
| 486-29-1786 | Locksley | Charlene |
| 724-80-9391 | MacFeather | Stearns |
| 893-72-1158 | McBadden | Heather |
| 267-41-2394 | O'Leary | Michael |
| 807-91-6654 | Panteley | Sylvia |
| 998-72-3567 | Ringer | Albert |
| 899-46-2035 | Ringer | Anne |
| 341-22-1782 | Smith | Meander |
| 274-80-9391 | Straight | Dean |
| 724-08-9931 | Stringer | Dirk |
| 172-32-1176 | White | Johnson |
| 672-71-3249 | Yokomoto | Akiko |

Understand that the row order is still not guaranteed, even with ORDER BY in place. Parallel data gathering and other operations by SQL Server could cause the rows to be returned out of sequence. To guarantee the order, use an ORDER BY clause with the SELECT that queries the view.

### ANSI_NULLS and QUOTED_IDENTIFIER

Like stored procedures, the status of SET QUOTED_IDENTIFIER and SET ANSI_NULLS is saved with each view. This means that individual session settings for these options are ignored by the view when it's queried. It also means that you can localize special quoted identifier or NULL handling to a particular view without affecting anything else.

### DML Restrictions

An UPDATE to the view without an INSTEAD OF trigger is not allowed to affect more than one underlying base table at a time. If the view joins two or more tables together, an UPDATE to it may only change one of them. Likewise, an INSERT into such a view must only modify one table at a time. This means that values can be supplied for only one table—the columns in the other tables must have DEFAULT constraints, allow NULLs, or otherwise be optional. Unless an INSTEAD OF trigger is present, DELETE can only be used with single-table views. It can't be used with multitable views at all.

## ANSI SQL Schema Views

SQL Server provides a number of views for accessing the system catalogs. These objects provide an ANSI SQL-92 compliant means of retrieving meta-data and system-level information from the server. You should use these rather than querying system catalog tables for two reasons:

1. You can depend on them not to change across releases of SQL Server, even though their underlying system tables may change.
2. The ANSI SQL-92 specification defines these views, so they should work similarly between different DBMS platforms.

The SQL-92-compliant views that SQL Server provides are as follows:

- CHECK_CONSTRAINTS
- COLUMN_DOMAIN_USAGE
- COLUMN_PRIVILEGES
- COLUMNS
- CONSTRAINT_COLUMN_USAGE
- CONSTRAINT_TABLE_USAGE
- DOMAIN_CONSTRAINTS
- DOMAINS
- KEY_COLUMN_USAGE
- PARAMETERS
- REFERENTIAL_CONSTRAINTS
- ROUTINE_COLUMNS
- ROUTINES
- SCHEMATA
- TABLE_CONSTRAINTS
- TABLE_PRIVILEGES
- TABLES
- VIEW_COLUMN_USAGE
- VIEW_TABLE_USAGE
- VIEWS

Note that you must refer to these objects using the INFORMATION_ SCHEMA database schema. In SQL Server parlance, a schema and an owner are synonymous. This means that you must use

```
SELECT * FROM INFORMATION_SCHEMA.TABLES
```

rather than

```
SELECT * FROM TABLES
```

Even though the views themselves reside only in the master database, they run in the context of the current database. This makes them similar to system stored procedures. On a related note, if you check an INFORMATION_SCHEMA view's IsMSShipped property, you'll find that SQL Server considers it a system object. (See Chapter 22 for more info on system objects).

## Creating Your Own INFORMATION_SCHEMA Views

The ability to create a view in the master database and have it run in the context of the current database has lots of practical applications. For example, if you had a large number of customer-specific databases with the same set of views in each one, you could lessen your administrative headaches and disk space requirements if you could keep them in master (instead of in each customer database) and have them run in the proper database context when queried. Fortunately, there is a way to do this, but it's undocumented. So, as with all undocumented techniques, keep in mind that it may change or not be available in future releases.

To create your own system views, follow these steps:

1. Enable updates to the system tables through a call to sp_configure:

```
sp_configure 'allow updates',1
RECONFIGURE WITH OVERRIDE
```

2. Enable automatic system object creation by calling the undocumented procedure sp_MS_upd_sysobj_category (you must be the database owner or a member of the setupadmin role):

```
sp_MS_upd_sysobj_category 1
```

This procedure turns on trace flag 1717 to cause all objects created to have their IsMSShipped bits turned on automatically. This is necessary because you can't create a nonsystem object that belongs to INFORMATION_SCHEMA. If you could, you could simply call sp_MS_marksystemobject (covered in Chapter 22) after creating each view to enable its system bit. Instead, because SQL Server won't create nonsystem INFORMATION_SCHEMA objects, we have to enable a special server mode wherein each object created is automatically flagged as a system object.

3. Create your view in the master database, specifying INFORMATION_SCHEMA as the owner, as demonstrated in Listing 9–4.

**4.** Disable automatic system object creation by calling sp_MS_upd_
sysobj_category again:

```
sp_MS_upd_sysobj_category 2
```

**5.** Disable 'allow updates' by calling sp_configure:

```
sp_configure 'allow updates',0
RECONFIGURE WITH OVERRIDE
```

Here's the code for a new INFORMATION_SCHEMA view called
DIRECTORY. It lists the objects and data types in a database in a format similar to the OS DIR command:

**Listing 9–4** A user-defined INFORMATION_SCHEMA view.

```
USE master
GO
EXEC sp_configure 'allow', 1
GO
RECONFIGURE WITH OVERRIDE
GO
EXEC sp_MS_upd_sysobj_category 1
GO
IF OBJECT_ID('INFORMATION_SCHEMA.DIRECTORY') IS NOT NULL
 DROP VIEW INFORMATION_SCHEMA.DIRECTORY
GO
CREATE VIEW INFORMATION_SCHEMA.DIRECTORY

/*

Object: DIRECTORY
Description: Lists object catalog information similarly to the OS DIR
command.

Usage: SELECT * FROM INFORMATION_SCHEMA.DIRECTORY
 WHERE Name LIKE name mask AND Type LIKE object type ORDER BY T, Name

name mask=pattern of object names to list
object type=type of objects to list

The following object types are listed:

 U=User tables
```

```
   S=System tables
   V=Views
   P=Stored procedures
   X=Extended procedures
   RF=Replication filter stored procedures
   TR=Triggers
   D=Default objects
   R=Rule objects
   T=User-defined data types
   IF=Inline user-defined function
   TF=Table-valued user-defined function
   FN=Scalar user-defined function


Created by: Ken Henderson. Email: khen@khen.com


Version: 8.0


Example usage:

 SELECT * FROM INFORMATION_SCHEMA.DIRECTORY
 WHERE Name LIKE 'ORD%' AND Type='U'
 ORDER BY T, Name


Created: 1992-06-12. Last changed: 2000-11-12.

*/
AS


SELECT TOP 100 PERCENT CASE GROUPING(T) WHEN 1 THEN '*' ELSE T END AS T,
       Name, Type, DateCreated,
       SUM(Rows) AS Rows,
       SUM(RowLenInBytes) AS RowLenInBytes,
       SUM(TotalSizeInKB) AS TotalSizeInKB,
       SUM(DataSpaceInKB) AS DataSpaceInKB,
       SUM(IndexSpaceInKB) AS IndexSpaceInKB,
       SUM(UnusedSpaceInKB) AS UnusedSpaceInKB,
        Owner
 FROM (
SELECT -- Get regular objects
 ' ' AS T,
Name=LEFT(o.name,30),
Type=o.type,
DateCreated=o.crdate,
```

```
    Rows=ISNULL(rows,0),
    RowLenInBytes=ISNULL((SELECT SUM(length)
         FROM syscolumns
         WHERE id=o.id AND o.type in ('U','S')),0),
    TotalSizeInKB=ISNULL((SELECT SUM(reserved)
         FROM sysindexes
         WHERE indid in (0, 1, 255) AND id=o.id),0)*2,
    DataSpaceInKB=ISNULL(((SELECT SUM(dpages)
         FROM sysindexes
         WHERE indid < 2 AND id=o.id)+
         (SELECT ISNULL(SUM(used), 0)
         FROM sysindexes
         WHERE indid=255 AND id=o.id)),0)*2,
    IndexSpaceInKB=ISNULL(((SELECT SUM(used)
         FROM sysindexes
         WHERE indid in (0, 1, 255) AND id=o.id) -
         ((SELECT SUM(dpages)
         FROM sysindexes
         WHERE indid < 2 AND id=o.id)+
         (SELECT ISNULL(SUM(used), 0)
         FROM sysindexes
         WHERE indid=255 AND id=o.id))),0)*2,
    UnusedSpaceInKB=ISNULL(((SELECT SUM(reserved)
         FROM sysindexes
         WHERE indid in (0, 1, 255) AND id=o.id) -
         (SELECT SUM(used)
         FROM sysindexes
         WHERE indid in (0, 1, 255) AND id=o.id)),0)*2,
         Owner=USER_NAME(o.uid)
    FROM sysobjects o, sysindexes i
    WHERE o.id*=i.id AND i.indid<=1
    UNION ALL -- Get user-defined data types
    SELECT ' ',
    LEFT(name,30), 'T', NULL, NULL,
    NULL, NULL, NULL, NULL, NULL, USER_NAME(uid)
    FROM systypes st
    WHERE (usertype & 256)<>0
    ) D
    GROUP BY T, Name,Type, DateCreated, Owner WITH ROLLUP
    HAVING (T+Name+Type+Owner IS NOT NULL)
    OR (COALESCE(T,Name,Type,Owner) IS NULL)
    ORDER BY T,name
```

```
GO
EXEC sp_MS_upd_sysobj_category 2
GO
EXEC sp_configure 'allow', 0
GO
RECONFIGURE WITH OVERRIDE
GO
```

Once the view is created, you can query it like any other INFORMA-
TION_SCHEMA view (Listing 9–5):

**Listing 9–5** Our new INFORMATION_SCHEMA view in action.

```
USE pubs
GO
SELECT * FROM INFORMATION_SCHEMA.DIRECTORY
GO
```

(Results abridged)

| T | Name | Type | DateCreated | Rows | RowLe |
|---|------|------|-------------|------|-------|
| | authors | U | 2000-03-21 12:02:24.057 | 30 | 151 |
| | byroyalty | P | 2000-03-21 12:02:26.510 | 0 | 0 |
| | CK__authors__au_id__77BFCB91 | C | 2000-03-21 12:02:24.077 | 0 | 0 |
| | CK__authors__zip__79A81403 | C | 2000-03-21 12:02:24.077 | 0 | 0 |
| | DF__publisher__count__7D78A4E7 | D | 2000-03-21 12:02:24.097 | 0 | 0 |
| | DF__titles__pubdate__023D5A04 | D | 2000-03-21 12:02:24.197 | 0 | 0 |
| | DF__titles__type__00551192 | D | 2000-03-21 12:02:24.107 | 0 | 0 |
| | discounts | U | 2000-03-21 12:02:24.247 | 3 | 53 |
| | empid | T | NULL | NULL | NULL |
| | employee | U | 2000-03-21 12:02:24.277 | 43 | 75 |
| | employee_insupd | TR | 2000-03-21 12:02:24.287 | 0 | 0 |
| | FK__discounts__stor__0F975522 | F | 2000-03-21 12:02:24.247 | 0 | 0 |
| | FK__employee__job_id__1BFD2C07 | F | 2000-03-21 12:02:24.277 | 0 | 0 |
| | FK__employee__pub_id__1ED998B2 | F | 2000-03-21 12:02:24.277 | 0 | 0 |
| | FK__pub_info__pub_id__173876EA | F | 2000-03-21 12:02:24.267 | 0 | 0 |
| | id | T | NULL | NULL | NULL |
| | jobs | U | 2000-03-21 12:02:24.257 | 14 | 54 |
| | PK__jobs__117F9D94 | K | 2000-03-21 12:02:24.257 | 0 | 0 |

| | | | | | |
|---|---|---|---|---|---|
| roysched | U | 2000-03-21 12:02:24.237 | 86 | 18 |
| sales | U | 2000-03-21 12:02:24.227 | 21 | 52 |
| stores | U | 2000-03-21 12:02:24.217 | 6 | 111 |
| tid | T | NULL | NULL | NULL |
| titleauthor | U | 2000-03-21 12:02:24.207 | 25 | 22 |
| titles | U | 2000-03-21 12:02:24.107 | 18 | 334 |
| titleview | V | 2000-03-21 12:02:26.500 | 0 | 0 |
| UPK_storeid | K | 2000-03-21 12:02:24.217 | 0 | 0 |
| UPKCL_auidind | K | 2000-03-21 12:02:24.057 | 0 | 0 |
| UPKCL_pubind | K | 2000-03-21 12:02:24.097 | 0 | 0 |
| UPKCL_pubinfo | K | 2000-03-21 12:02:24.267 | 0 | 0 |
| UPKCL_sales | K | 2000-03-21 12:02:24.227 | 0 | 0 |
| UPKCL_taind | K | 2000-03-21 12:02:24.207 | 0 | 0 |
| UPKCL_titleidind | K | 2000-03-21 12:02:24.107 | 0 | 0 |
| * NULL | NULL NULL | | 2424 | 88784 |

As with system stored procedures, you can prefix a system view with a database name (even databases other than the one in which is resides), and it will run in the context of that database. For example, we can do this (Listing 9–6):

**Listing 9–6** INFORMATION_SCHEMA views behave similar to system procedures.

```
USE pubs
GO
/* other code goes here */
SELECT * FROM Northwind.INFORMATION_SCHEMA.DIRECTORY
GO
```

(Results abridged)

| T | Name | Type | DateCreated | Rows | RowLe |
|---|---|---|---|---|---|
| | Alphabetical list of products | V | 2000-08-06 01:34:09.420 | 0 | 0 |
| | Categories | U | 2000-08-06 01:34:05.077 | 8 | 66 |
| | Category Sales for 1997 | V | 2000-08-06 01:34:11.530 | 0 | 0 |
| | CK_Birthdate | C | 2000-08-06 01:34:04.653 | 0 | 0 |
| | CK_Discount | C | 2000-08-06 01:34:08.470 | 0 | 0 |
| | CK_Products_UnitPrice | C | 2000-08-06 01:34:07.700 | 0 | 0 |

| | | | | | |
|---|---|---|---|---|---|
| CK_Quantity | C | 2000-08-06 | 01:34:08.470 | 0 | 0 |
| ... | | | | | |
| Shippers | U | 2000-08-06 | 01:34:06.060 | 3 | 132 |
| Summary of Sales by Quarter | V | 2000-08-06 | 01:34:12.187 | 0 | 0 |
| Summary of Sales by Year | V | 2000-08-06 | 01:34:12.403 | 0 | 0 |
| Suppliers | U | 2000-08-06 | 01:34:06.187 | 29 | 546 |
| Ten Most Expensive Products | P | 2000-08-06 | 01:34:12.623 | 0 | 0 |
| Territories | U | 2000-08-06 | 01:34:54.077 | 53 | 144 |
| * NULL | NULL | NULL | | 6860 | 73623 |

Even though the current database is pubs, the view runs in the context of Northwind because of our prefix.

### Creating Your Own INFORMATION_SCHEMA User-Defined Function

We're not limited to building INFORMATION_SCHEMA views. We can also build INFORMATION_SCHEMA UDFs. The two concepts are similar because table-valued UDFs can provide a kind of parameterized view functionality. Here's an INFORMATION_SCHEMA UDF that works like a parameterized view and can be executed from any database context (Listing 9–7):

**Listing 9–7** You can create INFORMATION_SCHEMA functions as well as views.

```
USE master
GO
EXEC sp_configure 'allow', 1
GO
RECONFIGURE WITH OVERRIDE
GO
EXEC sp_MS_upd_sysobj_category 1
GO
IF OBJECT_ID('INFORMATION_SCHEMA.OBJECTS') IS NOT NULL
 DROP FUNCTION INFORMATION_SCHEMA.OBJECTS
GO
CREATE FUNCTION INFORMATION_SCHEMA.OBJECTS(@mask sysname='%', @obtype
varchar(3)='%', @orderby varchar(1000)='/N')

/*
```

```
Object: OBJECTS
Description: Lists object catalog information similarly to the OS DIR command.

Usage: SELECT * FROM INFORMATION_SCHEMA.OBJECTS()
 WHERE Name LIKE name mask AND Type LIKE object type ORDER BY T, Name

name mask=pattern of object names to list
object type=type of objects to list

The following object types are listed:

 U=User tables
 S=System tables
 V=Views
 P=Stored procedures
 X=Extended procedures
 RF=Replication filter stored procedures
 TR=Triggers
 D=Default objects
 R=Rule objects
 T=User-defined data types
 IF=Inline user-defined function
 TF=Table-valued user-defined function
 FN=Scalar user-defined function

Created by: Ken Henderson. Email: khen@khen.com

Version: 8.0

Example usage:

 SELECT * FROM INFORMATION_SCHEMA.OBJECTS('ORD%','U',DEFAULT)
 ORDER BY T, Name

Created: 1992-06-12. Last changed: 2000-11-12.

The following orderings are supported:

/N  =  by name
/R  =  by number of rows
/S  =  by total object size
/D  =  by date created
/A  =  by total size of data pages
/X  =  by total size of index pages
```

```
/U  =  by total size of unused pages
/L  =  by maximum row length
/O  =  by owner
/T  =  by type

*/
RETURNS TABLE
AS
RETURN(
SELECT TOP 100 PERCENT CASE GROUPING(T) WHEN 1 THEN '*' ELSE T END AS T,
       Name, Type, DateCreated,
       SUM(Rows) AS Rows,
       SUM(RowLenInBytes) AS RowLenInBytes,
       SUM(TotalSizeInKB) AS TotalSizeInKB,
       SUM(DataSpaceInKB) AS DataSpaceInKB,
       SUM(IndexSpaceInKB) AS IndexSpaceInKB,
       SUM(UnusedSpaceInKB) AS UnusedSpaceInKB,
        Owner
 FROM (
SELECT -- Get regular objects
' ' AS T,
Name=LEFT(o.name,30),
Type=o.type,
DateCreated=o.crdate,
Rows=ISNULL(rows,0),
RowLenInBytes=ISNULL((SELECT SUM(length)
       FROM syscolumns
       WHERE id=o.id AND o.type in ('U','S')),0),
TotalSizeInKB=ISNULL((SELECT SUM(reserved)
       FROM sysindexes
       WHERE indid in (0, 1, 255) AND id=o.id),0)*2,
DataSpaceInKB=ISNULL(((SELECT SUM(dpages)
       FROM sysindexes
       WHERE indid < 2 AND id=o.id)+
       (SELECT ISNULL(SUM(used), 0)
       FROM sysindexes
       WHERE indid=255 AND id=o.id)),0)*2,
IndexSpaceInKB=ISNULL(((SELECT SUM(used)
       FROM sysindexes
       WHERE indid in (0, 1, 255) AND id=o.id) -
       ((SELECT SUM(dpages)
       FROM sysindexes
       WHERE indid < 2 AND id=o.id)+
       (SELECT ISNULL(SUM(used), 0)
```

```
        FROM sysindexes
        WHERE indid=255 AND id=o.id))),0)*2,
UnusedSpaceInKB=ISNULL(((SELECT SUM(reserved)
        FROM sysindexes
        WHERE indid in (0, 1, 255) AND id=o.id) -
        (SELECT SUM(used)
        FROM sysindexes
        WHERE indid in (0, 1, 255) AND id=o.id)),0)*2,
        Owner=USER_NAME(o.uid)
FROM sysobjects o, sysindexes i
WHERE o.name LIKE @mask
AND o.Type LIKE @obtype
AND o.id*=i.id AND i.indid<=1
UNION ALL -- Get user-defined data types
SELECT ' ',
LEFT(name,30), 'T', NULL, NULL,
NULL, NULL, NULL, NULL, NULL, USER_NAME(uid)
FROM systypes st
WHERE name LIKE @mask
AND 'T' LIKE @obtype
AND (usertype & 256)<>0
) D
GROUP BY T, Name,Type, DateCreated, Owner WITH ROLLUP
HAVING (T+Name+Type+Owner IS NOT NULL)
OR (COALESCE(T,Name,Type,Owner) IS NULL)
ORDER BY T, CASE UPPER(LEFT(@orderby,2))
            WHEN '/D' THEN CONVERT(CHAR(30),DateCreated,121)
            WHEN '/R' THEN REPLACE(STR(SUM(Rows),10,0),' ','0')
            WHEN '/A' THEN REPLACE(STR(SUM(DataSpaceInKB),10,0),' ','0')
            WHEN '/S' THEN REPLACE(STR(SUM(TotalSizeInKB),10,0),' ','0')
            WHEN '/X' THEN REPLACE(STR(SUM(IndexSpaceInKB),10,0),' ','0')
            WHEN '/U' THEN REPLACE(STR(SUM(UnusedSpaceInKB),10,0),' ','0')
            WHEN '/L' THEN REPLACE(STR(SUM(RowLenInBytes),10,0),' ','0')
            WHEN '/T' THEN Type
            WHEN '/O' THEN Owner
            END,
            Name -- Always sort by Name to break ties
)
GO
EXEC sp_MS_upd_sysobj_category 2
GO
EXEC sp_configure 'allow', 0
GO
RECONFIGURE WITH OVERRIDE
```

```
GO
SELECT *
FROM Northwind.INFORMATION_SCHEMA.OBJECTS('Ord%',DEFAULT,'/N')
```

(Results abridged)

| T | Name | Type | DateCreated | Rows | RowLen |
|---|------|------|-------------|------|--------|
|   | Order Details | U | 2000-08-06 01:34:08.470 | 2155 | 22 |
|   | Order Details Extended | V | 2000-08-06 01:34:10.873 | 0 | 0 |
|   | Order Subtotals | V | 2000-08-06 01:34:11.093 | 0 | 0 |
|   | Orders | U | 2000-08-06 01:34:06.610 | 830 | 364 |
|   | Orders Qry | V | 2000-08-06 01:34:09.780 | 0 | 0 |
| * | NULL | NULL | NULL | 2985 | 386 |

(6 row(s) affected)

This code exhibits several techniques worth discussing. First, note the method I used to merge the sysobjects and systypes tables. I used a UNION ALL to join the two tables, supplying constants and dummy values for systypes as necessary. This union was then wrapped in a derived table so that I could order the result set using my SELECT TOP 100 PERCENT trick. As I've said, the row ordering isn't guaranteed when you use ORDER BY from inside a view, derived table, or function, but at least it's a start. In my initial tests, it *is* preserved when returned to the client, and that's better than no order at all.

Next, take a look at the special handling given the **T** column. **T** is a sorting placeholder. It allows us to force the totals row to the bottom of the listing. Here's how it works: We use GROUP BY...WITH ROLLUP to have SQL Server compute totals for the numeric columns in the listing. Next, we use a HAVING clause to filter out all the ROLLUP rows except the grand total. We then wrap the **T** column in a CASE expression so that it can detect when it's being grouped (i.e., the grand total is being computed). When it's being grouped, we return an asterisk; otherwise, we just return a space. The query's ORDER BY then includes T as the high-order sort key, regardless of the chosen sort order. Because an asterisk sorts after a space (ASCII 42 versus 32), this has the effect of forcing the totals row to the bottom of the listing while still allowing the user to specify a different sort order for the other rows.

Let's finish up by examining the CASE expression used to formulate the ORDER BY clause. It allows us to specify the default sort order as a parameter to the function. Notice that we converted all the columns to the same data type and left-padded the numeric columns with zeros. This is necessary because a CASE expression that involves multiple data types assumes the type with the highest precedence (see the Books Online topic, "Data Type Precedence"). In this case, the data type with the highest precedence is datetime (of the **Date-Created** column). Once the CASE expression has assumed a given data type, it evaluates the conditional expressions that make it up, and if it attempts to return a result that's incompatible with this chosen data type, you'll see a syntax or type conversion error. Here, for example, sorting on Name would have caused an error if datetime had not already been cast as a char type.

What the ORDER BY...CASE combo gives us is a flexible way to change the default order of a result set via a parameter to the routine without having to resort to dynamic T-SQL. I include it here for demonstration purposes only—it would be preferable just to supply the order you want using an ORDER BY clause when you query the function.

## Calling a Stored Procedure from a View

Although some DBMSs allow you to SELECT from a stored procedure as though it were a table, SQL Server doesn't. You can probably think of times when this ability would have been very handy. Using a stored procedure, you can do pretty much anything you want with respect to the data in your databases; having it accessible in an object you can query like a table would make it all the more useful.

There's no direct way to do this, but there is a workaround: You can call a stored procedure from a view. To do so, follow these steps:

1. Create a linked server entry on your server that refers back to itself. That is, on an instance named Foo, create a linked server entry whose **Data source** property references Foo. Here are the specific steps:

    a. Right-click the Linked Servers node under your server's Securities node and select New Linked Server.

    b. In the Linked Server Properties dialog, click the **Other data source** radio button and select the **Microsoft OLEDB Provider for SQL Server** entry manually because, by default, SQL Server tries to keep you from configuring a local server as a linked server.

    c. For clarity, supply a name in the **Linked server** entry box that indicates the server is a loopback server (I named mine "Loopback"). This will keep you from mistaking it for a remote server down the road.

    d. Set the new linked server's **Data source** property to your current server name and instance or to an alias you've created for it in the Client Network utility.

    **e.** Set the security information correctly on the Security tab (I usually skip the local-to-remote server login mappings and select the **Be made using the login's security context** option.

    **f.** Because your new linked server will be talking to a server that couldn't be any more like it—itself—check the first five check boxes on the **Server options** tab. This will make your linked server entry as compatible with itself as possible.

    **g.** Click OK to exit the dialog—your new linked server is defined.

2. Once the linked server entry is created, click the Tables node under the new linked server entry in Enterprise Manager. If the tables display in the right pane, you're ready to use the loopback connection. Behind the scenes, Enterprise Manager runs sp_tables_ex against a linked server to list its tables.

3. Create a view that uses your new linked server and the OPENQUERY() rowset function to execute the desired stored procedure. Listing 9–8 provides some sample code:

**Listing 9–8** You can use OPENQUERY() to call a stored procedure from a view.

```
USE Northwind
GO
DROP VIEW ViewActivity
GO
CREATE VIEW ViewActivity AS
SELECT * FROM OPENQUERY(Loopback,'EXEC dbo.sp_who')
GO
SELECT * FROM ViewActivity
```

(Results abridged)

| spid | ecid | status | loginame | hostname | blk |
|------|------|--------|----------|----------|-----|
| 1 | 0 | background | sa | | 0 |
| 2 | 0 | sleeping | sa | | 0 |
| 3 | 0 | background | sa | | 0 |
| 4 | 0 | background | sa | | 0 |
| 5 | 0 | background | sa | | 0 |
| 6 | 0 | background | sa | | 0 |
| 7 | 0 | sleeping | sa | | 0 |
| 8 | 0 | background | sa | | 0 |
| 9 | 0 | background | sa | | 0 |
| 10 | 0 | background | sa | | 0 |
| 11 | 0 | background | sa | | 0 |

| 12 | 0 | background | sa | | 0 |
| 51 | 0 | sleeping | HENDERSON\khen | KHEN | 0 |
| 52 | 0 | sleeping | HENDERSON\khen | KHEN | 0 |

**NOTE:** You could use OPENROWSET() here instead of OPENQUERY(). This would alleviate the need for the loopback linked server, but would necessitate that you hard-code connection info into your T-SQL—a very poor practice, to say the least. Hard-wiring connection specifics into your code means that the code will break if that connection info ever changes. For example, if you use a regular SQL Server login account to connect to the server and you hard code its password into your T-SQL, not only are you creating the possibility that someone might discover the password who shouldn't, but you're also virtually guaranteeing that that code will break in the future. How many passwords never need changed? OPENQUERY() is the preferred tool because it uses SQL Server's answer to the problem of hard-coded passwords and system security. With a linked server definition, SQL Server stores this info in system tables and provides a graphical tool (Enterprise Manager) to edit it.

One of the many drawbacks to this approach is that there's no way to send parameters to the stored procedure. The query string in the OPENQUERY() call must be a string literal; it cannot be a variable. Another drawback has to do with distributed transactions. Because we're circumventing SQL Server's own mechanisms for managing distributed transactions, we run the risk of causing deadlocks or resource issues on the server because we are using it in ways it was not intended to be used. That said, the ability to call a stored procedure from a view is a powerful feature and should not be completely ruled out. If you run into a situation where you absolutely have to be able to query a stored procedure in the same way that you'd query a table, this is a good technique to know about.

Note that you can extend this technique to uses outside of views. For example, because OPENQUERY() returns a rowset, you can open a cursor against it, like this (Listing 9–9):

**Listing 9–9** You can extend the OPENQUERY() technique to create cursors on stored procedures.

```
USE Northwind
GO
DECLARE c CURSOR FOR
SELECT * FROM OPENQUERY(Loopback, 'EXEC dbo.sp_who')

OPEN c
```

```
FETCH c
WHILE @@FETCH_STATUS=0 BEGIN
  FETCH c
END
CLOSE c
DEALLOCATE c
```

(Results abridged)

```
spid   ecid   status       loginame
------ ------ ------------ --------------
11     0      background   sa


spid   ecid   status       loginame
------ ------ ------------ --------------
12     0      background   sa


spid   ecid   status       loginame
------ ------ ------------ --------------
51     0      sleeping     HENDERSON\KHEN


spid   ecid   status       loginame
------ ------ ------------ --------------
52     0      sleeping     HENDERSON\KHEN


spid   ecid   status       loginame
------ ------ ------------ --------------
53     0      sleeping     HENDERSON\KHEN


spid   ecid   status       loginame
------ ------ ------------ --------------
54     0      runnable     HENDERSON\KHEN


spid   ecid   status       loginame
------ ------ ------------ --------------
55     0      runnable     HENDERSON\KHEN
```

# Updatable Views

As mentioned earlier, there are a number of factors that affect whether a view without an INSTEAD OF trigger is updatable. Because you control how updates occur with views that have INSTEAD OF triggers, these restrictions don't apply to them. Otherwise, for a view to allow updates, the following criteria must be met:

- Aggregate functions, the TOP, GROUP BY, UNION, or DISTINCT clauses/keywords, are not allowed.
- Derived columns (columns constructed from complex expressions) cannot be updated.
- SELECT lists consisting entirely of nontabular expressions are not allowed.

Again, the bottom line is that the server must be able to translate an update to a row in the view into an update to a row in a base table. If it can't do this, you can't update the view.

## The WITH CHECK OPTION Clause

An updatable view can be created so that it checks updates for compliance with its WHERE clause, if it has one. This prevents rows added via the view from "vanishing" when the view is requeried because they don't meet its selection criteria. To set up a view this way, use the WITH CHECK OPTION clause when you create it (Listing 9–10):

**Listing 9–10** WITH CHECK OPTION controls the type of data a view will accept.

```
CREATE VIEW CALIFORNIA_AUTHORS AS
SELECT *
FROM authors
WHERE State='CA'
WITH CHECK OPTION
```

This particular example ensures that any author that's added via the view resides in California. For example, the statement in Listing 9–11 fails because of WITH CHECK OPTION:

**Listing 9–11** WITH CHECK OPTION refuses rows that fall outside the view's filter criteria.

```
INSERT CALIFORNIA_AUTHORS
VALUES ('867-53-09EI','Henderson','Ken',
```

```
'972 555-1212','57 Riverside','Dallas','TX','75080',1)

Server: Msg 550, Level 16, State 1, Line 1
The attempted insert or update failed because the target view either
specifies WITH CHECK OPTION or spans a view that specifies WITH CHECK
OPTION and one or more rows resulting from the operation did not qualify
under the CHECK OPTION constraint.
The statement has been terminated.
```

This also applies to updates. If an update you make through a view that has WITH CHECK OPTION enabled would cause the row to fail the view's WHERE criteria, the update will be rejected.

# Derived Tables

Derived tables are SELECT statements that you embed within the FROM clause of other SELECTs in place of table references. I include coverage of them here for completeness and because they resemble implicit or automatic views. Derived tables make certain types of queries possible that previously required separate view objects. Listing 9–12 presents an example:

**Listing 9–12** A derived table can be used in many instances when you'd use a temporary view.

```
CREATE TABLE #1996_POP_ESTIMATE (Region char(7), State char(2), Population int)

INSERT #1996_POP_ESTIMATE VALUES ('West',    'CA',31878234)
INSERT #1996_POP_ESTIMATE VALUES ('South',   'TX',19128261)
INSERT #1996_POP_ESTIMATE VALUES ('North',   'NY',18184774)
INSERT #1996_POP_ESTIMATE VALUES ('South',   'FL',14399985)
INSERT #1996_POP_ESTIMATE VALUES ('North',   'NJ', 7987933)
INSERT #1996_POP_ESTIMATE VALUES ('East',    'NC', 7322870)
INSERT #1996_POP_ESTIMATE VALUES ('West',    'WA', 5532939)
INSERT #1996_POP_ESTIMATE VALUES ('Central','MO', 5358692)
INSERT #1996_POP_ESTIMATE VALUES ('East',    'MD', 5071604)
INSERT #1996_POP_ESTIMATE VALUES ('Central','OK', 3300902)

SELECT * FROM (SELECT TOP 5 WITH TIES State,
         Region, Population=Population/1000000
       FROM #1996_POP_ESTIMATE
       ORDER BY Population/1000000) p
```

```
ORDER BY Population DESC

State Region Population
----- ------- -----------
NJ    North   7
NC    East    7
WA    West    5
MO    Central 5
MD    East    5
OK    Central 3
```

This query uses a derived table to return the five states with the lowest population among those listed in the table. It then uses the ORDER BY in the outer SELECT to sort them in descending order. Were it not for derived table support, this approach would require a separate stand-alone view or a temporary table.

One subtlety worth mentioning here is the requirement of a table alias when using derived tables. Note the inclusion of the table alias in Listing 9–12 even though it's not used. This is a requirement of derived tables, regardless of whether your code actually uses the alias.

# Parameterized Views

On SQL Server, an inline table-valued function is as close as you can get to a parameterized view. Like a view, an inline function doesn't have a body. It consists of a SELECT statement only. Of course, the SELECT may include unions and complex joins, but regardless it's still just a single SELECT. What an inline table gives you is a way to pass parameters into the SELECT. That is, instead of having to construct a WHERE clause every time you want to filter the view, with an inline function, you just pass in parameters. This is syntactically more concise and less error prone, and it gives you greater control over the query plan that will be produced. Oftentimes, when applying complex filter criteria in a SELECT that accesses a view that has its *own* complex filter criteria, you simply have to cross your fingers and pray that you'll get a good query plan—you're at the mercy of the optimizer. With an inline function, the filter conditions are applied in exactly one place. You can control how and where this happens. Listing 9–13 demonstrates an inline UDF playing the role of a parameterized view:

**Listing 9–13** An inline function can play the role of a parameterized function.

```
CREATE FUNCTION dbo.ContactCustomersv (@CompanyName nvarchar(80),
@ContactName nvarchar(60))
RETURNS TABLE
AS
RETURN(SELECT * FROM dbo.Customers
        WHERE
         CASE
        WHEN @CompanyName IS NULL AND @ContactName IS NOT NULL THEN ContactName
        WHEN @ContactName IS NULL AND @CompanyName IS NOT NULL THEN CompanyName
        ELSE '%'
        END LIKE COALESCE(@CompanyName, @ContactName, '%')
)
GO
SELECT * FROM dbo.ContactCustomersv(DEFAULT,'Ale%')
```

(Results abridged)

| CustomerID | CompanyName | ContactName | ContactTitle |
| --- | --- | --- | --- |
| MORGK | Morgenstern Gesundkost | Alexander Feuer | Marketing Assistant |
| ROMEY | Romero y tomillo | Alejandra Camino | Accounting Manager |

Because we can pass parameters into the function, we can essentially combine two queries into one. The function filters on different columns based on what parameters are passed in to it. Although this sort of "hoop-jumping" isn't necessarily conducive to an efficient query plan being generated, it does demonstrate the notion that an inline function playing the role of a parameterized view can do things a regular view could never do.

## Dynamic Views

When you access a view, a query plan is constructed by combining the original SELECT statement that was used to create the view with the one you're using to query it. Normally, the selection criteria you specified when you built the view are combined with any specified by your query, and the composite is passed on to the server engine for further processing.

Most views that include selection criteria impose static (or deterministic) criteria—the selection logic that's combined with the SELECT statement accessing the view never changes, regardless of how many times the view is queried.

The dynamic portion of the composite query usually comes from the user-supplied SELECT, not the view. With the exception of views that use joins to link other views and tables, the criteria the view supplies to filter the result set remains the same from use to use. Most of the time this is adequate, but there are times when it's handy to be able to set up a dynamic (or nondeterministic) view—a view with selection criteria that vary based on factors external to it.

A dynamic view is simply one with selection criteria that can change based on the evaluation of the expressions in its WHERE or HAVING clauses. This is an easy concept that can come in quite handy. Rather than evaluating to constants, these expressions are nondeterministic: they return different values from execution to execution, based on environmental or session conditions. The best example of such a view is one that returns a result set based on a nontabular expression. Listing 9–14 presents one that lists the sales for the current date using the nontabular GETDATE() function:

**Listing 9–14** A dynamic query allows you to use nondeterminism to your advantage.

```
CREATE VIEW DAILY_SALES AS
SELECT *
FROM sales
WHERE ord_date BETWEEN CONVERT(char(8),GETDATE(),112) AND
CONVERT(char(8),GETDATE(),112)+' 23:59:59.999'
```

You can add some rows to **sales** to see how this works:

```
INSERT sales
VALUES ('8042','QA879.1',GETDATE(),30,'Net 30','BU1032')
INSERT sales
VALUES ('6380','D4482',GETDATE(),11,'Net 60','PS2091')
INSERT sales
VALUES ('6380','D4492',GETDATE()+1,53,'Net 30','PS2091')

SELECT * FROM DAILY_SALES
```

| stor_id | ord_num | ord_date | qty | payterms | title_id |
|---------|---------|----------|-----|----------|----------|
| 6380 | D4482 | 1999-06-24 19:14:33.657 | 30 | Net 60 | PS2091 |
| 8042 | QA879.1 | 1999-06-24 19:13:26.230 | 30 | Net 30 | BU1032 |

This view uses GETDATE() to limit the sales returned to those whose ord_date is today. The criteria actually processed by the server will vary based on the current date. Today, its WHERE clause will be expanded to today's date and the first two rows that were inserted will show up. Tomorrow, it will evaluate to tomorrow's date and the third row will show up. This is the nature of dynamic views: The criteria that are actually processed by the server change from use to use based on external factors.

Here's another example that uses CASE to make the view even more dynamic. This code improves on the previous example by making it aware of weekends. Because no sales occur on weekends, this code returns the sales for either the previous Friday or the upcoming Monday when the current date falls on a weekend (Listing 9–15):

**Listing 9–15** A dynamic view that uses a nondeterministic function and CASE.

```
CREATE VIEW DAILY_SALES AS
SELECT *
FROM sales
WHERE ord_date BETWEEN
                (CASE DATEPART(DW,CONVERT(char(8),GETDATE(),112))
            WHEN 1 THEN CONVERT(char(8),GETDATE()+1,112)
            WHEN 7 THEN CONVERT(char(8),GETDATE()-1,112)
            ELSE CONVERT(char(8),GETDATE(),112)
            END)
AND              (CASE DATEPART(DW,CONVERT(char(8),GETDATE(),112))
            WHEN 1 THEN CONVERT(char(8),GETDATE()+1,112)
            WHEN 7 THEN CONVERT(char(8),GETDATE()-1,112)
            ELSE CONVERT(char(8),GETDATE(),112)
            END+' 23:59:59.999')
```

You can use other nontabular functions to create similar sliding or dynamic views. For example, SUSER_SNAME() could be used to limit the rows returned according to user name. HOST_NAME() could be used to filter based on machine name. Whatever the case, the SELECT statement used to query the view doesn't change (in the previous examples, it's always a simple SELECT *); only the criteria that the view provides to filter the result set do.

# Partitioned Views

**NOTE:** As of this writing (December 2000), SQL Server 2000 produces inefficient execution plans for some of the queries presented in this section. SQL Server 7.0, by contrast, produces good plans with nearly all the examples.

Microsoft has been alerted to the problem and promises a fix in SQL Server 2000, Service Pack 1, which is due sometime in the spring of 2001. I demonstrate both types of plans on the assumption that the inefficient plans currently produced by SQL Server 2000 are the result of bugs that you may encounter yourself. If you run into one of these, you may want to check with Microsoft to see whether a patch or service pack has been released that addresses the issue.

Simply put, a partitioned view is a view that unions tables together that serve as partitions (or sections) of a larger set of data. For example, a partitioned view over the activity on a Web site might union together separate tables for each month of the year. Each of these tables would store the activity data for a particular month. By unioning them together, the partitioned view would allow them to be treated as a single table while still keeping their sizes manageable.

There are two types of partitioned views: local partitioned views (LPVs) and distributed partitioned views (DPVs). An LPV is one in which all the underlying tables reside on the same SQL Server instance. A DPV is one in which they live on separate instances. These instances don't have to be on different machines, but usually are. Spreading a DPV across multiple machines helps "scale out" large SQL Server implementations. It can effectively bring the processing power and resources of many machines together to process a single query.

A partitioned view is a normal view object that unions together tables with certain attributes. It is characterized by tables with the same structure being combined to provide a unified view of a set of data, but that are segmented on a clearly defined "partitioning column." This partitioning column is set up using a CHECK constraint. In addition to doing what CHECK constraints always do—namely, controlling the type of data a column will accept—the partitioning column of a local or distributed partitioned view provides a means for the SQL Server query optimizer to be able to determine in which partition a given column value resides as it creates a query plan. This allows it to eliminate searches for the other partitions from the query plan when optimizing a query that includes the partitioning column. This is best understood by way of example (Listing 9–16):

**Listing 9–16** A basic partitioned view.

```
CREATE TABLE CustomersUS (
      CustomerID nchar (5) NOT NULL,
      CompanyName nvarchar (40) NOT NULL ,
      ContactName nvarchar (30) NULL ,
```

```
        ContactTitle nvarchar (30) NULL ,
        Address nvarchar (60) NULL ,
        City nvarchar (15) NULL ,
        Region nvarchar (15) NULL ,
        PostalCode nvarchar (10) NULL ,
        Country nvarchar (15) NOT NULL CHECK (Country='US'),
        Phone nvarchar (24) NULL ,
        Fax nvarchar (24) NULL,
 CONSTRAINT PK_CustUS PRIMARY KEY (Country, CustomerID)
)

CREATE TABLE CustomersUK (
        CustomerID nchar (5) NOT NULL,
        CompanyName nvarchar (40) NOT NULL ,
        ContactName nvarchar (30) NULL ,
        ContactTitle nvarchar (30) NULL ,
        Address nvarchar (60) NULL ,
        City nvarchar (15) NULL ,
        Region nvarchar (15) NULL ,
        PostalCode nvarchar (10) NULL ,
        Country nvarchar (15) NOT NULL CHECK (Country='UK'),
        Phone nvarchar (24) NULL ,
        Fax nvarchar (24) NULL,
CONSTRAINT PK_CustUK PRIMARY KEY (Country, CustomerID)
)

CREATE TABLE CustomersFrance (
        CustomerID nchar (5) NOT NULL,
        CompanyName nvarchar (40) NOT NULL ,
        ContactName nvarchar (30) NULL ,
        ContactTitle nvarchar (30) NULL ,
        Address nvarchar (60) NULL ,
        City nvarchar (15) NULL ,
        Region nvarchar (15) NULL ,
        PostalCode nvarchar (10) NULL ,
        Country nvarchar (15) NOT NULL CHECK (Country='France'),
        Phone nvarchar (24) NULL ,
        Fax nvarchar (24) NULL,
CONSTRAINT PK_CustFR PRIMARY KEY (Country, CustomerID)
)

GO

DROP VIEW CustomersV
GO
```

```
CREATE VIEW CustomersV
AS
SELECT * FROM dbo.CustomersUS
UNION ALL
SELECT * FROM dbo.CustomersUK
UNION ALL
SELECT * FROM dbo.CustomersFrance
GO
```

As you can see, we create three tables to store partitions, or slices, of a customer table. We then union those tables back together using a partitioned view. What's the point? Why not store the data as a single table? There are two advantages to this approach: One, by segmenting the customer data, we keep the tables more manageable—the individual partitions will be a fraction of the size of the entire customer table; two, SQL Server's query optimizer can recognize partitioned views and automatically determine the right underlying table to query based on the filter criteria and the CHECK constraint on the partitioning column. For example, have a look at the execution plan of the following query:

```
SELECT * FROM dbo.Customersv WHERE Country='US'
```

(Results abridged)

```
StmtText
-------------------------------------------------------------------------
  SELECT CompanyName=CompanyName FROM dbo.CustomersV WHERE Country=@1
    |--Compute Scalar(DEFINE:(CustomersUS.CompanyName=CustomersUS.CompanyName))
    |--Clustered Index Scan(OBJECT:(Northwind.dbo.CustomersUS.PK_Cust))
```

Even though we reference the view in our query, the optimizer figures out that the data we're requesting could only reside in one of the view's underlying tables, so it queries that table directly and omits the others from the query plan. It uses the WHERE clause criteria and the partitioning column in each table (its primary key) to make this determination.

There are a number of requirements that a view and its base tables must meet in order for it to be a partitioned view in the first place and for the optimizer to be able to optimize queries against it in this way. The number and significance of these requirements have, in fact, discouraged many users from taking advantage of partitioned views, especially LPVs. Whether you use them is a judgment call you'll have to make. You can read up on the requirements and limitations associated with partitioned views in the Books Online. Regarding the optimizer's ability to use the partitioning column to identify the correct base table to search for data, it's been my experience that the partitioning column should be the leftmost in the primary key. This bears further examination. Consider this partitioned view and query (Listing 9–17):

**Listing 9–17** A partitioning column/primary key mismatch.

```
CREATE TABLE Orders1996 (
        OrderID int PRIMARY KEY NOT NULL ,
        CustomerID nchar (5) NULL ,
        EmployeeID int NULL ,
        OrderDate datetime NOT NULL CHECK (Year(OrderDate)=1996),
        OrderYear int NOT NULL CHECK (OrderYear=1996),
        RequiredDate datetime NULL ,
        ShippedDate datetime NULL ,
        ShipVia int NULL
)
GO


CREATE TABLE Orders1997 (
        OrderID int PRIMARY KEY NOT NULL ,
        CustomerID nchar (5) NULL ,
        EmployeeID int NULL ,
        OrderDate datetime NOT NULL CHECK (Year(OrderDate)=1997),
        OrderYear int NOT NULL CHECK (OrderYear=1997),
        RequiredDate datetime NULL ,
        ShippedDate datetime NULL ,
        ShipVia int NULL
)
GO


CREATE TABLE Orders1998 (
        OrderID int PRIMARY KEY NOT NULL ,
        CustomerID nchar (5) NULL ,
        EmployeeID int NULL ,
        OrderDate datetime NOT NULL CHECK (Year(OrderDate)=1998),
        OrderYear int NOT NULL CHECK (OrderYear=1998),
        RequiredDate datetime NULL ,
        ShippedDate datetime NULL ,
        ShipVia int NULL
)
GO
```

```
CREATE VIEW OrdersV
AS
SELECT * FROM Orders1996
UNION ALL
SELECT * FROM Orders1997
UNION ALL
SELECT * FROM Orders1998
GO

SELECT * FROM OrdersV WHERE OrderYear=1997
```

Will the optimizer be able to narrow its search to just the Orders1997 partition? Let's look at the execution plan:

(Results abridged)

```
--------------------------------------------------------------------------
SELECT * FROM OrdersV WHERE OrderYear=@1
 |--Concatenation
  |--Filter(WHERE:(STARTUP EXPR(Convert(@1)=1996)))
  |  |--Clustered Index Scan(OBJECT:(master.dbo.Orders1996.PK__O1996), WHERE
  |--Filter(WHERE:(STARTUP EXPR(Convert(@1)=1997)))
  |  |--Clustered Index Scan(OBJECT:(master.dbo.Orders1997.PK__O1997), WHERE
  |--Filter(WHERE:(STARTUP EXPR(Convert(@1)=1998)))
    |--Clustered Index Scan(OBJECT:(master.dbo.Orders1998.PK__O1998), WHERE
```

Even though we're only querying data from one of the partitions, the query plan includes searches for all three of them. Why is that? Because the partitioning column is not part of each table's primary key. Let's add the partitioning column to the primary key and see if that makes any difference (Listing 9–18):

**Listing 9–18** A partitioned view/query combo that yields an inefficient query plan.

```
CREATE TABLE Orders1996 (
        OrderID int NOT NULL ,
        CustomerID nchar (5) NULL ,
        EmployeeID int NULL ,
        OrderDate datetime NOT NULL CHECK (Year(OrderDate)=1996),
         OrderYear int NOT NULL DEFAULT 1996 CHECK (OrderYear=1996),
        RequiredDate datetime NULL ,
        ShippedDate datetime NULL ,
```

```
        ShipVia int NULL,
        CONSTRAINT PK_Orders1996
        PRIMARY KEY (OrderYear, OrderID)
)
GO

CREATE TABLE Orders1997 (
        OrderID int NOT NULL ,
        CustomerID nchar (5) NULL ,
        EmployeeID int NULL ,
        OrderDate datetime NOT NULL CHECK (Year(OrderDate)=1997),
         OrderYear int NOT NULL DEFAULT 1997 CHECK (OrderYear=1997),
        RequiredDate datetime NULL ,
        ShippedDate datetime NULL ,
        ShipVia int NULL,
        CONSTRAINT PK_Orders1997
        PRIMARY KEY (OrderYear, OrderID)
)
GO

CREATE TABLE Orders1998 (
        OrderID int NOT NULL ,
        CustomerID nchar (5) NULL ,
        EmployeeID int NULL ,
        OrderDate datetime NOT NULL CHECK (Year(OrderDate)=1998),
        OrderYear int NOT NULL DEFAULT 1998 CHECK (OrderYear=1998),
        RequiredDate datetime NULL ,
        ShippedDate datetime NULL ,
        ShipVia int NULL,
        CONSTRAINT PK_Orders1998
        PRIMARY KEY (OrderYear, OrderID)
)
GO

CREATE VIEW OrdersV
AS
SELECT * FROM Orders1996
UNION ALL
SELECT * FROM Orders1997
UNION ALL
SELECT * FROM Orders1998
GO

SELECT * FROM OrdersV WHERE OrderYear=1997
```

(Results abridged)

```
-------------------------------------------------------------------
SELECT * FROM OrdersV WHERE OrderYear=@1
 |--Concatenation
 |--Filter(WHERE:(STARTUP EXPR(Convert(@1)=1996)))
 |  |--Clustered Index Scan(OBJECT:(master.dbo.Orders1996.PK__O1996), WHERE
 |--Filter(WHERE:(STARTUP EXPR(Convert(@1)=1997)))
 |  |--Clustered Index Scan(OBJECT:(master.dbo.Orders1997.PK__O1997), WHERE
 |--Filter(WHERE:(STARTUP EXPR(Convert(@1)=1998)))
    |--Clustered Index Scan(OBJECT:(master.dbo.Orders1998.PK__O1998), WHERE
```

Once again, the plan includes all three base tables. Why? We've met the requirement of having the partitioning column be part of the primary key, correct? The reason we're still getting an inefficient execution plan for this particular query is that, contrary to what logic might suggest, we need to include all the columns from the primary key in the query's filter criteria. Here's a revision that does this and its resultant execution plan (Listing 9–19):

**Listing 9–19** Matching up the partitioning column and primary key solves the problem.

```
SELECT * FROM OrdersV WHERE OrderYear=1997 AND OrderID=1000
```

(Results abridged)

```
StmtText
-----------------------------------------------------------------------
SELECT * FROM OrdersV WHERE OrderYear=@1 AND OrderID=@2
|-Compute Scalar(DEFINE:(Orders1997.OrderID=Orders1997.OrderID, Orders1997.Cust
  |-Clustered Index Scan(OBJECT:(Northwind.dbo.Orders1997.PK_Orders1997),
```

Now we get an efficient query plan. Not only is the partitioning column included in its host table's primary key, but all the columns in the primary key are included in the query's search criteria. In this case, merely matching query columns to primary key columns left to right wasn't enough. The query had to include *all* the columns in the primary key or the optimizer produced an inefficient plan. Listing 9–20 is a variation on our partitioned view and query that demonstrates the same quirk:

**Listing 9–20** Adding a column to the primary key again yields a poor plan.

```
CREATE TABLE Orders1996 (
        OrderID int NOT NULL ,
        CustomerID nchar (5) NOT NULL ,
        EmployeeID int NULL ,
        OrderDate datetime NOT NULL CHECK (Year(OrderDate)=1996),
        OrderYear int NOT NULL DEFAULT 1996 CHECK (OrderYear=1996),
        RequiredDate datetime NULL ,
        ShippedDate datetime NULL ,
        ShipVia int NULL,
        CONSTRAINT PK_Orders1996
        PRIMARY KEY (OrderYear, OrderID, CustomerId)
)
GO


CREATE TABLE Orders1997 (
        OrderID int NOT NULL ,
        CustomerID nchar (5) NOT NULL ,
        EmployeeID int NULL ,
        OrderDate datetime NOT NULL CHECK (Year(OrderDate)=1997),
        OrderYear int NOT NULL DEFAULT 1997 CHECK (OrderYear=1997),
        RequiredDate datetime NULL ,
        ShippedDate datetime NULL ,
        ShipVia int NULL,
        CONSTRAINT PK_Orders1997
        PRIMARY KEY (OrderYear, OrderID, CustomerId)
)
GO


CREATE TABLE Orders1998 (
        OrderID int NOT NULL ,
        CustomerID nchar (5) NOT NULL ,
        EmployeeID int NULL ,
        OrderDate datetime NOT NULL CHECK (Year(OrderDate)=1998),
        OrderYear int NOT NULL DEFAULT 1998 CHECK (OrderYear=1998),
        RequiredDate datetime NULL ,
        ShippedDate datetime NULL ,
        ShipVia int NULL,
        CONSTRAINT PK_Orders1998
        PRIMARY KEY (OrderYear, OrderID, CustomerId)
)
GO
```

```
CREATE VIEW OrdersV
AS
SELECT * FROM Orders1996
UNION ALL
SELECT * FROM Orders1997
UNION ALL
SELECT * FROM Orders1998
GO

SELECT * FROM OrdersV WHERE OrderYear=1997 AND OrderID=1000
```

(Results abridged)

```
-------------------------------------------------------------------------
SELECT * FROM OrdersV WHERE OrderYear=@1
 |--Concatenation
 |--Filter(WHERE:(STARTUP EXPR(Convert(@1)=1996)))
 | |--Clustered Index Scan(OBJECT:(master.dbo.Orders1996.PK__O1996), WHERE
 |--Filter(WHERE:(STARTUP EXPR(Convert(@1)=1997)))
 | |--Clustered Index Scan(OBJECT:(master.dbo.Orders1997.PK__O1997), WHERE
 |--Filter(WHERE:(STARTUP EXPR(Convert(@1)=1998)))
    |--Clustered Index Scan(OBJECT:(master.dbo.Orders1998.PK__O1998), WHERE
```

Here, we've added the **CustomerID** column to each partition's primary key, but we haven't changed the query to include this new column in its search criteria. The result is an inefficient query plan once again. Let's see what happens when we add CustomerID to the query's search criteria (Listing 9–21):

**Listing 9–21** Adding CustomerID to the search criteria remedies the problem.

```
SELECT * FROM OrdersV
WHERE OrderYear=1997 AND OrderID=1000 AND CustomerID = 'AAAAA'
StmtText
-------------------------------------------------------------------------
SELECT * FROM OrdersV WHERE OrderYear=@1 AND OrderID=@2 AND CustomerID=@3
 |-Compute Scalar(DEFINE:(Orders1997.OrderID=Orders1997.OrderID, Orders1997.Cus
  |-Clustered Index Scan(OBJECT:(Northwind.dbo.Orders1997.PK_Orders1997), WHERE
```

Once again, we're getting an optimal plan because we've matched the query criteria with the primary key columns of the partitioned view one to one. In this case, we achieved an optimal plan by adding columns to the search criteria. We could just as easily have removed columns from the primary key of each partition.

As the very first example in this section illustrated, it's not a requirement that you must always filter by the entire primary key to get an efficient execution plan when querying a partitioned view. Just be aware that this is sometimes the workaround when you're getting a bad plan with a partitioned view query.

## BETWEEN and Partitioned View Queries

In addition to the primary key-partition column relationship, another thing to watch out for with partitioned views is the use of theta (nonequality) operators. Even if the operators in the partitioning CHECK constraint and the query match exactly, the optimizer may be unable to identify the partition correctly to search when theta operators are used. This means that it may have to search all partitions and concatenate the results. For example, consider the partitioned view and query in Listing 9–22:

**Listing 9–22** Another problematic partitioned view/query combo.

```
CREATE TABLE CustomersUS (
        CustomerID nchar (5) NOT NULL,
        CompanyName nvarchar (40) NOT NULL ,
        ContactName nvarchar (30) NULL ,
        ContactTitle nvarchar (30) NULL ,
        Address nvarchar (60) NULL ,
        City nvarchar (15) NULL ,
        Region nvarchar (15) NULL ,
        PostalCode nvarchar (10) NULL ,
        Country nvarchar (15) NOT NULL CHECK (Country='US'),
        Phone nvarchar (24) NULL ,
        Fax nvarchar (24) NULL,
PRIMARY KEY (Country, CustomerID)
)

CREATE TABLE CustomersUK (
        CustomerID nchar (5) NOT NULL,
        CompanyName nvarchar (40) NOT NULL ,
        ContactName nvarchar (30) NULL ,
        ContactTitle nvarchar (30) NULL ,
        Address nvarchar (60) NULL ,
        City nvarchar (15) NULL ,
        Region nvarchar (15) NULL ,
        PostalCode nvarchar (10) NULL ,
        Country nvarchar (15) NOT NULL CHECK (Country='UK'),
        Phone nvarchar (24) NULL ,
```

```
        Fax nvarchar (24) NULL,
PRIMARY KEY (Country, CustomerID)
)

CREATE TABLE CustomersFrance (
        CustomerID nchar (5) NOT NULL,
        CompanyName nvarchar (40) NOT NULL ,
        ContactName nvarchar (30) NULL ,
        ContactTitle nvarchar (30) NULL ,
        Address nvarchar (60) NULL ,
        City nvarchar (15) NULL ,
        Region nvarchar (15) NULL ,
        PostalCode nvarchar (10) NULL ,
        Country nvarchar (15) NOT NULL CHECK (Country='France'),
        Phone nvarchar (24) NULL ,
        Fax nvarchar (24) NULL,
PRIMARY KEY (Country, CustomerID)
)

GO

DROP VIEW CustomersV
GO
CREATE VIEW CustomersV
AS
SELECT * FROM dbo.CustomersUS
UNION ALL
SELECT * FROM dbo.CustomersUK
UNION ALL
SELECT * FROM dbo.CustomersFrance
GO

SELECT * FROM dbo.CustomersV WHERE Country BETWEEN 'UK' AND 'US'
```

Even though the view's partitioning column is each underlying table's primary key, and even though the query filter criteria and the partitioning CHECK constraint match exactly, here's the execution plan we get:

(Results abridged)

```
StmtText
-------------------------------------------------------------------------
SELECT * FROM dbo.CustomersV WHERE Country>=@1 AND Country<=@2
```

```
|-Concatenation
 |-Filter(WHERE:(STARTUP EXPR(Convert(@1)<='US' AND Convert(@2)>='UK')))
  |-Clustered Index Seek(OBJECT:(Northwind.dbo.CustomersUKUS.PK__CustomersUKUS
 |-Filter(WHERE:(STARTUP EXPR(Convert(@1)<='France' AND Convert(@2)>='France')
  |-Clustered Index Seek(OBJECT:(Northwind.dbo.CustomersFrance.PK_CustomersFra
```

The CustomersFrance base table is being searched even though it's not logically possible that CustomersFrance contains the data we're seeking.

The issue isn't the range of data we're seeking, it's the BETWEEN operator itself and the way that the optimizer optimizes it. Even though the optimizer should be able to determine that the partition values in the CustomersUKUS and CustomersFrance base tables cannot overlap by inspecting their CHECK constraints, it appears to fail in doing so. It searches the CustomersFrance base table for values that logically fall outside those allowed by its CHECK constraint. Listing 9–23 presents a variation on the query that further establishes that the problem has to do with how the optimizer handles the BETWEEN operator in the query itself:

**Listing 9–23** Even when searching for a single value, the presence of BETWEEN is giving us grief.

```
SELECT * FROM dbo.CustomersV WHERE Country BETWEEN 'UK' AND 'UK'
```

(Results abridged)

```
StmtText
---------------------------------------------------------------------------
SELECT * FROM dbo.CustomersV WHERE Country>=@1 AND Country<=@2
 |-Concatenation
  |-Filter(WHERE:(STARTUP EXPR(Convert(@1)<='US' AND Convert(@2)>='UK')))
   |-Clustered Index Seek(OBJECT:(Northwind.dbo.CustomersUKUS.PK__CustomersUKUS
  |-Filter(WHERE:(STARTUP EXPR(Convert(@1)<='France' AND Convert(@2)>='France')
   |-Clustered Index Seek(OBJECT:(Northwind.dbo.CustomersFrance.PK_CustomersFra
```

Here we've changed the query to specify the same value for both terms of the BETWEEN operator. Notice that the query plan is the same as in the earlier query. Why is this? The cause of this is right in front of us. Look at the first line of the query plan (in bold type). The reason the optimizer fails to find the most efficient plan even though simple logic indicates that it should be possible has to do with the way in which the BETWEEN operator is optimized. Early in the optimization process, **Column BETWEEN @1 AND @2** is translated to **Column >= @1 AND Column <= @2**, a compound expression. Later, the optimizer searches for the terms of the compound expression separately and concatenates them. This optimization allows other types of theta operators (e.g., <>, !>, LIKE) to be serviced with indexes, so it's normally a good thing. In this case, it causes a table to be searched that shouldn't be, so it's something to be aware of. When you write code that will query a partitioned view, keep this in mind. If your intent is to avoid touching any more partitions than absolutely necessary, don't use theta operators.

Note that the issue isn't one of search argument (SARG) identification. Both branches of the compound plan use index seeks to locate their data. The problem is one of timing: It relates to when the transformations occur that enable certain normally "non-SARG-able" expressions to be searched. Obviously, they occur early enough in the optimization process that they can negatively affect later phases of the process when partitioned views are involved. Here's the query changed to use an equality test (Listing 9–24):

**Listing 9–24** Switching to an equality test fixes the problem.

```
SELECT * FROM dbo.CustomersV WHERE Country='US'
StmtText
----------------------------------------------------------------------------
SELECT * FROM dbo.CustomersV WHERE Country=@1
  |-Compute Scalar(DEFINE:(CustomersUKUS.CustomerID=CustomersUKUS.CustomerID, Cu
    |-Clustered Index Seek(OBJECT:(Northwind.dbo.CustomersUKUS.PK__CustomersUKUS)
```

Even though we continue to use a BETWEEN operator in the CHECK constraint of the CustomersUKUS base table, the query itself uses an equality test, so we get an efficient plan from the optimizer.

### Distributed Partitioned Views

A distributed partitioned view is a partitioned view with base tables that are scattered across a federation (a group) of autonomous servers. These remote base tables are accessed via linked server definitions. To set up a distributed partitioned view, follow these steps:

1.  Create linked server definitions for the servers on which the remote tables you want to access reside.

2. Enable the **lazy schema validation** server option for each linked server. This option cannot be set using the Linked Server Properties dialog in Enterprise Manager, so you must use sp_serveroption.

3. Create a partitioned view that references the remote partitions using four part names.

4. Repeat these steps on each of the linked servers referenced by the partitioned view. Doing this will allow you to load balance your SQL Server environment by routing users to different versions of the same view.

Here's our earlier partitioned view converted to a distributed partitioned view (Listing 9–25):

**Listing 9–25** A distributed partitioned view in the wild.

```
CREATE VIEW OrdersV
AS
SELECT * FROM Orders1996
UNION ALL
SELECT * FROM HOMER.Northwind.dbo.Orders1997
UNION ALL
SELECT * FROM MARGE.Northwind.dbo.Orders1998
GO
SELECT CustomerID FROM OrdersV WHERE OrderYear=1997 AND OrderID=1000
StmtText
---------------------------------------------------------------------
SELECT CustomerID=CustomerID FROM OrdersV WHERE OrderYear=@1 AND OrderID=@2
  |-Compute Scalar(DEFINE:(HOMER.Northwind.dbo.Orders1997.CustomerID=HOMER.nort
    |-Remote Query(SOURCE:(HOMER),QUERY:(SELECT Col1024 FROM (SELECT Tbl1003.
      "OrderID" Col1023,Tbl1003."CustomerID" Col1024,Tbl1003."OrderYear" Col1027
      FROM "northwind"."dbo"."Orders1997" Tbl1003) Qry1031 WHERE Col1023=(1000)))
```

As you can see, given that we've properly matched up the query's filter criteria with the partitioned view's primary key, the optimizer correctly focuses the search on just one of the partitions. Because that partition resides on a linked server, the optimizer adds a Remote Query step to the plan and sends the query to the remote server. Note that the WHERE clause of the remote query (in bold type) does not include the partition column even though the original query does. This is because it isn't needed. Once the correct partition has been identified, the partition column itself isn't needed to locate the data in the remote table. By virtue of the CHECK constraint, the optimizer knows that Orders1997 only contains data for one partition, 1997.

# Indexed Views

Typically, a view is a conceptual table only—it does not actually store any of the data it returns. It's a virtual table—you query it, and, behind the scenes, SQL Server runs its SELECT statement and returns the results. This is the way views have always worked on SQL Server.

Indexed views change this. By indexing a view you can materialize its result set permanently so that querying it in the future is much faster. Given a table with a large number of rows and a view over it that only returns a few of them, the difference an index over the view could make in execution time may well be dramatic.

As with partitioned views, there are a number of restrictions on the types of views that may be indexed. You can read up on these in the Books Online. To easily check whether you can create an index on an existing view, use the **IsIndexable** property of the OBJECTPROPERTY() function, as I mentioned earlier in the chapter. Be aware that **IsIndexable** can take a while to return because of all the criteria it must check to determine whether an object can be indexed. The purpose of this section is to discuss general design considerations when working with indexed views.

## Indexed View Usage by the Optimizer

That the optimizer may use an index that was built over a view when you query the view should be obvious. As with indexes on tables, this is the whole point of having the index in the first place. However, the SQL Server optimizer can also use indexed views when you *don't* refer to them directly—when you query their underlying tables. Take, for example, this view and index (Listing 9–26):

**Listing 9–26**  A basic indexed view.

```
USE pubs
GO
DROP VIEW dbo.SalesByMonth
GO
CREATE VIEW dbo.SalesByMonth
WITH SCHEMABINDING
AS
SELECT LEFT(CONVERT(char(8),ord_date,112),6) AS SalesMonth,
       COUNT_BIG(*) AS TotalNumSales
FROM dbo.sales
GROUP BY LEFT(CONVERT(char(8),ord_date,112),6)
GO
CREATE UNIQUE CLUSTERED INDEX MonthlySales ON dbo.SalesByMonth (SalesMonth)
```

A query over the sales table that aggregates on the year and month, as the view does, may indeed benefit from the view's index. For example, consider what happens when we run a query that's very similar to the one that composes the view (Listing 9–27):

**Listing 9–27** SQL Server can use view indexes even when not querying the view.

```
SELECT  LEFT(CONVERT(char(8),ord_date,112),6) AS SalesMonth,
        COUNT(*) AS TotalNumSales
FROM dbo.sales s JOIN dbo.titles t ON (s.title_id=s.title_id)
GROUP BY LEFT(CONVERT(char(8),ord_date,112),6)
```

On the Enterprise Edition of SQL Server, the query plan looks like this:

```
|-Compute Scalar(DEFINE:([Expr1003]=Convert([SalesByMonth].[TotalNumSales])))
|--Clustered Index Scan(OBJECT:([pubs].[dbo].[SalesByMonth].[MonthlySales]))
```

The index we built over the view is being used to service a query on its base table.

## Using Indexed Views on Other Editions of SQL Server

Normally, you can't create or use indexed views on versions of SQL Server other than the Enterprise Edition (EE) and the Developer Edition (DE), but there is a way around this. To "create" an indexed view on the Personal, Standard, or MSDE editions of SQL Server, first create the indexed view on SQL Server EE or DE, then back up the database and load it onto your target server. This will get the object onto your server, but it won't cause the optimizer to use it. To do that, use the NOEXPAND query hint. You can specify the NOEXPAND hint with an indexed view to force the optimizer to consider the indexes on the view. This works on any version of SQL Server. In conjunction with the INDEX hint, you can force the use of a view index, regardless of the SQL Server edition. Listing 9–28 presents an example of the use of the NOEXPAND hint:

**Listing 9–28** You can force the optimizer to consider your view indexes via the NOEXPAND hint.

```
SELECT  SalesMonth,
        TotalNumSales
FROM dbo.SalesByMonth (NOEXPAND)
```

# Designing Modular Indexed Views

Because of the many restrictions on indexed views (no unions, no outer joins, no aggregates other than SUM() and COUNT_BIG(), and so on), you won't find a lot of complex queries that you can cover completely with a single indexed view. However, you will likely find many simpler ones—aggregations and joins that your code repeats often—and this is where the best use of indexed views comes in: modular preprocessing. Indexed views are best suited to simpler queries that take a considerable amount of time to run because of the amount of data they traverse. By materializing the result sets that are produced by these queries, you create the possibility that the optimizer may use an indexed view to avoid having to reproduce a result set that's potentially very expensive. The performance gains can be dramatic.

Indexed views work best when the underlying data doesn't change much. The overhead associated with keeping an indexed view up to date during frequent updates may make them cost more than they're worth. Obviously, this means indexed views probably won't be used much in OLTP environments, but could very well prove quite useful with data warehouses.

Indexed views give SQL Server the ability to create and maintain automatically what people have been building manually for years: static summary and rollup tables. With large amounts of data, it's a common practice to summarize that data into static tables in ways that make it the most useful to the largest number of queries, and use those tables when possible to service requests from the database. It's a common practice, but it requires care and feeding from both the developer and the DBA—the DBA must create and manage the tables over time and the developer must change her app to use them. Indexed views, on the other hand, can be created and left alone. The DBA isn't tasked with making sure they stay up to date. SQL Server takes care of that. On the proper editions of SQL Server, they'll be used automatically if the optimizer thinks they'll reduce the overall cost of a query, so the developer doesn't have to do anything special to take advantage of them. They can't be used in as many situations as summary or rollup tables, but there is overlap between the two strategies. If you are currently creating and maintaining summary tables, you may want to review your physical database design to see whether it could benefit from indexed views.

## Indexed View Maintenance

Because the clustered index on a view actually stores the data returned by the view in its leaf nodes, it can become corrupted just like a table can. To check an indexed view for corruption, use DBCC CHECKTABLE. As with tables,

DBCC CHECKTABLE can scan an indexed view for corruption and optionally fix it. Likewise, DBCC CLEANTABLE can reclaim space from dropped variable-length columns and text columns in a view as well as a table. DBCC INDEXDEFRAG can defragment indexes on views just as it does table indexes, and DBCC SHOWCONTIG can report fragmentation info for indexed views. Most DBCC commands that operate specifically on tables will also work on indexed views. Check the Books Online for more info.

## Summary

You learned about view objects in this chapter. There are a number of different kinds of views—updatable views and read-only views, indexed and nonindexed views, local and distributed partitioned views, and so forth. You learned about the situations in which different types of views work best, you learned how to create and administer them, and you learned about some things to watch out for as you use them.

# CHAPTER 10

# User-Defined Functions

*Great designers have a relentless desire to create—to make things.*

*—Steve McConnell*[1]

A UDF is a special type of subroutine that can be used in expressions. UDFs are very much like Transact-SQL's built-in functions—you pass them the parameters they require and they return a result of some type.

UDFs come in three varieties: scalar functions, multistatement table-valued functions, and inline table-valued functions. A scalar function is one that returns a single value. It can be used in expressions just like regular system functions. A multistatement table-valued function (what I'll usually just refer to as a *table-valued function*) is a UDF that returns a table data type as its result. You can use it in the FROM clause of a SELECT statement similarly to Transact-SQL's built-in rowset functions (e.g., OPENXML(), OPENQUERY(), and so on). An inline table-valued function (what I'll usually refer to as an *inline function*) returns the results of a SELECT statement as its result—it has no function body. It can also be used in the FROM clause of the SELECT statement.

## Scalar Functions

Listing 10–1 presents an example of a simple scalar function:

**Listing 10–1** A basic scalar function.

```
CREATE FUNCTION dbo.Proper(@Name sysname)
RETURNS sysname
AS
```

---

1. McConnell, Steve. *After the Gold Rush*. Redmond, WA: Microsoft Press, 1999.

```
BEGIN
  DECLARE @len int, @i int, @Outname sysname, @LastSpc bit
  SET @len=DATALENGTH(@Name)
  SET @i=1
  SET @LastSpc=1
  SET @Outname=''
  WHILE @i<@len BEGIN
    SET @Outname=@Outname+
      CASE @Lastspc
      WHEN 1 THEN UPPER(SUBSTRING(@Name,@i,1))
      ELSE LOWER(SUBSTRING(@Name,@i,1))
      END
    SET @LastSpc=CASE SUBSTRING(@Name,@i,1) WHEN ' ' THEN 1 ELSE 0 END
    SET @i=@i+1
  END
  RETURN(@Outname)
END
GO
SELECT dbo.Proper('thomas a. edison')
```

(Results)

```
---------------------------------------------------------------------------
Thomas A. Edison
```

The function in Listing 10–1 converts a string into "proper" case. Each alphabetic character following a space is uppercased; the rest are lowercased. This is useful with many proper nouns, hence the name.

## Table-Valued Functions

Table-valued functions are also quite powerful and relatively easy to use. Table-valued functions return a table data type as their function result (UDFs do not support output parameters). With a few exceptions, you can perform the same operations on this table that you can perform on a regular table, including inserting, deleting, and updating (you can't use INSERT...EXEC or use user-defined data types). Text columns are automatically flagged as **text in row** columns. Here's an example of a multistatement table-valued UDF (Listing 10–2):

**Listing 10–2** A basic table-valued function.

```
CREATE TABLE staff (employee int PRIMARY KEY, employee_name varchar(10),
supervisor int NULL REFERENCES staff (employee))

INSERT staff VALUES (1,'GROUCHO',1)
INSERT staff VALUES (2,'CHICO',1)
INSERT staff VALUES (3,'HARPO',2)
INSERT staff VALUES (4,'ZEPPO',2)
INSERT staff VALUES (5,'MOE',1)
INSERT staff VALUES (6,'LARRY',5)
INSERT staff VALUES (7,'CURLY',5)
INSERT staff VALUES (8,'SHEMP',5)
INSERT staff VALUES (9,'JOE',8)
INSERT staff VALUES (10,'CURLY JOE',9)

GO
DROP FUNCTION dbo.ORGTABLE
GO
CREATE FUNCTION dbo.ORGTABLE(@employee_name varchar(10)='%')
RETURNS @orgtable TABLE (sequence int,

supervisor varchar(10),

supervises varchar(10),

employee_name varchar(10))
AS
BEGIN
     DECLARE @worktable TABLE (seq int identity,
            chartdepth int,
            employee int,
            supervisor int)

     INSERT @worktable (chartdepth, employee, supervisor)
     SELECT chartdepth=1, employee=o2.employee, supervisor=o1.employee
     FROM staff o1 INNER JOIN staff o2 ON (o1.employee=o2.supervisor)
     WHERE o1.employee_name LIKE @employee_name

     WHILE (@@rowcount > 0) BEGIN
       INSERT @worktable (chartdepth, employee, supervisor)
       SELECT DISTINCT o1.chartdepth+1, o2.employee, o1.supervisor
       FROM @worktable o1 INNER JOIN @worktable o2 ON
       (o1.employee=o2.supervisor)
```

```
            WHERE o1.chartdepth=(SELECT MAX(chartdepth) FROM @worktable)
            AND o1.supervisor<>o1.employee
        END
        INSERT @orgtable
        SELECT seq, s.employee_name, supervises='supervises', e.employee_name
        FROM @worktable o INNER JOIN staff s ON (o.supervisor=s.employee)
        INNER JOIN staff e ON (o.employee=e.employee)
        WHERE o.supervisor<>o.employee
        ORDER BY seq
        RETURN
END
GO
SELECT * FROM ORGTABLE(DEFAULT) ORDER BY Sequence
GO
DROP TABLE staff
```

(Results)

```
sequence     supervisor supervises employee_name
----------   ---------- ---------- -------------
2            GROUCHO    supervises CHICO
3            CHICO      supervises HARPO
4            CHICO      supervises ZEPPO
5            GROUCHO    supervises MOE
6            MOE        supervises LARRY
7            MOE        supervises CURLY
8            MOE        supervises SHEMP
9            SHEMP      supervises JOE
10           JOE        supervises CURLY JOE
11           GROUCHO    supervises HARPO
12           GROUCHO    supervises ZEPPO
13           GROUCHO    supervises LARRY
14           GROUCHO    supervises CURLY
15           GROUCHO    supervises SHEMP
16           MOE        supervises JOE
17           SHEMP      supervises CURLY JOE
18           GROUCHO    supervises JOE
19           GROUCHO    supervises CURLY JOE
20           MOE        supervises CURLY JOE
21           GROUCHO    supervises CURLY JOE
```

This routine creates an organizational chart from the staff table, then returns it as the function result. Note the use of an identity column on the internal worktable and the insert and joins with it later in the routine. From a usage standpoint, table variables are nearly identical to temporary tables, but they're far more scalable in terms of concurrency.

Note the absence of the owner qualifier on the call to the function. Only scalar functions require owner qualification; table-valued functions and inline functions do not.

The routine ends with a RETURN statement—a requirement of all UDFs. Because the table variable has already been loaded with data, the end result is that this table is returned to the caller.

# Inline Functions

Inline functions are also quite powerful. They provide a "parameterized view" type of functionality; something many of us have been requesting of Microsoft for years. An inline table-valued function has no body, so there's no BEGIN…END requirement with it. It consists only of a SELECT query, happily ensconced in a RETURN statement. Because the SELECT defines what type of table is actually returned, the RETURNS clause of an inline function simply lists TABLE as the return type, with no accompanying table definition. This differs from regular table-valued functions in which the entire table definition must be included in the RETURNS clause.

Here's an example that demonstrates an inline function (Listing 10–3):

**Listing 10–3** A basic inline function.

```
CREATE TABLE tempdb..singles (band int, single int, title varchar(30))

INSERT tempdb..singles VALUES(0,0,'LITTLE BIT O'' LOVE')
INSERT tempdb..singles VALUES(0,1,'FIRE AND WATER')
INSERT tempdb..singles VALUES(0,2,'ALL RIGHT NOW')
INSERT tempdb..singles VALUES(1,0,'BAD COMPANY')
INSERT tempdb..singles VALUES(1,1,'SHOOTING STAR')
INSERT tempdb..singles VALUES(1,2,'FEEL LIKE MAKIN'' LOVE')
INSERT tempdb..singles VALUES(1,3,'ROCK AND ROLL FANTASY')
INSERT tempdb..singles VALUES(1,4,'BURNING SKY')
INSERT tempdb..singles VALUES(2,0,'SATISFACTION GUARANTEED')
INSERT tempdb..singles VALUES(2,1,'RADIOACTIVE')
INSERT tempdb..singles VALUES(2,2,'MONEY CAN''T BUY')
INSERT tempdb..singles VALUES(2,3,'TOGETHER')
INSERT tempdb..singles VALUES(3,0,'GOOD MORNING LITTLE SCHOOLGIRL')
```

```
INSERT tempdb..singles VALUES(3,1,'HOOCHIE-COOCHIE MAN')
INSERT tempdb..singles VALUES(3,2,'MUDDY WATER BLUES')
INSERT tempdb..singles VALUES(3,3,'THE HUNTER')
GO
DROP FUNCTION PaulRodgersSingles
GO
CREATE FUNCTION PaulRodgersSingles(@title varchar(50)='%')
RETURNS TABLE
AS
RETURN(SELECT Free=MIN(CASE band WHEN 0 THEN CAST(title AS char(18))
                  ELSE NULL END),
          BadCompany=MIN(CASE band WHEN 1 THEN CAST(title AS char(21))
                      ELSE NULL END),
          TheFirm=MIN(CASE band WHEN 2 THEN CAST(title AS char(23))
                    ELSE NULL END),
          Solo=MIN(CASE band WHEN 3 THEN title ELSE NULL END)
      FROM tempdb..singles
      WHERE title LIKE @title
      GROUP BY single)
GO
SELECT * FROM PaulRodgersSingles(DEFAULT)
```

(Results abridged)

| Free | BadCompany | TheFirm | Solo |
|------|-----------|---------|------|
| LITTLE BIT O' LOVE | BAD COMPANY | SATISFACTION GUARANTEED | GOOD MORNING LITTLE SCHOOLGIRL |
| FIRE AND WATER | SHOOTING STAR | RADIOACTIVE | HOOCHIE-COOCHIE MAN |
| ALL RIGHT NOW | FEEL LIKE MAKIN' LOVE | MONEY CAN'T BUY | MUDDY WATER BLUES |
| NULL | ROCK AND ROLL FANTASY | TOGETHER | THE HUNTER |
| NULL | BURNING SKY | NULL | NULL |

This routine takes a linear data set—the singles table—and produces a cross tab that's broken out by band. The function takes single parameter, @title, that can be specified to limit the rows returned by the cross tab. In this sense, the function operates as a kind of parameterized view.

# Limitations

There are a number of limitations and restrictions that apply exclusively to UDFs:

- Except for inline functions, the outer BEGIN...END pair is required with UDFs. This differs from procedures and triggers. Curiously, the outer BEGIN...END enclosure is not only *not* required with inline functions, it's not allowed; you'll get a syntax error if you try to include it.
- Calls to scalar UDFs must be owner qualified. Note the **dbo.** prefix on the call to the Proper() function used earlier. There's an undocumented way around this requirement that we'll discuss momentarily.
- The last statement in a UDF must be RETURN.
- There are a number of restrictions on the T-SQL you can use inside a function. Basically, you aren't allowed to do anything that might have a side effect. For example, you can't create permanent objects of any type, you can't reference temporary tables in any way (even preexisting ones), and you can't call stored procedures. You can create table variables, but they have limitations (for example, you can't use user-defined data types in table variables and you can't use INSERT...EXEC or SELECT...INTO with them). You can call extended procedures, but only those that are named with the prefix **xp**. Some extended procedures (e.g., sp_executesql and sp_xml_preparedocument) are extended procedures from the perspective of Enterprise Manage, but they're prefixed with **sp** instead of **xp**. You can't call these from a UDF. My xp_exec extended procedure can work around this to some extent because it allows you to run a T-SQL command batch of your choosing via an extended procedure interface. See the section entitled, "Parameterized UDFs" for more info.
- You cannot call RAISERROR() from a UDF to report errors or to set @@ERROR.
- Many environmental settings cannot be changed from within a UDF, even those that you can normally use in a stored procedure and that only last for the duration of the procedure. SET NOCOUNT ON, for example, is not allowed.
- You cannot call a UDF using a four-part name. For example, you can't do this.

**Listing 10–4** A workaround for calling remote functions.

```
SELECT kufnahte...calc_interest(100000,7.6,30)
```

You can work around this limitation to some extent using rowset functions such as OPENQUERY(), like this:

```
SELECT *
FROM OPENQUERY(kufnahte, 'SELECT dbo.calc_interest(100000,7.6,30)')
```

However, OPENQUERY and its siblings do not allow a variable to be supplied as the query text—it must be a literal string—therefore, you can't pass parameters to the queries you execute—a horrible limitation. The only suitable workaround I've found is to use sp_executesql with an output parameter, like this (Listing 10–4):

```
DECLARE @interest int
EXEC kufnahte...sp_executesql N'SELECT
@int=dbo.calc_interest(@prin,@rate,@years)',
N'@prin int, @rate int, @years int, @int int OUT', 100000, 7.6, 30,
@interest OUT
SELECT @interest


-----------

210000
```

This is quite a bit of work just to call a function. You'd probably be better off either using a stored procedure instead or copying the function to the local server.

■ Optional UDF parameters are not truly optional—you can't actually omit them. If you want to leave out a parameter to a UDF, you must supply the DEFAULT keyword, even if it's the only parameter to the function. This can be a bit of a pain when a function has lots of optional arguments. Listing 10–5 illustrates:

**Listing 10–5** Optional UDF parameters are not truly optional.

```
CREATE FUNCTION dbo.Sprintf(@FmtStr varchar(255)
,@Parm0 varchar(255)
,@Parm1 varchar(255)=''
,@Parm2 varchar(255)=''
,@Parm3 varchar(255)=''
,@Parm4 varchar(255)=''
,@Parm5 varchar(255)=''
,@Parm6 varchar(255)=''
,@Parm7 varchar(255)=''
,@Parm8 varchar(255)=''
,@Parm9 varchar(255)=''
)
RETURNS VARCHAR(255)
AS
BEGIN
```

```
DECLARE @Result varchar(255)
EXEC master..xp_sprintf @Result OUT, @FmtStr, @Parm0, @Parm1,
@Parm2, @Parm3, @Parm4, @Parm5, @Parm6, @Parm7, @Parm8, @Parm9
RETURN(@Result)
END
GO
DECLARE @Artist varchar(30), @Song varchar(30), @Band varchar(30)
SELECT @Artist='Paul Rodgers', @Song='Fire and Water', @Band='Free'
SELECT dbo.Sprintf('%s sang the song "%s" for the band %s',@Artist,
@Song, @Band, DEFAULT, DEFAULT, DEFAULT, DEFAULT, DEFAULT, DEFAULT,
DEFAULT)
```
(Results)

```
-------------------------------------------------------------------

Paul Rodgers sang the song "Fire and Water" for the band Free
```

See the difficulty? Because Sprintf() may take as many as nine optional string parameters, we have to supply DEFAULT repeatedly—we can't simply omit the extra parameters. In C/C++ terms, we can't create a "varargs" routine even though xp_sprintf, the internal routine that's doing the real work here, allows a variable number of parameters to be specified to it.

---

**NOTE:** You may have noticed that the maximum length of Sprintf()'s parameters and return value is only 255 bytes. This is because the extended procedure it calls to format the string, SQL Server's xp_sprintf, has the same limitation. Xp_sprintf, like many older extended procedures, makes use of the deprecated srv_paramdata() and srv_paramlen() ODS functions to retrieve the contents and length of the parameters passed into it. Unlike the newer srv_paraminfo() function, these routines do not support the newer (post-SQL Server 6.5) data types or their increased capacities. I've limited Sprintf() to 255 bytes because strings longer than that are clipped by xp_sprintf when returned.

---

■ You may not call nondeterministic system functions from UDFs. A *deterministic* function is one that returns the same results each time it's called with the same parameters. A *nondeterministic* function is one that may not—it may return different results from execution to execution even when called with the same parameters. You aren't allowed to call nondeterministic system functions from UDF's, nor are you allowed to use nondeterministic computed columns (e.g., one

**Table 10–1**  OBJECTPROPERTY() Options for UDFs

| Option | Use | sysobjects type value |
|---|---|---|
| IsInlineFunction | Returns 1 for inline table-valued functions | IF |
| IsTableFunction | Returns 1 for multistatement table-valued functions | TF |
| IsScalarFunction | Returns 1 for scalar UDFs | FN |
| IsDeterministic | Returns 1 for deterministic UDFs | |
| IsSchemaBound | Returns 1 for schema-bound UDFs | |

based on a nondeterministic system or user function) as index keys. Examples of nondeterministic system functions include GETDATE(), @@CONNECTIONS, NEWID(), and RAND(). See the Books Online for the complete list.

■ You cannot create a PRIMARY KEY constraint on a computed column based on a UDF that may return NULL. A numeric UDF, for example, may return a NULL result because of an overflow or divide-by-zero error. The workaround is to wrap the computed column's expression in ISNULL() so that it's impossible for the expression to return NULL.

## Meta-data

Transact-SQL provides a handful of OBJECTPROPERTY() options for retrieving info about UDFs. They allow you to determine the specific type of UDF as well as whether a function is deterministic and/or schema bound. Table 10–1 summarizes these options:

Here's a query that demonstrates how these are used (Listing 10–6):

**Listing 10–6**  OBJECTPROPERTY() returns meta-data about UDFs.

```
SELECT LEFT(name,20) AS [Function],
OBJECTPROPERTY(id,'IsScalarFunction') AS Scalar,
OBJECTPROPERTY(id,'IsTableFunction') AS [Table],
OBJECTPROPERTY(id,'IsInlineFunction') AS Inline,
OBJECTPROPERTY(id,'IsDeterministic') AS Determ,
OBJECTPROPERTY(id,'IsSchemaBound') AS SchemaBound
FROM sysobjects
```

```
WHERE type in ('IF','TF','FN')
ORDER BY name
```

(Results)

| Function | Scalar | Table | Inline | Determ | SchemaBound |
|---|---|---|---|---|---|
| OrgTable | 0 | 1 | 0 | 0 | 0 |
| PaulRodgersSingles | 0 | 0 | 1 | 0 | 0 |
| Proper | 1 | 0 | 0 | 0 | 0 |
| Sprintf | 1 | 0 | 0 | 0 | 0 |

Notice that none of these is deterministic. Recall the earlier discussion on determinism. What is it about the Proper() function, for example, that makes it nondeterministic? For a given input, it will always return the same result. The same is true of Sprintf(). Given a specific input, it will always return the same string. Why then aren't these two scalar functions deterministic?

The reason is simple: schema binding. SQL Server flags a function as nondeterministic in these situations:

- The function is not schema-bound.
- At least one function called by the function is nondeterministic.
- The function references database objects outside its scope.
- The function calls an extended stored procedure.

So, in the case of the Proper() function, it's flagged as nondeterministic because it was not created with schema binding. For its part, the Sprintf() function breaks two of the rules: It's not schema-bound, and it calls an extended procedure.

What exactly is schema binding? Schema binding links a function (or a view) to the objects it references in such a way that they cannot be changed in a manner that affects it structurally. Take, for example, an inline function with a return type that is entirely dependent on the data types and columns of the tables it references. What happens if one of those tables is changed? What happens if a column's data type is changed so that the SELECT statement that makes up the inline function causes an error when run? Your code breaks, that's what. The SCHEMABINDING option of the CREATE FUNCTION and CREATE VIEW statements was designed to address this inevitability. It prevents changes that affect the structure of other objects. In some respects, it's analogous to SQL Server's referential integrity constraint facility: It ensures the structural integrity of dependent objects.

Before you can specify CREATE FUNCTION's SCHEMABINDING option, these conditions must be met:

- If the function references any view or UDFs, they must also be schema-bound.
- The function must spell out any column lists it references. It may not use * in place of a column list.
- If the function references outside objects, they must be in the same database and cannot be referenced with three- or four-part names.
- The function may not define local variables.
- If the function references outside objects, you must have REFERENCES permission on those objects.

See any problems? Proper() can't be deterministic because it's not schema-bound, and it can't be schema-bound because it defines local variables. Because we can't make Proper() a deterministic function, let's try the inline function we created earlier. Here it is again with the SCHEMABINDING option added (Listing 10–7):

**Listing 10–7** A schema-bound inline function.

```
CREATE FUNCTION PaulRodgersSingles(@title varchar(50)='%')
RETURNS TABLE
WITH SCHEMABINDING
AS
RETURN(SELECT Free=MIN(CASE band WHEN 0 THEN CAST(title AS char(18))
                    ELSE NULL END),
          BadCompany=MIN(CASE band WHEN 1 THEN CAST(title AS char(21))
                    ELSE NULL END),
          TheFirm=MIN(CASE band WHEN 2 THEN CAST(title AS char(23))
                    ELSE NULL END),
          Solo=MIN(CASE band WHEN 3 THEN title ELSE NULL END)
     FROM dbo.singles
     WHERE title LIKE @title
     GROUP BY single)
```

There are two differences between this version of the function and the previous one. First, of course, we added the SCHEMABINDING option to the function header. Second, we changed the reference to the singles table to use a two-part name. Previously, it used a three-part name. Even though both versions referred to the same table, three- and four-part names are not permitted in deterministic functions, as I mentioned earlier.

Now that the function is schema-bound, is it deterministic? Let's check:

| Function | Scalar | Table | Inline | Determ | SchemaBound |
|----------|--------|-------|--------|--------|-------------|
| OrgTable | 0 | 1 | 0 | 0 | 0 |
| PaulRodgersSingles | 0 | 0 | 1 | 0 | 1 |
| Proper | 1 | 0 | 0 | 0 | 0 |
| Sprintf | 1 | 0 | 0 | 0 | 0 |

It's still not deterministic. Why not? Because inline table-valued functions cannot be deterministic. By definition, what they return depends entirely on the data in the tables they reference—they cannot be assumed to be deterministic at any point in time. This is why OBJECTPROPERTY's IsDeterministic option applies only to scalar and table-valued functions. Just for kicks (or, just for pig iron, as an Irish friend of mine likes to say), let's create a deterministic function so that we can see what it looks like (Listing 10–8):

**Listing 10–8** A function that's both deterministic and schema-bound.

```
CREATE FUNCTION dbo.FortuneCookie(@Date datetime='20010101')
RETURNS varchar(255)
WITH SCHEMABINDING
AS
BEGIN
  RETURN(CASE DATEPART(mm,@Date)
    WHEN 1 THEN 'Where ever you go, there you are.'
    WHEN 2 THEN 'Ask not what I can do for you, ask what you can do for me.'
    WHEN 3 THEN 'Why do we drive on a parkway and park on a driveway?'
    WHEN 4 THEN 'I see lots of cobwebs in my basement. What is a cob?'
    WHEN 5 THEN 'To see in the dark, you must turn on the light.'
    WHEN 6 THEN 'That's one giant leap for man, one small step on a landmine.'
    WHEN 7 THEN 'In the words of the immoral Monica, "Close, but no cigar."'
    WHEN 8 THEN 'If a tree falls in the woods, does anyone feel sad for the
      grass it pulverizes?'
    WHEN 9 THEN 'Four score and seven years ago, the Rangers actually had a
      baseball team.'
    WHEN 10 THEN 'The paperless office is about as likely as the paperless
      bathroom. -- Joe Celko'
    WHEN 11 THEN 'An ounce of technique is with worth a pound of technology.'
    WHEN 12 THEN 'If you think education is expensive, try ignorance. -- Derek Bok'
  END)
END
```

This function takes a date as a parameter, and, based on its month, returns a one-liner. It references no external objects and declares no internal variables. It consistently returns the same value for the same input. It was created with SCHEMABINDING, but is it deterministic? Let's check:

```
Function             Scalar      Table        Inline       Determ SchemaBound
-------------------- ----------- ------------ ----------- ------ --------
FortuneCookie        1           0            0            1      1
OrgTable             0           1            0            0      0
PaulRodgersSingles   0           0            1            0      1
Proper               1           0            0            0      0
Sprintf              1           0            0            0      0
```

So now we've got a function that is both schema-bound and deterministic. If we wanted, FortuneCookie could serve as an index key or participate in an indexed view. This isn't true of the other functions.

## Creating Your Own System Functions

You'll recall the discussion in Chapter 9 regarding creating our own system views—views that can be queried from any database and run within the context of that database. You can do something similar with system functions. You can create functions that reside in master, but that can be queried from any database without a database name prefix.

Here's how it works: SQL Server creates a number of system UDFs during installation (e.g., fn_varbintohexstr(), fn_chariswhitespace(), and so on). Some of these are owned by the system_function_schema, and some aren't. Those that are owned by system_function_schema can be accessed from any database using a one-part name. You can find out which ones these are by running the query in Listing 10–9:

**Listing 10–9** SQL Server's system functions.

```
USE master
GO
SELECT name
FROM sysobjects
WHERE uid=USER_ID('system_function_schema')
AND   (OBJECTPROPERTY(id, 'IsScalarFunction')=1
      OR OBJECTPROPERTY(id, 'IsTableFunction')=1
      OR OBJECTPROPERTY(id, 'IsInlineFunction')=1)
```

(Results)

```
name
---------------------------------------------------
fn_chariswhitespace
fn_dblog
fn_generateparameterpattern
fn_getpersistedservernamecasevariation
fn_helpcollations
fn_listextendedproperty
fn_removeparameterwithargument
fn_replbitstringtoint
fn_replcomposepublicationsnapshotfolder
fn_replgenerateshorterfilenameprefix
fn_replgetagentcommandlinefromjobid
fn_replgetbinary8lodword
fn_replinttobitstring
fn_replmakestringliteral
fn_replprepadbinary8
fn_replquotename
fn_replrotr
fn_repltrimleadingzerosinhexstr
fn_repluniquename
fn_serverid
fn_servershareddrives
fn_skipparameterargument
fn_trace_geteventinfo
fn_trace_getfilterinfo
fn_trace_getinfo
fn_trace_gettable
fn_updateparameterwithargument
fn_virtualfilestats
fn_virtualservernodes
```

Chapter 22 covers creating system functions as well as other types of system objects. For now, just understand that because they belong to system_function_schema, they can be called across databases using one-part names.

To create your own system UDF, follow these steps:

1. Enable updates to the system tables. You can do that with this code:

```
sp_configure 'allow updates', 1
RECONFIGURE WITH OVERRIDE
```

2. Create the function in master, being sure to owner-qualify it. The function name must begin with fn_ and must be entirely in lowercase.

3. Disable updates to the system tables (as a rule, you should leave the **allow updates** switch turned off, especially on production systems):

```
sp_configure 'allow updates', 0
RECONFIGURE WITH OVERRIDE
```

Here's an example of couple of very simple system UDFs (Listing 10–10):

**Listing 10–10** Two user-defined system functions: fn_greatest() and fn_least().

```
USE master
GO
exec sp_configure 'allow updates',1
GO
reconfigure with override
GO
DROP FUNCTION system_function_schema.fn_greatest,
system_function_schema.fn_least
GO
CREATE FUNCTION system_function_schema.fn_greatest(@x bigint, @y bigint)
RETURNS bigint
AS
BEGIN
  RETURN(CASE WHEN @x>@y THEN @x ELSE @y END)
END
GO
CREATE FUNCTION system_function_schema.fn_least(@x bigint, @y bigint)
RETURNS bigint
AS
BEGIN
  RETURN(CASE WHEN @x<@y THEN @x ELSE @y END)
END
GO
exec sp_configure 'allow updates',0
GO
reconfigure with override
GO
use northwind
GO
SELECT fn_greatest(2156875324698752,2156875323698752), fn_least(989, 998)
```

(Results)

```
DBCC execution completed. If DBCC printed error messages, contact your system
administrator.
Configuration option 'allow updates' changed from 0 to 1. Run the RECONFIGURE
statement to install.
DBCC execution completed. If DBCC printed error messages, contact your system
administrator.
Configuration option 'allow updates' changed from 1 to 0. Run the RECONFIGURE
statement to install.


-------------------- --------------------
2156875324698752     989
```

Here we've created a couple of new system functions: fn_greatest() and fn_least(). These correspond to Oracle's GREATEST and LEAST functions. They return the larger or smaller of two 8-byte integers. You can create your own system UDFs by following the steps listed earlier. Note that table-valued system UDFs must be qualified with a double colon regardless of whether you created the function or it was created during the installation process.

# UDF Cookbook

The section that follows is a cookbook of UDFs I've written to address various business needs. These types of sections are always a lot of fun for me because I get to roll out some of my homegrown code and show the world what I've been up to. One of the design goals of this book is to provide you with code that has intrinsic value apart from the book—code that you could drop into place on your own systems and put to work. That's what this section is about. It's about demonstrating some of the techniques we've been talking about (and even a few we haven't) by working through some real-world code.

## An Improved SOUNDEX() Function

The built-in SOUNDEX() function is certainly a handy tool, but it uses a fairly primitive soundex algorithm, one that could be easily improved. The UDF that follows is fn_soundex(), a custom replacement for the stock SOUNDEX() function. It returns a larger number of unique soundex codes and is generally more functional than SOUNDEX(). Here's the code (Listing 10–11):

**Listing 10–11** A UDF that implements a better soundex routine.

```
USE master
GO
EXEC sp_configure 'allow updates',1
GO
RECONFIGURE WITH OVERRIDE
GO
DROP FUNCTION system_function_schema.fn_soundex
GO
CREATE FUNCTION system_function_schema.fn_soundex(@instring varchar(50))
RETURNS varchar(50)
/*

Object: fn_soundex
Description: Returns the soundex of a string (Russell optimization)

Usage: SELECT fn_soundex(@instring=string to translate)

Returns: string containing the soundex code

Created by: Ken Henderson. Email: khen@khen.com

Version: 8.0

Example: SELECT fn_soundex('Rodgers')

Created: 1998-05-15. Last changed: 2000-05-20.

Notes:
Based on the soundex algorithm published by Robert Russell and Margaret O'Dell, 1918,
extended to incorporate Russell's optimizations for finer granularity.

*/
AS
BEGIN

        DECLARE @workstr varchar(10), @soundex varchar(50)
        SET @instring=UPPER(@instring)
        -- Put all but the 1st char in a work buffer (we always return 1st char)
        SET @soundex=RIGHT(@instring,LEN(@instring)-1)

        /*
```

Translate characters to numbers per the following table:

```
Char              Number
B,F,P,V                 1
C,G,J,K,Q,S,X,Z         2
D,T               3
L                 4
M,N               5
R                 6
A,E,H,I,O,U,W,Y         9
*/

SET @workstr='BFPV'
WHILE (@workstr<>'') BEGIN
  SET @soundex=REPLACE(@soundex,LEFT(@workstr,1),'1')
  SET @workstr=RIGHT(@workstr,LEN(@workstr)-1)
END

SET @workstr='CGJKQSXZ'
WHILE (@workstr<>'') BEGIN
  SET @soundex=REPLACE(@soundex,LEFT(@workstr,1),'2')
  SET @workstr=RIGHT(@workstr,LEN(@workstr)-1)
END

SET @workstr='DT'
WHILE (@workstr<>'') BEGIN
  SET @soundex=REPLACE(@soundex,LEFT(@workstr,1),'3')
  SET @workstr=RIGHT(@workstr,LEN(@workstr)-1)
END

SET @soundex=replace(@soundex,'L','4')

SET @workstr='MN'
WHILE (@workstr<>'') BEGIN
  SET @soundex=REPLACE(@soundex,LEFT(@workstr,1),'5')
  SET @workstr=RIGHT(@workstr,LEN(@workstr)-1)
END

set @soundex=replace(@soundex,'R','6')

SET @workstr='AEHIOUWY'
WHILE (@workstr<>'') BEGIN
  SET @soundex=REPLACE(@soundex,LEFT(@workstr,1),'9')
```

```
      SET @workstr=RIGHT(@workstr,LEN(@workstr)-1)
    END

    -- Now replace repeating digits (e.g., '11' or '22') with single digits
    DECLARE @c int
    SET @c=1
    WHILE (@c<10) BEGIN
      -- Multiply by 11 to produce repeating digits
      SET
    @soundex=REPLACE(@soundex,CONVERT(char(2),@c*11),CONVERT(char(1),@c))
      SET @c=@c+1
    END
    SET @soundex=REPLACE(@soundex,'00','0') -- Get rid of double zeros

    SET @soundex=REPLACE(@soundex,'9','') -- Get rid of 9's

    SET @soundex=LEFT(@soundex,3)
    WHILE (LEN(@soundex)<3) SET @soundex=@soundex+'0' -- Pad with zero

    SET @soundex=LEFT(@instring,1)+@soundex -- Prefix first char and return
    RETURN @soundex
END
GO
EXEC sp_configure 'allow updates',0
GO
RECONFIGURE WITH OVERRIDE
GO
SELECT fn_soundex('Rodgers')
```

(Results)

```
--------------------------------------------------
R326
```

This function uses a better algorithm than SOUNDEX() and should perform about as well. Because it's a system function, you can use it any place that you are currently using SOUNDEX().

Although fn_soundex() is an improvement over the built-in SOUNDEX() function, it's still not as functional as it could be. Because it uses numerals in three of the four digits it returns, its total number of possible codes is only 26,000 ($26 * 10^3$). Contrast this with fn_soundex_ex (Listing 10–12), which uses alphabetic letters for each digit, for a total of 456,976 ($26^4$) possible codes. Here's the function:

**Listing 10–12** fn_soundex_ex—a vast improvement over SOUNDEX().

```
USE master
GO
EXEC sp_configure 'allow updates',1
GO
RECONFIGURE WITH OVERRIDE
GO
IF OBJECT_ID('fn_soundex_ex') IS NOT NULL
  DROP FUNCTION system_function_schema.fn_soundex_ex
GO
CREATE FUNCTION system_function_schema.fn_soundex_ex(@instring varchar(50))
RETURNS varchar(50)
/*

Object: fn_soundex_ex
Description: Returns the soundex of a string

Usage: fn_soundex_ex(@instring=string to translate)

Returns: string containing soundex code

Created by: Ken Henderson. Email: khen@khen.com

Version: 8.0

Example: SELECT dbo.fn_soundex_ex('Rodgers')

Created: 1998-05-15. Last changed: 2000-11-21.

Notes: Original source unknown.

Translation to Transact-SQL by Ken Henderson.

*/
AS
BEGIN
        DECLARE @workstr varchar(10), @soundex varchar(50)

        SET @instring=UPPER(@instring)
        -- Put all but the 1st char in a work buffer (we always return 1st char)
        SET @soundex=RIGHT(@instring,LEN(@instring)-1)

        SET @workstr='EIOUY' -- Replace vowels with A
```

```
WHILE (@workstr<>'') BEGIN
  SET @soundex=REPLACE(@soundex,LEFT(@workstr,1),'A')
  SET @workstr=RIGHT(@workstr,LEN(@workstr)-1)
END

/*

Translate word prefixes using this table
From       To
MAC        MCC
KN         NN
K          C
PF         FF
SCH        SSS
PH         FF

*/

-- Reaffix first char
SET @soundex=LEFT(@instring,1)+@soundex

IF (LEFT(@soundex,3)='MAC')
      SET @soundex='MCC'+RIGHT(@soundex,LEN(@soundex)-3)
IF (LEFT(@soundex,2)='KN')
      SET @soundex='NN'+RIGHT(@soundex,LEN(@soundex)-2)
IF (LEFT(@soundex,1)='K')
      SET @soundex='C'+RIGHT(@soundex,LEN(@soundex)-1)
IF (LEFT(@soundex,2)='PF')
      SET @soundex='FF'+RIGHT(@soundex,LEN(@soundex)-2)
IF (LEFT(@soundex,3)='SCH')
      SET @soundex='SSS'+RIGHT(@soundex,LEN(@soundex)-3)
IF (LEFT(@soundex,2)='PH')
      SET @soundex='FF'+RIGHT(@soundex,LEN(@soundex)-2)
-- Remove first char
SET @instring=@soundex
SET @soundex=RIGHT(@soundex,LEN(@soundex)-1)

/*

Translate phonetic prefixes (following the 1st char) using this table:

From       To
DG         GG
CAAN       TAAN
```

```
     D          T
     NST        NSS
     AV         AF
     Q          G
     Z          S
     M          N
     KN         NN
     K          C
     H          A (unless part of AHA)
     AW         A
     PH         FF
     SCH        SSS
*/
SET @soundex=REPLACE(@soundex,'DG','GG')
SET @soundex=REPLACE(@soundex,'CAAN','TAAN')
SET @soundex=REPLACE(@soundex,'D','T')
SET @soundex=REPLACE(@soundex,'NST','NSS')
SET @soundex=REPLACE(@soundex,'AV','AF')
SET @soundex=REPLACE(@soundex,'Q','G')
SET @soundex=REPLACE(@soundex,'Z','S')
SET @soundex=REPLACE(@soundex,'M','N')
SET @soundex=REPLACE(@soundex,'KN','NN')
SET @soundex=REPLACE(@soundex,'K','C')

-- Translate H to A unless it's part of "AHA"
SET @soundex=REPLACE(@soundex,'AHA','~~~')
SET @soundex=REPLACE(@soundex,'H','A')
SET @soundex=REPLACE(@soundex,'~~~','AHA')

SET @soundex=REPLACE(@soundex,'AW','A')
SET @soundex=REPLACE(@soundex,'PH','FF')
SET @soundex=REPLACE(@soundex,'SCH','SSS')

-- Truncate ending A or S
IF (RIGHT(@soundex,1)='A' or RIGHT(@soundex,1)='S')
     SET @soundex=LEFT(@soundex,LEN(@soundex)-1)

-- Translate ending "NT" to "TT"
IF (RIGHT(@soundex,2)='NT')
     SET @soundex=LEFT(@soundex,LEN(@soundex)-2)+'TT'
-- Remove all As
SET @soundex=REPLACE(@soundex,'A','')

-- Reaffix first char
```

```
          SET @soundex=LEFT(@instring,1)+@soundex
          -- Remove repeating characters
          DECLARE @c int
          SET @c=65
          WHILE (@c<91) BEGIN
            WHILE (CHARINDEX(char(@c)+CHAR(@c),@soundex)<>0)
              SET @soundex=REPLACE(@soundex,CHAR(@c)+CHAR(@c),CHAR(@c))
            SET @c=@c+1
          end

          SET @soundex=LEFT(@soundex,4)

          -- Pad with spaces
          IF (LEN(@soundex)<4) SET @soundex=@soundex+SPACE(4-LEN(@soundex))

          RETURN(@Soundex)
END
GO
EXEC sp_configure 'allow updates',0
GO
RECONFIGURE WITH OVERRIDE
GO
USE Northwind
GO


SELECT fn_soundex_ex(LastName) AS ex_Last,
       fn_soundex_ex(FirstName) AS ex_First,
SOUNDEX(LastName) AS bi_Last, SOUNDEX(FirstName) AS bi_First
FROM employees
```

(Results)

| ex_Last | ex_First | bi_Last | bi_First |
| --- | --- | --- | --- |
| DFL | NC | D140 | N520 |
| FLR | ANTR | F460 | A536 |
| LFRL | JNT | L164 | J530 |
| PC | MRGR | P220 | M626 |
| BCN | STFN | B255 | S315 |
| SN | MCL | S500 | M240 |
| CNG | RBRT | K520 | R163 |
| CLHN | LR | C450 | L600 |
| DTSW | AN | D326 | A500 |

As you can see, UDFs can be passed values from columns directly. This is the chief advantage of a UDF over a stored procedure: You can use it in DML statements to refer directly to table data.

## Statistical Functions

With the advent of UDF support in SQL Server, Transact-SQL has become much more capable as a statistics computation language. Given its set orientation and direct access to data, you may find that it outperforms traditional statistics computational packages in certain specific circumstances. There is a learning curve associated with most commercial statistics tools, so it makes sense to do operations that Transact-SQL can easily handle in UDFs and stored procedures, and only resort to industrial-strength statistics packages for the really heavy lifting.

### Clipping

The process of removing the topmost and bottommost values from a distribution set is called *clipping*. In statistics computations, we frequently want to toss out the highest and lowest members of a set so that we can focus on more typical values. The function in Listing 10–13, MiddleTemperatures(), shows you how to do this. It starts with a list of temperature samples and removes a user-specified section of the head and tail. It's implemented as an inline function so that you don't have the overhead of storing the slimmed-down version of the distribution anywhere. It simply acts as a parameterized view—you supply the size of the clipped region, and it takes care of the rest. Here's the code:

**Listing 10–13** You can use a UDF to perform statistical clipping.

```
USE tempdb
GO
CREATE TABLE tempdb..TemperatureReadings (MiddayTemp int)
INSERT tempdb..TemperatureReadings VALUES (75)
INSERT tempdb..TemperatureReadings VALUES (90)
INSERT tempdb..TemperatureReadings VALUES (76)
INSERT tempdb..TemperatureReadings VALUES (81)
INSERT tempdb..TemperatureReadings VALUES (98)
INSERT tempdb..TemperatureReadings VALUES (68)
GO
DROP FUNCTION dbo.MiddleTemperatures
GO
CREATE FUNCTION dbo.MiddleTemperatures(@ClipSize int = 2)
```

```
RETURNS TABLE
AS
    RETURN(SELECT v.MiddayTemp
    FROM tempdb..TemperatureReadings v CROSS JOIN tempdb..TemperatureReadings a
    GROUP BY v.MiddayTemp
    HAVING COUNT(CASE WHEN a.MiddayTemp <=v.MiddayTemp THEN 1 ELSE NULL END)
    >@ClipSize
    AND COUNT(CASE WHEN a.MiddayTemp >= v.MiddayTemp THEN 1 ELSE NULL END)
    >@ClipSize)
GO
SELECT * FROM dbo.MiddleTemperatures(2) ORDER BY MiddayTemp
```

(Results)

```
MiddayTemp
-----------
76
81
Warning: Null value is eliminated by an aggregate or other SET operation.
```

The @ClipSize parameter specifies the size of the clipped region. It indicates how many rows to remove from the top and bottom of the distribution before returning it.

### Histograms

Histograms—a kind of bar chart in which the lengths or widths of its bars represent data values—are a popular business reporting tool. You see them on everything from your utility bill to the stock prospectus brochures of the largest companies. The best reporting and charting tools have built-in features for producing histograms from relational data. Usually they can group, summarize, and extrapolate histogram data in numerous ways. That said, there are times when you need to compute your own histograms—to produce cross tabs from linear data that could function as the source to a histogram chart or be fed into a more complex routine for further processing. The following code shows you how to create histogram-oriented data using a UDF. It produces a two-dimensional histogram cross tab using the data from the pubs..sales table. You supply a filtering condition, and it takes care of the rest:

```
USE pubs
GO
DROP FUNCTION dbo.SalesHistogram
GO
```

```
CREATE FUNCTION dbo.SalesHistogram(@payterms varchar(12)='%')
RETURNS TABLE
AS
RETURN(
SELECT
PayTerms=isnull(s.payterms,'NA'),
"Less than 10"=COUNT(CASE WHEN s.sales >=0 AND s.sales <10 THEN 1 ELSE NULL END),
"10-19"=COUNT(CASE WHEN s.sales >=10 AND s.sales <20 THEN 1 ELSE NULL END),
"20-29"=COUNT(CASE WHEN s.sales >=20 AND s.sales <30 THEN 1 ELSE NULL END),
"30-39"=COUNT(CASE WHEN s.sales >=30 AND s.sales <40 THEN 1 ELSE NULL END),
"40-49"=COUNT(CASE WHEN s.sales >=40 AND s.sales <50 THEN 1 ELSE NULL END),
"50 or more"=COUNT(CASE WHEN s.sales >=50 THEN 1 ELSE NULL END)
FROM (SELECT t.title_id, s.payterms, sales=ISNULL(SUM(s.qty),0) FROM titles t LEFT
OUTER JOIN sales s ON (t.title_id=s.title_id) GROUP BY t.title_id, payterms) s
WHERE s.payterms LIKE @payterms
GROUP BY s.payterms
)
GO
SELECT * FROM dbo.SalesHistogram(DEFAULT)
```

(Results)

| PayTerms | Less than 10 | 10-19 | 20-29 | 30-39 | 40-49 | 50 or more |
| --- | --- | --- | --- | --- | --- | --- |
| Net 30 | 0 | 0 | 5 | 1 | 1 | 1 |
| Net 60 | 1 | 4 | 3 | 0 | 0 | 0 |
| ON invoice | 0 | 2 | 0 | 1 | 0 | 1 |

Warning: Null value is eliminated by an aggregate or other SET operation.

Here we specify the pay terms we're interested in seeing, and SalesHistogram() creates a cross tab representing unit sales organized by ranges. In the previous example, we allowed all pay terms to be displayed because we supplied the DEFAULT parameter. We could just as easily have listed just one set of pay terms data (Listing 10–14):

**Listing 10–14** A UDF that implements a basic histogram table.

```
SELECT * FROM dbo.SalesHistogram('Net 30')
```

(Results)

| PayTerms | Less than 10 | 10-19 | 20-29 | 30-39 | 40-49 | 50 or more |
| --- | --- | --- | --- | --- | --- | --- |
| Net 30 | 0 | 0 | 5 | 1 | 1 | 1 |

Warning: Null value is eliminated by an aggregate or other SET operation.

### Time Series Fluctuation

It's common to need to track the fluctuation of a value across a time series. An obvious example of this is stock price fluctuation. The various exchanges report stock prices on a regular basis throughout the business day, with each stock having a daily opening and closing price. The function presented in Listing 10–15, StockPriceFluctuation(), shows how to report time series fluctuation using stock prices as sample data. It consists of an inline UDF that joins the stock prices table with itself and matches opening and closing dates for (approximate) weekly periods, then reports on the fluctuation of the stock price over each period. The sample data lists the actual weekly closing prices for Microsoft (MSFT) and Oracle (ORCL) over a six-month period of time beginning in early July 2000 and ending in early January 2001. Here's the data and code:

**Listing 10–15** A UDF that reports time series fluctuation.

```
USE tempdb
go
CREATE TABLE dbo.stockprices (Symbol varchar(4), TradingDate smalldatetime,
ClosingPrice decimal(10,4))
INSERT dbo.stockprices (Symbol, TradingDate, ClosingPrice)
VALUES ('MSFT','20000706',  82.000)
INSERT dbo.stockprices (Symbol, TradingDate, ClosingPrice)
VALUES ('MSFT','20000710',  78.938)
INSERT dbo.stockprices (Symbol, TradingDate, ClosingPrice)
VALUES ('MSFT','20000717',  72.313)
INSERT dbo.stockprices (Symbol, TradingDate, ClosingPrice)
VALUES ('MSFT','20000724',  69.688)
INSERT dbo.stockprices (Symbol, TradingDate, ClosingPrice)
VALUES ('MSFT','20000731',  69.125)
INSERT dbo.stockprices (Symbol, TradingDate, ClosingPrice)
VALUES ('MSFT','20000807',  72.438)
INSERT dbo.stockprices (Symbol, TradingDate, ClosingPrice)
VALUES ('MSFT','20000814',  71.000)
INSERT dbo.stockprices (Symbol, TradingDate, ClosingPrice)
VALUES ('MSFT','20000821',  70.625)
INSERT dbo.stockprices (Symbol, TradingDate, ClosingPrice)
VALUES ('MSFT','20000828',  70.188)
INSERT dbo.stockprices (Symbol, TradingDate, ClosingPrice)
VALUES ('MSFT','20000905',  69.313)
INSERT dbo.stockprices (Symbol, TradingDate, ClosingPrice)
VALUES ('MSFT','20000911',  64.188)
INSERT dbo.stockprices (Symbol, TradingDate, ClosingPrice)
```

```
VALUES ('MSFT','20000918',  63.250)
INSERT dbo.stockprices (Symbol, TradingDate, ClosingPrice)
VALUES ('MSFT','20000925',  60.313)
INSERT dbo.stockprices (Symbol, TradingDate, ClosingPrice)
VALUES ('MSFT','20001002',  55.563)
INSERT dbo.stockprices (Symbol, TradingDate, ClosingPrice)
VALUES ('MSFT','20001009',  53.750)
INSERT dbo.stockprices (Symbol, TradingDate, ClosingPrice)
VALUES ('MSFT','20001016',  65.188)
INSERT dbo.stockprices (Symbol, TradingDate, ClosingPrice)
VALUES ('MSFT','20001023', 67.688)
INSERT dbo.stockprices (Symbol, TradingDate, ClosingPrice)
VALUES ('MSFT','20001030',  68.250)
INSERT dbo.stockprices (Symbol, TradingDate, ClosingPrice)
VALUES ('MSFT','20001106',  67.375)
INSERT dbo.stockprices (Symbol, TradingDate, ClosingPrice)
VALUES ('MSFT','20001113',  69.063)
INSERT dbo.stockprices (Symbol, TradingDate, ClosingPrice)
VALUES ('MSFT','20001120',  69.938)
INSERT dbo.stockprices (Symbol, TradingDate, ClosingPrice)
VALUES ('MSFT','20001127',  56.625)
INSERT dbo.stockprices (Symbol, TradingDate, ClosingPrice)
VALUES ('MSFT','20001204',  54.438)
INSERT dbo.stockprices (Symbol, TradingDate, ClosingPrice)
VALUES ('MSFT','20001211',  49.188)
INSERT dbo.stockprices (Symbol, TradingDate, ClosingPrice)
VALUES ('MSFT','20001218',  46.438)
INSERT dbo.stockprices (Symbol, TradingDate, ClosingPrice)
VALUES ('MSFT','20001226',  43.375)
INSERT dbo.stockprices (Symbol, TradingDate, ClosingPrice)
VALUES ('MSFT','20010102',  49.125)
INSERT dbo.stockprices (Symbol, TradingDate, ClosingPrice)
VALUES ('MSFT','20010108',  53.500)

INSERT dbo.stockprices (Symbol, TradingDate, ClosingPrice)
VALUES ('ORCL','20000706',  37.938)
INSERT dbo.stockprices (Symbol, TradingDate, ClosingPrice)
VALUES ('ORCL','20000710',  38.063)
INSERT dbo.stockprices (Symbol, TradingDate, ClosingPrice)
VALUES ('ORCL','20000717',  37.719)
INSERT dbo.stockprices (Symbol, TradingDate, ClosingPrice)
VALUES ('ORCL','20000724',  36.188)
INSERT dbo.stockprices (Symbol, TradingDate, ClosingPrice)
VALUES ('ORCL','20000731',  40.781)
```

```
INSERT dbo.stockprices (Symbol, TradingDate, ClosingPrice)
VALUES ('ORCL','20000807',  40.563)
INSERT dbo.stockprices (Symbol, TradingDate, ClosingPrice)
VALUES ('ORCL','20000814',  40.656)
INSERT dbo.stockprices (Symbol, TradingDate, ClosingPrice)
VALUES ('ORCL','20000821',  42.313)
INSERT dbo.stockprices (Symbol, TradingDate, ClosingPrice)
VALUES ('ORCL','20000828',  46.313)
INSERT dbo.stockprices (Symbol, TradingDate, ClosingPrice)
VALUES ('ORCL','20000905',  43.281)
INSERT dbo.stockprices (Symbol, TradingDate, ClosingPrice)
VALUES ('ORCL','20000911',  39.156)
INSERT dbo.stockprices (Symbol, TradingDate, ClosingPrice)
VALUES ('ORCL','20000918',  40.367)
INSERT dbo.stockprices (Symbol, TradingDate, ClosingPrice)
VALUES ('ORCL','20000925',  39.375)
INSERT dbo.stockprices (Symbol, TradingDate, ClosingPrice)
VALUES ('ORCL','20001002',  33.813)
INSERT dbo.stockprices (Symbol, TradingDate, ClosingPrice)
VALUES ('ORCL','20001009',  35.625)
INSERT dbo.stockprices (Symbol, TradingDate, ClosingPrice)
VALUES ('ORCL','20001016',  35.250)
INSERT dbo.stockprices (Symbol, TradingDate, ClosingPrice)
VALUES ('ORCL','20001023',  34.188)
INSERT dbo.stockprices (Symbol, TradingDate, ClosingPrice)
VALUES ('ORCL','20001030',  30.313)
INSERT dbo.stockprices (Symbol, TradingDate, ClosingPrice)
VALUES ('ORCL','20001106',  25.438)
INSERT dbo.stockprices (Symbol, TradingDate, ClosingPrice)
VALUES ('ORCL','20001113',  28.813)
INSERT dbo.stockprices (Symbol, TradingDate, ClosingPrice)
VALUES ('ORCL','20001120',  24.125)
INSERT dbo.stockprices (Symbol, TradingDate, ClosingPrice)
VALUES ('ORCL','20001127',  26.438)
INSERT dbo.stockprices (Symbol, TradingDate, ClosingPrice)
VALUES ('ORCL','20001204',  30.063)
INSERT dbo.stockprices (Symbol, TradingDate, ClosingPrice)
VALUES ('ORCL','20001211',  28.563)
INSERT dbo.stockprices (Symbol, TradingDate, ClosingPrice)
VALUES ('ORCL','20001218',  31.875)
INSERT dbo.stockprices (Symbol, TradingDate, ClosingPrice)
VALUES ('ORCL','20001226',  29.063)
INSERT dbo.stockprices (Symbol, TradingDate, ClosingPrice)
```

```
VALUES ('ORCL','20010102', 30.125)
INSERT dbo.stockprices (Symbol, TradingDate, ClosingPrice)
VALUES ('ORCL','20010108', 32.313)

DROP FUNCTION dbo.StockPriceFluctuation
GO
CREATE FUNCTION StockPriceFluctuation(@Symbol varchar(10),
        @StartDate smalldatetime='19900101',
        @EndDate smalldatetime='20100101')
RETURNS TABLE
AS
RETURN(
        SELECT
        v.Symbol,
        StartDate=CONVERT(char(8),v.TradingDate,112),
        EndDate=CONVERT(char(8), a.TradingDate,112),
        StartingPrice=v.ClosingPrice,
        EndingPrice=a.ClosingPrice,
        Change=SUBSTRING('- +',
                CAST(SIGN(a.ClosingPrice-v.ClosingPrice)+2 AS
                int),1)+CAST(ABS(a.ClosingPrice-v.ClosingPrice) AS varchar)
        FROM
          (SELECT Symbol, TradingDate, ClosingPrice,
                ranking=(SELECT COUNT(DISTINCT TradingDate)
                    FROM dbo.stockprices u
                    WHERE u.TradingDate <= l.TradingDate)
              FROM dbo.stockprices l) v
          LEFT OUTER JOIN
          (SELECT Symbol, TradingDate, ClosingPrice,
                ranking=(SELECT COUNT(DISTINCT TradingDate)
                    FROM dbo.stockprices u
                    WHERE u.TradingDate <= l.TradingDate)
              FROM dbo.stockprices l) a
          ON (a.ranking=v.ranking+1)
          WHERE v.Symbol = @Symbol AND a.Symbol = @Symbol
          AND a.TradingDate IS NOT NULL
          AND v.TradingDate BETWEEN @StartDate AND @EndDate
          AND a.TradingDate BETWEEN @StartDate AND @EndDate
)
GO
SELECT * FROM StockPriceFluctuation('ORCL',DEFAULT,DEFAULT)
ORDER BY StartDate
```

(Results)

| Symbol | StartDate | EndDate | StartingPrice | EndingPrice | Change |
|--------|-----------|---------|---------------|-------------|--------|
| ORCL | 20000706 | 20000710 | 37.9380 | 38.0630 | +0.1250 |
| ORCL | 20000710 | 20000717 | 38.0630 | 37.7190 | -0.3440 |
| ORCL | 20000717 | 20000724 | 37.7190 | 36.1880 | -1.5310 |
| ORCL | 20000724 | 20000731 | 36.1880 | 40.7810 | +4.5930 |
| ORCL | 20000731 | 20000807 | 40.7810 | 40.5630 | -0.2180 |
| ORCL | 20000807 | 20000814 | 40.5630 | 40.6560 | +0.0930 |
| ORCL | 20000814 | 20000821 | 40.6560 | 42.3130 | +1.6570 |
| ORCL | 20000821 | 20000828 | 42.3130 | 46.3130 | +4.0000 |
| ORCL | 20000828 | 20000905 | 46.3130 | 43.2810 | -3.0320 |
| ORCL | 20000905 | 20000911 | 43.2810 | 39.1560 | -4.1250 |
| ORCL | 20000911 | 20000918 | 39.1560 | 40.3670 | +1.2110 |
| ORCL | 20000918 | 20000925 | 40.3670 | 39.3750 | -0.9920 |
| ORCL | 20000925 | 20001002 | 39.3750 | 33.8130 | -5.5620 |
| ORCL | 20001002 | 20001009 | 33.8130 | 35.6250 | +1.8120 |
| ORCL | 20001009 | 20001016 | 35.6250 | 35.2500 | -0.3750 |
| ORCL | 20001016 | 20001023 | 35.2500 | 34.1880 | -1.0620 |
| ORCL | 20001023 | 20001030 | 34.1880 | 30.3130 | -3.8750 |
| ORCL | 20001030 | 20001106 | 30.3130 | 25.4380 | -4.8750 |
| ORCL | 20001106 | 20001113 | 25.4380 | 28.8130 | +3.3750 |
| ORCL | 20001113 | 20001120 | 28.8130 | 24.1250 | -4.6880 |
| ORCL | 20001120 | 20001127 | 24.1250 | 26.4380 | +2.3130 |
| ORCL | 20001127 | 20001204 | 26.4380 | 30.0630 | +3.6250 |
| ORCL | 20001204 | 20001211 | 30.0630 | 28.5630 | -1.5000 |
| ORCL | 20001211 | 20001218 | 28.5630 | 31.8750 | +3.3120 |
| ORCL | 20001218 | 20001226 | 31.8750 | 29.0630 | -2.8120 |
| ORCL | 20001226 | 20010102 | 29.0630 | 30.1250 | +1.0620 |
| ORCL | 20010102 | 20010108 | 30.1250 | 32.3130 | +2.1880 |

As you can see, this routine plays the role of a parameterized view, just as the SalesHistogram() function did. As with all inline and table-valued functions, you can aggregate the results returned by the function as though they resided in a table:

```
SELECT SUM(CAST(Change AS decimal(10,2)))
FROM StockPriceFluctuation('ORCL',DEFAULT,DEFAULT)
```

(Results)

```
----------------------------------------
-5.63
```

So the value of Oracle Corporation's stock declined by approximately $5.63/share over the six-month period between July 2000 and January 2001. Because we also have data for Microsoft, let's see how it did (Listing 10–16):

**Listing 10–16** Time series fluctuation for Microsoft stock in 2H 2000.

```
SELECT *
FROM StockPriceFluctuation('MSFT',DEFAULT,DEFAULT)
ORDER BY StartDate
```

(Results)

| Symbol | StartDate | EndDate | StartingPrice | EndingPrice | Change |
| ------ | --------- | -------- | ------------- | ----------- | -------------------- |
| MSFT | 20000706 | 20000710 | 82.0000 | 78.9380 | -3.0620 |
| MSFT | 20000710 | 20000717 | 78.9380 | 72.3130 | -6.6250 |
| MSFT | 20000717 | 20000724 | 72.3130 | 69.6880 | -2.6250 |
| MSFT | 20000724 | 20000731 | 69.6880 | 69.1250 | -0.5630 |
| MSFT | 20000731 | 20000807 | 69.1250 | 72.4380 | +3.3130 |
| MSFT | 20000807 | 20000814 | 72.4380 | 71.0000 | -1.4380 |
| MSFT | 20000814 | 20000821 | 71.0000 | 70.6250 | -0.3750 |
| MSFT | 20000821 | 20000828 | 70.6250 | 70.1880 | -0.4370 |
| MSFT | 20000828 | 20000905 | 70.1880 | 69.3130 | -0.8750 |
| MSFT | 20000905 | 20000911 | 69.3130 | 64.1880 | -5.1250 |
| MSFT | 20000911 | 20000918 | 64.1880 | 63.2500 | -0.9380 |
| MSFT | 20000918 | 20000925 | 63.2500 | 60.3130 | -2.9370 |
| MSFT | 20000925 | 20001002 | 60.3130 | 55.5630 | -4.7500 |
| MSFT | 20001002 | 20001009 | 55.5630 | 53.7500 | -1.8130 |
| MSFT | 20001009 | 20001016 | 53.7500 | 65.1880 | +11.4380 |
| MSFT | 20001016 | 20001023 | 65.1880 | 67.6880 | +2.5000 |
| MSFT | 20001023 | 20001030 | 67.6880 | 68.2500 | +0.5620 |
| MSFT | 20001030 | 20001106 | 68.2500 | 67.3750 | -0.8750 |
| MSFT | 20001106 | 20001113 | 67.3750 | 69.0630 | +1.6880 |
| MSFT | 20001113 | 20001120 | 69.0630 | 69.9380 | +0.8750 |
| MSFT | 20001120 | 20001127 | 69.9380 | 56.6250 | -13.3130 |
| MSFT | 20001127 | 20001204 | 56.6250 | 54.4380 | -2.1870 |
| MSFT | 20001204 | 20001211 | 54.4380 | 49.1880 | -5.2500 |
| MSFT | 20001211 | 20001218 | 49.1880 | 46.4380 | -2.7500 |
| MSFT | 20001218 | 20001226 | 46.4380 | 43.3750 | -3.0630 |
| MSFT | 20001226 | 20010102 | 43.3750 | 49.1250 | +5.7500 |
| MSFT | 20010102 | 20010108 | 49.1250 | 53.5000 | +4.3750 |

And, because we've listed fluctuation from week to week within the series, let's look at the total change over the entire six-month period, as we did with Oracle:

```
SELECT SUM(CAST(Change AS decimal(10,2)))
FROM StockPriceFluctuation('MSFT',DEFAULT,DEFAULT)
```

(Results)

```
----------------------------------------
-28.52
```

Looks like Microsoft had a bad six-month run at the end of 2000 as well. Fortunately, both stocks appeared to be climbing at the end of the sampling period.

### Trend Analysis

Beyond listing fluctuation from sample point to sample point, we often want to identify trends in data, especially time series data. The function that follows in Listing 10–17, StockPriceTrends(), shows you how to identify trends in series-oriented data.

Technically, a trend is simply a sequential region or subsection of the data that conforms to some predetermined criteria. For example, we may be looking for members of the distribution that have the same absolute value or the same value relative to one another, or that qualify in some other way. Identifying these regions helps us analyze the trends they represent. StockPriceTrends() identifies regions within stock price data where the price increased from week to week. It uses a variation on the earlier StockPrices table that includes an identity column. Here's the code:

**Listing 10–17** You can use UDFs to identify complex data trends.

```
DROP FUNCTION dbo.StockPriceTrend
GO
CREATE FUNCTION StockPriceTrend(@Symbol varchar(10),
        @StartDate smalldatetime='19900101',
        @EndDate smalldatetime='20100101')
RETURNS TABLE
AS
RETURN(
        SELECT v.TradingDate, v.ClosingPrice
```

```
            FROM dbo.StockPrices v JOIN dbo.StockPrices a
            ON ((a.ClosingPrice >= v.ClosingPrice) AND (a.SampleId = v.SampleId+1))
            OR ((a.ClosingPrice <= v.ClosingPrice) AND (a.SampleId = v.SampleId-1))
            WHERE a.Symbol=@Symbol AND v.Symbol=@Symbol
            AND v.TradingDate BETWEEN @StartDate AND @EndDate
            AND a.TradingDate BETWEEN @StartDate AND @EndDate
            GROUP BY v.TradingDate, v.ClosingPrice
)
GO
SELECT * FROM dbo.StockPriceTrend('MSFT',DEFAULT,DEFAULT)
ORDER BY TradingDate
```

(Results)

| TradingDate | ClosingPrice |
| --- | --- |
| 2000-07-31 00:00:00 | 69.1250 |
| 2000-08-07 00:00:00 | 72.4380 |
| 2000-10-09 00:00:00 | 53.7500 |
| 2000-10-16 00:00:00 | 65.1880 |
| 2000-10-23 00:00:00 | 67.6880 |
| 2000-10-30 00:00:00 | 68.2500 |
| 2000-11-06 00:00:00 | 67.3750 |
| 2000-11-13 00:00:00 | 69.0630 |
| 2000-11-20 00:00:00 | 69.9380 |
| 2000-12-26 00:00:00 | 43.3750 |
| 2001-01-02 00:00:00 | 49.1250 |
| 2001-01-08 00:00:00 | 53.5000 |

If you look back at the data itself, you'll see that each of the sample points listed here belongs to a sequence of data in which the stock price increased from week to week. You can infer the length of the trend by computing the number of sequential weeks each region spans. For example, the first price increase trend begins on July 31st and runs through August 7th. Then we have a gap of a couple months, and then another increase trend starting on October 10th. This trend runs through November 20th. Encapsulating the code in a UDF makes identifying the trends as easy as querying a table.

### *Least Squares Linear Regression*

When the relationship between two variables is approximately linear, it can be summarized with a straight line. A statistical modeling technique for establishing this relationship is known as *least sum of squares linear regression*. It's what most people mean when they say they're using *least squares, regression,* or *linear regression* to fit a model to their data.

Least squares regression allows us to draw a regression line through the points on a two-dimensional plot of the data points in a series. It allows us to establish the relationship between the x- and y-coordinates on the plot.

The function in Listing 10–18, LSLR_StockPrices() extends our stock price metaphor a bit further and computes the slope intercept and coefficient on the stock data we've been working with. In this example, the week of the year is the x-coordinate and the stock price is the y-coordinate, although you could extend the code to work with any two-dimensional data. I've included the week of the year as a computed column in the table to make the routine easier to follow. Here's the code:

**Listing 10–18** A linear squares UDF.

```
DROP FUNCTION dbo.LSLR_StockPrices
GO

CREATE FUNCTION dbo.LSLR_StockPrices()
RETURNS @LSLR TABLE (SlopeCoefficient decimal(38,4),
                     SlopeIntercept decimal(38,3))
AS
BEGIN
  DECLARE @MeanX decimal (38,4),
          @MeanY decimal (38,4),
          @Count decimal (38,4),
          @SlopeCoefficient decimal (38,4)

  DECLARE @WorkTable
  TABLE (x decimal(38,4),
         y decimal(38,4),
         XDeviation decimal(38,4),
         YDeviation decimal(38,4),
         CrossProduct decimal(38,4),
         XDevSquared decimal(38,4),
         YDevSquared decimal(38,4)
  )

  -- Get the means of x and y, and the total number of values
  SELECT  @MeanX=AVG(TradingWeek),
          @MeanY=AVG(ClosingPrice),
          @Count=COUNT(*)
  FROM dbo.StockPrices
```

```
-- Store the deviations for each point,
-- the cross product of the deviations,
-- and the squares of the deviations
INSERT @WorkTable
SELECT
  TradingWeek,
  ClosingPrice,
  TradingWeek-@MeanX,
  ClosingPrice-@MeanY,
  (TradingWeek-@MeanX)*(ClosingPrice-@MeanY),
  POWER(TradingWeek-@MeanX, 2),
  POWER(ClosingPrice-@MeanY, 2)
FROM dbo.StockPrices

-- Compute the slope coefficient
SELECT @SlopeCoefficient =
((@Count * SUM(CrossProduct)) - SUM(x) * SUM(y))     /
((@Count * SUM(XDevSquared)) - POWER(SUM(x), 2))
FROM @WorkTable

-- Insert the slope coefficient and the slope intercept
-- into the table to return
INSERT @LSLR SELECT @SlopeCoefficient,
(@MeanY - (@SlopeCoefficient * @MeanX))
  AS SlopeIntercept -- (For clarity)
RETURN
END
GO

SELECT 'Slope-intercept equation is y = '
      +CAST(SlopeCoefficient AS varchar(10))+'x + '
      +CAST(SlopeIntercept AS varchar(10))
FROM LSLR_StockPrices()
```

(Results)

```
------------------------------------------------------
Slope-intercept equation is y = 1.7903x + -2.811
```

This presents us with a picture of the relationship between x (the week of the year) and y (the stock price). It's expressed in the form of y = mx + b, the slope-intercept formula. Using it, we can predict future values for y (stock prices) if we have x. Of course, there's no strong correlation between the week of the year and the stock price. Nothing about the passage of time makes stock go up or down in value. For that matter, there's no concrete way to predict stock prices with certainty using *any* formula, but this function at least gives a semblance of an analysis tool.

## Recursion

As with stored procedures and triggers, Transact-SQL UDFs support recursion. A UDF can call itself without having to worry about stack management issues or reentrancy. Listing 10–19 is a simple function that uses recursion to compute a number's factorial:

**Listing 10–19** Transact-SQL UDFs support recursion.

```
USE tempdb
GO
IF OBJECT_ID('dbo.Factorial') IS NOT NULL
  DROP FUNCTION dbo.Factorial
GO
CREATE FUNCTION dbo.Factorial(@base_number decimal(38,0))
RETURNS decimal(38,0)
AS
BEGIN
     DECLARE @previous_number decimal(38,0), @factorial decimal(38,0)

     IF ((@base_number>26) and (@@MAX_PRECISION<38)) OR (@base_number>32)
        RETURN(NULL)

     IF (@base_number<0)
       RETURN(NULL)              .

     IF (@base_number<2) SET @factorial=1 -- Factorial of 0 or 1=1
     ELSE BEGIN
       SET @previous_number=@base_number-1
       SET @factorial=dbo.Factorial(@previous_number) -- Recursive call
       IF (@factorial=-1) RETURN(NULL) -- Got an error, return
       SET @factorial=@factorial*@base_number
       IF (@@ERROR<>0) RETURN(NULL) -- Got an error, return
     END
  RETURN(@factorial)
END
GO
```

```
SELECT dbo.Factorial(32) AS Factorial

Factorial
----------------------------------------
263130836933693530167218012160000000
```

Note the bold line in Listing 10–19. It's the recursive call of the function to itself. Factorial() continues to call itself until the entire computation is complete.

## Parameterized UDFs

One of the limitations of UDFs is that you cannot parameterize the objects they work with. That is, if a UDF is coded to work with the StockPrices table, there's no way to have it work with a different table—there's no way to generalize the function. You can't pass the table name in as a parameter to the UDF. If you have ten StockPrice tables named StockPrice0 through StockPrice9, you'll need ten LSLR_StockPrices() functions to work with them.

Because you can't call stored procedures from UDFs or use INSERT… EXEC with table variables, there's no out-of-the-box method for generalizing a UDF so that it can work with any table. Microsoft has made this fairly airtight, but they did leave one backdoor—extended stored procedures. You can execute them from UDFs. This is where xp_exec comes in. Xp_exec is an extended procedure that you can call to execute ad hoc Transact-SQL. You can call it from a UDF. It takes three parameters: a string containing the query to run, a Yes/No flag indicating whether to enlist in the caller's transaction, and the name of the database in which to run the query. You can find the complete discussion of xp_exec in Chapter 20. For now, let's look at a technique that addresses the UDF shortcomings I just mentioned through the use of xp_exec (Listing 10–20):

**Listing 10–20** A UDF that breaks all the UDF rules.

```
USE tempdb
GO
CREATE TABLE dist
(c1 int)
GO
INSERT dist VALUES (1)
INSERT dist VALUES (2)
INSERT dist VALUES (2)
```

```
INSERT dist VALUES (3)
INSERT dist VALUES (3)

INSERT dist VALUES (4)
INSERT dist VALUES (5)
INSERT dist VALUES (8)

GO
DROP FUNCTION MEDIAN
GO
CREATE FUNCTION dbo.MEDIAN(@Tablename sysname, @Colname sysname)
RETURNS @Median Table (Median sql_variant)
AS
BEGIN
  DECLARE @funcsql varchar(8000)
  SET @funcsql='
CREATE FUNCTION dbo.MedianPrim()
RETURNS @MedianTab Table(Median sql_variant)
AS
BEGIN
INSERT @MedianTab
SELECT Median=AVG(c1) FROM (
      SELECT MIN(c1) AS c1 FROM (
      SELECT TOP 50 PERCENT '+@Colname+' AS c1 FROM '+@Tablename+'
      ORDER BY c1 DESC) t
UNION ALL
      SELECT MAX(c1) FROM (
      SELECT TOP 50 PERCENT '+@Colname+' AS c1 FROM '+@Tablename+'
      ORDER BY c1) t
) M
RETURN
END
'

  EXEC master..xp_exec 'DROP FUNCTION dbo.MEDIANPRIM','N','tempdb'
  EXEC master..xp_exec @funcsql,'N','tempdb'
  INSERT @median SELECT * FROM MEDIANPRIM()
  RETURN
END
GO

SELECT * FROM Median('dist','c1')
```

(Results)

```
Median
-----------
3
```

In this example, we create a table-valued function named Median() that takes two parameters: the name of the table on which to compute the median and the name of the column to use to compute it. Let's examine the Median() function to see how it works.

Note the large @funcsql varchar at the top of the function. What is it? It stores the text of a second UDF, called MedianPrim(), that Median() creates via xp_exec. Median() has to create MedianPrim() for two reasons:

1. So that it can INSERT...SELECT the dist table's median into its return result. UDFs can't INSERT...EXEC, but they can INSERT... SELECT.
2. There's no other way for it to dynamically specify the table and column to use for its calculation.

From a performance standpoint, the technique that MedianPrim() uses to compute the median of the table is very efficient. It should execute almost instantly on even very large sets of data.

So, Median() creates MedianPrim() via xp_exec, then INSERT... SELECTs its result. This value is then returned as Median()'s function result. We could have coded both functions to return numeric values instead of tables, but using a table allows us to return multiple values should we decide to (e.g., for vectored medians, and so on).

So. There you have it. A means of getting around most UDF restrictions and making a function that can run any Transact-SQL you specify. Just build a function that follows the general pattern laid out in the Median() routine and— *voila!*—you have a UDF that can do almost anything.

You could rewrite most of the table-valued functions in this chapter to take tables/columns as parameters. Many of them would benefit immensely from this flexibility. For example, the StockPriceFluctuation() and StockPrice-Trend() functions would benefit enormously from being able to refer to other objects.

Before you jump in and start coding every function like Median(), keep these caveats in mind:

1. As mentioned in Chapter 20, xp_exec connects back to the server using an ODBC connection. It connects using the LocalServer system DSN, so this will need to exist on the SQL Server machine.

2. Never specify Y for xp_exec's second parameter when calling xp_exec from a UDF. This parameter specifies whether to join the transaction of the caller. You should not try to enlist in the transaction space of a UDF—it does not work consistently and Microsoft has recommended against it.

3. Queries you run with xp_exec must be less than 8000 bytes in size. This isn't a huge limitation, but it's something to be aware of. The reason for this is obvious. I'm using a varchar to define the parameter within the procedure, and varchars are limited to 8000 bytes.

4. If you want to run your query in a database other than the default specified by the LocalServer DSN or for your login name, you must pass it as xp_exec's third parameter. This parameter is a varchar(128). It doesn't support Unicode types such as nvarchar or sysname.

5. By its very nature, this technique is not multiuser, reentrant, or thread safe. Obviously, if two users try to create MedianPrim() at the same time with two different tables, you've got a problem. If SQL Server calls multiple instances of Median() in parallel threads, you've also got a problem because these calls may well collide with one another. You can disable parallel query execution for a query via the MAXDOP query hint. And, of course, you can't nest recursive calls to this type of function. If MedianPrim() were to call Median(), it would fail because the server would not allow it to drop itself. There's a workaround for the multiuser issue that I'll show you in a moment, but given that UDFs can't reference temporary objects, there's really no seamless solution. It's best to save functions like this for use only in very unusual circumstances.

So, now that we have a working generalized UDF, let's try it out against a different table:

```
SELECT * FROM Median('StockPrices','ClosingPrice')
```

(Results)

```
Median
---------
67.531500
```

Of course, this is the StockPrices table we created in some of the earlier examples. We specify the name of the table and the column on which to compute the median, and the UDF takes care of the rest.

What happens if we want to filter the data in some way? As currently coded, the UDF examines the entirety of the table you pass in. What if you wanted to specify some filter criteria or grouping that should occur before the UDF does its magic? Very simple. Pass a derived table expression into the UDF, like this:

```
SELECT *
FROM Median('(SELECT * FROM StockPrices WHERE Symbol=''MSFT'') AS sp',
'ClosingPrice')
```

The bold string in the previous query is a derived table expression. Have a look at the @funcsql variable in the Median() function, and you'll understand why this works. Because of how we've laid out the function, either a table name or a complete derived table expression can be dropped in place in the Median-Prim() function. You can use this technique to filter or group the data that the UDF sees however you want.

I mentioned earlier that the parameterized UDF technique is inherently a single-user approach. The main reason for this is that the technique depends on the ability to drop and recreate an object while it executes, and it cannot use a unique name or temporary table for this object because UDFs do not allow it. So, every execution of the Median() function drops and recreates the same object: the MedianPrim() function. This means that multiple simultaneous executions would likely collide. What can you do about this? The obvious thing is not to use it in situations in which multiple users may execute it at the same time. Depending on your situation, this may not be practical, so I'll give you a workaround.

Given that we control the code that's generated to create MedianPrim(), we can owner-qualify the function with the name of the current user, then leave off the owner in the INSERT...SELECT back in the Median() function. If we're logged in as, say, JoeUser and we're not a db_owner, MedianPrim() will be created as JoeUser.MedianPrim(), and, as long as no one else logs in with the same account, we won't have to worry about the multiuser collisions I spoke of earlier. Because the owner qualification is omitted in Median(), SQL Server looks first to see whether user JoeUser owns an object named MedianPrim(), and, because he does, that's the function that Median() will end up executing.

Obviously, this workaround requires that your users use different login names and restricts them from being db_owners (a db_owner's database name always reports as "dbo"; hence, we're right back where we started in terms of name collisions). This workaround also requires that you specifically grant rights on both the underlying table that MedianPrim() will be querying and the Median() function. Listing 10–21 provides code that demonstrates this:

**Listing 10–21** You can work around the multiuser issue using the USER_NAME() function.

```
SET NOCOUNT ON
USE tempdb
go
DROP TABLE dbo.StockPrices
GO
CREATE TABLE dbo.StockPrices (Symbol varchar(4), TradingDate smalldatetime,
ClosingPrice decimal(10,4))
/*
Code abridged
*/
INSERT dbo.StockPrices (Symbol, TradingDate, ClosingPrice)
VALUES ('MSFT','20010108',  53.500)
GO
GRANT SELECT ON dbo.StockPrices TO public
GO
DROP FUNCTION MEDIAN
GO
CREATE FUNCTION dbo.MEDIAN(@Tablename sysname, @Colname sysname)
RETURNS @Median Table (Median sql_variant)
AS
BEGIN
  DECLARE @funcsql varchar(8000), @cmd varchar(255)
   SET @funcsql='
CREATE FUNCTION '+USER_NAME()+'.MedianPrim()
RETURNS @MedianTab Table(Median sql_variant)
AS
BEGIN
INSERT @MedianTab
SELECT Median=AVG(c1) FROM (
       SELECT MIN(c1) AS c1 FROM (
       SELECT TOP 50 PERCENT '+@Colname+' AS c1 FROM '+@Tablename+'
       ORDER BY c1 DESC) t
UNION ALL
       SELECT MAX(c1) FROM (
       SELECT TOP 50 PERCENT '+@Colname+' AS c1 FROM '+@Tablename+'
       ORDER BY c1) t
) M
RETURN
END
'
   SET @cmd='DROP FUNCTION '+USER_NAME()+'.MEDIANPRIM'
```

```
    EXEC master..xp_exec @cmd,'N','tempdb'
    EXEC master..xp_exec @funcsql,'N','tempdb'
    INSERT @median SELECT * FROM MEDIANPRIM()
    RETURN
END
GO
GRANT SELECT ON dbo.Median TO public
GO
```

This code creates the table and the Median() function and grants SELECT access on both of them to the public group. Note the use of the USER_NAME() function within the Median() function. For non-db_owners, this provides a modicum of isolation between concurrent executions of parameterized functions—a kind of namespace, if you will.

Once this is complete, the stage is set for other users to compute medians using the parameterized UDF. They query just as the dbo or any other user would:

```
USE tempdb
GO
SELECT * FROM Median('dbo.TemperatureData','HiTemp')
```

# Summary

In this chapter you learned how UDFs work, how to create your own, and what to watch out for when building them. You learned how to create system functions, and you learned how to use the xp_exec extended procedure to get around many of the limitations UDFs bring with them.

# PART III

# HTML, XML, and .NET

# CHAPTER 11

# HTML

*People often ask me what I think about the downfall of the so-called new economy and the end of the new world order doing business on the Internet was supposed to have ushered in. Frankly, I'm glad about it. I'm glad it still takes hard work to succeed. I'm glad it takes more than a good idea to acquire long-term wealth. I'm glad you still have to run a business intelligently to make it last. These are all good things. That the speculators and snake oil salesmen of the dotcom craze have been largely silenced is the best thing to happen to the Net since the invention of the browser.*

—*H. W. Kenton*

This chapter is not about Hypertext Markup Language (HTML), per se, but about how you can translate data stored in SQL Server databases into HTML. HTML is the subject of (many) other books; we'll focus on SQL Server topics in this one. The subject of translating XML into HTML via style sheets is covered in Chapter 12.

## Origins

The Web experience, as we know it, was officially born when Tim Berners-Lee at CERN (*le Conseil Européen pour la Recherche Nucléaire,* or the European Laboratory for Particle Physics) in Geneva designed HTML to allow people in the physics community to communicate with each other. In December 1990, HTML was released within CERN, and it became available to the public in the summer of 1991. In the grand tradition of Internet share-and-enjoy, CERN and Berners-Lee gave away the specifications for HTML, Hypertext Transfer Protocol (HTTP), and uniform resource locators (URLs).

Berners-Lee based HTML on the Standard Generalized Markup Language (SGML). Like XML, SGML is a *meta-language* and can be used to define other languages. Each language that's defined this way is called an SGML *application*. HTML is an SGML application.

For its part, SGML came about from research at IBM in the late 1960s into the generalized representation of text documents. Out of that research came GML (General Markup Language), a predecessor to SGML. In 1978, ANSI produced the first version of SGML. ANSI released the draft of the first SGML standard in 1985, and the standard itself in 1986. In a portent of things to come, CERN's Anders Berglund developed the SGML system that published the first SGML standard. CERN, of course, is the organization that later gave us HTML and the Web.

The US Department of Defense, many other government entities, and numerous large industries and corporations have settled on SGML as a document standard. Although SGML is complex and difficult to work with, its flexibility makes it attractive to industries in which document needs are complex and vary widely.

By most accounts, the reason SGML hasn't been adopted on a grander scale is its complexity. It's too complex for most people to work with successfully, in my opinion. HTML, on the other hand, is very simple and *not* very sophisticated. Unfortunately, for many needs, it's too simple.

## Producing HTML from Transact-SQL

Because of its basic simplicity, HTML isn't terribly hard to produce. That's why, to this day, many hard-core HTML coders prefer simple tools like Notepad to all-encompassing products like Frontpage. Compared with its forerunner SGML, HTML is very basic indeed. As such, it's easy to program and easy to produce. In fact, you can emit HTML from Transact-SQL with very little effort at all.

### Tables

Tables represent a natural display format for relational data. Because HTML offers direct support for tabular data display, it only makes sense to explore producing HTML tables from SQL Server data. HTML tables are delimited by <TABLE> tags and each row is delimited with <TR> tags. Each piece of data within a table is delimited with <TD> tags. Given that these tags and the data they enclose consist of plain text, you can easily produce an HTML table using a simple Transact-SQL query. Listing 11–1 illustrates one way of doing this:

**Listing 11–1** Transact-SQL that produces HTML.

```
SET NOCOUNT ON
USE Northwind
GO
SELECT
'<TABLE BORDER="1">','','',''
UNION ALL
SELECT TOP 10
'<TR>','<TD>'+CompanyName+'</TD>','<TD>'+CustomerId+'</TD>','</TR>'
FROM customers
UNION ALL
SELECT
'</TABLE>','','',''
```

(Results)

```
---------------- ----------------------------------------- -------------------
<TABLE BORDER="1">
<TR>            <TD>Alfreds Futterkiste</TD>               <TD>ALFKI</TD> </TR>
<TR>            <TD>Ana Trujillo Emparedados y helados</TD> <TD>ANATR</TD> </TR>
<TR>            <TD>Antonio Moreno Taquería</TD>            <TD>ANTON</TD> </TR>
<TR>            <TD>Around the Horn</TD>                    <TD>AROUT</TD> </TR>
<TR>            <TD>Berglunds snabbköp</TD>                 <TD>BERGS</TD> </TR>
<TR>            <TD>Blauer See Delikatessen</TD>            <TD>BLAUS</TD> </TR>
<TR>            <TD>Blondesddsl père et fils</TD>           <TD>BLONP</TD> </TR>
<TR>            <TD>Bólido Comidas preparadas</TD>          <TD>BOLID</TD> </TR>
<TR>            <TD>Bon app'</TD>                           <TD>BONAP</TD> </TR>
<TR>            <TD>Bottom-Dollar Markets</TD>              <TD>BOTTM</TD> </TR>
</TABLE>
```

Like most kinds of tables, HTML tables have three basic parts: the header, the body, and the footer. This query produces all three through the use of UNIONs. The first SELECT produces the header—the obligatory <TABLE> tag, along with a width specification for the lines that make up the table grid. The second SELECT produces the body of the table, enveloping each column value in the required <TD> tags and surrounding each row with <TR> tags. The final SELECT produces the closing </TABLE> tag.

If you run this query in OSQL with column headers and line numbering disabled, it will produce an HTML table that can then be displayed in a browser. Figure 11–1 illustrates what it should look like:

| | |
|---|---|
| Alfreds Futterkiste | ALFKI |
| Ana Trujillo Emparedados y helados | ANATR |
| Antonio Moreno Taquerja | ANTON |
| Around the Horn | AROUT |
| Berglunds snabbk"p | BERGS |
| Blauer See Delikatessen | BLAUS |
| Blondesddsl pŠre et fils | BLONP |
| B¢lido Comidas preparadas | BOLID |
| Bon app' | BONAP |
| Bottom-Dollar Markets | BOTTM |

**Figure 11–1** The table produced by our Transact-SQL.

Given that the script does all the real work of producing the HTML, it's trivial to generalize the call to OSQL by placing it in a .CMD file. Listing 11–2 illustrates a .CMD file that you can use to create and open an HTML document produced by OSQL:

**Listing 11–2** TSQL2HTML.CMD—a command file that produces HTML from T-SQL.

```
@echo off
OSQL -E -h-1 -n -i%1.sql -o%1.html %2
%1.html
```

TSQL2HTML.CMD takes two parameters: the name of the script to run and an optional OSQL command-line parameter (for example, to specify the server name, as in -Sservername). If the script you pass in renders valid HTML, it will be displayed once it's been written to an .HTML file.

## Column Headings

You may have noticed that our HTML table contains no column headings. This is easily remedied. Here's a variation on the earlier query that includes column headings (Listing 11–3):

**Listing 11–3** A revision of the Customers query that includes column headings.

```
SET NOCOUNT ON
USE Northwind
GO
SELECT
'<TABLE BORDER="1">','<TH>Company Name</TH>','<TH>Customer ID</TH>',''
UNION ALL
SELECT TOP 10
'<TR>','<TD>'+CompanyName+'</TD>','<TD>'+CustomerId+'</TD>','</TR>'
FROM customers
UNION ALL
SELECT
'</TABLE>','','',''
```

(Results)

```
------------------  ---------------------------------------------  ---------------- ----
<TABLE BORDER="1">  <TH>Company Name</TH>                           <TH>CustomerID</TH>
<TR>                <TD>Alfreds Futterkiste</TD>                    <TD>ALFKI</TD>   </TR>
<TR>                <TD>Ana Trujillo Emparedados y helados</TD>     <TD>ANATR</TD>   </TR>
<TR>                <TD>Antonio Moreno Taquería</TD>                 <TD>ANTON</TD>   </TR>
<TR>                <TD>Around the Horn</TD>                         <TD>AROUT</TD>   </TR>
<TR>                <TD>Berglunds snabbköp</TD>                      <TD>BERGS</TD>   </TR>
<TR>                <TD>Blauer See Delikatessen</TD>                 <TD>BLAUS</TD>   </TR>
<TR>                <TD>Blondesddsl père et fils</TD>                <TD>BLONP</TD>   </TR>
<TR>                <TD>Bólido Comidas preparadas</TD>               <TD>BOLID</TD>   </TR>
<TR>                <TD>Bon app'</TD>                                <TD>BONAP</TD>   </TR>
<TR>                <TD>Bottom-Dollar Markets</TD>                   <TD>BOTTM</TD>   </TR>
</TABLE>
```

The only real change here is the addition of <TH> tags and column heading text to the first SELECT statement. These appear in the first row of output from the query. HTML <TH> tags specify headings for table columns, so if you save this result set to an .HTML file and open it in a browser, you should see something like the table in Figure 11–2.

Of course, you can produce more than just HTML tables using this technique. You can produce any valid HTML you want, and you can use the SQL Server query processor to help you iterate through the data as you do.

| Company Name | Customer ID |
|---|---|
| Alfreds Futterkiste | ALFKI |
| Ana Trujillo Emparedados y helados | ANATR |
| Antonio Moreno Taquerja | ANTON |
| Around the Horn | AROUT |
| Berglunds snabbk"p | BERGS |
| Blauer See Delikatessen | BLAUS |
| Blondesddsl pŠre et fils | BLONP |
| B¢lido Comidas preparadas | BOLID |
| Bon app' | BONAP |
| Bottom-Dollar Markets | BOTTM |

**Figure 11–2** The table with column headings.

## Producing HTML from sp_makewebtask

Up to this point we've been exploring emitting HTML the old-fashioned way—through Transact-SQL and OSQL. SQL Server includes a much better way of translating data from a database into HTML: sp_makewebtask. Sp_makewebtask exposes a full-blown HTML production engine that you can use to create tasks that produce Web pages from SQL Server data.

One of the challenges of writing a SQL Server book is in trying to avoid replicating what's already covered in the Books Online while remaining thorough enough to be comprehensive and to reassure those who've purchased the book that their money was well spent. SQL Server's online documentation has long been one of its strong points. It's far more extensive, cohesive, and generally more useful than the online documentation of the other DBMS products I regularly work with. That said, its thoroughness makes writing about topics it covers in depth challenging for those who don't want to simply rephrase what it says quite well already. Rather than rehash the info that comes in the box with the product, I'd rather spend the limited number of pages in this book teaching you things that don't.

So, rather than list the syntax and parameter list for sp_makewebtask, I'll let you research that in the Books Online. I'll explain in general terms how sp_makewebtask works, then provide some examples that should get you started using it yourself.

Sp_makewebtask is a stored procedure that creates a SQL Server job that produces HTML from data stored in a SQL Server database. It can schedule this job, run it immediately, or both. For scheduled jobs, sp_runwebtask can be used to invoke them manually.

There are nearly three dozen parameters that you can pass to sp_makewebtask. The two most important ones are @query and @outputfile. The @query parameter specifies a query to produce the data you want to display, and @outputfile specifies the name of the file in which to save the newly generated HTML. Here's a call to sp_makewebtask that produces the same table we built ourselves using plain Transact-SQL (Listing 11–4):

**Listing 11–4** sp_makewebtask produces our table with one line of code.

```
EXEC sp_makewebtask @outputfile = 'C:\temp\cust_table.HTML',
@query='SELECT CompanyName, CustomerID FROM Northwind..Customers ORDER BY
CompanyName'
, @lastupdated=0,@resultstitle='  '
```

(Results abridged)

| CompanyName | CustomerID |
|---|---|
| Alfreds Futterkiste | ALFKI |
| Ana Trujillo Emparedados y helados | ANATR |
| Antonio Moreno Taquería | ANTON |
| Around the Horn | AROUT |
| Berglunds snabbköp | BERGS |
| Blauer See Delikatessen | BLAUS |
| Vaffeljernet | VAFFE |
| Victuailles en stock | VICTE |
| Vins et alcools Chevalier | VINET |
| Wartian Herkku | WARTH |
| Wellington Importadora | WELLI |
| White Clover Markets | WHITC |
| Wilman Kala | WILMK |
| Wolski Zajazd | WOLZA |

In addition to the @query and @outputfile parameters, we also specify the @lastupdated and @resultstitle parameters. The @lastupdated parameter takes a 1 or 0 indicating whether you want a "Last Updated" line included on the Web page. Here we disable it by specifying 0. The @resultstitle parameter specifies a page heading string. We pass two spaces to it in order to disable the display of a results title. The default is "Query Results."

One parameter that we didn't specify is the @whentype parameter. It takes an integer specifying when to create the Web page. The page can be created immediately (the default), when requested, when scheduled, or some combination of the three. By not specifying the parameter, we leave it at its default (1) which simply creates the page immediately.

### Hyperlinks

Sp_makewebtask can also include hyperlinks on the pages it creates. You can specify a single URL directly or supply a query that provides a list of them. Here's an example that adds a single URL to the bottom of a generated page (Listing 11–5):

**Listing 11–5** sp_makewebtask can optionally include hyperlinks on the pages it creates.

```
EXEC sp_makewebtask @outputfile = 'C:\temp\cust_table.HTML',
@query='SELECT CompanyName, CustomerID FROM Northwind..Customers ORDER BY
CompanyName',
@lastupdated=0, @resultstitle=' ',
@URL='http://www.khen.com',@reftext='Ken Henderson''s Home Page'
```

(Results abridged)

| CompanyName | CustomerID |
|---|---|
| Alfreds Futterkiste | ALFKI |
| Ana Trujillo Emparedados y helados | ANATR |
| Antonio Moreno Taquería | ANTON |
| Around the Horn | AROUT |
| Berglunds snabbköp | BERGS |
| Blauer See Delikatessen | BLAUS |
| Vaffeljernet | VAFFE |
| Victuailles en stock | VICTE |
| Vins et alcools Chevalier | VINET |
| Wartian Herkku | WARTH |
| Wellington Importadora | WELLI |
| White Clover Markets | WHITC |
| Wilman Kala | WILMK |
| Wolski Zajazd | WOLZA |

Ken Henderson's Home Page

Note the hyperlink at the bottom of the page. Sp_makewebtask can also retrieve URLs from a query that you supply. This query needs to supply both the URL and the display text for each hyperlink you want to include. An example is presented in Listing 11–6:

**Listing 11–6** You can supply a table of hyperlinks for sp_makewebtask to use.

```
CREATE TABLE WebSites(URL varchar(100), URL_text varchar(100) NULL)
GO
INSERT WebSites VALUES ('http://www.awl.com', 'Addison-Wesley')
INSERT WebSites VALUES ('http://www.khen.com','Ken Henderson''s Home Page')
GO
EXEC sp_makewebtask @outputfile = 'C:\temp\cust_table.HTML',
@query='SELECT CompanyName, CustomerID FROM Northwind..Customers ORDER BY
CompanyName',
@lastupdated=0, @resultstitle=' ',
@table_urls = 1, @url_query= 'SELECT URL, URL_text FROM WebSites'
```

(Results abridged)

| CompanyName | CustomerID |
|---|---|
| Alfreds Futterkiste | ALFKI |
| Ana Trujillo Emparedados y helados | ANATR |
| Antonio Moreno Taquería | ANTON |
| Around the Horn | AROUT |
| Berglunds snabbköp | BERGS |
| Blauer See Delikatessen | BLAUS |
| Vaffeljernet | VAFFE |
| Victuailles en stock | VICTE |
| Vins et alcools Chevalier | VINET |
| Wartian Herkku | WARTH |
| Wellington Importadora | WELLI |
| White Clover Markets | WHITC |
| Wilman Kala | WILMK |
| Wolski Zajazd | WOLZA |

Addison-Wesley
Ken Henderson's Home Page

Note the hyperlinks at the bottom of the page. These are added to the page through two key parameters: @table_urls and @url_query. @table_urls tells sp_makewebtask to generate a list of URLs using the query specified in @url_query. Note that @URL and @reftext are mutually exclusive of @table_urls and @urll_query. You can specify one pair or the other, but not both.

## Templates

The ability to configure most of what sp_makewebtask does through parameters is nice, but an even more powerful and more flexible approach is to use HTML templates. Sp_makewebtask supports the use of HTML templates with placeholders indicating where to insert data. This gives you complete control over formatting and placement of data, and allows you to create sophisticated "data-driven" Web pages. Here's an example of an HTML template (Listing 11–7):

**Listing 11–7** A basic HTML template.

```
<HTML>

<HEAD>

<TITLE>An HTML template that displays Customer data</TITLE>

<BODY>

<H1>Customers</H1>

<P>
<%insert_data_here%>
<P>

<A HREF = "http://www.awl.com">Addison-Wesley</A><P>
<A HREF = "http://www.khen.com">Ken Henderson's Home Page</A><P>

</BODY>

</HTML>
```

The key here is the <%insert_data_here%> placeholder. It specifies where sp_makewebtask inserts the data returned by the query supplied in @query. Here's a query (Listing 11–8) that makes use of the template:

**Listing 11–8** The Customers table listed using a template.

```
EXEC sp_makewebtask @outputfile = 'C:\temp\cust_table.HTML',
@query='SELECT CompanyName, CustomerID FROM Northwind..Customers ORDER BY
CompanyName',
@templatefile='c:/temp/cust_table.htp',
@lastupdated=0, @resultstitle='  '
```

(Results abridged)

## Customers

| CompanyName | CustomerID |
|---|---|
| Alfreds Futterkiste | ALFKI |
| Ana Trujillo Emparedados y helados | ANATR |
| Antonio Moreno TaquerÃa | ANTON |
| Around the Horn | AROUT |
| Berglunds snabbkÃ¶p | BERGS |
| Blauer See Delikatessen | BLAUS |
| Vaffeljernet | VAFFE |
| Victuailles en stock | VICTE |
| Vins et alcools Chevalier | VINET |
| Wartian Herkku | WARTH |
| Wellington Importadora | WELLI |
| White Clover Markets | WHITC |
| Wilman Kala | WILMK |
| Wolski Zajazd | WOLZA |

Addison-Wesley
Ken Henderson's Home Page

Although the ability to control the HTML completely that precedes and
follows the query result set certainly affords a great deal of flexibility, for sophisticated, professional-looking Web pages you need the ability to control the formatting of the result set itself. You can use templates to do this as well. Rather
than simply inserting the result set as one contiguous monolithic piece, you can
specify formatting for each column in the result set. Listing 11–9 presents a
template that does this:

**Listing 11–9** A more sophisticated template that allows row and column formatting.

```
<HTML>

<HEAD>

<TITLE>An HTML template that displays Customer data</TITLE>

<BODY>

<H1>Customers</H1>

<P>
<TABLE BORDER>
<TR> <TH><B>Company Name</B></TH><TH><B>Customer ID</B></TH></TR>
<%begindetail%>
<TR><TD><%insert_data_here%></TD><TD><I><%insert_data_here%></I></TD></TR>
<%enddetail%>
</TABLE>
<P>
<A HREF = "http://www.awl.com">Addison-Wesley</A><P>
<A HREF = "http://www.khen.com">Ken Henderson's Home Page</A><P>

</BODY>
</HTML>
```

Notice the <%begindetail%> and <%enddetail%> placeholders. They envelop the body of the table that sp_makewebtask generates. Specifically, they allow you to control the formatting of the rows in the table. Notice that we've used HTML <I> tags to italicize the second column. Using standard HTML tags, you can bold columns, underline them, change the display font or color, and so forth. The <%insert_date_here%> placeholder we used earlier indicates where to insert each column (columns are inserted in the order they're returned by the query). Listing 11–10 is the query that uses this template and the resulting Web page:

**Listing 11–10** The table produced by the custom template.

```
EXEC sp_makewebtask @outputfile = 'C:\temp\cust_table.HTML',
@query='SELECT CompanyName, CustomerID FROM Northwind..Customers ORDER BY
CompanyName',
```

```
@templatefile='c:\temp\cust_table2.htp',
@lastupdated=0, @resultstitle='  '
```

(Results abridged)

## Customers

| CompanyName | CustomerID |
|---|---|
| Alfreds Futterkiste | ALFKI |
| Ana Trujillo Emparedados y helados | ANATR |
| Antonio Moreno TaquerÃa | ANTON |
| Around the Horn | AROUT |
| Berglunds snabbkÃ¶p | BERGS |
| Blauer See Delikatessen | BLAUS |
| Vaffeljernet | VAFFE |
| Victuailles en stock | VICTE |
| Vins et alcools Chevalier | VINET |
| Wartian Herkku | WARTH |
| Wellington Importadora | WELLI |
| White Clover Markets | WHITC |
| Wilman Kala | WILMK |
| Wolski Zajazd | WOLZA |

Addison-Wesley
Ken Henderson's Home Page

Using templates and HTML's ability to control text layout and formatting, you can create sophisticated pages with little or no coding. Moreover, by standardizing your Web page production using templates, you give your Web site a uniform look and feel, and can take advantage of more advanced features such as cascading style sheets, DHTML, and embedded controls.

## Summary

In this chapter you learned how to produce HTML documents (Web pages) using SQL Server's Web tools. You learned how to produce HTML using plain Transact-SQL, and you were introduced to the powerful and flexible sp_makewebtask stored procedure. You can read up on sp_makewebtask in the Books Online, but the introduction provided here should get you well on your way to generating complex Web pages containing SQL Server data.

# CHAPTER 12

# Introduction to XML

*He that will not apply new remedies must expect new evils for time is the greatest innovator.*

*—Francis Bacon*[1]

I'm including an introductory chapter on XML in this book for two reasons. One, because XML is now a core component of SQL Server, I think it deserves to be covered in books that cover SQL Server. Two, many Transact-SQL programmers are new to XML, and understanding how XML works is fundamental to understanding not only the other chapters in this book that cover XML, but also the current and future course that SQL Server is taking.

Unfortunately, there isn't time or space to discuss XML as completely as I'd like to. Whole books (many of them, in fact) have been written on the subject of XML and the XML family of technologies. I'll try to hit the high points of what you need to know about XML to be able to use SQL Server's XML-related features. That said, you should probably supplement the coverage here with research of your own. See the "Further Reading" section later in the chapter for some recommended resources.

## Wooden Nickels

The first thing you should know about XML is that *XML is not hard*. It is not difficult to learn. In its bare essence, XML is a programmable, hierarchical text file format—that's all. It will not cure cancer or walk your dog. It's simply a technology—a very powerful technology—that people are using to enable applications to work together and share data. It is *not* hard, and its syntax isn't even that complex, as you'll see in just a moment.

---

1. Bacon, Francis. *The Essays*, New York: Penguin, 1985. Page 132.

That said, XML does seem to be in a constant state of flux—its creators just can't seem to leave it alone. I'm reminded of what the French film director Marcel Pagnol once said, "One has to look out for engineers—they begin with sewing machines and end up with the atomic bomb." XML's extensibility has led to a dizzying array of initiatives based on it. It seems there's a new XML-related W3C draft specification or recommendation published every week. Just when you think you have your arms around the technology, a new XML application drops out of the sky that addresses a new problem you hadn't thought of, or addresses an old problem in a new way. How does one stay up with all this? How can you possibly make time to master all these XML technologies when all you want to do is share data between your company's SQL Server database and your supplier's UNIX order tracking system?

My advice? Relax. You don't need to know every XML application or technology in order to use XML for its primary purpose. The primary function of XML is to provide open data exchange between platforms and applications. An understanding of XML's purpose and syntax—neither of which is difficult to grasp—is all you need to use XML productively. The nice thing about XML is that technologies based on it, which are referred to as XML *applications*, are built with XML itself. So if you can read XML, you can read an XML style sheet, even if you've never seen one before and don't have the foggiest idea of what it will be used for. Of course, reading is one thing; understanding is another. Being able to read English doesn't mean that one can understand a physics textbook written in English. That said, most of the core members of the XML family of technologies are not difficult to grasp, even though they are capable of performing some very complex tasks.

My second recommendation is this: Don't let anyone sell you any wooden nickels, as my grandfather used to say each time I left his home. In the gold rush-like fever that has surrounded XML since it was first introduced, a number of XML "experts" have come out of the woodwork offering their services to the unwary. What they were doing before they became XML experts is anyone's guess, but oftentimes it turns out to have had little to do with the Web or even technology in general. Be very careful of this. Interest in a technology is not the same thing as expertise in it. Enthusiasm is good; experience is better. I'm enthusiastic about the NBA, but that doesn't qualify me to coach. If a person claims to be an expert in a particular technology—XML or some other—but hasn't actually used it to build anything, I'm not interested. You cannot master XML by studying W3C recommendations or reading MSDN. Sure, researching a technology to improve your knowledge of it is important. Of course it is. That's why you're reading this book. Read voraciously. Don't stop with W3C recommendations and MSDN. Read everything you can get your hands on regarding XML. This will only advance your overall knowledge of it. But to master any technology, you must use it, and I don't mean to build toy applications or strawman examples. To viscerally know something as broad and as deep as XML, you must build things with it—real things, complex things, useful things.

The situation reminds me of the early days of Java, during which it seemed there was a Java expert on every corner. It was cool to know Java. Java was the new "thing." The book *Teach Yourself Java* was outselling Stephen King (!), and Java was in the media more than any programming language had ever been. User groups were formed, seminars were conducted, books were written—Java was taking over the world. There was just one problem. Most of the people extolling all the virtues of Java to do everything from create safer programs to bring back the dinosaurs had never built anything of any significance with it. It was too new. How can you be an expert on something that just came out yesterday?

Since then, the overall level of expertise in the Java community has improved dramatically. Real Java applications are being built all over the world. We now have several years of experience with it under our belts. Now we *really* know what Java can do and what it cannot, what it does well and what it does not do so well. And Java itself has evolved. There's a whole new crop of Java experts, but these aren't the same people who were on the street corners five years ago. These are the old hands of other languages, the veterans who took a look at Java and realized its immense potential if used properly. They didn't dive into Java the moment it came out because they know better than to adopt a technology just because it's new or is the latest fad. They waited a little, let the standards settle a bit, then began studying Java to see whether it was any better at tackling the problems they'd been addressing for years with language like C++. Many determined that Java *could* improve the way they built applications—that it *was* an improvement over the old ways of doing things—and so they joined the revolution. This is how intelligent adoption of technology should work: It should not be based on fads or a desire to strike it rich. It should be based on experience, data, and reasoning that tells us that the technology in question is enough better than the technology we're using to justify its adoption, to make the overall price of putting it in place near zero because its benefits outweigh its costs.

So, be wary of the snake oil salesmen out there. If someone tells you XML is difficult to learn (and, therefore, you need their expensive consulting to help you understand it), run—don't walk—the other way. If they claim to be experts, but don't have the references to back it up, slam the door. Remember: Enthusiasm is good; experience is even better. There are two kinds of technologists in the world: those who aspire to technical prowess in some area but are not willing to put in the hours necessary to acquire it, and those who love their craft and work diligently everyday to hone it.

# XML: An Overview

Thanks to the World Wide Web, HTML has taken over the world. And yet, despite its ubiquity and popularity, HTML has always had a number of serious limitations. You don't have to build Web applications for very long before you run into some of them. HTML works reasonably well for formatting informal documents, but not so well for more complex tasks. It was never intended to describe the structure of data, but business needs have caused it to be used to do just that. The fact that it's being used to do things it was never intended to do has highlighted many of its shortcomings. It has created the need for a more powerful markup language—one that's data-centric rather than display-centric, one that doesn't just know how to format data, but that can give the data contextual meaning.

XML is the answer to many of the problems with HTML and with building extensible applications in general. XML is easy for anyone who understands HTML to learn, but is overwhelmingly more powerful. XML is more than just a markup language—it's a *meta-language*—a language that can be used to define new languages. With XML, you can create a language that's tailored to your particular application or business domain and use it to exchange data with your vendors, your trading partners, your customers, and anyone else that can speak XML.

Rather than replacing HTML, XML complements it. Beyond merely providing a means of formatting data, XML gives it contextual meaning. Once data has contextual meaning, displaying it is the easy part. But displaying it is just one of the many things you can do with the data once it has context. By correctly separating the presentation of the data from its storage and management, we open up an almost infinite number of opportunities for using the data and exchanging it with other parties.

In this chapter we'll explore the history of markup languages and how XML came into existence. We'll look at how data is presented in HTML and compare that with how XML improves on it. We'll discuss why you might want to set up your own XML dialect, and we'll explore how to go about it. We'll touch on the basics of XML notation, and how XML can be displayed through translation to HTML via XML style sheets. We'll talk about document validation using both

Document Type Definitions (DTDs) and XML schemas, and we'll discuss some of the nuances of each. We'll finish up by touching on the Document Object Model (DOM) and how it's used to manipulate XML documents as objects.

## HTML: Simplicity Comes at a Price

HTML's purpose is to format documents. It specifies display elements—titles, headings, fonts, captions, and so on. It's very presentation oriented. It's pretty good at laying out data. It's not good at describing that data or making it generally accessible.

Web site designers have worked around HTML's many shortcomings in some astonishingly novel ways. Still, HTML has serious flaws that make it ill suited for building complex, open information systems. Here are a few of them:

- HTML isn't extensible. Each browser supports a fixed set of tags, and you may not add your own.
- HTML is format-centric. Although it displays data reasonably well, HTML gives data no context. If the format of data a program is accessing via HTML changes, the program will likely break.
- Once generated, HTML is static and cannot be easily refreshed. DHTML and other technologies help alleviate this, but HTML, in its most basic essence, was never intended to serve up live data.
- HTML provides only a single view of data. Because it is display-centric, changing the view of the data is more difficult than it should be. Again, technologies like DHTML help to some extent, but the bottom line is that we need a markup language that *knows* about its data.
- HTML has little or no semantic structure. There's no facility for representing data by *meaning* rather than by layout. As I've said, HTML's forte is displaying data, and sometimes it's not even very good at that.

Although SGML doesn't have these faults, its vast flexibility makes it extremely complex, as I've said. DSSSL (Document Style Semantics and Specification Language), the language used to format SGML, is powerful and flexible, but this power comes at a price: It's extremely difficult to use. What we need is a language that's similar to HTML in terms of ease of use, but that features the flexibility of SGML.

# XML: A Brief History

With the explosion the Web and the massive amount of HTML development that consequently began to be undertaken, people began running into HTMLs many shortcomings very quickly. At the same time, SGML proponents, who'd been working in relative obscurity for many years, began looking for a way to use SGML itself on the Web, instead of just one application of it (HTML). They realized that SGML itself was too complex for the task. Most people couldn't or wouldn't use it, so they needed an alternative. Again, what they were looking for was something that blended the best aspects of HTML and SGML.

In mid-1996, Jon Bosak of Sun Microsystems approached the W3C about forming a committee on using SGML on the Web. The effort was given the green light by the W3C's Dan Connolly and, although organized, led, and underwritten by Sun Microsystems, the actual work was shared among Bosak and people from outside Sun Microsystems, including Tim Bray, C. M. Sperberg-McQueen, and Jean Paoli of Microsoft. By November of 1996, the committee had the beginnings of a simplified form of SGML that was no more difficult to learn and use than HTML, but that retained many of the best features of SGML. This was the birth of XML as we know it.

# XML versus HTML: An Example

I've mentioned that you can create your own tags in XML. This is such a powerful, vital part of XML that it bears further discussion. If you're used to working in HTML, this concept is probably very foreign to you because HTML does not allow you to define your own tags. Although various browser vendors have extended HTML with their own custom tags, the bottom line is that at some point you're stuck. You have to use the tags provided to you by your browser. You cannot make your own.

So how do you define a new tag in XML? The simplest answer is: You don't have to. You just use it. You can control which tags are valid in an XML document using DTD documents and XML schemas (we'll talk about each of these later), but the bottom line is that you simply use a tag to define it in XML. There is no **typedef** or similar construct.

To compare and contrast how HTML and XML represent data, let's look at the same data represented using each language. Here's some sample HTML that displays a recipe (Listing 12–1):

**Listing 12–1**  A basic HTML document.

```
<!-- The original html recipe -->
<HTML>
<HEAD>
<TITLE>Henderson's Hotter-than-Hell Haba?ero Sauce</TITLE>
</HEAD>
<BODY>
<H3>Henderson's Hotter-than-Hell Habañero Sauce</H3>
Homegrown from stuff in my garden (you don't want to know exactly what).
<H4>Ingredients</H4>
<TABLE BORDER="1">
<TR BGCOLOR="#308030"><TH>Qty</TH><TH>Units</TH><TH>Item</TH></TR>
<TR><TD>6</TD><TD>each</TD><TD>Habañero peppers</TD></TR>
<TR><TD>12</TD><TD>each</TD><TD>Cowhorn peppers</TD></TR>
<TR><TD>12</TD><TD>each</TD><TD>Jalapeño peppers</TD></TR>
<TR><TD></TD><TD>dash</TD><TD>Tequila (optional)</TD></TR>
</TABLE>
<P>
<H4>Instructions</H4>
<OL>
<LI>Chop up peppers, removing their stems, then grind to a liquid.</LI>
<!-- and so forth -->
</BODY>
</HTML>
```

If you read through the HTML in Listing 12–1, you'll no doubt notice that the recipe is stored in an HTML table. Figure 12–1 shows what it looks like in a browser.

There are several positive aspects of how HTML represents this data:

1. It's readable. If you look hard enough, you can tell what data the HTML contains.
2. It can be displayed by any browser, even nongraphical ones.
3. A cascading style sheet could be used to further control the formatting.

However, there's a really big negative aspect that outweighs the others insofar as data markup goes: There's nothing in the code to indicate the *meaning* of any of its elements. The data contained in the document has no context. A program could scan the document and pick out the items in the table, but it wouldn't know what they were. And although you could hard code assumptions about the data (column 1 is **Qty,** column 2 is **Units,** and so on), if the format of the page were changed, your app would break.

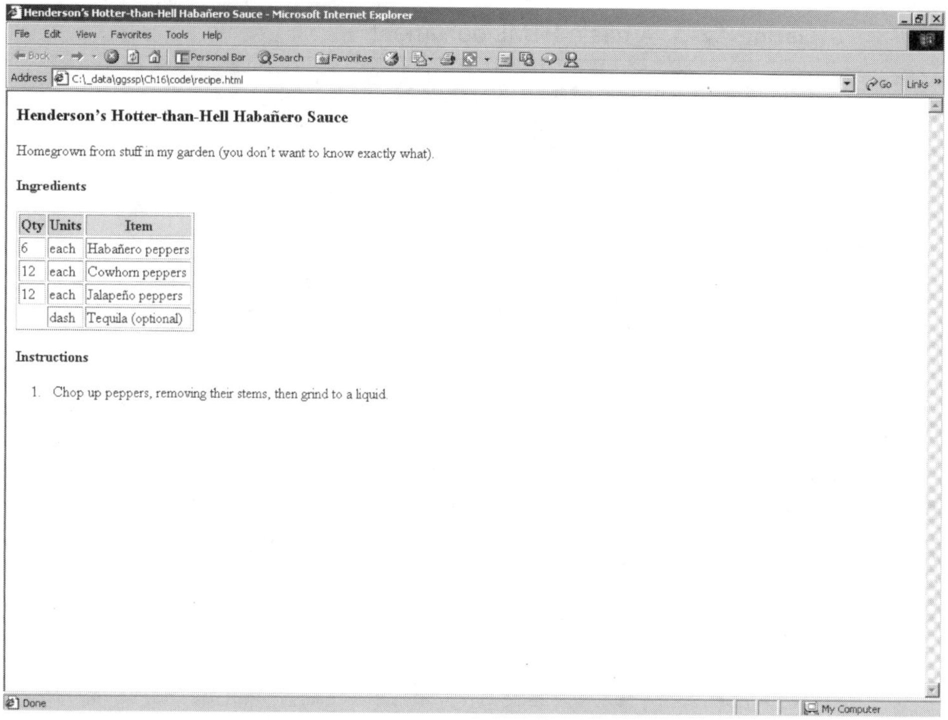

**Figure 12–1** A simple HTML page containing some data.

The problem is further exacerbated by attempting to extract the data and store it in a database. Because the semantic information about the data was stripped out when it was translated into HTML, we have to resupply this info in order to store it meaningfully in a database. In other words, we have to translate the data back out of HTML because HTML is not a suitable storage medium for semantic information.

Now let's take a look at the same data represented as XML. You'll notice that the markup has nothing to do with displaying the data—it is all about describing content. Here's the code (Listing 12–2):

**Listing 12–2** The recipe data stored as XML.

```
<?xml version="1.0" ?>
<Recipe>
        <Name>Henderson&apos;s Hotter-than-Hell Habañero Sauce</Name>
        <Description> Homegrown from stuff in my garden (you don&apos;t want
to know exactly what).</Description>
```

```
<Ingredients>
      <Ingredient>
            <Qty unit="each">6</Qty>
            <Item>Habanero peppers</Item>
      </Ingredient>
      <Ingredient>
            <Qty unit="each">12</Qty>
            <Item>Cowhorn peppers</Item>
      </Ingredient>
      <Ingredient>
            <Qty unit="each">12</Qty>
            <Item>Jalapeno peppers</Item>
      </Ingredient>
      <Ingredient>
            <Qty unit="dash" />
            <Item optional="1">Tequila</Item>
      </Ingredient>
</Ingredients>
<Instructions>
      <Step> Chop up peppers, removing their stems, then grind to a
liquid.</Step>
            <!-- and so forth... -->
      </Instructions>
</Recipe>
```

See the difference? The tags in this data relate to recipes, not formatting. The file remains readable, so it retains the simplicity of the HTML format, but the data now has context. A program that parses this file will know exactly what a Jalepeno is—it's an Item in an Ingredient in a Recipe.

And, regarding ease of use, I think you'll find that XML is actually more human readable, not less, than HTML. It accomplishes the goal of being at least as simple to use as HTML, yet it's orders of magnitude more powerful. It explains the information in a recipe in terms of recipes, *not* in terms of how to display recipes. We leave the display formatting for later and for tools better suited to it.

## Notational Nuances

It's important to get some of the nomenclature straight before we get too far into our discussion of XML. Let's reexamine part of our XML document:

```
<Item optional="1">Tequila</Item>
```

In this code:

1. Item is the tag name. As in HTML, tags mark the start of an *element* in XML. Elements are a key piece of the XML puzzle. XML documents consist mostly of elements and attributes.
2. optional is an attribute name. An attribute is a field that further describes an element. We could have called it something besides optional. The name we've come up with is entirely of our own choosing. Notice that the other elements in the document do not have this attribute.
3. "1" is the value of the optional attribute, and the portion from optional through "1" comprises the attribute.
4. /Item is the end tag of the Item element.
5. The portion from Item through /Item is the Item element.

XML tags do not always contain text. They can be empty or contain just attributes. For example, have a look at this excerpt:

```
<Qty unit="dash" />
```

Here, Qty is the element name, and unit is its only attribute. The forward slash at the end of the text indicates that the element itself is empty and therefore does not require a closing tag. It's shorthand for this:

```
<Qty unit="dash"></Qty>
```

Empty tags may or may not have attributes.

In addition to these basic structure rules, XML documents require stricter formatting than HTML. XML documents must be well formed in order for an XML parser to be able to process them. In mathematics, equations have particular forms they must follow in order to be logical. The ones that don't aren't well formed and aren't terribly useful for anything. XML has a similar requirement. In order for a parser to be able to parse an XML document, it must meet certain rules. The most important of these are the following:

- Every document must have a root element that envelops the rest of the document. It need not be named "root." In our earlier example, Recipe is the root element.
- All tags must have closing tags, either in the form of an end tag or via the empty tag symbol (/). HTML often doesn't enforce this rule. Browsers typically try to guess where a closing tag should go if it's missing.

- All tags must be properly nested. If Qty is contained within Ingredient, you must close Qty before you close Ingredient. This is, again, not something that's rigorously enforced by HTML, but an XML parser will not parse tags that are improperly nested.
- Unlike element text, attribute values must always be enclosed in single or double quotes.
- The characters <, >, and " cannot be represented literally; you must use character entities instead. A character entity is a string that begins with an ampersand (&) and ends with a semicolon and takes the place of a special symbol to avoid confusing the parser. Because <, >, and " all have special meaning in XML, you must represent them using the special character entities **&lt;**, **&gt;**, and **&quot;** respectively. There are two other predefined special character entities that you may use when necessary: **&amp;** and **&apos;**. The **&amp;** entity takes the place of an ampersand. Because ampersands typically denote character entities in an XML document, using them in your data can confuse the parser. Similarly, **&apos;** represents a single-quote—an apostrophe. Because attribute values can be enclosed in single quotes, a stray apostrophe can confuse the parser.
- Unlike HTML, if you wish to use character entities other than the predefined five we just talked about, you must first declare them in a DTD. We'll discuss DTDs shortly.
- Element and attribute names may not begin with the letters "XML" in any casing. XML reserves these for its own use.
- XML is case sensitive. This means that an element named Customer is a different element than one named customer.

There's a difference between a well-formed XML document and a valid one. A valid XML document is a well-formed document that has had additional validation criteria applied to it. Being well formed is only the beginning. Beyond being able to be parsed, an XML document will typically have certain data relationships and requirements that make it sensible. A document that breaks these rules, although well formed, is not valid. For example, consider this XML fragment (Listing 12–3):

**Listing 12–3** A well-formed but invalid XML fragment.

```
<Car Name="Mustang" Make="Ford" Model="1966" LicensePlate="OU812">
    <Engine Type="Cleveland">341</Engine>
    <Engine Type="Winchester">302</Engine>
</Car>
```

Is it well formed? Yes. Is it valid? Perhaps not. Most cars don't have two engines. Consider this modified excerpt from our example document:

```
<Ingredient>
    <Qty unit="each">12</Qty>
    <Qty unit="each">10</Qty>
    <Item>Jalapeno peppers</Item>
</Ingredient>
```

Does it make sense for an ingredient to include two Qty specifications? No, probably not. Although the document is well formed, it's most likely invalid.

How do you establish the validity rules for a document? Through DTDs and XML schemas. We'll discuss each of these in the sections that follow.

## Document Type Definitions

There are two types of XML parsers: validating and nonvalidating parsers. A nonvalidating parser checks an XML document to be sure that it's well formed, and returns it to you as a tree of objects. A validating parser, on the other hand, ensures the document is well formed, *then* checks it against its DTD or schema to determine whether it's valid. In this section, we'll discuss the first of these validation methods—the DTD.

A DTD is a somewhat antiquated although still widely used method of validating documents. DTDs have a peculiar and rather limited syntax, but are still found in lots of XML implementations. Over time, it's likely that XML schemas will become the tool of choice for setting up data validation. That said, there's still plenty of DTD code out there (and there are a few things that DTDs can do that XML schemas can't), so DTDs are still worth knowing about.

A DTD can formalize and codify the tags used in a particular type of document. Because XML itself allows you to use virtually any tags you want as long as the document itself is well formed, a facility is needed to bring structure to documents, to ensure that they make sense. DTDs were the first attempt at doing this. And because DTDs define which tags can and cannot be used in a document, as well as certain characteristics of those tags, they're also used to define new XML *dialects*, formalized subsets of XML tags and validation rules. Originally, DTDs put the X in XML: They were the means by which new applications of XML were designed.

Let's have a look at a DTD for our earlier Recipe example. Here's what it might look like (Listing 12–4):

**Listing 12–4** A DTD for our recipe data.

```
<!-- Recipe.DTD, an example DTD for Recipe.XML -->
<!ELEMENT Recipe (Name, Description?, Ingredients?, Instructions?, Step?)>
<!ELEMENT Name (#PCDATA)>
<!ELEMENT Description (#PCDATA)>
<!ELEMENT Ingredients (Ingredient)*>
<!ELEMENT Ingredient (Qty, Item)>
<!ELEMENT Qty (#PCDATA)>
<!ATTLIST Qty unit CDATA #REQUIRED>
<!ELEMENT Item (#PCDATA)>
<!ATTLIST Item optional CDATA "0">
<!ELEMENT Instructions (Step)+>
<!ELEMENT Step (#PCDATA)>
```

This DTD defines several characteristics of the document that are worth discussing. First, note the topmost noncomment line in the file (in bold type). It indicates the elements that can be represented by a document that uses this DTD. A question mark after an element indicates that it's optional.

Second, notice the #PCDATA flags. They indicate that the element or attribute can contain character data and nothing else.

Third, take note of the #REQUIRED flag. This indicates that the unit attribute of the Qty element is required. Documents that use this DTD may not omit it.

Fourth, note the default value supplied for the Item element's optional attribute. Rather than being required, this attribute can be omitted, as its name suggests. Moreover, for elements that omit the attribute, it defaults to "0."

From Listing 12–4, you can see that DTD syntax is not an XML dialect, nor is it terribly intuitive. That's why people are increasingly using schemas instead. We'll discuss XML schemas shortly.

You link a DTD and a document together using a document type declaration element at the top of the document (immediately after the <?xml...> line). The document type declaration can contain either an inline copy of the DTD or a reference to its filename using a URI (Universal Resource ID). The one for recipe.xml looks like this:

```
<!DOCTYPE Recipe SYSTEM "recipe.dtd">
```

Here's the document again with the DTD line included (Listing 12–5):

**Listing 12–5** The recipe XML document with the DTD reference included.

```
<?xml version="1.0" ?>
<!DOCTYPE Recipe SYSTEM "recipe.dtd">
<Recipe>
        <Name>Henderson&apos;s Hotter-than-Hell Habaero Sauce</Name>
        <Description> Homegrown from stuff in my garden (you don&apos;t want
to know exactly what).</Description>
        <Ingredients>
                <Ingredient>
                        <Qty unit="each">6</Qty>
                        <Item>Habanero peppers</Item>
                </Ingredient>
                <Ingredient>
                        <Qty unit="each">12</Qty>
                        <Item>Cowhorn peppers</Item>
                </Ingredient>
                <Ingredient>
                        <Qty unit="each">12</Qty>
                        <Item>Jalapeno peppers</Item>
                </Ingredient>
                <Ingredient>
                        <Qty unit="dash" />
                        <Item optional="1">Tequila</Item>
                </Ingredient>
        </Ingredients>
        <Instructions>
                <Step> Chop up peppers, removing their stems, then grind to a
liquid.</Step>
                <!-- and so forth... -->
        </Instructions>
</Recipe>
```

Validating the data against the DTD can be done through a number of means. If you're using Internet Explorer 5.0 or later, you can use Microsoft's built-in DTD validator simply by loading an XML document into the browser, right-clicking it, and selecting Validate. A number of GUI and command-line tools exist to do the same thing. Several of them are listed on the World Wide Web Consortium site (http://www.w3c.org).

# XML Schemas

> **NOTE:** As I write this (January 2001), the XML Schema syntax is still in the process of being approved. The W3C is currently considering input from several sources and will likely publish a standard later this year. It's likely that the final XML Schema syntax will differ semantically from XML Data-Reduced (XDR) schemas, the schema syntax currently supported by Microsoft's XML-enabled products (including SQL Server). Microsoft has announced that it will support whatever the final syntax is, so keep an eye out for changes in the technology.

I mentioned earlier that DTDs were somewhat old-fashioned. The reason for this is that there's a newer, better technology for validating XML documents. It's called XML Schema. Unlike DTDs, you build XML Schema documents using XML. They consist of elements and attributes, just like the XML documents they validate. They have a number of other advantages over DTDs, including the following:

- DTDs cannot control the kind of information a given element or attribute can contain. Merely being able to specify that an element stores text is not precise enough for most business needs. We may want to specify the format that text should have, or whether the text is a date or a number. XML Schema has extensive support for data domain control.
- DTDs feature only ten stock data types. XML Schema features more than 44 base data types, plus you can create your own.
- All declarations in a DTD are global. This means that you can't define multiple elements with the same name, even if they exist in completely different contexts.
- Because DTD syntax is not XML, it requires special handling. It cannot be processed by an XML parser. This adds complexity to documents with associated DTDs and potentially slows down their processing.

A complete discussion on XML Schema is outside the scope of this book, but we should still touch on a few of the high points. Let's have a look at a validation schema for the recipe.xml document we built earlier. Here's what it might look like (Listing 12–6):

**Listing 12–6** An XML schema for our recipe document.

```
<?xml version="1.0" ?>
<xsd:schema xmlns:xsd="http://www.w3.org/2000/10/XMLSchema" elementFormDefault="qualified">
```

```xml
<xsd:element name="Recipe">
    <xsd:complexType>
        <xsd:sequence>
            <xsd:element name="Name" type="xsd:string"/>
            <xsd:element name="Description" type="xsd:string"/>
            <xsd:element name="Ingredients">
                <xsd:complexType>
                    <xsd:sequence>
                        <xsd:element name="Ingredient" maxOccurs="unbounded">
                            <xsd:complexType>
                                <xsd:sequence>
                                    <xsd:element name="Qty">
                                        <xsd:complexType>
                                            <xsd:simpleContent>
                                                <xsd:restriction base="xsd:byte">
                                                    <xsd:attribute name="unit" use="required">
                                                        <xsd:simpleType>
                                                            <xsd:restriction base="xsd:NMTOKEN">
                                                                <xsd:enumeration value="dash"/>
                                                                <xsd:enumeration value="each"/>
                                                                <xsd:enumeration value="dozen"/>
                                                                <xsd:enumeration value="cups"/>
                                                                <xsd:enumeration value="teasp"/>
                                                                <xsd:enumeration value="tbls"/>
                                                            </xsd:restriction>
                                                        </xsd:simpleType>
                                                    </xsd:attribute>
                                                </xsd:restriction>
                                            </xsd:simpleContent>
                                        </xsd:complexType>
                                    </xsd:element>
                                    <xsd:element name="Item">
                                        <xsd:complexType>
                                            <xsd:simpleContent>
                                                <xsd:restriction base="xsd:string">
                                                    <xsd:attribute name="optional" type="xsd:boolean"/>
                                                </xsd:restriction>
                                            </xsd:simpleContent>
                                        </xsd:complexType>
                                    </xsd:element>
                                </xsd:sequence>
                            </xsd:complexType>
                        </xsd:element>
                    </xsd:sequence>
```

```
        </xsd:complexType>
      </xsd:element>
      <xsd:element name="Instructions">
        <xsd:complexType>
          <xsd:sequence>
            <xsd:element name="Step" type="xsd:string"/>
          </xsd:sequence>
        </xsd:complexType>
      </xsd:element>
    </xsd:sequence>
  </xsd:complexType>
</xsd:element>
</xsd:schema>
```

Look a little daunting? It's a bit longer than the DTD we looked at earlier, isn't it?!

It's not as bad as it might seem. Most of the document consists of opening and closing tags. The schema itself is not that complex.

The first thing you should notice is that each of the elements and attributes in the XML document is assigned a data type. When the document is validated with this schema, each piece of data in the document is checked to see whether it's valid for its assigned data type. If it isn't, the document fails the validation test.

Next, take a look at the maxOccurs element. Via a schema, you can specify a number of ancillary properties for elements, including how many (or how few) times an element can appear in a document. The default for both minOccurs and maxOccurs is 1. You can make an element optional by setting its minOccurs attribute to 0.

Next, notice the xsd:enumeration elements under the unit attribute. In an XML schema, you can specify a list of valid values for an element or attribute. If an element or attribute attempts to store a value not in the list, the document fails validation.

Last, notice the new data type for the Item element's optional attribute. I've changed it from an integer to a Boolean value—one of the stock data types supported by XML Schema. I point this out because I want you to realize the very rich data type set that XML Schema offers. Not only that, but understand that you can create new types by extending the existing one. Furthermore, you can create complex types—elements that contain other elements and attributes. In the schema listed earlier, the **Qty** data type is a complex data type, as are the **Ingredients** and **Instructions** types. Any schema element that contains other elements or attributes is, by definition, a complex data type.

You may be wondering how you associate a schema with an XML document. You do so by adding a couple of attributes to the document's root element. For example, the root element in our recipe.xml document now looks like this:

```
Recipe xmlns:xsi="http://www.w3.org/2000/10/XMLSchema-instance"
xsi:noNamespaceSchemaLocation="C:\_data\ggssp\Ch12\code\recipe.xsd">
```

The first attribute makes the elements in the xsi (the XML Schema Instance) namespace available to the document. A namespace is a collection of names identified by a URI reference. You can define your own, or you can do as we've done here and refer to a namespace defined on the W3C Web site. As in many programming disciplines, an XML namespace provides name scoping to an application so that names from different sources do not collide with one another. Unlike traditional namespaces, the names within an XML namespace do not have to be unique. Without veering off into why this is, for now, just understand that a namespace gives scope to the names you use in XML. In this particular case, it provides access to the names in the xsi namespace, which is where XML Schema Instance elements reside. By referring to the namespace in this way, we can use XML Schema Instance elements in the document by prefixing them with **xsi:**.

The second attribute describes the location of the XML Schema document. This is the document listed earlier. It contains the schema info for our document.

Once these attributes are in place, "XML Schema-aware" tools will validate the document using the schema identified by the attribute.

# Extensible Stylesheet Language Transformation (XSLT)

In the same way that Cascading Style Sheets are commonly used to transform HTML documents, XSLT transforms XML documents. It can transform XML documents from one document format to another, into other XML dialects, or into completely different file formats such as PostScript, RTF, and TeX.

The best part about XSLT is that it's XML. An XSLT document is a regular XML document. "How can that be?" you ask. "Wouldn't you have issues with circular references?" No. XSLT is just another XML dialect. Modern XML parsers are intelligent enough to know how to use the instructions encoded in an XSLT document (which are just ordinary XML tags and attributes and the like) to transform or provide structure to another document.

## XML to HTML: An Example

An XSLT style sheet is XML document that's made up of a series of rules, called *templates*, that are applied to another XML document to produce a third document. These templates are written in XML using specific tags with defined meanings. Each time a template matches something in the source XML document, a new structure is produced in the output. This is often HTML, as the example we're about to examine demonstrates, but it does not have to be.

Here's an XSLT style sheet (Listing 12–7) that transforms our Recipe XML document into an HTML document that closely resembles the HTML document we built by hand earlier in the chapter:

**Listing 12–7** An XSLT style sheet that transforms our XML document into HTML.

```
<?xml version='1.0'?>
<xsl:stylesheet version="1.0"
xmlns:xsl="http://www.w3.org/1999/XSL/Transform">
<xsl:template match="/">
  <html>
   <HEAD>
   <TITLE>Henderson&apos;s Hotter-than-Hell Habanero Sauce</TITLE>
   </HEAD>
  <body>
    <H3>Henderson&apos;s Hotter-than-Hell Habanero Sauce</H3>
Homegrown from stuff in my garden (you don&apos;t want to know exactly
what).
     <H4>Ingredients</H4>
    <table border="2">
     <tr BGCOLOR="#00FF00">
      <TH>Qty</TH>
      <TH>Units</TH>
      <TH>Item</TH>
     </tr>
     <xsl:for-each select="Recipe/Ingredients/Ingredient">
     <tr>
       <td><xsl:value-of select="Qty"/></td>
       <td><xsl:value-of select="Qty/@unit"/></td>
       <td><xsl:value-of select="Item"/></td>
     </tr>
     </xsl:for-each>
    </table>
<P/>
    <H4>Instructions</H4>
```

```
<OL>
  <xsl:for-each select="Recipe/Instructions">
    <LI><xsl:value-of select="Step"/></LI>
  </xsl:for-each>
</OL>
</body>
</html>
</xsl:template>
</xsl:stylesheet>
```

This style sheet does several interesting things. First, note the xsl:template match="/" element. As I've said, XSLT transformations occur by applying templates to specific parts of the XML document. The match attribute of this element specifies, via what's known as XML Path (XPath) syntax, to which part of the document the template should apply. In this case, it's the root element. So what the style sheet is saying is: Locate the root element of the document, and when you find it, insert the following text into the output document. What follows are several lines of standard HTML that set up the header of the Web page.

Note the **xsl:** prefix on the template element. It refers to the xsl namespace. The xsl namespace is where the template element and the other **xsl:**-prefixed names are defined. Adding the namespace reference makes the **xsl:** prefix available to the document so that it can reference those names. The URI reference is at the top of the style sheet. It has the form

```
<xsl:stylesheet version="1.0"
xmlns:xsl="http://www.w3.org/1999/XSL/Transform">
```

Next, notice the HTML table header info that's generated by the style sheet. It contains three sets of HTML <TH> tags that set up the column headers for the table. This section of the code matches that of the original HTML document we created earlier.

The most interesting part of the document is the looping it does. This is where the real power of XSLT lies. Notice the first xsl:for-each loop (in bold type). An XSLT for-each loop does exactly what it sounds like: It iterates through a collection of nodes at the same level in a document. The base node from which it works is identified by its select attribute. In this case, it's the Recipe/Ingredients/Ingredient node. As with the earlier match attribute, this is an XPath to the node we want to access. What this means is that we're going to loop through the ingredients for the recipe. For each one we find, we'll generate a new row in the table.

Note the way in which the nodes within each Ingredient are referenced. We use the xsl:value-of element to insert the value of each field in each ingredient as we come to it. To access the unit attribute of the Qty element, we use the XPath attribute syntax, /@name, where name is the attribute we want to access.

Note the paragraph tag <P/> that follows the looping code. Traditional HTML would permit this tag to be specified without a matching closing tag, but not XML. And this brings up an important point: When you provide HTML code for a style sheet to generate, it must be well formed. That is, it must comply with the rules that dictate whether an XML document is well formed. Remember: A style sheet is an XML document in every sense of the word. It must be well formed or it cannot be parsed.

The code finishes up with another for-each loop. This one lists the Steps in each Instructions element. Note use of the HTML Ordered List (<OL>) and List Item (<LI>) tags. These work just like they do in standard HTML—they produce a numbered list.

You have several options for using this style sheet to transform the Recipe.xml document. You could use Microsoft's stand-alone XSLT transformer, you could use a third-party XSLT transformer, or you could use the one that's built into your browser, if your browser supports direct XSLT transformations. See the Tools section later in the chapter for more info, but, in my case, I'm using Internet Explorer's built-in XSLT transformer. This requires the addition of an <?xml-stylesheet> element to the XML document itself, just beneath the <?XML VERSION> tag. Here's the complete element:

```
<?xml-stylesheet type="text/xsl" href="recipe3.xsl"?>
```

As you can see, the element contains an href attribute that references the style sheet using a URI. Now, every time I view the XML document in Internet Explorer, the style sheet will automatically be applied to transform it. Here's the HTML code that's generated using the style sheet (Listing 12–8):

**Listing 12–8** The HTML code generated by the transformation.

```
<html>
<HEAD>
<TITLE>Henderson's Hotter-than-Hell Habanero Sauce</TITLE>
</HEAD>
<body>
<H3>Henderson's Hotter-than-Hell Habanero Sauce</H3>
Homegrown from stuff in my garden (you don't want to know exactly what).
    <H4>Ingredients</H4>
```

```
<table border="2">
<tr BGCOLOR="#00FF00">
<TH>Qty</TH>
<TH>Units</TH>
<TH>Item</TH>
</tr>
<tr>
<td>6</td>
<td>each</td>
<td>Habanero peppers</td>
</tr>
<tr>
<td>12</td>
<td>each</td>
<td>Cowhorn peppers</td>
</tr>
<tr>
<td>12</td>
<td>each</td>
<td>Jalapeno peppers</td>
</tr>
<tr>
<td></td>
<td>dash</td>
<td>Tequila</td>
</tr>
</table>
<P />
<H4>Instructions</H4>
<OL>
<LI>Chop up peppers, removing their stems, then grind to a liquid.</LI>
</OL>
</body>
</html>
```

And here's what it looks like when viewed from a browser (Figure 12–2):

Although it's nifty to be able to translate the XML document into well-formed HTML that matches our original example, what does this really buy us? Wouldn't it have been easier just to have created the document using HTML in the first place?

Perhaps it would have been easier to have created *this* document in HTML without using XML and a style sheet. However, by separating the storage of the data from its presentation, we can radically alter its formatting without affect-

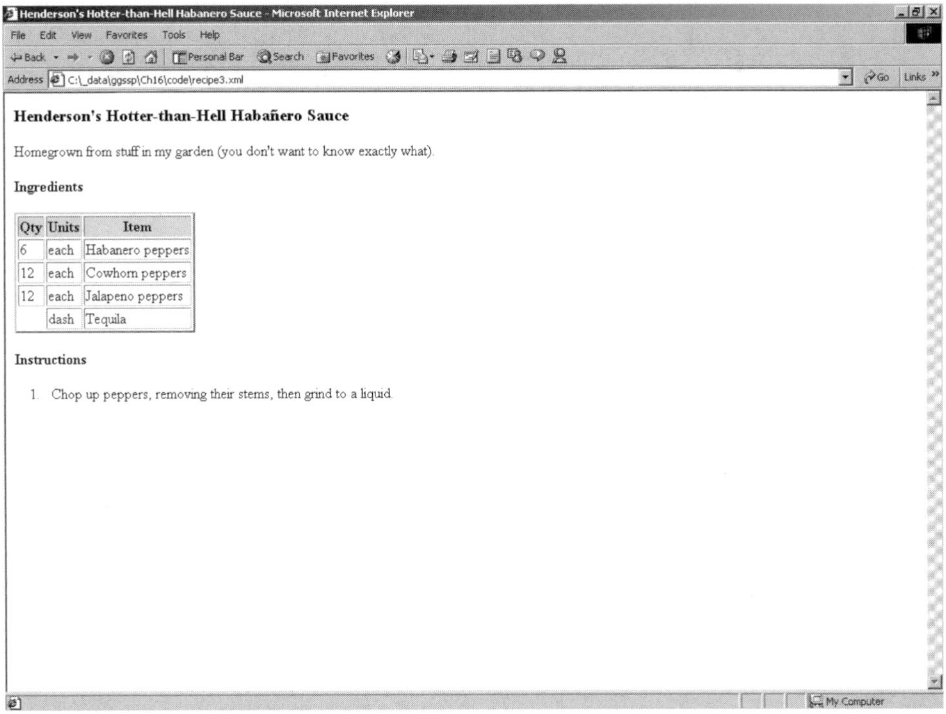

**Figure 12–2** The HTML document in a browser.

ing the data. This is not true of HTML. To understand this, check out the style sheet in Listing 12–9:

**Listing 12–9** A completely different transformation for the same XML document.

```
<?xml version='1.0'?>
<xsl:stylesheet version="1.0"
xmlns:xsl="http://www.w3.org/1999/XSL/Transform">
<xsl:template match="/">
  <html>
   <HEAD>
   <TITLE>Henderson&apos;s Hotter-than-Hell Habanero Sauce</TITLE>
   </HEAD>
   <body>
    <H3>Henderson&apos;s Hotter-than-Hell Habanero Sauce</H3>
Homegrown from stuff in my garden (you don&apos;t want to know exactly what).
    <H4>Ingredients</H4>
```

```
      <UL>
      <xsl:for-each select="Recipe/Ingredients/Ingredient">
        <LI>
        <xsl:value-of select="Qty"/>&#9;<xsl:value-of select="Qty/@unit"/> of
<xsl:value-of select="Item"/>
        </LI>
      </xsl:for-each>
      </UL>
      <P/>
   <H4>Instructions</H4>
   <table border="2">
     <tr BGCOLOR="#00FF00">
     <TH>#</TH>
     <TH>Step</TH>
     </tr>
     <xsl:for-each select="Recipe/Instructions">
     <tr>
       <td><xsl:value-of select="position()"/></td>
       <td><xsl:value-of select="Step"/></td>
     </tr>
     </xsl:for-each>
     </table>
 </body>
 </html>
</xsl:template>
</xsl:stylesheet>
```

We can use this style sheet to transform the XML document into a completely different HTML layout than the first one (you can specify a new style sheet for a document by changing the document's <?xml-stylesheet> element or by overriding it in your XSLT transformation tool). Figure 12–3 shows what the new Web page looks like in a browser:

As you can see, the page formatting is completely different. The ingredients table is gone, replaced by a bulleted list. Conversely, the Instruction steps have been moved from an ordered list into a table. The formatting has changed completely, but the data is the same. The XML document didn't change at all.

Because the data now has context, we can access it directly. There's no need to hard code table column or table row references to the HTML and translate the data out of HTML into a usable data format. The data is already in such a format. And, regardless of how we decide to transform or format the data, this will always be true. Because it's stored in XML, the data can be manipulated in virtually any way we see fit.

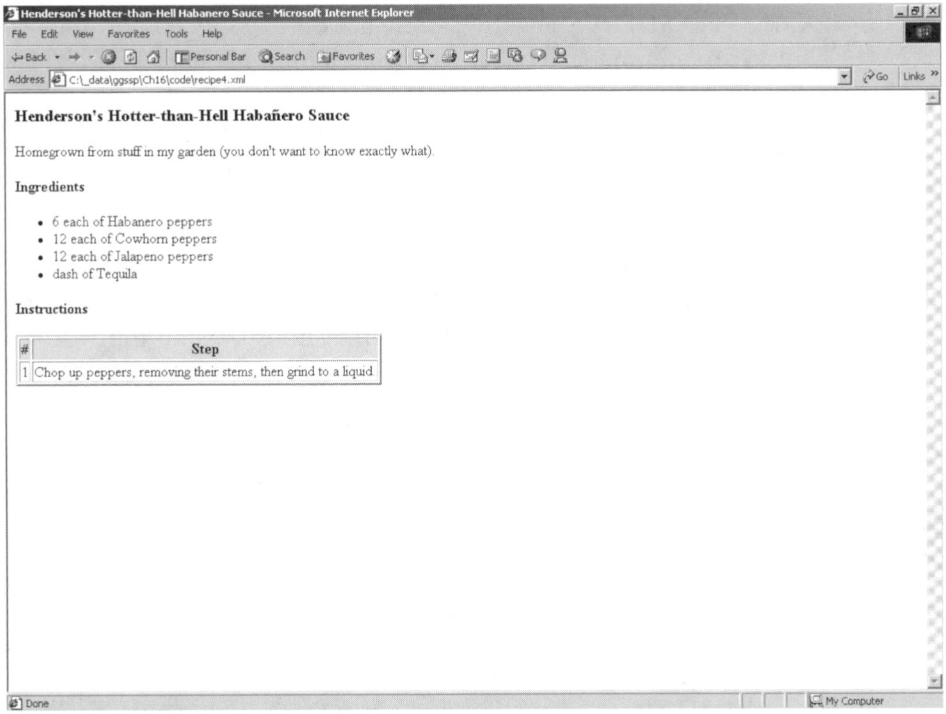

**Figure 12–3** The transformed document in a browser.

The xsl:for-each element in our style sheets gave us a glimpse of some of XSLT's power. Like most languages, much of its utility can be found in its ability to perform a task repetitively. XSLT defines a number of constructs that are similarly powerful. Among them are

- xsl:if
- xsl:choose
- xsl:sort
- xsl:attribute
- Embedded scripting. IBM's LotusXSL package provides most of the functionality of XSLT, including the ability to call embedded ECMAScript, the European standard JavaScript, from XSLT templates.

You can check the XSLT specification itself for the full list, but suffice it to say, XSLT brings to bear some of the real power and extensibility of XML. It's an example of what I like to refer to as the "programmable data" aspect of

XML. Via XSLT, we have the ability not only to specify how data is formatted, but to programmatically change it *from within the data itself*. This is powerful stuff indeed.

Because we've been performing formatting-related tasks with XSLT and XML, it may appear that XML is just a content management technology. This is not the case. It's far more than that. Certainly, from the perspective of Webmasters, XML and XSLT offer huge advancements over HTML. However, XML is about more than just formatting data or managing content. It is about *data,* and giving that data sufficient context to be useful in a wide variety of situations. There's a whole world of applications outside the realm of browsers and Web pages. To add the power of XML to those types of applications, we can use something called the *Document Object Model.*

# Document Object Model

Thus far we've explored XML from the standpoint of generalizing document formats. But XML's real power comes into play when it is used to structure information.

All XML documents consist of nested sets of elements. Every document is wrapped in a root element, which in turn houses other elements. The structure is a natural tree—a tree of elements, objects that represent the content of the document. The DOM goes beyond the simple text stream approach and provides a language-neutral means of working with an XML document as a tree of objects.

This object-oriented access to XML documents opens the door to a whole host of other uses for XML. It makes it trivial to incorporate XML as an interprocess or interapplication data interchange mechanism because all you deal with are objects in your programming language of choice. It doesn't matter whether that language is Visual Basic, Java, or C#, you can read, manipulate, and generally process XML documents by calling methods on objects and accessing their properties.

Think of all the possibilities this brings with it. For example, imagine a database system in which the entire database was represented as an XML document. Need a schema of the database? No problem. Extract the XML schema from the DOM and run it through an XSLT transformation and you've got yourself a "browsable" database schema that's always current. Want to write a unified tool that can administer objects on SQL Server, Oracle, DB2, and all the other big players in the DBMS space without having to code to each of the administrative APIs separately? Have them expose their database schemas as

DOM trees, and you should be able to build a single tool that works with all of them.

Already, vendors are putting DOM and XML to use in scenarios like the ones I've just described. SQL Server has certainly done its fair share of this, as we'll discuss in the next few chapters.

## Further Reading

- I've found Liz Castro's book *XML for the World Wide Web Visual Quickstart Guide* to be a concise yet thorough treatment of the subject. Liz writes good books, and I've found this one particularly useful.
- O'Reilly's *XML in a Nutshell* also offers a concise treatment of the subject material. Unfortunately, it does not cover schemas, but it does cover most of the other important topics adequately.
- Steve Holzner's *Inside XML* is also a good read. It's comprehensive and covers many key XML subjects in great detail.
- *Learning XML,* another book by O'Reilly, is another good introductory text. It contains a nice introduction to the many XML parsers out there and delves into a few topics omitted by some of the other books (for example, XML Schema).
- The *XSLT Programmer's Reference* by Michael Kay will tell you everything you need to know about XSLT. Michael is also the author of SAXON, one of the best XSLT processors out there.
- The Web site of the W3C (http://www.w3c.org) is as valuable a source on XML, HTML, and all things Web-related as you'll find. The specifications documents can be a little dry at times, but they're worth reading if you can get through them. The site also has a number of links to XML-related tutorials, free tools, and other resources.
- Most of the major software vendors have a large XML portal of some type available from their sites. I've found the Microsoft and Sun Microsystems sites to be the most informative.

## Tools

- You should begin by getting yourself a good XML/XSLT/XSD editor. I like XML Spy (http://www.xmlspy.com), but there are several good ones out there. Don't let anyone tell you that GUIs are for wimps. Using

Notepad to spend hours doing what a GUI tool will do for you in seconds simply makes no sense. You end up spending lots of time trudging around in clunky tools that would be better spent mastering the technology.

- You'll also want an XML Schema/DTD validator. I've had the best luck with Henry Thompson and Richard Tobin's XSV tool, particularly with schema validation, but there are several available.
- Depending on your other tools, you may need a separate XSLT transformation tool. I use Microsoft's built-in transformer in Internet Explorer, as well as James Clark's XT tool. Again, there are several freebies out there.
- If you run on Windows, get the latest version of the MSXML parser. It's the best one for Windows. IBM also has a nice product.
- Michael Kay's SAXON tool is worth having even if you have other XSLT processors. It's a nice piece of software written by a master of the technology.
- The MSXML SDK is also worth having if you're on Windows. It contains some good sample code and documentation that will come in handy if you build applications using the MSXML APIs.

## Summary

In this chapter you learned about XML. We had a brief history lesson, then went on a guided tour through some of XML's key tenets: XML documents, DTDs, schemas, and XSLT. You learned that XML is not just one technology—it's a whole family of technologies, and these technologies continue to evolve and to be adopted by more people around the world each day. It's crucial to learn as much as you can about XML now, so that you can make the best use of SQL Server's XML-related features—both those it has today and those coming in the future. Here's a bold prediction for you: The day will come when XML will be at least as important to SQL Server application development as Transact-SQL is today. It's definitely time to dive in.

# CHAPTER 13

# XML and SQL Server: HTTP Queries

*Generally, he who occupies the field of battle first and waits his enemy is at ease; he who comes later to the scene and rushes into the fight is weary.*

—*Sun Tzu*[1]

As I mentioned in the previous chapter, XML is taking over the world. Someday it will probably even supplant HTML as the most widely used markup language on the Internet. So it's no surprise that SQL Server has built-in support for working with XML. Like most modern DBMSs, SQL Server regularly needs to work with and store data that may have originated in an XML document. Without this built-in support, getting XML to and from SQL Server would require the application developer to translate XML data before sending it to SQL Server and again after receiving it back. Obviously, this could quickly become very tedious, given the ubiquity and growing popularity of the language.

SQL Server is an XML-enabled database. This means that it can read and write XML data. It can return data from databases in XML format, and it can read and update data stored in XML documents. As Table 13–1 illustrates, out of the box, SQL Server's XML features can be broken down into four general categories. (The beta version of SQL-XML Web Release 1 promises to add to this list. See the section titled "Web Release 1" at the end of Chapter 15 for more information.)

---

[1]Tzu, Sun. *The Art of War*. Cambridge, England: Oxford University Press, 1963. Page 96.

**Table 13–1**  SQL Server's XML Features

| Feature | Purpose |
| --- | --- |
| FOR XML | An extension to the SELECT command that allows result sets to be returned as XML |
| OPENXML() | Allows reading and writing of data in XML documents |
| XPath queries | Allows SQL Server databases to be queried using XPath syntax |
| XDR schemas | Supports XDR schemas and XPath queries against them |

# Accessing SQL Server over HTTP

The first thing you should do to begin working with XML data in Transact-SQL is to set up an IIS virtual directory using the **Configure SQL XML Support in IIS** menu option in the SQL Server program folder. Note that you can use ADO to process XML data from SQL Server without setting up a virtual directory. You may take this approach, for example, when building components that provide business processing functionality on top of processing the documents themselves.

Configuring a virtual directory allows you to work with SQL Server's XML features via HTTP. This opens up all sorts of possibilities. To begin with, it allows you to create data-driven Web sites with far less work than technologies such as ASP and JSP would require. Furthermore, you can use XSL style sheets to translate XML data returned from SQL Server into other document formats such as HTML and WML (Wireless Markup Language). Additionally, internal and external clients can work directly with your SQL Server-produced XML data via simple HTTP requests.

You use a virtual directory to establish a link between a SQL Server database and a segment of a URL. It provides a navigation path from the root directory on your Web server to a database on your SQL Server.

SQL Server's ability to publish data over HTTP is made possible through SQLISAPI, an ISAPI application that ships with the product. SQLISAPI uses SQLOLEDB, SQL Server's native OLE-DB provider, to access the database associated with a virtual directory and return results to the client.

Client applications have four methods of requesting data from SQL Server over HTTP. These can be broken down into two general types: those more suitable for private intranet access because of security concerns, and those safe to use on the public Internet:

### Private intranet

1. Post an XML query template to SQLISAPI.
2. Send a SELECT...FOR XML query string in a URL.

### Public Internet

3. Specify a server-side XML schema in a virtual root.
4. Specify a server-side XML query template in a virtual root.

Because of their open-ended nature, methods 1 and 2 could pose security risks over the public Internet, but are perfectly valid on corporate or private intranets. Normally, Web applications use server-side schemas and query templates to make XML data accessible to the outside world in a controlled fashion.

## Configuring a Virtual Directory

As I mentioned earlier, you set up virtual directories using the Configure SQL XML **Support in IIS** utility. It's in the Microsoft SQL Server folder under Start|Programs. Load it and you should see the IIS servers configured on the current machine. Click the plus sign to the left of your server to expand it. (If your server isn't listed, for example if it's a remote server, right-click the IIS Virtual Directory Manager node and select Connect to connect to it.) To add a new virtual directory, right-click the Default Web Site node and select New|Virtual Directory. You should then see the New Virtual Directory Properties dialog.

### Specifying a Virtual Directory Name and Path

The **Virtual Directory Name** entry box is where you specify the name of the new virtual directory. This is the name that users will include in a URL to access the data exposed by the virtual directory, so it's important to make it descriptive. A common convention is to name virtual directories after the databases they reference. To work through the rest of the examples in the chapter, specify Northwind as the name of the new virtual directory.

Although Local Path will sometimes not be used, it's required nonetheless. In a normal ASP or HTML application, this would be the path where the source files themselves reside. In SQLISAPI applications, this folder does not necessarily need to contain anything, but it must exist nevertheless. On NTFS partitions, you must also make sure that users have at least read access to this folder to use the virtual directory. You configure which user accounts will be used to access the application (and thus will need access to the folder) in the dialog's Security page.

Click the Security tab to select the authentication mode you'd like to use. You can use a specific user account, Windows Integrated Authentication, or Basic (clear text) Authentication. Select the option that matches your usage scenario most closely; Windows Integrated Authentication will likely be the best choice for working through the examples in this chapter.

Next, click the Data Source page tab. This is where you set the server and the database that the virtual directory references. Select your SQL Server from the list and specify Northwind as the database name.

Go to the Virtual Names table and set up two virtual names, templates and schemas. Create two folders under Northwind named Templates and Schemas so that each of these virtual names can have its own local folder. Set the Type of schemas to **schema** and the type of templates to **template**. Each of these provides a navigation path from a URL to the files in its local folder. We'll use them later.

The last dialog page with which we're concerned is the Settings page. Click it, then make sure every check box on it is checked. We want to enable all of these options so that we may test them later in the chapter. The following is a brief description of each of the options on the Settings page.

### Allow URL Queries

URL queries allow users to specify a complete Transact-SQL query via a URL. Special characters are replaced with placeholders, but essentially the query is sent to the server as is and its results are returned over HTTP. Because allowing URL queries permits a user to run any query he wishes against a database, this option is usually disabled on production systems. For now, enable it so that we can try it out later.

### Allow Template Queries

Template queries are by far the most pervasive method of retrieving XML data from SQL Server. XML documents that store query "templates"—generic parameterized queries with placeholders for parameters—reside on the server and provide a controlled access to the underlying data. The results from template queries are returned over HTTP to the user.

### Allow XPath

When Allow XPath is enabled, users can use a subset of the XPath language to retrieve data from SQL Server based on an annotated schema. Annotated schemas are stored on a Web server as XML documents, and map XML elements and attributes to the data in the database referenced by a virtual directory. XPath queries allow the user to specify the data defined in an annotated schema to return.

### *Allow POST*

HTTP supports the notion of sending data to the Web server via its POST command. When Allow POST is enabled, you can post a query template (usually implemented as a hidden form field on a Web page) to a Web server via HTTP. This causes the query to be executed and returns the results back to the client.

For this to work, not only must Allow POST be enabled, but Allow URL queries must also be turned on. As I mentioned earlier, the open-endedness of this usually limits its use to private intranets. A malicious user could form up her own template and post it over HTTP to retrieve data to which she isn't supposed to have access, or, worse yet, make changes to it.

Once you've enabled these options, click the OK button to create the virtual directory.

---

**TIP:** A handy option on the Advanced tab is Disable caching of mapping schemas. Normally, mapping schemas are cached in memory the first time they're used, and are accessed from the cache thereafter. While developing a mapping schema, you'll likely want to disable this so that the schema will be reloaded each time you test it.

---

## URL Queries

The easiest way to test your new virtual directory is to submit a URL query that uses it from an XML-enabled browser such as Internet Explorer. URL queries take this form:

```
http://localhost/Northwind?sql=SELECT+*+FROM+Customers+FOR+XML+AUTO
&root=Customers
```

---

**NOTE:** As with all URLs, the URL listed here should be typed on one line. Page width restrictions may force some of the URLs listed in this book to span multiple lines, but a URL should always be typed on a single line.

---

Here, localhost is the name of the Web server. It could just as easily be a fully qualified DNS domain name such as www.nkandescent.com. Northwind is the virtual directory name we created earlier.

A question mark separates the URL from its parameters. Multiple parameters are separated by ampersands. The first parameter we pass here is named sql. It specifies the query to run. The second parameter specifies the name of the root element for the XML document that will be returned. By definition, you get just one of these per document. Failure to specify a root element results in an error if your query returns more than one top-level element.

To see how this works, submit the following URL from your Web browser (be sure to change localhost to the correct name of your Web server if it resides on a different machine):

```
http://localhost/Northwind?sql=SELECT+*+FROM+Customers+WHERE+CustomerId='ALFKI'
+FOR+XML+AUTO
```

(Results)

```
<Customers CustomerID="ALFKI" CompanyName="Alfreds Futterkiste"
ContactName="Maria Anders" ContactTitle="Sales Representative" Address="Obere Str.
57" City="Berlin" PostalCode="12209" Country="Germany"
Phone="030-0074321" Fax="030-0076545" />
```

Notice that we left off the root element specification. Look at what happens when we bring back more than one row:

```
http://localhost/Northwind?sql=SELECT+*+FROM+Customers+
WHERE+CustomerId='ALFKI'+OR+CustomerId='ANATR'+FOR+XML+AUTO
```

(Results abridged)

```
The XML page cannot be displayed
Only one top level element is allowed in an XML document. Line 1, Position 243
```

Because we're returning multiple top-level elements (two, to be exact), our XML document has two root elements named Customers, which, of course, isn't allowed because it isn't well-formed XML. To remedy the situation, we need to specify a root element. This element can be named anything. It serves only to wrap the rows returned by FOR XML so that we have a well-formed document. Here's an example:

```
http://localhost/Northwind?sql=SELECT+*+FROM+Customers+WHERE+CustomerId='ALFKI'
+OR+CustomerId='ANATR'+FOR+XML+AUTO&root=CustomerList
```

(Results)

```
<?xml version="1.0" encoding="utf-8" ?>
  <CustomerList>
    <Customers CustomerID="ALFKI" CompanyName="Alfreds Futterkiste"
```

```
        ContactName="Maria Anders" ContactTitle="Sales Representative"
        Address="Obere Str. 57" City="Berlin" PostalCode="12209"
        Country="Germany" Phone="030-0074321" Fax="030-0076545" />
    <Customers CustomerID="ANATR" CompanyName="Ana Trujillo Emparedados y
        helados" ContactName="Ana Trujillo" ContactTitle="Owner" Address="Avda.
        de la Constituci?n 2222" City="M?xico D.F." PostalCode="05021"
        Country="Mexico" Phone="(5) 555-4729" Fax="(5) 555-3745" />
</CustomerList>
```

You can also supply the root element yourself as part of the sql parameter, like this:

```
http://localhost/Northwind?sql=SELECT+'<CustomerList>';
SELECT+*+FROM+Customers+WHERE+CustomerId='ALFKI'+OR+CustomerId='ANATR'+FOR+XML+AUTO;
SELECT+'</CustomerList>';
```

(Results formatted)

```
_   <CustomerList>
      <Customers CustomerID="ALFKI" CompanyName="Alfreds Futterkiste"
          ContactName="Maria Anders" ContactTitle="Sales Representative"
          Address="Obere Str. 57" City="Berlin" PostalCode="12209"
          Country="Germany" Phone="030-0074321" Fax="030-0076545" />
      <Customers CustomerID="ANATR" CompanyName="Ana Trujillo Emparedados y
          helados" ContactName="Ana Trujillo" ContactTitle="Owner" Address="Avda.
          de la Constituci?n 2222" City="M?xico D.F." PostalCode="05021"
          Country="Mexico" Phone="(5) 555-4729" Fax="(5) 555-3745" />
</CustomerList>
```

The sql parameter of this URL actually contains three queries. It uses the same technique as the UNION examples we built in the HTML chapter to generate three distinct pieces of data: It uses multiple queries. The first one generates an opening tag for the root element, the second is the query itself, and the third generates a closing tag for the root element. We separate the individual queries with semicolons.

As you can see, FOR XML returns XML document fragments, so you'll need to provide a root element to produce a well-formed document.

## Special Characters

Certain characters that are perfectly valid in Transact-SQL can cause problems in URL queries because they have special meanings within a URL. You've already noticed that we're using "+" to signify a space character. Obviously, this

**Table 13–2** Characters that Have Special Meaning in a URL Query and Their Hexadecimal Values

| Character | Hexadecimal value |
|---|---|
| + | 2B |
| & | 26 |
| ? | 3F |
| % | 25 |
| / | 2F |
| # | 23 |

precludes the direct use of "+" in the query itself. Instead, you must encode characters that have special meaning within a URL query so that SQLISAPI can properly translate them before passing on the query to SQL Server. Encoding a special character amounts to specifying a percent sign (%) followed by the character's ASCII value in hexadecimal. Table 13–2 lists the special characters recognized by SQLISAPI and their corresponding values:

Here's a URL query that illustrates how to encode special characters:

```
http://localhost/Northwind?sql=SELECT+'<CustomerList>';SELECT+*+FROM+Customers+
WHERE+CustomerId+LIKE+'A%25'+FOR+XML+AUTO;SELECT+'</CustomerList>';
```

This query specifies a LIKE predicate that includes an encoded percent sign, Transact-SQL's wildcard symbol. Hexadecimal 25 (decimal 37) is the ASCII value of the percent sign, so we encode it as %25.

## Style Sheets

In addition to the sql and root parameters, a URL query can also include the xsl parameter to specify an XML style sheet to use to translate the XML document that's returned by the query into a different format. The most common use of this feature is to translate the document into HTML. This allows you to view the document using browsers that aren't XML aware, and gives you more control over the display of the document in those that are. Here's a URL query that includes the xsl parameter:

```
http://localhost/Northwind?sql=SELECT+CustomerId,+CompanyName+FROM+
    Customers+FOR+XML+AUTO&root=CustomerList&xsl=CustomerList.xsl
```

Here's the XSL style sheet it references and the output that's produced:

```
<?xml version="1.0"?>
<xsl:stylesheet xmlns:xsl="http://www.w3.org/1999/XSL/Transform" version="1.0">
    <xsl:template match="/">
        <HTML>
            <BODY>
                <TABLE border="1">
                    <TR>
                        <TD><B>Customer ID</B></TD>
                        <TD><B>Company Name</B></TD>
                    </TR>
                    <xsl:for-each select="CustomerList/Customers">
                        <TR>
                            <TD>
                            <xsl:value-of select="@CustomerId"/>
                            </TD>
                            <TD>
                            <xsl:value-of select="@CompanyName"/>
                            </TD>
                        </TR>
                    </xsl:for-each>
                </TABLE>
            </BODY>
        </HTML>
    </xsl:template>
</xsl:stylesheet>
```

(Results abridged)

| Customer ID | Company Name |
|---|---|
| ALFKI | Alfreds Futterkiste |
| ANATR | Ana Trujillo Emparedados y helados |
| ANTON | Antonio Moreno TaquerÃa |
| AROUT | Around the Horn |
| BERGS | Berglunds snabbkÃ¶p |
| BLAUS | Blauer See Delikatessen |
| BLONP | Blondesddsl pÃ¨re et fils |
| WARTH | Wartian Herkku |
| WELLI | Wellington Importadora |
| WHITC | White Clover Markets |
| WILMK | Wilman Kala |
| WOLZA | Wolski Zajazd |

## Content Type

By default, SQLISAPI returns the results of a URL query with the appropriate type specified in the header so that a browser can properly render it. When FOR XML is used in the query, this is text/xml unless the xsl attribute specifies a style sheet that translates the XML document into HTML. In that case, text/html is returned.

You can force the content type using the contenttype URL query parameter, like this:

```
http://localhost/Northwind?sql=SELECT+CustomerId,+CompanyName+FROM+Customers+
    FOR+XML+AUTO&root=CustomerList&xsl=CustomerList.xsl&contenttype=text/xml
```

Here we've specified the style sheet from the previous example to cause the content type to default to text/html. Then we override this default by specifying a contenttype parameter of text/xml. The result is an XML document containing the translated result set:

```
- <HTML>
-     <BODY>
          - <TABLE border="1">
              - <TR>
                  - <TD>
                          <B>Customer ID</B>
                    </TD>
                  - <TD>
                          <B>Company Name</B>
                    </TD>
                </TR>
              - <TR>
                    <TD>ALFKI</TD>
                    <TD>Alfreds Futterkiste</TD>
                </TR>
              - <TR>
                    <TD>ANATR</TD>
                    <TD>Ana Trujillo Emparedados y helados</TD>
                </TR>
                <TR>
                    <TD>WILMK</TD>
                    <TD>Wilman Kala</TD>
                </TR>
              - <TR>
                    <TD>WOLZA</TD>
                    <TD>Wolski Zajazd</TD>
```

```
                    </TR>
                </TABLE>
            </BODY>
    </HTML>
```

So, even though the document consists of well-formed HTML, it's rendered as an XML document because we've forced the content type.

## Non-XML Results

Being able to specify the content type comes in particularly handy when working with XML fragments in an XML-aware browser. As I mentioned earlier, executing a FOR XML query with no root element results in an error. You can, however, work around this by forcing the content to HTML, like this:

```
http://localhost/Northwind?sql=SELECT+*+FROM+Customers+WHERE+
    CustomerId='ALFKI'+OR+CustomerId='ANATR'+FOR+XML+AUTO
    &contenttype=text/html
```

If you load this URL in a browser, you'll probably see a blank page because most browsers ignore tags they don't understand. However, you can view the source of the Web page and you'll see the XML fragment returned as you'd expect. This would be handy in situations when you're communicating with SQLISAPI using HTTP from outside a browser—from an application of some sort. You could return the XML fragment to the client, then use client-side logic to apply a root element and/or process the XML further.

SQLISAPI also allows you to omit the FOR XML clause to return a single column from a table, view, or table-valued function as a plain text stream, like this:

```
http://localhost/Northwind?sql=SELECT+CAST(CustomerId+AS+char(10))+AS+
    CustomerId+FROM+Customers+ORDER+BY+CustomerId&contenttype=text/html
```

(Results)

```
ALFKI ANATR ANTON AROUT BERGS BLAUS BLONP BOLID BONAP BOTTM BSBEV CACTU CENTC
CHOPS COMMI CONSH DRACD DUMON EASTC ERNSH FAMIA FISSA FOLIG FOLKO FRANK FRANR FRANS
FURIB GALED GODOS GOURL GREAL GROSR HANAR HILAA HUNGC HUNGO ISLAT KOENE LACOR LAMAI
LAUGB LAZYK LEHMS LETSS LILAS LINOD LONEP MAGAA MAISD MEREP MORGK NORTS OCEAN OLDWO
OTTIK PARIS PERIC PICCO PRINI QUEDE QUEEN QUICK RANCH RATTC REGGC RICAR RICSU ROMEY
SANTG SAVEA SEVES SIMOB SPECD SPLIR SUPRD THEBI THECR
TOMSP TORTU TRADH TRAIH VAFFE VICTE VINET WANDK WARTH WELLI WHITC WILMK WOLZA
```

Note that SQLISAPI doesn't support returning multicolumn results. That said, this is still a handy way to quickly return a simple data list.

## Stored Procedures

You can execute stored procedures via URL queries just as you can other types of Transact-SQL queries. Of course, this procedure needs to return its result set as XML if you intend to process it as XML in the browser or client application. Here's a stored procedure that illustrates:

```
CREATE PROC ListCustomersXML
@CustomerId varchar(10)='%',
@CompanyName varchar(80)='%'
AS
SELECT CustomerId, CompanyName
FROM Customers
WHERE CustomerId LIKE @CustomerId
AND CompanyName LIKE @CompanyName
FOR XML AUTO
```

Once your procedure correctly returns results in XML format, you can call it from a URL query using the Transact-SQL EXEC command. Here's an example of a URL query that calls a stored procedure using EXEC:

```
http://localhost/Northwind?sql=EXEC+ListCustomersXML+@CustomerId='A%25',
   @CompanyName='An%25'&root=CustomerList
```

(Results)

```
<?xml version="1.0" encoding="utf-8" ?>
_ <CustomerList>
        <Customers CustomerId="ANATR" CompanyName="Ana Trujillo Emparedados y
helados" />
        <Customers CustomerId="ANTON" CompanyName="Antonio Moreno Taquer?a" />
   </CustomerList>
```

Notice that we specify the Transact-SQL wildcard character "%" using its encoded equivalent, %25. This is necessary, as I said earlier, because % has special meaning in a URL query.

---

**TIP:** You can also use the ODBC CALL syntax to call a stored procedure from a URL query. Because you have no way of binding RPC parameters from a URL query, if you supply any parameters to the procedure, it's translated to a regular language event on the server. However, if the procedure takes no parameters, the procedure will execute as an RPC call on the server, which is generally faster and more efficient than normal T-SQL language events. On high-volume Web sites, the small difference in performance this makes can add up quickly.

Here's a URL query that uses the ODBC CALL syntax:

```
http://localhost/Northwind?sql={CALL+ListCustomersXML}+
    &root=CustomerList
```

If you submit this URL from your Web browser while you have a Profiler trace running that includes all RPC events, you should see an RPC:Starting event for the procedure. This indicates that the procedure is being called via the more efficient RPC mechanism rather than via a language event, as I mentioned in Chapter 1.

See the Template Queries section later in this chapter for information on making RPCs that support parameters from XML.

## Template Queries

A safer and more widely used technique for retrieving data over HTTP is to use server-side XML templates that encapsulate Transact-SQL queries. Because these templates are stored on the Web server and are referenced via a virtual name, the end user never sees their source code. They are XML documents based on the XML-SQL namespace and function as a mechanism for translating a URL into a query that SQL Server can process. As with plain URL queries, results from template queries are returned as either XML or HTML.

Here's a simple XML query template:

```
<?xml version='1.0' ?>
<CustomerList xmlns:sql='urn:schemas-microsoft-com:xml-sql'>
    <sql:query>
        SELECT CustomerId, CompanyName
        FROM Customers
        FOR XML AUTO
    </sql:query>
</CustomerList>
```

Note the use of the **sql** namespace prefix with the query itself. This is made possible by the namespace reference on the second line of the template (in bold type).

Here we're merely returning two columns from the Northwind Customers table, as we've been doing for most of the chapter. We include FOR XML AUTO to return the data as XML. Here's a URL that uses the template, along with the data it returns:

```
http://localhost/Northwind/templates/CustomerList.XML
```

(Results abridged)

```
<?xml version="1.0" ?>
_ <CustomerList xmlns:sql="urn:schemas-microsoft-com:xml-sql">
       <Customers CustomerId="ALFKI" CompanyName="Alfreds Futterkiste" />
       <Customers CustomerId="VAFFE" CompanyName="Vaffeljernet" />
       <Customers CustomerId="VICTE" CompanyName="Victuailles en stock" />
       <Customers CustomerId="VINET" CompanyName="Vins et alcools Chevalier" />
       <Customers CustomerId="WARTH" CompanyName="Wartian Herkku" />
       <Customers CustomerId="WELLI" CompanyName="Wellington Importadora" />
       <Customers CustomerId="WHITC" CompanyName="White Clover Markets" />
       <Customers CustomerId="WILMK" CompanyName="Wilman Kala" />
       <Customers CustomerId="WOLZA" CompanyName="Wolski Zajazd" />
</CustomerList>
```

Notice that we're using the templates virtual name that we created under the Northwind virtual directory earlier.

## Parameterized Templates

You can also create parameterized XML query templates that permit the user to supply parameters to the query when it's executed. You define parameters in the header of the template, which is contained in its sql:header element. Each parameter is defined using the sql:param tag and can include an optional default value. Here's an example:

```
<?xml version='1.0' ?>
<CustomerList xmlns:sql='urn:schemas-microsoft-com:xml-sql'>
    <sql:header>
        <sql:param name='CustomerId'>%</sql:param>
    </sql:header>
    <sql:query>
        SELECT CustomerId, CompanyName
        FROM Customers
        WHERE CustomerId LIKE @CustomerId
        FOR XML AUTO
```

```
       </sql:query>
</CustomerList>
```

Note the use of sql:param to define the parameter. Here we give the parameter a default value of "%" because we're using it in a LIKE predicate in the query. This means that we list all customers if no value is specified for the parameter.

Note that SQLISAPI is smart enough to submit a template query to the server as an RPC when you define query parameters. It binds the parameters you specify in the template as RPC parameters and sends the query to SQL Server using RPC API calls. This is more efficient than using T-SQL language events and should result in better performance, particularly on systems with high throughput.

Here's an example of URL that specifies a parameterized template query, along with its results:

```
http://localhost/Northwind/Templates/CustomerList2.XML?CustomerId=A%25
```

(Results)

```
<?xml version="1.0" ?>
- <CustomerList xmlns:sql="urn:schemas-microsoft-com:xml-sql">
      <Customers CustomerId="ALFKI" CompanyName="Alfreds Futterkiste" />
      <Customers CustomerId="ANATR" CompanyName="Ana Trujillo Emparedados
y helados" />
      <Customers CustomerId="ANTON" CompanyName="Antonio Moreno Taquería"
/>
      <Customers CustomerId="AROUT" CompanyName="Around the Horn" />
</CustomerList>
```

## Style Sheets

As with regular URL queries, you can specify a style sheet to apply to a template query. You can do this in the template itself or in the URL that accesses it. Here's an example of a URL that applies a style sheet to a template query:

```
http://localhost/Northwind/Templates/CustomerList3.XML
    ?xsl=Templates/CustomerList3.xsl&contenttype=text/html
```

Note the use of the contenttype parameter to force the output to be treated as HTML (in bold type). We do this because we know that the style sheet we're applying translates the XML returned by SQL Server into an HTML table.

We include the relative path from the virtual directory to the style sheet because it's not automatically located in the Templates folder even though the XML document is located there. The path specifications for a template query and its parameters are separate from one another.

As I've mentioned, the XML-SQL namespace also supports specifying the style sheet in the template itself. Here's a template that specifies a style sheet:

```
<?xml version='1.0' ?>
<CustomerList xmlns:sql='urn:schemas-microsoft-com:xml-sql'
sql:xsl='CustomerList3.xsl'>
    <sql:query>
        SELECT CustomerId, CompanyName
        FROM Customers
        FOR XML AUTO
    </sql:query>
</CustomerList>
```

Here's the style sheet the template references:

```
<?xml version="1.0"?>
<xsl:stylesheet xmlns:xsl="http://www.w3.org/1999/XSL/Transform" version="1.0">
    <xsl:template match="/">
        <HTML>
            <BODY>
                <TABLE border="1">
                    <TR>
                        <TD><I>Customer ID</I></TD>
                        <TD><I>Company Name</I></TD>
                    </TR>
                    <xsl:for-each select="CustomerList/Customers">
                        <TR>
                            <TD><B>
                            <xsl:value-of select="@CustomerId"/>
                            </B></TD>
                            <TD>
                            <xsl:value-of select="@CompanyName"/>
                            </TD>
                        </TR>
                    </xsl:for-each>
                </TABLE>
            </BODY>
        </HTML>
    </xsl:template>
</xsl:stylesheet>
```

Here's a URL that uses the two of them, along with the results it produces:

```
http://localhost/Northwind/Templates/CustomerList4.XML?contenttype=text/html
```

(Results abridged)

| Customer ID | Company Name |
|---|---|
| **ALFKI** | Alfreds Futterkiste |
| **ANATR** | Ana Trujillo Emparedados y helados |
| **ANTON** | Antonio Moreno TaquerÃa |
| **AROUT** | Around the Horn |
| **VICTE** | Victuailles en stock |
| **VINET** | Vins et alcools Chevalier |
| **WARTH** | Wartian Herkku |
| **WELLI** | Wellington Importadora |
| **WHITC** | White Clover Markets |
| **WILMK** | Wilman Kala |
| **WOLZA** | Wolski Zajazd |

Note that, once again, we specify the contenttype parameter to force the output to be treated as HTML. This is necessary because XML-aware browsers such as Internet Explorer automatically treat the output returned by XML templates as text/xml. Because the HTML we're returning is also well-formed XML, the browser doesn't know to render it as HTML unless we tell it to. That's what the contenttype specification is for: It causes the browser to render the output of the template query as it would any other HTML document.

---

**TIP:** While developing XML templates and similar documents that you then test in a Web browser, you may run into problems with the browser caching old versions of documents, even when you click the Refresh button or hit the Refresh key (F5). In Internet Explorer, you can press Ctrl-F5 to cause a document to be completely reloaded, even if the browser doesn't think it needs to be. Usually, this resolves problems with an old version persisting in memory after you've changed the one on disk.

---

## Applying Style Sheets on the Client

If the client is XML enabled, you can also apply style sheets to template queries on the client side. This off-loads a bit of the work of the server, but requires a separate round-trip to download the style sheet to the client. If the client is not XML enabled, the style sheet will be ignored, making this approach more suitable to situations in which you know for certain whether your clients are XML enabled, such as with private intranet or corporate applications.

Here's a template that specifies a client-side style sheet translation:

```
<?xml version='1.0' ?>
<?xml-stylesheet type='text/xsl' href='CustomerList3.xsl'?>
<CustomerList xmlns:sql='urn:schemas-microsoft-com:xml-sql'>
    <sql:query>
        SELECT CustomerId, CompanyName
        FROM Customers
        FOR XML AUTO
    </sql:query>
</CustomerList>
```

Note the xml-stylesheet specification at the top of the document (in bold type). This tells the client-side XML processor to download the style sheet specified in the href attribute and apply it to the XML document rendered by the template. Here's the URL and results:

```
http://localhost/Northwind/Templates/CustomerList5.XML?contenttype=text/html
```

(Results abridged)

| Customer ID | Company Name |
|-------------|--------------|
| ALFKI | Alfreds Futterkiste |
| ANATR | Ana Trujillo Emparedados y helados |
| ANTON | Antonio Moreno Taqueria |
| AROUT | Around the Horn |
| VICTE | Victuailles en stock |
| VINET | Vins et alcools Chevalier |
| WARTH | Wartian Herkku |
| WELLI | Wellington Importadora |
| WHITC | White Clover Markets |
| WILMK | Wilman Kala |
| WOLZA | Wolski Zajazd |

## Client-side Templates

As I mentioned earlier, it's far more popular (and safer) to store templates on your Web server and route users to them via virtual names. That said, there are times when allowing the user the flexibility to specify templates on the client side is very useful. Specifying client-side templates in HTML or in an application alleviates the necessity to set up the templates in advance or the virtual names that reference them. Although this is certainly easier from an administration standpoint, it's potentially unsafe on the public Internet because it allows clients to specify the code they run against your SQL Server. Use of this technique should probably be limited to private intranets and corporate networks.

Here's a Web page that embeds a client-side template:

```
<HTML>
    <HEAD>
        <TITLE>Customer List</TITLE>
    </HEAD>
    <BODY>
        <FORM action='http://localhost/Northwind' method='POST'>
            <B>Customer ID Number</B>
            <INPUT type=text name=CustomerId value='%'>
            <INPUT type=hidden name=xsl value=Templates/CustomerList2.xsl>
            <INPUT type=hidden name=template value='
            <CustomerList xmlns:sql="urn:schemas-microsoft-com:xml-sql">
                <sql:header>
                    <sql:param name="CustomerId">%</sql:param>
                </sql:header>
                <sql:query>
                    SELECT CompanyName, ContactName
                    FROM Customers
                    WHERE CustomerId LIKE @CustomerId
                    FOR XML AUTO
                </sql:query>
            </CustomerList>
            '>
            <P><input type='submit'>
        </FORM>
    </BODY>
</HTML>
```

The client-side template (in bold type) is embedded as a hidden field in the Web page. If you open this page in a Web browser, you should see an entry box for a Customer ID and a Submit button. Entering a customer ID or mask and clicking Submit Query will post the template to the Web server. SQLISAPI will then extract the query contained in the template and run it against SQL Server's Northwind database (because of the template's virtual directory reference). The CustomerList2.xsl style sheet will then be applied to translate the XML document that SQL Server returns into HTML, and the result will be returned to the client. Here's an example:

**Customer ID Number** | A%

Submit Query

(Results)

| Company Name | Contact Name |
|---|---|
| Alfreds Futterkiste | Maria Anders |
| Ana Trujillo Emparedados y helados | Ana Trujillo |
| Antonio Moreno Taqueria | Antonio Moreno |
| Around the Horn | Thomas Hardy |

As with server-side templates, client-side templates that include parameters are sent to SQL Server using an RPC.

## Summary

In this chapter you learned to access SQL Server over HTTP. You learned how to configure SQL Server's HTTP access facility, you learned how it works behind the scenes, and you learned how to submit queries and receive results over HTTP. You also learned about template queries and why they're generally preferred to URL queries. In the next chapter we'll build on this to access more of SQL Server's XML features.

# CHAPTER 14

# XML and SQL Server: Retrieving Data

*The process of preparing programs for a digital computer is especially attractive, not only because it can be economically and scientifically rewarding, but also because it can be an aesthetic experience much like composing poetry or music.*

*—Donald Knuth*[1]

Thus far, we've used FOR XML AUTO to return SQL Server data in a basic XML format so that we could work with it from a Web browser. Transact-SQL's FOR XML syntax is much richer than this, though. It supports several options that extend its usefulness in numerous ways. In this chapter, we'll discuss a few of these and work through examples that illustrate them.

## SELECT...FOR XML

As the examples in the previous chapter demonstrated, you can retrieve XML data from SQL Server using the FOR XML option of the SELECT command. FOR XML causes SELECT to return query results as an XML stream rather than a traditional rowset. This stream can have one of three formats: RAW, AUTO, or EXPLICIT. The basic FOR XML syntax looks like this:

```
SELECT column list
FROM table list
WHERE filter criteria
FOR XML RAW | AUTO | EXPLICIT [, XMLDATA] [, ELEMENTS] [, BINARY BASE64]
```

---

[1]Knuth, Donald. *The Art of Computer Programming Vol. 1 Fundamental Algorithms*. Reading, MA: Addison-Wesley, 1997. Page v.

Although I'll discuss these options separately, let's go over them briefly now.

RAW returns column values as attributes and wraps each row in a generic row element. AUTO returns column values as attributes and wraps each row in an element named after the table from which it came. (There's actually more to this than simply naming each row after the table, view, or UDF that produced it. SQL Server uses a set of heuristics to decide what the actual element names are with FOR XML AUTO.) EXPLICIT lets you completely control the format of the XML returned by a query.

XMLDATA causes an XDR schema to be returned for the document being retrieved. ELEMENTS causes the columns in XML AUTO data to be returned as elements rather than attributes. BINARY BASE64 specifies that binary data is to be returned using BASE64 encoding.

# RAW Mode

RAW mode is the simplest of the three basic FOR XML modes. It performs a very basic translation of the result set into XML. Here's an example:

```
SELECT CustomerId, CompanyName
FROM Customers FOR XML RAW
```

(Results abridged)

```
XML_F52E2B61-18A1-11d1-B105-00805F49916B
--------------------------------------------------------------------------
<row CustomerId="ALFKI" CompanyName="Alfreds Futterkiste"/><row
CustomerId="ANATR" CompanyName="Ana Trujillo Emparedados y helados"/><row
CustomerId="ANTON" CompanyName="Antonio Moreno Taquer?a"/><row
CustomerId="AROUT" CompanyName="Around the Horn"/><row CustomerId="BERGS"
CompanyName="Berglunds snabbk?p"/><row CustomerId="BLAUS"
CompanyName="Blauer See Delikatessen"/><row CustomerId="BLONP"
CompanyName="Blondesddsl père et fils"/><row CustomerId="WELLI"
CompanyName="Wellington Importadora"/><row CustomerId="WHITC"
CompanyName="White Clover Markets"/><row CustomerId="WILMK"
CompanyName="Wilman Kala"/><row CustomerId="WOLZA"
CompanyName="Wolski Zajazd"/>
```

Each column becomes an attribute in the result set, and each row becomes an element with the generic name of row.

As I've mentioned before, keep in mind that the XML that's returned by FOR XML is not well formed because it lacks a root element. It's technically an XML fragment, and you must supply a root element in order for the document to be usable by an XML parser.

# AUTO Mode

FOR XML AUTO gives you more control than RAW mode over the XML fragment that's produced. To begin with, each row in the result set is named after the table, view, or table-valued UDF that produced it. For example, here's a basic FOR XML AUTO query:

```
SELECT CustomerId, CompanyName
FROM Customers FOR XML AUTO
```

(Results abridged)

```
XML_F52E2B61-18A1-11d1-B105-00805F49916B
------------------------------------------------------------------------
<Customers CustomerId="ALFKI" CompanyName="Alfreds Futterkiste"/><Customers
CustomerId="ANATR" CompanyName="Ana Trujillo Emparedados y helados"/><Customers
CustomerId="ANTON" CompanyName="Antonio Moreno Taquer?a"/><Customers
CustomerId="AROUT" CompanyName="Around the Horn"/><Customers CustomerId="VINET"
CompanyName="Vins et alcools Chevalier"/><Customers CustomerId="WARTH"
CompanyName="Wartian Herkku"/><Customers CustomerId="WELLI"
CompanyName="Wellington Importadora"/><Customers CustomerId="WHITC"
CompanyName="White Clover Markets"/><Customers CustomerId="WILMK"
CompanyName="Wilman Kala"/><Customers CustomerId="WOLZA"
CompanyName="Wolski Zajazd"/>
```

Notice that each row is named after the table from whence it came: Customers. For results with more than one row, this amounts to having more than one top-level (root) element in the fragment, which isn't allowed in XML.

One big difference between AUTO and RAW mode is the way in which joins are handled. In RAW mode, a simple one-to-one translation occurs between columns in the result set and attributes in the XML fragment. Each row becomes an element in the fragment named row. These elements are technically empty themselves. They contain no values or subelements; they only contain attributes. Think of attributes as specifying characteristics of an element, whereas data and subelements compose its contents. In AUTO mode, each row is named after the source from which it came, and the rows from joined tables are nested within one another. Here's an example:

```
SELECT Customers.CustomerID, CompanyName, OrderId
FROM Customers JOIN Orders
ON (Customers.CustomerId=Orders.CustomerId)
FOR XML AUTO
```

(Results abridged and formatted)

```
XML_F52E2B61-18A1-11d1-B105-00805F49916B
-------------------------------------------------------------------------
<Customers CustomerID="ALFKI" CompanyName="Alfreds Futterkiste">
        <Orders OrderId="10643"/><Orders OrderId="10692"/>
        <Orders OrderId="10702"/><Orders OrderId="10835"/>
        <Orders OrderId="10952"/><Orders OrderId="11011"/>
</Customers>
<Customers CustomerID="ANATR" CompanyName="Ana Trujillo Emparedados y helados">
        <Orders OrderId="10308"/><Orders OrderId="10625"/>
        <Orders OrderId="10759"/><Orders OrderId="10926"/></Customers>
<Customers CustomerID="FRANR" CompanyName="France restauration">
        <Orders OrderId="10671"/><Orders OrderId="10860"/>
        <Orders OrderId="10971"/>
</Customers>
```

I've formatted the XML fragment to make it easier to read. If you run the query yourself from Query Analyzer, you'll see an unformatted stream of XML text.

Note the way in which the Orders for each customer are contained within each Customer element. As I said, AUTO mode nests the rows returned by joins. Note my use of the full table name in the join criterion. Why didn't I use a table alias? Because AUTO mode uses the table aliases you specify to name the elements it returns. If you use shortened monikers for a table, its elements will have that name in the resulting XML fragment. Although useful in traditional Transact-SQL, this makes the fragment difficult to read if the alias isn't sufficiently descriptive.

## ELEMENTS

The ELEMENTS option of the FOR XML AUTO clause causes AUTO mode to return nested elements instead of attributes. Depending on your business needs or those of your clients, element-centric mapping may be preferable to the default attribute-centric mapping. Here's an example of a FOR XML query that returns elements instead of attributes:

```
SELECT CustomerID, CompanyName
FROM Customers
FOR XML AUTO, ELEMENTS
```

(Results abridged and formatted)

```
XML_F52E2B61-18A1-11d1-B105-00805F49916B
---------------------------------------------------------------------------
<Customers>
        <CustomerID>ALFKI</CustomerID>
        <CompanyName>Alfreds Futterkiste</CompanyName>
</Customers>
<Customers>
        <CustomerID>ANATR</CustomerID>
        <CompanyName>Ana Trujillo Emparedados y helados</CompanyName>
</Customers>
<Customers>
        <CustomerID>ANTON</CustomerID>
        <CompanyName>Antonio Moreno Taquería</CompanyName>
</Customers>
<Customers>
        <CustomerID>AROUT</CustomerID>
        <CompanyName>Around the Horn</CompanyName>
</Customers>
<Customers>
        <CustomerID>WILMK</CustomerID>
        <CompanyName>Wilman Kala</CompanyName>
</Customers>
<Customers>
        <CustomerID>WOLZA</CustomerID>
        <CompanyName>Wolski Zajazd</CompanyName>
</Customers>
```

Notice that the ELEMENTS option has caused what were being returned as attributes of the Customers element to instead be returned as subelements. Each attribute is now a pair of element tags that enclose the value from a column in the table.

---

**NOTE:** Currently, AUTO mode does not support GROUP BY or aggregate functions. The heuristics it uses to determine element names are incompatible with these constructs, so you cannot use them in AUTO mode queries. Additionally, FOR XML itself is incompatible with COMPUTE, so you can't use it in FOR XML queries of any kind.

---

# EXPLICIT Mode

If you need more control over the XML that FOR XML produces, EXPLICIT mode is more flexible (and therefore more complicated to use) than either RAW mode or AUTO mode. EXPLICIT mode queries define XML documents in terms of a "universal table"—a mechanism for returning a result set from SQL Server that *describes* what you want the document to look like, rather than composing the document itself. A universal table is just a SQL Server result set with special column headings that tell SQL Server how to produce an XML document from your data. Think of it as a set-oriented method of making an API call and passing parameters to it. You use the facilities available in Transact-SQL to make the call and pass it parameters.

A universal table consists of one column for each table column that you want to return in the XML fragment, plus two additional columns: Tag and Parent. Tag is a positive integer that uniquely identifies each tag that is to be returned by the document; Parent establishes parent-child relationships between tags.

The other columns in a universal table—the ones that correspond to the data you want to include in the XML fragment—have special names that actually consist of multiple segments delimited by exclamation points. These special column names pass muster with SQL Server's parser and provide specific instructions regarding the XML fragment to produce. They have the format of

```
Element!Tag!Attribute!Directive
```

We'll see some examples of these shortly.

The first thing you need to do to build an EXPLICIT mode query is to determine the layout of the XML document with which you want to end up. Once you know this, you can work backward from there to build a universal table that will produce the desired format. For example, let's say we want a simple customer list based on the Northwind Customers table that returns the customer ID as an attribute and the company name as an element. The XML fragment we're after might look like this:

```
<Customers CustomerId="ALFKI">Alfreds Futterkiste</Customers>
```

Here's a Transact-SQL query that returns a universal table that specifies this layout:

```
SELECT 1 AS Tag,
NULL AS Parent,
CustomerId AS [Customers!1!CustomerId],
CompanyName AS [Customers!1]
FROM Customers
```

(Results abridged)

```
Tag          Parent          Customers!1!CustomerId Customers!1
----------   -----------     ---------------------- -----------------------------
1            NULL            ALFKI                  Alfreds Futterkiste
1            NULL            ANATR                  Ana Trujillo Emparedados y
1            NULL            ANTON                  Antonio Moreno Taquería
```

The first two columns are the extra columns I mentioned earlier. **Tag** specifies an identifier for the tag we want to produce. Because we only want to produce one element per row, we hard code this to 1. The same is true of **Parent.** There's only one element, and a top-level element doesn't have a parent, so we return NULL for **Parent** in every row.

Because we want to return the customer ID as an attribute, we specify an attribute name in the heading of column 3 (in bold type). And because we want to return CompanyName as an element rather than an attribute, we omit the attribute name in column 4.

By itself, this table accomplishes nothing. We have to add FOR XML EXPLICIT to the end of it in order for the odd column names to have any special meaning. Add FOR XML EXPLICIT to this query and run it from Query Analyzer. Here's what you should see:

```
SELECT 1 AS Tag,
NULL AS Parent,
CustomerId AS [Customers!1!CustomerId],
CompanyName AS [Customers!1]
FROM Customers
FOR XML EXPLICIT
```

(Results abridged and formatted)

```
XML_F52E2B61-18A1-11d1-B105-00805F49916B
-------------------------------------------------------------------
<Customers CustomerId="ALFKI">Alfreds Futterkiste</Customers>
<Customers CustomerId="ANATR">Ana Trujillo Emparedados y helados</Customers>
<Customers CustomerId="WHITC">White Clover Markets</Customers>
<Customers CustomerId="WILMK">Wilman Kala</Customers>
<Customers CustomerId="WOLZA">Wolski Zajazd</Customers>
```

As you can see, each CustomerId value is returned as an attribute, and each CompanyName is returned as the element data for the Customers element, just as we specified.

## Directives

The fourth part of the multivalue column headings supported by EXPLICIT mode queries is the directive segment. You use it to further control how data is represented in the resulting XML fragment. The directive segment supports eight values (Table 14–1).

Of these, element is the most frequently used. It causes data to be rendered as a subelement rather than an attribute. For example, let's say that, in addition to CustomerId and CompanyName, we wanted to return ContactName in our

**Table 14–1** Values of the Directive Segment

| Value | Function |
| --- | --- |
| element | Causes data in the column to be encoded and represented as a subelement. |
| xml | Causes data to be represented as a subelement without encoding it. |
| xmltext | Retrieves data from an overflow column and appends it to the document. |
| cdata | Causes data in the column to be represented as a CDATA section in the resulting document. |
| hide | Hides (omits) a column that appears in the universal table from the resulting XML fragment. |
| id, idref, idrefs | In conjunction with XMLDATA, the id, idref, and idrefs directives can establish relationships between elements across multiple XML fragments. |

XML fragment and we wanted it to be a subelement rather than an attribute. Here's what the query would look like:

```
SELECT 1 AS Tag,
NULL AS Parent,
CustomerId AS [Customers!1!CustomerId],
CompanyName AS [Customers!1],
ContactName AS [Customers!1!ContactName!element]
FROM Customers
FOR XML EXPLICIT
```

(Results abridged and formatted)

```
XML_F52E2B61-18A1-11d1-B105-00805F49916B
-------------------------------------------------------------------------
<Customers CustomerId="ALFKI">Alfreds Futterkiste
        <ContactName>Maria Anders</ContactName>
</Customers>
<Customers CustomerId="ANATR">Ana Trujillo Emparedados y
        <ContactName>Ana Trujillo</ContactName>
</Customers>
<Customers CustomerId="ANTON">Antonio Moreno Taquería
        <ContactName>Antonio Moreno</ContactName>
</Customers>
<Customers CustomerId="AROUT">Around the Horn
        <ContactName>Thomas Hardy</ContactName>
</Customers>
<Customers CustomerId="BERGS">Berglunds snabbköp
        <ContactName>Christina Berglund</ContactName>
</Customers>
<Customers CustomerId="WILMK">Wilman Kala
        <ContactName>Matti Karttunen</ContactName>
</Customers>
<Customers CustomerId="WOLZA">Wolski Zajazd
        <ContactName>Zbyszek Piestrzeniewicz</ContactName>
</Customers>
```

As you can see, ContactName is nested within each Customers element as a subelement. The elements directive encodes the data it returns. We can retrieve the same data using the xml directive without encoding like this:

```
SELECT 1 AS Tag,
NULL AS Parent,
CustomerId AS [Customers!1!CustomerId],
```

```
CompanyName AS [Customers!1],
ContactName AS [Customers!1!ContactName!xml]
FROM Customers
FOR XML EXPLICIT
```

The xml directive (in bold type) causes the column to be returned without encoding any special characters it contains.

## Establishing Data Relationships

Thus far, we've been listing the data from a single table, so our EXPLICIT queries haven't been terribly complex. That would still be true even if we queried multiple tables, as long as we didn't mind repeating the data from each table in each top-level element in the XML fragment. Just as the column values from joined tables are often repeated in the result sets of Transact-SQL queries, we could create an XML fragment that contained data from multiple tables repeated in each element. However, this wouldn't be the most efficient way to represent the data in XML. Remember: XML supports hierarchical relationships between elements. You can establish these hierarchies using EXPLICIT mode queries and T-SQL UNIONs. Here's an example:

```
SELECT 1 AS Tag,
NULL AS Parent,
CustomerId AS [Customers!1!CustomerId],
CompanyName AS [Customers!1],
NULL AS [Orders!2!OrderId],
NULL AS [Orders!2!OrderDate!element]
FROM Customers
UNION
SELECT 2 AS Tag,
1 AS Parent,
CustomerId,
NULL,
OrderId,
OrderDate
FROM Orders
ORDER BY [Customers!1!CustomerId], [Orders!2!OrderDate!element]
FOR XML EXPLICIT
```

This query does several interesting things. First, it links the Customers and Orders tables using the **CustomerId** column that they share. Notice the third column in each SELECT statement. It returns the **CustomerId** column from each table. The **Tag** and **Parent** columns establish the details of the relationship between the two tables. The Tag and Parent values in the second query

link it to the first. They establish that ORDER records are children of CUS-
TOMER records. Lastly, note the ORDER BY clause. It arranges the elements
in the table in a sensible fashion—first by CustomerId and secondly by the
OrderDate of each Order. Here's the result set:

(Results abridged and formatted)

```
XML_F52E2B61-18A1-11d1-B105-00805F49916B
--------------------------------------------------------------------------
<Customers CustomerId="ALFKI">Alfreds Futterkiste
        <Orders OrderId="10643">
                <OrderDate>1997-08-25T00:00:00</OrderDate>
        </Orders>
        <Orders OrderId="10692">
                <OrderDate>1997-10-03T00:00:00</OrderDate>
        </Orders>
        <Orders OrderId="10702">
                <OrderDate>1997-10-13T00:00:00</OrderDate>
        </Orders>
        <Orders OrderId="10835">
                <OrderDate>1998-01-15T00:00:00</OrderDate>
        </Orders>
        <Orders OrderId="10952">
                <OrderDate>1998-03-16T00:00:00</OrderDate>
        </Orders>
        <Orders OrderId="11011">
                <OrderDate>1998-04-09T00:00:00</OrderDate>
        </Orders>
</Customers>
<Customers CustomerId="ANATR">Ana Trujillo Emparedados y helados
        <Orders OrderId="10308">
                <OrderDate>1996-09-18T00:00:00</OrderDate>
        </Orders>
        <Orders OrderId="10625">
                <OrderDate>1997-08-08T00:00:00</OrderDate>
        </Orders>
        <Orders OrderId="10759">
                <OrderDate>1997-11-28T00:00:00</OrderDate>
        </Orders>
        <Orders OrderId="10926">
                <OrderDate>1998-03-04T00:00:00</OrderDate>
        </Orders>
</Customers>
```

As you can see, each customer's orders are nested within its element.

### The hide Directive

You use the hide directive to omit a column you've included in the universal table from the resulting XML document. One use of this functionality is to order the result by a column that you don't want to include in the XML fragment. When you aren't using UNION to merge tables, this isn't a problem because you can order by any column you choose. However, the presence of UNION in a query requires order by columns to exist in the result set. The hide directive gives you a way of satisfying this requirement without being forced to return data you don't want to. Here's an example:

```
SELECT 1 AS Tag,
NULL AS Parent,
CustomerId AS [Customers!1!CustomerId],
CompanyName AS [Customers!1],
PostalCode AS [Customers!1!PostalCode!hide],
NULL AS [Orders!2!OrderId],
NULL AS [Orders!2!OrderDate!element]
FROM Customers
UNION
SELECT 2 AS Tag,
1 AS Parent,
CustomerId,
NULL,
NULL,
OrderId,
OrderDate
FROM Orders
ORDER BY [Customers!1!CustomerId], [Orders!2!OrderDate!element],
[Customers!1!PostalCode!hide]
FOR XML EXPLICIT
```

Notice the hide directive (in bold type) that's included in the column 5 heading. It allows the column to be specified in the ORDER BY clause without actually appearing in the resulting XML fragment.

### The cdata Directive

It's not unusual for XML documents to need to include unparsed data. CDATA (as opposed to PCDATA, where "P" stands for "Parsed") is unparsed character data. A CDATA section is output by an XML parser in the same condition it was received. There's no encoding or other translation. CDATA sections allow you to include XML sections that might otherwise confuse the parser. To render a

CDATA section from an EXPLICIT mode query, include the cdata directive. Here's an example:

```
SELECT 1 AS Tag,
NULL AS Parent,
CustomerId AS [Customers!1!CustomerId],
CompanyName AS [Customers!1],
Fax AS [Customers!1!!cdata]
FROM Customers
FOR XML EXPLICIT
```

(Results abridged and formatted)

```
XML_F52E2B61-18A1-11d1-B105-00805F49916B
-------------------------------------------------------------------------
<Customers CustomerId="ALFKI">Alfreds Futterkiste
     <![CDATA[030-0076545]]>
</Customers>
<Customers CustomerId="ANATR">Ana Trujillo Emparedados y helados
     <![CDATA[(5) 555-3745]]>
</Customers>
<Customers CustomerId="ANTON">Antonio Moreno Taquería
</Customers>
<Customers CustomerId="AROUT">Around the Horn
     <![CDATA[(171) 555-6750]]>
</Customers>
<Customers CustomerId="BERGS">Berglunds snabbköp
     <![CDATA[0921-12 34 67]]>
</Customers>
```

As you can see, each value in the **Fax** column is returned as a CDATA section in the XML fragment. Note the omission of the attribute name in the **cdata** column heading (in bold type). This is because attribute names aren't allowed for CDATA sections. Again, they represent unparsed sections in a document, so the XML parser can't process any attribute or element names they may contain.

### The id, idref, and idrefs Directives

The id, idref, and idfrefs directives can be used to represent relational data in an XML document. Set up in a DTD or XML-Data schema, they establish relationships between elements. They're handy in situations when you need to exchange complex data and want to minimize the amount of data duplication in the document.

EXPLICIT mode queries can use the id, idref, and idrefs directives to specify relational fields in an XML document. Naturally, this approach is only workable if a schema is used to define the document and identify the columns used to establish links between entities. FOR XML's XMLDATA option provides a means of generating an inline schema for its XML fragment. In conjunction with the id directives, it can identify relational fields in the XML fragment. Here's an example:

```
SELECT 1 AS Tag,
       NULL AS Parent,
       CustomerId AS [Customers!1!CustomerId!id],
       CompanyName AS [Customers!1!CompanyName],
       NULL AS [Orders!2!OrderID],
       NULL AS [Orders!2!CustomerId!idref]
FROM Customers
UNION
SELECT 2,
       NULL,
       NULL,
       NULL,
       OrderID,
       CustomerId
FROM Orders
ORDER BY [Orders!2!OrderID]
FOR XML EXPLICIT, XMLDATA
```

(Results abridged and formatted)

```
XML_F52E2B61-18A1-11d1-B105-00805F49916B
-------------------------------------------------------------------------
<Schema name="Schema2" xmlns="urn:schemas-microsoft-com:xml-data"
xmlns:dt="urn:schemas-microsoft-com:datatypes">
       <ElementType name="Customers" content="mixed" model="open">
             <AttributeType name="CustomerId" dt:type="id"/>
             <AttributeType name="CompanyName" dt:type="string"/>
             <attribute type="CustomerId"/>
             <attribute type="CompanyName"/>
       </ElementType>
<ElementType name="Orders" content="mixed" model="open">
             <AttributeType name="OrderID" dt:type="i4"/>
             <AttributeType name="CustomerId" dt:type="idref"/>
```

```
            <attribute type="OrderID"/>
            <attribute type="CustomerId"/>
        </ElementType>
</Schema>
<Customers xmlns="x-schema:#Schema2" CustomerId="ALFKI"
        CompanyName="Alfreds Futterkiste"/>
<Customers xmlns="x-schema:#Schema2" CustomerId="ANATR"
        CompanyName="Ana Trujillo Emparedados y helados"/>
<Customers xmlns="x-schema:#Schema2" CustomerId="ANTON"
        CompanyName="Antonio Moreno Taquería"/>
<Customers xmlns="x-schema:#Schema2" CustomerId="AROUT"
        CompanyName="Around the Horn"/>
<Orders xmlns="x-schema:#Schema2" OrderID="10248" CustomerId="VINET"/>
<Orders xmlns="x-schema:#Schema2" OrderID="10249" CustomerId="TOMSP"/>
<Orders xmlns="x-schema:#Schema2" OrderID="10250" CustomerId="HANAR"/>
<Orders xmlns="x-schema:#Schema2" OrderID="10251" CustomerId="VICTE"/>
<Orders xmlns="x-schema:#Schema2" OrderID="10252" CustomerId="SUPRD"/>
<Orders xmlns="x-schema:#Schema2" OrderID="10253" CustomerId="HANAR"/>
<Orders xmlns="x-schema:#Schema2" OrderID="10254" CustomerId="CHOPS"/>
<Orders xmlns="x-schema:#Schema2" OrderID="10255" CustomerId="RICSU"/>
```

Note the use of the id and idref directives to in the **CustomerId** columns of the Customers and Orders tables (in bold type). These directives link the two tables using the **CustomerId** column that they share.

If you examine the XML fragment returned by the query, you'll see that it starts off with the XML-Data schema that the xmldata directive created. This schema is then referenced in the XML fragment that follows.

# Mapping Schemas

We discussed XML schemas in Chapter 12, so I won't go back into them here. Suffice it to say that XML schemas are XML documents that define the type of data that other XML documents may contain. They are a replacement for the old DTD technology originally used for that purpose, and are easier to use and more flexible because they consist of XML themselves.

By their very nature, schemas also define document exchange formats. Because they define what a document may and may not contain, companies wishing to exchange XML data need to agree on a common schema definition to do so. XML schemas allow companies with disparate business needs and cultures to exchange data seamlessly.

The syntax for XML Schemas is still in the process of being approved as I write this (January 2001). The W3C is currently considering input from several sources and will likely publish a standard later this year. For now, Microsoft, along with several other companies, has proposed that a subset of the W3C XML-Data syntax be used to define schemas for document interchange. XML-Data Reduced (XDR) is an XML-Data subset that can be used to define schemas. SQL Server and Microsoft's other XML-enabled products support XDR schemas.

It's likely that the final syntax for XML Schemas will differ semantically from XDR. Microsoft has announced that it will support whatever the final syntax is, so you should keep your eyes open for changes in the technology.

Listing 14–1 presents an example of an XDR schema:

**Listing 14–1** ProductsCat.xdr.

```
<?xml version="1.0"?>
<Schema name="NorthwindProducts"
    xmlns="urn:schemas-microsoft-com:xml-data"
    xmlns:dt="urn:schemas-microsoft-com:datatypes">

    <ElementType name="Description" dt:type="string"/>
    <ElementType name="Price" dt:type="fixed.19.4"/>

    <ElementType name="Product" model="closed">
        <AttributeType name="ProductCode" dt:type="string"/>
        <attribute type="ProductCode" required="yes"/>
        <element type="Description" minOccurs="1" maxOccurs="1"/>
        <element type="Price" minOccurs="1" maxOccurs="1"/>
    </ElementType>

    <ElementType name="Category" model="closed">
        <AttributeType name="CategoryID" dt:type="string"/>
        <AttributeType name="CategoryName" dt:type="string"/>
        <attribute type="CategoryID" required="yes"/>
        <attribute type="CategoryName" required="yes"/>
        <element type="Product" minOccurs="1" maxOccurs="*"/>
    </ElementType>

    <ElementType name="Catalog" model="closed">
        <element type="Category" minOccurs="1" maxOccurs="1"/>
    </ElementType>
</Schema>
```

This schema defines what a product catalog might look like (we're using the sample tables and data from the Northwind database). It uses the datatypes namespace (in bold type) to define the valid data types for elements and attributes in the document. Every place you see dt:, it is a reference to the datatypes namespace. The use of the closed model guarantees that only elements that exist in the schema can be used in a document based on it.

Listing 14–2 presents an XML document that uses ProductsCat.xdr:

**Listing 14–2**  ProductsCat.xml.

```
<?xml version="1.0"?>
<Catalog xmlns=
    "x-schema:http://localhost/ProductsCat.xdr">
    <Category CategoryID="1" CategoryName="Beverages">
        <Product ProductCode="1">
            <Description>Chai</Description>
            <Price>18</Price>
        </Product>
        <Product ProductCode="2">
            <Description>Chang</Description>
            <Price>19</Price>
        </Product>
    </Category>
    <Category CategoryID="2" CategoryName="Condiments">
        <Product ProductCode="3">
            <Description>Aniseed Syrup</Description>
            <Price>10</Price>
        </Product>
    </Category>
</Catalog>
```

If you copy both of these files to the root folder of your Web server and type the following URL

```
http://localhost/ProductsCat.xml
```

into your browser, you should see this output:

```
  <?xml version="1.0" ?>
- <Catalog xmlns="x-schema:http://localhost/ProductsCat.xdr">
- <Category CategoryID="1" CategoryName="Beverages">
    _ <Product ProductCode="1">
            <Description>Chai</Description>
```

```
                    <Price>18</Price>
           </Product>
         - <Product ProductCode="2">
                    <Description>Chang</Description>
                    <Price>19</Price>
           </Product>
   </Category>
 _ <Category CategoryID="2" CategoryName="Condiments">
       _ <Product ProductCode="3">
                    <Description>Aniseed Syrup</Description>
                    <Price>10</Price>
           </Product>
   </Category>
   </Catalog>
```

You've already seen that XML data can be extracted and formatted in a variety of ways. One of the challenges in exchanging data using XML is this flexibility. However, mapping schemas help us overcome this challenge. They allow us to return data from a database in a particular format. They allow us to map columns and tables to attributes and elements.

The easiest way to use a schema to map data returned by SQL Server into XML entities is to assume the default mapping returned by SQL Server. That is, every table becomes an element, and every column becomes an attribute. Here's a schema that does this:

```
<?xml version="1.0"?>
<Schema name="customers"
    xmlns="urn:schemas-microsoft-com:xml-data">
    <ElementType name="Customers">
        <AttributeType name="CustomerId"/>
        <AttributeType name="CompanyName"/>
    </ElementType>
</Schema>
```

Here we retrieve only two columns, each of them from the Customers table. If you store this schema under the schemas virtual name that we created earlier and retrieve it via a URL, you'll see a simple XML document with the data from the Customers table in an attribute-centric mapping, as we've seen several times throughout this chapter.

You use XML-Data's ElementType to map a column in a table to an element in the resulting XML document. Here's an example:

```
<?xml version="1.0"?>
```

```
<Schema name="customers"
    xmlns="urn:schemas-microsoft-com:xml-data">
    <ElementType name="Customers">
        <ElementType name="CustomerId" content="textOnly"/>
        <ElementType name="CompanyName" content="textOnly"/>
    </ElementType>
</Schema>
```

Note the use of the content="textOnly" attribute with each element. In conjunction with the ElementType element, this maps a column to an element in the resulting XML document. Note that the elements corresponding to each column are actually empty. They contain attributes only; no data.

## Annotated Schemas

An annotated schema is a mapping schema with special annotations (from the XML-SQL namespace) that link elements and attributes with tables and columns. Here's some code that uses our familiar Customer list example:

```
<?xml version="1.0"?>
<Schema name="customers"
    xmlns="urn:schemas-microsoft-com:xml-data">
    xmlns:sql="urn:schemas-microsoft-com:xml-sql">
    <ElementType name="Customer" sql:relation="Customers">
        <AttributeType name="CustomerNumber" sql:field="CustomerId"/>
        <AttributeType name="Name" sql:field="CompanyName"/>
    </ElementType>
</Schema>
```

First, note the reference to the XML-SQL namespace at the top of the schema. Because we'll be referencing it later in the schema, we begin with a reference to XML-SQL so that we can use the sql: namespace shorthand for it later. Next, notice the sql:relation attribute of the first ElementType element. It establishes that the Customer element in the resulting document relates to the Customers table in the database referenced by the virtual directory. This allows you to call the element whatever you want. Last, notice the sql:field references. They establish, for example, that the CustomerNumber element refers to the **CustomerId** column in the referenced table. Things get more complicated when multiple tables are involved, but you get the picture—an annotated schema allows you to establish granular mappings between document entities and database entities.

# Summary

In this chapter we explored FOR XML in detail, and also took a look at mapping schemas. FOR XML allows us to translate a SQL Server result set into XML, giving us a great deal of control over how that XML is formatted. Mapping schemas also provide a mechanism for retrieving SQL Server data in XML format. They provide a greater degree of control than FOR XML, but they're also more complicated to use.

# CHAPTER 15

# XML and SQL Server: OPENXML

*Generally, in battle, use the normal force to engage; use the extraordinary to win.*

*—Sun Tzu*[1]

In this chapter we'll talk about SQL Server's OPENXML() function and how it's used to read XML documents. We'll also touch on the new features and changes coming in the forthcoming XML for SQL Server Web Release 1. This will be the final chapter in our coverage of SQL Server's XML functionality.

OPENXML() is a built-in Transact-SQL function that can return an XML document as a rowset. In conjunction with sp_xml_preparedocument and sp_xml_removedocument, OPENXML() allows you to break down (or shred) nonrelational XML documents into relational pieces than can be inserted into tables.

The Books Online documents OPENXML() well, so I won't repeat it here. Here's a basic example of how to use OPENXML():

```
DECLARE @hDoc int
EXEC sp_xml_preparedocument @hDoc output,
'<songs>
        <song><name>Somebody to Love</name></song>
        <song><name>These Are the Days of Our Lives</name></song>
        <song><name>Bicycle Race</name></song>
        <song><name>Who Wants to Live Forever</name></song>
        <song><name>I Want to Break Free</name></song>
        <song><name>Friends Will Be Friends</name></song>
</songs>'
```

---

[1]Tzu, Sun. *The Art of War.* Cambridge, England: Oxford University Press, 1963. Page 91.

```
SELECT * FROM OPENXML(@hdoc, '/songs/song', 2) WITH (name varchar(80))
EXEC sp_xml_removedocument @hDoc
```

(Results)

```
name
--------------------------------------------------------------------------
Somebody to Love
These Are the Days of Our Lives
Bicycle Race
Who Wants to Live Forever
I Want to Break Free
Friends Will Be Friends
```

To use OPENXML(), you follow these basic steps:

1. Call sp_xml_preparedocument to load the XML document into memory. MSXML's DOM parser is called to translate the document into a tree of nodes that you can then access with an XPath query. A pointer to this tree is returned by the procedure as an integer.
2. Issue a SELECT from OPENXML(), passing in the handle you received in step 1.
3. Include XPath syntax in the call to OPENXML() in order to specify exactly what nodes you want to access.
4. Optionally include a WITH clause that maps the XML document into a specific table schema. This can be a full table schema as well as a reference to a table itself.

OPENXML() is extremely flexible, so several of these steps have variations and alternatives, but this is the basic process you follow to shred and use an XML document with OPENXML().

Here's a variation of the earlier query that uses a table to define the schema used to map the document:

```
USE tempdb
GO
create table songs (name varchar(80))
go
DECLARE @hDoc int
EXEC sp_xml_preparedocument @hDoc output,
'<songs>
      <song><name>Somebody to Love</name></song>
      <song><name>These Are the Days of Our Lives</name></song>
```

```
        <song><name>Bicycle Race</name></song>
        <song><name>Who Wants to Live Forever</name></song>
        <song><name>I Want to Break Free</name></song>
        <song><name>Friends Will Be Friends</name></song>
</songs>'
SELECT * FROM OPENXML(@hdoc, '/songs/song', 2) WITH songs
EXEC sp_xml_removedocument @hDoc
GO
DROP TABLE songs
```

(Results)

```
name
--------------------------------------------------------------------------
Somebody to Love
These Are the Days of Our Lives
Bicycle Race
Who Wants to Live Forever
I Want to Break Free
Friends Will Be Friends
```

You can also use the WITH clause to set up detailed mappings between the XML document and the tables in your database. Here's an example:

```
DECLARE @hDoc int
EXEC sp_xml_preparedocument @hDoc output,
'<songs>
        <artist name="Johnny Hartman">
        <song> <name>It Was Almost Like a Song</name></song>
        <song> <name>I See Your Face Before Me</name></song>
        <song> <name>For All We Know</name></song>
        <song> <name>Easy Living</name></song>
        </artist>
        <artist name="Harry Connick, Jr.">
        <song> <name>Sonny Cried</name></song>
        <song> <name>A Nightingale Sang in Berkeley Square</name></song>
        <song> <name>Heavenly</name></song>
        <song> <name>You Didn''t Know Me When</name></song>
        </artist>
</songs>'
SELECT * FROM OPENXML(@hdoc, '/songs/artist/song', 2)
WITH (artist varchar(30) '../@name',
      song varchar(50) 'name')
EXEC sp_xml_removedocument @hDoc
```

(Results)

```
artist                          song
----------------------------    ------------------------------------------
Johnny Hartman                  It Was Almost Like a Song
Johnny Hartman                  I See Your Face Before Me
Johnny Hartman                  For All We Know
Johnny Hartman                  Easy Living
Harry Connick, Jr.              Sonny Cried
Harry Connick, Jr.              A Nightingale Sang in Berkeley Square
Harry Connick, Jr.              Heavenly
Harry Connick, Jr.              You Didn't Know Me When
```

Note that attribute references are prefixed with the "@" symbol. In this example we supply an XPath query that navigates the tree down to the Song element, then reference an attribute called Name in song's parent element, Artist. For the second column, we retrieve a child element of song that's also called Name.

Here's another example:

```
DECLARE @hDoc int
EXEC sp_xml_preparedocument @hDoc output,
'<songs>
      <artist> <name>Johnny Hartman</name>
      <song> <name>It Was Almost Like a Song</name></song>
      <song> <name>I See Your Face Before Me</name></song>
      <song> <name>For All We Know</name></song>
      <song> <name>Easy Living</name></song>
      </artist>
      <artist> <name>Harry Connick, Jr.</name>
      <song> <name>Sonny Cried</name></song>
      <song> <name>A Nightingale Sang in Berkeley Square</name></song>
      <song> <name>Heavenly</name></song>
      <song> <name>You Didn''t Know Me When</name></song>
      </artist>
</songs>'
SELECT * FROM OPENXML(@hdoc, '/songs/artist/name', 2)
WITH (artist varchar(30) '.',
      song varchar(50) '../song/name')
EXEC sp_xml_removedocument @hDoc
```

(Results)

```
artist                           song
-----------------------------    ------------------------------------------------
Johnny Hartman                   It Was Almost Like a Song
Harry Connick, Jr.               Sonny Cried
```

Notice that we only get two rows. Why is that? It's because our XPath pattern navigated to the Artist/Name node, of which there are only two. In addition to getting each artist's Name element, we also grabbed the name of its first Song element. In the previous query, the XPath pattern navigated us to the Song element, of which there were eight, then referenced each song's parent node (it's Artist) via the XPath ".." designator.

Note the use in the previous query of the XPath "." specifier. This merely references the current element. We need it here because we are changing the name of the current element from name to artist. Keep this technique in mind when you want to rename an element you're returning via OPENXML().

## The Flags Parameter

OPENXML()'s flags parameter allows you to specify whether OPENXML() should process the document in an attribute-centric fashion, an element-centric fashion, or some combination of the two. Thus far, we've been specifying 2 for the flags parameter, which specifies element-centric mapping. Here's an example of attribute-centric mapping:

```
DECLARE @hDoc int
EXEC sp_xml_preparedocument @hDoc output,
'<songs>
        <artist name="Johnny Hartman">
        <song name="It Was Almost Like a Song"/>
        <song name="I See Your Face Before Me"/>
        <song name="For All We Know"/>
        <song name="Easy Living"/>
        </artist>
        <artist name="Harry Connick, Jr.">
        <song name="Sonny Cried"/>
        <song name="A Nightingale Sang in Berkeley Square"/>
        <song name="Heavenly"/>
        <song name="You Didn''t Know Me When"/>
        </artist>
</songs>'
SELECT * FROM OPENXML(@hdoc, '/songs/artist/song', 1)
```

```
WITH (artist varchar(30) '../@name',
      song varchar(50) '@name')
EXEC sp_xml_removedocument @hDoc
```

(Results)

```
artist                        song
----------------------------  -------------------------------------------
Johnny Hartman                It Was Almost Like a Song
Johnny Hartman                I See Your Face Before Me
Johnny Hartman                For All We Know
Johnny Hartman                Easy Living
Harry Connick, Jr.            Sonny Cried
Harry Connick, Jr.            A Nightingale Sang in Berkeley Square
Harry Connick, Jr.            Heavenly
Harry Connick, Jr.            You Didn't Know Me When
```

# Edge Table Format

You can completely omit OPENXML()'s WITH clause to retrieve a portion of an XML document in "edge table format"—essentially a two-dimensional representation of the XML tree. Here's an example:

```
DECLARE @hDoc int
EXEC sp_xml_preparedocument @hDoc output,
'<songs>
      <artist name="Johnny Hartman">
      <song> <name>It Was Almost Like a Song</name></song>
      <song> <name>I See Your Face Before Me</name></song>
      <song> <name>For All We Know</name></song>
      <song> <name>Easy Living</name></song>
      </artist>
      <artist name="Harry Connick, Jr.">
      <song> <name>Sonny Cried</name></song>
      <song> <name>A Nightingale Sang in Berkeley Square</name></song>
      <song> <name>Heavenly</name></song>
      <song> <name>You Didn''t Know Me When</name></song>
      </artist>
</songs>'
SELECT * FROM OPENXML(@hdoc, '/songs/artist/song', 2)
EXEC sp_xml_removedocument @hDoc
```

(Results abridged)

| id | parentid | nodetype | localname |
| --- | --- | --- | --- |
| 4 | 2 | 1 | song |
| 5 | 4 | 1 | name |
| 22 | 5 | 3 | #text |
| 6 | 2 | 1 | song |
| 7 | 6 | 1 | name |
| 23 | 7 | 3 | #text |
| 8 | 2 | 1 | song |
| 9 | 8 | 1 | name |
| 24 | 9 | 3 | #text |
| 10 | 2 | 1 | song |
| 11 | 10 | 1 | name |
| 25 | 11 | 3 | #text |
| 14 | 12 | 1 | song |
| 15 | 14 | 1 | name |
| 26 | 15 | 3 | #text |
| 16 | 12 | 1 | song |
| 17 | 16 | 1 | name |
| 27 | 17 | 3 | #text |
| 18 | 12 | 1 | song |
| 19 | 18 | 1 | name |
| 28 | 19 | 3 | #text |
| 20 | 12 | 1 | song |
| 21 | 20 | 1 | name |
| 29 | 21 | 3 | #text |

# Inserting Data with OPENXML()

Given that it's a rowset function, it's natural that you'd want to insert the results of a SELECT against OPENXML() into another table. There are a couple of ways of approaching this. First, you could execute a separate pass against the XML document for each piece of it that you wanted to extract. You would execute an INSERT...SELECT FROM OPENXML() for each database table that you wanted to insert rows into, grabbing a different section of the XML document with each pass. Here's an example of this approach:

```
USE tempdb

GO
```

```
CREATE TABLE Artists
(ArtistId varchar(5),
 Name varchar(30))
GO
CREATE TABLE Songs
(ArtistId varchar(5),
 SongId int,
 Name varchar(50))
GO

DECLARE @hDoc int
EXEC sp_xml_preparedocument @hDoc output,
'<songs>
        <artist id="JHART" name="Johnny Hartman">
        <song id="1" name="It Was Almost Like a Song"/>
        <song id="2" name="I See Your Face Before Me"/>
        <song id="3" name="For All We Know"/>
        <song id="4" name="Easy Living"/>
        </artist>
        <artist id="HCONN" name="Harry Connick, Jr.">
        <song id="1" name="Sonny Cried"/>
        <song id="2" name="A Nightingale Sang in Berkeley Square"/>
        <song id="3" name="Heavenly"/>
        <song id="4" name="You Didn''t Know Me When"/>
        </artist>
</songs>'
INSERT Artists (ArtistId, Name)
SELECT id,name
FROM OPENXML(@hdoc, '/songs/artist', 1)
WITH (id varchar(5) '@id',
      name varchar(30) '@name')
INSERT Songs (ArtistId, SongId, Name)
SELECT artistid, id,name
FROM OPENXML(@hdoc, '/songs/artist/song', 1)
WITH (artistid varchar(5) '../@id',
      id int '@id',
      name varchar(50) '@name')
EXEC sp_xml_removedocument @hDoc
GO
SELECT * FROM Artists
SELECT * FROM Songs
GO
DROP TABLE Artists, Songs
```

(Results)

```
ArtistId Name
-------- ------------------------------
JHART    Johnny Hartman
HCONN    Harry Connick, Jr.
ArtistId SongId      Name
-------- ----------- -------------------------------------------------
JHART    1           It Was Almost Like a Song
JHART    2           I See Your Face Before Me
JHART    3           For All We Know
JHART    4           Easy Living
HCONN    1           Sonny Cried
HCONN    2           A Nightingale Sang in Berkeley Square
HCONN    3           Heavenly
HCONN    4           You Didn't Know Me When
```

As you can see, we make a separate call to OPENXML() for each table. The tables are normalized; the XML document is not, so we shred it into multiple tables. Here's another way to accomplish the same thing that doesn't require multiple calls to OPENXML():

```
USE tempdb
GO
CREATE TABLE Artists
(ArtistId varchar(5),
 Name varchar(30))
GO
CREATE TABLE Songs
(ArtistId varchar(5),
 SongId int,
 Name varchar(50))
GO
CREATE VIEW ArtistSongs AS
SELECT      a.ArtistId,
     a.Name AS ArtistName,
     s.SongId,
     s.Name as SongName
FROM Artists a JOIN Songs s
ON (a.ArtistId=s.ArtistId)
GO
CREATE TRIGGER ArtistSongsInsert ON ArtistSongs INSTEAD OF INSERT AS
INSERT Artists
```

```
SELECT DISTINCT ArtistId, ArtistName FROM inserted
INSERT Songs
SELECT ArtistId, SongId, SongName FROM inserted
GO


DECLARE @hDoc int
EXEC sp_xml_preparedocument @hDoc output,
'<songs>
        <artist id="JHART" name="Johnny Hartman">
        <song id="1" name="It Was Almost Like a Song"/>
        <song id="2" name="I See Your Face Before Me"/>
        <song id="3" name="For All We Know"/>
        <song id="4" name="Easy Living"/>
        </artist>
        <artist id="HCONN" name="Harry Connick, Jr.">
        <song id="1" name="Sonny Cried"/>
        <song id="2" name="A Nightingale Sang in Berkeley Square"/>
        <song id="3" name="Heavenly"/>
        <song id="4" name="You Didn''t Know Me When"/>
        </artist>
</songs>'
INSERT ArtistSongs (ArtistId, ArtistName, SongId, SongName)
SELECT artistid, artistname, songid, songname
FROM OPENXML(@hdoc, '/songs/artist/song', 1)
WITH (artistid varchar(5) '../@id',
      artistname varchar(30) '../@name',
      songid int '@id',
      songname varchar(50) '@name')

EXEC sp_xml_removedocument @hDoc
GO
SELECT * FROM Artists
SELECT * FROM Songs
GO
DROP VIEW ArtistSongs
GO
DROP TABLE Artists, Songs
```

(Results)

```
ArtistId Name
-------- -----------------------------
HCONN    Harry Connick, Jr.
JHART    Johnny Hartman
```

```
ArtistId SongId      Name
-------- ----------- ------------------------------------------------
JHART    1           It Was Almost Like a Song
JHART    2           I See Your Face Before Me
JHART    3           For All We Know
JHART    4           Easy Living
HCONN    1           Sonny Cried
HCONN    2           A Nightingale Sang in Berkeley Square
HCONN    3           Heavenly
HCONN    4           You Didn't Know Me When
```

This technique uses a view and an INSTEAD OF trigger to alleviate the need for two passes with OPENXML(). We use a view to simulate the denormalized layout of the XML document, then set up an INSTEAD OF trigger to insert the data in the XML document "into" this view. The trigger performs the actual work of shredding, only it does it much more efficiently than calling OPENXML() twice. It makes two passes over the logical inserted table and splits the columns contained therein (which mirror those of the view) into two separate tables.

# Web Release 1

Microsoft has announced its intentions to update the XML support in SQL Server via periodic updates called *Web releases*. The first of these is in beta test as I write this. It should be out later this year. It promises to add significant functionality to SQL Server's XML support. Among the new features Microsoft has announced are:

- Updategram support—Updategrams are templatelike documents that you can use to insert, update, and delete SQL Server data. An option will be added to the Configure SQL XML Support In IIS tool to allow you to enable updategrams to be posted to a virtual directory.
- XML bulk load—This will be a COM component that you can use to load XML data quickly into a database in a manner analogous to the T-SQL BULK INSERT command. This will be more efficient than doing so via OPENXML().
- Additional data type support in schemas—Currently, SQL Server's annotated schemas allow you to use the sql:datatype annotation for BLOB data types such as text and image. Web Release 1 will add support for all SQL Server data types (e.g., int, varchar).

- Enhanced templates—Microsoft has announced that templates will be enhanced through several additions to the XML-SQL namespace. The details are a little sketchy at this point, but it appears that these features are geared toward making templates easier to use.

One of frustrating things about writing technical books is that the technology literally changes as you write. What follows is a brief discussion of the two biggest features in the beta version of Web Release 1 that I'm currently using: updategrams and the XML Bulk Load components. Keep in mind that this is beta software. Some details may have changed—perhaps dramatically—by the time you read this.

## Updategrams

Updategrams provide an XML-based method of updating data in a SQL Server database. They are basically templates with special attributes and elements that allow you to specify the data you want to update and how you want to update it. An updategram contains a before-and-after image of the data you want to change. You submit updategrams to SQL Server in much the same way you submit templates. All the execution mechanisms available with templates work equally well with updategrams. You can post updategrams via HTTP, save updategrams to files and execute them via URLs, and you can execute updategrams directly via ADO and OLEDB.

### Details

Updategrams are based on the xml-updategram namespace. You reference this namespace via the xmlns:updg qualifier. Each updategram contains at least one Sync element. This Sync element contains the data changes you wish to make in the form of Before and After elements. The Before element contains the before image of the data you wish to change. Normally, it will also contain a primary key or candidate key reference so that SQL Server will be able to locate the row you wish to change. Note that only one row can be selected for update by the Before element. If the elements and attributes included in the Before element identify more than one row, you'll receive an error message.

For row deletions, an updategram will have a before image, but no after image. For insertions, it will have an after image, but no before image. And, of course, for updates, an updategram will have both before and after images. Here's an example:

```
<?xml version="1.0"?>
<employeeupdate xmlns:updg="urn:schemas-microsoft-com:xml-updategram">
```

```
<updg:sync>
    <updg:before>
        <Employees EmployeeID="4"/>
    </updg:before>
    <updg:after>
        <Employees City="Scotts Valley" Region="CA"/>
    </updg:after>
</updg:sync>
</employeeupdate>
```

In this example, we change the **City** and **Region** columns for **Employee 4** in the Northwind Employees table. The EmployeeID attribute in the Before element identifies the row to change, and the City and Region attributes in the After element identify which columns to change and what values to assign to them.

Each batch of updates within a Sync element is considered a transaction. Either all the updates in the Sync element succeed or none of them do. You can include multiple Sync elements to break updates into multiple transactions.

### Mapping Data

Of course, when sending data to the server for updates, deletions, and insertions via XML, we need a means of linking values in the XML document to columns in the target database table. SQL Server sports two facilities for doing this: default mapping and mapping schemas.

#### Default Mapping

Naturally, the easiest way to map data in an updategram to columns in the target table is to use default mapping (a.k.a., intrinsic mapping). With default mapping, a Before or After element's top-level tag is assumed to refer to the target database table, and each subelement or attribute it contains refers to a column of the same name in the table.

Here's an example that shows how to map the **OrderID** column in the Orders table:

```
<Orders OrderID="10248"/>
```

This example maps XML attributes to table columns. You could also map subelements to table columns, like this:

```
<Orders>
    <OrderID>10248</OrderID>
```

```
</Orders>
```

You need not select either attribute-centric or element-centric mapping. You can freely mix them within a given Before or After element. Here's an example:

```
<Orders OrderID="10248">
    <ShipCity>Reims</ShipCity>
</Orders>
```

Use the four-digit hexadecimal UCS-2 code for characters in table names that are illegal in XML elements (e.g., spaces). For example, to reference the Northwind Order Details table, do this:

```
<Order_x0020_Details OrderID="10248"/>
```

### Mapping Schemas

You can also use mapping schemas to map data in an updategram to tables and columns in a database. We talked about mapping schemas earlier in the book, so I won't go back into them here except to say that you use a *sync*'s *updg:mapping-schema* attribute to specify the mapping schema for an updategram. Here's an example that specifies a mapping schema for the Orders table:

```
<?xml version="1.0"?>
<orderupdate xmlns:updg="urn:schemas-microsoft-com:xml-updategram">
    <updg:sync updg:mapping-schema="OrderSchema.xml">
        <updg:before>
            <Order OID="10248"/>
        </updg:before>
        <updg:after>
            <Order City="Reims"/>
        </updg:after>
    </updg:sync>
</orderupdate>
```

And here's its mapping schema:

```
<?xml version="1.0"?>
<Schema xmlns="urn:schemas-microsoft-com:xml-data"
        xmlns:sql="urn:schemas-microsoft-com:xml-sql">
    <ElementType name="Order" sql:relation="Orders">
        <AttributeType name="OID"/>
        <AttributeType name="City"/>
```

```
            <attribute type="OID" sql:field="OrderID"/>
            <attribute type="City" sql:field="ShipCity"/>
        </ElementType>
</Schema>
```

As you can see, the mapping schema helps translate the layout of the XML document into the layout of the Northwind Orders table.

### NULLs

It's common to represent missing or inapplicable data as NULL in a database. To represent or retrieve NULL data in an updategram, you use the *sync* element's *nullvalue* attribute to specify a placeholder for NULL. This placeholder is then used everywhere in the updategram that you need to specify a NULL value. Here's an example:

```
<?xml version="1.0"?>
<employeeupdate xmlns:updg="urn:schemas-microsoft-com:xml-updategram">
    <updg:sync updg:nullvalue="NONE">
        <updg:before>
            <Orders OrderID="10248"/>
        </updg:before>
        <updg:after>
      <Orders ShipCity-"Reims" ShipRegion="NONE"
            ShipName="NONE"/>
        </updg:after>
    </updg:sync>
</employeeupdate>
```

As you can see, we define a placeholder for NULL named "NONE." We then use this placeholder to assign a NULL value to the **ShipRegion** and **ShipName** columns.

### Parameters

Curiously, parameters work slightly different with updategrams than with templates. Rather than using at (@) symbols to denote updategram parameters, you use dollar ($) symbols, like this:

```
<?xml version="1.0"?>
<orderupdate xmlns:updg="urn:schemas-microsoft-com:xml-updategram">
    <updg:header>
        <updg:param name="OrderID"/>
```

```
        <updg:param name="ShipCity"/>
    </updg:header>
    <updg:sync>
        <updg:before>
            <Orders OrderID="$OrderID"/>
        </updg:before>
        <updg:after>
            <Orders ShipCity="$ShipCity"/>
        </updg:after>
    </updg:sync>
</orderupdate>
```

This nuance has interesting implications for passing currency values as parameters. To pass a currency parameter value to a table column (e.g., the **Freight** column in the Orders table), you must map the data using a mapping schema.

To pass a parameter with a NULL value to an updategram, include the null value placeholder attribute in the updategram's Header element. You can then pass this placeholder value into the updategram to signify a NULL parameter value. This is similar to the way in which you specify a NULL value for a column in an updategram, the difference being that you specify nullvalue within the Sync element for column values, but within the Header element for parameters. Here's an example:

```
<?xml version="1.0"?>
<orderupdate xmlns:updg="urn:schemas-microsoft-com:xml-updategram">
    <updg:header nullvalue="NONE">
        <updg:param name="OrderID"/>
        <updg:param name="ShipCity"/>
    </updg:header>
    <updg:sync>
        <updg:before>
            <Orders OrderID="$OrderID"/>
        </updg:before>
        <updg:after>
            <Orders ShipCity="$ShipCity"/>
        </updg:after>
    </updg:sync>
</orderupdate>
```

This updategram accepts two parameters. Passing a value of "NONE" will cause the **ShipCity** column to be set to NULL for the specified order.

Note that we don't include the xml-updategram (updg:) qualifier when specifying the nullvalue placeholder for parameters in the updategram's Header.

### Multiple Rows

I mentioned earlier that each Before element can identify at most one row. This means that to update multiple rows, you must include an element for each row you wish to change.

#### The Id Attribute

When you specify multiple subelements within your Before and After elements, SQL Server requires that you provide a means of matching each Before element with its corresponding After element. One way to do this is through the Id attribute. The Id attribute allows you to specify a unique string value that you can use to match a Before element with an After element. Here's an example:

```
<?xml version="1.0"?>
<orderupdate xmlns:updg="urn:schemas-microsoft-com:xml-updategram">
    <updg:sync>
        <updg:before>
            <Orders updg:id="ID1" OrderID="10248"/>
            <Orders updg:id="ID2" OrderID="10249"/>
        </updg:before>
        <updg:after>
            <Orders updg:id="ID2" ShipCity="Munster"/>
            <Orders updg:id="ID1" ShipCity="Reims"/>
        </updg:after>
    </updg:sync>
</orderupdate>
```

Here, we use the Updg:id attribute to match up subelements in the Before and After elements. Even though these subelements are specified out of sequence, SQL Server is able to apply the updates to the correct rows.

#### Multiple Before and After Elements

Another way to do this is to specify multiple Before and After elements, rather than multiple subelements. For each row you want to change, specify a separate Before/After element pair. Here's an example:

```
<?xml version="1.0"?>
<orderupdate xmlns:updg="urn:schemas-microsoft-com:xml-updategram">
```

```
<updg:sync>
    <updg:before>
        <Orders OrderID="10248"/>
    </updg:before>
    <updg:after>
        <Orders ShipCity="Reims"/>
    </updg:after>
    <updg:before>
        <Orders OrderID="10249"/>
    </updg:before>
    <updg:after>
        <Orders ShipCity="Munster"/>
    </updg:after>
</updg:sync>
</orderupdate>
```

As you can see, this updategram updates two rows. It includes a separate *before/after* element pair for each update.

### Results

The result returned to a client application that executes an updategram is normally an XML document containing the empty root element specified in the updategram. For example, we would expect to see this result returned by the orderupdate updategram:

```
<?xml version="1.0"?>
<orderupdate xmlns:updg="urn:schemas-microsoft-com:xml-updategram">
</orderupdate>
```

Any errors that occur during updategram exection are returned as <?MSSQLError> elements within the updategram's root element.

### Identity Column Values

In real applications, you're often going to need to be able to retrieve an identity value that's generated by SQL Server for one table and insert it into another. This is especially true when you need to insert data into a table with a primary key that is an identity column and a table that references this primary key via a foreign key constraint. Take the example of inserting orders in the Northwind Orders and Order Details tables. As its name suggests, Order Details stores detailed information for the orders in the Orders table. Part of Order Details' primary key is the Orders table's **OrderID** column. When we insert a new row into the Orders table, we need to be able to retrieve that value and insert it into the Order Details table.

From Transact-SQL, we'd usually handle this situation with an INSTEAD OF insert trigger or a stored procedure. To handle it with an updategram, you use the *at-identity* attribute. Similarly to the *id* attribute, *at-identity* serves as a placeholder: Everywhere you use its value in the updategram, SQL Server supplies the identity value for the corresponding table (each table can have just one identity column). Here's an example:

```
<?xml version="1.0"?>
<orderinsert xmlns:updg="urn:schemas-microsoft-com:xml-updategram">
    <updg:sync>
        <updg:before>
        </updg:before>
        <updg:after>
            <Orders updg:at-identity="ID" ShipCity="Reims"/>
            <Order_x0020_Details OrderID="ID" ProductID="11"
                UnitPrice="$14.00" Quantity="12"/>
            <Order_x0020_Details OrderID="ID" ProductID="42"
                UnitPrice="$9.80" Quantity="10"/>
        </updg:after>
    </updg:sync>
</orderinsert>
```

Here we use the string "ID" to signify the identity column in the Orders table. Once ID is assigned, we can use it in the insertions for the Order Details table.

In addition to being able to use an identity column value elsewhere in an updategram, it's quite likely that you'll want to be able to return it to the client. To do this, use the *after* element's *returnid* attribute and specify the at-identity placeholder as its value, like this:

```
<?xml version="1.0"?>
<orderinsert xmlns:updg="urn:schemas-microsoft-com:xml-updategram">
    <updg:sync>
        <updg:before>
        </updg:before>
        <updg:after updg:returnid="ID">
            <Orders updg:at-identity="ID" ShipCity="Reims"/>
            <Order_x0020_Details OrderID="ID" ProductID="11"
                UnitPrice="$14.00" Quantity="12"/>
            <Order_x0020_Details OrderID="ID" ProductID="42"
```

```
                UnitPrice="$9.80" Quantity="10"/>
            </updg:after>
        </updg:sync>
</orderinsert>
```

Executing this updategram will return an XML document that looks like this:

```
<?xml version="1.0"?>
<orderinsert xmlns:updg="urn:schemas-microsoft-com:xml-updategram">
    <returnid>
        <ID>10248</ID>
    </returnid>
</orderinsert>
```

### *Globally Unique Identifiers (GUIDs)*

It's not unusual to see GUIDs used as key values across a partitioned view or other distributed system. Normally, you use the Transact-SQL NEWID() function to generate new GUIDs. The updategram equivalent of NEWID() is the Guid attribute. You can specify the Guid attribute to generate a GUID for use elsewhere in a Sync element. As with Id, Nullvalue, and the other attributes presented in this section, the Guid attribute establishes a placeholder that you can then supply to other elements and attributes in the updategram to use the generated GUID. Here's an example:

```
<orderinsert>
    xmlns:updg="urn:schemas-microsoft-com:xml-updategram">
    <updg:sync>
        <updg:before>
        </updg:before>
        <updg:after>
            <Orders updg:guid="GUID">
                <OrderID>GUID</OrderID>
                <ShipCity>Reims</ShipCity>
            </Orders>
            <Order_x0020_Details OrderID="GUID" ProductID="11"
                UnitPrice="$14.00" Quantity="12"/>
            <Order_x0020_Details OrderID="GUID" ProductID="42"
                UnitPrice="9.80" Quantity="10"/>
        </updg:after>
    </updg:sync>
</orderinsert>
```

## XML Bulk Load

As we saw in the earlier discussions of updategrams and OPENXML(), inserting XML data into a SQL Server database is relatively easy. However, both of these methods of loading data have one serious drawback: They're not suitable for loading large amounts of data. In the same way that using the Transact-SQL INSERT statement is suboptimal for loading large numbers of rows, using updategrams and OPENXML() to load large volumes of XML data into SQL Server is slow and resource intensive.

Web release 1 will introduce a new facility intended specifically to address this problem. It's called the XML Bulk Load component, and it is a COM component that you can call from OLE Automation-capable languages/tools such as Visual Basic, Delphi, and even Transact-SQL. It presents an object-oriented interface to loading XML data in bulk in a manner similar to the Transact-SQL BULK INSERT command.

### Using the Component

The first step in using the XML Bulk Load component is to define a mapping schema that maps the XML data you're importing to tables and columns in your database. When the component loads your XML data, it will read it as a stream and use the mapping schema to decide where the data goes in the database.

The mapping schema determines the scope of each row added by the Bulk Load component. As the closing tag for each row is read, its corresponding data is written to the database.

You access the bulk load component itself via the SQLXMLBulkLoad interface on the SQLXMLBulkLoad COM object. The first step in using it is to connect to the database using an OLE-DB connection string or by setting its ConnectionCommand property to an existing ADO Command object. The second step is to call its Execute method. Here's some VBScript code that illustrates:

```
Set objBulkLoad = CreateObject("SQLXMLBulkLoad.SQLXMLBulkLoad")
objBulkLoad.ConnectionString = _
    "provider=SQLOLEDB;data source=KUFNATHE;database=Northwind;" & _
    "Integrated Security=SSPI;"
objBulkLoad.Execute d:\xml\OrdersSchema.xml, d:\xml\OrdersData.xml
Set objBulkLoad = Nothing
```

You can also specify an XML stream (rather than a file) to load, making cross-DBMS data transfers (from platforms that feature XML support) fairly easy.

### XML Fragments

Setting the XMLFragment property to TRUE allows the Bulk Load component to load data from an XML fragment (an XML document with no root element, similar to the type returned by Transact-SQL's FOR XML extension). Here's an example:

```
Set objBulkLoad = CreateObject("SQLXMLBulkLoad.SQLXMLBulkLoad")
objBulkLoad.ConnectionString = _
    "provider=SQLOLEDB;data source=KUFNATHE;database=Northwind;" & _
    "Integrated Security=SSPI;"
objBulkLoad.XMLFragment = True
objBulkLoad.Execute d:\xml\OrdersSchema.xml, d:\xml\OrdersFrag.xml
Set objBulkLoad = Nothing
```

### Enforcing Constraints

Be default, the XML Bulk Load component does not enforce check and referential integrity constraints. Enforcing constraints as data is loaded slows down the process significantly, so the component doesn't enforce them unless you tell it to do so. One situation in which you might want to do that is when you're loading data directly into production tables and you want to ensure that the integrity of your data is not compromised. To cause the component to enforce your constraints as it loads data, set the CheckConstraints property to TRUE, like this:

```
Set objBulkLoad = CreateObject("SQLXMLBulkLoad.SQLXMLBulkLoad")
objBulkLoad.ConnectionString = _
    "provider=SQLOLEDB;data source=KUFNATHE;database=Northwind;" & _
    "Integrated Security=SSPI;"
objBulkLoad.CheckConstraints = True
objBulkLoad.Execute d:\xml\OrdersSchema.xml, d:\xml\OrdersData.xml
Set objBulkLoad = Nothing
```

### Duplicate Keys

Normally, you'd want to stop a bulk load process when you encounter a duplicate key. Usually, this means you've got unexpected data values or data corruption of some type and you need to have a look at the source data before proceeding. There are, however, exceptions. Say, for example, that you get a daily data feed from an external source that contains the entirety of a table. Each day, a few new rows show up, but for the most part, the data in the XML document already exists in your table. Your interest is in loading the new rows, but the external source who provides you the data may not know which rows you have and which ones you don't. They may provide data to lots of companies, and what your particular database contains may be unknown to them.

In this situation, you can set the IgnoreDuplicateKeys property before the load, and the component will ignore the duplicate key values it encounters. The bulk load won't halt when it encounters a duplicate key. It will simply ignore the row containing the duplicate key, and the rows with nonduplicate keys will be loaded as you'd expect. Here's an example:

```
Set objBulkLoad = CreateObject("SQLXMLBulkLoad.SQLXMLBulkLoad")
objBulkLoad.ConnectionString = _
    "provider=SQLOLEDB;data source=KUFNATHE;database=Northwind;" & _
    "Integrated Security=SSPI;"
objBulkLoad.IgnoreDuplicateKeys = True
objBulkLoad.Execute d:\xml\OrdersSchema.xml, d:\xml\OrdersData.xml
Set objBulkLoad = Nothing
```

When IgnoreDuplicateKeys is set to TRUE, inserts that would cause a duplicate key will still fail, but the bulk load process will not halt. The remainder of the rows will be processed as though no error occurred.

### Identity Columns

SQLXMLBulkLoad's KeepIdentity property is TRUE by default. This means that values for identity columns in your XML data will be loaded into the database rather than being generated on-the-fly by SQL Server. Normally, this is what you'd want, but you can set KeepIdentity to FALSE if you'd rather have SQL Server generate these values.

There are a couple of caveats regarding the KeepIdentity property. First, when KeepIdentity is set to TRUE, SQL Server uses SET IDENTITY_INSERT to enable identity value insertion into the target table. SET IDENTITY_INSERT has specific permissions requirements: execute permission defaults to the sysadmin role, the db_owner and db_ddladmin fixed database roles, and the table owner. This means that a user who does not own the target table and who also is not a sysadmin, dbo, or DDL administrator will likely have trouble loading data with the XML Bulk Load component. Merely having bulk admin rights is not enough.

Another caveat is that you would normally want to preserve identity values when bulk loading data into a table with dependent tables. Allowing these values to be regenerated by the server could be disastrous. You could break parent-child relationships between tables with no hope of reconstructing them. If a parent table's primary key is its identity column and KeepIdentity is set to

FALSE when you load it, you may not be able to resynchronize it with the data you load for its child table. Fortunately, KeepIdentity is enabled by default, so normally this isn't a concern, but be sure you know what you're doing if you choose to set KeepIdentity to FALSE.

Here's some code that illustrates setting the KeepIdentity property:

```
Set objBulkLoad = CreateObject("SQLXMLBulkLoad.SQLXMLBulkLoad")
objBulkLoad.ConnectionString = _
    "provider=SQLOLEDB;data source=KUFNATHE;database=Northwind;" & _
    "Integrated Security=SSPI;"
objBulkLoad.KeepIdentity = False
objBulkLoad.Execute d:\xml\OrdersSchema.xml, d:\xml\OrdersData.xml
Set objBulkLoad = Nothing
```

Another thing to keep in mind is that KeepIdentity is a very binary option—either it's on or it's not. Whether you set it to TRUE or FALSE, this setting affects every object into which it inserts rows within a given bulk load. You can't retain identity values for some tables and allow SQL Server to generate them for others.

### NULL Values

For a column not mapped in the schema, SQLXMLBulkLoad inserts the column's default value. If the column doesn't have a default, NULL is inserted. If the column doesn't allow NULLs, the bulk load halts with an error message.

The KeepNulls property allows you to tell the bulk load facility to insert a NULL value rather than a column's default when the column is not mapped in the schema. Here's some code that demonstrates:

```
Set objBulkLoad = CreateObject("SQLXMLBulkLoad.SQLXMLBulkLoad")
objBulkLoad.ConnectionString = _
    "provider=SQLOLEDB;data source=KUFNATHE;database-Northwind;" & _
    "Integrated Security=SSPI;"
objBulkLoad.KeepNulls = True
objBulkLoad.Execute d:\xml\OrdersSchema.xml, d:\xml\OrdersData.xml
Set objBulkLoad = Nothing
```

### Table Locks

As with SQL Server's other bulk load facilities, you can configure SQLXML-BulkLoad to lock the target table before it begins loading data into it. This is more efficient and faster than using more granular locks, but it has the disadvantage of preventing other users from accessing the table while the bulk load runs. To force a table lock during an XML bulk load, set the ForceTableLock property to TRUE, like this:

```
Set objBulkLoad = CreateObject("SQLXMLBulkLoad.SQLXMLBulkLoad")
objBulkLoad.ConnectionString = _
    "provider=SQLOLEDB;data source=KUFNATHE;database=Northwind;" & _
    "Integrated Security=SSPI;"
objBulkLoad.ForceTableLock = True
objBulkLoad.Execute d:\xml\OrdersSchema.xml, d:\xml\OrdersData.xml
Set objBulkLoad = Nothing
```

### Transactions

By default, XML bulk load operations are not transactional. That is, if an error occurs during the load process, the rows loaded up to that point will remain in the database. This is the fastest way of doing things, but it has the disadvantage of possibly leaving a table in a partially loaded state. To force a bulk load operation to be handled as a single transaction, set SQLXMLBulkLoad's Transaction property to TRUE before calling Execute.

When Transaction is TRUE, all inserts are cached in a temporary file before being loaded onto SQL Server. You can control where this file is written by setting the TempFilePath property. TempFilePath has no meaning unless Transaction is TRUE. If TempFilePath is not otherwise set, it defaults to the folder specified by the **temp** environmental variable on the server.

I should point out that bulk loading data within a transaction is much slower than loading it outside of one. That's why the component doesn't load data within a transaction by default. Also, you can't bulk load binary XML data from within a transaction, so keep that in mind.

Here's some code that illustrates a transactional bulk load:

```
Set objBulkLoad = CreateObject("SQLXMLBulkLoad.SQLXMLBulkLoad")
objBulkLoad.ConnectionString = _
    "provider=SQLOLEDB;data source=KUFNATHE;database=Northwind;" & _
    "Integrated Security=SSPI;"
objBulkLoad.Transaction = True
objBulkLoad.TempFilePath = "c:\temp\xmlswap"
objBulkLoad.Execute d:\xml\OrdersSchema.xml, d:\xml\OrdersData.xml
Set objBulkLoad = Nothing
```

In this example, SQLXMLBulkLoad establishes its own connection to the server over OLE-DB, so it operates within its own transaction context. If an error occurs during the bulk load, the component rolls back its own transaction.

When SQLXMLBulkLoad uses an existing OLE-DB connection via its ConnectionCommand property, the transaction context belongs to that connection and is controlled by the client application. When the bulk load completes, the client application must explicitly commit or roll back the transaction. Here's an example:

```
On Error Resume Next
Err.Clear
Set objCmd = CreateObject("ADODB.Command")
objCmd.ActiveConnection= _
    "provider=SQLOLEDB;data source=KUFNATHE;database=Northwind;" &
    "Integrated Security=SSPI;"
Set objBulkLoad = CreateObject("SQLXMLBulkLoad.SQLXMLBulkLoad")
objBulkLoad.Transaction = True
objBulkLoad.ConnectionCommand = objCmd
objBulkLoad.Execute d:\xml\OrdersSchema.xml, d:\xml\OrdersData.xml
If Err.Number = 0 Then
    objCmd.ActiveConnection.CommitTrans
Else
    objCmd.ActiveConnection.RollbackTrans
End If
Set objBulkLoad = Nothing
Set objCmd = Nothing
```

Note that when using the ConnectionCommand property, Transaction is required. It must be set to TRUE.

### Errors

The XML Bulk Copy component supports logging error messages to a file via its ErrorLogFile property. This file is an XML document itself that lists any errors that occurred during the bulk load. Here's some code that demonstrates using it:

```
Set objBulkLoad = CreateObject("SQLXMLBulkLoad.SQLXMLBulkLoad")
objBulkLoad.ConnectionString = _
    "provider=SQLOLEDB;data source=KUFNATHE;database=Northwind;" & _
    "Integrated Security=SSPI;"
objBulkLoad.ErrorLogFile = "c:\temp\xmlswap\errors.xml"
objBulkLoad.Execute d:\xml\OrdersSchema.xml, d:\xml\OrdersData.xml
Set objBulkLoad = Nothing
```

The file you specify will contain a Record element for each error that occurred during the last bulk load. The most error message will be listed first.

### Generating Database Schemas

In addition to loading data into existing tables, the XML Bulk Copy component can also create target tables for you if they do not already exist, or drop and recreate them if they do exist. To create nonexistent tables, set the component's SchemaGen property to TRUE, like this:

```
Set objBulkLoad = CreateObject("SQLXMLBulkLoad.SQLXMLBulkLoad")
objBulkLoad.ConnectionString = _
    "provider=SQLOLEDB;data source=KUFNATHE;database=Northwind;" & _
    "Integrated Security=SSPI;"
objBulkLoad.SchemaGen = True
objBulkLoad.Execute d:\xml\OrdersSchema.xml, d:\xml\OrdersData.xml
Set objBulkLoad = Nothing
```

Because SchemaGen is set to TRUE, any tables in the schema that don't already exist will be created when the bulk load starts. For tables that already exist, data is simply loaded into them as it normally would be.

If you set the BulkLoad property of the component to FALSE, no data is loaded. So, if SchemaGen is set to TRUE, but BulkLoad is FALSE, you'll get empty tables for those in the mapping schema that did not already exist in the database, but you'll get no data. Here's an example:

```
Set objBulkLoad = CreateObject("SQLXMLBulkLoad.SQLXMLBulkLoad")
objBulkLoad.ConnectionString = _
    "provider=SQLOLEDB;data source=KUFNATHE;database=Northwind;" & _
    "Integrated Security=SSPI;"
objBulkLoad.SchemaGen = True
objBulkLoad.BulkLoad = False
objBulkLoad.Execute d:\xml\OrdersSchema.xml, d:\xml\OrdersData.xml
Set objBulkLoad = Nothing
```

When XML Bulk Load creates tables, it uses the information in the mapping schema to define the columns in each table. The sql:datatype annotation defines column data types, and the Dt:type attribute further defines column type information. To define a primary key within the mapping schema, set a column's Dt:type attribute to Id and set the SGUseID property of the XML Bulk Load component to True. Here's a mapping schema that illustrates:

```
<ElementType name="Orders" sql:relation="Orders">
    <AttributeType name="OrderID" sql:datatype="int" dt:type="id"/>
    <AttributeType name="ShipCity" sql:datatype="nvarchar(30)"/>

    <attribute type="OrderID" sql:field="OrderID"/>
    <attribute type="ShipCity" sql:field="ShipCity"/>
</ElementType>
```

And here's some VBScript code that sets the SGUseID property so that a primary key will automatically be defined for the table that's created on the server:

```
Set objBulkLoad = CreateObject("SQLXMLBulkLoad.SQLXMLBulkLoad")
objBulkLoad.ConnectionString = _
    "provider=SQLOLEDB;data source=KUFNATHE;database=Northwind;" & _
    "Integrated Security=SSPI;"
objBulkLoad.SchemaGen = True
objBulkLoad.SGUseID = True
objBulkLoad.Execute d:\xml\OrdersSchema.xml, d:\xml\OrdersData.xml
Set objBulkLoad = Nothing
```

Here's the Transact-SQL that results when the bulk load executes:

```
CREATE TABLE Orders
(
    OrderID int NOT NULL,
    ShipCity nvarchar(30) NULL,
    PRIMARY KEY CLUSTERED (OrderID)
)
```

In addition to being able to create new tables from those in the mapping schema, SQLXML BulkLoad can also drop and recreate tables. Set the SGDropTables property to TRUE to cause the component to drop and recreate the tables mapped in the schema. Here's an example:

```
Set objBulkLoad = CreateObject("SQLXMLBulkLoad.SQLXMLBulkLoad")
objBulkLoad.ConnectionString = _
    "provider=SQLOLEDB;data source=KUFNATHE;database=Northwind;" & _
    "Integrated Security=SSPI;"
objBulkLoad.SchemaGen = True
objBulkLoad.SGDropTables = True
objBulkLoad.Execute d:\xml\OrdersSchema.xml, d:\xml\OrdersData.xml
Set objBulkLoad = Nothing
```

## Limitations

Even with the new features in the forthcoming Web Release 1, SQL Server's XML support has some fundamental limitations that make it difficult to use in certain situations. In this section we'll explore a couple of these and look at ways of working around them.

## sp_xml_concat

Given that sp_xml_preparedocument accepts document text of virtually any length (up to 2GB), you'd think that SQL Server's XML facilities would be able to handle long documents just fine, but this is not the case. Although sp_xml_preparedocument's xmltext parameter accepts text as well as varchar parameters, the problem is that Transact-SQL doesn't support local text *variables*. About the closest you can get to a local text variable in Transact-SQL is to set up a procedure with a text *parameter*. However, this parameter cannot be assigned to nor can it be the recipient of the text data returned by the READTEXT command. About the only thing you can do with it is insert it into a table.

The problem is painfully obvious when you try to store a large XML document in a table and process it with sp_xml_preparedocument. Once the document is loaded into the table, how do you extract it to pass it into sp_xml_preparedocument? Unfortunately, there's no easy way to do this. Because we can't declare local text variables, about the only thing we can do is break the document into multiple 8,000-byte varchar variables and use parameter concatenation when we call sp_xml_preparedocument. This is a ridiculously difficult task, so I've written a stored procedure to do it for you. It's called sp_xml_concat, and you can use it to process large XML documents stored in a table in a text, varchar, or char column.

Sp_xml_concat takes three parameters: the names of the table and column in which the document resides, and an output parameter that returns the document handle as generated by sp_xml_preparedocument. You can take the handle that's returned by sp_xml_concat and use it with OPENXML() and sp_xml_unpreparedocument.

The table parameter can either be an actual table or view name, or it can be a derived table complete with a table alias. The ability to specify a derived table allows you to filter the table that the procedure sees. So, if you want to process a specific row in the table or otherwise restrict the procedure's view of the table, you can do so using a derived table expression.

Here's the full source code to sp_xml_concat:

```
USE master
GO
IF OBJECT_ID('sp_xml_concat','P') IS NOT NULL
  DROP PROC sp_xml_concat
GO
CREATE PROC sp_xml_concat
```

```
        @hdl int OUT,
        @table sysname,
        @column sysname
AS
EXEC('
SET TEXTSIZE 4000
DECLARE
        @cnt int,
        @c nvarchar(4000)
DECLARE
        @declare varchar(8000),
        @assign varchar(8000),
        @concat varchar(8000)

SELECT @c = CONVERT(nvarchar(4000),'+@column+') FROM '+@table+'

SELECT @declare = ''DECLARE'',
                  @concat = '''''''''''''''''',
                  @assign = '''',
                  @cnt = 0

WHILE (LEN(@c) > 0) BEGIN
   SELECT @declare = @declare + '' @c''+CAST(@cnt as nvarchar(15))+''
             nvarchar(4000),'',
        @assign = @assign + ''SELECT @c''+CONVERT(nvarchar(15),@cnt)+''
             = SUBSTRING(' + @column+',''+CONVERT(nvarchar(15), 1+@cnt*4000)+
             '', 4000) FROM '+@table+' '',
        @concat = @concat + ''+@c''+CONVERT(nvarchar(15),@cnt)
   SET @cnt = @cnt+1
   SELECT @c = CONVERT(nvarchar(4000),SUBSTRING('+@column+',1+@cnt*4000,4000))
FROM '+@table+'
END

IF (@cnt = 0) SET @declare = ''''
ELSE SET @declare = SUBSTRING(@declare,1,LEN(@declare)-1)

SEt @concat = @concat + ''+''''''''''''''

EXEC(@declare+'' ''+@assign+'' ''+
''EXEC(
''''DECLARE @hdl_doc int
EXEC sp_xml_preparedocument @hdl_doc OUT, ''+@concat+''
   DECLARE hdlcursor CURSOR GLOBAL FOR SELECT @hdl_doc AS DocHandle'''')''
)
```

```
')
OPEN hdlcursor
FETCH hdlcursor INTO @hdl
DEALLOCATE hdlcursor
GO
```

What this procedure does is dynamically generate the necessary DECLARE and SELECT statements to break up a large text column into nvarchar(4,000) pieces (e.g., DECLARE @c1 nvarchar(4000) SELECT @c1=...). As it does this, it also generates a concatenation expression that includes all of these variables (e.g., @c1+@c2+@c3,...). Since the EXEC() function supports concatenation of strings up to 2GB in size, we pass this concatenation expression into it dynamically and allow EXEC() to perform the concatenation on-the-fly. This basically reconstructs the document that we extracted from the table. This concatenated string is then passed into sp_xml_preparedocument for processing. The end result is a document handle that you can use with OPENXML(). Here's an example:

```
(Code abridged)
USE Northwind
GO
CREATE TABLE xmldoc
(id int identity,
 doc text)
INSERT xmldoc VALUES('<Customers>
<Customer CustomerID="VINET" ContactName="Paul Henriot">
   <Order CustomerID="VINET" EmployeeID="5" OrderDate="1996-07-04T00:00:00">
      <OrderDetail OrderID="10248" ProductID="11" Quantity="12"/>
      <OrderDetail OrderID="10248" ProductID="42" Quantity="10"/>
//More code lines here...
   </Order>
</Customer>
<Customer CustomerID="LILAS" ContactName="Carlos Gonzlez">
   <Order CustomerID="LILAS" EmployeeID="3" OrderDate="1996-08-16T00:00:00">
      <OrderDetail OrderID="10283" ProductID="72" Quantity="3"/>
   </Order>
</Customer>
</Customers>')

DECLARE @hdl int
EXEC sp_xml_concat @hdl OUT, '(SELECT doc FROM xmldoc WHERE id=1) a', 'doc'

SELECT * FROM OPENXML(@hdl, '/Customers/Customer') WITH (CustomerID
```

```
nvarchar(50))

EXEC sp_xml_removedocument @hdl
SELECT DATALENGTH(doc) from xmldoc
GO
DROP TABLE xmldoc
```

(Results)

```
CustomerID
--------------------------------------------------
VINET
LILAS
-----------
36061
```

You'll find the full test query on the CD accompanying this book. Although I've abridged the XML document in the test query, the one on the CD is more than 36,000 bytes, as the DATALENGTH() query at the end of the test code reports.

We pass a derived table expression into sp_xml_concat along with the column name we want to extract, and the procedure does the rest. As you can see, it's able to extract the nodes for which we're searching, even though one of them is near the end of a fairly large document.

### sp_run_xml_proc

Another limitation of SQL Server's XML support is that XML results are not returned as traditional rowsets. This has many advantages, but one of the disadvantages is that you can't call a stored procedure that returns an XML result using a four-part name or OPENQUERY() and get a useful result. The result set you'll get will be an unrecognizable binary result set because SQL Server's linked server architecture doesn't support XML streams.

You'll run into similar limitations if you try to insert the result of a FOR XML query into a table or attempt to trap it in a variable. SQL Server simply won't let you do either of these? Why? Because the XML documents returned by SQL Server are not traditional rowsets, as I mentioned earlier.

To work around this, I wrote a stored procedure called sp_run_xml_proc. You can use it to call linked server stored procedures (it needs to reside on the linked server) that return XML documents, as well as local XML procedures with results that you'd like to store in a table or trap in a variable. It does its magic by opening its own connection into the server (it assumes Windows authentication) and running your procedure. Once your procedure completes, sp_run_xml_proc processes the XML stream it returns using SQL-DMO calls, then translates it into a traditional rowset and returns that rowset. This result set can be inserted into a table or processed further just like any other result set. Here's the source code to sp_run_xml_proc:

```
USE master
GO
IF OBJECT_ID('sp_run_xml_proc','P') IS NOT NULL
  DROP PROC sp_run_xml_proc
GO
CREATE PROC sp_run_xml_proc
     @procname sysname   -- Proc to run
AS

DECLARE @dbname sysname,
       @sqlobject int,    --SQL Server object
       @object int, -- Work variable for accessing COM objects
       @hr int,     -- Contains HRESULT returned by COM
  @results int, -- QueryResults object
  @msgs varchar(8000) -- Query messages

IF (@procname='/?') GOTO Help

-- Create a SQLServer object
EXEC @hr-sp_OACreate 'SQLDMO.SQLServer', @sqlobject OUT
IF (@hr <> 0) BEGIN
    EXEC sp_displayoaerrorinfo @sqlobject, @hr
    RETURN
END

-- Set SQLServer object to use a trusted connection
EXEC @hr = sp_OASetProperty @sqlobject, 'LoginSecure', 1
IF (@hr <> 0) BEGIN
    EXEC sp_displayoaerrorinfo @sqlobject, @hr
    RETURN
END

-- Turn off ODBC prefixes on messages
EXEC @hr = sp_OASetProperty @sqlobject, 'ODBCPrefix', 0
IF (@hr <> 0) BEGIN
    EXEC sp_displayoaerrorinfo @sqlobject, @hr
    RETURN
```

```
END

-- Open a new connection (assumes a trusted connection)
EXEC @hr = sp_OAMethod @sqlobject, 'Connect', NULL, @@SERVERNAME
IF (@hr <> 0) BEGIN
    EXEC sp_displayoaerrorinfo @sqlobject, @hr
    RETURN

-- Get a pointer to the SQLServer object's Databases collection
EXEC @hr = sp_OAGetProperty @sqlobject, 'Databases', @object OUT
IF @hr <> 0 BEGIN
    EXEC sp_displayoaerrorinfo @sqlobject, @hr
    RETURN
END

-- Get a pointer from the Databases collection for the current database
SET @dbname=DB_NAME()
EXEC @hr = sp_OAMethod @object, 'Item', @object OUT, @dbname
IF @hr <> 0 BEGIN
    EXEC sp_displayoaerrorinfo @object, @hr
    RETURN
END

-- Call the Database object's ExecuteWithResultsAndMessages2 method to run
the proc
EXEC @hr = sp_OAMethod @object, 'ExecuteWithResultsAndMessages2',@results
OUT,
@procname, @msgs OUT
IF @hr <> 0 BEGIN
    EXEC sp_displayoaerrorinfo @object, @hr
    RETURN
END

-- Display any messages returned by the proc
PRINT @msgs

DECLARE @rows int, #cols int, @x int, @y int, @col varchar(8000), @row
varchar(8000)

-- Call the QueryResult object's Rows method to get the number of rows in
the result set
EXEC @hr = sp_OAMethod @results, 'Rows',@rows OUT
IF @hr <> 0 BEGIN
```

```
        EXEC sp_displayoaerrorinfo @object, @hr
        RETURN
END


-- Call the QueryResult object's Columns method to get the number of
columns in the result set
EXEC @hr = sp_OAMethod @results, 'Column',@cols OUT
IF @hr <> 0 BEGIN
        EXEC sp_displayoaerrorinfo @object, @hr
        RETURN
END


DECLARE @table TABLE (XMLText varchar(8000))


-- Retrieve the result set column by column using the GetColumnString
method
SET @y=1
WHILE (@y<=@rows) BEGIN
   SET @x=1
   SET @row=''
   WHILE (@x<=@cols) BEGIN
           EXEC @hr = sp_OAMethod @results, 'GetColumnString',@col OUT, @y,
           @x
             IF @hr <> 0 BEGIN
                   EXEC sp_displayoaerrorinfo @object, @hr
                   RETURN
             END
     SET @row=@row+@col+' '
     SET @x=@x+1
   END
   INSERT @table VALUES (@row)
   SET @y=@y+1
END


SELECT * FROM @table


EXEC sp_OADestroy @sqlobject      -- For cleanliness


RETURN 0


Help:
PRINT 'You must specify a procedure name to run'
RETURN -1
```

```
GO
```

Although the prospect of having to open a separate connection into the server to translate the document is not a particularly pretty one, it is unfortunately the only way to do this without resorting to client-side processing—at least for now. Here's some test code that shows how to use sp_run_xml_proc:

```
USE pubs
GO
DROP PROC testxml
GO
CREATE PROC testxml as
PRINT 'a message here'
SELECT * FROM pubs..authors FOR XML AUTO
GO
EXEC [BUC\FRYIN].pubs.dbo.sp_run_xml_proc 'testxml'
```

(Results abridged)

```
a message here
XMLText
---------------------------------------------------------------------
<pubs..authors au_id="172-32-1176" au_lname="White" au_fname="Johnson"
<pubs..authors au_id="672-71-3249" au_lname="Yokomoto" au_fname="Akiko"
```

Although I've clipped the resulting document down considerably, if you run this code from Query Analyzer (replace the linked server reference in the example with your own), you'll see that the entire document is returned as a result set. You can then insert this result set into a table using INSERT...EXEC for further processing. For example, you could use this technique to assign the document that's returned to a variable (up to the first 8,000 bytes) or to change it in some way using Transact-SQL. And once the document is modified to your satisfaction, you could call sp_xml_concat (listed earlier in the chapter) to return a document handle for it so that you can query it with OPENXML(). Here's an example that does just that:

```
SET NOCOUNT ON
GO
USE pubs
GO
DROP PROC testxml
GO
CREATE PROC testxml as
```

```
SELECT au_lname, au_fname FROM authors FOR XML AUTO
GO

CREATE TABLE #XMLText1
(XMLText varchar(8000))
GO

-- Insert the XML document into a table
-- using sp_run_xml_proc
INSERT #XMLText1
EXEC sp_run_xml_proc 'testxml'

-- Put the document in a variable
-- and add a root element
DECLARE @doc varchar(8000)
SET @doc=''

SELECT @doc=@doc+XMLText FROM #XMLText1
SET @doc='<root>'+@doc+'</root>'

-- Put the document back in a table
-- so that we can pass it into sp_xml_concat
SELECT @doc AS XMLText INTO #XMLText2

GO
DECLARE @hdl int
EXEC sp_xml_concat @hdl OUT, '#XMLText2', 'XMLText'
SELECT * FROM OPENXML(@hdl, '/root/authors') WITH (au_lname nvarchar(40))
EXEC sp_xml_removedocument @hdl
GO
DROP TABLE #XMLTEXT1, #XMLTEXT2
```

After the document is returned by sp_run_xml_proc and stored in a table, we load it into a variable, wrap it in a root element, and store it in a second table so that we may pass it into sp_xml_concat. Once sp_xml_concat returns, we pass the document handle it returns into OPENXML() and extract part of the document:

(Results abridged)

```
au_lname
----------------------------------------
Bennet
Blotchet-Halls
```

```
Carson
DeFrance
. . .
Ringer
Ringer
Smith
Straight
Stringer
White
Yokomoto
```

So, using sp_xml_concat and sp_run_xml_proc in conjunction with SQL Server's built-in XML tools, we're able to run the entire XML processing gamut. We start with an XML fragment returned by FOR XML AUTO, then we store this in a table, retrieve it from the table, wrap it in a root node, and pass it into OPENXML() to extract a small portion of the original document as a rowset. You should find that these two procedures enhance SQL Server's own XML abilities significantly.

## Summary

In this chapter you learned about OPENXML(). You learned how to "shred" or break down nonrelational XML data into relational pieces that you can manipulate with Transact-SQL. You learned to supply basic XPath strings to navigate an XML document via OPENXML(), and you learned to insert data into a table using OPENXML() as your data source. You also learned about the forthcoming Web Release 1, and the impact it will have on SQL Server's XML functionality, and you were introduced to a couple of handy stored procedures that should make life easier for you if you end up doing much with SQL Server's XML facilities.

# CHAPTER 16

# .NET and the Coming Revolution

*Organizations bloated with inefficient processes produce piggy, sluggish software.*

*—Steve McConnell[1]*

---

**NOTE:** I've included a discussion of .NET in this book because Microsoft has announced that SQL Server will include support for .NET's Common Language Runtime in its next version. Even if this wasn't the case, it makes sense to get up to speed now with .NET. It's coming, and it's coming very soon.

At the time of this writing, the .NET Framework and Visual Studio.NET have not yet been released. Some of the details may have changed between the time this was written and the present.

---

I've had this feeling at least three other times. It usually goes away eventually, but sometimes it lingers. It's not a pleasant feeling. It's really one of exasperation, of isolation, of incredulity. Sometimes the sensation makes me look around and ask: *Has the whole world gone mad? How could we have gone so wrong?*

The first time I can remember feeling it was when I was introduced to user-interface programming on an IBM mainframe. I walked into a colleague's office only to find the entire team crowded around his terminal. "Come here, come here!" one of the guys said excitedly, "Look at what Neil's done!"

Neil had built a spreadsheet—and on a dumb terminal, no less. Because the terminal was essentially a display device for the computer in the data center, this was no mean feat. To execute program logic, one had to submit the screen to the mainframe, let it generate a new screen, and await results. This meant that Neil's program couldn't do something as simple as, say, scrolling around on

---

[1]McConnell, Steve. *After the Gold Rush*. Redmond, WA: Microsoft Press, 1999. Page 67.

a spreadsheet using the arrow keys or updating a formula result when its referenced cells changed. No, the Submit key had to be pressed each time the screen was to be repainted. Each screen was essentially dead: The terminal would get a screen and display it, the user would type some things onto it and resubmit, and the whole screen would be sent back to the mainframe for further processing. In many ways, it wasn't unlike today's Web browsing model.

I came away from the impromptu demo seriously underwhelmed. *You have got to be kidding,* I thought. *Surely there's a better way to build a spreadsheet for such a powerful machine. My little PC's spreadsheet is an order of magnitude better than that mainframe concoction will ever be!*

It was a feeling I would experience again—that of being astonished at the nonsense people will put up with to get ill-fitting or poorly chosen technology to do what they want.

The second time the feeling came over me was in May of 1990. I will never forget it. It was a perfect spring day in the mountains of southwest Missouri when a package arrived for me from Microsoft. I picked up the box at the receptionist's desk and looked it over. I shook it a bit. *What could it be?* I wondered. *There could be a thousand different things in there!*

Back in my office, I ripped the outer shipping box to pieces and tossed it aside. I yanked out the shipping paper and manifest—they flew behind me in a frenzy. I picked up the box inside, shook off the Styrofoam packing and held it up to the light. There it was in all its wondrous, effervescent glory: the Windows 3.0 SDK!

I opened the box and dumped its contents on to my desk. *I will build a Windows app,* I thought. *I'll build one right now!*

I had watched Windows over the years and was particularly excited about the 3.0 release. Microsoft had combined the Windows, Windows 286, and Windows 386 lines into a single product, and had published a uniform API for writing apps for it. The display and fonts were smoother, the stark MS-DOS Executive had been replaced by the friendlier Program Manager. At long last, Windows seemed like more than just a toy. I decided it was time to see what the Macintosh-inspired user interface was all about, and I would use the SDK to build my first GUI app.

So I installed the software and quickly located one of the sample applications. It was a simple little program, really, a multiwindow text editor, similar to Notepad in terms of complexity. I fired up the Microsoft C compiler and compiled the sample. A few minutes later, it had finished—a whopping 80,000 lines of code! *Why do we need so much code for such a simple app?* I wondered. My worse fears were soon confirmed as I loaded the source into a text editor. What appeared before me was some of the most repulsive code I'd ever seen. Header file after header file, after header file. Message loop after message loop, after message loop. One level of indirection after another. Not really procedural code, but not object-oriented either. *What a huge mess,* I thought. *There has to be a better way.*

Over the next couple of years I kept looking for that better way. I looked at lots of products from lots of vendors. All had the same flaw: They all wanted you to wade through thousands of lines of code to produce a Windows app of even modest complexity. To be fair, some of them began generating much of this code for you, but you still had to wait while tens of thousands of lines of code were pored over by a multipass compiler. And God help you if you had to modify any of that generated code. It was some of the ugliest gobbledygook the programming world had ever seen.

Unfortunately for those of us creating those early Windows apps, this Rube Goldberg-way of building things came with the territory. It was the state of the technology at that time. We had no choice but to work with it. In earlier days, if a DOS-based technology was poorly conceived or difficult to work with, we'd simply not use it. So you don't like Lattice C and Panels? Fine, use Turbo Pascal. You don't like database management in Turbo Pascal? No problem. Use Clipper or Quicksilver. Many DOS tools had completely different programming paradigms, and if you didn't like one or it was ill-suited to your task, you could just use something else. Somewhere along the road to Windows uniformity we lost our sense of taste regarding programming tools. Everything turned to dog food, and we just let it happen.

Just about the time I'd given up on my quest to find a reasonable way to build Windows apps, along came Visual Basic. It changed everything. Although far from perfect, Visual Basic made great strides toward that ideal I'd been chasing—namely, that simple apps ought to be simple to build, regardless of the operating system, and that apps of greater complexity should be only linearly, not exponentially, more difficult. Over the years, tools like Delphi and Power-Builder improved on the Visual Basic model, and rapid application development (RAD) came into its own. My original disdain for the tediousness of early Windows development had been well founded. The success of RAD tools had vindicated me.

The third time I had the sensation was when I was first introduced to system administration on UNIX. Thanks to regular and repeated corruption problems with SQL Server on OS/2, my team was forced to migrate a large system off of it onto Sybase running under Solaris. I had only *thought* that administration was primitive and unnecessarily difficult on OS/2. For me, UNIX redefined unnecessary convolution. I was stunned to learn that the progenitors of UNIX actually expected people to manage critical line-of-business apps with arcane OS commands and cryptic tools that looked like they'd been put together by a couple of graduate students intent on unleashing a torrent of unbridled obfuscation on the world.

Like the C programming language, I discovered that UNIX has been assailed by short-sighted neophytes, that every CompSci graduate since Dyson had played pin the tail on the donkey with it, cheerily tacking on one disjointed feature after another, until it was about to collapse under its own weight. I wondered: *Do you people really manage systems this way? Who could keep up with all this? Who would want to? This is way too much complexity for what it is. We're not landing on the moon here; we're managing a database!*

Over time, the OS vendors themselves realized this shortcoming and began to try to put a friendlier, more systematic face on UNIX. The first to do so successfully was IBM with its AIX offering. Shortly after it came out, the other vendors followed suit. Soon, UNIX was an order of magnitude easier to install, use, and administer than it ever had been. Today, it's a mature OS offered on a number of platforms by many different vendors. In my opinion, it's still not as easy to use as it could be, and I doubt that Linux will supplant Windows as the dominant desktop OS anytime soon, but things are much improved over yesteryear. My astonishment at its needless complexity has subsided to a large extent.

The fourth and most recent time I experienced the sensation was when I saw my first complex Web application. I had just taken over as the CIO of a small Internet-oriented software development company when the CTO gave me a two-hour tour of the company's source code. He covered not only our products, but also the then-current, state-of-the-art in Web development—HTML, JavaScript, cookies, and so forth. I sat there in silent bewilderment. The old feeling was back. *Surely no one would go to this much trouble to build relatively simple applications. Surely no one would use such primitive, ill-fitting technologies to build critical software.*

Sure they would. They certainly had before.

To begin with, I was stunned at how primitive the development tools were. There seemed to be just two varieties: the do-it-all tools that built entire Web sites but came at the expense of cookie-cutter blandness and an annoying imprecision, and the do-it-yourself tools that basically consisted of someone's idea of an HTML-oriented Notepad. There was little middle ground, and technology fragmentation and competing standards made the situation all the worse.

I was also stunned at how weak and inflexible much of the technology itself was. I was disappointed in HTML as a language, in its general intransigence and lack of power. I was shocked that people were willing to go back to the days of running production apps under an interpreter and of having syntax errors show up in live code. I couldn't believe that they'd be willing to give up the visual development model that had made Visual Basic so popular or that they would stand for tools that forced you to hand-code anything of any complexity.

Moreover, I couldn't help but notice the enormous amount of effort that had gone into *working around* the Web's deficiencies. No one thought of state management? No problem. We'll handle it through cryptic URLs, cookies, and hidden fields. So we underestimated how much people would miss interactive content? Not to worry. We'll write interpretive scripts that run under the browser (perhaps different ones for each browser). We'll create spiffy UI controls in Java, C++, VB, or some other language and download them to the user's machine, and, to deal with the long download times that will then result, we'll cache these controls on users' machines without any sort of version management or upgrade path. To deal with the possibility of malicious code, we'll take a step backward and go back to application-based security. We'll add security mechanisms to the Web browser to supplement those of the operating system. Because, technically, everyone using a Web server is the same operating system user, we'll move the security and authentication mechanisms for these controls to the browser itself. And when we're done, we'll present a user-interface experience that's perhaps half as rich as what people already enjoyed long before the Web came into vogue. We'll literally spend years coming up with one workaround after another—many necessitated by shortcomings that should never have existed in the first place.

Because the world had settled on a markup language as the primary tool for building programs and had embraced a document-centric view of software, we were being forced to give up many of the hard-fought gains we'd spent years achieving: object-oriented programming; active, vibrant user interfaces; client-side intelligence and state management; network domain-based security; the speed and stability of compiled rather than interpretive code; readable, supportable programs; code reuse; centralization of application binaries; and so forth. I was astounded that people were willing to build critical applications using clunky text files produced by a mainframe-style, submit-and-generate interface. I thought we'd left that model behind because we discovered it didn't work very well. I thought we'd outgrown it.

As I sat there that day, it became apparent to me that, thanks to the Web, user interfaces had been dumbed-down a great deal, that applications had become less (not more) usable, and that developing software that was powerful, user-friendly, and extensible had become exponentially more difficult. In the narrow-minded interest of internetworking, it seemed the advent of the Web had set the entire software industry back a good two to three years in a number of areas, particularly with respect to applications development and user-interface design.

So, since that time, I've been looking for an answer—a technology or set of technologies that would make building simple Web apps easy and that would make building more complex apps only linearly more complex. I've been looking for technology that's fully object-oriented, and that lets me use inheritance, encapsulation, and polymorphism to my heart's content. I want something that's compiled, not interpreted; that catches my typos and syntax errors at compile time, not at runtime; and that runs at native code speed.

I want to be able to use one language for everything. I don't want to have to build pages in one language, controls in another, and scripts in yet another. I want to have to master just one language, and I want it to be orthogonal and systematic enough to be *worth* mastering.

I want to be able to build as rich a user interface as I can conceive. I don't want to be limited by my tools. I want my tools to enable me, not hinder me, so that I can focus on what it is my apps are supposed to do, not on the ugly details of making it happen.

I want a tool that takes care of state management for me, but that's still based on HTTP and connectionless application design. I want a tool with a rich suite of data-bound controls that can display themselves in a Web page without my having to generate HTML from a database or otherwise manually populate them.

I want a tool set that allows me to build Web pages visually, similarly to the way that RAD tools work. I want to drop a button onto a form, double-click it, and attach some code to it. I don't want to have to think about form submission or form variables; I want to code to objects and let system-level software take care of the rest.

I want a tool that's not language-centric, that lets me select from a wide range of programming languages without losing functionality or running into weird cross-language data conversion issues. If I want to build a class in one language, and someone else wants to inherit from that class into another, I want the technology to make it happen.

I want a tool that lets me develop any kind of application I want. I don't want to have to use one type of tool for GUI building and another for system-level development. I want to be able to build any type of app I need to—from a console application, to a service, to a Windows app, to a Web app—with a single tool. And I don't want a least common denominator approach. I want the technology to be powerful, easy to use, and extensible on every platform it supports.

I want the safety and security of an advanced framework around my apps. I want to use technology that manages resources for me, that keeps me from accessing memory I shouldn't, and that generally lets me focus on the business problems my applications are designed to address, not on the hair-splitting details of how it all happens behind the scenes.

I want a technology that lets me build multitier applications that are lightweight, scalable, and easy to build. I want a technology that allows me to exchange data easily with applications and code that I did not write.

I want a tool that's reasonably backward compatible with the existing code base out there, that will preserve my investment in the apps I've built thus far, and that will allow me to easily find programming talent that's already skilled in it.

In short, I want everything. I want to revolutionize the way that applications—particularly Web applications—are built.

Fortunately, somebody out there has already thought of all this and has been working on it for some time now. And fortunately, that somebody is Microsoft.

# .NET: The Future of Applications Development

Those who know me well know that I'm not a bandwagon person. I don't chase after the latest fads and never have. When Java first came out, I didn't join the party immediately. I waited for the hype to settle down a bit, then explored Java for myself and drew my own conclusions regarding its usefulness. When Linux first began making headlines, I didn't spend much of my time trying to use it or find tools that would allow me to build software for it. And when XML became all the rage, I waited until some of the standards settled down a bit before I made my first foray into it. That's just the way I am—a little conservative, perhaps, but it has served me well.

So, when I tell you that Microsoft's .NET initiative is going to change the way that applications are built, you can assume that I thought a lot about the statement before I made it, and that I at least *believe* that what I'm saying is the truth. I believe that .NET will transform Web applications development from a haven for hackers to a place where software craftsmanship and sound engineering can flourish. A good number of expert developers have stayed away from Web development because it's such a revolting mess. I think .NET will change this. The best developers in the world will be attracted to Web development with .NET because it will feature tools and technologies that finally make sense, that don't feel half-baked, and that provide the power and flexibility that experts demand.

I believe .NET will especially be a boon to novice and intermediate developers. I believe it will keep rookie coders from shooting themselves (or their customers) in the foot quite so often. I believe it will protect us from ourselves while our development skills improve over time. It will make the easy things easy and the harder things only incrementally harder. It will alleviate the need to master ten different technologies just to build scalable applications, and will allow us to focus on solving business problems rather than on the trivialities of constructing programs.

# What Is .NET?

That's a really good question. Microsoft has branded so many things with the .NET label that it's difficult to tell sometimes. Let me tell you what it means to me. First, the high-level view:

.NET is a set of technologies that

- Pulls together the best of the many disparate application development technologies, particularly those related to Web development.
- Unifies today's isolated Web applications and platforms.
- Dramatically improves developer productivity.
- Makes the same software design best practices available to Web developers that have been used successfully on other platforms for years.
- Provides a safe environment in which applications can run without having to concern themselves as much with resource management or low-level programming details.
- Corrects longstanding deficiencies in Microsoft's family of programming tools. Although Microsoft had a larger share of the developer tools market than anyone else, until .NET came to be, I do not believe they had the best products. In my opinion, that distinction clearly belonged to Borland. Having used both company's products for many years, I think I can say this, although I'm sure there are many who would disagree.
- Provides the tools to build apps that fulfill the stated vision of making information available anytime, anywhere, and on any device.

And now the specifics:

- .NET consists of a class framework, a family of programming languages, and the system-level facilities necessary to produce and run executable code and to share data between applications. The languages include Visual Basic.NET, C++, JScript, and a brand new language called C# (pronounced "C sharp"), an easier-to-use member of the C/C++ family.
- The .NET class framework (the .NET Framework) is an all-encompassing, extremely rich, object-oriented RTL (RunTime Library) that greatly simplifies and standardizes application development for any of the target platforms that .NET supports. It puts an object-oriented face on virtually anything you can do in a program. For example, rather than calling CreateWindow to create a window, or waiting in a message loop to process keys under Windows, you simply add a new WinForm to your project and drop controls onto it visually, as with Visual Basic. Unlike Visual

Basic, though, the code behind the form is a true OOP class in every sense of the word. When you attach code to a button, you're coding a method of the form class. The WinForms architecture uses the same form-based delegation model that was originally pioneered in Delphi. You get object orientation and visual development in one tool—something the current shipping version of Visual Studio does not have.

- All .NET languages are object-oriented. All support inheritance, encapsulation, and polymorphism, and all support interfaces as a separate language construct apart from classes.

- .NET languages are cross-compatible. You can create a class in one language and inherit from it in another. This is something we've never had before in the Microsoft family of development tools. You could *use* objects in one language tool that were created in another, but you could not *extend* an object created in another language through inheritance.

- All .NET languages support the same data types. The conversion issues we often run into now with sharing data between, say, a VB app and a C++ program are gone.

- All .NET languages support structured exception handling. If an exception is raised by a class, it's communicated properly to its caller, regardless of what language each is written in.

- In addition to the languages that will ship with .NET, Microsoft has provided an open API (the Common Language Specification) that allows third parties to build their own .NET-compliant languages. Several third parties have announced plans to do so. (I've seen probably a dozen or so third-party .NET languages announced in the trades. I know that both a Perl.NET and a COBOL.NET are planned, for example.) Each .NET language, regardless of who produces it, will have the same rich feature set as the others.

- Programs are compiled into MSIL (Microsoft Intermediate Language) by the .NET language compilers. This code is known as *managed code*. Managed code brings with it a number of intrinsic benefits:
  - Automatic garbage collection. Like the Java Virtual Machine, .NET's Common Language RunTime (CLR) automatically disposes of objects when they're no longer needed and the system needs to free physical memory. Unlike the Java VM, though, the CLR provides methods of controlling exactly what it does and when it does it. Objects can be excluded from garbage collection, and the frequency and scope of garbage collection can be controlled by the developer.
  - Bounds and range checking. You aren't allowed to overwrite memory you don't own.

- The potential for the CLR to be ported to other platforms. Although this isn't high on most Wintel developers' lists, it would certainly be something most would like to have.
- When executed, a program is automatically translated to native code by .NET's just-in-time (JIT) compiler. This approach has a number of positive aspects, among them:
  - The compiler can generate different instructions for different processor chips. Instead of having to take a one-size-fits-all approach, the JIT compiler is free to generate code that's optimized for the chip on which it's currently running. For example, the JIT may produce different code for an Intel chip than for an AMD or Cyrix chip.
  - By waiting to produce native code until an app executes, the possibility exists that updates to the framework could improve the quality and performance of the native code that's generated without necessitating even a recompile of end-user apps. That is, as Microsoft's JIT compiler technology improves, your apps can improve with it without requiring you to recompile or redistribute your apps.
- .NET provides facilities for backward compatibility and interoperability with COM and unmanaged code.
- .NET makes creating distributed applications as easy as creating a GUI. .NET Web Services are XML and SOAP (Simple Object Access Protocol) based, but you do not have to deal directly with either of them unless you want to. You code to classes, and .NET takes care of the rest. Web Services are automatically discoverable across a network, and .NET will create the code necessary for you to use them as though they were local classes.
- .NET supports the creation of rich user interfaces for both the Web and Windows:
  - You design forms for either platform using a visual designer similar to the one in Visual Basic. You drop controls onto a form and attach code to them.
  - You can create your own controls that are descendents or composites of others.
  - For Web forms, you can decide in the visual designer whether a control resides on the server or on the client.
  - You can use ActiveX controls alongside .NET controls on the same form.
- The .NET forms architectures supports visual form inheritance. You can create a Web or Windows form and inherit from it to create other similar forms. You can override methods, treat the forms polymorphically, and so forth. This capability was, again, pioneered in Delphi (I don't count

PowerBuilder Data Windows here because they weren't object-oriented). However, .NET improves on the Delphi approach by keeping the form inheritance based entirely in code. In Delphi, a complicated form-differencing algorithm determines the appearance of descendent forms at runtime because, as in Visual Basic, property settings are stored in a separate resource file for each form. Each member in an inheritance tree has to be examined and have his property settings checked to determine the impact on descendent forms. The process doesn't always work, and it's not hard to break it. In .NET, all property settings are stored in the class itself, so if you drop a button onto a form and set its caption, code is generated automatically that assigns the caption the value you specified. However, the Visual Studio 7 IDE is smart enough to fold that code out of view, so you don't have to wade through it while working. You get the best of both worlds: true OOP-based form inheritance without the headaches of having to trudge through reams of autogenerated code.

- Because .NET does not rely on the system registry, the deployment of applications has been greatly simplified. You may have heard of the fabled "XCOPY deployment." It's not a fable. It works. I've tried it. Because there's no registration requirement for .NET assemblies (.NET parlance for compiled binaries—DLLs and EXEs), you simply XCOPY an application assembly and the assemblies it depends on to deploy it. Unlike COM, you can have multiple copies of the same .NET object assembly on the same machine. This doesn't require any special hoop jumping or the kludges of side-by-side COM deployment and DLL redirection. It's not an afterthought—it's the way the framework was designed to work in the first place. This greatly reduces the potential for the installation of one app to break another—what we commonly refer to as *DLL Hell*.

- Although you would typically deploy an application's required assemblies to the folders under its root folder, you can also share an assembly across all applications by putting it in the Global Assembly Cache.

- .NET provides direct support for object versioning. The framework includes built-in support for ensuring that installing a new version of an object does not break applications that depend on older versions and that you can easily determine which versions of which assemblies an application depends on.

- .NET does away with many silly, obsolete, and problematic C/C++ "features" such as include files, macros, multiple inheritance, mutable/immutable classes, and other language gobbledygook. C#, in particular, is as elegant and powerful as any programming language I have ever used.

- Pointers in .NET are automatically dereferenced, another technique borrowed from Delphi. So, although you get the performance advantage of using a 4-byte pointer to an object rather than, say, storing it in a variant, you have none of the hassles associated with pointers and pointer arithmetic.

- .NET supports a true string type. You concatenate and work with strings as easily in any .NET language as you can in Visual Basic now.

- Every data type in .NET is an object. This also true of Java, but .NET improves on the Java approach in many ways. For example, .NET supports the concept of boxing and unboxing—a behind-the-scenes method of achieving the performance benefits of primitive data types without losing the ability to treat them as objects. Another advantage .NET has in this regard is that its base types' virtual method tables are relatively lean because a number of lesser-used methods have been relegated to separate helper classes. In other words, rather than including a method on every base type to translate it to every other base type, .NET has moved most of these routines to separate conversion classes. Each base type carries with it the methods needed to perform common tasks; lesser-used code is centralized in helper classes.

- .NET assemblies provide extensive meta-data to the outside world. Any class, field, method, property, or event that the code in the assembly exposes to the outside world is available from the binary itself. You do not need source code or symbol files. This is actually how cross-language inheritance works in .NET: You inherit directly from assemblies, not from source code or header files. So, in truth, what you're inheriting from is MSIL, rather than the language with which the assembly was originally built. This meta-data is more extensive than a type library and is inseparable from the assembly. It's stored in binary format and is used for everything from cross-language inheritance to the IntelliSense features of the Visual Studio 7 IDE.

- .NET cleans up the horrendous mess that is modern-day Web development. Instead of having to code an HTML file, then embed VBScript or JavaScript within it, and occasionally reference an ActiveX control or Java applet, you simply design Web forms visually. The code behind the Web form is a class. You don't have to deal with the spaghetti code normally associated with complex Web pages. .NET's Web technologies are known collectively as ASP.NET, a natural evolution of ASP. When you build a Web page in the Visual Studio 7 IDE, you drop the controls you want onto the form, designate where they should reside (server or client), and attach any code you want to their events (e.g., a button's

Click event). The code necessary to provide your form's functionality within a browser is generated for you automatically and deployed when you use the Visual Studio 7 IDE to deploy the app to your Web server. (Visual Studio 7 supports the notion of deploying directly to a Web server just as InterDev and Frontpage have for some time.)

- ASP.NET supports data-bound controls and the automatic population of them by data sources. You can use grid controls as well as single-row controls, and can bind them to any data source that .NET supports.

- The code behind ASP.NET Web forms is compiled rather than interpreted. Your ASP.NET apps will execute at native code speed. This is a vast improvement over current ASP technology, which is interpreted and relies heavily on variant data types.

- .NET also supports an evolutionary upgrade to ADO known as ADO.NET. ADO.NET is heavily XML based. In fact, XML is the native file format for ADO.NET data sets. The notion of disconnected data sets is not an afterthought in ADO.NET; it's a core feature. ADO.NET consists of a sensible class hierarchy that resembles the classic ADO framework in some ways and differs from it in others. It provides a scalable, lightweight, connectionless data services layer that was designed from the ground up to be as powerful and easy to use on the Web as it is in desktop applications. By being XML based, ADO.NET provides a ready means of exchanging data with non-.NET applications. It allows the developer to build applications that heavily leverage XML without having to deal with the XML itself any more than absolutely necessary. You code to the class framework, and .NET takes care of the rest.

- .NET's data access is language neutral. It works the same in any .NET language. Unlike classic ADO, in which there's an obvious advantage to using Visual Basic, all .NET languages work equally well with ADO.NET. It uses the same data types as the CLR (they're both based on XML data types) and provides the entirety of its functionality through regular .NET classes.

- ADO.NET supports advanced XML features such as XML transformations and schemas. It supports connecting directly to OLEDB providers such as SQL Server's SQLOLEDB and to XML-based sources. It makes building apps that pull together data from lots of different sources a snap.

- Visual Studio.NET features the most intelligent, most productive software development environment ever created. It has all the basics covered with features like IntelliSense hints while you type, syntax highlighting, and a versatile project manager. It also has a number of advanced features that you don't see often in mainstream development environments. One of my favorites is the code editor. It's probably the best I've seen in a mainstream tool, and sports features like code folding (the ability to collapse code nodes so that they don't display)—a great feature when you're focusing on a particular method and want to clear the edit window of distractions. Another nice feature is dynamic help: The IDE watches what you type and displays help from the MSDN Library in an unobtrusive panel on the right of the screen (à la Office-XP). Control toolboxes are hidden on the left of the screen. They display when you hover the mouse over them, or you can pin them in place. Web Service and other types of external references can be made right from the IDE. A few clicks of the mouse and the reference is added along with any code necessary to support it. The IDE features a Web-like interface, complete with a start-up page, links to recent projects, and Microsoft developer content on the Web.

No discussion of .NET would be complete without at least a little dabbling in code. Listing 16–1 shows the source to a Hello World application in Visual Basic.NET. Note that I only wrote one line of code—the call to MsgBox() (in bold type). The rest was autogenerated by the IDE. I've left out the autogenerated property settings and form setup code because it's normally not displayed.

**Listing 16–1** A simple Visual Basic.NET application.

```
Public Class Form1
    Inherits System.Windows.Forms.Form
    Private Sub Button1_Click(ByVal sender As System.Object, ByVal e As
System.EventArgs) Handles Button1.Click
        MsgBox("Hello world!")
    End Sub
End Class
```

As you can see, Visual Basic now supports object orientation and inheritance. Our form class (Form1) inherits from the base form class in the .NET Framework, System.Windows.Forms.Form. This base form class in actually written in C#, so you're seeing cross-language inheritance in action—something COM has never had.

The method Button1_Click() is a method of Form1. Clicking Button1 causes this method to execute and passes in a reference to the control that triggered it via the sender parameter.

Now here's the same app in C# (Listing 16–2):

**Listing 16–2** A Hello World app in C#.

```csharp
using System;
using System.Drawing;
using System.Collections;
using System.ComponentModel;
using System.Windows.Forms;
using System.Data;
namespace HelloWorldCS
{
    /// <summary>
    /// Summary description for Form1.
    /// </summary>
    public class Form1 : System.Windows.Forms.Form
    {
        private System.Windows.Forms.Button button1;
        /// <summary>
        /// Required designer variable.
        /// </summary>
        private System.ComponentModel.Container components;
        public Form1()
        {
            //
            // Required for Windows Form Designer support
            //
            InitializeComponent();
            //
            // TODO: Add any constructor code after
            // InitializeComponent call
            //
        }
        /// <summary>
        /// Clean up any resources being used.
        /// </summary>
        public override void Dispose()
        {
            base.Dispose();
            if(components != null)
                components.Dispose();
        }
        /// <summary>
        /// The main entry point for the application.
        /// </summary>
        [STAThread]
```

```
        static void Main()
        {
                Application.Run(new Form1());
        }
        private void button1_Click(object sender,System.EventArgs e)
        {
                MessageBox.Show("Hello world!");
        }
    }
}
```

Although there's a bit more code here than there was in the Visual Basic listing, I only wrote one line of it (in bold type). The rest was automatically created. If you're familiar with C and C++, the syntax probably looks very familiar to you. C# does not need or use header files—all definitions are inline—that is, the implementation also serves as the interface. You decide what is or isn't visible to the outside world via modifiers (e.g., private, public, and so on).

## On Microsoft Bashing

I'm fully expecting the Microsoft bashing to begin in earnest as Microsoft's competitors begin to learn more about .NET. They'll likely be worried—very worried—that this could be another home run for Microsoft, and rightfully so. I think it will be. .NET is going to change the way that people build software. It will revolutionize Web development the same way that Visual Basic revolutionized Windows development.

People who fear or compete with Microsoft are not going to like this. I expect the propaganda machine to kick into high gear once .NET is released. There will be a certain crowd (hopefully the minority) who will eschew the benefits of .NET simply because it comes from Microsoft. They'll never give the technology itself a fair hearing. They'd prefer just about anything over a Microsoft product, particularly enterprise software like .NET.

To me, shunning technology simply because it comes from Microsoft is like going to France and refusing to learn or speak French because you don't care for the French. Microsoft technologies are the *lingua franca* of the computing world. Refusing fluency in them only hurts us as developers; it doesn't affect them at all. None of us is big enough to impact their bottom line, regardless of what we might like to think.

People who know me know that I'm no one's lackey and that I've crossed swords with Microsoft more than once. I do not agree with everything they do, nor do I think their products are always the best of breed. It depends on the product—I use what works. That's why I use SQL Server, and that's why I've embraced .NET.

When I hear of developers rejecting technology solely because it's produced by Microsoft, I envision the tiny chicken hawk going after the rooster in the Warner Brothers cartoons. It's silly and is doomed to failure. How do I know? Because it's been tried before, over and over, and it has failed miserably each and every time. Just ask WordPerfect. Or Novell. Or Lotus. The road is lined with companies who got into a shoving match with Microsoft rather than focusing on giving customers what they wanted when they wanted it.

I think developers should choose technology based on its suitability to their work. Certainly, we can't be shortsighted and pick technologies that are here today and gone tomorrow or that don't play well with others. Nor can we follow every fad that comes along. However, allowing an anti-Microsoft bias to cause us to disregard whatever innovations they may come up with simply because we don't like *them* is foolhardy. It's counterproductive and bad for us as well as the industry. If we follow this fatuous course long enough, we'll soon find ourselves out-engineered and out-competed in the grand contest to win and retain customers. It's a tech-eat-tech world out there, and only the fittest technologies survive. Sometimes they happen to come from Microsoft.

## Microsoft Bigotry?

Trying to provoke me in a meeting recently, someone said, "OK, if you're going to be a Microsoft bigot, let's just get that on the table right now so we can start fighting about it." To which I replied, "I'm not a Microsoft bigot, but I'm also not an anti-Microsoft bigot. I'm a good technology bigot. I use whatever works, regardless of who produced it."

There is a romanticism that seems to have attached itself to rejecting Microsoft technology on moral grounds, but it is a false one. There's a school of thought that believes that refusing to work with Microsoft technology actually helps the world in some tangible way, in the same way that dedicating one's life to public service, or to working in third-world countries might. I think this borders on pretentiousness. Any perceived benefits to humankind that come from rejecting technologies because they're produced by Microsoft are spurious at best. The fact is: There are plenty of developers out there who will use Microsoft technologies if we elect not to, just as there are plenty of mechanics who will service General Motors vehicles if some of the grease monkeys of the world decried the inhumanity and tactics of large corporations and switched exclusively to Yugos.

It's important to guard against moral vanity here, and it's important not to let one's lack of knowledge of a technology result in rejecting that technology out-of-hand, without having even tried it. Refusing even to consider technology simply because it comes from Microsoft disrespects all those who work hard to make it good. Even if you don't like Microsoft's business practices, the people who build its software are, for the most part, not responsible for them. They're people like you and me. They build things; they work for a living. They aren't any more or less evil than the technologists in any company are. Sometimes they come up with great ideas; sometimes they don't. It pays to know when they do.

## Summary

In this chapter you learned about .NET. You learned what .NET entails and what some of its strengths are. You learned why .NET was so badly needed and the types of problems it was designed to solve. More than anything else, you learned about the coming .NET revolution. .NET is coming. Soon. It's time to get ready.

# PART IV

# Advanced Topics

# CHAPTER 17

# Performance Considerations

*Happiness isn't anything more than having something to look forward to, and, conversely, unhappiness is borne of dread, of things you don't look forward to. The trick is in arranging things so that you have more of the former than the latter.*

—*H. W. Kenton*

Normally, when I approach the subject of performance tuning, I attack it from the perspective of things you can do to speed up your code. People love stuff like that—often it's why they buy books like this in the first place. There are few things as satisfying as seeing a simple technique dramatically speed up your code.

It seems these days that everyone's in a hurry. We all want fast-food-style technology tidbits as quickly as we can get them. Never mind depth of understanding or a grasp of the overall philosophy employed in a technology. We just want the goods, and we want them yesterday.

So, I suppose the most direct approach to discussing SQL Server performance tuning might be to list common performance problems and their resolutions. We could go through the various mistakes people make when writing Transact-SQL code and designing SQL Server databases, and talk about ways of remedying them. In short order, we could come up with a fairly full "toolbox" of techniques that you could whip out on a moment's notice to address a variety of performance tuning scenarios.

This is certainly the approach I took in the Performance Tuning chapter of my previous book, *The Guru's Guide to Transact-SQL*. I think there's a place for this, and I find solutions cookbooks just as useful as the best textbooks. That said, it seems to me that understanding the reasoning behind the how-to is actually more important and will benefit you more in the long run than simply having a truckload of tips dumped on you, particularly when it comes to performance tuning. As I said in the Preface, understanding the philosophy behind a technology is more important than learning its syntax. Your ability to tune your Transact-SQL stored procedures is a product of your knowledge and understanding of SQL Server itself—how it works, what it does when it processes a query, what resources it needs to formulate an efficient plan, and so forth. So, in this chapter, I'll discuss the internals of SQL Server query processing. I'll talk about the various query stages and what happens at each one. As you come to understand how SQL Server query processing works for yourself, you'll develop your own methods of speeding up T-SQL code. And you'll use techniques that are sensible and safe because you'll have a good understanding of how SQL Server was designed to work.

# Indexing

There are few more beneficial things you can do to speed up query performance than to construct usable, efficient indexes. The name of the game with large data banks is I/O. You want to avoid as much of it as you can. Caching helps. Processing power helps. Fast hard drives help. But nothing affects query performance as fundamentally or as profoundly as indexing.

Without a useful index, SQL Server has little choice but to scan the entire table or tables to find the data you need. If you're joining two or more tables, SQL Server may have to scan some of them multiple times to find all the data needed to satisfy the query. Indexes can dramatically speed up the process of finding data as well as the process of joining tables together.

## Storage

The sysindexes system table stores system-level information about SQL Server indexes. Every index has a row in sysindexes. Each index is identified by its **indid** column, a 1-based integer—the clustered index is always indid 1. If a table has no clustered index, sysindexes will contain a row for the table itself with an indid value of 0.

### The Index Allocation Map

SQL Server tracks the extents that belong to a table or index using IAM (Index Allocation Map) pages. A heap or index will have at least one IAM for each file on which has allocated extents. An IAM is a bitmap that maps extents to objects. Each bit indicates whether the corresponding extent belongs to the object that owns the IAM. Each IAM bitmap covers a range of 512,000 pages (8,000 pages

* 8 bits/byte * 8 pages/extent = 512,000). The first IAM page for an index is stored in sysindexes' **FirstIAM** column. IAM pages are allocated randomly in a database file and linked together in a chain. Even though the IAM permits SQL Server to efficiently prefetch a table's extents, individual rows must still be examined. The IAM just serves as an access method to the pages themselves.

### Index Types

SQL Server supports two types of indexes: clustered and nonclustered. Both types have a number of features in common. Both consist of pages stored in balanced (B)-trees. The node levels of each type contain pointers to pages at the next level, whereas the leaf level contains the key values.

### B-Trees

SQL Server indexes are stored physically as B-trees. B-trees support the notion of searching through data using a binary search-type algorithm. B-tree indexes store keys with similar values close together, with the tree itself being continually rebalanced to ensure that a given value can be reached with a minimum of page traversal. Because B-trees are balanced, the cost of finding a row is fairly constant, regardless of which row it is.

The first node in a B-tree index is the root node. A pointer to each index's root node is stored in sysindexes' **root** column. When searching for data using an index, SQL Server begins at the root node, then traverses any intermediate levels that may exist, finally either finding or not finding the data in the bottom-level leaf nodes of the index. The number of intermediate levels will vary based on the size of the table, the size of the index key, and the number of columns in the key. Obviously the more data there is or the larger each key is, the more pages you need.

Index pages above the leaf level are known as *node pages*. Each row in a node page contains a key or keys and a pointer to a page at the next level whose first key row matches it. This is the general structure of a B-tree. SQL Server navigates these linkages until it locates the data for which it's searching or reaches the end of the linkage in a leaf-level node. The leaf level of a B-tree contains key values, and, in the case of nonclustered indexes, bookmarks to the underlying clustered index or heap. These key values are stored sequentially and can be sorted in either ascending or descending order on SQL Server 2000 and later.

Unlike nonclustered indexes, the leaf node of a clustered index actually stores the data itself. There is no bookmark, nor is there a need for one. When a clustered index is present, the data itself lives in the leaf level of the index.

The data pages in a table are stored in a *page chain*, a doubly linked list of pages. When a clustered index is present, the order of the rows on each page and the order of the pages within the chain are determined by the index key. Given that the clustered index key causes the data to be sorted, it's important to choose it wisely. The key should be selected with several considerations in mind, among them:

- The key should be as small as possible because it will serve as the bookmark in every nonclustered index
- The key should be chosen such that it aligns well with common ORDER BY and GROUP BY queries
- It should match reasonably well with common range queries (queries in which a range of rows is requested based on the values in a column or columns)

Beginning with SQL Server 7.0, all clustered indexes have unique keys. If a clustered index is created without the UNIQUE keyword, SQL Server forces the index to be unique by appending a 4-byte value called a *uniqueifier* to key values as necessary to differentiate identical key values from one another.

Leaf-level pages in a nonclustered index contain index keys and bookmarks to the underlying clustered index or table. A bookmark can take one of two forms. When a clustered index exists on the table, the bookmark is the clustered index's key. If the clustered index and the nonclustered index share a common key column, it's stored just once. When a clustered index isn't present, the bookmark consists of a RID (a row identifier) made up of the file number, the page number, and the slot number of the row referenced by the nonclustered key value.

The fact that a heap (a table without a clustered index) forces nonclustered indexes to reference it using physical location information is a good enough reason alone to create a clustered index on every table you build. Without it, changes to the table that cause page splits will have a ripple effect on the table's nonclustered indexes because the physical location of the rows they reference will change, perhaps quite often. This was, in fact, one of the major disadvantages of SQL Server indexing prior to version 7.0: Nonclustered indexes always stored physical row locator information rather than the clustered key value, and were thus susceptible to physical row location changes in the underlying table.

Nonclustered indexes are best at singleton selects—queries that return a single row. Once the nonclustered B-tree is navigated, the actual data can be accessed with just one page I/O—the read of the page from the underlying table.

## Covering Indexes

A nonclustered index is said to "cover" a query when it contains all the columns requested by the query. This allows it to skip the bookmark lookup step and simply return the data the query seeks from its own B-tree. When a clustered index is present, a query can be covered using a combination of nonclustered and clustered key columns because the clustered key is the nonclustered index's bookmark. That is, if the nonclustered index is built on the **LastName** and **FirstName** columns, and the clustered index key is built on **CustomerID**, a query that requests the **CustomerID** and **LastName** columns can be covered by the nonclustered index. A covering nonclustered index is the next best thing to having multiple clustered indexes on the same table.

## Performance Issues

Generally speaking, keep your index keys as narrow as possible. Wider keys cause more I/O and permit fewer key rows to fit on each B-tree page. This results in the index requiring a larger number of pages than it otherwise would, and causes it to take up more disk space. In practice, you'll probably find yourself tailoring your indexing strategy to meet specific business requirements. For example, if you have a query that takes an extremely long time to return because it needs an index with key columns none of your current indexes have, you may indeed want to widen an existing index or create a new one.

Naturally, there's a tradeoff with adding additional indexes or index columns—namely, update performance. Because the indexes on a table have to be maintained and updated as you add or change data, each new index you add brings with it a certain amount of overhead. The more indexes you add, the slower the updates against the underlying tables become, so it's important to keep your indexes as compact and narrow as possible, while still meeting the business needs your system was designed to address.

## Index Intersection

Prior to version 7.0, the SQL Server query optimizer would use just one index per table to resolve a query. SQL Server 7.0 and later can use multiple indexes per table, intersecting their sets of bookmarks before incurring the expense of retrieving data from the underlying table. This has some implications on index design and key selection, as I'll discuss in a moment.

## Index Fragmentation

You can control the amount of fragmentation in an index through its fillfactor setting and through regular defragmenting operations. An index's fillfactor affects performance in several ways. First, creating an index with a relatively low fillfactor helps avoid page splits during inserts. Obviously, with pages only partially full, the potential for needing to split one of them to insert new rows is lower than it would be with completely full pages. Second, a high fillfactor can help compact pages so that less I/O is required to service a query. This is a common technique with data warehouses. Because SQL Server performs I/O operations at the extent level, and extents are themselves collections of pages, retrieving pages that are only partially full wastes I/O bandwidth.

An index's fillfactor setting only affects the leaf-level pages in the index. SQL Server normally reserves enough empty space on intermediate index pages to store at least one row of the index's maximum size. If you want your fillfactor specification applied to intermediate as well as leaf-level pages, supply the PAD_INDEX option of the CREATE TABLE statement. PAD_INDEX instructs SQL Server to apply the fillfactor to the intermediate-level pages of the index. If your fillfactor setting is so high that there isn't room on the intermediate pages for even a single row (e.g., a fillfactor of 100%), SQL Server will override the percentage so that at least one row fits. If your fillfactor setting is so low that the intermediate pages cannot store at least two rows, SQL Server will override the fillfactor percentage on the intermediate pages so that at least two rows fit on each page.

Understand that an index's fillfactor setting isn't maintained over time. It's applied when the index is first created, but is not enforced afterward. DBCC SHOWCONTIG is the tool of choice for determining how full the pages in a table and/or index really are. The key indicators you want to examine are "Logical Scan Fragmentation" and "Avg. Page Density." DBCC SHOWCONTIG shows three types of fragmentation: extent scan fragmentation, logical scan fragmentation, and scan density. Use DBCC INDEXDEFRAG to fix logical scan fragmentation; rebuild indexes to defrag the table and/or index completely.

Listing 17–1 shows some sample DBCC SHOWCONTIG output from the Northwind Customers table:

**Listing 17–1** DBCC SHOWCONTIG.

```
DBCC SHOWCONTIG (Customers)
```

(Results)

```
DBCC SHOWCONTIG scanning 'Customers' table...
Table: 'Customers' (2073058421); index ID: 1, database ID: 6
TABLE level scan performed.
- Pages Scanned................................: 5
```

```
- Extents Scanned.............................: 3
- Extent Switches.............................: 4
- Avg. Pages per Extent.......................: 1.7
- Scan Density [Best Count:Actual Count].......: 20.00% [1:5]
- Logical Scan Fragmentation ..................: 40.00%
- Extent Scan Fragmentation ...................: 66.67%
- Avg. Bytes Free per Page....................: 3095.2
- Avg. Page Density (full)....................: 61.76%
```

As you can see, the Customer table is a bit fragmented. Logical Scan Fragmentation is sitting at 40% and Avg. Page Density is at 61.76%. In other words, the pages in the table are, on average, approximately 40% empty. Let's defrag the table's clustered index and see if things improve any (Listing 17–2):

**Listing 17–2** The Customer table after defragmentation.

```
DBCC INDEXDEFRAG(Northwind,Customers,1)
```

(Results)

```
Pages Scanned Pages Moved Pages Removed
------------- ----------- -------------
1             0           1
```

(Results)

```
DBCC SHOWCONTIG (Customers)
```

(Results)

```
DBCC SHOWCONTIG scanning 'Customers' table...
Table: 'Customers' (2073058421); index ID: 1, database ID: 6
TABLE level scan performed.
- Pages Scanned...............................: 4
- Extents Scanned.............................: 3
- Extent Switches.............................: 2
- Avg. Pages per Extent.......................: 1.3
- Scan Density [Best Count:Actual Count].......: 33.33% [1:3]
- Logical Scan Fragmentation ..................: 25.00%
- Extent Scan Fragmentation ...................: 66.67%
- Avg. Bytes Free per Page....................: 1845.0
- Avg. Page Density (full)....................: 77.21%
```

As you can see, DBCC INDEXDEFRAG helped considerably. Logical Scan Fragmentation has dropped to 25% and Avg. Page Density is now at a little more than 77%—an improvement of approximately 15%.

By default, DBCC SHOWCONTIG reports leaf-level info only. To scan the other levels of the table/index, specify the ALL_LEVELS option (Listing 17–3):

**Listing 17–3** DBCC SHOWCONTIG can show fragmentation at all levels.

```
DBCC SHOWCONTIG (Customers) WITH TABLERESULTS, ALL_LEVELS
```

(Results abridged)

```
ObjectName IndexName    AveragePageDensity  ScanDensity        LogicalFragmenta
---------- -----------  ------------------  -----------------  ----------------
Customers  PK_Customers 77.205337524414063  33.333333333333329 25.0
Customers  PK_Customers 0.95132195949554443 0.0                0.0
```

Table 17–1 lists the key data elements reported by DBCC SHOWCONTIG and what they mean:

I use the Logical Scan Fragmentation and Avg. Page Density fields to determine overall table/index fragmentation. You should see them change in tandem as fragmentation increases or decreases over time.

**Table 17–1** DBCC SHOWCONTIG FIELDS

| SHOWCONTIG field | Meaning |
|---|---|
| Avg. Bytes Free per Page | Average number of bytes free on each page |
| Pages Scanned | Number of pages accessed |
| Extents Scanned | Number of extents accessed |
| Out of order pages (not displayed, but used to compute Logical Scan Fragmentation) | Number of times a page had a lower page number than the previous page in the scan |
| Extent Switches | Number of times a page in the scan was on a different extent than the previous page in the scan |

## Defragmenting

As you just saw, DBCC INDEXDEFRAG is a handy way to defragment an index. It's an online operation, so the index is still usable while it works. That said, it only reorganizes the index at the leaf level, performing a kind of bubble sort on the leaf-level pages. To fully defrag an index, you must rebuild it. You have several ways of doing this. First, you could simply drop and recreate it using DROP/CREATE INDEX. The drawback to this, though, is that you have to take the index offline while you rebuild it, and you aren't allowed to drop indexes that support constraints. You could use DBCC DBREINDEX or the DROP_EXISTING clause of CREATE INDEX, but, again, the index is unavailable until it's rebuilt. The one upside is that the index can be created in parallel if you're running on the Enterprise Edition of SQL Server. Because SQL Server's parallel index creation scales almost linearly on multiple processors, the length of time that an index is offline while being recreated can be decreased significantly by simply adding more processors.

Generally speaking, DBCC INDEXDEFRAG is the best tool for the job unless you find widespread fragmentation in the nonleaf levels of the index and you feel this fragmentation is unacceptably affecting query performance. As I mentioned, you can check the fragmentation of the other levels of an index by passing the ALL_LEVELS option to DBCC SHOWCONTIG.

In addition to defragmenting the leaf-level pages, DBCC INDEXDE-FRAG also features a compaction phase in which it compacts the index's pages using the original fillfactor as its target. It attempts to leave enough space for at least one row on each page when it finishes. If it can't obtain a lock on a particular page during compaction, it skips the page. It removes any pages that end up completely empty as a result of the compaction.

## Indexes on Views and Computed Columns

Creating an index on a view or a computed column persists data that would otherwise exist only in a logical sense. Normally, the data returned by a view exists only in the tables the view queries. When you query the view, your query is combined with the one comprising the view and the data is retrieved from the underlying objects. The same is true for computed columns. Normally, the data returned by a computed column does not actually exist independently of the columns or expressions it references. Every time you request it from its host table, the expression that comprises it is reevaluated and its data is generated "on the fly."

When you begin building indexes on a view, you must start with a clustered index. This is where the real data persistence happens. Just as with tables, a

**Table 17–2** Indexed View/Computed Column Required Settings

| Setting | Required value |
| --- | --- |
| ARITHABORT | ON |
| CONCAT_NULL_YIELDS_NULL | ON |
| QUOTED_IDENTIFIER | ON |
| ANSI_NULLS | ON |
| ANSI_PADDING | ON |
| ANSI_WARNING | ON |
| NUMERIC_ROUNDABORT | OFF |

clustered index created on a view actually stores the data itself in its leaf-level nodes. Once the clustered index exists, you're free to created nonclustered indexes on the view as well.

This differs from computed columns in tables. With computed columns, you're not required first to create a clustered index to build nonclustered indexes. Because the column will serve merely as an index key value, a nonclustered index works just fine.

## Prerequisites

SQL Server requires that seven specific SET options be specified correctly to create an index on a view or a computed column. Table 17–2 lists the settings and their required values. As you can see from the table, all settings except NUMERIC_ROUNDABORT must be set to ON.

Only deterministic expressions can be used with indexed views and indexes on computed columns. A deterministic expression is one that when supplied a given input, always returns the same output. SELECT SUBSTRING('He who loves money more than truth will end up poor',23,7) is a deterministic expression; GETDATE() isn't.

You can check to see whether a view or column can be indexed using Transact-SQL's OBJECTPROPERTY() and COLUMNPROPERTY() functions (Listing 17–4):

**Listing 17–4** Not all views can be indexed.

```
SELECT OBJECTPROPERTY (OBJECT_ID('Invoices'), 'IsIndexable')
SELECT COLUMNPROPERTY (OBJECT_ID('syscomments'), 'text' , 'IsIndexable')
SELECT COLUMNPROPERTY (OBJECT_ID('syscomments'), 'text' ,
'IsDeterministic')
```

(Results)

```
-----------
0
-----------
0

-----------
0
```

One final prerequisite for views is that a view can only be indexed if it was created with the SCHEMABINDING option. Creating a view with SCHEMABINDING causes SQL Server to prevent the objects it references from being dropped unless the view is first dropped or changed so that the SCHEMABINDING option is removed. Also, ALTER TABLE statements on tables referenced by the view will fail if they affect the view definition.

In the previous example, the Invoice view cannot be indexed because it was not created with SCHEMABINDING. Here's a version of it that was, along with a subsequent check of IsIndexable (Listing 17–5):

**Listing 17–5** The Invoices2 view can now be indexed.

```
CREATE VIEW Invoices2
WITH SCHEMABINDING
AS
SELECT Orders.ShipName, Orders.ShipAddress, Orders.ShipCity,
       Orders.ShipRegion,
       Orders.ShipPostalCode, Orders.ShipCountry, Orders.CustomerID,
       Customers.CompanyName AS CustomerName, Customers.Address,
       Customers.City,
       Customers.Region, Customers.PostalCode, Customers.Country,
       Orders.OrderID, Orders.OrderDate, Orders.RequiredDate,
       Orders.ShippedDate, Shippers.CompanyName As ShipperName,
       [Order Details].ProductID, Products.ProductName,
       [Order Details].UnitPrice, [Order Details].Quantity,
       [Order Details].Discount,
       Orders.Freight
       FROM   dbo.Shippers INNER JOIN
           (dbo.Products INNER JOIN
               (
```

```
          (dbo.Employees INNER JOIN
            (dbo.Customers INNER JOIN dbo.Orders
              ON Customers.CustomerID = Orders.CustomerID)
          ON Employees.EmployeeID = Orders.EmployeeID)
        INNER JOIN dbo.[Order Details]
          ON Orders.OrderID = [Order Details].OrderID)
      ON Products.ProductID = [Order Details].ProductID)
    ON Shippers.ShipperID = Orders.ShipVia
GO
SELECT OBJECTPROPERTY (OBJECT_ID('Invoices2'), 'IsIndexable')
```

(Results)

```
-----------
1
```

Note that all the object references now use two-part names (they don't in the original Invoices view). Creating a view with SCHEMABINDING requires all object references to use two-part names.

Once a view has been indexed, the optimizer can make use of the index when the view is queried. In fact, on SQL Server EE, the optimizer will even use the index to service a query on the view's underlying tables if it thinks this would yield the least cost in terms of execution time.

Normally, indexed views are not used at all by the optimizer unless you're running on EE. For example, consider this index and query:

```
CREATE UNIQUE CLUSTERED INDEX inv ON invoices2 (orderid, productid)
GO
SELECT * FROM invoices2 WHERE orderid=10844 AND productid=22
```

(Results abridged)

| ShipName | ShipAddress | ShipCity | ShipRegion | ShipPostalCode |
| --- | --- | --- | --- | --- |
| Piccolo und mehr | Geislweg 14 | Salzburg | NULL | 5020 |

Here's an excerpt from its query plan (Listing 17–6):

**Listing 17–6** View indexes aren't used by default on non-EE versions of SQL Server.

StmtText

```
- - - - - - - - - - - - - - - - - - - - - - - - - - - - - - - - - - - - - - - - -
SELECT * FROM [invoices2] WHERE [orderid]=@1 AND [productid]=@2
  |--Nested Loops(Inner Join)
      |--Nested Loops(Inner Join)
      |   |--Nested Loops(Inner Join, OUTER REFERENCES:([Orders].[ShipVia]))
      |   |   |--Nested Loops(Inner Join, OUTER REFERENCES:([Orders].[Employ
      |   |   |   |--Nested Loops(Inner Join, OUTER REFERENCES:([Orders].[C
      |   |   |   |   |--Clustered Index Seek(OBJECT:([Northwind].[dbo].[O
      |   |   |   |   |--Clustered Index Seek(OBJECT:([Northwind].[dbo].[C
      |   |   |   |--Clustered Index Seek(OBJECT:([Northwind].[dbo].[Employ
      |   |   |--Clustered Index Seek(OBJECT:([Northwind].[dbo].[Shippers].[
      |   |--Clustered Index Seek(OBJECT:([Northwind].[dbo].[Order Details].[
      |--Clustered Index Seek(OBJECT:([Northwind].[dbo].[Products].[PK_Product
```

Although the plan text is clipped on the right, you can tell that the view index obviously isn't being used, even though it contains both the columns on which the query filters. On versions of SQL Server other than EE, this is completely expected. Out of the box, only SQL Server EE will consider view indexes when formulating an execution plan. There is, however, a workaround. You can use the NOEXPAND query hint on non-EE versions of SQL Server to force the consideration of a view's index. Here's the query again (Listing 17–7), this time with the NOEXPAND keyword and the resultant query plan:

**Listing 17–7** NOEXPAND forces the use of a view's index.

```
SELECT * FROM invoices2 (NOEXPAND) WHERE orderid=10844 AND productid=22
StmtText
- - - - - - - - - - - - - - - - - - - - - - - - - - - - - - - - - - - - - - - - -
SELECT * FROM invoices2 (NOEXPAND) WHERE orderid=10844 AND productid=22
|--Clustered Index Seek(OBJECT:([Northwind].[dbo].[Invoices2].[inv]), SEEK:([
```

Notice that the index is now used. In conjuction with the INDEX hint, NOEXPAND can force the optimizer to use a view's index, even if doing so yields a suboptimal plan, so regard it with the same skepticism that you do other query hints. It's best to let the optimizer do its job and override it only when you have no other choice.

## Locking and Indexes

One telltale sign that a table lacks a clustered index is when you notice that it has RID locks taken out on it. SQL Server will never take out RID locks on a table with a clustered index; it will always take out key locks instead.

Generally speaking, you should let SQL Server control locking of all types, including locking with indexes. Normally, it makes good decisions and will do the best job of managing its own resources.

You can use the sp_indexoption system procedure to control manually the types of locks that are allowed on an indexed table. You can use it to disable row and/or page locks, which can come in handy when SQL Server's locking facilities refuse to work correctly, particularly with regard to lock escalation.

Note that sp_indexoption only applies to indexes, so you can't control the locking with the pages in a heap. That said, when a table has a clustered index, it *is* affected by the settings specified via sp_indexoption.

# Statistics

You've probably heard the term *statistics* bandied about in discussions of SQL Server query performance. Statistics are meta-data that SQL Server maintains about index keys and, optionally, nonindexed column values. SQL Server uses statistics to determine whether using an index could speed up a query. In conjunction with indexes, statistics are the single most important source of data for helping the optimizer develop optimum execution plans. When statistics are missing or out-of-date, the optimizer's ability to formulate the best execution plan for a query is seriously impaired.

Let's cover a few basic statistics-related terms before we discuss statistics in more depth.

### Cardinality

The cardinality of data refers to how many unique values exist in the data. In strict relational database theory, duplicate rows (tuples) are not permitted within a relation (a table), so cardinality would refer to the total number of tuples. That said, SQL Server *does* permit duplicate rows to exist in a table, so for our purposes the term *cardinality* refers to the number of *unique* values within a data set.

### Density

Density refers to the uniqueness of values within a data set. An index's density is computed by dividing the number of rows that would correspond to a given key value by the number of rows in the table. For a unique index, this amounts to dividing 1 by the table's total row count. Density values range from 0 through 1; lower densities are better.

## Selectivity

Selectivity is a measure of the number of rows that will be returned by a particular query criterion. It expresses a relationship between your query criteria and the key values in an index. It is computed by dividing the number of keys being requested by the number of rows they access. Query criteria (usually specified in a WHERE clause) that are highly selective are the most useful to the optimizer because they allow it to predict with certainty how much I/O is required to satisfy a query.

## Performance Issues

Indexes with high densities will likely be ignored by the optimizer. The most useful indexes to the optimizer have density values of 0.10 or less. Let's take the example of a table called VoterRegistration with 10,000 rows, no clustered index, and a nonclustered index on its **PartyAffiliation** column. If there are three political parties registered in the voting precinct and they each have about the same representation across the voter base, **PartyAffiliation** will likely contain only three unique values. This means that a given key value in the index could identify as many as 3,333 rows in the table, perhaps more. This gives the index a density of 0.33 (3,333 ÷ 10,000), and virtually ensures that the optimizer will not use the index when formulating an execution plan for queries that require columns not covered by the index.

To understand this better, let's compare the cost of using the index versus not using it to satisfy a simply query. If we wanted to list all the voters in the precinct affiliated with the Democratic Party, we'd be talking about hitting approximately a third of the table, or 3,333 rows. If we use the PartyAffiliation index to access these rows, we're faced with 3,333 separate logical page reads from the underlying table. In other words, as we found each key value in the index, we'd have to look up its bookmark in the underlying table to get the columns not contained in the index, and each time we did this, we'd incur the overhead of a logical (and possibly physical) page I/O. All told, we may incur as much as 26MB of page I/O overhead to look up these bookmark values (3,333 keys * 8K/page). Now consider the cost of simply scanning the table sequentially. If an average of 50 rows fits on each data page and we have to read the entire table to find all the ones affiliated with the Democratic Party, we're still only looking at about 200 logical page I/Os (10,000 rows ÷ 50 rows/page = 200 pages). This is a big difference and is the chief reason you'll see nonclustered indexes ignored in favor of table/clustered index scans.

At what point does a nonclustered index become sufficiently selective to be useful to the optimizer? In our example, 200 is the magic number. Specifically, the optimizer would have to believe that retrieving data via the index would require fewer than 200 page I/Os in order for it to consider the index a more efficient access path than simply scanning the entire table. The original 3,333 estimate could be lowered by adding columns to the index (and also to the query) that make it more selective. There is a point of diminishing returns here, though. As you add columns to the index in an attempt to make it more selective, you increase the amount of overhead that comes with traversing the index's B-tree. By making the index larger, you also make it more expensive to navigate. At some point, it becomes cheaper just to scan the data itself than to incur the overhead of walking through the B-tree.

## Storage

SQL Server stores statistics for an index key or a column in the **statblob** column of sysindexes. **Statblob** is an image data type that stores a histogram containing a sampling of the values in the index key or column. For composite indexes, only the first column is sampled, but density values are maintained for the other columns.

During the index selection phase of query optimization, the optimizer decides whether an index matches up with the columns in the filter criteria, determines index selectivity as it relates to that criteria, and estimates the cost of accessing the data the query seeks.

If an index only has one column, its statistics consist of one histogram and one density value. If an index has multiple columns, a single histogram is maintained, as well as density values for each prefix (left to right) combination of key columns. The optimizer uses this combination of an index's histogram and densities—its statistics—to determine how useful the index is in resolving a particular query.

The fact that a histogram is only stored for the first column of a composite index is one of the reasons you should position the most selective columns first in a multicolumn index: The histogram will be more useful to the optimizer. Moreover, this is also the reason that splitting up composite indexes into multiple single-column indexes is sometimes advisable. Because the server can intersect and join multiple indexes on a single table, you retain the benefits of having the columns indexed, and you get the added benefit of having a histogram for each column (column statistics can help out here, as well). This isn't a blanket statement. Don't run out and drop all your composite indexes. Just keep in mind that breaking down composite indexes is sometimes a viable performance tuning option.

## Columns Statistics

Besides index statistics, SQL Server can also create statistics on nonindexed columns (which happens automatically when you query a nonindexed column while AUTO_CREATE_STATISTICS is enabled for the database). Being able to determine the likelihood that a given value may occur in a column gives the optimizer valuable information in determining how best to service a query. It allows the optimizer to estimate the number of rows that will qualify from a given table involved in a join, allowing it to select join order more accurately. Also, the optimizer can use column statistics to provide histogram-type information for the other columns in a multicolumn index. Basically, the more information you can give the optimizer about your data, the better.

## Listing Statistics

SQL Server uses statistics to track the distribution of key values across a table. The histogram that's stored as part of an index's statistics contains a sampling of as many as 200 values for the index's first key column. Besides the histogram, **statblob** also contains:

- The number of rows on which the histogram and densities are based
- The average length of the index key
- The date and time of the last statistics generation
- Density values for other prefix combinations of key columns

The range of key values between each of the 200 histogram sample values is called a *step*. Each sample value denotes the end of a step, and each step stores three values:

1. EQ_ROWS—The number of rows with a key value matching the sample value
2. RANGE_ROWS—The number of other values inside the range
3. RANGE_DENSITY—A density computation for the range itself

DBCC SHOW_STATISTICS lists the EQ_ROWS and RANGE_ROWS values verbatim and uses RANGE_DENSITY to compute DISTINCT_RANGE_ROWS and AVG_RANGE_ROWS for the step. It computes DISTINCT_RANGE_ROWS (the total number of distinct rows within the step's range) by dividing 1 by RANGE_DENSITY, and computes AVG_RANGE_ ROWS (the average number of rows per distinct key value) by multiplying RANGE_ROWS by RANGE_DENSITY.

## Updating Statistics

Statistics can be updated in a couple of ways. The first and most obvious is through the AUTO_UPDATE_STATISTICS database option (you can turn this on via ALTER DATABASE or sp_dboption). When statistics are generated automatically, SQL Server uses sampling (as opposed to scanning the entire table) to speed up the process. This works in the vast majority of cases, but can sometimes lead to statistics that are less useful than they could be.

Closely related to automatic statistics updating is automatic statistics creation. This occurs when the AUTO_CREATE_STATISTICS database option has been enabled and you issue a query that filters on a nonindexed column. SQL Server will automatically create a set of column statistics for you.

The second method of updating statistics is through the UPDATE STATISTICS command. UPDATE STATISTICS was the only way to update statistics prior to SQL Server 7.0. UPDATE STATISTICS can either use sampling, as happens with automatic updating, or it can do a full scan of the table, resulting in better statistics, but likely taking longer.

Closely related to UPDATE STATISTICS is the CREATE STATISTICS command. You use CREATE STATISTICS to create column statistics manually. Once created, these statistics can be updated through automatic updating or via UPDATE STATISTICS, just as regular index statistics can.

SQL Server provides a few stored procedures to make creating and updating statistics easier. Sp_updatestats runs UPDATE STATISTICS against all user-defined tables in the current database. Unlike the UPDATE STATISTICS command itself, though, sp_updatestats cannot issue a full scan of a table to build statistics—it always uses sampling. If you want full-scan statistics, you have to use UPDATE STATISTICS.

Sp_createstats is similarly handy. It can automate the creation of column statistics for all eligible columns in all eligible tables in a database. Eligible columns include noncomputed columns with data types other than **text, ntext,** or **image** that do not already have column or first-column index statistics. Eligible tables include all user (nonsystem) tables.

Sp_autostats allows you to control automatic statistics updating at the table and index levels. Rather than simply relying on the AUTO_UPDATE_STATISTICS database option, you can enable/disable automatic statistics generation at a more granular level. For example, if you run a nightly job on a large table to update its statistics using a full scan, you may want to disable automatic statistics updates for the table. Using sp_autostats, you can disable automatic statistics updates on this one table, and leave it enabled for the rest of the database. Statistics updates on large tables, even those that use sampling, can take a while to run and can use significant CPU and I/O resources.

Keep in mind that the negative impact on performance of not having statistics or having out-of-date statistics far outweighs the performance benefits of avoiding automatic statistics updates/creation. You should only disable auto update/create stats when thorough testing has shown that there's no other way to achieve the performance or scalability you require.

### sp_showstatdate

Listing 17–8 shows a stored procedure that you can use to stay on top of statistics updates. It shows the statistics type, the last time it was updated, and a wealth of other information that you may find useful in managing index and column statistics. Here's the code:

**Listing 17–8** The sp_showstatdate procedure helps stay on top of statistics updates.

```
CREATE PROC sp_showstatdate @tabmask sysname='%', @indmask sysname='%'
AS
  SELECT
  LEFT(CAST(USER_NAME(uid)+'.'+o.name AS sysname),30) AS TableName,
  LEFT(i.name,30) AS IndexName,
  CASE WHEN INDEXPROPERTY(o.id,i.name,'IsAutoStatistics')=1 THEN
'AutoStatistics'
       WHEN INDEXPROPERTY(o.id,i.name,'IsStatistics')=1 THEN 'Statistics'
   ELSE 'Index'
   END AS Type,
  STATS_DATE(o.id, i.indid) AS StatsUpdated,
  rowcnt,
  rowmodctr,
  ISNULL(CAST(rowmodctr/CAST(NULLIF(rowcnt,0) AS decimal(20,2))*100 AS int),0)
AS PercentModifiedRows,
  CASE i.status & 0x1000000
  WHEN 0 THEN 'No'
  ELSE 'Yes'
  END AS [NoRecompute?],
  i.status
FROM dbo.sysobjects o JOIN dbo.sysindexes i ON (o.id = i.id)
WHERE o.name LIKE @tabmask
 AND i.name LIKE @indmask
 AND OBJECTPROPERTY(o.id,'IsUserTable')=1
```

```
 AND i.indid BETWEEN 1 AND 254
ORDER BY TableName, IndexName
GO
USE pubs
GO
EXEC sp_showstatdate
```

(Results abridged)

```
TableName          IndexName        Type        StatsUpdated
----------------   --------------   ----------  -------------------------
dbo.authors        au_fname         Statistics  2000-07-02 19:42:04.487
dbo.authors        aunmind          Index       2000-06-30 20:54:56.737
dbo.authors        UPKCL_auidind    Index       2000-06-30 20:54:56.737
dbo.dtproperties   pk_dtproperties  Index       NULL
dbo.employee       employee_ind     Index       2000-06-30 20:54:45.280
dbo.employee       PK_emp_id        Index       2000-06-30 20:54:45.297
```

# Query Optimization

When you submit a query to SQL Server, it begins by optimizing your query for execution. Using the statistics and indexes at its disposal, the SQL Server query optimizer develops an execution plan that it believes is the most efficient way to service your query. This optimization is cost-based, with plans that cost less in terms of estimated execution time winning out over those that cost more. The costing process leans heavily toward reducing I/O operations because they are the typical bottleneck when accessing large amounts of data.

As illustrated by Figure 17–1, query plan development consists of several phases or steps:

1. Identify trivial plans.
2. Simplify plan.
3. Load statistics.
4. Evaluate plans based on cost.
5. Optimize for parallelism.
6. Output plan.

Let's discuss each of these in more depth.

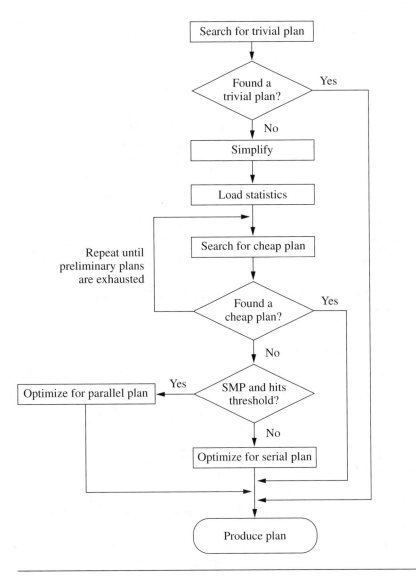

**Figure 17–1** The query optimization process.

## Trivial Plan Optimization

Because query plans can be expensive to evaluate, SQL Server includes a special optimization for creating plans for queries that really only have one possible plan anyway. A SELECT against a table with a single unique covering index is one example. An INSERT statement with a VALUES clause is another. SQL Server uses built-in heuristics to identify candidates for trivial plans. If a query plan can be trivialized without giving up performance, it saves the optimizer from having to evaluate all the possible plans for the query.

## Simplification

If the trivial plan optimizer is unable to find a plan for the query, the optimizer simplifies the query through syntactic transformations by doing things like folding constants, converting HAVING to WHERE when possible, translating !=@parm to < @parm OR >@parm, and so forth. These optimizations do not require examining cost, index, or statistics info, but they can result in a more efficient query plan being developed.

## Statistics Loading

Once the plan has been simplified, the optimizer loads index and column statistics as well as other support info so that cost-based plan generation can begin. This means that it accesses sysindexes and other system tables and loads up the pertinent info for the tables involved in the query.

## Cost-based Optimization

Cost-based optimization is divided into a series of phases that allow plans to be generated in pieces. Because of the number of options available to SQL Server for optimizing a plan, the optimizer tries simpler plan optimizations first in order to minimize the time spent formulating a plan. Each successive phase tries transformations of the query that are more costly that the previous one, but that hopefully yield a more efficient plan. This process is repeated until a plan that meets the optimizer's threshold for cost is reached.

The preliminary phases of cost-based optimization are the most basic. The optimizer is designed so that the vast majority of plans can be formulated during the preliminary cost-based optimization phases. This keeps the cost of generating plans relatively low and ensures that the more advanced phases of optimization are reserved for advanced queries.

Each time an execution plan is generated, SQL Server examines it to see whether the plan is sufficiently cheap to execute based on an internal threshold.

If the plan is sufficiently cheap, the optimizer outputs it. If not, it keeps looking.

The preliminary phases usually find simple plans involving nested loops for tables with just one usable index. These simpler plans can resolve a good number of queries fairly well, so the optimizer is designed to generate them in a wide variety of circumstances.

Every optimization phase consists of applying a set of rules to transform the query into a resolvable series of steps. When the optimizer believes that the cost of executing these steps would be sufficiently cheap, it emits the plan to be executed.

## Full Optimization

If, during the preliminary phases, the optimizer doesn't find a suitable plan, it puts the query through a full optimization phase. It's during this phase that a parallel plan can be developed. It bases the decision to do this on whether the cost threshold for parallelism has been reached. This threshold refers to the number of seconds required to execute the plan in a serial (nonparallel) fashion on a specific hardware configuration. If SQL Server is running on an SMP machine and the optimizer estimates that executing the serial version of a plan would exceed the cost threshold, it builds a parallel plan for the query. The optimizer assumes that the query is sufficiently long or complex to benefit from being run in parallel. It believes that the overall gains in performance from executing the plan in parallel will offset the expense of initializing, synchronizing, and terminating the parallel plan. Even though the plan may end up running serially because of other factors on the server, if conditions are right, the optimizer still targets a parallel plan. Sometimes a parallel plan is chosen even though the query's cost ends up being less than the cost threshold because the decision regarding whether to use a parallel plan is based on the optimizer's estimate of query time before the full optimization process has completed.

## Selectivity Estimation

To correctly determine the relative cost of a query plan, the optimizer needs to be able to precisely estimate the number of rows returned by the query. As I mentioned earlier, this is known as *selectivity*, and it's crucial for the optimizer to be able to accurately estimate it.

Selectivity estimates come from comparing query criteria with the statistics for the index key or column they reference. Selectivity tells us to expect a single row for a given key value, or 10,000 rows for a different one. It gives us an idea of how many rows correspond to the key or column value for which we're searching. This, in turn, helps us determine the type of approach that would be the most efficient for accessing those rows. Obviously, you take a different approach to access one row than you would for 10,000.

If the optimizer discovers that you don't have index or column statistics for a column in the query's filter criteria, it may automatically create column-level statistics for the column if you have the AUTO_CREATE_STATISITCS database option enabled. You'll incur the cost of creating the statistics the first time around, but subsequent queries should be sped up by the new statistics.

## Optimizing Search Arguments

A SARG, or search argument, is a clause in a query that the optimizer can potentially use in conjunction with an index to limit the results returned by the query. The optimizer attempts to identify SARGs in a query's criteria so that it can determine the best indexes to use to service the query. SARGs have the form

```
Column op Constant/Variable
```

(the terms can be reversed) where Column is a table column; op is one of the following operators: =, >=, <=, >, <, <>, !=, !>, !<, BETWEEN, and LIKE (some LIKE clauses can be translated to SARGs; some can't); and Constant/Variable is a constant value, variable reference, or one of a handful of functions.

Even though some of these operators do not lend themselves to becoming SARGs, the optimizer can translate them into expressions that do. For example, consider the query in Listing 17–9:

**Listing 17–9** The optimizer can translate != to something SARG-able.

```
SELECT * FROM authors
WHERE au_lname != 'Greene'
```

Is the WHERE clause SARG-able? Yes. Look at the translation that occurs in this excerpt from the query plan:

```
SEEK:([authors].[au_lname] < 'Greene' OR [authors].[au_lname] > 'Greene')
```

The optimizer is smart enough to know that x != @parm is the same as x < @parm OR x > @parm, and translates it accordingly. Because the two branches of the OR clause can be executed in parallel and merged, this affords the use of an index to service the WHERE.

How about this one (Listing 17–10):

**Listing 17–10** LIKE expressions can also be SARG-able.

```
SELECT * FROM authors
WHERE au_lname LIKE 'Gr%'
```

Is it SARG-able? Yes. Once again, the optimizer translates the WHERE clause criteria to something it finds more palatable:

```
SEEK:([authors].[au_lname] >= 'GQ_' AND [authors].[au_lname] < 'GS')
```

Here's another (Listing 17–11):

**Listing 17–11** The optimizer can translate !> to something more usable.

```
SELECT * FROM authors
WHERE au_lname !> 'Greene'
```

Can the optimizer use an index to satisfy the query? Yes it can. Here's an excerpt from the plan:

```
SEEK:([authors].[au_lname] <= 'Greene')
```

Here's one more query (Listing 17–12):

**Listing 17–12** The optimizer can use expressions involving !<.

```
SELECT * FROM authors
WHERE au_lname !< 'Greene'
```

And here's its plan:

```
SEEK:([authors].[au_lname] >= 'Greene')
```

See the pattern? The optimizer attempts to translate seemingly un-SARG-able expressions into ones it can deal with more easily.

SARGs can be joined together with AND to form compound clauses. The rule of thumb for identifying SARGs is that a clause can be a useful search argument if the optimizer can detect that it's a comparison between an index key value and a constant or variable. A clause that compares two columns or one that compares two expressions is not a SARG clause. A common beginner's error is to involve a column in an expression when comparing it with a constant or variable. For the most part, this prevents the clause from being a SARG because the optimizer doesn't know what the expression actually evaluates to—it's not known until runtime. The trick, then, is to isolate the column in these types of expressions so that it's not modified or encapsulated in any way. Use commonsense algebra to put the modifiers in the clause on the value/constant side of the expression and leave the column itself unmodified.

## Join Order and Type Selection

In addition to choosing indexes and identifying SARGs, the optimizer also selects a join order and picks a join strategy. The selection of indexes and join strategy go hand-in-hand: Indexes influence the types of join strategies that are viable, and the join strategy influences the types of indexes the optimizer needs to produce an efficient plan.

SQL Server supports three types of joins:

1. Nested loop—Works well with a smaller outer table and an index on the inner table.
2. Merge—Works well when both inputs are sorted on the joining column (the optimizer can sort one of the inputs if necessary).
3. Hash—Performs well in situations in which there are no usable indexes. Usually, creating an index (so that a different join strategy can be chosen) will provide better performance.

The optimizer determines the join strategy to use to service a query. It evaluates the cost of each strategy and selects the one it thinks will cost the least. It reserves the right to reorder tables in the FROM clause if doing so will improve the performance of the query. You can always tell whether this has happened by inspecting the execution plan. The order of the tables in the execution plan is the order the optimizer thought would perform best.

You can override the optimizer's ability to determine join order using the OPTION (FORCE ORDER) clause for a query and using the SET FORCE-PLAN ON session option. Each of these forces the optimizer to join tables in the order specified by the FROM clause.

Note that forcing join order may have the side effect of also forcing a particular join strategy. For example, consider the query in Listing 17–13:

**Listing 17–13** Right outer joins often result in table reordering by the optimizer.

```
SELECT o.OrderId, p.ProductId
FROM [Order Details] o RIGHT JOIN Products p
ON (o.ProductId=p.ProductId)
```

Here's its execution plan (Listing 17–14):

**Listing 17–14** The optimizer switches the order of the Order Details and Products tables.

```
StmtText
----------------------------------------------------------------------
SELECT o.OrderId, p.ProductId
FROM [Order Details] o RIGHT JOIN Products p
ON (o.ProductId=p.ProductId)
  |--Nested Loops(Left Outer Join, OUTER REFERENCES:(p.ProductID))
     |--Index Scan(OBJECT:(Northwind.dbo.Products.SuppliersProducts AS p))
     |--Index Seek(OBJECT:(Northwind.dbo.[Order Details].ProductID AS o),
        SEEK:(o.ProductID=p.ProductID) ORDERED FORWARD)
```

Notice that it uses a nested loop join and that it reorders the tables (Products is listed first in the plan, even though Order Details is listed first in the FROM clause). Now let's force the join order using the FORCE ORDER query hint (Listing 17–15):

**Listing 17–15** You can force the join order using the FORCE ORDER hint.

```
SELECT o.OrderId, p.ProductId
FROM [Order Details] o RIGHT JOIN Products p ON (o.ProductId=p.ProductId)
OPTION(FORCE ORDER)
```

Look what happens to the query plan (Listing 17–16):

**Listing 17–16** Forcing the join order sometimes changes the join strategy.

```
StmtText
----------------------------------------------------------------------
SELECT o.OrderId, p.ProductId
FROM [Order Details] o RIGHT JOIN Products p ON (o.ProductId=p.ProductId)
OPTION(FORCE ORDER)
  |--Merge Join(Right Outer Join, MANY-TO-MANY MERGE:(o.ProductID)=
     (p.ProductID), RESIDUAL:(o.ProductID=p.ProductID))
        |--Index Scan(OBJECT:(Northwind.dbo.[Order Details].
           ProductsOrder_Details AS o), ORDERED FORWARD)
        |--Clustered Index Scan(OBJECT:(Northwind.dbo.Products.
           PK_Products AS p), ORDERED FORWARD)
```

Because it can't reorder the tables, the optimizer switches to a merge join strategy. This is less efficient than letting the optimizer order the tables as it sees fit and join the tables using a nested loop.

### Nested Loop Joins

Nested loop joins consist of a loop within a loop. A nested loop join designates one table in the join as the outer loop and the other as the inner loop. For each iteration of the outer loop, the entire inner loop is traversed. This works fine for small to medium-sized tables, but as the loops grow larger, this strategy becomes increasingly inefficient. The general process is as follows:

1.  Find a row in the first table.
2.  Use values from that row to find a row in the second table.
3.  Repeat the process until there are no more rows in the first table that match the search criteria.

The optimizer evaluates at least four join combinations even if those combinations are not specified in the join predicate. It balances the cost of evaluating additional combinations with the need to keep down the overall cost of the producing the query plan.

Nested loop joins perform much better than merge joins and hash joins when working with small to medium-sized amounts of data. The query optimizer uses nested loop joins if the outer input is quite small and the inner input is indexed and quite large. It orders the tables so that the smaller input is the outer table and requires a useful index on the inner table. The optimizer always uses the nested loop strategy with theta (nonequality) joins.

### Merge Joins

Merge joins perform much more efficiently with large data sets than nested loop joins. Both tables must be sorted on the merge column in order for the join to work. The optimizer usually chooses a merge join when working with large data sets that are already sorted on the join columns. The optimizer can use index trees to provide the sorted inputs and can also leverage the sort operations of GROUP BY, CUBE, and ORDER BY—the sorting only needs to occur once. If an input is not already sorted, the optimizer may opt to first sort it so that a merge join can be performed if it thinks a merge join is more efficient than a nested loop join. This happens very rarely and is denoted by the SORT operator in the query plan.

A merge join entails the following five steps:

1. Get the first input values from each table.
2. Compare them.
3. If the values are equal, return the rows.
4. If the values are not equal, toss the lower value and use the next input value from that table for the next comparison.
5. Repeat the process until all the rows from one of the tables have been processed.

The optimizer only makes one pass per table. The operation terminates after all the input values from one of the tables have been evaluated. Any values remaining in the other table are not processed.

The optimizer can perform a merge join operation for every type of relational join operation except CROSS JOIN and FULL JOIN. Merge operations can also be used to UNION tables together (because they must be sorted to eliminate duplicates).

### Hash Joins

Hash joins are also more efficient with large data sets than nested loop joins. Additionally, they work well with tables that are not sorted on the join columns. The optimizer typically opts for a hash join when dealing with large inputs, and no index exists to join them or an index exists but is unusable.

SQL Server performs hash joins by hashing the rows from the smaller of the two tables (designated the "build" table) and inserting them into a hash table, then processing the larger table (the "probe" table) a row at a time and scanning the hash table for matches. Because the smaller of the two tables supplies the values in the hash table, the table size is kept to a minimum, and because hashed values rather than real values are used, comparisons can be made between the tables very quickly.

Hash joins are a variation on the concept of hashed indexes that have been available in a handful of advanced DBMS products for several years. With hashed indexes, the hash table is stored permanently—it *is* the index. Data is hashed into slots that have the same hashing value. If the index has a unique contiguous key, what is known as a *minimal perfect hashing function* exists: Every value hashes to its own slot and there are no gaps between slots in the index. If the index is unique but noncontiguous, the next best thing—a *perfect hashing function*—can exist in which every value hashes to its own slot, but there are potentially gaps between them.

If the build and probe inputs are chosen incorrectly (for example, because of inaccurate density estimates), the optimizer reverses them dynamically using a process called *role reversal*.

Hash join operations can service every type of relational join (including UNION and DIFFERENCE operations) except CROSS JOINs. Hashing can also be used to group data and remove duplicates (for example, with vector aggregates—SUM(Quantity) GROUP BY ProductId). When it uses hashing in this fashion, the optimizer uses the same table for both the build and probe roles.

When join inputs are large and of a similar size, a hash join performs comparably with a merge join. When join inputs are large, but differ significantly in size, a hash join will usually outperform a merge join by a fair margin.

## Subqueries and Join Alternatives

A subquery is a query nested within a larger one. Typically, a subquery supplies values for predicate operators such as IN, ANY, and EXISTS, or a single value for a derived column or variable assignment. Subqueries can be used in lots of places, including a query's WHERE and HAVING clauses.

Understand that joins are not inherently better than subqueries. Often the optimizer will normalize a subquery into a join, but this doesn't mean that the subquery was an inefficient coding choice.

When attempting to rework a query to avoid the performance overhead of joins, remember that you can use table variables and temporary tables to store work data for further processing. For extremely complex queries, this may be the best alternative because it affords you complete control over the optimization process. You can break the query into several steps and can control what executes when.

For simple to moderately complex queries, derived tables provide a similar benefit in that they allow you to serialize the order of query processing to some extent. Derived tables work like parentheses in expression evaluation (and are, in fact, delimited with parentheses)—they establish an order of events. When you demote part of a complex SELECT to a derived table, against which you then apply the remainder of the SELECT, you're in effect saying, Do this first, then hand its results to the outer SELECT. This ability alone—the capability to serialize the processing of the query—gives you some of the power of a stored procedure in terms of query evaluation without the complexities or code maintenance.

## Logical and Physical Operators

Physical operators describe what SQL Server is doing to execute the query. Logical operators describe the relational operation used to process the statement. They correspond to the operations in your code that caused particular physical operators to be used. Oftentimes a logical operator maps to multiple physical operators. Because execution plans consist of physical operations, this means that all execution plan steps will have physical operators, but not all will have logical ones.

Each step in an execution plan corresponds to a physical operator: Execution plans consist of a series of physical operators. Query Analyzer's graphical execution plan displays these operations in the title area of its yellow pop-up hint windows. If a step has a logical operator in addition to the physical operator, it will also be displayed in the title area of the window to the right of the physical operator, separated by a slash. For the textual show plan, the **PhysicalOp** column stores the physical operator, whereas the **LogicalOp** column stores the logical operator for a step.

This is best understood by way of example. Consider the query in Listing 17–17:

**Listing 17–17** This query requests a relational inner join.

```
SELECT *
FROM Orders o JOIN [Order Details] d ON (o.OrderID = d.OrderID)
```

The optimizer chooses a merge join for it, although the query itself obviously doesn't ask for one. Relationally, the query is performing an inner join between the two tables. Here's an excerpt from its textual show plan (Listing 17–18):

**Listing 17–18** The logical operation is INNER JOIN; the physical one is MERGE JOIN.

```
PhysicalOp          LogicalOp            Argument
------------------- -------------------- -------------------------------
Merge Join          Inner Join           MERGE:([o].[OrderID])=([d].[Or
Clustered Index Scan Clustered Index Scan OBJECT:([Northwind].[dbo].[Ord
Clustered Index Scan Clustered Index Scan OBJECT:([Northwind].[dbo].[Ord
```

Notice that the **PhysicalOp** column lists MERGE JOIN as the operator. This is what happens behind the scenes to service the operation spelled out in the **LogicalOp** column: INNER JOIN. An inner join is what we requested via our query. The server chose a MERGE JOIN as the physical operator to carry out our request.

Besides deciding which index to use and which join strategy to apply, the optimizer has additional decisions to make regarding other types of operations. A few of them are presented in the following pages:

### DISTINCT

When the optimizer encounters DISTINCT or UNION in a query, it must remove duplicates from the inputs before returning a result set. It has a couple of options here. It can sort the data to remove duplicates, or it can hash it. The optimizer may service the DISTINCT or UNION logical operation using a hash or sort physical operator. (Stream Aggregate—the same physical operator often used for GROUP BY queries—is also a popular choice here.)

### GROUP BY

The optimizer can service GROUP BY queries using plain sorts or by hashing. Again, the physical operator may be HASH or SORT, but the logical operator remains AGGREGATE OR something similar. Also, STREAM AGGREGATE is a popular choice for GROUP BY operations.

Because the optimizer may choose to perform a HASH operation to group the data, the result set may not come back in sorted order. You can't rely on GROUP BY to sort data automatically. If you want the result set sorted, include an ORDER BY clause.

### ORDER BY

Even with ORDER BY, the optimizer has a decision to make. Assuming no clustered index exists that has already sorted the data, the optimizer has to come up with a way to return the result set in the requested order. It can sort the data, as we'd naturally expect, or it can traverse the leaf level of an appropriately keyed nonclustered index. Whether it does this depends on a number of factors. The biggest one is selectivity: How many rows will be returned by the query? Equally relevant is index covering: Can the nonclustered index cover the query? If the number of rows is relatively low, it may be cheaper to use the nonclustered index than to sort the entire table. Likewise, if the index can cover the query, you've got the next best thing to having a second clustered index, and the optimizer will likely use it.

### Spooling

The Spooling operator in a query plan indicates that the optimizer is saving the results from an intermediate query in a table for further processing. With a lazy spool, the worktable is populated as needed. With an eager spool, the table is populated in one step. The optimizer favors lazy spools over eager spools because of the possibility that it may be able to avoid having to fill the worktable completely based on logic deeper in the query plan. There are cases when eager

**Table 17–3** The Optimizer's Physical Operators

| PhysicalOp | Meaning |
|---|---|
| ASSERT | Indicates a subquery is being used in a situation in which it is only allowed to return one row (use SELECT TOP 1 in the subquery to eliminate the Assert). |
| BOOKMARK LOOKUP | Indicates that the RID or clustered index key stored in a nonclustered index is being used to look up data in the underlying table or clustered index. |
| CONSTANT SCAN | Indicates that the optimizer knows in advance that a condition will never be true. |
| CURSOR OPERATIONS | Indicates operations with server-side cursors. |
| FILTER | Indicates that data is being reduced (probably using WHERE clause criteria) before being passed on. |
| JOINS | A nested loop, merge, or hash join is occurring. |
| SCAN | Indicates a sequential search of the leaf-level nodes of an index. |
| SEEK | Indicates a binary (nonsequential) search of an index B-tree. |
| SORT | Indicates data is being sorted before being passed to the next step. |
| SPOOL | Indicates that the optimizer is saving the results from an intermediate query plan step in a worktable for further processing. |
| STREAM AGGREGATE | Indicates vector aggregation or grouping is occurring. |

spools are necessary—for example, to protect against the Halloween problem—but, generally, the optimizer prefers lazy spools because of their reduced overhead.

Spool operations can be performed on tables as well as indexes. The optimizer uses a rowcount spool when all it needs to know is whether a row exists.

Table 17–3 lists the physical operators the SQL Server optimizer uses and their meanings.

## Summary

You've just toured the way in which SQL Server processes and optimizes query plans. Understanding how this process works is key to designing efficient databases and writing speedy queries. Once you have a grasp of the internal mechanics of SQL Server query processing, you have the tools you need to develop your own best practices and tuning methodologies.

# Debugging and Profiling

*The program may not be broken, but it does hurt.*

*—Martin Fowler*[1]

In this chapter we'll talk about debugging and profiling Transact-SQL stored procedures. We'll also talk about how to stress test SQL Server using Transact-SQL queries and a free stress testing tool that you'll find on the book's CD.

## Debugging

The best tool for debugging Transact-SQL stored procedures comes right in the SQL Server box. Query Analyzer now includes a full-featured stored procedure debugger. You can set breakpoints, establish watches, and generally do what debuggers are designed to do—debug code. You can debug procedures from the current version of SQL Server back through SQL Server 6.5 Service Pack 2.

The interface by which this occurs is known as the SQL Server Debug Interface, or SDI for short. It was originally introduced with SQL Server 6.5 and has since been completely integrated with Visual Studio and, now, Query Analyzer.

### Setup and Security Issues

You should run SQL Server under a user account, not the LocalSystem account, when debugging. Running under LocalSystem disables breakpoints. If you attempt to debug a procedure and it executes without letting you step through code and without stopping at breakpoints, the SQL Server service is probably set up to log in as LocalSystem.

On a machine with multiple instances of SQL Server, if you do not have a default (unnamed) instance, the debugger won't work properly. Your procedure

---

[1]Fowler, Martin. *Refactoring: Improving the Design of Existing Code*. Reading, MA; Addison-Wesley, 1999. Page 7.

will simply execute without stopping for breakpoints. It will behave as though SQL Server is running under the LocalSystem account even when it isn't. This is because it erroneously uses the credentials from the default instance for debugging on *any* instance. The workaround is to create a default instance and set up its login info to match that of the named instance.

If you're debugging under a named instance on a machine that has a default instance, debugging will fail to work if the login info of the *default* instance does not allow it. Again, this is because SQL Server uses the login info of the *default* instance regardless of which instance you're actually debugging under. For example, even if you have your named instance set up to use a domain account for the SQL Server service, T-SQL debugging won't work properly if the default instance logs in with LocalSystem. If the account info differs between your named instance and the default instance, the debugger will use the wrong login credentials and may fail to work properly.

## General Advice and Caveats

- On Windows NT and 2000, SDI messages are written to the event log under MSDEVSDI.
- You can only debug one stored procedure at a time. If you try to debug another routine while one is currently being debugged, you'll be asked whether to terminate the current debugging session.
- Try not to debug stored procedures on a production server. Debugging can tie up system resources, blocking other users and reducing concurrency.
- Debugging stored procedures over a Windows Terminal Server session does not work properly. The best workaround is to use a different remote control technology such as PC Anywhere, NetMeeting, or Laplink.
- Raising an error within a stored procedure with a severity of 16 or higher while debugging seems to break the debugger. On my server, all debugging options suddenly become unavailable once the message is raised, and the debugger begins to behave erratically.
- Although the debugger's Local Variables window can display **sql_variant, cursor, image, text,** and **ntext** variables, you cannot modify them.
- You can't modify a stored procedure while it's being debugged.
- The debugger's Watch window displays only the first 255 characters of a **char** or **varchar** variable, regardless of how long it actually is.
- You cannot place a table variable in the debugger's Watch window.
- You can't debug extended stored procedures using Query Analyzer's debugger. Extended stored procedures reside in DLLs and are usually written in C or C++. See Chapter 20 for instructions on how to debug them.

- You can't open a new connection (from within a single instance of Query Analyzer) while debugging. If you need another connection, start another instance of Query Analyzer.

## Steps

To debug a procedure, follow these steps:

1. Open the Query Analyzer Object Browser and find the stored procedure you want to debug.
2. Right-click it and select Debug from the pop-up menu.
3. Supply any required parameters for the stored procedure and click OK.
4. The debugger will then start, and you can set breakpoints, add watch variables, and so forth, using the menus or via the keyboard.
5. Note that you can also start a debugging session from the Object Search tool.

## Debugging Without a Net

If you're ever forced to debug stored procedures without using the built-in debugger—either at gunpoint or at a remote site where they can't spare enough disk space for Query Analyzer—here are a few tips to help you survive:

- You can lace your code with PRINT statements to send debug info to the results window. PRINT can display any scalar variable and also supports string concatenation and other basic expressions.
- You can use xp_logevent to log diagnostic info in the system error and event logs.
- You can use sp_trace_generate_event to add a user-defined event to a Profiler trace.
- You can use the undocumented sp_user_counter*N* procedures to set user-defined Perfmon/Sysmon counter values from within Transact-SQL. For example, this would allow you to trace the changes over time in the value of a stored procedure variable in a Perfmon chart or log.
- There are several undocumented trace flags that aid with debugging complex Transact-SQL. Have a look at Chapter 22 for a list of some of them.
- A technique I often use to debug complex stored procedures is to take the code from the procedure and put it in a command batch. Then I can run it a section at a time and comment/uncomment parts of it as I work through the problem.

### Debugging Triggers and User-Defined Functions

To debug a trigger or UDF, debug a stored procedure that uses it, even if you have to create one for that express purpose. For example, to debug a trigger, you could first set up a stored procedure that modifies the trigger's table such that the trigger fires. When you debug the procedure, you'll be able to step into the trigger (by stepping into the DML statement). The same is true with UDFs. Set up a stored procedure that calls the function, then debug the stored procedure.

# Profiling

SQL Server's Profiler is also a fairly capable tool. It could be a lot better, but it provides the basic functionality you need, and it's a vast improvement over the SQL Trace facility in releases of SQL Server prior to 7.0. It presents a graphical interface wherein you specify the events for which you'd like to watch on the server. You can trace virtually anything that happens on the server—from T-SQL batches to stored procedures to sort warnings and error log entries.

### Starting a Trace

To start a new trace using Profiler, follow these steps:

1. Click File|New|Trace in the Profiler GUI to bring up the Trace Properties dialog.
2. Specify the trace attributes you want, selecting the elements that make the most sense in your particular situation. As a rule, select all columns.
3. Click the Run button. You should see the trace start.

### Tracing versus Viewing

I strongly encourage you to use stored procedures to run traces. The traces you generate via stored procedures can still be viewed in Profiler, so you lose nothing in terms of analyzing a trace file once it's collected. What you gain is a means of gathering trace information that will be much less burdensome on your SQL Server.

### Command-Line Parameters

In addition to its GUI interface, SQL Profiler supports a few command-line parameters that can be used to control how it works. Table 18–1 summarizes them.

**Table 18-1** SQL Profiler Command-line Options

| Option | Meaning |
|--------|---------|
| /S | Specifies a trace definition to start. |
| /F | Specifies a trace file to open. |
| /D | Specifies a trace definition file to open. |

## General Advice and Caveats

- If possible, don't run Profiler on your SQL Server machine. Run it on a different machine and connect across the network. I've seen Profiler take as much as 80% of the CPU time on a reasonably fast machine. This doesn't leave much for SQL Server.

- Never trace to a table. Tracing to a table forces Profiler to open a loopback connection over ODBC to the SQL Server to work with the table. Tracing to a table has been known to eat up resources on the server and is generally a bad idea.

- Don't trace events you don't need, especially statement-level events. Tracing too many events can have a noticeable performance impact on your server and will bloat your trace files.

- As a rule, include all columns in your traces. It's not that much more expensive to do so, and some events depend on certain columns being present to return useful info or ancillary details. For example, Profiler's showplan events won't display correctly unless the **BinaryData** column is included. If you don't want to include every column in the trace, I think a good standard set would include at least the following ones:
  - **BinaryData**
  - **ClientProcessID**
  - **CPU**
  - **Duration**
  - **EndTime**
  - **EventClass**
  - **EventSubClass**
  - **HostName**
  - **IntegerData**
  - **LoginName**
  - **NTUserName**
  - **Reads**
  - **SPID**
  - **StartTime**

- **TextData**
- **Writes**

Keep in mind that the event classes use the various ancillary fields in different ways. Often, fields like EventSubClass and IntegerData contain information that further defines a particular type of event.

- Remember that you can place bookmarks (Ctrl-F2) in a trace file as you browse through it in Profiler and can jump (F2) from bookmark to bookmark.

- When you can, use the sp_trace_XXXX extended procedures to start and stop traces. See the sp_start_trace routine in Chapter 21 for an example of how to do this. Using the sp_trace_XXXX procedures can greatly reduce the performance impact of running Profiler traces on your system.

- You can use the File|Script Trace menu option to generate a T-SQL batch that will start the currently defined trace using extended procedure calls. If nothing else, this is a great way to learn how to build these kinds of routines, even if you don't end up using the generated script. Listing 18–1 shows what one of these scripts looks like:

**Listing 18–1** Profiler will generate T-SQL tracing code for you.

```
*******************************************************/
/* Created by: SQL Profiler                          */
/* Date: 09/10/2000 00:14:40 AM                      */
/*******************************************************/

-- Create a Queue
declare @rc int
declare @TraceID int
declare @maxfilesize bigint
set @maxfilesize = 5

-- Please replace the text InsertFileNameHere, with an appropriate
-- filename prefixed by a path, e.g., c:\MyFolder\MyTrace. The .trc
-- extension will be appended to the filename automatically. If you are
-- writing from remote server to local drive, please use UNC path and make
-- sure server has write access to your network share

exec @rc = sp_trace_create @TraceID output, 0, N'InsertFileNameHere',
@maxfilesize, NULL
if (@rc != 0) goto error
```

```
-- Client-side File and Table cannot be scripted

-- Set the events
declare @on bit
set @on = 1
exec sp_trace_setevent @TraceID, 10, 1, @on
exec sp_trace_setevent @TraceID, 10, 6, @on
exec sp_trace_setevent @TraceID, 10, 9, @on
exec sp_trace_setevent @TraceID, 10, 10, @on
exec sp_trace_setevent @TraceID, 10, 11, @on
exec sp_trace_setevent @TraceID, 10, 12, @on
exec sp_trace_setevent @TraceID, 10, 13, @on
exec sp_trace_setevent @TraceID, 10, 14, @on
exec sp_trace_setevent @TraceID, 10, 16, @on
exec sp_trace_setevent @TraceID, 10, 17, @on
exec sp_trace_setevent @TraceID, 10, 18, @on
exec sp_trace_setevent @TraceID, 12, 1, @on
exec sp_trace_setevent @TraceID, 12, 6, @on
exec sp_trace_setevent @TraceID, 12, 9, @on
exec sp_trace_setevent @TraceID, 12, 10, @on
exec sp_trace_setevent @TraceID, 12, 11, @on
exec sp_trace_setevent @TraceID, 12, 12, @on
exec sp_trace_setevent @TraceID, 12, 13, @on
exec sp_trace_setevent @TraceID, 12, 14, @on
exec sp_trace_setevent @TraceID, 12, 16, @on
exec sp_trace_setevent @TraceID, 12, 17, @on
exec sp_trace_setevent @TraceID, 12, 18, @on
exec sp_trace_setevent @TraceID, 14, 1, @on
exec sp_trace_setevent @TraceID, 14, 6, @on
exec sp_trace_setevent @TraceID, 14, 9, @on
exec sp_trace_setevent @TraceID, 14, 10, @on
exec sp_trace_setevent @TraceID, 14, 11, @on
exec sp_trace_setevent @TraceID, 14, 12, @on
exec sp_trace_setevent @TraceID, 14, 13, @on
exec sp_trace_setevent @TraceID, 14, 14, @on
exec sp_trace_setevent @TraceID, 14, 16, @on
exec sp_trace_setevent @TraceID, 14, 17, @on
exec sp_trace_setevent @TraceID, 14, 18, @on
exec sp_trace_setevent @TraceID, 15, 1, @on
exec sp_trace_setevent @TraceID, 15, 6, @on
exec sp_trace_setevent @TraceID, 15, 9, @on
exec sp_trace_setevent @TraceID, 15, 10, @on
exec sp_trace_setevent @TraceID, 15, 11, @on
exec sp_trace_setevent @TraceID, 15, 12, @on
```

```
exec sp_trace_setevent @TraceID, 15, 13, @on
exec sp_trace_setevent @TraceID, 15, 14, @on
exec sp_trace_setevent @TraceID, 15, 16, @on
exec sp_trace_setevent @TraceID, 15, 17, @on
exec sp_trace_setevent @TraceID, 15, 18, @on
exec sp_trace_setevent @TraceID, 17, 1, @on
exec sp_trace_setevent @TraceID, 17, 6, @on
exec sp_trace_setevent @TraceID, 17, 9, @on
exec sp_trace_setevent @TraceID, 17, 10, @on
exec sp_trace_setevent @TraceID, 17, 11, @on
exec sp_trace_setevent @TraceID, 17, 12, @on
exec sp_trace_setevent @TraceID, 17, 13, @on
exec sp_trace_setevent @TraceID, 17, 14, @on
exec sp_trace_setevent @TraceID, 17, 16, @on
exec sp_trace_setevent @TraceID, 17, 17, @on
exec sp_trace_setevent @TraceID, 17, 18, @on
-- Set the Filters
declare @intfilter int
declare @bigintfilter bigint

exec sp_trace_setfilter @TraceID, 10, 0, 7, N'SQL Profiler'

-- Set the trace status to start
exec sp_trace_setstatus @TraceID, 1

-- display trace id for future references
select TraceID=@TraceID
goto finish

error:
select ErrorCode=@rc

finish:
go
```

Note the use of the @On bit variable. Many extended procedures, including those used to manage Profiler traces, have parameters that are very strongly typed. Because there's no way to tell sp_trace_setevent to cast the 1 that's passed into it as a bit, the script is forced to put the 1 in a bit variable and pass it to the extended procedure instead. You'll notice that the sp_start_trace routines in Chapter 21 do the same thing.

■ Remember that you can use filters to reduce the amount and type of data that's traced. Again, overtracing will slow down your server measurably.

- If you do end up managing traces using Profiler and discover that you use a given collection of events, columns, and filters repeatedly, set up a trace definition file to package them together so that you can use it to define your traces easily and consistently. Profiler comes with a number of trace definition files already set up.
- You can feed Profiler trace files into the Index Tuning wizard in order to receive automated help regarding index tuning and design.
- Profiler trace events can be used to audit security-related activities on the server. Add the Security Audit group of event classes to a trace to see how this works. As pointed out in Chapter 22, you can generate auditing events from your own applications using DBCC AUDITEVENT(). These will show up in a Profiler trace as Security Audit events.
- Make sure your TEMP folder has plenty of space. Profiler uses this area for a variety of things, and the files it creates there can be huge.
- The search facility in Profiler is case sensitive. If you search for something that you know is there, but it isn't found, check the case of your search string.
- Keep in mind that you can save Profiler traces as Transact-SQL. This allows you to play back those traces in any tool that can run T-SQL, including Query Analyzer and OSQL.

## Replaying Traces

One of the more powerful aspects of having events collected by Profiler is that they can be played back. Once the trace file is created, just load it into Profiler and press F5 to replay it. There are some events that Profiler is simply incapable of playing back (the Attention event is one of them), but this works pretty well for the most part.

## Loading a Trace File into a Table

Something that's really handy when you're working with large trace files is to load them into a table and use Transact-SQL to query, aggregate, pivot them, and so forth. The ::fn_trace_gettable() system function allows you to do this very easily. It's a rowset function that you can use to read a Profiler trace file from within a SELECT statement (Listing 18–2):

**Listing 18–2** The ::fn_trace_gettable() system function lists the contents of a trace file.

```
SELECT * FROM ::fn_trace_gettable('c:\temp\test.trc',DEFAULT)
```

(Results abridged)

```
TextData
-----------------------------------------------------------------------
network protocol: Named Pipes
set quoted_identifier off
set implicit_transactions off
set cursor_close_on_commit off
set ansi_warnings on
set ansi_padding on
set ansi_nulls on
set concat_null_yields_null on
set language us_english
set dateformat mdy
set datefirst 7
```

Of course, you can insert the results of a SELECT FROM ::fn_trace_get-table() query into a separate table for permanent storage or further analysis. Keep in mind that any trace file you open using ::fn_trace_gettable() must be accessible from the server, and remember that the path you specify is relevant to the server, *not* your local machine.

## Emitting a Trace File as XML

If you'd rather work with a trace file as an XML document instead of a SQL Server table, this is easy enough to do. A nifty side benefit of the fact that Transact-SQL can translate SELECT results into XML is that you can translate a Profiler trace file into an XML document with a single command (Listing 18–3):

**Listing 18–3** It's easy to translate a trace file to XML.

```
SELECT TextData,
       DatabaseID,
       TransactionID,
       NTUserName,
       NTDomainName,
       HostName,
       ClientProcessID,
       ApplicationName,
       LoginName,
       SPID,
```

```
        Duration,
        StartTime,
        EndTime,
        Reads,
        Writes,
        CPU,
        Permissions,
        Severity,
        EventSubClass,
        ObjectID,
        Success,
        IndexID,
        IntegerData,
        ServerName,
        EventClass,
        ObjectType,
        NestLevel,
        State,
        Error,
        Mode,
        Handle,
        ObjectName,
        DatabaseName,
        FileName,
        OwnerName,
        RoleName,
        TargetUserName,
        DBUserName,
        TargetLoginName,
        ColumnPermissions
FROM ::fn_trace_gettable('c:\_temp\test.trc',DEFAULT)
FOR XML AUTO
```

Note the FOR XML AUTO clause at the end of the SELECT. This is what's responsible for the SELECT result being translated into XML. Once the data is in XML format, you can use an XML style sheet to translate it into virtually any other format.

## Grouping Profiler Data

Profiler can group the data in a trace display based on a column or columns. This allows for easier navigation and analysis of trace info. To group on a set of columns:

1. Bring up the Trace Properties dialog.
2. Switch to the Data Columns tab.
3. Use the Up and Down buttons to move columns in and out of the Groups branch on the right side of the dialog.

## ODBC Tracing

If you connect to SQL Server over ODBC and you're having trouble getting the info you need from Profiler, you can set up a separate ODBC trace at the driver level. You do this from the Tracing tab in the ODBC Administrator. This will at least tell you what's being sent to the server and what's being returned. Be sure to turn off the ODBC trace when you're finished with it.

# Stress Testing

There are a number of powerful third-party tools available for stress testing SQL Server. Many of these are quite expensive. What I'm about to show isn't as advanced as these types of tools, nor does it have the extensive feature set that many of them have. But it does have one advantage over them: It's free. STRESS.CMD, my SQL Server stressing tool, is a poor man's robo-test—you give it a T-SQL script to run and it runs the script a specified number of times against a SQL Server. STRESS.CMD has five main features:

1. It can run a specified T-SQL script repetitively against a SQL Server.
2. It can run one script multiple times or run many scripts once, or some combination of the two.
3. It can route output to the console or it can log each script's output individually.
4. It can display, hide, or minimize each script window.
5. It can run all scripts concurrently or it can run them one after the other.

**NOTE:** Microsoft publishes a tool called SQL70IOStress that tests the performance of a disk subsystem for use with SQL Server. This is not the kind of stress test I'm talking about here. What I'm referring to here is a tool that's capable of simulating multiple users connected to a SQL Server simultaneously, each running Transact-SQL queries against the server that stress it in some way.

Listing 18–4 shows the full source code to STRESS.CMD. This is a routine I originally wrote many years ago (on OS/2, no less) and have gradually developed over the years. You'll need the Windows 2000 command extensions enabled (they're on by default in Windows 2000) to use this code:

**Listing 18–4** STRESS.CMD, a homegrown SQL Server stress test tool.

```
@echo off

REM Check for too few or too many parms and error
IF (%1)==() GOTO ERROR
IF NOT (%9)==() GOTO ERROR

REM Set some default values

SET ggmask=%1
SET ggtimes=1
SET ggwait=NO
SET ggserv=(local)
SET gguser=-E
SET ggwaitparm=/NORMAL
SET ggwin=NORMAL
SET ggout=YES

REM Move parameters to variables

IF NOT (%2)==() SET ggtimes=%2
IF NOT (%3)==() SET ggwait=%3
IF NOT (%4)==() SET ggwin=%4
IF NOT (%5)==() SET ggout=%5
IF NOT (%6)==() SET ggserv=%6
IF NOT (%7)==() SET gguser=%7

REM Set this to empty if not supplied

SET ggpwd=%8

REM Set this to empty

SET ggoutparm=%9

REM Further process some of the parameters

IF NOT (%ggpwd%)==() SET ggpwd=-P%ggpwd%
IF /i %ggwait%==YES SET ggwaitparm=/WAIT
IF NOT %gguser%==-E SET gguser=-U%gguser%
```

```
IF /i %ggout%==YES SET ggoutparm=-o%%~nf.OUT

REM Run the script(s) using a nested loop
REM
REM The inner loop iterates through the files matching the mask and runs
them
REM The outer loop executes the inner loop the number of times specified

FOR /L %%i in (1,1,%ggtimes%) DO FOR %%f IN (%ggmask%) DO START "%%f"
     %ggwaitparm% /%ggwin% OSQL.EXE -S%ggserv% %gguser% %ggpwd% -i%%f
     %ggoutparm%

GOTO NOERROR

:ERROR
echo You must specify a script to run
SET ERRORLEVEL=1
ECHO STRESS.CMD
ECHO .
ECHO Runs specified Transact-SQL script(s) multiple times simultaneously
ECHO .
ECHO Copyright (c) 1992, Ken Henderson. All rights reserved.
ECHO Based on my code in User-to-User, PC Magazine, March 26, 1991.
ECHO .
ECHO USAGE: STRESS script [N] [wait] [windowstyle] [saveoutput] [server]
[user] [password]
ECHO .
ECHO where:
ECHO    script = the script or mask you want to run
ECHO    N = the number of times you want to run it (default 1)
ECHO    wait = YES to wait for each script to finish before running next
(default NO)
ECHO    windowstyle = type of window to create for each script execution:
ECHO .
ECHO          MIN = minimized MAX = maximized B = no window NORMAL = normal
window
ECHO .
ECHO    saveoutput = YES to save output to file using -o OSQL parameter
(default YES)
ECHO    server = the server to run it on (default (local) )
ECHO    user = your SS user name (default - use trusted connection)
ECHO    password = your SS password (default - use trusted connection)
:NOERROR
```

STRESS.CMD takes up to eight parameters. These parameters are positional (in other words, to specify parameter five, you must also specify parameters one through four) and have the meanings detailed in Table 18–2:

**Table 18–2** STRESS.CMD Command-line Parameters

| Parameter | Meaning |
| --- | --- |
| SCRIPT | The script or mask you want to run |
| N | The number of times you want to run it (default, 1) |
| WAIT | YES to wait for each script to finish before running the next one (default, NO) |
| WINDOWSTYLE | Type of window to create for each script execution: MIN, minimized; MAX, maximized; B, no window; NORMAL, normal window (default, normal) |
| SAVEOUTPUT | YES to save output to file using OSQL -o parameter (default, YES) |
| SERVER | The server on which to run it (default, **local**)) |
| USER | Your SS user name (default, use trusted connection) |
| PASSWORD | Your SS password (default, use trusted connection) |

A call to STRESS.CMD might look like this:

```
stress stress.sql 10 no normal no dragonzlair
```

In this example, the script stress.sql will be executed ten times. We won't wait for each execution to finish before starting another, nor are we interested in saving the output to a file. The name of the server we're connecting to is dragonzlair, and we'll use a trusted connection to log in.

Another STRESS.CMD might look like this:

```
stress stress*.sql 100 no min yes dragonzlair monty python
```

Here we're going to execute all the scripts that match the mask stress°.sql in the current directory. Second, we're going to execute any scripts we find 100 times asynchronously. Third, we're going to minimize each script window and save the output of each execution to a file (using OSQL's -o option). Last, we'll connect to SQL Server dragonzlair using user name monty and password python.

As you can see, you can come up some pretty exotic combinations to throw at your servers. Anything you can put in a T-SQL script, you can run via

STRESS.CMD. You can run multiple scripts or just one, and you can run them as many times as you want.

You can run scripts concurrently or synchronously and can direct their results to the screen or to text files. You can cause Attention events on the server by pressing Ctrl-C to stop a running script, and you can stop the whole process by pressing Ctrl-C repeatedly until you're asked whether to terminate the command batch.

STRESS.CMD takes much of the tedium out of stress testing SQL Server. And it does so with a very small .CMD file that you can customize or use in conjunction with other operating system commands.

Some years ago I wrote a tool like this in C. It used the DB-Library API to do much of what this command file does. It was a handy tool, but the problem was that it seemed I was never done with it. People kept asking me to add "just one more feature" to it. I'd find myself still up at five o'clock in the morning working on "just one more feature" just to keep my users happy. Finally, I decided to scrap it and publish something people could change themselves if they wanted to. So I blew the dust off something I'd written for a magazine, changed it a bit, and STRESS.CMD was born. These days, when someone wants "just one more feature," I say, "Hey, you've got the source—have at it!" Now, if I could only find a way to get them to work for free on *the rest* of my code.

## Summary

In this chapter you learned how to debug, profile, and test Transact-SQL stored procedure code. SQL Server has several nice tools for debugging, profiling, and stress testing end-user code. And as STRESS.CMD demonstrates, it isn't hard to come up with your own when what comes in the box doesn't quite meet your needs.

# CHAPTER 19

# Automation

*Whether we are building a plane in the living room, writing a book at two o'clock in the morning, or developing components, most of our time and energy is spent on thousands of details.*

*—Dale Rogerson[1]*

In this chapter we'll talk about automating (in other words, controlling) COM objects with Transact-SQL. Before we do this, though, let's review a bit about COM itself and discuss why we might want to control a COM object from Transact-SQL.

## A Brief Overview of COM

If you've built many Windows applications, you probably have at least a passing familiarity with OLE and ActiveX. OLE originally stood for Object Linking and Embedding and represented the first generation of cross-application object access and manipulation in Windows. The idea was to have a document-centric view of the world where an object from one application could happily reside in and interact with another. OLE 1.0 used DDE (dynamic data exchange) to facilitate communication between objects. DDE is a message-based inter-process communication mechanism that's based on the Windows messaging architecture. DDE has a number of shortcomings (it's slow, inflexible, difficult to program, and so on), so the second version of OLE was moved away from it.

The second iteration of OLE was rewritten to depend entirely on COM. And even though COM is more efficient and faster than DDE, OLE is still a bit of a bear to deal with. Why? Because it was the first-ever implementation of COM. We've learned a lot since then. That said, OLE provides functionality that's very powerful and very rich. It may be big, slow, and hard to code to, but that's not COM's fault—that has to do with how OLE itself was built.

---

[1]Rogerson, Dale. *Inside COM*. Redmond, WA: Microsoft Press, 2000. Page 128.

ActiveX is also built on COM. The original and still primary focus of ActiveX is on Internet-enabled components. ActiveX is a set of technologies whose primary mission is to enable interactive content (hence, the "Active" designation) on Web pages. Formerly known as OLE controls or OCX controls, ActiveX controls are components you can insert into a Web page or Windows application to make use of packaged functionality provided by a third party.

COM is the foundation on which OLE and ActiveX controls are built. Through COM, an object can expose its functionality to other components and applications. In addition to defining an object's life cycle and how the object exposes itself to the outside world, COM also defines how this exposure works across processes and networks.

COM is Microsoft's answer to the fundamental questions: How do I expose the classes in my code to other applications in a language-neutral fashion? How do I provide an object-oriented way for users of my DLL to use it? How can people make use of my work without needing source code or header files?

## Before COM

There was a time not so long ago in software development when it was quite normal to distribute full source code and/or header files with third-party libraries. To make use of these libraries, people simply compiled them (or included their header files) into applications. The end result was a single executable that might contain code from many different vendors. Because it was common for many developers to use the same third-party library, a version of the library might exist in the executables deployed with numerous products. Executables tended to be relatively large and there was little or no code sharing between them. Updating one of these third-party libraries required recompilation and/or relinking because the library was incorporated directly into the executable at compile time.

This all changed with Windows' introduction of DLLs. Almost overnight, it became quite common for third-party vendors to ship only header files and binaries. Instead of being able to deploy a single executable, the developer would end up distributing a sometimes sizeable collection of DLLs with his application. At runtime, it was up to the application to load—either implicitly or explicitly—the DLLs provided by the third-party vendor. As applications became more complex, it was not uncommon to see executables that required dozens of DLLs with complex interdependencies between them.

**NOTE:** This is, in fact, how Windows itself works. Windows is an executable with a large collection of DLLs. Windows apps make calls to the functions exposed by these DLLs.

This approach worked reasonably well, but it had several drawbacks. One of the main ones was that the interfaces to these DLLs weren't object-oriented, and therefore were difficult to extend and susceptible to being broken by even minor changes to an exposed function. If a vendor added a new parameter to a function in his third-party library, he might well break the code of everyone currently using that library. The approach most vendors took to address this was simply to create a new version of the function (often with an "Ex" suffix or something similar) that included the new parameter. The end result was call-level interfaces (CLIs) that became unmanageable very quickly. It was common for third-party libraries (and even Windows itself) to include multiple versions of the same function call in an attempt to be compatible with every version of the library that had ever existed. The situation quickly grew out of control and was exacerbated by the fact that there was no easy, direct method for users of these libraries to know which of the many versions of a given function should be used. Coding to these interfaces became a trial-and-error exercise that involved lots of scouring API manuals and guesswork.

Another big problem with this approach was the proliferation of multiple copies of the same DLL across a user's computer. Hard drive space was once much more expensive than it is now, so having multiple copies of a library in different places on an end user's system was something vendors sought to avoid. Unfortunately, their solution to the problem wasn't really very well thought out. Their answer was to put the DLLs their apps needed in the Windows system directory. This addressed the problem of having multiple copies of the same DLL, but introduced a whole host of others.

Chief among these were the problems inherent with conflicting versions of the same DLL. If vendor A and vendor B depended on different versions of a DLL produced by vendor C, there was a strong likelihood that one of their products would be broken by the other's version of the DLL. If the interface to the DLL changed even slightly between versions, it was quite likely that at least one of the apps would misbehave (if it worked at all) when presented with a version of the DLL it wasn't expecting.

Another problem with centralizing DLLs was the trouble that arose from centralized, yet unmanaged configuration information. In the days before the Windows registry, it was common to have a separate configuration file (usually with an .INI extension) for every application (and even multiple configuration files for some applications). These configuration files might include paths to DLLs of which the application made use, further complicating the task of unraveling DLL versioning problems. Because these configuration files were not managed by Windows itself, there was nothing to stop an application from completely wiping out a needed configuration file, putting entries into it that might break other applications, or completely ignoring it. These .INI files were simply text files that an application could use or not use as it saw fit.

The progression used by Windows to locate DLLs was logical and well documented; however, the fact that an application might use Windows' LoadLibrary and grab a DLL from anywhere it pleased on a user's hard drive meant that this might not mean anything in terms of knowing what code an application actually depended on. The app might pick up a load path from a configuration file that no one else even knew about, or it might just search the hard drive and load what it thought was the best version of the library. It was common for applications to have subtle interdependencies that made the applications themselves rather brittle. We had come full circle from the days of bloated executables and little or no code sharing: Now everyone depended on everyone else, with the installation of one app frequently breaking another.

## The Dawn of COM

Microsoft's answer to these problems was COM. Simply put, COM provides an interface to third-party code that is:

- Object-oriented
- Centralized
- Versioned
- Language-neutral

Because it uses the system registry, the days of unmanaged/improperly used configuration information are gone. When an application instantiates a COM object (usually through a call to CreateObject()), Windows checks the system registry to find the object's location on disk and loads it. There's no guesswork and multiple copies of the same object aren't allowed—each COM object lives in exactly one place on the system.

---

**NOTE:** Microsoft has recently introduced the concept of COM redirection and side-by-side deployment. This allows multiple versions of the same COM object to reside happily on the same system. This functionality has all the hallmarks of an afterthought and is only applicable in limited circumstances. (You can't, for example, use COM redirection to load different copies of an object into different Web applications on an IIS implementation. Although the Web pages may seem like different apps to users, there's actually just one application—IIS—in the scenario, and COM still limits a given app to just one copy of a particular object version.) The vast majority of COM applications still abide by the standard COM versioning constraints.

---

This isn't to say that you can't have multiple versions of an object on a system. COM handles this through multiple interfaces. Each new version of an object has its own interface and may as well be a completely separate object as far as its users are concerned. There may or may not be code sharing between the versions of the object. As an application developer, you try not to worry about this—you just code to the interface.

Lest I omit a very fundamental detail, an interface is similar to a class without a body or implementation. It's a programming construct that defines a functionality contract—a contract between the provider of the functionality and its users. By implementing an interface, the author of the object ensures that clients of the object can depend on a fixed set of functionality being present in the object. Regardless of what the object actually is, the client can code to the interface without being concerned about the details. If the author of the object ever needs to enhance his code in a way that might break client applications that depend on it, he can simply define a new interface and leave the old one intact.

COM has its limitations (most of which are addressed in the forthcoming .NET Framework), but it is ubiquitous and fairly standardized. The world has embraced COM, so SQL Server includes a mechanism for working with COM objects from Transact-SQL.

## Basic Architecture

The fundamental elements of COM are

- Interfaces
- Reference counting
- QueryInterface
- IUnknown
- Aggregations
- Marshaling

Let's talk about each of these separately.

### Interfaces

From an OOP standpoint and also from the perspective of COM, an interface is a mechanism for exposing functionality, as I mentioned earlier. Typically, an object uses an interface to make its capabilities available to the outside world. When an object uses an interface, the object is said to *implement* that interface. Users of the object can interact with the interface without knowing what the object actually is, and a single object can implement multiple interfaces.

Generally speaking, to implement an interface, the methods exposed by the interface are linked to an object's methods. The interface itself requires no memory and really just specifies the functionality that an object implementing it must have.

Each COM interface is based on IUnknown, the fundamental COM interface. IUnknown allows navigation to the other interfaces exposed by the object.

Each interface has a unique interface ID (IID). This makes it is easy to support interface versioning. A new version of a COM interface is actually a separate interface, with its own IID. The IIDs for the standard ActiveX, OLE, and COM interfaces are predefined.

### Reference Counting

Unlike .NET and the Java Runtime, COM does not perform automatic garbage collection. Disposing of objects that are no longer needed is left to the developer. You use an object's reference count to determine whether the object can be destroyed.

The IUnknown methods AddRef and Release manage the reference count of interfaces on a COM object. When a client receives a pointer to a COM interface (a descendent of IUnknown), AddRef must be called on the interface. When the client has finished using the interface, it must call Release.

In its most primitive form, each AddRef call increments a counter variable inside its object and each Release call decrements it. When this count reaches zero, the interface no longer has any clients and can be destroyed.

You can also implement reference counting such that each reference to an object (as opposed to an interface implemented by the object) is counted. In this scenario, calls to AddRef and Release are delegated to a central reference count implementation. Release frees the whole object when its reference count reaches zero.

### QueryInterface/IUnknown

The fundamental COM mechanism used to access an object's functionality is the QueryInterface method of the IUnknown interface. Because every COM interface is derived from IUnknown, every COM interface has an implementation of QueryInterface. QueryInterface queries an object using the IID of the interface to which the caller wants a pointer. If the object implements IUnknown, QueryInterface retrieves a pointer to it and also calls AddRef. If the object does not implement IUnknown, QueryInterface returns the E_NOINTERFACE error code.

### Aggregations

For those situations when an object's implementer wants to make use of the services offered by another (e.g., a third party) object and wants this second object to function as a natural part of the first one, COM supports the concepts of containment and aggregation.

By aggregation, I mean that the containing object creates the contained object as part of its construction process and exposes the interfaces of the contained object within its own interface. Some objects can be aggregated; some can't. An object must follow a specific set of rules to participate in aggregation.

### Marshaling

Marshaling enables the COM interfaces exposed by an object in one process to be accessed by another process. Through marshaling, COM either provides code or uses code provided by the implementer of the interface to pack a method's parameters into a format that can be shipped across processes or across the network to other machines and to unpack those parameters during the call. When the call returns, the process is reversed.

Marshaling is usually unnecessary when an interface is being used in the same process as the object that provides it. However, marshaling can still be required between threads.

## COM at Work

Practically speaking, COM objects are used through two basic means: early and late binding. When an application makes object references that are resolvable at compile time, the object is early bound. To early bind an object in Visual Basic, you add a reference to the library containing the object during development, then "Dim" specific instances of it. To early bind an object in tools like Visual C++ and Delphi, you import the object's type library and work with the interfaces it provides. In either case, you code directly to the interfaces exposed by the object as though they were interfaces you created yourself. The object itself may live on a completely separate machine and may be accessed via Distributed COM (DCOM) or may be marshaled by a transaction manager such as Microsoft Transaction Server or Component Services. Generally speaking, you don't care; you just code to the interface.

When references to an object aren't known until runtime, the object is late bound. You normally instantiate late bound objects via a call to CreateObject() and store the object instance in a variant. Because the compiler didn't know what object you were referencing at compile time, you may encounter bad method calls or nonexistent properties at runtime. This is the tradeoff with late binding: It's more flexible in that you can decide at runtime what objects to create and can even instantiate objects that didn't exist on the development system, but it's also more error prone. It's easy to make mistakes when you late bind objects because your development environment can't provide the same level of assistance that it can when it knows the objects you're dealing with.

Once you have an instance of an object, you call methods and access properties on it like any other object. COM supports the notion of events (although they're a bit more trouble to use than they should be), so you can subscribe and respond to events on COM objects as well.

## SQL Server and COM Automation

SQL Server provides a set of stored procedures that allows you to automate COM objects from Transact-SQL. Automation is a language-independent method of controlling and using COM objects. Lots of applications expose functionality via COM objects. Many of Microsoft's retail products, as well as many from other vendors, expose some type of functionality via COM objects. You can use these objects to manipulate the host application through an automation controller—a facility that knows how to interact with COM interfaces. The most popular automation controller is Visual Basic, followed closely by VBScript. SQL Server's ODSOLE facility is an automation controller in its own right and is exposed via a set of system procedures that you can access from Transact-SQL.

### The sp_OA Procedures

Transact-SQL's automation stored procedures are named using the convention sp_OA*Function*, where *Function* indicates what the procedure does (for example, sp_OACreate creates COM objects, sp_OAMethod calls a method, sp_OAGetProperty and sp_OASetProperty get and set object properties, and so on). These procedures make Transact-SQL considerably more powerful because they give you full access to the world of COM.

### sp_checkspelling

The code that follows illustrates a simple procedure that uses the sp_OA procedures to automate a COM object. The procedure instantiates the Microsoft Word Application object and calls its CheckSpelling method to check the spelling of a word you pass the procedure. Here's the code:

```
USE master
GO
IF (OBJECT_ID('sp_checkspelling') IS NOT NULL)
  DROP PROC sp_checkspelling
GO
CREATE PROC sp_checkspelling
        @word varchar(30),          -- Word to check
        @correct bit OUT            -- Returns whether word is correctly spelled
/*
Object: sp_checkspelling
Description: Checks the spelling of a word using the Microsoft Word Application
automation object

Usage: sp_checkspelling
        @word varchar(128),         -- Word to check
        @correct bit OUT            -- Returns whether word is correctly spelled


Returns: (None)

$Author: Ken Henderson $. Email: khen@khen.com
Example: EXEC sp_checkspelling 'asdf', @correct OUT
Created: 2000-10-14. $Modtime: 2001-01-13 $.
*/
AS
IF (@word='/?') GOTO Help
DECLARE @object int,         -- Work variable for instantiating COM objects
        @hr int         -- Contains HRESULT returned by COM

-- Create a Word Application object
EXEC @hr=sp_OACreate 'Word.Application', @object OUT
IF (@hr <> 0) BEGIN
    EXEC sp_displayoaerrorinfo @object, @hr
    RETURN
END

-- Call its CheckSpelling method
EXEC @hr = sp_OAMethod @object, 'CheckSpelling', @correct OUT, @word
IF (@hr <> 0) BEGIN
    EXEC sp_displayoaerrorinfo @object, @hr
    RETURN @hr
END

-- Destroy it
EXEC @hr = sp_OADestroy @object
```

```
IF (@hr <> 0) BEGIN
    EXEC sp_displayoaerrorinfo @object, @hr
    RETURN @hr
END

RETURN 0

Help:

EXEC sp_usage @objectname='sp_checkspelling',
@desc='Checks the spelling of a word using the Microsoft Word Application automation
object',
@parameters='
        @word varchar(30),         -- Word to check
        @correct bit OUT           -- Returns whether word is correctly spelled
',
@author='Ken Henderson', @email='khen@khen.com',
@datecreated='20001014',@datelastchanged='20010113',
@example='EXEC sp_checkspelling ''asdf'', @correct OUT',
@returns='(None)'
RETURN -1
GO
```

Sp_checkspelling exposes two parameters—the word whose spelling you wish to check and an output parameter to receive a 1 or 0 indicating whether the word is spelled correctly. A call to the procedure looks like this:

```
DECLARE @cor bit
EXEC sp_checkspelling 'asdf', @cor OUT
SELECT @cor
```

(Results)

```
----
0
```

There are three key elements of this procedure: the creation of the COM object, the method call, and the disposal of the object. Let's begin with the call to sp_OACreate. Calling sp_OACreate instantiates a COM object. "Word.Application" is what is known in COM as a ProgID—a programmatic identifier. A programmatic identifier is a string that identifies a COM object so that applications can access it by name. How do we know to specify Word.Application here? Several ways. First, we could check the Word object interface as documented in MSDN. Second, we could fire up Visual Basic and add a Reference to the Microsoft Word Object Library to a project, then allow Visual Studio's IntelliSense technology to show us the objects and methods available from Word (you can do the same thing via Delphi's Project|Import Type Library option). Third, we could simply check the system registry and scan for all the interfaces involving Microsoft Word. The registry, for example, tells us that Word.Application is Word's VersionIndependentProgID string. This means that instantiating Word.Application should work regardless of the version of Word that's installed.

We store the object handle that's returned by sp_OACreate in @object. This handle is then passed into sp_OAMethod when we call methods on the Word.Application interface. In this case, we call just one method—Check-Spelling—and pass @word as the word for which to check spelling and @correct to receive the 1 or 0 returned by the method.

When we're finished with the object, we destroy it by calling sp_OADestroy. Again, we pass in the @object handle we received earlier from sp_OACreate.

---

**TIP:** You can control whether objects created with sp_OACreate run inside the SQL Server process or outside it. COM objects that run inside the SQL Server process are known as *in-proc servers*; those that run outside are known as *out-of-proc servers*. When possible, build COM objects that can run out of process (.EXEs). These are far less likely to cause SQL Server itself problems because they run outside the SQL Server process space. When your object is capable of running out-of-process, you can instruct SQL Server to load it out of process using sp_OACreate's third parameter, *context*. A value of 1 tells SQL Server to load the object in process, 4 says to load it out of process, and 5 says to allow either type of server.

---

This is what it's like to work with COM objects in Transact-SQL. As with many languages and technologies, you create the object, do some things with it, then clean up after yourself when you're through.

## sp_exporttable

Here's another stored procedure that makes use of the sp_OA routines to control a COM object. Sp_exporttable instantiates SQL Server's own SQL-DMO objects to export a table by name. It works analogously to the built-in BULK INSERT command, providing an interface to the BCP API from Transact-SQL. Here's the code:

```
USE master
GO
IF (OBJECT_ID('sp_exporttable') IS NOT NULL)
  DROP PROC sp_exporttable
GO
CREATE PROC sp_exporttable
        @table sysname,              -- Table to export
        @outputpath sysname=NULL,    -- Output directory, terminate with a "\"
        @outputname sysname=NULL,    -- Output filename (defaults to @table+'.BCP')
        @server sysname='(local)',       -- Name of the server to connect to
        @username sysname='sa',          -- Name of the user (defaults to 'sa')
        @password sysname=NULL,          -- User's password
        @trustedconnection bit=1         -- Use a trusted connection to connect
to the server
/*
Object: sp_exporttable
Description: Exports a table in a manner similar to BULK INSERT

Usage: sp_exporttable
        @table sysname,              -- Table to export
        @outputpath sysname=NULL,    -- Output directory, terminate with a '\'
        @outputname sysname=NULL,    -- Output filename (defaults to @table+'.BCP')
        @server sysname='(local)',       -- Name of the server to connect to
        @username sysname='sa',          -- Name of the user (defaults to 'sa')
        @password sysname=NULL,          -- User's password
        @trustedconnection bit=1         -- Use a trusted connection to connect to
the server

Returns: Number of rows exported

$Author: Ken Henderson $. Email: khen@khen.com

Example: EXEC sp_exporttable 'authors', 'C:\TEMP\'

Created: 1999-06-14. $Modtime: 2000-12-01 $.
*/
AS
IF (@table='/?') OR (@outputpath IS NULL) GOTO Help
DECLARE @srvobject int,          -- Server object
        @object int,         -- Work variable for instantiating COM objects
        @hr int,             -- Contains HRESULT returned by COM
        @bcobject int,           -- Stores pointer to BulkCopy object
        @TAB_DELIMITED int, -- Will store a constant for tab-delimited output
        @logname sysname,    -- Name of the log file
```

```
         @errname sysname,     -- Name of the error file
         @dbname sysname,      -- Name of the database
         @rowsexported int     -- Number of rows exported

SET @TAB_DELIMITED=2 -- SQL-DMO constant for tab-delimited exports
SET @dbname=ISNULL(PARSENAME(@table,3),DB_NAME()) -- Extract the DB name
SET @table=PARSENAME(@table,1)    -- Remove extraneous stuff from table name
IF (@table IS NULL) BEGIN
   RAISERROR('Invalid table name.',16,1)
   GOTO Help
END
IF (RIGHT(@outputpath,1)<>'\')
   SET @outputpath=@outputpath+'\'     -- Append a "\" if necessary
SET @logname=@outputpath+@table+'.LOG' -- Construct the log file name
SET @errname=@outputpath+@table+'.ERR' -- Construct the error file name

IF (@outputname IS NULL)
  SET @outputname=@outputpath+@table+'.BCP' -- Construct the output name
ELSE
  IF (CHARINDEX('\',@outputname)=0)
    SET @outputname=@outputpath+@outputname

-- Create a SQLServer object
EXEC @hr=sp_OACreate 'SQLDMO.SQLServer', @srvobject OUTPUT
IF (@hr <> 0) GOTO ServerError

-- Create a BulkCopy object
EXEC @hr=sp_OACreate 'SQLDMO.BulkCopy', @bcobject OUTPUT
IF (@hr <> 0) GOTO BCPError

-- Set BulkCopy's DataFilePath property to the output filename
EXEC @hr = sp_OASetProperty @bcobject, 'DataFilePath', @outputname
IF (@hr <> 0) GOTO BCPError

-- Tell BulkCopy to create tab-delimited files
EXEC @hr = sp_OASetProperty @bcobject, 'DataFileType', @TAB_DELIMITED
IF (@hr <> 0) GOTO BCPError

-- Set BulkCopy's LogFilePath property to the log filename
EXEC @hr = sp_OASetProperty @bcobject, 'LogFilePath', @logname
IF (@hr <> 0) GOTO BCPError

-- Set BulkCopy's ErrorFilePath property to the error filename
EXEC @hr = sp_OASetProperty @bcobject, 'ErrorFilePath', @errname
```

```
IF (@hr <> 0) GOTO BCPError

-- Connect to the server
IF (@trustedconnection=1) BEGIN
  EXEC @hr = sp_OASetProperty @srvobject, 'LoginSecure', 1
       IF (@hr <> 0) GOTO ServerError
  EXEC @hr = sp_OAMethod @srvobject, 'Connect', NULL, @server
END ELSE BEGIN
 IF (@password IS NOT NULL)
   EXEC @hr =sp_OAMethod @srvobject,'Connect',NULL,@server, @username, @password
       ELSE
          EXEC @hr = sp_OAMethod @srvobject, 'Connect', NULL, @server, @username
END
IF (@hr <> 0) GOTO ServerError

-- Get a pointer to the SQLServer object's Databases collection
EXEC @hr = sp_OAGetProperty @srvobject, 'Databases', @object OUT
IF (@hr <> 0) GOTO ServerError

-- Get a pointer from the Databases collection for the specified database
EXEC @hr = sp_OAMethod @object, 'Item', @object OUT, @dbname
IF (@hr <> 0) GOTO Error

-- Get a pointer from the Database object's Tables collection for the table
IF (OBJECTPROPERTY(OBJECT_ID(@table),'IsTable')=1) BEGIN
  EXEC @hr = sp_OAMethod @object, 'Tables', @object OUT, @table
  IF (@hr <> 0) GOTO Error
END ELSE -- Get a pointer from the Database object's View collection for the view
IF (OBJECTPROPERTY(OBJECT_ID(@table),'IsView')=1) BEGIN
  EXEC @hr = sp_OAMethod @object, 'Views', @object OUT, @table
  IF (@hr <> 0) GOTO Error
END ELSE BEGIN
  RAISERROR('Source object must be either a table or view.',16,1)
  RETURN -1
END

-- Call the object's ExportData method to export the table/view using BulkCopy
EXEC @hr = sp_OAMethod @object, 'ExportData', @rowsexported OUT, @bcobject
IF (@hr <> 0) GOTO Error

EXEC sp_OADestroy @srvobject -- Dispose of the server object
EXEC sp_OADestroy @bcobject -- Dispose of the bcp object
RETURN @rowsexported
```

```
Error:

EXEC sp_displayoaerrorinfo @object, @hr

GOTO ErrorCleanUp

BCPError:

EXEC sp_displayoaerrorinfo @bcobject, @hr

GOTO ErrorCleanUp

ServerError:

EXEC sp_displayoaerrorinfo @srvobject, @hr

GOTO ErrorCleanUp

ErrorCleanUp:

IF @srvobject IS NOT NULL
  EXEC sp_OADestroy @srvobject -- Dispose of the server object
IF @bcobject IS NOT NULL
  EXEC sp_OADestroy @bcobject  -- Dispose of the bcp object

RETURN -2

Help:

EXEC sp_usage @objectname='sp_exporttable',
@desc='Exports a table in a manner similar to BULK INSERT',
@parameters='
      @table sysname,                -- Table to export
      @outputpath sysname=NULL,   -- Output directory, terminate with a ''\''
      @outputname sysname=NULL,   -- Output filename (default: @table+''.BCP'')
      @server sysname=''(local)'',-- Name of the server to connect to
      @username sysname=''sa'',   -- Name of the user (defaults to ''sa'')
      @password sysname=NULL,     -- User''s password
       @trustedconnection bit=1    -- Use a trusted connection
',
@author='Ken Henderson', @email='khen@khen.com',
@datecreated='19990614',@datelastchanged='20001201',
@example='EXEC sp_exporttable ''authors'', ''C:\TEMP\''',
@returns='Number of rows exported'
```

```
RETURN -1
GO
```

Sp_exporttable follows this general plan of attack:

1. Create a SQLServer object. We'll use this object to connect to the server. Most DMO applications require a SQLServer object. We access the other objects on the server by drilling into the SQLServer object just as you do in Enterprise Manager.
2. Create a BulkCopy object. We'll use this object to export the table. Ultimately, we'll call the ExportData method of the specified table or view to "bulk copy" its contents to an operating system file. ExportData requires a BulkCopy object to do its work.
3. Set various properties on the BulkCopy object that will control the export.
4. Connect to the server using the SQLServer object.
5. Locate the table or view to be exported using nested object collections exposed by the SQLServer object.
6. Call the ExportData method of the view or table object, passing it the required BulkCopy object as a parameter
7. Once the export finishes, dispose of the SQLServer and BulkCopy objects.

The comments in the stored procedure detail how it works. It's pretty straightforward. You run sp_exporttable using this syntax:

```
DECLARE @rc int
EXEC @rc=pubs..sp_exporttable @table='pubs..authors',
@outputpath='c:\temp\'
SELECT RowsExported=@rc


RowsExported
------------
23
```

Note the use of the **pubs..** prefix on the procedure call. Because sp_exporttable uses the OBJECTPROPERTY() function (which does not work across databases), in order for the procedure to work correctly with objects in other databases, the database context must be temporarily changed to the correct one for the object specified. As I mentioned earlier in this book, prefixing a system procedure call with a database name temporarily changes the database context. The previous call is the equivalent of:

```
USE pubs
GO
EXEC @rc=sp_exporttable @table='pubs..authors', @outputpath='c:\temp\'
GO
USE master -- or some other database
GO
SELECT RowsExported=@rc
```

You may have noticed the calls to the sp_DisplayOAErrorInfo system procedure. We use sp_displayoaerrorinfo to display more verbose error info for error codes returned by the sp_OA procedures. Sp_DisplayOAErrorInfo calls sp_OAGetErrorInfo to get extended error info for object automation error codes. Sp_DisplayOAErrorInfo isn't created by default, but you can find it in the Books Online. It depends on sp_hexadecimal (also in the Books Online) to convert binary values to hexadecimal strings. See the topic "OLE Automation Return Codes and Error Information" in the Books Online for the source code to both procedures.

This example and the ones that follow illustrate how to use the sp_OA stored procedures to automate COM objects (SQL-DMO, in this case) exposed by SQL Server itself. These objects provide much of Enterprise Manager's underlying functionality and are a handy way of managing the server via program code. Of course, you aren't limited to accessing objects exposed by SQL Server. You can automate objects exposed by any application—PowerBuilder, Excel, Oracle, and so forth—and can even create your own COM objects and use them with SQL Server.

The comments in sp_exporttable explain how it works. It does a number of interesting things that are too extensive to get into here in detail. Using COM automation, the procedure is able to perform a fairly involved task with ease. The amount of Transact-SQL code required to accomplish the task is no more than that required by a comparable Delphi or Visual Basic program.

### sp_importtable

Despite the fact that we have the Transact-SQL BULK INSERT command for bulk loading data, here's the source to sp_importtable, the bulk load counterpart to sp_exporttable for completeness:

```
USE master
GO
IF (OBJECT_ID('sp_importtable') IS NOT NULL)
  DROP PROC sp_importtable
GO
```

```
CREATE PROC sp_importtable
       @table sysname,            -- Table to import
       @inputpath sysname=NULL,   -- input directory, terminate with a "\"
       @inputname sysname=NULL,   -- input filename (defaults to @table+'.BCP')
       @server sysname='(local)', -- Name of the server to connect to
       @username sysname='sa',    -- Name of the user (defaults to 'sa')
       @password sysname=NULL,        -- User's password
        @trustedconnection bit=1      -- Use a trusted connection

/*
Object: sp_importtable
Description: Imports a table similarly to BULK INSERT

Usage: sp_importtable
       @table sysname,            -- Table to import
       @inputpath sysname=NULL,   -- input directory, terminate with a '\'
       @inputname sysname=NULL,   -- input filename (defaults to @table+'.BCP')
       @server sysname='(local)', -- Name of the server to connect to
       @username sysname='sa',    -- Name of the user (defaults to 'sa')
       @password sysname=NULL,        -- User's password
       @trustedconnection bit=1       -- Use a trusted connection

Returns: Number of rows imported

 $Author: Ken Henderson $. Email: khen@khen.com

Example: EXEC sp_importtable 'authors', 'C:\TEMP\'

Created: 1999-06-14. $Modtime: 2000-12-03 $.
*/
AS
IF (@table='/?') OR (@inputpath IS NULL) GOTO Help
DECLARE @srvobject int,  -- Server object
        @object int, -- Work variable for instantiating COM objects
        @hr int,     -- Contains HRESULT returned by COM
        @bcobject int,      -- Stores pointer to BulkCopy object
        @TAB_DELIMITED int, -- Will store a constant for tab-delimited input
        @logname sysname,   -- Name of the log file
        @errname sysname,   -- Name of the error file
        @dbname sysname,    -- Name of the database
        @rowsimported int   -- Number of rows imported

SET @TAB_DELIMITED=2 -- SQL-DMO constant for tab-delimited imports
SET @dbname=ISNULL(PARSENAME(@table,3),DB_NAME()) -- Extract the DB name
```

```
SET @table=PARSENAME(@table,1)    -- Remove extraneous stuff from table name
IF (@table IS NULL) BEGIN
   RAISERROR('Invalid table name.',16,1)
   RETURN -1
END
IF (RIGHT(@inputpath,1)<>'\')
   SET @inputpath=@inputpath+'\' -- Append a "\" if necessary
SET @logname=@inputpath+@table+'.LOG' -- Construct the log file name
SET @errname=@inputpath+@table+'.ERR' -- Construct the error file name

IF (@inputname IS NULL)
  SET @inputname=@inputpath+@table+'.BCP' -- Construct the input name
ELSE
  SET @inputname=@inputpath+@inputname    -- Prefix source path


-- Create a SQLServer object
EXEC @hr=sp_OACreate 'SQLDMO.SQLServer', @srvobject OUT
IF (@hr <> 0) GOTO ServerError


-- Create a BulkCopy object
EXEC @hr=sp_OACreate 'SQLDMO.BulkCopy', @bcobject OUT
IF (@hr <> 0) GOTO BCPError


-- Set BulkCopy's DataFilePath property to the input filename
EXEC @hr = sp_OASetProperty @bcobject, 'DataFilePath', @inputname
IF (@hr <> 0) GOTO BCPError


-- Tell BulkCopy to create tab-delimited files
EXEC @hr = sp_OASetProperty @bcobject, 'DataFileType', @TAB_DELIMITED
IF (@hr <> 0) GOTO BCPError


-- Set BulkCopy's LogFilePath property to the log filename
EXEC @hr = sp_OASetProperty @bcobject, 'LogFilePath', @logname
IF (@hr <> 0) GOTO BCPError


-- Set BulkCopy's ErrorFilePath property to the error filename
EXEC @hr = sp_OASetProperty @bcobject, 'ErrorFilePath', @errname
IF (@hr <> 0) GOTO BCPError


-- Set BulkCopy's UseServerSideBCP property to TRUE
EXEC @hr = sp_OASetProperty @bcobject, 'UseServerSideBCP', 1
IF (@hr <> 0) GOTO BCPError


-- Connect to the server
```

```
IF (@trustedconnection=1) BEGIN
  EXEC @hr = sp_OASetProperty @srvobject, 'LoginSecure', 1
      IF (@hr <> 0) GOTO ServerError
  EXEC @hr = sp_OAMethod @srvobject, 'Connect', NULL, @server
END ELSE BEGIN
      IF (@password IS NOT NULL)
        EXEC @hr = sp_OAMethod @srvobject, 'Connect', NULL, @server, @username,
@password
      ELSE
        EXEC @hr = sp_OAMethod @srvobject, 'Connect', NULL, @server, @username
END
IF (@hr <> 0) GOTO ServerError

-- Get a pointer to the SQLServer object's Databases collection
EXEC @hr = sp_OAGetProperty @srvobject, 'Databases', @object OUT
IF (@hr <> 0) GOTO ServerError

-- Get a pointer from the Databases collection for the specified database
EXEC @hr = sp_OAMethod @object, 'Item', @object OUT, @dbname
IF (@hr <> 0) GOTO Error

-- Get a pointer to the specified table
IF (OBJECTPROPERTY(OBJECT_ID(@table),'IsTable')<>1) BEGIN
  RAISERROR('Target object must be a table.',16,1)
  RETURN -1
END BEGIN
  EXEC @hr = sp_OAMethod @object, 'Tables', @object OUT, @table
  IF (@hr <> 0) GOTO Error
END

-- Call the Table object's ImportData method to import the table using BulkCopy
EXEC @hr = sp_OAMethod @object, 'ImportData', @rowsimported OUT, @bcobject
IF (@hr <> 0) GOTO Error

EXEC sp_OADestroy @srvobject -- Dispose of the server object
EXEC sp_OADestroy @bcobject  -- Dispose of the bcp object
RETURN @rowsimported

Error:

EXEC sp_displayoaerrorinfo @object, @hr

GOTO ErrorCleanUp

BCPError:
```

```
EXEC sp_displayoaerrorinfo @bcobject, @hr

GOTO ErrorCleanUp

ServerError:

EXEC sp_displayoaerrorinfo @srvobject, @hr

GOTO ErrorCleanUp

ErrorCleanUp:

IF @srvobject IS NOT NULL
  EXEC sp_OADestroy @srvobject -- Dispose of the server object
IF @bcobject IS NOT NULL
  EXEC sp_OADestroy @bcobject  -- Dispose of the bcp object

RETURN -2

Help:

EXEC sp_usage @objectname='sp_importtable',
@desc='Imports a table similarly to BULK INSERT',
@parameters='
     @table sysname,            -- Table to import
     @inputpath sysname=NULL,   -- input directory, terminate with a ''\''
     @inputname sysname=NULL,   -- input filename (default: @table+''.BCP'')
     @server sysname=''(local)'', -- Name of the server to connect to
     @username sysname=''sa'',   -- Name of the user (defaults to ''sa'')
     @password sysname=NULL      -- User''s password
',
@author='Ken Henderson', @email='khen@khen.com',
@datecreated='19990614',@datelastchanged='20001203',
@example='EXEC sp_importtable ''authors'', ''C:\TEMP\''',
@returns='Number of rows imported'
RETURN -1
GO
```

Similarly to the built-in BULK INSERT command, sp_importtable loads external files into SQL Server tables. As with sp_exporttable, sp_importtable assumes that file is tab delimited, but you can change this if you wish. Here's an example of sp_exporttable and sp_importtable being used together:

```
SET NOCOUNT ON
USE pubs
```

```
DECLARE @rc int

-- First, export the rows
EXEC @rc=pubs..sp_exporttable @table='pubs..authors',
@outputpath='c:\temp\'
SELECT @rc AS RowsExported

-- Second, create a new table to store the rows
SELECT * INTO authorsimp FROM authors WHERE 1=0

-- Third, import the exported rows
EXEC pubs..sp_importtable @table='authorsimp', @inputpath=
'c:\temp\',@inputname='authors.bcp'

SELECT COUNT(*) AS RowsLoaded FROM authorsimp
GO
DROP TABLE authorsimp
```

The script starts by exporting the authors table from the pubs sample database to a tab-delimited text file. It creates an empty copy of the table and then imports the exported file using sp_importtable. As with BULK INSERT, any file that sp_importtable is to load must be accessible from the SQL Server machine.

### sp_getSQLregistry

SQL Server's SQL-DMO provides access to a wealth of Enterprise Manager-type services and server info. Given that SQL-DMO is a COM-based technology, this functionality is exposed via COM objects. One of these objects is the Registry object. SQL-DMO's Registry object provides access to the portion of the system registry used by SQL Server. You can use this object to get at such things as the default SQL Mail login name, the default SQL Server installation path, the number of processors installed on the server, and so forth. Here's a stored procedure that shows how to use the Registry object:

```
USE master
GO
IF OBJECT_ID('sp_getSQLregistry') IS NOT NULL
  DROP PROC sp_getSQLregistry
GO
CREATE PROC sp_getSQLregistry
        @regkey varchar(128),          -- Registry key to extract
        @regvalue varchar(8000)=NULL OUT, -- Value from SQL Server registry
```

```
        @server varchar(128)='(local)',   -- Name of the server to connect to
        @username sysname='sa',    -- Name of the user (defaults to 'sa')
        @password sysname=NULL,    -- User's password
   @trustedconnection bit=1       -- Use a trusted connection


/*

Object: sp_getSQLregistry
Description: Retrieves a value from the SQL Server branch in the system registry
Usage: sp_getSQLregistry
        @regkey varchar(128),         -- Registry key to extract
        @regvalue varchar(8000) OUT,  -- Value from SQL Server registry tree
        @server varchar(128)="(local)", -- Name of the server to connect to
        @username varchar(128)="sa",    -- Name of the user (Default: "sa")
        @password varchar(128)=NULL   -- User's password
        @trustedconnection bit=1      -- Use a trusted connection

Returns: Data length of registry value

$Author: Ken Henderson $. Email: khen@khen.com

$Revision: 6.4 $

Example: sp_getSQLregistry "SQLRootPath", @sqlpath OUT

Created: 1996-09-03. $Modtime: 2000-11-14 $.

*/
AS
SET NOCOUNT ON
IF (@regkey='/?') GOTO Help

DECLARE @srvobject int, -- Server object
@object int, -- Work variable for instantiating COM objects
@hr int -- Contains HRESULT returned by COM

-- Create a SQLServer object
EXEC @hr=sp_OACreate 'SQLDMO.SQLServer', @srvobject OUTPUT
IF (@hr <> 0) GOTO ServerError

-- Connect to the server
IF (@trustedconnection=1) BEGIN
  EXEC @hr = sp_OASetProperty @srvobject, 'LoginSecure', 1
     IF (@hr <> 0) GOTO ServerError
```

```
      EXEC @hr = sp_OAMethod @srvobject, 'Connect', NULL, @server
END ELSE BEGIN
 IF (@password IS NOT NULL)
   EXEC @hr =sp_OAMethod @srvobject,'Connect',NULL,@server, @username, @password
 ELSE
   EXEC @hr = sp_OAMethod @srvobject, 'Connect', NULL, @server, @username
END
IF (@hr <> 0) GOTO ServerError

-- Get a pointer to the SQLServer object's Registry object
EXEC @hr = sp_OAGetProperty @srvobject, 'Registry', @object OUT
IF (@hr <> 0) GOTO Error

-- Get the registry value
EXEC @hr = sp_OAGetProperty @object, @regkey, @regvalue OUT
IF (@hr <> 0) GOTO ServerError

EXEC sp_OADestroy @srvobject -- Dispose of the server object
RETURN datalength(@regvalue)

Error:

EXEC sp_displayoaerrorinfo @object, @hr

GOTO ErrorCleanUp

ServerError:

EXEC sp_displayoaerrorinfo @srvobject, @hr

GOTO ErrorCleanUp

ErrorCleanUp:

IF @srvobject IS NOT NULL
   EXEC sp_OADestroy @srvobject -- Dispose of the server object

RETURN -2

Help:
EXEC sp_usage @objectname='sp_getSQLregistry',
@desc='Retrieves a value from the SQL Server branch in the system registry',
@parameters='
```

```
        @regkey varchar(128),              -- Registry key to extract
        @regvalue varchar(8000)   OUTPUT, -- Value from SQL Server registry
        @server varchar(128)="(local)", -- Name of the server to connect to
        @username varchar(128)="sa",      -- Name of the user (Default: "sa")
        @password varchar(128)=NULL      -- User''s password',
@author='Ken Henderson', @email='khen@khen.com',
@datecreated='19960903', @datelastchanged='20001114',
@version='6', @revision='4',
@returns='Data length of registry value',
@example='sp_getSQLregistry "SQLRootPath", @sqlpath OUTPUT'

GO
```

You can use sp_getSQLregistry to retrieve values from the SQL Server portion of the system registry via the SQL-DMO Registry object. Here's an example:

```
SET NOCOUNT ON
DECLARE @numprocs varchar(10), @installedmemory varchar(20), @rootpath varchar(8000)

EXEC sp_getSQLregistry 'PhysicalMemory', @installedmemory OUT
EXEC sp_getSQLregistry 'NumberOfProcessors', @numprocs OUT
EXEC sp_getSQLregistry 'SQLRootPath', @rootpath OUT

SELECT @numprocs AS NumberOfProcessors, @installedmemory AS InstalledRAM, @rootpath
AS RootPath

DECLARE @charset varchar(100), @sortorder varchar(100)
EXEC sp_getSQLregistry 'CharacterSet', @charset OUT

SELECT @charset AS CharacterSet

EXEC sp_getSQLregistry 'SortOrder', @sortorder OUT

SELECT @sortorder AS SortOrder
NumberOfProcessors InstalledRAM         RootPath
------------------ -------------------- ---------------------------------------
2                  223                  C:\Program Files\Microsoft SQL
                                        Server\MSSQL$SS2000


CharacterSet
------------------------------------------------------------------------------
Latin1-General
```

```
SortOrder

---------------------------------------------------------------------------

case-insensitive, accent-sensitive, kanatype-insensitive, width-insensitive for
Unicode Data, SQL Se
```

## Summary

COM is a powerful and ubiquitous technology that enables applications to interoperate in a wide variety of ways. Though imperfect, COM addressed a number of the shortcomings in the technologies that preceded it. Thanks to the sp_OA procedures, Transact-SQL can access COM object interfaces exposed by other applications and even by SQL Server itself, such as SQL-DMO. By combining the power of a relational database with the flexibility and ubiquity of COM, you can build applications that are very powerful indeed.

# CHAPTER 20

# Extended Stored Procedures

*Programming in machine code is like eating with a toothpick. The bites are so small and the process so laborious that dinner takes forever.*

*—Charles Petzold*[1]

In addition to regular Transact-SQL-based stored procedures, you can also write stored procedures in C, C++, and other languages that can communicate with the ODS API. These types of procedures are known as *extended stored procedures*, and they receive parameters and return results via the ODS framework. They reside in DLLs and behave similarly to regular stored procedures. You create a reference to them in SQL Server by calling the sp_addextendedproc stored procedure (or through Enterprise Manager, which calls sp_addextendedproc). Sp_addextendedproc calls DBCC ADDEXTENDEDPROC() to add the reference to the sysobjects and syscomments system tables (sysobjects stores the object name, type, and so forth, as it does with all objects; syscomments stores the name of the DLL that hosts the extended procedure). This reference is the means by which you call the procedure from Transact-SQL. In this sense, it's very much like a regular stored procedure. From the perspective of SQL Server, extended procedures reside in the master database (they cannot be created in other databases) and run within the SQL Server process space.

There's nothing about extended procedures that requires them to be written in C or C++, but writing them in a different language would require you to first translate the ODS header files from C into your chosen language. I've written extended procedures in Delphi's Object Pascal—so it can be done—but it's not for the timid.

---

[1]Petzold, Charles. *Code*. Redmond, WA: Microsoft Press, 2000. Page 349.

If you want a stored procedure-like interface to routines written in a language other than C or C++ or for which you don't have source code, a reasonable alternative is to create a "wrapper" extended procedure using a C++ compiler, and call your routines (residing in a DLL or EXE) from it. This way, you leverage existing code and the language tools with which you prefer to work against the power of the ODS API. You get the best of both without having to translate code from one language to another.

Beyond the obvious language differences, there are some other important differences between extended procedures and regular procedures. Extended procedures aren't automatically located in the master database when called from other databases, and they don't assume the context of the current database when executed. To execute an extended procedure from a database other than the master, you must fully qualify the reference.

Another quirk I've discovered with extended procedures is that the DBCC command that unloads a DLL in which an extended procedure resides (DBCC dllname(FREE)) doesn't work consistently when the DLL initially resides in a folder other than the one containing sqlservr.exe—the main SQL Server executable. I don't know why this is, but oftentimes the DLL will fail to unload if it was initially specified with a path. No error message is returned, but the DLL often remains loaded nonetheless. If you try to overwrite it, you'll find that it's still in use. The workaround, of course, is to copy the DLL to the SQL Server BINN folder (home of sqlservr.exe) and specify it to sp_addextendedproc without a path.

Internally, SQL Server uses the Windows API LoadLibrary() and FreeLibrary() routines to load and unload DLLs, and they certainly support fully qualified DLL filenames, so the path shouldn't be an issue. Nevertheless, I've seen the problem on several different systems, so it's something to watch out for.

## Open Data Services

The ODS API is discussed at length in the Books Online, so I won't rehash it, but here's a broad overview:

- ODS is a Call Level Interface (CLI) for building extended procedures and database gateways. Microsoft has deprecated database gateways in favor of linked servers, so these days ODS is used primarily for building extended procedures.
- By CLI, I mean that the interface is non-COM. It's just a traditional DLL interface. The DLL exports functions that applications can call.

- The ODS API is implemented in a DLL named OPENDS60.DLL. In SQL Server 2000 and later, this DLL is merely a proxy for the ODS routines themselves, which are implemented internally by the server. If you compare the size of the OPENDS60.DLL for SQL Server 7.0 with that for 2000, you'll see that the 2000 version is much smaller. This is because ODS is no longer implemented in the DLL itself.
- To make use of the ODS API, you typically link OPENDS60.LIB into a C++ project. If you use the Visual C++ Extended Procedure wizard, this is taken care of for you.

## Start-up Code

Every extended procedure is passed a handle to the server process that called it. The interface to an extended procedure looks like this in C (Listing 20–1):

**Listing 20–1** The interface to an extended procedure.

```
RETCODE __declspec(dllexport) xp_foo(SRV_PROC *srvproc)
{
...
}
```

The dllexport directive makes the routine visible to the outside world. It will be exported from the DLL using the name of the function itself. When you execute the procedure from Transact-SQL, SQL Server calls the Win32 API LoadLibrary() routine to load the DLL (if it's not already loaded) and uses GetProcAddress() to retrieve the procedure's address in the DLL. Once it locates this address, SQL Server casts it to a function pointer matching the specification in Listing 20–1.

SRV_PROC is a C structure defined in the ODS header file srvstruc.h that looks like this (Listing 20–2):

**Listing 20–2** The SRV_PROC structure.

```
typedef struct srv_proc
{
WORD            tdsversion;
WORD            status;
SRV_IO          srvio;
SRV_LOGINREC    login;
void            *langbuff;
```

```
unsigned long      langlen;
unsigned int       event;
void               *server;
char               *threadstack;
THREAD             threadID;
HANDLE             threadHDL;
HANDLE             iowakeup;
HANDLE             exited;
DBINT              rowsent;
SRV_COLDESC        *coldescp;
DBUSMALLINT        coldescno;
BYTE               *colnamep;
WORD               colnamelen;
void               *userdata;
void               *event_data;
BYTE               serverlen;
BYTE               *servername;
BYTE               rpc_active;
BYTE               rpc_server_len;
BYTE               *rpc_server;
BYTE               rpc_database_len;
BYTE               *rpc_database;
BYTE               rpc_owner_len;
BYTE               *rpc_owner;
BYTE               rpc_proc_len;
BYTE               *rpc_proc_name;
unsigned int       rpc_proc_number;
unsigned int       rpc_linenumber;
unsigned short     rpc_options;
unsigned short     rpc_num_params;
SRV_RPCp           **rpc_params;
BYTE               non_rpc_active;
unsigned short     non_rpc_num_params;
SRV_RPCp           **non_rpc_params;
char               temp_buffer[100];
SRV_SUBCHANNEL     *(*subprocs);
TRANSLATION_INFO   translation_info;
struct             srv_listentry IOListEntry;
struct             srv_listentry CommandListEntry;
PSRV_LISTHEAD      pNetListHead;
BOOL               bNewPacket;
long               StatusCrit;
void               *serverdata;
```

```
SRV_SUBCHANNEL        *subchannel;
SRV_PEVENTS           *pre_events;
SRV_PEVENTS           *post_events;
void                  *p_langbuff;
BOOL                  fSecureLogin;
BOOL                  fInExtendedProc;
Unsigned              fLocalPost:1;
unsigned              fMadeBoundCall:1;
unsigned              uFill1:30;
SRV_COMPORT_QUEUE     comport_queue;
void                  *pSF1;
void                  *pSF2;
HANDLE                hPreHandlerMutex;
HANDLE                hPostHandlerMutex;
BOOL                  bSAxp;
}                     SRV_PROC;
```

You can review srvstruc.h yourself for details, but, suffice it to say, every server process structure carries with it a large and diverse collection of data.

## Extended Procedure Activities

Extended procedures usually take a parameter or parameters and return a result set or output variable to the calling connection. Often, extended procedures also generate messages that they send back to the client. Although it's possible to create extended procedures that take no parameters and produce no output, these are really pretty rare.

## Sending Messages

You use the ODS srv_sendmsg() function to send a message from an extended procedure to the calling connection. Calls to srv_sendmsg() look like this (Listing 20–3):

**Listing 20–3** Sending a message using ODS.

```
srv_sendmsg(srvproc, SRV_MSG_ERROR, LISTFILE_ERROR,
    SRV_INFO, (DBTINYINT) 0,
    NULL, 0, 0,
    "Error executing procedure: Invalid number of parameters.",
    SRV_NULLTERM);
```

The text string you see in the middle of the call is the actual message. The other parameters specify attributes such as the message state, the line on which it occurred, and the message's type. See the Books Online for details.

## Processing Parameters

You process the parameters passed to an extended procedure using srv_paraminfo(), srv_paramdata(), srv_paramtype(), and similar ODS API functions. The srv_paramtype() function allows you to check the data type of a given parameter, whereas srv_paramdata() retrieves the parameter's value. Here's an example of how these two functions are used (Listing 20–4):

---

**NOTE:** The srv_paraminfo() function can return all the info that srv_paramtype(), srv_paramlen(), and srv_paramdata() return in a single call. Moreover, it supports the new data types available in SQL Server 7.0 and later. Because of this, using srv_paraminfo() is preferable to calling these other functions. See the Books Online for details.

---

**Listing 20–4** Processing parameters with ODS.

```
// Check parameter for correct type.
if (srv_paramtype(srvproc, 1) != SRVVARCHAR) {
    // Send error message and return.
    srv_sendmsg(srvproc, SRV_MSG_ERROR, LISTFILE_ERROR,
        SRV_INFO, (DBTINYINT) 0,
        NULL, 0, 0,
        "Error executing extended procedure: Invalid parameter type.",
        SRV_NULLTERM);
    // A SRV_DONE_MORE instead of a SRV_DONE_FINAL must complete the
    // result set of an Extended Stored Procedure.
    srv_senddone(srvproc, (SRV_DONE_ERROR | SRV_DONE_MORE), 0, 0);
    return(XP_ERROR);
}

// Terminate parameter string with NULL.
memcpy(FileName, srv_paramdata(srvproc, 1), srv_paramlen(srvproc, 1));
FileName[srv_paramlen(srvproc, 1)] = '\0';
```

In each of the calls in bold type, the first parameter passed into the function is the server process handle. This is the convention with ODS API calls: The server process handle is usually the first (and sometimes the only) parameter passed into the routine. The second parameter in both examples is the parameter number for which to retrieve info. In both of the examples here, we're inquiring about the first parameter passed into the procedure.

## Returning Data

Every column that is to be returned by an extended procedure must first be described using the srv_describe() function. Here's an example:

```
srv_describe(srvproc, 1, ColName, SRV_NULLTERM, SRVINT4, sizeof(DBINT),
             SRVINT4, sizeof(DBINT), 0);
```

Here we provide, among other things, the name and data type of the first result set column. The second parameter (in bold type) is the ordinal position of the column in the result set—the column number.

Before each row can be sent back to the server, srv_setcoldata is called to assign individual column values. Here's an example of a call to srv_setcoldata():

```
srv_setcoldata(srvproc, 2, LineText);
```

Here, LineText is a string variable that contains the data we want to assign to the column. Because a string in C and C++ is really a pointer to an array of characters, what we're really passing to srv_setcoldata() is the address of that array. The first two parameters passed to srv_setcoldata() should be familiar by now: They're the server process handle and the column number respectively.

Once all the column values have been set, each result set row is sent back to the server using srv_sendrow(). Listing 20–5 provides an example:

**Listing 20–5** Sending result rows with ODS.

```
if (srv_sendrow(srvproc) == FAIL) {
    srv_sendmsg(srvproc, SRV_MSG_ERROR, LISTFILE_ERROR,
    SRV_INFO, (DBTINYINT) 0,
    NULL, 0, 0,
    "Error executing extended stored procedure: Unable to send results.",
    SRV_NULLTERM);
    return (XP_ERROR);
}
```

We begin by calling srv_sendrow() and checking its return value. Notice that its only parameter is the server process handle. By the time it's called, all column values have already been added to the process structure. If the function fails, we send a message to the server indicating the problem, and return an error code from the extended procedure. If the function succeeds, we continue to send result rows to the server until we're finished, then we call srv_senddone() like this:

```
srv_senddone(srvproc, SRV_DONE_MORE | SRV_DONE_COUNT, (DBUSMALLINT)0, i);
```

Notice the bitmap value that's passed as the second parameter to the function (in bold type). Typically, extended procedures should always include SRV_DONE_MORE when calling srv_senddone(). SRV_DONE_MORE indicates that more results are pending; SRV_DONE_FINAL indicates that no more remain. It might seem that SRV_DONE_FINAL should be passed when the extended procedure has no more rows to send; however, SRV_DONE_FINAL is only used for ODS gateway applications, not extended procedures (the ODS API can be used to construct either; however, ODS gateway applications have been deprecated in favor of linked servers). When an extended procedure completes, the server itself sends SRV_DONE_FINAL, so the procedure itself must not.

## A Simple Example

If you're new to C/C++ development, the preceding overview of extended procedure development may have been a bit daunting. It's really not as bad as it might seem, though. Studying the source code to a simple extended procedure will likely allay any concerns you might have, so that's what we'll do shortly.

Creating your own extended stored procedure is as easy as selecting File|New|Extended Proc wizard in the Visual C++ development environment. The wizard will construct an extended procedure workspace for you, complete with INCLUDE statements for the ODS header files and a sample extended stored procedure. You can then modify this code to do what you need.

The routine that follows in Listing 20–6 is an extended procedure that returns the contents of a text file as a result set. It takes one parameter—the name of the file—and returns a result set containing two columns: a line number and the text for each line. Here's the code:

**Listing 20–6** The entire xp_listfile routine.

```
RETCODE __declspec(dllexport) xp_listfile(SRV_PROC *srvproc)
{

    DBINT i = 0;
```

```
DBCHAR ColName[MAXCOLNAME];
   DBCHAR LineText[MAXTEXT];
   DBCHAR FileName[MAXFILENAME];
   FILE *f;

// STEP 1: Process parameters
// Check number of parameters.
 if ( srv_rpcparams(srvproc) != 1) {
    // Send error message and return.
    srv_sendmsg(srvproc, SRV_MSG_ERROR, LISTFILE_ERROR,
        SRV_INFO, (DBTINYINT) 0,
        NULL, 0, 0,
        "Error executing extended proc: Invalid number of parameters.",
        SRV_NULLTERM);

    // A SRV_DONE_MORE instead of a SRV_DONE_FINAL must complete the
    // result set of an Extended Stored Procedure.
    srv_senddone(srvproc, (SRV_DONE_ERROR | SRV_DONE_MORE), 0, 0);
    return(XP_ERROR);
    }

// Check parameter for correct type.
if (srv_paramtype(srvproc, 1) != SRVVARCHAR) {
    // Send error message and return.
    srv_sendmsg(srvproc, SRV_MSG_ERROR, LISTFILE_ERROR,
        SRV_INFO, (DBTINYINT) 0,
        NULL, 0, 0,
        "Error executing extended proc: Invalid parameter type.",
        SRV_NULLTERM);
    // A SRV_DONE_MORE instead of a SRV_DONE_FINAL must complete the
    // result set of an Extended Stored Procedure.
    srv_senddone(srvproc, (SRV_DONE_ERROR | SRV_DONE_MORE), 0, 0);
    return(XP_ERROR);
    }

// Terminate parameter string with NULL.
memcpy(FileName, srv_paramdata(srvproc, 1), srv_paramlen(srvproc, 1));
FileName[srv_paramlen(srvproc, 1)] = '\0';

//STEP 2: Set up the column names

wsprintf(ColName, "LineNo");
    srv_describe(srvproc, 1, ColName, SRV_NULLTERM, SRVINT4, sizeof(DBINT), SRVINT4,
sizeof(DBINT), 0);
```

```
      wsprintf(ColName, "Text");
      srv_describe(srvproc, 2, ColName, SRV_NULLTERM, SRVCHAR, MAXTEXT, SRVCHAR, 0,
NULL);

          // STEP 3: Read the text file and send back results, line by line
          if( (f = fopen( FileName, "r" )) != NULL ) {
                while (!feof(f)) {
                      if (fgets(LineText,MAXTEXT,f) != NULL) {
                            srv_setcoldata(srvproc, 1, (void *)&++i);

                            // Remove CR/LF at EOL
                            if (LineText[strlen(LineText)-1]=='\n') {
                                  LineText[strlen(LineText)-1]='\0';
                            }
                            if (LineText[strlen(LineText)-1]=='\r') {
                                  LineText[strlen(LineText)-1]='\0';
                            }

                            if (strlen(LineText)==0) { //Filter out NULLs
                                  LineText[0]=' ';
                                  LineText[1]='\0';
                            }
                            srv_setcoldata(srvproc, 2, LineText);
                            srv_setcollen(srvproc, 2, strlen(LineText));
                            // Send the row
                            if (srv_sendrow(srvproc) == FAIL) {
                                  srv_sendmsg(srvproc, SRV_MSG_ERROR,
                                  LISTFILE_ERROR,
                                        SRV_INFO, (DBTINYINT) 0,
                                        NULL, 0, 0,
                                        "Error sending extended proc results.",
                                        SRV_NULLTERM);
                                  return (XP_ERROR);
                            }
                      }
                }
                fclose(f);
          }
          else {
            // Send error message and return.
            srv_sendmsg(srvproc, SRV_MSG_ERROR, LISTFILE_ERROR,
                  SRV_INFO, (DBTINYINT) 0,
                  NULL, 0, 0,
                  "Error executing extended stored procedure: Unable to open file.",
```

```
        SRV_NULLTERM);
    // A SRV_DONE_MORE instead of a SRV_DONE_FINAL must complete the
    // result set of an Extended Stored Procedure.
    srv_senddone(srvproc, (SRV_DONE_ERROR | SRV_DONE_MORE), 0, 0);
    return(XP_ERROR);
    }
    // STEP 4: Return the number of rows processed
    srv_senddone(srvproc, SRV_DONE_MORE | SRV_DONE_COUNT, (DBUSMALLINT)0, i);

    return XP_NOERROR ;

}
```

I've broken the code into four distinct steps. Examine the comments in the source code to see where each step begins and ends.

In step 1 we process the parameters passed into the routine. If we receive the wrong number of parameters, or one that's an unexpected type, we send the client an error message and abort.

In step 2 we set up the column names for the result set. As I mentioned earlier, we do this in ODS using the srv_describe() function. Once we've set up the columns, we're ready to start loading them with data and sending that data back to the client.

In step 3 we iterate through the text file, loading each line into a row and sending that row to the client as we go. We also send a line number with each row to make ordering the result set easy for the client.

In step 4 we return the total number of rows processed to the client. All we have to do here is send the final value of the line count variable we incremented as we processed the file.

Once we compile and link the extended procedure, we copy its DLL to SQL Server's BINN folder. We can then add the procedure to the master database using sp_addextendedproc, like this (Listing 20–7):

**Listing 20–7** Adding an extended procedure.

```
USE master
GO
EXEC sp_addextendedproc 'xp_listfile','xp_listfile.dll'
```

Once the procedure is available in the master, we can call it from Transact-SQL like any other procedure:

```
EXEC master.dbo.xp_listfile 'C:\WINNT\sqlstp.log'
```

(Results abridged)

```
LineNo       Text
----------   ---------------------------------------------------------------
1            23:44:44 Begin Setup
2            23:44:44 8.00.194
3            23:44:44 Mode = Normal
4            23:44:44 ModeType = NORMAL
5            23:44:44 GetDefinitionEx returned: 0, Extended: 0x0
6            23:44:44 ValueFTS returned: 1
7            23:44:44 ValuePID returned: 1
8            23:44:44 ValueLic returned: 0
9            23:44:44 System: Windows NT WorkStation
10           23:44:44 SQL Server ProductType: Personal Edition [0x2]
11           23:44:44 Begin Action: SetupInitialize
12           23:44:44 End Action SetupInitialize
13           23:44:44 Begin Action: SetupInstall
14           23:44:44 Reading Software\Microsoft\Windows\...
15           23:44:44 CommonFilesDir=C:\Program Files\Common Files
16           23:44:44 Windows Directory=C:\WINNT\
17           23:44:44 Program Files=C:\Program Files\
18           23:44:44 TEMPDIR=C:\WINNT\TEMP\
19           23:44:44 Begin Action: SetupInstall
20           23:44:44 digpid size : 256
21           23:44:45 digpid size : 164
22           23:44:45 Begin Action: CheckFixedRequirements
23           23:44:45 Platform ID: 0xf000000
24           23:44:45 Version: 5.0.2195
25           23:44:45 File Version - C:\WINNT\System32\shdocvw.dll: 5.0.2920.0
26           23:44:45 End Action: CheckFixedRequirements
27           23:44:45 Begin Action: ShowDialogs
```

Dropping the procedure is as easy as adding it. You just call sp_dropextendedproc (Listing 20–8):

**Listing 20–8**  Dropping an extended procedure.

```
USE master
GO
EXEC sp_dropextendedproc 'xp_listfile'
```

If you need to replace an extended procedure after it has been loaded by SQL Server, you'll first have to free the DLL that hosts it using DBCC dllname(FREE), like this (Listing 20–9):

**Listing 20–9** Unloading an extended procedure's DLL.

```
USE master
GO
DBCC xp_listfile(FREE)
```

**NOTE:** The undocumented procedure xp_readerrorlog can also read a plain text file (not just an error log) and return it as a result set. See Chapter 22 for more info.

# A Better Example

Now that you've seen how easy it is to put together a simple extended procedure, let's try one that's a little more complex. The code that follows in Listing 20–10 implements an extended procedure named xp_exec. As I mentioned in the chapter on UDFs, you aren't allowed to call EXEC() from within a UDF. Only extended procedures can be called, and only ones that begin with **xp** (sp_executesql isn't allowed even though it's an extended procedure because it doesn't begin with **xp**). Xp_exec works around this. You pass it a query you'd like to run, and it returns a result set, if there is one. Although you can't insert this result into a table variable (INSERT…EXEC isn't supported with table variables), you can manipulate tables and data, perform administrative tasks, and do most of the other things Transact-SQL allows you to do.

Because xp_exec needs to execute queries apart from the calling connection, it must initiate its own connection (over ODBC) to the server using the connection info from the caller. SQLAllocHandle() and SQLConnect() are the key functions we'll use. Here's the code:

**Listing 20–10** Connecting from ODBC.

```
// STEP 1: Allocate an ODBC environment handle
sret = SQLAllocHandle(SQL_HANDLE_ENV, NULL, &henv);
if (sret != SQL_SUCCESS) {
    handle_odbc_err("SQLAllocHandle:Env",
        sret,
        (DBINT) REMOTE_FAIL,
        henv,
        SQL_HANDLE_ENV,
```

```
                srvproc);
            return(XP_ERROR);
            }
    SQLSetEnvAttr(henv, SQL_ATTR_ODBC_VERSION, (SQLPOINTER) SQL_OV_ODBC3,
        SQL_IS_INTEGER);


    // STEP 2: Allocate an ODBC connection handle
    sret = SQLAllocHandle(SQL_HANDLE_DBC, henv, &hdbc);
    if (sret != SQL_SUCCESS) {
        handle_odbc_err("SQLAllocHandle:Dbc",
            sret,
            (DBINT)REMOTE_FAIL,
            henv,
            SQL_HANDLE_ENV,
            srvproc);

        SQLFreeHandle(SQL_HANDLE_ENV, henv);
        return(XP_ERROR);
        }


    // STEP 3: Check for integrated security.
    if (strcmp(srv_pfield(srvproc, SRV_LSECURE, (int *)NULL), "TRUE") == 0) {
        // Client has accessed using some form of integrated security
        // Impersonate client and set SQL_INTEGRATED_SECURITY option
        bImpersonated = srv_impersonate_client(srvproc);

        // Connect to DSN using integrated security
        SQLSetConnectAttr(hdbc, SQL_INTEGRATED_SECURITY,
            (SQLPOINTER) SQL_IS_ON, SQL_IS_INTEGER);
        _tcscpy(acUID, _T(""));
        _tcscpy(acPWD, _T(""));
        }
    else {
        // Client used standard login. Set the user name and password.
#ifdef UNICODE
        MultiByteToWideChar(CP_ACP, 0, srv_pfield(srvproc, SRV_USER, NULL),
            -1, acUID, MAXNAME);
        MultiByteToWideChar(CP_ACP, 0, srv_pfield(srvproc, SRV_PWD, NULL),
-1, acPWD, MAXNAME);
#else
        strncpy(acUID, srv_pfield(srvproc, SRV_USER, NULL),
            MAXNAME);
        strncpy(acPWD, srv_pfield(srvproc, SRV_PWD, NULL),
            MAXNAME);
```

```
#endif
        }

// STEP 4: Connect
if (!SQL_SUCCEEDED(
    sret = SQLConnect(hdbc, (SQLTCHAR*) szDSN, SQL_NTS,
    (SQLTCHAR*) acUID, SQL_NTS, (SQLTCHAR*) acPWD, SQL_NTS)
    )) {
    handle_odbc_err("SQLConnect",
        sret,
        (DBINT)REMOTE_FAIL,
        hdbc,
        SQL_HANDLE_DBC,
        srvproc);
    goto SAFE_EXIT;
    }
```

As you can see, I've broken this down into four steps. First, we get an ODBC environment handle. We then use this handle to allocate an ODBC connection handle. Once we have a connection handle, we check the security of the calling connection and set ours to match it. Lastly, we take the connection handle and connect to the specified ODBC DSN (xp_exec assumes you've created a *system* DSN named LocalServer, but you can change that if you like). Once connected, we'll be able to execute SQL batches.

Obviously, starting a new connection within xp_exec complicates things a bit because it means that locks held by the caller will block xp_exec. To get around this, you can instruct xp_exec to call sp_bindsession to enlist in the caller's transaction block. This keeps xp_exec from blocking or being blocked by transactions initiated by the caller. You pass Y as xp_exec's second parameter to cause it to enlist in the caller's transaction. The code is presented in Listing 20–11:

**Listing 20–11** Joining the caller's transaction block.

```
// STEP 1: Get the client session token
if ((szShareTran[0]=='Y') || (szShareTran[0]=='y')) {
    rc = srv_getbindtoken(srvproc, acBindToken);
    if (rc == FAIL) {
        srv_sendmsg(srvproc,
            SRV_MSG_ERROR,
            EXECSQL_ERROR,
            SRV_INFO,
```

```
                    (DBTINYINT) 0,
                    NULL,
                    0,
                    0,
                    "Error with srv_getbindtoken",
                    SRV_NULLTERM);
            srv_senddone(srvproc, (SRV_DONE_ERROR | SRV_DONE_MORE), 0, 0);
            return(XP_ERROR);
            }


    // STEP 2: Bind it as a param for the proc call
    _tcscpy(szQuery, _T("{call sp_bindsession(?)}"));
    sret = SQLBindParameter(hstmt, 1, SQL_PARAM_INPUT, SQL_C_CHAR,
        SQL_VARCHAR, 255, 0, acBindToken, 256, NULL);
    if (sret != SQL_SUCCESS) {
        handle_odbc_err("SQLBindParameter",
            sret,
            (DBINT)REMOTE_FAIL,
            hstmt,
            SQL_HANDLE_STMT,
            srvproc);
        return(XP_ERROR);
        }


    // STEP 3: Bind our session to the client's session
    sret = SQLExecDirect(hstmt, (SQLTCHAR*) szQuery, SQL_NTS);
    if (!((sret == SQL_SUCCESS) ||(sret == SQL_SUCCESS_WITH_INFO))) {
        handle_odbc_err("SQLExecDirect",
            sret,
            (DBINT) EXECSQL_ERROR,
            hstmt,
            SQL_HANDLE_STMT,
            srvproc);
        return(XP_ERROR);
        }
    }
```

I've broken this down into three steps. First we get the token for the cur-rent client session by calling srv_getbindtoken(). Next we bind this value as an ODBC procedure parameter so that we can pass it to sp_bindsession. Last we call sp_bindsession and pass it the session token from the calling connection. This enlists the calling connection and our new ODBC connection in the same transaction. To verify that xp_exec has enlisted in the caller's transaction, you can begin a transaction in the caller and have xp_exec check @@TRAN-COUNT, like this:

```
BEGIN TRAN
PRINT 'Joining the transaction of the caller'
EXEC master..xp_exec 'SELECT @@TRANCOUNT','Y','master'
PRINT 'Running independently'
EXEC master..xp_exec 'SELECT @@TRANCOUNT','N','master'
GO
ROLLBACK
```

(Results abridged)

```
Joining the transaction of the caller
-----------
1


Running independently
-----------
0
```

Xp_exec's third parameter specifies the database context in which to run your code. It's an optional parameter. The previous example specifies the master database as the target context.

Once we've decided whether to enlist in the caller's transaction, the next order of business is to execute the query. That code looks like this (Listing 20–12):

**Listing 20–12** Using ODBC to execute the query.

```
// STEP 4: Execute the query
    _tcscpy(szQuery, szTSQL);
    sret = SQLExecDirect(hstmt, (SQLTCHAR*) szQuery, SQL_NTS);
    if (!((sret == SQL_SUCCESS)||(sret == SQL_NO_DATA))) {
        handle_odbc_err("SQLExecDirect",
            sret,
            (DBINT) EXECSQL_ERROR,
            hstmt,
            SQL_HANDLE_STMT,
            srvproc);
        return(XP_ERROR);
        }
```

SQLExecDirect() is the key function here. We pass it a statement handle (allocated earlier), the query to execute, and the type of string (null-terminated) that contains the query.

Because it doesn't know what type of result set (if any) it might receive, xp_exec makes some ODS calls to determine the characteristics of the result set. The key function call is SQLColAttribte(). Here's the code (Listing 20–13):

**Listing 20–13** You can use ODBC calls to interpret a result set.

```
for (nCol = 0; nCol < nCols; nCol++) {
    // Get the column name, length, and data type.
        SQLColAttribute(hstmt,
                (SQLSMALLINT) (nCol + 1),
                SQL_DESC_NAME,
                (SQLTCHAR*) acColumnName, // returned column name
                MAXNAME, // max length of rgbDesc buffer
                &cbAttr, // number of bytes returned in rgbDesc
                &iNumAttr);

        SQLColAttribute(hstmt,
                (SQLSMALLINT) (nCol + 1),
                SQL_DESC_OCTET_LENGTH,
                NULL,
                0,
                NULL,
                &cbColData);

    // Get the column's SQL Server data type, then reset the length
    // of the data retrieved as required.
    SQLColAttribute(hstmt,
                (SQLSMALLINT) (nCol + 1),
                SQL_CA_SS_COLUMN_SSTYPE,
                NULL,
                0,
                NULL,
                &eSQLType);

    // Overwrite the column length returned by ODBC
        // with the correct value to be used by ODS
        switch( eSQLType ) {
                case SQLMONEYN:
                case SQLMONEY:
            cbColData = sizeof(DBMONEY);
            break;
```

```
                    case SQLDATETIMN:
                    case SQLDATETIME:
                            cbColData = sizeof(DBDATETIME);
                            break;

                    case SQLNUMERIC:
                    case SQLDECIMAL:
                            cbColData = sizeof(DBNUMERIC);
                            break;

                    case SQLMONEY4:
                cbColData = sizeof(DBMONEY4);
                break;

                    case SQLDATETIM4: //smalldatetime
                            cbColData = sizeof(DBDATETIM4);
                            break;
                }
// ...
```

Once we've found out what columns we have in the result set, we can begin
sending them back to the client. As with xp_listfile, we call srv_describe() to set
up each result set column and srv_sendrow() to send each row back to the
client (Listing 20–14):

**Listing 20–14** Once we have the ODBC result set in hand, we use ODS to
transmit it.

```
        // Allocate memory for row data.
        if ((ppData[nCol] = (PBYTE) malloc(cbColData)) == NULL)
            goto SAFE_EXIT;
        memset(ppData[nCol], 0, cbColData);

            // Bind column
            SQLBindCol(hstmt,
                    (SQLSMALLINT) (nCol + 1),
                    SQL_C_BINARY, // No data conversion.
                    ppData[nCol],
                    cbColData,
                    &(pIndicators[nCol]));

            // Prepare structure that will be sent via ODS back to
            // the caller of the extended procedure
```

```
        srv_describe(srvproc,
            nCol + 1,
            acColumnName,
            SRV_NULLTERM,
            eSQLType, // Dest data type.
            (DBINT) cbColData,// Dest data length.
            eSQLType, // Source data type.
            (DBINT) cbColData, // Source data length.
            (PBYTE) NULL);
    }

// Initialize the row counter
rows = 0;

// Get each row of data from ODBC
// until there are no more rows
while((sret = SQLFetch(hstmt)) != SQL_NO_DATA_FOUND) {
    if (!SQL_SUCCEEDED(sret)) {
        handle_odbc_err("SQLFetch",
            sret,
            (DBINT) EXECSQL_ERROR,
            hstmt,
            SQL_HANDLE_STMT,
            srvproc);
        goto SAFE_EXIT;
        }

    // For each data field in the current row,
    // fill the structure
    // that will be sent back to the caller.
     for (nCol = 0; nCol < nCols; nCol++) {
        cbColData = (pIndicators[nCol] == SQL_NULL_DATA ?
            0 : pIndicators[nCol]);
        srv_setcollen(srvproc, nCol+1, (int) cbColData);
        srv_setcoldata(srvproc, nCol+1, ppData[nCol]);
        }

    // Send the data row back to SQL Server via ODS.
    if (srv_sendrow(srvproc) == SUCCEED)
        rows++;
    }
```

As you can see, building even a moderately complex extended procedure is pretty straightforward.

## Making Extended Procedures Easier to Use

One technique for making an extended procedure a bit handier is to wrap it in a system procedure. This allows it to be easily called from any database context without having to be prefixed with **master..** A good number of SQL Server's own extended procedures are wrapped in system stored procedures. Here's an example using the undocumented routine xp_varbintohexstr (Listing 20–15):

**Listing 20–15**  "Wrapping" extended procedures makes them easier to use.

```
USE master
IF (OBJECT_ID('dbo.sp_hexstring') IS NOT NULL)
  DROP PROC dbo.sp_hexstring
GO
CREATE PROC dbo.sp_hexstring @int varchar(10)=NULL, @hexstring
varchar(30)=NULL OUT
/*
Object: sp_hexstring
Description: Return an integer as a hexadecimal string

Usage: sp_hexstring @int=Integer to convert, @hexstring=OUTPUT parm to
receive hex string

Returns: (None)

Created by: Ken Henderson. Email: khen@khen.com

Version: 1.0

Example: sp_hexstring 23, @myhex OUT

Created: 1999-08-02. Last changed: 1999-08-15.
*/
AS
IF (@int IS NULL) OR (@int = '/?') GOTO Help
DECLARE @i int, @vb varbinary(30)
SELECT @i=CAST(@int as int), @vb=CAST(@i as varbinary)
EXEC master..xp_varbintohexstr @vb, @hexstring OUT
RETURN 0
Help:
EXEC sp_usage @objectname='sp_hexstring',
      @desc='Return an integer as a hexadecimal string',
      @parameters='@int=Integer to convert, @hexstring=OUTPUT parm to
receive hex string',
```

```
            @example='sp_hexstring "23", @myhex OUT',
            @author='Ken Henderson',
            @email='khen@khen.com',
            @version='1', @revision='0',
            @datecreated='19990802', @datelastchanged='19990815'
RETURN -1

GO
DECLARE @hex varchar(30)
EXEC sp_hexstring 10, @hex OUT
SELECT @hex
```

(Results)

```
------------------------------
0x0000000A
```

Sp_hexstring validates the parameters to be passed to the extended procedure xp_varbintohexstr before calling it. Because sp_hexstring is a system procedure, it can be called from any database without referencing the extended
stored procedure directly.

## Debugging Extended Procedures

You debug extended stored procedures the same way you debug any other
DLL-based routine—by supplying a host application that loads the DLL and
placing a breakpoint in the routine you wish to debug. In the case of extended
procedures, the host application is SQL Server itself.

You can't debug extended procedures using the service version of SQL
Server, so you have to use its console version instead. How do you start SQL
Server as a console application? First, shut down the SQL Server service, then
run sqlservr.exe (in the SQL Server BINN folder) directly and pass -c as a parameter. Additionally, if you wish to start a named instance of SQL Server, specify the -s command-line parameter and specify the name of the instance you
wish to start.

---

**NOTE:** This section assumes that you're using Microsoft's Visual C++ to code
and debug your extended procedures. If you're using some other language tool,
you'll need to set it up to debug your extended procedure as a DLL using
sqlservr.exe as its host executable. Most modern Windows development tools
allow you to debug DLLs and specify alternate host executables.

---

You set up SQL Server as the host application for your DLL via a setting in your development environment. If you're using Visual C++, find the edit box titled **Executable for debug session:** on the Debug tab in the Project Settings dialog. Key in the full path to sqlservr.exe, along with the -c parameter. Include the -s parameter if necessary.

Place a breakpoint in your extended procedure code, then "run" your application. You should see SQL Server start in a console window. Once it has finished starting up (you can determine this by watching for the Recovery Complete message in the console window), open a Query Analyzer window and run your extended procedure. You should see execution stop at your breakpoint in Visual C++. From here, you can debug your extended procedure just as you would any other routine. You can step through the code line by line, trace into subroutines, view watch variables, and terminate the debugging session whenever you like.

---

**NOTE:** If you wish to debug using a named instance of SQL Server, be sure to include the -s parameter followed by the name of the instance (don't include the machine name) you wish to start. Failing to do this can cause a spurious error message to display indicating that your SQL Server installation is corrupt. If you see this message when you start SQL Server as a console application, check to see whether you've specified the -s option correctly.

---

## Isolating Extended Procedures

Because extended procedures run in the SQL Server process space, they can wreak havoc when ill-behaved. Of particular concern is the possibility that an extended procedure can leak memory, eventually exhausting the entire MemToLeave pool. SQL Server memory is organized into two basic memory pools: the buffer pool, from which the data and procedure caches are allocated, as well as most other memory allocations; and the MemToLeave pool, which defaults to 256MB in SQL Server 2000 (128MB in SQL Server 7.0) and is the area from which extended procedure and COM in-process (e.g., OLE-DB) allocations come. You can set the size of the MemToLeave pool via SQL Server's -g command-line option.

If an extended procedure that leaks memory is called frequently, it will eventually exhaust the entire MemToLeave pool. When this happens, the server will likely begin to crash or otherwise behave erratically, and the error log will begin to receive 17800-series errors along with, possibly, 8645 errors. At this point, the only real answer is to shut down and restart the SQL Server. If the extended procedure isn't fixed, the problem will continue to occur and the server will have to be regularly stopped and restarted to keep performance acceptable.

What if you could isolate extended procedures so that they ran outside the SQL Server process (à la out-of-process COM servers)? Well, you can. Sort of. The technique is really very simple. It amounts to creating a named instance of SQL Server whose purpose is to run extended procedures. Just follow these steps to set it up:

1.  Make sure your server machine has plenty of RAM.
2.  On the same machine as your primary SQL Server 2000 or later instance, install a second named SQL Server instance for the express purpose of hosting extended procedures.
3.  Register your extended procedures with this new instance, but not with the primary instance.
4.  Create system stored procedures on the primary instance that call the extended procedures on the other instance using four-part names.
5.  Code your application to call these system procedures rather than the extended procedures.

Using this technique allows you to set up an entire process just for extended procedures to run in. They are isolated from your production server by the operating system, and even if one of them is ill behaved, it's unlikely to be able to take down your primary SQL Server.

Remember that you can set the size of the MemToLeave pool using the -g command-line option on the extended procedure instance. You may wish to set it higher than the primary instance because it will house your application's extended procedures.

## xp_setpriority

In closing out this chapter, I'll leave you with an extended procedure that I think could change the way you work, especially if you manage a SQL Server installation in which long-running batch jobs and shorter, time-critical jobs regularly compete for system resources. Earlier, I mentioned that extended procedures run in the SQL Server process space. They also run in the context of the calling thread. That is, unless fiber mode has been enabled on the server, each connection gets its own Win32 thread. This thread is taken from the pool of worker threads that SQL Server creates on start-up and can change from query to query on the same connection. When an extended procedure runs, it runs within the context of this thread. This means that it has full access to the thread and can change certain characteristics of the thread if it so chooses. Whatever changes the extended procedure makes are retained by the thread after it finishes executing.

Xp_setpriority takes advantage of this nuance to allow you to adjust the thread priority of a SQL Server connection. Because SQL Server threads are already created with the highest priority setting permitted by their thread class, you can't raise the initial priority of a connection's thread, but you can lower it. Why would you want to lower it? Why would you want to slow a job down? Very simple: To allow other concurrent jobs to complete more quickly. That is, if you have a batch-type job that normally runs for many hours and often doesn't finish until the middle of the night, slowing it down so that other time-critical routines can execute more quickly may indeed be a viable option for you. If these jobs normally run concurrently anyway, slowing down the batch job a bit will have the net effect of speeding up the other jobs—perhaps dramatically.

Let's begin with the source code to xp_setpriority. There isn't much of it:

```
RETCODE xp_setpriority(srvproc)
SRV_PROC *srvproc;
{

    int threadpriority = THREAD_PRIORITY_TIME_CRITICAL;

    int        nParams;
    DBINT      paramtype;

    TCHAR          szPriority[20] = "";
    BYTE pbType;
    ULONG pcbMaxLen;
    ULONG pcbActualLen;
    BOOL pfNull;

    RETCODE    rcXP = XP_ERROR;    // Assume failure until shown otherwise.

    // Get number of parameters.
    nParams = srv_rpcparams(srvproc);

    // Check number of parameters
    if (nParams != 1) {
    // Send error message and return
        srv_sendmsg(srvproc, SRV_MSG_ERROR, XP_SETPRIORITY_ERROR, SRV_INFO,
        (DBTINYINT)0,
```

```
              NULL, 0, 0, "Error executing extended stored procedure: Invalid
              number of parameters.",
              SRV_NULLTERM);

               // A SRV_DONE_MORE instead of a SRV_DONE_FINAL must complete the
               // result set of an Extended Stored Procedure.
               srv_senddone(srvproc, (SRV_DONE_ERROR | SRV_DONE_MORE), 0, 0);
               return(XP_ERROR);
               }

      // If parameter is not varchar (should be HIGHEST/LOWEST/etc.), send an
      // error and return.
      paramtype = srv_paramtype(srvproc, 1);
      if (paramtype != SRVVARCHAR) {
         srv_sendmsg(srvproc, SRV_MSG_ERROR, XP_SETPRIORITY_ERROR, SRV_INFO,
         (DBTINYINT)0,
         NULL, 0, 0,
         "Error executing extended stored procedure: Invalid Parameter Type",
         SRV_NULLTERM);
          // A SRV_DONE_MORE instead of a SRV_DONE_FINAL must complete the
          // result set of an Extended Stored Procedure.
          srv_senddone(srvproc, (SRV_DONE_ERROR | SRV_DONE_MORE), 0, 0);
          return(XP_ERROR);
          }

              // Terminate parameter string with NULL.
              srv_paraminfo(srvproc,1,&pbType, &pcbMaxLen, &pcbActualLen,
              szPriority, &pfNull);
              szPriority[pcbActualLen] = '\0';

          if (stricmp(szPriority,"HIGHEST")==0)
            {
                  threadpriority=THREAD_PRIORITY_TIME_CRITICAL;
            }
            else if (stricmp(szPriority,"HIGH")==0)
            {
                  threadpriority=THREAD_PRIORITY_ABOVE_NORMAL;
            }
            else if (stricmp(szPriority,"LOW")==0)
            {
                  threadpriority=THREAD_PRIORITY_BELOW_NORMAL;
            }
            else if (stricmp(szPriority,"LOWEST")==0)
            {
```

```
                threadpriority=THREAD_PRIORITY_LOWEST;
        }
        else if (stricmp(szPriority,"NORMAL")==0)
        {
                threadpriority=THREAD_PRIORITY_NORMAL;
        }
        SetThreadPriority(GetCurrentThread(),threadpriority);
        srv_senddone(srvproc, SRV_DONE_MORE, (DBUSMALLINT)0,
        (DBINT)0);
        // We got here successfully, let the client know.
        return XP_NOERROR ;
}
```

Other than the usual boilerplate parameter processing code, there's really only one significant line of code in xp_setpriority: the call to the Windows API SetThreadPriority() routine. It nests a call to GetCurrentThread() to get the handle of the current connection's thread, then sets its priority to that specified by the user. The routine supports five priority settings: HIGHEST, HIGH, NORMAL, LOW, and LOWEST. These are all relevant to the thread's base class.

To grasp the practical usefulness of this routine, let's have a look at some code. You'll need a SQL Server with little or no activity on it for the following tests to be meaningful. Begin by copying the xp_setpriority.dll file to your SQL Server instance's BINN folder (be sure this is the BINN folder under the instance and not the one associated with the SQL Server Tools folder). Once the DLL is copied, run this script to make xp_setpriority available on your server:

```
USE master
GO


EXEC sp_addextendedproc 'xp_setpriority', 'xp_setpriority.dll'
GO
```

Once you've added the extended procedure, load the following query into Query Analyzer and run it one time. It initiates a CPU-intensive operation—a loop that counts from 1 to 1 million—then returns. Run it once and note its execution time (Query Analyzer displays the execution time in the bottom frame of each query window):

```
SELECT GETDATE()
go
--EXEC master..xp_setpriority 'LOWEST'
```

```
DECLARE @i int
SET @i=0
WHILE @i<1000000 BEGIN
  SET @i=@i+1
END
EXEC master..xp_setpriority 'NORMAL'
GO
SELECT GETDATE()
```

On the ancient laptop on which I'm writing this book, this code takes about 23 seconds to run.

Now open a second window in Query Analyzer and load the query into it as well. Once it loads, run it and the first instance of the query simultaneously. This will tell us how much resource contention (in this case, CPU time) affects the execution time of our query. On my laptop, each instance of the query now takes about 42 seconds to run—an increase of almost 100%. This makes sense. After all, there's only so much CPU to go around.

But wait a minute: What if you could adjust the execution priority of one of the jobs so that the other one could finish more quickly? What if only one of the jobs was time-critical? What if slowing down one query so that the other could finish more quickly would help your business? That's easily done with xp_setpriority. Simply uncomment the call to it in one (but not both) of the query windows and rerun both of them. On my machine, the query that's still running at NORMAL priority now finishes in 23 seconds even though the other query is competing with it for CPU bandwidth. This means that it takes no longer to run while the second query runs than it did to run it by itself. This is because of the fact that it has a higher thread priority than the query that called xp_setpriority to slow itself down. We've effectively sped up the first query by nearly 50% by simply slowing down its competition. Moreover, the slower query only takes a little longer to run than it did when it was running at NORMAL priority. On my machine, it now takes 58 seconds to run. That's about a 33% reduction in performance by one query to speed up another by nearly 50%—a pretty good trade. The trade isn't a wash because, by allowing the higher priority query to finish, the second query is preempted less often than it would be were both queries competing vigorously for CPU time.

Note that a query's thread priority need not be permanent. You can raise it back to normal status or lower it again whenever you want during the execution of the query. Moreover, you can wrap critical sections of code in calls that raise the thread priority momentarily back to normal for the query, then lower it again, so that those particular sections get all the CPU time they possibly can. Using xp_setpriority, you have as much control over your thread's execution time as SQL Server will allow.

A nice feature for a future release of SQL Server would be the ability to set a connection's execution priority via Transact-SQL code. It's reasonable that administrators and developers would want to be able to customize the execution priority for individual connections rather than taking a one-size-fits-all approach and using the same setting for all of them. Until this functionality is added, though, you can use xp_setpriority to accomplish the same thing. If you have long-running, batch-oriented jobs with execution times that are not something you're terribly concerned about, consider lowering their execution time to allow your more critical jobs to run more quickly. You could go so far as to partition your users into classes based on business needs, and allow some to run at a higher priority than others. By tailoring the thread priorities of your SQL Server connections, you may well see an increase in overall performance and efficiency on your server.

---

**WARNING:** *It's very important that you read through this warning completely before using xp_setpriority.* In fact, it's so important that I almost pulled the coverage of xp_setpriority from this book out of concern that people would cause themselves problems by misusing it. Like most powerful tools, xp_setpriority can wreak havoc when used improperly. Please read the following warning completely and be sure you understand it thoroughly before using xp_setpriority on a production server.

Because SQL Server regularly rotates the worker threads that service user connections, it's possible—in fact, likely—that changes you make to a thread via xp_setpriority will affect other connections if you're not careful. I once saw a sign that said, "Your mother does not work here. Please clean up after yourself." It's *extremely important* that you undo any changes you make to a thread context with xp_setpriority before your query returns. That is, the last statement *in any query batch* that uses xp_setpriority should be

```
EXEC master..xp_setpriority 'NORMAL'
```

This ensures that another connection will not inherit the temporary changes you make to the thread priority. And you'll want to be sure that errors that might occur before the final call to xp_setpriority are properly handled so that it's not bypassed. Failing to reset the thread priority properly after lowering it could have the effect of, say, randomly slowing down other connections on your system—something you probably wouldn't like, and that would be nigh impossible to troubleshoot.

To see how this works, run the following query several times in a row on a server with lots of activity:

```
SELECT kpid FROM master..sysprocesses WHERE spid=@@spid
```

The **kpid** column in sysprocesses is the Win32 thread ID assigned to the connection. Run the query several times in succession on a busy server, and you'll see that this thread ID fluctuates. The thread you used last time may be in use by someone else now, and the thread you have currently may have last been used by a completely different connection. This is why it's important to clean up after yourself. Because SQL Server uses thread pooling, changes you make to a thread can affect other connections.

## Summary

In this chapter you learned how to create and use extended procedures. You were introduced to the ODS API as well as to how basic memory and thread management works on SQL Server. Extended procedures can provide rich functionality when used properly, but can take down a server when used unwisely.

# CHAPTER 21

# Administrative Stored Procedures

*Generally, management of many is the same as management of few. It is a matter of organization.*

*—Sun Tzu*[1]

In this chapter we'll explore building administrative stored procedures. Although SQL Server comes with a large number of documented and undocumented stored procedures, there always seems to be a need for one more. That's what this chapter is about. It shows you some of the techniques you can use to build administrative code by taking you on a tour of several administrative routines that I've built. These routines demonstrate techniques that you can use in your own work and provide code that you may find useful as well. Several of them build on one another. For example, sp_generate_script uses sp_readtextfile, and sp_diffdb uses sp_generate_script and sp_diff. Many of these routines are connected in some way. Study them, run them yourself, and see if you can think of similar routines you might build on your own. Take some of the techniques I've used in these procedures and build new procedures that make your life as a SQL Server practitioner easier.

## sp_readtextfile

Sp_readtextfile allows you to read a text file on the SQL Server machine (or a machine accessible to it on the network) and either return it as a result set or store the first 8,000 bytes of it in an output parameter. The code is presented in Listing 21–1.

---

[1]Tzu, Sun. *The Art of War*. Cambridge, England: Oxford University Press, 1963. Page 90.

**Listing 21–1** sp_readtextfile.

```
USE master
GO
IF OBJECT_ID('sp_readtextfile') IS NOT NULL
  DROP PROC sp_readtextfile
GO
CREATE PROC sp_readtextfile @textfilename sysname,
@contents varchar(8000)='Results Only' OUT
/*

Object: sp_readtextfile
Description: Reads the contents of a text file into a SQL result set

Usage: sp_readtextfile @textfilename=name of file to read,
@contents=optional output var to receive contents of file (up to 8000
bytes)

Returns: (None)

$Author: Ken Henderson $. Email: khen@khen.com

$Revision: 8.0 $

Example: sp_readtextfile 'D:\MSSQL7\LOG\errorlog'

Created: 1996-05-01. $Modtime: 2000-01-20 $.

*/
AS
SET NOCOUNT ON
IF (@textfilename='/?') GOTO Help

CREATE TABLE #lines (lno int identity, line varchar(8000))

DECLARE @cmd varchar(8000), @crlf char(2)
SET @cmd='TYPE '+@textfilename
SET @crlf=CHAR(13)+CHAR(10)

INSERT #lines (line)
EXEC master.dbo.xp_cmdshell @cmd

IF ISNULL(@contents,'')='Results Only'
  SELECT ISNULL(line,'') AS line
```

```
   FROM #lines
   ORDER BY lno
ELSE
   SELECT @contents=CASE lno WHEN 1 THEN ISNULL(RTRIM(line),'')+@crlf ELSE
@contents+ISNULL(RTRIM(line),'')+@crlf END
   FROM #lines
   ORDER BY lno

DROP TABLE #lines
RETURN 0

Help:
EXEC sp_usage @objectname='sp_readtextfile',
@desc='Reads the contents of a text file into a SQL result set',
@parameters='@textfilename=name of file to read, @contents=optional output
var to receive contents of file (up to 8000 bytes)',
@author='Ken Henderson', @email='khen@khen.com',
@version='8',@revision='0',
@datecreated='19960501', @datelastchanged='20000120',
@example='sp_readtextfile ''D:\MSSQL7\LOG\errorlog'' '
RETURN -1
GO
EXEC sp_readtextfile 'c:\readme.txt'
```

(Results)

```
line
-----------------------------------------------------------------------------
README.TXT

Use this at your own risk. I don't warranty this software to do anything in
particular, useful or otherwise. I particularly disclaim any responsibility
for the software working at all. If my new Whizbang Calendar Doowop Control
doesn't meet your needs, please return it. You won't get a refund, but at
least you won't be bothered by bad software anymore :-p
-----------------------------------------------------------------------------
```

This routine employs a couple of interesting techniques. First, notice the use of a default value for the output parameter. This makes the parameter optional. It's not unusual for input parameters to be optional, but you may not have considered doing the same thing for output parameters. I've done it this way to allow the procedure to be used two different ways. If all you want is the text file as a result set, you can omit the output parameter. The procedure will simply insert the text file into a table, then clean up the text a bit as it returns the rows as a result set. If, instead, you need the contents of the file loaded into a variable, you can pass in a varchar, and the procedure will fill it with the first 8,000 bytes of the file. We can't use a text field here because local text variables are not supported by Transact-SQL. Here's what the call would look like with an output parameter:

```
DECLARE @txt varchar(8000)
EXEC sp_readtextfile 'c:\readme.txt', @txt OUT
SELECT @txt
```

Another interesting technique in the routine is the use of xp_cmdshell to list the file. All we do to load the text file into a temporary table is pass xp_cmdshell a call to the operating system TYPE command. Because xp_cmdshell can be redirected to a table via INSERT...EXEC, this serves as a simple mechanism for reading the file. We load the file into a table because xp_cmdshell replaces empty lines in the file with NULL—unnecessary and not terribly aesthetic. Putting the data in a table allows us to use ISNULL() to filter out those unsightly NULLs.

---

**NOTE:** SQL Server's xp_readerrorlog routine can also read plain text files. To get xp_readerrorlog to read a text file other than an errorlog, pass -1 as its first parameter, followed by a comma and the name of the file you'd like to read. Sp_readtextfile provides a means of reading text files without requiring an extended procedure, but xp_readerrorlog works well if you don't mind dealing with extended procedures.

---

## sp_diff

You may recall from Chapter 4 that we wired VSS's difference-checking tool into Query Analyzer's tools menu so that you could difference check T-SQL scripts. Sp_diff takes a similar approach. It calls VSS's command-line interface, SS.EXE, and accesses its differencing engine to check the differences between two files that you supply. It returns the differences VSS finds between the files as a result set. Here's the code (Listing 21–2):

**Listing 21–2** sp_diff.

```
USE master
GO
```

```
IF OBJECT_ID('sp_diff') IS NOT NULL
  DROP PROC sp_diff
GO
CREATE PROC sp_diff @file1 sysname='/?', @file2 sysname=NULL
/*

Object: sp_diff
Description: Returns the differences between two text files as a result set (uses
VSS)

Usage: sp_diff @file1=full path to first file, @file2=fullpath to second file

Returns: (None)

$Author: Ken Henderson $. Email: khen@khen.com

$Revision: 1.0 $

Example: sp_diff 'c:\customers.sql', 'c:\customers2.sql'

Created: 2001-01-14. $Modtime: 2001-01-16 $.

*/
AS
SET NOCOUNT ON

IF (COALESCE(@file1+@file2,'/?')='/?') GOTO Help

DECLARE @cmd varchar(1000)
SET @cmd='SS diff '+@file1+' '+@file2+' -Yadmin'
CREATE TABLE #diffs (line int identity, diff varchar(8000))
INSERT #diffs (diff)
EXEC master..xp_cmdshell @cmd

SELECT ISNULL(diff,'') AS diff FROM #diffs
ORDER BY line

DROP TABLE #diffs

RETURN 0
Help:
EXEC sp_usage @objectname='sp_diff',
@desc='Returns the differences between two text files as a result set (uses VSS)',
@parameters='@file1=full path to first file, @file2=fullpath to second file',
```

```
@author='Ken Henderson', @email='khen@khen.com',
@version='1',@revision='0',
@datecreated='20010114', @datelastchanged='20010116',
@example='sp_diff ''c:\customers.sql'', ''c:\customers2.sql'' '
RETURN -1
GO
EXEC sp_diff 'c:\customers.sql', 'c:\customers2.sql'
```

(Results)

```
diff
--------------------------------------------------------------------------------
Diffing: c:\customers.sql
Against: c:\customers2.sql

  6 Change:   [CompanyName] [nvarchar] (40) COLLATE SQL_Latin1_General_CP1_CI_A
       To:   [Company] [nvarchar] (40) COLLATE SQL_Latin1_General_CP1_CI_AS NO
 15   Del:   [Fax] [nvarchar] (24) COLLATE SQL_Latin1_General_CP1_CI_AS NULL ,
```

Here, I've supplied two scripts to sp_diff to difference check. It returns the two filenames at the top of the listing, then lists the differences between them. It shows that the **CompanyName** column was shortened to just **Company** in the second table, and that line 15 was deleted in the second table. How do we know which table the differences apply to? Look closely at the verbiage at the top of the listing "Diffing...Against." This means that Customer2.SQL is being treated as the master copy of the code, and the listing is displaying the steps you would need to take to make Customer.SQL match it exactly.

As with sp_readtextfile, sp_diff calls on xp_cmdshell to do the real work of the procedure. It uses xp_cmdshell to call SS.EXE, the VSS command-line utility, and passes the two files to it so they can be difference checked. Notice the -Y parameter. This is the user name with which you want to log into VSS. Here I've just supplied the admin user with no password for simplicity's sake—you'll likely use a different one.

We trap the output from xp_cmdshell in a temporary table, and, as with sp_readtextfile, cleanse the data of NULLs as we return it. The end result is a basic, yet very functional, difference-checking facility from Transact-SQL.

## sp_generate_script

Sp_generate_script provides a handy utility for scripting out objects from a database. It originally appeared in my last book, *The Guru's Guide to Transact-*

*SQL*, and has been updated for the latest release of the product and enhanced a bit since then.

You use sp_generate_script by passing it the name of the object you want to script. You can supply a mask with wildcards, if you like, or you can omit the name altogether and the current database will be scripted.

Sp_generate_script uses the SQL-DMO API to do its work. It creates DMO COM objects using sp_OACreate and calls methods on them using sp_OAMethod. Because DMO requires a connection to the server to do any type of scripting, you must pass login information into sp_generate_script so that it can instantiate a new connection to the server using DMO method calls. Once the connection is established, the procedure finds the object or objects for which you want to generate scripts, and adds them to a DMO Transfer object so that they can be written out to a disk file. If you opt to receive a result set (enabled by default), sp_generate_script calls sp_readtextfile to read the script file produced by DMO and returns it as a result set.

The one quirk about the routine is that the DMO Transfer object generates a partial result set that cannot (as far as I can tell) be disabled. So, regardless of whether you ask for a result set, you get a small one after every call to sp_generate_script. I've put a PRINT message in the code just after the call to the Transfer object's ScriptTransfer method telling you to ignore this spurious output, but that's about all I can do. Fortunately, it seems completely harmless: The script is produced despite the message. Here's the code (Listing 21–3):

**Listing 21–3** sp_generate_script.

```
USE master
GO
IF OBJECT_ID('sp_generate_script') IS NOT NULL
  DROP PROC sp_generate_script
GO
CREATE PROC sp_generate_script
        @objectname sysname=NULL,   -- Object mask to copy
        @outputname sysname=NULL,   -- Output file to create (default:
@objectname+'.SQL')
        @scriptoptions int=NULL,    -- Options bitmask for Transfer
        @resultset bit=1,    -- Determines whether the script is returned as a result
set
        @server sysname='(local)',       -- Name of the server to connect to
        @username sysname='sa',          -- Name of the user to connect as (defaults
to 'sa')
        @password sysname=NULL,          -- User's password
   @trustedconnection bit=1,       -- Use a trusted connection to connect to the server
```

```
    @IncludeHeaders bit=1 -- Determines whether descriptive headers are included with
scripts
/*

Object: sp_generate_script
Description: Generates a creation script for an object or collection of objects

Usage: sp_generate_script [@objectname='Object name or mask (defaults to all object
in current database)']
                          [,@outputname='Output file name' (Default: @objectname+'.SQL', or
GENERATED_SCRIPT.SQL for entire database)]
                          [,@scriptoptions=bitmask specifying script generation options]
                          [,@resultset=bit specifying whether to generate a result set
                          [,@includeheaders=bit specifying whether to generate discriptive
headers for scripts
                          [,@server='server name'] [, @username='user name'] [,
@password='password'] [, @trustedconnection=1]

Returns: (None)

$Author: Ken Henderson $. Email: khen@khen.com

$Revision: 8.0 $

Example: sp_generate_script @objectname='authors', @outputname='authors.sql'

Created: 1998-04-01. $Modtime: 2000-12-16 $.

*/
AS


-- SQLDMO_SCRIPT_TYPE vars
DECLARE @SQLDMOScript_Default int
DECLARE @SQLDMOScript_Drops int
DECLARE @SQLDMOScript_ObjectPermissions int
DECLARE @SQLDMOScript_PrimaryObject int
DECLARE @SQLDMOScript_ClusteredIndexes int
DECLARE @SQLDMOScript_Triggers int
DECLARE @SQLDMOScript_DatabasePermissions int
DECLARE @SQLDMOScript_Permissions int
DECLARE @SQLDMOScript_ToFileOnly int
DECLARE @SQLDMOScript_Bindings int
DECLARE @SQLDMOScript_AppendToFile int
DECLARE @SQLDMOScript_NoDRI int
```

```
DECLARE @SQLDMOScript_UDDTsToBaseType int
DECLARE @SQLDMOScript_IncludeIfNotExists int
DECLARE @SQLDMOScript_NonClusteredIndexes int
DECLARE @SQLDMOScript_Indexes int
DECLARE @SQLDMOScript_Aliases int
DECLARE @SQLDMOScript_NoCommandTerm int
DECLARE @SQLDMOScript_DRIIndexes int
DECLARE @SQLDMOScript_IncludeHeaders int
DECLARE @SQLDMOScript_OwnerQualify int
DECLARE @SQLDMOScript_TimestampToBinary int
DECLARE @SQLDMOScript_SortedData int
DECLARE @SQLDMOScript_SortedDataReorg int
DECLARE @SQLDMOScript_TransferDefault int
DECLARE @SQLDMOScript_DRI_NonClustered int
DECLARE @SQLDMOScript_DRI_Clustered int
DECLARE @SQLDMOScript_DRI_Checks int
DECLARE @SQLDMOScript_DRI_Defaults int
DECLARE @SQLDMOScript_DRI_UniqueKeys int
DECLARE @SQLDMOScript_DRI_ForeignKeys int
DECLARE @SQLDMOScript_DRI_PrimaryKey int
DECLARE @SQLDMOScript_DRI_AllKeys int
DECLARE @SQLDMOScript_DRI_AllConstraints int
DECLARE @SQLDMOScript_DRI_All int
DECLARE @SQLDMOScript_DRIWithNoCheck int
DECLARE @SQLDMOScript_NoIdentity int
DECLARE @SQLDMOScript_UseQuotedIdentifiers int

-- SQLDMO_SCRIPT2_TYPE vars
DECLARE @SQLDMOScript2_Default int
DECLARE @SQLDMOScript2_AnsiPadding int
DECLARE @SQLDMOScript2_AnsiFile int
DECLARE @SQLDMOScript2_UnicodeFile int
DECLARE @SQLDMOScript2_NonStop int
DECLARE @SQLDMOScript2_NoFG int
DECLARE @SQLDMOScript2_MarkTriggers int
DECLARE @SQLDMOScript2_OnlyUserTriggers int
DECLARE @SQLDMOScript2_EncryptPWD int
DECLARE @SQLDMOScript2_SeparateXPs int

-- SQLDMO_SCRIPT_TYPE values
SET @SQLDMOScript_Default = 4
SET @SQLDMOScript_Drops = 1
SET @SQLDMOScript_ObjectPermissions = 2
SET @SQLDMOScript_PrimaryObject = 4
```

```
SET @SQLDMOScript_ClusteredIndexes = 8
SET @SQLDMOScript_Triggers = 16
SET @SQLDMOScript_DatabasePermissions = 32
SET @SQLDMOScript_Permissions = 34
SET @SQLDMOScript_ToFileOnly = 64
SET @SQLDMOScript_Bindings = 128
SET @SQLDMOScript_AppendToFile = 256
SET @SQLDMOScript_NoDRI = 512
SET @SQLDMOScript_UDDTsToBaseType = 1024
SET @SQLDMOScript_IncludeIfNotExists = 4096
SET @SQLDMOScript_NonClusteredIndexes = 8192
SET @SQLDMOScript_Indexes = 73736
SET @SQLDMOScript_Aliases = 16384
SET @SQLDMOScript_NoCommandTerm = 32768
SET @SQLDMOScript_DRIIndexes = 65536
SET @SQLDMOScript_IncludeHeaders = 131072
SET @SQLDMOScript_OwnerQualify = 262144
SET @SQLDMOScript_TimestampToBinary = 524288
SET @SQLDMOScript_SortedData = 1048576
SET @SQLDMOScript_SortedDataReorg = 2097152
SET @SQLDMOScript_TransferDefault = 422143
SET @SQLDMOScript_DRI_NonClustered = 4194304
SET @SQLDMOScript_DRI_Clustered = 8388608
SET @SQLDMOScript_DRI_Checks = 16777216
SET @SQLDMOScript_DRI_Defaults = 33554432
SET @SQLDMOScript_DRI_UniqueKeys = 67108864
SET @SQLDMOScript_DRI_ForeignKeys = 134217728
SET @SQLDMOScript_DRI_PrimaryKey = 268435456
SET @SQLDMOScript_DRI_AllKeys = 469762048
SET @SQLDMOScript_DRI_AllConstraints = 520093696
SET @SQLDMOScript_DRI_All = 532676608
SET @SQLDMOScript_DRIWithNoCheck = 536870912
SET @SQLDMOScript_NoIdentity = 1073741824
SET @SQLDMOScript_UseQuotedIdentifiers = -1

-- SQLDMO_SCRIPT2_TYPE values
SET @SQLDMOScript2_Default = 0
SET @SQLDMOScript2_AnsiPadding = 1
SET @SQLDMOScript2_AnsiFile = 2
SET @SQLDMOScript2_UnicodeFile = 4
SET @SQLDMOScript2_NonStop = 8
SET @SQLDMOScript2_NoFG = 16
SET @SQLDMOScript2_MarkTriggers = 32
SET @SQLDMOScript2_OnlyUserTriggers = 64
```

```
SET @SQLDMOScript2_EncryptPWD = 128
SET @SQLDMOScript2_SeparateXPs = 256

DECLARE @dbname sysname,
        @srvobject int,       -- SQL Server object
        @object int,  -- Work variable for accessing COM objects
        @hr int,          -- Contains HRESULT returned by COM
        @tfobject int,        -- Stores pointer to Transfer object
   @res int

SET @res=0

IF (@objectname='/?') GOTO Help

IF (@objectname IS NOT NULL) AND (CHARINDEX('%',@objectname)=0) AND
(CHARINDEX('_',@objectname)=0) BEGIN
  SET @dbname=ISNULL(PARSENAME(@objectname,3),DB_NAME()) -- Extract the DB name;
default to current
  SET @objectname=PARSENAME(@objectname,1)    -- Remove extraneous stuff from table
name
  IF (@objectname IS NULL) BEGIN
     RAISERROR('Invalid object name.',16,1)
     RETURN -1
  END
  IF (@outputname IS NULL)
     SET @outputname=@objectname+'.SQL'
END ELSE BEGIN
  SET @dbname=DB_NAME()
  IF (@outputname IS NULL)
     SET @outputname='GENERATED_SCRIPT.SQL'
END

-- Create a SQLServer object
EXEC @hr=sp_OACreate 'SQLDMO.SQLServer', @srvobject OUTPUT
IF (@hr <> 0) BEGIN
    EXEC sp_displayoaerrorinfo @srvobject, @hr
    RETURN
END

-- Create a Transfer object
EXEC @hr=sp_OACreate 'SQLDMO.Transfer', @tfobject OUTPUT
IF (@hr <> 0) BEGIN
    EXEC sp_displayoaerrorinfo @tfobject, @hr
    RETURN
```

```
END

-- Set Transfer's CopyData property
EXEC @hr = sp_OASetProperty @tfobject, 'CopyData', 0
IF (@hr <> 0) BEGIN
    EXEC sp_displayoaerrorinfo @tfobject, @hr
    RETURN
END

-- Tell Transfer to copy the schema
EXEC @hr = sp_OASetProperty @tfobject, 'CopySchema', 1
IF (@hr <> 0) BEGIN
    EXEC sp_displayoaerrorinfo @tfobject, @hr
    RETURN
END

IF (@objectname IS NULL) BEGIN -- Get all objects in the database

  -- Tell Transfer to copy all objects
  EXEC @hr = sp_OASetProperty @tfobject, 'CopyAllObjects', 1
  IF (@hr <> 0) BEGIN
     EXEC sp_displayoaerrorinfo @tfobject, @hr
     RETURN
  END

  -- Tell Transfer to get groups as well
  EXEC @hr = sp_OASetProperty @tfobject, 'IncludeGroups', 1
  IF (@hr <> 0) BEGIN
     EXEC sp_displayoaerrorinfo @tfobject, @hr
     RETURN
  END

  -- Tell it to include users
  EXEC @hr = sp_OASetProperty @tfobject, 'IncludeUsers', 1
  IF (@hr <> 0) BEGIN
     EXEC sp_displayoaerrorinfo @tfobject, @hr
     RETURN
  END

  -- Tell it to include logins
  EXEC @hr = sp_OASetProperty @tfobject, 'IncludeLogins', 1
  IF (@hr <> 0) BEGIN
     EXEC sp_displayoaerrorinfo @tfobject, @hr
     RETURN
```

```
      END

      -- Include object dependencies too
      EXEC @hr = sp_OASetProperty @tfobject, 'IncludeDependencies', 1
      IF (@hr <> 0) BEGIN
          EXEC sp_displayoaerrorinfo @tfobject, @hr
          RETURN
      END

      IF (@scriptoptions IS NULL) BEGIN
        SET @scriptoptions=@SQLDMOScript_OwnerQualify | @SQLDMOScript_Default |
@SQLDMOScript_Triggers |
                       @SQLDMOScript_Bindings | @SQLDMOScript_DatabasePermissions |
                       @SQLDMOScript_Permissions | @SQLDMOScript_ObjectPermissions |
                       @SQLDMOScript_ClusteredIndexes | @SQLDMOScript_Indexes |
@SQLDMOScript_Aliases |
                       @SQLDMOScript_DRI_All
        IF @includeheaders=1 SET @scriptoptions=@scriptoptions |
@SQLDMOScript_IncludeHeaders
      END

END ELSE BEGIN
   DECLARE @obname sysname,
           @obtype varchar(2),
           @obowner sysname,
           @OBJECT_TYPES varchar(50),
           @obcode int

   -- Used to translate sysobjects.type into the bitmap that Transfer requires
   SET @OBJECT_TYPES='T     V  U  P     D  R  TR          FN TF IF '

   -- Find all the objects that match the supplied mask and add them to Transfer's
   -- list of objects to script
   DECLARE ObjectList CURSOR FOR
        SELECT name,CASE type WHEN 'TF' THEN 'FN' WHEN 'IF' THEN 'FN' ELSE type END AS
type,USER_NAME(uid) FROM sysobjects
        WHERE (name LIKE @objectname)
     AND (CHARINDEX(type+' ',@OBJECT_TYPES)<>0)
     AND (OBJECTPROPERTY(id,'IsSystemTable')=0)
     AND (status>0)
        UNION ALL -- Include user-defined data types
        SELECT name,'T',USER_NAME(uid)
        FROM SYSTYPES
        WHERE (usertype & 256)<>0
```

```
        AND (name LIKE @objectname)

   OPEN ObjectList

   FETCH ObjectList INTO @obname, @obtype, @obowner
   WHILE (@@FETCH_STATUS=0) BEGIN
     SET @obcode=POWER(2,(CHARINDEX(@obtype+' ',@OBJECT_TYPES)/3))

     EXEC @hr = sp_OAMethod @tfobject, 'AddObjectByName', NULL, @obname, @obcode,
@obowner
     IF (@hr <> 0) BEGIN
        EXEC sp_displayoaerrorinfo @tfobject, @hr
        RETURN
     END

     FETCH ObjectList INTO @obname, @obtype, @obowner
   END
   CLOSE ObjectList
   DEALLOCATE ObjectList

   IF (@scriptoptions IS NULL)
     SET @scriptoptions=@SQLDMOScript_Default -- Keep it simple when not scripting the
entire database
END

-- Set Transfer's ScriptType property
EXEC @hr = sp_OASetProperty @tfobject, 'ScriptType', @scriptoptions
IF (@hr <> 0) BEGIN
   EXEC sp_displayoaerrorinfo @tfobject, @hr
   RETURN
END

-- Connect to the server
IF (@trustedconnection=1) BEGIN
  EXEC @hr = sp_OASetProperty @srvobject, 'LoginSecure', 1
       IF (@hr <> 0) GOTO ServerError
  EXEC @hr = sp_OAMethod @srvobject, 'Connect', NULL, @server
END ELSE BEGIN
       IF (@password IS NOT NULL)
         EXEC @hr = sp_OAMethod @srvobject, 'Connect', NULL, @server, @username,
@password
       ELSE
         EXEC @hr = sp_OAMethod @srvobject, 'Connect', NULL, @server, @username
END
```

```
IF (@hr <> 0) GOTO ServerError

-- Get a pointer to the SQLServer object's Databases collection
EXEC @hr = sp_OAGetProperty @srvobject, 'Databases', @object OUT
IF @hr <> 0 BEGIN
    EXEC sp_displayoaerrorinfo @srvobject, @hr
    RETURN
END

-- Get a pointer from the Databases collection for the specified database
EXEC @hr = sp_OAMethod @object, 'Item', @object OUT, @dbname
IF @hr <> 0 BEGIN
    EXEC sp_displayoaerrorinfo @object, @hr
    RETURN
END

-- Call the Database object's ScriptTransfer method to create the script
EXEC @hr = sp_OAMethod @object, 'ScriptTransfer',NULL, @tfobject, 2, @outputname
IF @hr <> 0 BEGIN
    EXEC sp_displayoaerrorinfo @object, @hr
    RETURN
END

PRINT 'NOTE: Ignore the code displayed above. It''s a remnant of the SQL-DMO method
used to produce
the script file'

IF (@resultset=1) EXEC sp_readtextfile @outputname
GOTO ExitPoint

ServerError:
SET @res=-2

ExitPoint:
EXEC sp_OADestroy @srvobject        -- For cleanliness
EXEC sp_OADestroy @tfobject         -- For cleanliness

RETURN @res

Help:
EXEC sp_usage @objectname='sp_generate_script',@desc='Generates a creation script for
an object or collection of objects',
                @parameters='[@objectname=''Object name or mask (defaults to all
object in current database)'']'
```

```
                   [,@outputname=''Output file name'' (Default:
@objectname+''.SQL'', or GENERATED_SCRIPT.SQL for entire database)]
                   [,@scriptoptions=bitmask specifying script generation options]
                   [,@resultset=bit specifying whether to generate a result set
                   [,@includeheaders=bit specifying whether to generate descriptive
headers for scripts
                   [,@server=''server name''][, @username=''user name''][,
@password=''password''][, @trustedconnection=1]',
@author='Ken Henderson', @email='khen@khen.com',
@version='8', @revision='0',
@datecreated='19980401', @datelastchanged='20001216',
@example='sp_generate_script @objectname=''authors'', @outputname=''authors.sql'' '
RETURN -1


GO
USE Northwind
GO
EXEC sp_generate_script 'Customers', @server='khenmp\ss2000'
```

(Results)

```
Column1
-------------------------------------------------------------------------------
set quoted_identifier OFF
GO

CREATE TABLE [Customers] (
   [CustomerID] [nchar] (5) COLLATE SQL_Latin1_General_CP1_CI_AS NOT NULL ,
   [CompanyName] [nvarchar] (40) COLLATE SQL_Latin1_General_CP1_CI_AS NOT NULL ,
   [ContactName] [nvarchar] (30) COLLATE SQL_Latin1_General_CP1_CI_AS NULL ,
   [ContactTitle] [nvarchar] (30) COLLATE SQL_Latin1_General_CP1_CI_AS NULL ,
   [Address] [nvarchar] (60) COLLATE SQL_Latin1_General_CP1_CI_AS NULL ,
   [City] [nvarchar] (15) COLLATE SQL_Latin1_General_CP1_CI_AS NULL ,
   [Region] [nvarchar] (15) COLLATE SQL_Latin1_General_CP1_CI_AS NULL ,
   [PostalCode] [nvarchar] (10) COLLATE SQL_Latin1_General_CP1_CI_AS NULL ,
   [Country] [nvarchar] (15) COLLATE SQL_Latin1_General_CP1_CI_AS NULL ,
   [Phone] [nvarchar] (24) COLLATE SQL_Latin1_General_CP1_CI_AS NULL ,
   [Fax] [nvarchar] (24) COLLATE SQL_Latin1_General_CP1_CI_AS NULL ,
   [rowguid] uniqueidentifier ROWGUIDCOL NOT NULL CONSTRAINT
[DF__Customers__rowgu__0EF836A4] DEFAULT (newid()),
   CONSTRAINT [PK_Customers] PRIMARY KEY CLUSTERED
   (
     [CustomerID]
   ) ON [PRIMARY]
```

```
) ON [PRIMARY]
GO

(1 row(s) affected)
```

**NOTE: Ignore the code displayed above. It's a remnant of the SQL-DMO method used to produce the script file**
```
line
----------------------------------------------------------------------------
set quoted_identifier OFF
GO

CREATE TABLE [Customers] (
    [CustomerID] [nchar] (5) COLLATE SQL_Latin1_General_CP1_CI_AS NOT NULL ,
    [CompanyName] [nvarchar] (40) COLLATE SQL_Latin1_General_CP1_CI_AS NOT NULL ,
    [ContactName] [nvarchar] (30) COLLATE SQL_Latin1_General_CP1_CI_AS NULL ,
    [ContactTitle] [nvarchar] (30) COLLATE SQL_Latin1_General_CP1_CI_AS NULL ,
    [Address] [nvarchar] (60) COLLATE SQL_Latin1_General_CP1_CI_AS NULL ,
    [City] [nvarchar] (15) COLLATE SQL_Latin1_General_CP1_CI_AS NULL ,
    [Region] [nvarchar] (15) COLLATE SQL_Latin1_General_CP1_CI_AS NULL ,
    [PostalCode] [nvarchar] (10) COLLATE SQL_Latin1_General_CP1_CI_AS NULL ,
    [Country] [nvarchar] (15) COLLATE SQL_Latin1_General_CP1_CI_AS NULL ,
    [Phone] [nvarchar] (24) COLLATE SQL_Latin1_General_CP1_CI_AS NULL ,
    [Fax] [nvarchar] (24) COLLATE SQL_Latin1_General_CP1_CI_AS NULL ,
    [rowguid] uniqueidentifier ROWGUIDCOL NOT NULL CONSTRAINT
    [DF__Customers__rowgu__0EF836A4] DEFAULT (newid()),
    CONSTRAINT [PK_Customers] PRIMARY KEY CLUSTERED
    (
        [CustomerID]
    ) ON [PRIMARY]
) ON [PRIMARY]
GO
```

Everything above the PRINT message (in bold type) is spurious output that you can safely ignore. The output below the message is the actual script. Here I've scripted the Customers table from the Northwind database. I could just as easily have scripted the entire database, or supplied a mask to generate a script of several objects at once.

The procedure begins by instantiating the DMO SQLServer and Transfer objects. DMO's SQLServer object is its root-level access path; you use it to connect to the server and to access other objects on the server. The Transfer object encapsulates DMOs server-to-server or server-to-file object and data transfer facility. Sp_generate_script uses it to generate SQL scripts.

If you've done any DMO programming, you may be wondering why I'm using a Transfer object instead of calling the Script method on individual objects. The reason for this is simple: object dependencies. The Transfer object writes object schema info to the script in order of dependency. Because it was originally intended to support transferring one database to another, it has to be mindful of object creation order; otherwise, CREATE statements for objects that depended on other objects will fail if the objects they require haven't yet been created. Consider a foreign key constraint. If the Order Details table makes a foreign key reference to the Products table, the Products table must exist before the Order Details table can be created. The CREATE TABLE statement will fail if it doesn't. The Transfer object ensures this by checking object dependencies when it scripts out a database.

Once the Transfer object is created, the procedure determines whether the user wants to script the entire database or only selected objects. This distinction is important because DMO lists objects in order of dependency when scripting an entire database, as I've said. If only a subset of the objects in a database is to be scripted, the procedure opens a cursor on the sysobjects and systypes tables (via UNION ALL) and calls Transfer's AddObjectByName method to set them up for scripting, one by one.

The procedure next uses the SQLServer object to locate the database housing the objects it needs to script. It finds this database by accessing the object's Databases collection. DMO objects often expose collections of other objects. Items in these collections can be accessed by name or by ordinal index. In the case of sp_generate_script, collection items are always accessed by name.

Once the procedure retrieves a pointer to the correct database, it calls that database's ScriptTransfer method, passing it the previously created Transfer object as a parameter. This generates a SQL script containing the objects we've specified.

The final step in the procedure is to return the script as a result set. Usually, the caller will expect to see the script immediately. If @resultset = 1 (the default), sp_generate_script calls sp_readtextfile to return the newly generated script file to the caller via a result set. A useful variation of this would be to return a cursor pointer to the script, but that's an exercise best left to the reader.

# Sp_start_trace

SQL Server's Profiler utility is a powerful tool and a vast improvement over the SQL Trace facility that came with releases prior to 7.0. However, it's also a resource-intensive and sometimes painfully slow application. Because I often need to trace the activity on SQL Server in situations where I don't wish to incur the overhead of the Profiler GUI, I wrote my own set of stored procedures to manage Profiler traces. They allow you to start, stop, and list Profiler traces without actually using Profiler itself. How do they work? By calling SQL Server's sp_trace_% extended procedures, the same way that Profiler itself does. These procedures are documented in the Books Online and are considerably easier to use than previous versions.

My trace management code consists of three procedures: sp_start_trace, sp_stop_trace, and sp_list_trace. They each do what their names imply. Here's the code for sp_start_trace (Listing 21–4):

**Listing 21–4** sp_start_trace.

```
USE master
GO
IF OBJECT_ID('sp_start_trace') IS NOT NULL
  DROP PROC sp_start_trace
GO
CREATE PROC sp_start_trace @FileName sysname=NULL,
@TraceName sysname='tsqltrace',
@Options int=2,
@MaxFileSize bigint=5,
@StopTime datetime=NULL,
@Events varchar(300)=
--  11 - RPC:Starting
--  13 - SQL:BatchStarting
--  14 - Connect
--  15 - Disconnect
--  16 - Attention
--  17 - Existing Connection
--  33 - Exception
--  42 - SP:Starting
--  43 - SP:Completed
--  45 - SP:StmtCompleted
--  55 - Hash Warning
--  67 - Execution Warnings
--  69 - Sort Warnings
--  79 - Missing Column Statistics
--  80 - Missing Join Predicate
'11,13,14,15,16,17,33,42,43,45,55,67,69,79,80',
@Cols varchar(300)=
-- All columns
'1,2,3,4,5,6,7,8,9,10,11,12,13,14,15,16,17,18,19,20,21,22,23,24,25,26,27,28
,29,30,31,32,33,34,35,36,37,38,39,40,41,42,43,44,',
```

```
@IncludeTextFilter sysname=NULL, @ExcludeTextFilter sysname=NULL,
@IncludeObjIdFilter int=NULL, @ExcludeObjIdFilter int=NULL,
@TraceId int = NULL
AS
SET NOCOUNT ON

IF @FileName='/?' GOTO Help

-- Declare variables
DECLARE @OldQueueHandle int -- Queue handle of currently running trace
queue
DECLARE @QueueHandle int -- Queue handle for new running trace queue
DECLARE @On bit -- Necessary because of a bug in some of the sp_trace_xx
procs
DECLARE @OurObjId int -- Used to keep us out of the trace log
DECLARE @OldTraceFile sysname -- File name of running trace
DECLARE @res int -- Result var for sp calls
SET @On=1

-- Do some basic param validation
IF (@Cols IS NULL) BEGIN
  RAISERROR('You must specify the columns to trace.',16,10)
  RETURN -1
END

IF (@Events IS NULL) BEGIN
  RAISERROR('You must specify a list of trace events in @Events.',16,10)
  RETURN -1
END

-- Append the datetime to the file name to create a new, unique file name.
IF @FileName IS NULL
SELECT @FileName = 'c:\TEMP\tsqltrace_' + CONVERT(CHAR(8),getdate(),112) +
    REPLACE(CONVERT(varchar(15),getdate(),114),':','')

-- Create the trace queue

  EXEC @res=sp_trace_create @traceid=@QueueHandle OUT, @options=@Options,
    @tracefile=@FileName, @maxfilesize=@MaxFileSize, @stoptime=@StopTime
IF @res<>0 BEGIN
  IF @res=1 PRINT 'Trace not started. Reason: Unknown error.'
  ELSE IF @res=10 PRINT 'Trace not started. Reason: Invalid options.
Returned when options specified are incompatible.'
```

```
ELSE IF @res=12 PRINT 'Trace not started. Reason: Error creating file.
Returned if the file already exists, drive is out of space, or path does
not exist.'
   ELSE IF @res=13 PRINT 'Trace not started. Reason: Out of memory. Returned
when there is not enough memory to perform the specified action.'
   ELSE IF @res=14 PRINT 'Trace not started. Reason: Invalid stop time.
Returned when the stop time specified has already happened.'
   ELSE IF @res=15 PRINT 'Trace not started. Reason: Invalid parameters.
Returned when the user supplied incompatible parameters.'
   RETURN @res
END
PRINT 'Trace started.'
PRINT 'The trace file name is : '+@FileName+'.'

-- Specify the event classes and columns to trace
IF @Events IS NOT NULL BEGIN
-- Loop through the @Events and @Cols strings, parsing out each event &
column number and adding them to the trace definition
 IF RIGHT(@Events,1)<>',' SET @Events=@Events+',' -- Append comma for the
loop
   IF RIGHT(@Cols,1)<>',' SET @Cols=@Cols+',' -- Append comma for the loop
   DECLARE @i int, @j int, @Event int, @Col int, @ColStr varchar(300)
   SET @i=CHARINDEX(',',@Events)
   WHILE @i<>0 BEGIN
     SET @Event=CAST(LEFT(@Events,@i-1) AS int)
     SET @ColStr=@Cols
     SET @j=CHARINDEX(',',@ColStr)
     WHILE @j<>0 BEGIN
       SET @Col=CAST(LEFT(@ColStr,@j-1) AS int)
       EXEC sp_trace_setevent @traceid=@QueueHandle, @eventid=@Event,
         @columnid=@Col, @on=@On
       SET @ColStr=SUBSTRING(@ColStr,@j+1,300)
       SET @j=CHARINDEX(',',@ColStr)
     END
     SET @Events=SUBSTRING(@Events,@i+1,300)
     SET @i=CHARINDEX(',',@Events)
   END
END

-- Set filters (default values avoid tracing the trace activity itself)
-- You can specify other filters like application name, etc., by supplying
strings to the @IncludeTextFilter/@ExcludeTextFilter parameters, separated
by semicolons
```

```
SET @ExcludeTextFilter='sp_%trace%'+ISNULL(';'+@ExcludeTextFilter,'')
  -- By default, keep our own activity from showing up
SET @OurObjId=OBJECT_ID('master..sp_start_trace')
EXEC sp_trace_setfilter @traceid=@QueueHandle, @columnid=1,
  @logical_operator=0, @comparison_operator=7, @value=@ExcludeTextFilter
EXEC sp_trace_setfilter @traceid=@QueueHandle, @columnid=1,
  @logical_operator=0, @comparison_operator=7, @value=N'EXEC% sp_%trace%'
IF @IncludeTextFilter IS NOT NULL
    EXEC sp_trace_setfilter @traceid=@QueueHandle, @columnid=1,
    @logical_operator=0, @comparison_operator=6, @value=@IncludeTextFilter
IF @IncludeObjIdFilter IS NOT NULL
    EXEC sp_trace_setfilter @traceid=@QueueHandle, @columnid=22,
    @logical_operator=0, @comparison_operator=0, @value=@IncludeObjIdFilter
    EXEC sp_trace_setfilter @traceid=@QueueHandle, @columnid=22,
    @logical_operator=0, @comparison_operator=1, @value=@OurObjId
IF @ExcludeObjIdFilter IS NOT NULL
    EXEC sp_trace_setfilter @traceid=@QueueHandle, @columnid=22,
    @logical_operator=0, @comparison_operator=1, @value=@ExcludeObjIdFilter

-- Turn on the trace
EXEC sp_trace_setstatus @traceid=@QueueHandle, @status=1

-- Record the trace queue handle for subsequent jobs. (This allows us to
know how to stop the trace.)
IF OBJECT_ID('tempdb..TraceQueue') IS NULL BEGIN
  CREATE TABLE tempdb..TraceQueue
  (TraceID int, TraceName varchar(20), TraceFile sysname)
  INSERT tempdb..TraceQueue VALUES(@QueueHandle, @TraceName, @FileName)
END ELSE BEGIN
 IF EXISTS(SELECT * FROM tempdb..TraceQueue WHERE TraceName = @TraceName)
BEGIN
    UPDATE tempdb..TraceQueue SET TraceID = @QueueHandle,
TraceFile=@FileName
    WHERE TraceName = @TraceName
  END ELSE BEGIN
    INSERT tempdb..TraceQueue VALUES(@QueueHandle, @TraceName, @FileName)
  END
END
RETURN 0
Help:
/*
Code abridged
*/
RETURN -1
```

```
GO
exec sp_start_trace
```

(Results)

```
Trace started.
The trace file name is : c:\TEMP\tsqltrace_20001204011454350.
```

By default, sp_start_trace initiates a Profiler trace that includes all trace columns and a stock set of trace events, but you can change this by specifying the @Events and/or @Cols parameters. Both are comma-delimited lists of event/column numbers. You can look up these numbers in the Books Online.

If you don't specify your own trace output file name, sp_start_trace attempts to create one for you in C:\TEMP using the current date and time to label the file. Trace files can grow to be quite large, so you should be careful to direct the file to a drive where you have plenty of space. Understand that the path that sp_start_trace uses is relative to the SQL Server on which the trace will run, *not* your local machine. Unlike Profiler, sp_start_trace always runs traces exclusively on the server.

## sp_stop_trace

Starting a trace using a stored procedure is nifty enough, but how do we stop it so that we can analyze the trace file? We use sp_stop_trace. Here's its code (Listing 21–5):

**Listing 21–5** sp_stop_trace.

```
USE master
GO
IF OBJECT_ID('sp_stop_trace') IS NOT NULL
  DROP PROC sp_stop_trace
GO
CREATE PROC sp_stop_trace @TraceName sysname='tsqltrace'
/*
Object: sp_stop_trace
Description: Stops a Profiler-like trace using Transact-SQL eXtended
Procedure calls.

Usage: sp_stop_trace @TraceName sysname default: tsqltrace -- Specifies the
name of the trace
```

```
Returns: (None)

$Author: Ken Henderson $. Email: khen@khen.com

$Revision: 2.0 $

Example: EXEC sp_stop_trace -- Stops the default trace

Created: 1999-04-01. $Modtime: 2000-12-16 $
*/
AS
SET NOCOUNT ON
IF @TraceName='/?' GOTO Help

-- Declare variables
DECLARE @OldQueueHandle int -- Queue handle of currently running trace
queue
DECLARE @OldTraceFile sysname -- File name of running trace

-- Stop the trace if running
IF OBJECT_ID('tempdb..TraceQueue') IS NOT NULL BEGIN
  IF EXISTS(SELECT * FROM tempdb..TraceQueue WHERE TraceName = @TraceName)
BEGIN

    SELECT @OldQueueHandle = TraceID, @OldTraceFile=TraceFile
    FROM tempdb..TraceQueue
    WHERE TraceName = @TraceName

    IF @@ROWCOUNT<>0 BEGIN
      EXEC sp_trace_setstatus @traceid=@OldQueueHandle, @status=0
      EXEC sp_trace_setstatus @traceid=@OldQueueHandle, @status=2
      PRINT 'Deleted trace queue ' + CAST(@OldQueueHandle AS
varchar(20))+'.'
      PRINT 'The trace output file name is: '+@OldTraceFile
      DELETE tempdb..TraceQueue WHERE TraceName = @TraceName
    END
  END ELSE PRINT 'No active traces named '+@TraceName+'.'
END ELSE PRINT 'No active traces.'

RETURN 0

Help:
EXEC sp_usage @objectname='sp_stop_trace',@desc='Stops a Profiler-like
trace using Transact-SQL eXtended Procedure calls.',
                @parameters='@TraceName sysname default: tsqltrace --
                Specifies the name of the trace
```

```
',
@author='Ken Henderson', @email='khen@khen.com',
@version='2', @revision='0',
@datecreated='19990401', @datelastchanged='20001216',
@example='EXEC sp_stop_trace -- Stops the default trace
'
RETURN -1
GO
EXEC sp_stop_trace
```

Because you can name traces when you start them, sp_stop_trace allows you to pass a trace name as a parameter. If you don't specify a trace name, it attempts to stop the default trace—tsqltrace.

Note the use of the Tempdb..TraceQueue table by both routines. We need a way of tracking by name which traces are running, and we need one that will persist across disconnects. We could have used a plain temporary table, but it could be dropped as soon as we disconnected. We could have used a permanent table in a different database—master, for instance. However, that would unnecessarily clutter the server with unneeded permanent objects. After all, any traces we've started will stop automatically when the server stops. We don't need an object that persists across server shutdowns. What we need is a storage mechanism that persists as long as the currently running instance of SQL Server is running. We want one that goes away automatically when the server is restarted so that we don't mistakenly believe traces are running that, in fact, are not. This is why I chose to use a permanent table in Tempdb. Because Tempdb is recreated each time the server is restarted, it works perfectly for our purposes. The TraceQueue table represents the best of both worlds—a temporary object that persists across connections and other user activity.

## sp_list_trace

Because the trace routines are designed to allow you to start the trace and leave it running even if you close the connection, it's possible that you'll need a means of checking the status of the currently running traces. This is what sp_list_trace is for. Here's its code (Listing 21–6):

**Listing 21–6** sp_list_trace.

```
USE master
GO
IF OBJECT_ID('sp_list_trace') IS NOT NULL
```

```
  DROP PROC sp_list_trace
GO
CREATE PROC sp_list_trace @TraceId varchar(10)=NULL
/*
Object: sp_list_trace
Description: Lists the currently running traces.

Usage: sp_list_trace @TraceId -- the ID number of a previously started
trace (optional)

Returns: (None)

$Author: Ken Henderson $. Email: khen@khen.com

$Revision: 2.0 $

Example: EXEC sp_list_trace -- Lists the currently running traces

Created: 1999-04-01. $Modtime: 2000-12-16 $.
*/

AS
SET NOCOUNT ON

IF @TraceId='/?' GOTO Help

DECLARE @T int
SET @T=CAST(@TraceId AS int)

IF (OBJECT_ID('tempdb..TraceQueue') IS NOT NULL) BEGIN
      IF (@T IS NULL) BEGIN
            DECLARE tc CURSOR FOR SELECT * FROM tempdb..TraceQueue
            FOR READ ONLY
            DECLARE @tid int, @tname varchar(20), @tfile sysname
            OPEN tc
            FETCH tc INTO @tid, @tname, @tfile
      IF @@ROWCOUNT<>0 BEGIN
            WHILE @@FETCH_STATUS=0 BEGIN
                  SELECT TraceId, TraceName, TraceFile
                  FROM tempdb..TraceQueue
                  WHERE TraceId=@tid
                  SELECT * FROM ::fn_trace_getinfo(@tid)
                  FETCH tc INTO @tid, @tname, @tfile
            END
```

```
      END ELSE PRINT 'No traces in the trace queue.'
            CLOSE tc
            DEALLOCATE tc
      END ELSE BEGIN
          SELECT TraceId, TraceName, TraceFile FROM tempdb..TraceQueue
            WHERE TraceId=@T
          SELECT * FROM ::fn_trace_getinfo(@T)
  END
END ELSE PRINT 'No traces to list.'
RETURN 0

Help:
EXEC sp_usage @objectname='sp_list_trace',@desc='Lists the currently
running traces.',
@parameters='@TraceId -- the ID number of a previously started trace
(optional)',
@author='Ken Henderson', @email='khen@khen.com',
@version='2', @revision='0',
@datecreated='19990401', @datelastchanged='20001216',
@example='EXEC sp_list_trace -- Lists the currently running traces'
RETURN -1
GO
exec sp_list_trace
```

(Results)

```
TraceId     TraceName            TraceFile
----------  -------------------  ----------------------------------------
4           tsqltrace            c:\TEMP\tsqltrace_20001204012356767

traceid     property     value
----------  -----------  ----------------------------------------
4           1            2
4           2            c:\TEMP\tsqltrace_20001204012356767
4           3            5
4           4            NULL
4           5            1
```

Sp_list_trace calls the ::fn_trace_getinfo() system function to access key info for each trace. The table in Listing 21–6 with traceid as its first column is produced by ::fn_trace_getinfo(). You can take the trace name listed in the top table (which comes from Tempdb..TraceQueue) and pass it to sp_stop_trace to stop the trace if you like.

These routines present a viable alternative to the Profiler utility and may come in handy in your work. It wouldn't be difficult to combine the three of them into one master procedure so that you wouldn't have three procedures to keep track of. Again, this is an exercise best left to the reader.

## sp_proc_runner

Starting, stopping, and listing traces using stored procedures is handy, but what if you need to schedule these starts and stops? What if you wanted to trace until a given event on the server occurred or for a specified duration of time? Given how large trace files can become, you may want to schedule the tracing so that it doesn't run at all (or runs with a much slimmer event set) during periods of high system activity. This is what sp_proc_runner was designed to address. Sp_proc_runner runs other code. This other code can be a stored procedure, a T-SQL batch—you name it—sp_proc_runner doesn't care. It's a miniature scheduler that can run the code you supply for a given period of time or until a condition on the system becomes true (e.g., a long-running transaction or a blocked spid). Sp_proc_runner can also cycle repetitive commands. In other words, it can stop a running process at given intervals and restart it. It can continue to do this until the total duration you told it to run has elapsed or until a condition you've specified becomes true on the server.

Sp_proc_runner can also manage the files that a command you're running may be producing. You can tell it how many files to keep and where to put them. Assuming the routine you're running cooperates, sp_proc_runner can manage your code's output files automatically. For example, let's say you use sp_proc_runner to run sp_start_trace. At regular intervals you may want to stop the trace and restart it. You can either let sp_start_trace manage these files, or you can let sp_proc_runner. You can tell sp_proc_runner to keep only the last ten trace files and it will do exactly that. It will check as the files are being produced, and while cycling the trace, it will delete older files as necessary to keep under the limit you specified.

I originally built sp_proc_runner to run sp_start_trace, but it can actually run anything. You can specify your own code and a custom stop condition, and sp_proc_runner will take care of the rest. Here's its code (Listing 21–7):

**Listing 21–7** sp_proc_runner.

```
USE master
GO
```

```
IF OBJECT_ID('sp_proc_runner') IS NOT NULL
  DROP PROC sp_proc_runner
GO
CREATE PROC sp_proc_runner
      @StartCmd nvarchar(4000)='/?',
      @StartTime char(8)=NULL,
      @StopCondition nvarchar(4000)=NULL,
      @StopMessage nvarchar(4000)='Stop condition met.',
      @IterationTime char(8)=NULL,
      @Duration char(8)=NULL,
      @StopCmd nvarchar(4000)=NULL,
      @PollingInterval char(8)='00:00:10',
      @OutputDir sysname=NULL,
      @OutputFileMask sysname=NULL,
      @NumFiles int=16
/*
Object: sp_proc_runner
Description: Runs a specified TSQL command batch or stored procedure
repetitively for a specified period of time

Returns: (None)

$Author: Ken Henderson $. Email: khen@khen.com

$Revision: 2.0 $
Example:
EXEC sp_proc_runner @StartCmd=N'EXEC sp_start_trace ',
      @StopCondition=N'OBJECT_ID(''tempdb..stoptab'') IS NOT NULL',
      @StopMessage=N'Trace stopped', @IterationTime='00:30:00',
      @StopCmd=N'EXEC sp_stop_trace ',
      @OutputDir='c:\temp',@OutputFileMask='sp_trace*.trc', @NumFiles=16
EXEC sp_proc_runner @StartCmd=N'EXEC sp_start_trace ',
      @IterationTime='00:30:00', @Duration='12:00:00',
      @StopCmd=N'EXEC sp_stop_trace ',
      @OutputDir='c:\temp',@OutputFileMask='sp_trace*.trc', @NumFiles=10
Created: 1999-04-01. $Modtime: 2000-12-16 $.
*/
AS
SET NOCOUNT ON

IF @StartCmd='/?' GOTO Help

-- Do some minimal param checking
IF COALESCE(@Duration, @StopCondition) IS NULL BEGIN
```

```
  RAISERROR('You must supply either the @Duration or the @StopCondition
parameter.',16,10)
  RETURN -1
END
IF @OutputFileMask='*' BEGIN
  RAISERROR('You may not specify an empty file mask.',16,10)
  RETURN -1
END
IF (@OutputDir IS NOT NULL) AND (@OutputFileMask IS NULL) BEGIN
  RAISERROR('You must supply a file mask when supplying a
directory.',16,10)
  RETURN -1
END

-- Wait until the start time if there is one
IF @StartTime IS NOT NULL
  WAITFOR TIME @StartTime

-- Declare some variables and assign initial values
DECLARE @Stop int, @i int, @EndTime datetime, @CurDate datetime,
        @CurDateStr varchar(25),
        @FName sysname, @DelCmd varchar(255),
        @OutputDirCmd varchar(255), @SCmd nvarchar(4000),
        @IterationDateTime datetime
SET @CurDate=getdate()
SET @EndTime=@CurDate+@Duration

-- @Duration of 00:00:00, perhaps?
SET @Stop=CASE WHEN @CurDate >= @EndTime THEN 1 ELSE 0 END
SET @i=0
SET
  @StopCondition='IF ('+@StopCondition+')
RAISERROR('''+@StopMessage+''',11,1)'

-- If we're going to generate filenames, delete any old ones
IF @OutputDir IS NOT NULL BEGIN
  IF RIGHT(@OutputDir,1)<>'\' SET @OutputDir=@OutputDir+'\'
  SET @DelCmd='DEL '+@OutputDir+@OutputFileMask
  EXEC xp_cmdshell @DelCmd, no_output -- Delete all files matching the mask
  -- Prepare for Dir listing (below)
  SET @OutputDirCmd='DIR '+@OutputDir+@OutputFileMask+' /B /ON'
END

-- Check the stop condition - don't start if it's met
```

```
--IF (@Stop<>1) AND (@StopCondition IS NOT NULL)
--   EXEC @Stop=sp_executesql @StopCondition
WHILE (@Stop=0) BEGIN
  -- Gen a filename using the current date and time
  IF @OutputDir IS NOT NULL BEGIN
      SET @CurDateStr=CONVERT(CHAR(8),getdate(),112) +
      REPLACE(CONVERT(varchar(15),getdate(),114),':','')
      SET @FName=REPLACE(@OutputFileMask,'*',@CurDateStr)
      SET @SCmd=@StartCmd+', @FileName='''+CAST(@OutputDir+@FName as
      nvarchar(255))+''''
  END ELSE SET @SCmd=@StartCmd

  EXEC sp_executesql @SCmd -- Execute the start command

  SET @IterationDateTime=getdate()+ISNULL(@IterationTime,'23:59:59.999')
  WHILE (@Stop=0) AND (getdate()<@IterationDateTime) BEGIN

        IF @PollingInterval IS NOT NULL -- Do polling interval delay
      WAITFOR DELAY @PollingInterval

        -- Check the duration
        SET @Stop=CASE WHEN getdate() >= @EndTime THEN 1 ELSE 0 END
        -- Check the stop condition
        IF (@Stop<>1) AND (@StopCondition IS NOT NULL)
          EXEC @Stop=sp_executesql @StopCondition
      END
  IF @StopCmd IS NOT NULL -- Execute the stop command if there is one
    EXEC sp_executesql @StopCmd

SET @i=@i+1
-- Get rid of extra files
IF (@OutputDir IS NOT NULL) AND (@i>@NumFiles) BEGIN

  CREATE TABLE #files (fname varchar(255) NULL)

  INSERT #files
  EXEC master..xp_cmdshell @OutputDirCmd

  SELECT TOP 1 @DelCmd='DEL '+@OutputDir+fname FROM #files WHERE fname IS
NOT NULL ORDER BY fname
    IF @@ROWCOUNT<>0
      EXEC master..xp_cmdshell @DelCmd, no_output

  DROP TABLE #files
```

```
    END
END
END
RETURN 0
Help:
/*
Code abridged
*/
RETURN -1
GO

EXEC sp_proc_runner @StartCmd=N'EXEC sp_start_trace ',
    @IterationTime='00:30:00', @Duration='12:00:00',
    @StopCmd=N'EXEC sp_stop_trace ',
    @OutputDir='C:\TEMP',@OutputFileMask='sp_trace*.trc', @NumFiles=10
```

In this example we're using sp_proc_runner to execute sp_start_trace. It will run for a total duration of 12 hours and will stop and restart the trace every 30 minutes. It will store the trace files in C:\TEMP and will name the files sp_trace*.trc, where * is replaced with the current date and time. It will keep a maximum of ten files at any one time and will delete older ones as necessary to stay under the limit. Let's look at another example (Listing 21–8):

**Listing 21–8** sp_proc_runner can check for a stop condition on the server.

```
EXEC sp_proc_runner @StartCmd=N'EXEC sp_start_trace ',
    @StopCondition=N'EXISTS(SELECT * FROM sysprocesses WHERE blocked<>0
    and waittime>60000)',
    @StopMessage=N'Long-term block detected', @IterationTime='00:30:00',
    @StopCmd=N'EXEC sp_stop_trace ',
    @OutputDir='c:\temp',@OutputFileMask='sp_trace*.trc', @NumFiles=16
```

In this example, sp_proc_runner again runs sp_start_trace, but this time it watches for a long-term block on the server—one that lasts at least 60 seconds. When this event occurs, sp_proc_runner stops the trace, displays a message, and terminates:

```
Server: Msg 50000, Level 11, State 1, Line 1
Long-term block detected
Trace started.
The trace filename is : c:\temp\sp_trace20010704030737887.trc.
Deleted trace queue 1.
```

```
The trace output filename is: c:\temp\sp_trace20010704030737887.trc.
```

Between being able to run code for a given total duration and being able to run until a server-side condition comes true, sp_proc_runner affords a great deal of flexibility in scheduling your own jobs on SQL Server. Remember that you can use it to run any type of T-SQL or stored procedure you wish: You're not limited to running sp_start_trace.

## sp_create_backup_job

Sp_create_backup_job does what its name implies: It sets up a backup job for you. It uses SQL Server's SQLMAINT facility to set up a job that backs up the data and log files for a database you specify. The procedure takes six parameters, and these are summarized in Table 21–1.

**Table 21–1** sp_create_backup_job PARAMETERS

| Parameter | Type | Default | Purpose |
|---|---|---|---|
| @dbname | sysname | None | Specifies the name of the database to back up. |
| @OperatorNetSendAddress | sysname | None | Specifies the NET SEND address of the operator. |
| @ScheduledStart | int | 200000 | Specifies the start time of the job. |
| @PlanName | sysname | " | Specifies the name of the maintenance plan to create. |
| @DataBackupName | sysname | " | Names the data backup portion of the job. |
| @LogBackupName | sysname | " | Names the log portion of the job. |

Here's the source code (Listing 21–9):

**Listing 21–9** sp_create_backup_job.

```
USE master
GO
IF OBJECT_ID('dbo.sp_create_backup_job') IS NOT NULL
  DROP PROC dbo.sp_create_backup_job
```

```
GO
CREATE PROC dbo.sp_create_backup_job @dbname sysname,
@OperatorNetSendAddress sysname,
@ScheduledStart int=200000, @PlanName sysname='',
@DataBackupName sysname='', @LogBackupName sysname=''
AS
DECLARE @execstr varchar(8000), @JobID uniqueidentifier, @StepID int,
@devname sysname
DECLARE @PlanID uniqueidentifier, @DataCmd varchar(8000), @LogCmd
varchar(8000)

SET @PlanName='Daily Backup for '+ @dbname
SET @DataBackupName='Data backup for '+@dbname
SET @LogBackupName='Log backup for '+@dbname

-- Delete the operator if it already exists
IF EXISTS(SELECT * FROM msdb.dbo.sysoperators WHERE name = 'Oper')
EXEC msdb.dbo.sp_delete_operator 'Oper'

-- Add the operator
EXEC msdb.dbo.sp_add_operator @name = 'Oper',
    @enabled = 1,
    @email_address ='',
    @pager_address = '',
    @weekday_pager_start_time = 090000,
    @weekday_pager_end_time = 210000,
    @pager_days = 127,
    @netsend_address=@OperatorNetSendAddress

-- Delete the job from sysdbmaintplans and related tables if it exists
SELECT @PlanID = plan_id FROM msdb.dbo.sysdbmaintplans WHERE
plan_name=@PlanName;
IF @@ROWCOUNT<>0 BEGIN
  DECLARE job CURSOR FOR
  SELECT job_id FROM msdb.dbo.sysdbmaintplan_jobs
  WHERE plan_id=@PlanID

  OPEN job
  FETCH job INTO @JobID
  WHILE (@@FETCH_STATUS=0) BEGIN
    EXEC msdb.dbo.sp_delete_job @JOBID
    FETCH job INTO @JobID
  END
  DEALLOCATE job
```

```
      DELETE msdb.dbo.sysdbmaintplan_history WHERE plan_id =@PlanID
      DELETE msdb.dbo.sysdbmaintplan_jobs WHERE plan_id =@PlanID
      DELETE msdb.dbo.sysdbmaintplan_databases WHERE plan_id =@PlanID
      DELETE msdb.dbo.sysdbmaintplans WHERE plan_id =@PlanID
END

-- Gen a new GUID, then insert it into sysdbmaintplans
SELECT @PlanID = NEWID()
INSERT msdb.dbo.sysdbmaintplans (plan_id, plan_name, max_history_rows,
remote_history_server, max_remote_history_rows)
VALUES (@PlanID, @PlanName, 1000, N'', 0)

DELETE msdb.dbo.sysdbmaintplan_jobs WHERE plan_id = @PlanID

-- Setup generic Data and Log xp_sqlmaint calls that we'll use later
SET @DataCmd='EXEC master.dbo.xp_sqlmaint ''-PlanID '+CAST(@PlanID AS
varchar(36))+' -WriteHistory -VrfyBackup -BkUpMedia DISK -BkUpDB -UseDefDir
-BkExt "BAK" -DelBkUps 7days''';
SET @LogCmd='EXEC master.dbo.xp_sqlmaint ''-PlanID '+CAST(@PlanID AS
varchar(36))+' -WriteHistory -VrfyBackup -BkUpMedia DISK -BkUpLog -
UseDefDir -BkExt "TRN" -DelBkUps 7days''';

-- Delete the job if it already exists
SELECT @JobID = job_id FROM msdb.dbo.sysjobs WHERE name=@DataBackupName
IF (@@ROWCOUNT>0) BEGIN
        -- Don't delete if it's a multiserver job
        IF (EXISTS (SELECT * FROM msdb.dbo.sysjobservers
           WHERE (job_id=@JobID) AND (server_id <> 0))) BEGIN
              RAISERROR ('Unable to create job because there is already a
              multi-server job with the same name.',16,1)
        END ELSE -- Delete the job
              EXEC msdb.dbo.sp_delete_job @job_id=@JobID
END

-- Add the backup job
EXEC msdb.dbo.sp_add_job
    @job_name = @DataBackupName,
    @enabled = 1,
    @category_id=3,
    @description = @DataBackupName,
    @notify_level_eventlog = 2,
    @notify_level_netsend = 2,
    @notify_netsend_operator_name='Oper',
    @delete_level = 0
```

```
SELECT @JobID=job_id FROM msdb.dbo.sysjobs WHERE name=@DataBackupName

-- Add the job to sysdbmaintplan_jobs
INSERT msdb.dbo.sysdbmaintplan_jobs VALUES (@PlanID, @JobID)
-- Schedule the job
EXEC msdb.dbo.sp_add_jobschedule @job_id=@JobID,
    @name = 'ScheduledBackup',
    @freq_type = 4, -- everyday
    @freq_interval = 1,
    @active_start_time = @ScheduledStart

-- Add the database to sysdbmaintplan_databases
IF NOT EXISTS(SELECT * FROM msdb.dbo.sysdbmaintplan_databases WHERE plan_id
=
@PlanID AND database_name =    @dbname)
  INSERT msdb.dbo.sysdbmaintplan_databases (plan_id, database_name) VALUES
(@PlanID, @dbname)

-- Add a job step to back up the database
EXEC msdb.dbo.sp_add_jobstep @job_id=@JobID,
@step_name='DataBackup',
@subsystem='TSQL',
@command=@DataCmd,
@flags=4,@on_success_action=1

-- Associate the job with the job server
EXEC msdb.dbo.sp_add_jobserver @job_id=@JobID

-- Add a job and job step to back up its log
IF (@dbname<>'master') AND (DATABASEPROPERTY(@dbname,'IsTruncLog')=0) BEGIN
  -- Delete the job if it already exists
  SELECT @JobID = job_id FROM msdb.dbo.sysjobs WHERE name=@LogBackupName
  IF (@@ROWCOUNT>0) BEGIN
        -- Don't delete if it's a multiserver job
        IF (EXISTS (SELECT * FROM msdb.dbo.sysjobservers
            WHERE (job_id=@JobID) AND (server_id <> 0))) BEGIN
            RAISERROR ('Unable to create job because there is already a
            multi-server job with the same name.',16,1)
        END ELSE -- Delete the job
            EXEC msdb.dbo.sp_delete_job @job_id=@JobID
  END

  -- Add the backup job
  EXEC msdb.dbo.sp_add_job
```

```
        @job_name = @LogBackupName,
        @enabled = 1,
        @category_id=3,
        @description = @LogBackupName,
        @notify_level_eventlog = 2,
        @notify_level_netsend = 2,
        @notify_netsend_operator_name='Oper',
        @delete_level = 0

SELECT @JobID=job_id FROM msdb.dbo.sysjobs WHERE name=@LogBackupName

-- Add the job to sysdbmaintplan_jobs
INSERT msdb.dbo.sysdbmaintplan_jobs VALUES (@PlanID, @JobID)

-- Schedule the job
EXEC msdb.dbo.sp_add_jobschedule @job_id=@JobID,
    @name = 'ScheduledLogBackup',
    @freq_type = 4, -- everyday
    @freq_interval = 1,
    @active_start_time = @ScheduledStart

    -- Add the database to sysdbmaintplan_databases
    IF NOT EXISTS(SELECT * FROM msdb.dbo.sysdbmaintplan_databases
                WHERE plan_id = @PlanID AND database_name = @dbname)
        INSERT msdb.dbo.sysdbmaintplan_databases (plan_id,
        database_name)
        VALUES (@PlanID,    @dbname)

    EXEC msdb.dbo.sp_add_jobstep @job_id=@JobID,
    @step_name='LogBackup',
    @subsystem='TSQL',
    @command=@LogCmd,
    @flags=4,@on_success_action=1

    -- Associate the job with the job server
    EXEC msdb.dbo.sp_add_jobserver @job_id=@JobID
END
```

As you can see, the routine is a bit involved, but a certain amount of complexity is unavoidable because of the steps required to set up and manage a SQL Server maintenance plan. From a usability standpoint, you can call the procedure and forget about the details for the most part.

# sp_diffdb

This last example is kind of the grand finale (well, as close as we'll get) for this chapter. It makes use of a couple of the routines we looked at earlier in the chapter to provide a capability that is surprisingly absent from the SQL Server product itself—namely, the ability to check the differences between two databases. I probably get at least one e-mail message a week on this subject alone. People are always wanting to know how to determine the differences between two versions of a given database. Although there are third-party tools that provide this functionality, it tends to be a bit on the expensive side. I need this ability frequently myself, so I built a stored procedure that can check the schema of one database against that of another. It's completely automated and surprisingly functional.

How does it work? Recall the sp_diff and sp_generate_script procedures from earlier in the chapter. Sp_diffdb simply uses sp_generate_script to generate scripts for the databases you want to compare, then calls sp_diff to check them for differences. Clever, eh? Here's the code (Listing 21–10):

**Listing 21–10** sp_diffdb.

```
USE master
GO
IF OBJECT_ID('sp_diffdb') IS NOT NULL
  DROP PROC sp_diffdb
GO
CREATE PROC sp_diffdb @DB1 sysname='/?', @DB2 sysname=NULL,
       @TempPath sysname='C:\TEMP',
       @server sysname='(local)',        -- Name of the server to connect to
       @username sysname='sa',           -- Name of the user to connect as
       (defaults to 'sa')
       @password sysname=NULL,           -- User's password
  @trustedconnection bit=1        -- Use a trusted connection to connect to
the server
/*

Object: sp_diffdb
Description: Returns the differences between two text files as a result set
(uses VSS)

Usage: sp_diffdb @file1=full path to first file, @file2=fullpath to second
file
```

```
Returns: (None)

$Author: Ken Henderson $. Email: khen@khen.com

$Revision: 1.0 $

Example: sp_diffdb 'c:\customers.sql', 'c:\customers2.sql'

Created: 2001-01-14. $Modtime: 2001-01-16 $.

*/
AS
SET NOCOUNT ON

IF (COALESCE(@DB1+@DB2,'/?')='/?') GOTO Help
DECLARE @cmd varchar(1000), @cmdout varchar(1000), @trustcon char(1),
@file1 sysname, @file2 sysname

SET @trustcon=CAST(@trustedconnection AS char(1))
IF RIGHT(@TempPath,1)<>'\' SET @TempPath=@TempPath+'\'

SET @file1=@TempPath+@DB1+'.SQL'
SET @cmd=@DB1+'..sp_generate_script @includeheaders=0, @resultset=0,
@outputname='''+@file1+''', @server='''+@server+''',
@username='''+@username+''''+ISNULL(', @password='''+@password+'''','')+',
@trustedconnection='+@trustcon
EXEC(@cmd)
print @cmd

SET @file2=@TempPath+@DB2+'.SQL'
SET @cmd=@DB2+'..sp_generate_script @includeheaders=0, @resultset=0,
@outputname='''+@file2+''', @server='''+@server+''',
@username='''+@username+''''+ISNULL(', @password='''+@password+'''','')+',
@trustedconnection='+@trustcon
EXEC(@cmd)

EXEC sp_diff @file1, @file2
RETURN 0

Help:
EXEC sp_usage @objectname='sp_diffdb',
@desc='Returns the differences between two text files as a result set (uses
VSS)',
```

```
@parameters='@file1=full path to first file, @file2=fullpath to second
file',
@author='Ken Henderson', @email='khen@khen.com',
@version='1',@revision='0',
@datecreated='20010114', @datelastchanged='20010116',
@example='sp_diffdb ''c:\customers.sql'', ''c:\customers2.sql'' '
RETURN -1
GO
```

Because sp_diffdb calls sp_generate_script, which in turn connects to the server separately, we have to supply login info to the procedure. Other than that, the two key parameters to the routine are the names of the two databases you want to compare. Here's an example of a call to sp_diffdb (Listing 21–11):

**Listing 21–11** sp_diffdb can report the differences between two databases.

```
EXEC sp_diffdb 'northwind','northwind5'
diff
-----------------------------------------------------------------------------
Diffing: C:\TEMP\northwind.SQL
Against: C:\TEMP\northwind5.SQL

 94    Del: CREATE TABLE [dbo].[cust] (
 95    Del:   [CustNo] [int] IDENTITY (1, 1) NOT NULL ,
 96    Del:   [City] [varchar] (30) COLLATE SQL_Latin1_General_CP1_CI_AS NULL ,
 97    Del:   [State] [varchar] (10) COLLATE SQL_Latin1_General_CP1_CI_AS NULL
 98    Del: ) ON [PRIMARY]
 99    Del: GO
100    Del:
101    Del: CREATE CLUSTERED INDEX [citystate] ON [dbo].[cust]([City], [Sta
102    Del: GO
103    Del:
104    Del:
```

Here, we can see that the schema for Northwind5 is missing the cust table. As I said earlier in the discussion on sp_diff, the second of the two files passed to sp_diff is considered the master copy: The output from sp_diff lists the steps necessary to make the first file match the second one. From this output, we can infer that the Northwind database has a table named cust, whereas Northwind5 does not. Let's see what happens when we compare identical databases (Listing 21–12):

**Listing 21–12** sp_diffdb can detect when there are no differences between two databases.

```
EXEC sp_diffdb 'northwind','northwind4'

diff
----------------------------------------------------------------------
Diffing: C:\TEMP\northwind.SQL
Against: C:\TEMP\northwind4.SQL
No differences.
```

Although not a graphical tool, sp_diffdb's ability to check for differences between two different databases is a powerful capability and should come in handy in a good number of situations.

## Summary

You learned about creating administrative stored procedures in this chapter. Hopefully, the routines contained herein have inspired you to build some of your own administrative stored procedures. You've seen how versatile Transact-SQL can be, and how COM Automation and access to the operating system can give the language special abilities.

# Undocumented Transact-SQL

*To a great designer, not applying knowledge is tantamount to not
having obtained the knowledge in the first place.*

*—Steve McConnell*[1]

You're better off not using undocumented features unless there's just no other
way. Undocumented features are usually undocumented for good reason: They
may be unsafe to use in certain circumstances, or they may change or be
removed in future releases. Misuse of a product's undocumented features is a
fast ticket to lost data and indifference from the vendor.

So be careful with the undocumented stored procedures, commands, functions, and syntax I'm about to share with you. Use them at your own risk. The
elation one feels on discovering a hidden feature is nothing compared with the
humiliation that comes with the realization that, for no good reason, you've just
corrupted a production server on which lots of people depend. Take it from
someone who knows: The excruciating pain that comes from shooting yourself
in the foot is a lot more intense and long-lasting than that momentary *Eureka*
feeling you experience when you figure out some heretofore unknown keyword. Keep things in perspective. Using an undocumented feature in a production environment is usually not worth the risk.

If you evaluate the risks and decide to use undocumented features anyway,
realize that these features may change or be removed from the product without
notice. An example of such a feature is the PWDENCRYPT() function. It
changed between releases 6.5 and 7.0 of SQL Server, breaking code that
depended on the old behavior when it was migrated to 7.0.

In terms of support, understand that "undocumented" means "unsup-
ported." Don't expect vendor support for undocumented features. Microsoft
has intentionally left certain features out of the product documentation because
it knows they will be changing or will be removed in future releases of SQL
Server. It wants to be able to change these features without worrying about

---

[1]McConnell, Steve. *After the Gold Rush*. Redmond, WA: Microsoft Press, 1999. Page 27.

breaking customer code. If you base production code on undocumented features, you accept the fact that your code may break in the future because of changes in the product, or may even be unsafe in the present because you're using undocumented features in ways they were never intended to be used.

## What Defines Undocumented?

When I describe something as an undocumented SQL Server feature, I'm referring to a feature that is not mentioned in the product documentation, i.e., in the Books Online. Some of these can be found in other publicly available Microsoft documentation; some can't. From the perspective of this chapter, if it isn't in the Books Online, it isn't documented.

In addition to undocumented procedures, I'll also talk about undocumented DBCC command verbs, undocumented functions, and undocumented trace flags. None of these lists is exhaustive, but you're still likely to discover an undocumented feature or two that you didn't know about. Regardless of whether you use the features, it's still good to know about them, if for no other reason than to give you a glimpse of how SQL Server works behind the scenes. This is why I've included coverage of undocumented routines in this book—to help you master SQL Server.

## Undocumented Procedures

By my count, there are more than 100 undocumented stored procedures, not counting undocumented replication stored procedures. I've listed many of them in the section that follows. I haven't included every last one of them for several reasons:

1. There are simply too many to cover in any sort of depth. This is why I've intentionally left out the undocumented routines relating to replication. Replication is a world unto itself.
2. Some undocumented routines are so fragile and add so little value to the Transact-SQL command set that they are best left undocumented.
3. Some of the undocumented routines behave so erratically or are so dependent on code external to SQL Server (e.g., in Enterprise Manager or SQL-DMO) that they are either unusable or of little value to the Transact-SQL developer. The idea here is to provide complete coverage without getting carried away.

Each of the following procedures is not documented in the Books Online, but many of them provide useful functionality. You'll have to judge whether their functionality is worth the associated risk.

## sp_checknames [@mode]

Checks key system tables for non-ASCII names.

```
sp_checknames @mode='silent'
```

## sp_delete_backuphistory @oldest_date

Clears system backup history prior to a given date.

```
msdb..sp_delete_backuphistory @oldest_date datetime
```

## sp_enumerrorlogs

Enumerates the current server error log files.

```
master..sp_enumerrorlogs
```

(Results abridged)

```
Archive #    Date                   Log File Size (Byte)
----------   -------------------    --------------------
6            06/28/2000   23:13     3139
5            06/29/2000   11:19     3602
4            06/29/2000   11:35     3486
3            06/29/2000   22:55     15998
2            06/29/2000   23:10     3349
1            07/01/2000   12:49     120082
0            07/01/2000   12:51     3532
```

## sp_enumoledbdatasources

Enumerates the OLEDB data providers visible to the server.

```
sp_enumoledbdatasources
```

## sp_fixindex @dbname, @tabname, @indid

Allows indexes on system tables to be dropped/recreated.

```
USE northwind
EXEC sp_dboption 'northwind','single',true
EXEC sp_fixindex 'northwind', 'sysobjects', 2
EXEC sp_dboption 'northwind','single',false
```

## sp_gettypestring @tabid, @colid, @typestring output

Renders a textual description of a column's data type.

```
declare @tabid int, @typestr varchar(30)
SET @tabid=OBJECT_ID('authors')
EXEC sp_gettypestring @tabid, 1, @typestr OUT
SELECT @typestr
```

(Results)

```
----------------------------
varchar(11)
```

## sp_MS_marksystemobject @objname

Sets an object's system bit (0xC0000000). Several functions and DBCC command verbs do not work properly unless executed from a system object. Setting this bit will cause the IsMSShipped object property to return 1.

```
sp_Ms_marksystemobject 'sp_dir'
```

## sp_MS_upd_sysobj_category @pSeqMode integer

Enables/disables a special system mode wherein newly created objects are automatically system objects. Setting @pSeqMode to 1 enables this mode; setting it to 2 disables it. Among other things, sp_MS_upd_sysobj_category allows the creation of user-defined INFORMATION_SCHEMA views. See Chapter 9 for more information.

```
sp_MS_upd_sysobj_category 1
```

## sp_MSaddguidcol @source_owner, @source_table

Adds a **ROWGUIDCOL** column to a table. Also marks the table for replication (use EXEC sp_MSunmarkreplinfo to reverse this).

```
sp_MSaddguidcolumn dbo,testguid
```

### sp_MSaddguidindex @source_owner, @source_table

Creates an index on a table's **ROWGUIDCOL** column.

```
sp_MSaddguidindex dbo,testuid
```

### sp_MSaddlogin_implicit_ntlogin @loginname

Adds a SQL Server login that corresponds to an existing NT login.

```
sp_MSaddlogin_implicit_ntlogin 'GoofyTingler'
```

### sp_MSadduser_implicit_ntlogin @ntname

Adds a database user that corresponds to an existing NT login.

```
sp_MSadduser_implicit_ntlogin 'GoofyTingler'
```

### sp_MScheck_uid_owns_anything @uid

Returns 1 when a user owns any objects in the current database.

```
DECLARE @res int, @uid int
SELECT @uid=USER_ID()
EXEC @res=sp_MScheck_uid_owns_anything @uid
SELECT @res
```

(Results)

```
Server: Msg 15183, Level 16, State 1, Procedure
sp_MScheck_uid_owns_anything, Line 17
The user owns objects in the database and cannot be dropped.
Name type
-------------------------------------------------- ----
LastCustNo   U

-----------
1
```

### sp_MSdbuseraccess @mode='perm'|'db', @qual=db name mask

Returns a list of databases a user can access and a bitmap representing the access in each.

```
sp_MSdbuseraccess @mode='db'

name         version crdate                  owner
------------ ------- ----------------------- --------------------
distribution 539     2000-11-28 20:46:14.293 LEX\TALIONIS
master       539     2000-08-06 01:29:12.250 sa
model        539     2000-08-06 01:40:52.437 sa
msdb         539     2000-08-06 01:40:56.810 sa
Northwind    539     2000-08-06 01:41:00.310 sa
pubs         539     2000-05-06 14:34:09.720 LEX\TALIONIS
rentman      NULL    2000-06-30 16:32:11.813 LEX\TALIONIS
tempdb       539     2000-07-01 12:51:55.590 sa
```

### sp_MSdbuserpriv @mode='perm'|'serv'|'ver'|'role'

Returns a bitmap representing user privileges.

```
sp_MSdbuserpriv @mode='role'
```

(Results)

```
-----------
73855
```

### sp_MSdependencies @objname, @objtype, @flags int, @objlist

Shows object dependencies.

```
sp_MSdependencies @objname = 'titleauthor'
```

(Results abridged)

```
oType       oObjName    oOwner  oSequence
----------- ----------- ------- ---------
8           authors     dbo     1
8           publishers  dbo     1
8           titles      dbo     2
```

### sp_MSdrop_object [@object_id] [,@object_name] [,@object_owner]

Generically drops a table, view, trigger, or procedure.

```
sp_MSdrop_object @object_name='authors2'
```

## sp_MSexists_file @full_path, @filename

Checks for the existence of an operating system file (version 7.0 only).

```
DECLARE @res int
EXEC @res=sp_MSexists_file 'd:\readme.txt', 'readme.txt'
```

## sp_MSforeachdb @command1 @replacechar = '?' [,@command2] [,@command3] [,@precommand] [,@postcommand]

Executes up to three commands for every database on the system. @replacechar will be replaced with the name of each database. @precommand and @postcommand can be used to direct commands to a single result set.

```
EXEC sp_MSforeachdb 'DBCC CHECKDB(?)'
EXEC sp_MSforeachdb @command1='PRINT ''Listing ?''', @command2='USE ?
SELECT DB_NAME()'
```

(Results abridged)

```
DBCC results for 'Northwind'.
DBCC results for 'sysobjects'.
There are 232 rows in 5 pages for object 'sysobjects'.
DBCC results for 'sysindexes'.
There are 162 rows in 7 pages for object 'sysindexes'.
DBCC results for 'syscolumns'.
There are 1056 rows in 23 pages for object 'syscolumns'.
DBCC results for 'systypes'.
There are 26 rows in 1 pages for object 'systypes'.
DBCC results for 'syscomments'.
There are 232 rows in 25 pages for object 'syscomments'.
DBCC results for 'sysfiles1'.
There are 2 rows in 1 pages for object 'sysfiles1'.
DBCC results for 'syspermissions'.
There are 72 rows in 1 pages for object 'syspermissions'.
DBCC results for 'sysusers'.
There are 14 rows in 1 pages for object 'sysusers'.
DBCC results for 'sysproperties'.
There are 0 rows in 0 pages for object 'sysproperties'.
DBCC results for 'sysdepends'.
There are 760 rows in 4 pages for object 'sysdepends'.
```

```
DBCC results for 'sysreferences'.
There are 14 rows in 1 pages for object 'sysreferences'.
DBCC results for 'sysfulltextcatalogs'.
There are 0 rows in 0 pages for object 'sysfulltextcatalogs'.
DBCC results for 'sysfulltextnotify'.
There are 0 rows in 0 pages for object 'sysfulltextnotify'.
DBCC results for 'sysfilegroups'.
There are 1 rows in 1 pages for object 'sysfilegroups'.
DBCC results for 'Orders'.
There are 830 rows in 26 pages for object 'Orders'.
DBCC results for 'pubs'.
DBCC results for 'sysobjects'.
There are 108 rows in 3 pages for object 'sysobjects'.
DBCC results for 'sysindexes'.
There are 54 rows in 3 pages for object 'sysindexes'.
DBCC results for 'syscolumns'.
There are 440 rows in 5 pages for object 'syscolumns'.
DBCC results for 'systypes'.
There are 29 rows in 1 pages for object 'systypes'.
DBCC results for 'syscomments'.
There are 149 rows in 11 pages for object 'syscomments'.
DBCC results for 'sysfiles1'.
There are 2 rows in 1 pages for object 'sysfiles1'.
DBCC results for 'syspermissions'.
There are 69 rows in 1 pages for object 'syspermissions'.
DBCC results for 'sysusers'.
There are 13 rows in 1 pages for object 'sysusers'.
DBCC results for 'sysproperties'.
There are 0 rows in 0 pages for object 'sysproperties'.
DBCC results for 'sysdepends'.
There are 354 rows in 2 pages for object 'sysdepends'.
DBCC results for 'sysreferences'.
There are 10 rows in 1 pages for object 'sysreferences'.
DBCC results for 'sysfulltextcatalogs'.
There are 0 rows in 0 pages for object 'sysfulltextcatalogs'.
DBCC results for 'sysfulltextnotify'.
There are 0 rows in 0 pages for object 'sysfulltextnotify'.
DBCC results for 'sysfilegroups'.
There are 1 rows in 1 pages for object 'sysfilegroups'.
DBCC results for 'titleauthor'.
There are 25 rows in 1 pages for object 'titleauthor'.
DBCC results for 'stores'.
There are 6 rows in 1 pages for object 'stores'.
```

```
Listing distribution
--------------------
distribution
Listing master
--------------------
master
Listing model
--------------------
model
Listing msdb
--------------------
msdb
Listing Northwind
--------------------
Northwind
Listing pubs
--------------------
pubs
Listing rentman
--------------------
rentman
Listing tempdb
--------------------
tempdb
```

### sp_MSforeachtable @command1 @replacechar = '?' [,@command2] [,@command3] [,@whereand] [,@precommand] [,@postcommand]

Executes up to three commands for every table in a database (optionally matching the @whereand clause). @replacechar will be replaced with the name of each table. @precommand and @postcommand can be used to direct commands to a single result set.

```
EXEC sp_MSforeachtable @command1='EXEC sp_help [?]'

EXEC sp_MSforeachtable @command1='PRINT "Listing ?"', @command2='SELECT *
FROM ?',@whereand=' AND name like "title%"'
```

```
Name            Owner       Type         Created_datetime
--------------  ----------  -----------  ----------------------------
Orders          dbo         user table   2000-08-06 01:34:06.610
```

| Column_name | Type | Computed | Length | Prec | Scale | N |
|---|---|---|---|---|---|---|
| OrderID | int | no | 4 | 10 | 0 | n |
| CustomerID | nchar | no | 10 | | | y |
| EmployeeID | int | no | 4 | 10 | 0 | y |
| OrderDate | datetime | no | 8 | | | y |
| RequiredDate | datetime | no | 8 | | | y |
| ShippedDate | datetime | no | 8 | | | y |
| ShipVia | int | no | 4 | 10 | 0 | y |
| Freight | money | no | 8 | 19 | 4 | y |
| ShipName | nvarchar | no | 80 | | | y |
| ShipAddress | nvarchar | no | 120 | | | y |
| ShipCity | nvarchar | no | 30 | | | y |
| ShipRegion | nvarchar | no | 30 | | | y |
| ShipPostalCode | nvarchar | no | 20 | | | y |
| ShipCountry | nvarchar | no | 30 | | | y |

| Identity | Seed | Increment | Not For Replication |
|---|---|---|---|
| OrderID | 1 | 1 | 0 |

RowGuidCol
-----------------------------
No rowguidcol column defined.

Data_located_on_filegroup
-----------------------------
PRIMARY

| index_name | index_description |
|---|---|
| CustomerID | nonclustered located on PRIMARY |
| CustomersOrders | nonclustered located on PRIMARY |
| EmployeeID | nonclustered located on PRIMARY |
| EmployeesOrders | nonclustered located on PRIMARY |
| OrderDate | nonclustered located on PRIMARY |
| PK_Orders | clustered, unique, primary key located on PRIMARY |
| ShippedDate | nonclustered located on PRIMARY |
| ShippersOrders | nonclustered located on PRIMARY |
| ShipPostalCode | nonclustered located on PRIMARY |

| constraint_type | constraint_name | delete_action | updat |
|---|---|---|---|
| DEFAULT on column Freight | DF_Orders_Freight | (n/a) | (n/a) |

```
FOREIGN KEY                FK_Orders_Customers  No Action    No Ac

FOREIGN KEY                FK_Orders_Employees  No Action    No Ac

FOREIGN KEY                FK_Orders_Shippers   No Action    No Ac

PRIMARY KEY (clustered)    PK_Orders            (n/a)        (n/a)

Table is referenced by foreign key
------------------------------------------------------
Northwind.dbo.Order Details: FK_Order_Details_Orders
Table is referenced by views
------------------------------------------------------
V1
```

```
Listing [dbo].[Order Details]
OrderID      ProductID   UnitPrice              Quantity Discount
-----------  ----------- ---------------------  -------- --------------------
10248        11          14.0000                12       0.0
10248        42          9.8000                 10       0.0
10248        72          34.8000                5        0.0
10249        14          18.6000                9        0.0
10249        51          42.4000                40       0.0
10250        41          7.7000                 10       0.0
10250        51          42.4000                35       0.15000001
10250        65          16.8000                15       0.15000001
10251        22          16.8000                6        5.0000001E-2
10251        57          15.6000                15       5.0000001E-2
10251        65          16.8000                20       0.0
10252        20          64.8000                40       5.0000001E-2
10252        33          2.0000                 25       5.0000001E-2
10252        60          27.2000                40       0.0
10253        31          10.0000                20       0.0
10253        39          14.4000                42       0.0
10253        49          16.0000                40       0.0
10254        24          3.6000                 15       0.15000001
10254        55          19.2000                21       0.15000001
10254        74          8.0000                 21       0.0
10255        2           15.2000                20       0.0
10255        16          13.9000                35       0.0
10255        36          15.2000                25       0.0
10255        59          44.0000                30       0.0
10256        53          26.2000                15       0.0
10256        77          10.4000                12       0.0
```

```
10257        27           35.1000              25        0.0
10257        39           14.4000              6         0.0
10257        77           10.4000              15        0.0
10258        2            15.2000              50        0.2
```

```
Listing [dbo].[Orders]
OrderID CustomerID EmployeeID  OrderDate
------- ---------- ----------- -------------------
10248   VINET      5           1996-07-04 00:00:00
10249   TOMSP      6           1996-07-05 00:00:00
10250   HANAR      4           1996-07-08 00:00:00
10251   VICTE      3           1996-07-08 00:00:00
10252   SUPRD      4           1996-07-09 00:00:00
10253   HANAR      3           1996-07-10 00:00:00
10254   CHOPS      5           1996-07-11 00:00:00
10255   RICSU      9           1996-07-12 00:00:00
10256   WELLI      3           1996-07-15 00:00:00
10257   HILAA      4           1996-07-16 00:00:00
10258   ERNSH      1           1996-07-17 00:00:00
10259   CENTC      4           1996-07-18 00:00:00
10260   OTTIK      4           1996-07-19 00:00:00
10261   QUEDE      4           1996-07-19 00:00:00
10262   RATTC      8           1996-07-22 00:00:00
10263   ERNSH      9           1996-07-23 00:00:00
10264   FOLKO      6           1996-07-24 00:00:00
10265   BLONP      2           1996-07-25 00:00:00
10266   WARTH      3           1996-07-26 00:00:00
10267   FRANK      4           1996-07-29 00:00:00
10268   GROSR      8           1996-07-30 00:00:00
10269   WHITC      5           1996-07-31 00:00:00
10270   WARTH      1           1996-08-01 00:00:00
10271   SPLIR      6           1996-08-01 00:00:00
10272   RATTC      6           1996-08-02 00:00:00
10273   QUICK      3           1996-08-05 00:00:00
10274   VINET      6           1996-08-06 00:00:00
10275   MAGAA      1           1996-08-07 00:00:00
10276   TORTU      8           1996-08-08 00:00:00
10277   MORGK      2           1996-08-09 00:00:00
10278   BERGS      8           1996-08-12 00:00:00
10279   LEHMS      8           1996-08-13 00:00:00
10280   BERGS      2           1996-08-14 00:00:00
10281   ROMEY      4           1996-08-14 00:00:00
10282   ROMEY      4           1996-08-15 00:00:00
10283   LILAS      3           1996-08-16 00:00:00
10284   LEHMS      4           1996-08-19 00:00:00
```

## sp_MSget_oledbinfo @server [,@infotype] [,@login] [,@password]

Returns OLEDB provider information for a linked server.

```
sp_MSget_oledbinfo @server='pythia', @login='sa'
```

## sp_MSget_qualified_name @object_id, @qualified_name OUT

Translates an object ID into a fully qualified object name.

```
DECLARE @oid int, @obname sysname
SET @oid=OBJECT_ID('Customers')
EXEC sp_MSget_qualified_name @oid, @obname OUT
SELECT @obname
```

(Results)

```
-------------------------------------------------------------------
[dbo].[Customers]
```

## sp_MSget_type @tabid, @colid, @colname OUT, @type OUT

Returns the name and type of a table column.

```
DECLARE @tabid int, @colname sysname, @type nvarchar(4000)
SET @tabid=OBJECT_ID('Customers')
EXEC sp_MSget_type @tabid, 1, @colname OUT, @type OUT
SELECT @colname, @type
```

(Results)

```
------------ ----------
CustomerID   nchar(5)
```

## sp_MSguidtostr @guid, @mystr OUT

Returns a uniqueidentifier as a string.

```
DECLARE @guid uniqueidentifier, @guidstr sysname
SET @guid=NEWID()
EXEC sp_MSguidtostr @guid, @guidstr OUT
```

## sp_MShelpindex @tablename [,@indexname] [,@flags]

Lists index catalog info. Includes lots of info not returned by the stock sp_helpindex procedure.

```
sp_MShelpindex 'Customers'
```

(Results abridged)

```
name                        status       indid  OrigFillFactor
------------------------    -----------  ------ --------------
PK_Customers                18450        1      0
City                        2097152      2      0
CompanyName                 0            3      0
PostalCode                  2097152      4      0
Region                      2097152      5      0
ContactName                 2097152      6      0
index_2073058421            2            7      0
_WA_Sys_Country_7B905C75    10485856     8      0
ContactTitle                2097248      9      0
```

## sp_MShelptype [@typename] [,@flags='sdt'|'uddt' |NULL]

List data type catalog info.

```
EXEC sp_MShelptype 'id'
EXEC sp_MShelptype 'int','sdt'
EXEC sp_MShelptype
```

(Results abridged)

```
UserDatatypeName     owner   basetypename    defaultname    rulename
------------------   ------- --------------- -------------- -----------
id                   dbo     varchar         NULL           NULL
```

(1 row(s) affected)

```
SystemDatatypeName   ifvarlen_max allownulls  isnumeric   allowidentity
------------------   ------------ ----------- ----------- --------------
int                  NULL         1           0           1
```

```
SystemDatatypeName   ifvarlen_max allownulls  isnumeric   allowidentity
------------------   ------------ ----------- ----------- --------------
bigint               NULL         1           0           1
binary               8000         1           0           0
bit                  NULL         1           0           0
char                 8000         1           0           0
datetime             NULL         1           0           0
decimal              NULL         1           1           1
```

| | | | | |
|---|---|---|---|---|
| float | NULL | 1 | 0 | 0 |
| image | NULL | 1 | 0 | 0 |
| int | NULL | 1 | 0 | 1 |
| money | NULL | 1 | 0 | 0 |
| nchar | 8000 | 1 | 0 | 0 |
| ntext | NULL | 1 | 0 | 0 |
| numeric | NULL | 1 | 1 | 1 |
| nvarchar | 8000 | 1 | 0 | 0 |
| real | NULL | 1 | 0 | 0 |
| smalldatetime | NULL | 1 | 0 | 0 |
| smallint | NULL | 1 | 0 | 1 |
| smallmoney | NULL | 1 | 0 | 0 |
| sql_variant | NULL | 1 | 0 | 0 |
| sysname | NULL | 0 | 0 | 0 |
| text | NULL | 1 | 0 | 0 |
| timestamp | NULL | 1 | 0 | 0 |
| tinyint | NULL | 1 | 0 | 1 |
| uniqueidentifier | NULL | 1 | 0 | 0 |
| varbinary | 8000 | 1 | 0 | 0 |
| varchar | 8000 | 1 | 0 | 0 |

| UserDatatypeName | owner | basetypename | defaultname | rulename | tid |
|---|---|---|---|---|---|
| empid | dbo | char | NULL | NULL | 259 |
| id | dbo | varchar | NULL | NULL | 257 |
| tid | dbo | varchar | NULL | NULL | 258 |

## sp_MSindexspace @tablename [,@index_name]

Lists index size info.

```
EXEC sp_MSindexspace 'Customers'
```

| Index ID | Index Name | Size (KB) | Comments |
|---|---|---|---|
| 1 | PK_Customers | 16 | Size excludes actual data. |
| 2 | City | 16 | (None) |
| 3 | CompanyName | 16 | (None) |
| 4 | PostalCode | 16 | (None) |
| 5 | Region | 16 | (None) |
| 6 | ContactName | 16 | (None) |
| 7 | index_2073058421 | 16 | (None) |
| 8 | _WA_Sys_Country_7B905C75 | 0 | (None) |
| 9 | ContactTitle | 0 | (None) |

### sp_MSis_pk_col @source_table, @colname, @indid

Checks a column to see whether it's a primary key.

```
DECLARE @res int
EXEC @res=sp_MSis_pk_col 'Customers','CustomerId',1
SELECT @res
```

(Results)

```
-----------
1
```

### sp_MSkilldb @dbname

Uses DBCC DBREPAIR to drop a database (even if the database isn't damaged).

```
sp_MSkilldb 'northwind2'
```

### sp_MSloginmappings @loginname

Lists login, database, user, and alias mappings.

```
sp_MSloginmappings
```

(Results abridged)

| LoginName | DBName | UserName | AliasName |
| --- | --- | --- | --- |
| BUILTIN\Administrators | NULL | NULL | NULL |

| LoginName | DBName | UserName | AliasName |
| --- | --- | --- | --- |
| LEX\TALIONIS | statworld | dbo | NULL |
| LEX\TALIONIS | Northwind2 | dbo | NULL |
| LEX\TALIONIS | Northwind3 | dbo | NULL |
| LEX\TALIONIS | pubs | dbo | NULL |

| LoginName | DBName | UserName | AliasName |
| --- | --- | --- | --- |
| distributor_admin | NULL | NULL | NULL |

| LoginName | DBName | UserName | AliasName |
| --- | --- | --- | --- |
| sa | distribution | dbo | NULL |
| sa | master | dbo | NULL |

```
sa                    model          dbo         NULL
sa                    msdb           dbo         NULL
sa                    Northwind      dbo         NULL
sa                    tempdb         dbo         NULL
sa                    test           dbo         NULL


LoginName             DBName         UserName    AliasName
--------------------- -------------- ----------- ------------
puck                  Northwind      puck        NULL
puck                  pubs           puck        NULL
puck                  pubs2          puck        NULL


LoginName             DBName         UserName    AliasName
--------------------- -------------- ----------- ------------
farker                Northwind      farker      NULL
farker                pubs           farker      NULL
farker                pubs2          farker      NULL


LoginName             DBName         UserName    AliasName
--------------------- -------------- ----------- ------------
frank                 Northwind      frank       NULL
```

## sp_MStable_has_unique_index @tabid

Checks a table for a unique index.

```
DECLARE @objid int, @res int
SET @objid=OBJECT_ID('Customers')
EXEC @res=sp_MStable_has_unique_index @objid
SELECT @res
```

(Results)

```
-----------
1
```

## sp_MStablekeys [tablename] [,@colname] [,@type] [,@keyname] [,@flags]

Lists a table's keys.

```
sp_MStablekeys 'Orders'
cType cName                 cFlags      cColCount   cFillFactor
----- --------------------- ----------- ----------- -----------
1     PK_Orders             1           1           0
```

```
3       FK_Orders_Customers    2067        1           NULL
3       FK_Orders_Employees    2067        1           NULL
3       FK_Orders_Shippers     2067        1           NULL
```

## sp_MStablerefs @tablename,@type= N'actualtables',@direction= N'primary',@reftable

Lists the objects a table references or that reference it.

```
sp_MStablerefs 'Orders'
```

(Results)

```
candidate_table      candidate_key   referenced
------------------   -------------   ----------
[dbo].[Customers]    N/A             1
[dbo].[Employees]    N/A             1
[dbo].[Shippers]     N/A             1
```

## sp_MStablespace [@name]

Lists table space information.

```
sp_MStablespace 'Orders'
```

(Results)

```
Rows        DataSpaceUsed IndexSpaceUsed
-----------  ------------- --------------
830         208           328
```

## sp_MSunc_to_drive @unc_path, @local_server, @local_path OUT

Converts a UNC path to a drive.

```
DECLARE @path sysname
EXEC sp_MSunc_to_drive '\\PYTHIA\C$\', 'PYTHIA',@path OUT
SELECT @path
```

(Results)

```
---------------------------------------------------------------------------
C:\
```

### sp_MSuniquecolname table_name, @base_colname, @unique_colname OUT

Generates a unique column name for a specified table using a base name.

```
DECLARE @uniquename sysname
EXEC sp_MSuniquecolname 'Customers','CustomerId',@uniquename OUT
SELECT @uniquename
```

(Results)

```
------------------------------------------------------------------------
CustomerId13
```

### sp_MSuniquename @seed, @start

Returns a result set containing a unique object name for the current database using a specified seed name and start value.

```
sp_MSuniquename 'Customers',3
Name                                              Next
------------------------------------------------- -----------
Customers3__92
```

### sp_MSuniqueobjectname @name_in, @name_out OUT

Generates a unique object name for the current database.

```
DECLARE @outname sysname
SET @outname='' -- Can't be NULL
EXEC sp_MSuniqueobjectname 'Customers',@outname OUT
SELECT @outname
```

(Results)

```
------------------------------------------------------------------------
austomers
```

### sp_MSuniquetempname @name_in, @name_out OUT

Generates a unique temporary object (tempdb) name using a base name.

```
USE tempdb
CREATE TABLE livr_kp (c1 int)
```

```
DECLARE @name_out sysname
exec sp_Msuniquetempname 'livr_kp', @name_out OUT
SELECT @name_out
```

(Results)

```
------------------------------------------------
liar_kp
```

## sp_readerrorlog [@lognum]

Lists the system error log corresponding to lognum. Omit lognum to list the current error log.

```
sp_readerrorlog 2
```

(Results abridged)

```
ERRORLOG.2
-------------------------------------------------------------
2000-09-29 22:57:38.89 server    Microsoft SQL Server  2000 - 8
        Aug  6 2000 00:57:48
        Copyright (c) 1988-2000 Microsoft Corporation
        Personal Edition on Windows NT 5.0 (Build 2195: Service
2000-09-29 22:57:38.96 server    Copyright (C) 1988-2000 Micros
2000-09-29 22:57:38.96 server    All rights reserved.
2000-09-29 22:57:38.96 server    Server Process ID is 780.
2000-09-29 22:57:38.96 server    Logging SQL Server messages in
2000-09-29 22:57:45.73 server    SQL server listening on TCP, S
2000-09-29 22:57:45.73 server    SQL server listening on 192.16
2000-09-29 22:57:45.81 server    SQL Server is ready for client
2000-09-29 22:57:45.90 spid5     Clearing tempdb database.
2000-09-29 22:57:49.06 spid5     Starting up database 'tempdb'.
2000-09-29 22:57:51.07 spid4     Recovery complete.
```

## sp_remove_tempdb_file @filename

Removes a file on which tempdb is based.

```
master..sp_remove_tempdb_file 'tempdev02'
```

## sp_set_local_time [@server_name] [,@adjustment_in_minutes] (for Win9x)

Synchronizes the computer's local time with another server (if supplied).

```
msdb..sp_set_local_time
```

## sp_tempdbspace

Returns space usage info for tempdb.

```
sp_tempdbspace
```

(Results)

```
database_name database_size          spaceused
------------- ---------------------- -------------------------------------
tempdb        8.750000               .546875
```

## xp_dirtree 'rootpath'

Completely lists all the subdirectories (and their subdirectories) of a given path, including the node level of each directory.

```
master..xp_dirtree 'c:\'
```

(Results abridged)

```
subdirectory      depth
----------------- -----------
WINDOWS           1
SYSTEM            2
OOBE              3
MSNSETUP          4
SETUP             4
HTML              4
MOUSE             5
IMAGES            6
ISPSGNUP          5
IMAGES            4
ERROR             4
MSNHTML           4
ISPSGNUP          5
MOUSE             5
MSNERROR          4
MSN               4
PASSPORT          4
SHELLEXT          3
COLOR             3
VMM32             3
MACROMED          3
```

```
DIRECTOR        4
FLASH           4
Shockwave       4
XTRAS           5
IOSUBSYS        3
VIEWERS         3
WBEM            3
logs            4
MOF             4
bad             5
good            5
```

## xp_dsninfo @systemdsn

Lists ODBC DSN information for the specified system datasource.

```
master..xp_dsninfo 'pubsdsn'
```

## xp_enum_oledb_providers

Enumerates the OLEDB providers available on the server machine.

```
master..xp_enum_oledb_providers
```

(Results abridged)

```
Provider Name               Provider Description
--------------------------  -----------------------------------------------------
EMPOLEDB.1                  VSEE Versioning Enlistment Manager Proxy Data
Source
MediaCatalogDB.1            MediaCatalogDB OLE DB Provider
SQLOLEDB                    Microsoft OLE DB Provider for SQL Server
DTSPackageDSO               Microsoft OLE DB Provider for DTS Packages
SQLReplication.OLEDB        SQL Server Replication OLE DB Provider for DTS
MediaCatalogMergedDB.1      MediaCatalogMergedDB OLE DB Provider
MSDMine                     Microsoft OLE DB Provider For Data Mining Services
ADsDSOObject                OLE DB Provider for Microsoft Directory Services
MediaCatalogWebDB.1         MediaCatalogWebDB OLE DB Provider
MSDAIPP.DSO                 Microsoft OLE DB Provider for Internet Publishing
MSSearch.CollatorDSO.1      Microsoft OLE DB Provider for Microsoft Search
MSDASQL                     Microsoft OLE DB Provider for ODBC Drivers
MSUSP                       Microsoft OLE DB Provider for Outlook Search
Microsoft.Jet.OLEDB.4.0     Microsoft Jet 4.0 OLE DB Provider
MSDAOSP                     Microsoft OLE DB Simple Provider
```

```
MSDAORA                    Microsoft OLE DB Provider for Oracle
MSIDXS                     Microsoft OLE DB Provider for Indexing Service
```

## xp_enumdsn

Enumerates the system ODBC datasources available on the server machine.

```
master..xp_enumdsn
```

(Results abridged)

```
Data Source Name          Description
--------------------      -----------------------------------
DeluxeCD                  Microsoft Access Driver (*.mdb)
Visual FoxPro Database    Microsoft Visual FoxPro Driver
Visual FoxPro Tables      Microsoft Visual FoxPro Driver
dBase Files - Word        Microsoft dBase VFP Driver (*.dbf)
FoxPro Files - Word       Microsoft FoxPro VFP Driver (*.dbf)
SS7                       SQL Server
KHENSS2K                  SQL Server
MS Access Database        Microsoft Access Driver (*.mdb)
Excel Files               Microsoft Excel Driver (*.xls)
dBASE Files               Microsoft dBase Driver (*.dbf)
LocalServer               SQL Server
MQIS                      SQL Server
FoodMart                  Microsoft Access Driver (*.mdb)
ECDCMusic                 Microsoft Access Driver (*.mdb)
```

## xp_enumerrorlogs

Enumerates (lists) the current server error log files.

```
master..xp_enumerrorlogs
```

(Results abridged)

```
Archive # Date                  Log File Size (Byte)
--------- -------------------   --------------------
6         06/28/2000  23:13     3139
5         06/29/2000  11:19     3602
4         06/29/2000  11:35     3486
3         06/29/2000  22:55     15998
2         06/29/2000  23:10     3349
1         07/01/2000  12:49     120082
0         07/01/2000  12:51     31086
```

## xp_execresultset 'code query','database'

Allows you to supply a query that returns a T-SQL query to execute. This is handy for extremely large queries—those too large for varchar(8,000) variables. You can simply place your query in a table and reference the table in the query you pass to xp_execresultset:

```
exec master..xp_execresultset
'SELECT ''PRINT ''test'''','pubs'
```

(Results)

```
test
```

## xp_fileexist 'filename'

Returns a result set indicating whether a file exists.

```
exec master..xp_fileexist 'd:\winnt\readme.txt'
exec master..xp_fileexist 'c:\winnt\readme.txt'
exec master..xp_fileexist 'c:\winnt\odbc.ini'
exec master..xp_fileexist 'c:\winnt'
```

(Results)

```
File Exists File is a Directory Parent Directory Exists
----------- ------------------- -----------------------
0           0                   0


File Exists File is a Directory Parent Directory Exists
----------- ------------------- -----------------------
0           0                   1


File Exists File is a Directory Parent Directory Exists
----------- ------------------- -----------------------
1           0                   1


File Exists File is a Directory Parent Directory Exists
----------- ------------------- -----------------------
0           1                   1
```

## xp_fixeddrives

Returns a result set listing the fixed drives on the server machine.

```
master..xp_fixeddrives
```

(Results)

```
drive MB free
----- -----------
C     4743
```

### xp_get_MAPI_default_profile

Returns the default MAPI mail profile.

```
master..xp_get_MAPI_default_profile
```

(Results)

```
Profile name
--------------------------------
Microsoft Outlook Internet Setti
```

### xp_get_MAPI_profiles

Returns a result set listing the system's MAPI profiles.

```
master..xp_get_MAPI_profiles
```

(Results)

```
Profile name                     Is default profile
-------------------------------- ------------------
Microsoft Outlook Internet Setti 1
```

### xp_getfiledetails 'filename'

Returns a result set listing file details for the specified file.

```
master..xp_getfiledetails 'c:\winnt\odbc.ini'
```

(Results abridged)

```
Alternate Name Size   Creation Date Creation Time Last Written Date
-------------- ------ ------------- ------------- -----------------
NULL           2144   20000903      220228        20000628
```

## xp_getnetname

Returns the network name of the server computer.

```
master..xp_getnetname
```

(Results)

```
Server Net Name
---------------
TALIONIS
```

## xp_oledbinfo @providername, @datasource, @location, @providerstring, @catalog, @login, @password, @infotype

Returns a result set listing detailed OLEDB information about a specific linked server.

```
master..xp_oledbinfo 'SQLOLEDB', 'PYTHIA', NULL, NULL, NULL, 'sa',
'drkildare', NULL
```

(Results)

```
Information Type                   Value
--------------------------------   ------------------------------
DBMS Name                          Microsoft SQL Server
DBMS Version                       8.00.194
Database Name                      master
SQL Subscriber                     TRUE
```

## xp_readerrorlog [lognum][filename]

Returns a result set (c1 char(255) c2 int) containing the error log specified by lognum (omit to get the current error log).

```
master..xp_readerrorlog 3
```

(Results abridged)

```
ERRORLOG.3
-------------------------------------------------------------------------
2000-09-29 11:36:07.58 server   Microsoft SQL Server  2000 - 8.00.194 (I
        Aug  6 2000 00:57:48
```

```
                      Copyright (c) 1988-2000 Microsoft Corporation
                      Personal Edition on Windows NT 5.0 (Build 2195: Service Pack 2, R
2000-09-29 11:36:07.58 server      Copyright (C) 1988-2000 Microsoft Corpor
2000-09-29 11:36:07.60 server      All rights reserved.
2000-09-29 11:36:07.60 server      Server Process ID is 1080.
2000-09-29 11:36:07.60 server      Logging SQL Server messages in file 'C:\
2000-09-29 11:36:07.61 server      SQL Server is starting at priority class
2000-09-29 11:36:07.72 server      SQL Server configured for thread mode pr
2000-09-29 11:36:07.72 server      Using dynamic lock allocation. [500] Loc
2000-09-29 11:36:07.85 spid3       Starting up database 'master'.
2000-09-29 11:36:07.99 server      Using 'SSNETLIB.DLL' version '8.0.194'.
2000-09-29 11:36:07.99 spid5       Starting up database 'model'.
2000-09-29 11:36:08.02 spid3       Server name is 'KHENMP\SS2000'.
2000-09-29 11:36:08.02 spid3       Skipping startup of clean database id 4
2000-09-29 11:36:08.02 spid3       Skipping startup of clean database id 5
2000-09-29 11:36:08.18 spid5       Clearing tempdb database.
2000-09-29 11:36:08.51 spid5       Starting up database 'tempdb'.
2000-09-29 11:36:08.71 spid3       Recovery complete.
2000-09-29 22:55:28.36 server      SQL Server terminating because of system
2000-09-29 22:55:39.34 spid3       SQL Server is terminating due to 'stop'
```

You can also pass -1 as lognum and specify a second parameter containing the name of a file you want to read instead of an error log. That is, xp_readerrorlog can read any text file, not just error logs. For example, this command will read a file named README.TXT:

```
EXEC master..xp_readerrorlog -1, 'C:\README.TXT'
```

## xp_regenumvalues

Enumerates the values under a registry key.

```
CREATE TABLE #reg
(kv nvarchar(255) NOT NULL,
 kvdata nvarchar(255) null)

INSERT #reg
EXEC master..xp_regenumvalues 'HKEY_LOCAL_MACHINE',
'SOFTWARE\Microsoft\MSSQLServer\MSSQLServer'

SELECT * FROM #reg
```

(Results)

```
kv                    kvdata
-------------------   ---------------------------------------------------------
FullTextDefaultPath   C:\Program Files\Microsoft SQL Server\MSSQL$SS2000\FTData
ListenOn - Item #1    SSMSSH70
ListenOn - Item #2    SSNETLIB
SetHostName           0
AuditLevel            0
LoginMode             2
Tapeloadwaittime      -1
DefaultLogin          guest
Map_                  \
Map#                  -
Map$                  NULL
BackupDirectory       C:\Program Files\Microsoft SQL Server\MSSQL$SS2000\BACKUP
DefaultDomain         DAD
DefaultCollationName  SQL_Latin1_General_CP1_CI_AS
```

### xp_regaddmultistr, xp_regdeletekey, xp_regdeletevalue, xp_regread, xp_regremovemultistring, xp_regwrite

Allows addition, modification, and deletion of registry keys and key values.

```
DECLARE @df nvarchar(64)
EXEC master.dbo.xp_regread N'HKEY_CURRENT_USER', N'Control
  Panel\International', N'sShortDate', @df OUT, N'no_output'
SELECT @df
```

(Results)

```
----------------------------------------------------------------
M/d/yyyy
```

### xp_subdirs

Returns a result set containing a directory's immediate subdirectories.

```
master..xp_subdirs 'C:\Program Files\Microsoft SQL Server'
```

(Results)

```
subdirectory
--------------
MSSQL$SS2000
80
```

### xp_test_MAPI_profile 'profile'

Tests the specified MAPI profile to ensure that it's valid and can be connected to.

```
master..xp_test_MAPI_profile 'SQL'
```

### xp_varbintohexstr

Converts a varbinary variable to a hexadecimal string.

```
CREATE PROC sp_hex @i int, @hx varchar(30) OUT AS
DECLARE @vb varbinary(30)
SET @vb=CAST(@i as varbinary)
EXEC master..xp_varbintohexstr @vb, @hx OUT
GO
DECLARE @hex varchar(30)
EXEC sp_hex 343, @hex OUT
SELECT @hex
```

(Results)

```
------------------------------
0x00000157
```

# Creating INFORMATION_SCHEMA Views

You may be aware that you can query ANSI-style INFORMATION_SCHEMA views from any database even though they actually reside only in master. The ability to create a view in the master database and to be able to query it in the context of the current database can come in quite handy. Imagine all the object duplication you could avoid if you could create views that behaved like system procedures—that ran in the context of the current database even though they resided in master. As with most things SQL Server, if the system can create an object with special properties, so can you. The trick is in finding out how given that the precise technique usually undocumented. This is certainly the case with INFORMATION_SCHEMA views. The steps that I'm about to show you for creating them are not documented by Microsoft. As with all undocumented techniques, keep in mind that these steps may change or not work at all in future releases.

To create your own INFORMATION_SCHEMA view, follow these steps:

1. Enable updates to the system tables through a call to sp_configure:

```
sp_configure 'allow updates',1
RECONFIGURE WITH OVERRIDE
```

2. Enable automatic system object creation by calling the undocumented procedure sp_MS_upd_sysobj_category (you must be the database owner or a member of the setupadmin role):

```
sp_MS_upd_sysobj_category 1
```

This procedure turns on trace flag 1717 to cause all objects created to have their IsMSShipped bits turned on automatically. This is necessary because you can't create a nonsystem object that belongs to INFORMATION_SCHEMA. If you could, you could simply call sp_MS_marksystemobject (also covered in this chapter) after creating each view to enable its system bit. Instead, because SQL Server won't create nonsystem INFORMATION_SCHEMA objects, we have to enable a special server mode wherein each object created is automatically flagged as a system object.

3. Create your view in the master database, specifying INFORMATION_SCHEMA as the owner.

4. Disable automatic system object creation by calling sp_MS_upd_sysobj_category again:

```
sp_MS_upd_sysobj_category 2
```

5. Disable 'allow updates' by calling sp_configure:

```
sp_configure 'allow updates',0
RECONFIGURE WITH OVERRIDE
```

That's all there is to it. You can create views that behave just like SQL Server's built-in INFORMATION_SCHEMA views. See Chapter 9 for some examples of user-defined system views.

## Creating System Functions

Similar to creating system views, you can create functions that reside in master but can be queried from any database without a database name prefix.

Here's how it works: SQL Server creates a number of system UDFs during installation (for example, fn_varbintohexstr(), fn_chariswhitespace(), and so on). The ones that are created with system_function_schema as their owner can be accessed from any database using a one-part name. You can find out which ones these are by running the following query:

```
USE master
GO
SELECT name
FROM sysobjects
WHERE uid=USER_ID('system_function_schema')
AND    (OBJECTPROPERTY(id, 'IsScalarFunction')=1
       OR OBJECTPROPERTY(id, 'IsTableFunction')=1
       OR OBJECTPROPERTY(id, 'IsInlineFunction')=1)
```

(Results)

```
name
--------------------------------------------------
fn_chariswhitespace
fn_dblog
fn_generateparameterpattern
fn_getpersistedservernamecasevariation
fn_helpcollations
fn_listextendedproperty
fn_removeparameterwithargument
fn_replbitstringtoint
fn_replcomposepublicationsnapshotfolder
fn_replgenerateshorterfilenameprefix
fn_replgetagentcommandlinefromjobid
fn_replgetbinary8lodword
fn_replinttobitstring
fn_replmakestringliteral
fn_replprepadbinary8
fn_replquotename
fn_replrotr
fn_repltrimleadingzerosinhexstr
fn_repluniquename
fn_serverid
fn_serversharedrives
fn_skipparameterargument
fn_trace_geteventinfo
fn_trace_getfilterinfo
```

```
fn_trace_getinfo
fn_trace_gettable
fn_updateparameterwithargument
fn_virtualfilestats
fn_virtualservernodes
```

Because they belong to system_function_schema, they can be called across databases using one-part names.

Follow these steps to create your own system function:

1.  Enable updates to the system tables:

    ```
    sp_configure 'allow updates', 1
    RECONFIGURE WITH OVERRIDE
    ```

2.  Create your function using the CREATE FUNCTION command and be sure to create the function in the master database and owner-qualify it with system_function_schema. Be sure the functions name begins with **fn_** and consists only of lowercase letters.

3.  Set allow updates back off, especially on a production system:

    ```
    sp_configure 'allow updates', 0
    RECONFIGURE WITH OVERRIDE
    ```

You can create your own system UDFs by following these steps. Note that table-valued system functions must be qualified with a double colon regardless of whether you created the function or it was created during the installation process. See Chapter 10 for some examples of user-defined system functions.

## Undocumented DBCC Commands

The DBCC command originally exposed a small cadre of database maintenance routines that were outside the realm of traditional Transact-SQL. DBCC organized these routines into a versatile database administration Swiss army knife that DBAs used to manage routine maintenance and consistency checking.

Since then, DBCC's command verb list has grown to include dozens of things not related to database error checking. DBCC now handles everything from Profiler audit messages to database consistency checking to full-text index management. Many of the things DBCC can do are undocumented and are only called by Microsoft-supplied code. We'll talk about a few of them in a moment.

Before we delve into DBCC undocumented command verbs, here are a few things to keep in mind:

Include the WITH NO_INFOMSGS option to limit DBCC output to error messages. This makes the output from verbose commands like DBCC CHECKALLOC much more manageable without losing critical info.

DBCC HELP(*commandverb*) lists usage information for many DBCC command verbs. Naturally, most of the undocumented commands aren't listed, but it's still a good idea to check.

Use DBCC TRACEON(3604) to route DBCC output back to you rather than to the system console or error log. Although many of the undocumented commands send their output to the error log by default, you can route them to your client connection by enabling trace flag 3604.

**Table 22-1** Undocumented DBCC Command Verbs

| DBCC command verb and purpose | Example |
|---|---|
| ADDEXTENDEDPROC(procname,DLL) Adds an extended procedure to the list maintained by the server. It has the same basic functionality as the sp_addextendedproc stored procedure and is, in fact, called by the procedure. The procname parameter is the name of the extended procedure and DLL is the name of the DLL in which it resides. | `DBCC ADDEXTENDEDPROC('xp_mode','xp_stats.dll')` |
| ADDINSTANCE(object,instance) Adds an object instance to track in Performance Monitor. Stored procedures that initialize Performance Monitor counters use this to set up various areas of SQL Server for performance tracking. object is the name of the object that contains the instance (e.g., "SQL Replication Agents"). instance is the name of the instance to add (e.g., "Logreader"). | `DBCC ADDINSTANCE("SQL Replication Agents", "Snapshot")` |

*continued on page 660*

**Table 22–1** *(Continued)*

| DBCC Command verb and purpose | Example |
|---|---|
| AUDITEVENT(id, subclass, succeeded, loginame, username, grpname, sid) Generates a Security Audit trace event. You can trace Security Audit events in Profiler. Id is the event number you wish to generate. Subclass is the ID of the specific event subclass you wish to generate. Loginame is the login attempting the audited event. Username is the user name of the database user attempting the event. Grpname is the name of the group or role to which the user belongs. Sid is the security ID number of the login attempting the audited action. | <pre>DBCC AUDITEVENT (109, 1, 0, @loginame, @name_in_db, @grpname , NULL) /* Valid id/subclass values: ID    Sub      Event 104   1        Add login 104   2        Drop login 105   1        Grant login 105   2        Revoke login 105   3        Deny login 106   1        Change default database 106   2        Change default language 107   1        User change password 107   2        Admin. change password 108   1        Add server role member 108   2        Drop server role member 109   1        Add DB user 109   2        Drop DB user 109   3        Grant DB access 109   4        Revoke DB access 110   1        Add DB role member 110   2        Drop DB role member 110   3        Change DB role member 111   1        Add role 111   2        Drop role 112   1        App role change password */</pre> |
| BCPTABLOCK(dbid, tabid, setflag) Sets the **table lock on bulk load** option for a table. (It's called by sp_tableoption.) This can improve performance for bulk inserts because it avoids setting a row lock for every inserted row. Dbid is the database ID, tabid is the table's object ID, and setflag is a 1 or 0 indicating whether to set the option. | <pre>DECLARE @dbid int, @objid int SELECT @dbid=DB_ID('pubs'), @objid=OBJECT_ID('titles') DBCC BCPTABLOCK(@dbid,@objid,1)</pre> |
| BUFFER(dbid[,objid][,numberofbuffers][, printopt {0 \| 1 \| 2}]) Used to dump the contents of SQL Server memory buffers. Buffers can be listed for a specific object or for an entire database. | <pre>DECLARE @dbid int, @objid int SELECT @dbid=DB_ID('pubs'), @objid=OBJECT_ID('pubs..titles') SELECT COUNT(*) FROM pubs..titles -- Load buf DBCC TRACEON(3604) DBCC BUFFER(@dbid,@objid,1,2)</pre> |

**Table 22–1** *(Continued)*

| DBCC command verb and purpose | Example |
| --- | --- |
| BYTES(startingaddress,length) Lists the contents of the memory area beginning at startingaddress for length bytes. The address specified must be a valid address within the SQL Server process space. | `DBCC BYTES(0014767000,50)` |
| CALLFULLTEXT(funcid[ catid][,objid]) Valid function ID values ID Function (Parameters) 1 Creates a catalog (Catalog ID, path) 2 Drops a catalog (Catalog ID) 3 Populates a catalog (Catalog ID, 0 = full, 1 = incremental) 4 Stops a catalog population (Catalog ID) 5 Adds a table for FT indexing (Catalog ID, Object ID) 6 Removes a table from FT indexing (Catalog ID, Object ID) 7 Drops all catalogs (Database ID) 8 Performs catalog clean-up 9 Specifies the level of CPU resources allocated to Microsoft Search (Resource value: 1–5; 1 = background, 5 = dedicated – default: 3) 10 Sets FT connection timeout (Timeout value in seconds: 1–32,767) Used to perform a variety of full-text-related functions. Funcid specifies what function to perform and what parameters are valid. Catid is the full-text catalog ID. Objid is the object ID of the affected object. Note that CALLFULLTEXT is only valid within a system stored procedure. This procedure must have its system bit set (see the undocumented procedure sp_MS_marksystemobject for more info) and its name must begin with "sp_fulltext_." | ```USE master GO IF OBJECT_ID('sp_fulltext_resource') IS NOT NULL   DROP PROC sp_fulltext_resource GO CREATE PROC sp_fulltext_resource @value int -- value for 'resource_usage' AS       DBCC CALLFULLTEXT(9,@value)       -- FTSetResource (@value)       IF (@@error<>0) RETURN 1       -- SUCCESS -- RETURN 0       -- sp_fulltext_resource GO EXEC sp_MS_marksystemobject 'sp_fulltext_resource' EXEC sp_fulltext_resource 3``` |

*continued on page 662*

**Table 22–1** *(Continued)*

| DBCC Command verb and purpose | Example |
|---|---|
| DBCONTROL(dbname,option)<br>Sets database options. Performs many of the functions of sp_dboption and is, in fact, called by the procedure. Dbname is the name of the database. Option is a token specifying the option to set. | ```/* Supported options```<br>```multi Specifies multi-user mode```<br>```offline       Takes database offline```<br>```online Brings database back online```<br>```readonly      Makes database readonly```<br>```readwrite     Makes database readwrite```<br>```single Specifies single-user mode```<br>```*/```<br>```DBCC DBCONTROL('pubs',multi)``` |
| DBINFO(dbname)<br>Lists system-level information about the specified database, including its creation date, ID, status, next timestamp value, and so forth. | ```DBCC DBINFO('pubs')``` |
| DBRECOVER(dbname)<br>Manually recovers a database. Normally, databases are recovered at system start-up. If this did not occur—because of an error or because recovery was disabled (see trace flags 3607 and 3608—DBCC DBRECOVER can be used to attempt a manual recovery. Dbname is the name of the database to recover. | ```DBCC DBRECOVER('pubs')``` |
| DBREINDEXALL(dbname)<br>Rebuilds all the indexes in the current database. Only works for user (nonsystem) databases. | ```DBCC DBREINDEXALL('pubs') WITH NO_INFOMSGS``` |
| DBCC DBTABLE(dbid)<br>Lists DBT (DB Table) and FCB (File Control Block) information for the specified database. | ```DECLARE @dbid int```<br>```SET @dbid=DB_ID('pubs')```<br>```DBCC DBTABLE(@dbid)``` |

**Table 22–1** *(Continued)*

| DBCC Command verb and purpose | Example |
|---|---|
| **DELETEINSTANCE**(object,instance)<br>Deletes a Performance Monitor object instance previously set up with DBCC ADDINSTANCE. Object is the name of the Performance Monitor object. Instance is the name of the instance to delete. Specify a wildcard for instance to delete multiple instances. | `DBCC DELETEINSTANCE("SQL Replication Merge", "%")` |
| **DES**(dbid,objid)<br>Lists system-level descriptive information for the specified object. | `DECLARE @dbid int, @objid int`<br>`SELECT @dbid=DB_ID('pubs'),`<br>`@objid=OBJECT_ID('authors')`<br>`DBCC DES(@dbid, @objid)` |
| **DETACHDB**(dbname)<br>Detaches a database from the server. The database can then be moved to another server and can be reattached with sp_attach_db. This function is called by the sp_detach_db stored procedure. | `DBCC DETACHDB('northwind2')` |
| **DROPEXTENDEDPROC**(procname)<br>Drops an extended procedure. It's called by sp_dropextendedprocedure. | `USE master`<br>`DBCC DROPEXTENDEDPROC('xp_mode')` |
| **ERRORLOG**<br>Closes the current error log and starts another one, cycling the file extensions similarly to a server restart. It's called by the sp_cycle_errorlog stored procedure. | `DBCC ERRORLOG` |
| **EXTENTINFO**(dbname, tablename, indid)<br>Lists extent information for all the extents belonging to an object. Dbname is the name of the database, tablename is the name of the table, and indid is the index ID of the index to list. | `DBCC EXTENTINFO('pubs','titles',1)` |

*continued on page 664*

**Table 22–1** *(Continued)*

| DBCC Command verb and purpose | Example |
|---|---|
| **FLUSHPROCINDB(dbid)**<br>Forces a recompile of all the stored procedures in a database. Dbid is the database ID of the target database. This is handy when you've changed an option in the database that would materially affect the queries generated for its stored procedures. Sp_dboption, for example, uses DBCC FLUSHPROCINDB to ensure that changes to compile-time options are accommodated by a database's stored procedures. | `DECLARE @dbid int`<br>`SET @dbid=DB_ID('pubs')`<br>`DBCC FLUSHPROCINDB(@dbid)` |
| **IND(dbid, objid[,indid])**<br>Lists system-level index information for the specified object. | `DECLARE @dbid int, @objid int`<br>`SELECT @dbid=DB_ID('pubs'),`<br>`@objid=OBJECT_ID('pubs..authors')`<br>`DBCC IND(@dbid,@objid, 1)` |
| **INVALIDATE_TEXTPTR(@TextPtrVal)**<br>Invalidates the specified in-row text pointer in the transaction. If @TextPtrVal is NULL, invalidates all in-row text pointers in the current transaction. Called by sp_invalidate_textptr. | `CREATE TABLE #testtxt (c1 int, c2 text)`<br>`EXEC tempdb..sp_tableoption '#testtxt',`<br>`'text in row', 'on'`<br>`INSERT #testtxt VALUES ('1','Text lives`<br>`here')`<br>`BEGIN TRAN`<br>`DECLARE @ptr varbinary(16)`<br>`SELECT @ptr = TEXTPTR(c2)`<br>`FROM #testtxt`<br>`READTEXT #testtxt.c2 @ptr 0 5`<br>`DBCC INVALIDATE_TEXTPTR(@ptr)`<br>`READTEXT #testtxt.c2 @ptr 0 5 -- Fails`<br>`COMMIT TRAN` |
| **LOCKOBJECTSCHEMA (objname)**<br>Blocks schema changes by other connections until the caller commits the current transaction. It also increments the **schema_ver** column in sysobjects. This command has no effect if executed outside a transaction. | `USE pubs`<br>`BEGIN TRAN`<br>`DBCC LOCKOBJECTSCHEMA('titleauthor')` |

**Table 22–1** *(Continued)*

| DBCC Command verb and purpose | Example |
|---|---|
| LOG(dbid)<br>Displays log record information from the current database's transaction log. You can use INSERT..EXEC() to trap this output in a table for further processing. | ```CREATE TABLE #logrecs```<br>```(CurrentLSN varchar(30),```<br>```Operation varchar(20),```<br>```Context varchar(20),```<br>```TransactionID varchar(20))```<br>```INSERT #logrecs```<br>```EXEC('DBCC LOG(''pubs'')')``` |
| MEMORYSTATUS<br>Provides detailed info about SQL Server memory use. | ```DBCC MEMORYSTATUS``` |
| NO_TEXTPTR(@TabId, @InlineSize)<br>Marks a table as not supporting text pointers (16-byte pointers to text pages), thus allowing in-row text. @TabId is the object ID of the table. @InlineSize is the number of characters (24–7,000) to store inline. Called by sp_tableoption. | ```CREATE TABLE testtxt (c1 int, c2 text)```<br>```DECLARE @TabId int```<br>```SET @TabId=OBJECT_ID('testtxt')```<br>```DBCC NO_TEXTPTR(@TabId,500)```<br>```INSERT testtxt VALUES ('1','Text lives```<br>```here')```<br>```BEGIN TRAN```<br>```DECLARE @ptr varbinary(16)```<br>```SELECT @ptr = TEXTPTR(c2)```<br>```FROM testtxt```<br>```READTEXT testtxt.c2 @ptr 0 5```<br>```COMMIT TRAN``` |
| PAGE (dbid\|dbname, filenum, pagenum [,printopt])<br>Value    Meaning<br>0  (Default)—Print the page and buffer headers<br>1  Print the page and buffer headers, each row of the table, and the row offset table<br>2  Print the page and buffer headers, the page itself, and the row offset table<br>Dumps the contents of a specific database page. dbid\|dbname is the ID or name of the database, filenum is the database file number containing the page, pagenum is the number of the page, and printopt specifies what to print. | ```DBCC TRACEON(3604)```<br>```GO```<br>```DBCC PAGE('pubs',1,70,2)``` |

*continued on page 666*

**Table 22–1** *(Continued)*

| DBCC Command verb and purpose | Example |
|---|---|
| PRTIPAGE(dbid, objid, indexid[, printopt {0 \| 1 \| 2}]) <br> Lists page information for the specified index. | ```DECLARE @dbid int, @pagebin varchar(12), @pageid int, @fileid int, @objid int SELECT TOP 1 @dbid=DB_ID('pubs'), @objid=id, @pagebin=first FROM pubs..sysindexes WHERE id=OBJECT_ID('pubs..authors')``` <br><br> ```EXEC sp_decodepagebin @pagebin, @fileid OUT, @pageid OUT``` <br><br> ```DBCC PRTIPAGE(@dbid, @objid, 2, @pageid)``` |
| PSS <br> Dumps the process status structure (PSS) for a given connection. There is one PSS for every connection on the server, including system connections. The PSS includes info such as the transaction control block, the isolation level, and a host of other useful info. | ```DBCC PSS``` |
| RESOURCE <br> Lists resource utilization information for the server. | ```DBCC TRACEON(3604) DBCC resource DBCC TRACEOFF(3604)``` |
| SETINSTANCE(object,counter,instance, val) <br> Sets the value of a Performance Monitor instance counter. You can use this when benchmarking query and stored procedure performance to set a user-definable counter inside Performance Monitor. In fact, this is how the sp_user_counternn procedures work—they call DBCC SETINSTANCE. Object is the name of the Performance Monitor object, instance is the name of the object's instance to adjust, counter is the name of the performance counter to change, and val is the new value of the counter. | ```DBCC SETINSTANCE('SQLServer:User Settable', 'Query', 'User counter 1', 3)``` |

**Table 22-1** *(Continued)*

| DBCC Command verb and purpose | Example |
|---|---|
| STACKDUMP<br>Dumps the call stacks of all active connections, including their input buffers. Part of this info ends up in the error log; the rest is placed in a file with a .DMP extension in the SQL Server log folder. | `DBCC STACKDUMP` |
| TAB(dbid,objid[,printopt {0 \| 1 \| 2}}])<br>Lists system-level information for the specified table. | `DECLARE @dbid int, @objid int`<br>`SELECT @dbid=DB_ID('pubs'),`<br>`@objid=OBJECT_ID('pubs..authors')`<br>`DBCC TAB(@dbid, @objid, 2)` |
| UPGRADEDB(dbname)<br>Upgrades the system objects in the specified database to the current version of the database engine. | `DBCC UPGRADEDB('oldpubs')` |

# Undocumented Functions

Before the advent of UDFs, using undocumented functions was particularly tempting because if Transact-SQL didn't have a function you needed, there were certain things you simply couldn't do. With the addition of UDFs in SQL Server 2000, there's not nearly as much reason to use undocumented routines. In most cases you should be able to "roll your own" to provide functionality not found in Transact-SQL's documented routines.

That said, there may be times when undocumented functions provide capabilities or system internals info that you can't access by any other means. What follows in Table 22-2 is a list of some undocumented Transact-SQL functions. As I said before, use them at your own risk.

**Table 22-2** Undocumented Transact-SQL Functions

| Function and purpose | Example |
|---|---|
| **@@MICROSOFTVERSION**<br>Returns an internal tracking number used by Microsoft. | ```<br>SELECT @@MICROSOFTVERSION<br>-----------<br>117441211<br>``` |
| **ENCRYPT(string)**<br>Encrypts a string. It's used internally by the server to encrypt Transact-SQL code stored in syscomments (when WITH ENCRYPTION is specified). | ```<br>SELECT ENCRYPT('VALET')<br>------------------------------------------<br>0x4C0059004E00410052004400<br>``` |
| **GET_SID(username)**<br>Returns the current NT system ID for a specified user or group name as a varbinary(85). Prefix username with **\U** to search for an NT user ID; prefix it with **\G** to search for an NT group ID. Note that this function only works within system stored procedures that have their system bit set. See the undocumented procedure sp_MS_marksystemobject for more information. | ```<br>USE master<br>GO<br>IF (OBJECT_ID('sp_get_sid') IS NOT NULL)<br>  DROP PROC sp_get_sid<br>GO<br>CREATE PROCEDURE sp_get_sid<br>    @loginame sysname<br>AS<br>DECLARE @sid varbinary(85)<br>IF (charindex('\', @loginame) = 0)<br>      SELECT SUSER_SID(@loginame) AS 'SQL<br>User ID'<br>ELSE BEGIN<br>      SELECT @sid=get_sid('\U'+@loginame,<br>      NULL)<br>      IF @sid IS NULL<br>         SELECT @sid=get_sid('\G'+<br>         @loginame, NULL) -- Maybe it's<br>         a group<br>      IF @sid IS NULL BEGIN<br>        RAISERROR('Couldn''t find an ID<br>        for the specified<br>        loginame',16,10)<br>         RETURN -1<br>        END ELSE SELECT @sid AS 'NT User<br>ID'<br>      RETURN 0<br>END<br>GO<br>EXEC sp_MS_marksystemobject 'sp_get_sid'<br>EXEC sp_get_sid 'LEX_TALIONIS\KHEN'<br>``` |

**Table 22–2** *(Continued)*

| Function and purpose | Example |
|---|---|
| OBJECT_ID(..,'local')<br>Although the OBJECT_ID() function itself is of course documented, its optional second parameter isn't. Because you can pass a fully qualified object name as the first argument, OBJECT_ID() can return ID numbers for objects that reside in databases other than the current one. There may be times when you want to prevent this. For example, if you're performing a task on an object that requires access to catalog information in the current database, you may need to ensure that the object name not only translates to a valid object ID, but that it's also a local object. Pass 'local' as OBJECT_ID()'s second parameter to ensure that it sees objects in the current database only. | ```USE pubs SELECT OBJECT_ID('Northwind..Orders'), OBJECT_ID('Northwind..Orders','local') ----------- ----------- 357576312   NULL``` |
| PLATFORM()<br>Returns an integer representing the operating system and version of SQL Server on which you're running. | ```SELECT PLATFORM() ----------- 1025``` |
| PWDCOMPARE(str,pwd,oldenc)<br>Compares a string with an encrypted password. Str is the string to compare, pwd is the encrypted password to use, and oldenc is a 1 or 0 indicating whether old-style encryption was used to encrypt pwd. You can retrieve an encrypted password directly from the sysxlogins password column, or you can use the undocumented PWDENCRYPT() function to create one from a string. | ```SELECT PWDCOMPARE('enmity', password, (CASE WHEN xstatus&2048=2048 THEN 1 ELSE 0 END)) FROM sysxlogins WHERE name='k_reapr' ----------- 1``` |

*continued on page 670*

**Table 22–2** *(Continued)*

| Function and purpose | Example |
|---|---|
| PWDENCRYPT(str)<br><br>Encrypts a string using SQL Server's password encryption algorithm. Stored procedures that manage SQL Server passwords use this function to encrypt user passwords. You can use the undocumented PWDCOMPARE() function to compare an unencrypted string with the return value of PWDENCRYPT(). | ```
SELECT PWDENCRYPT('vengeance') AS
EncryptedString,PWDCOMPARE('vengeance',
PWDENCRYPT('vengeance'), 0) AS
EncryptedCompare
EncryptedString EncryptedCompare
EncryptedString EncryptedCompare
---------------- ----------------
--------        1
``` |
| TSEQUAL(ts1,ts2)<br><br>Compares two timestamp or rowversion values. Returns 1 if they're identical; raises an error if they're not. The TSEQUAL() function has been around for years. It dates back to the days when Microsoft SQL Server was merely an OS/2 port of Sybase SQL Server. It's not used as often any more, mainly because it's no longer necessary. You can compare two timestamp/rowversion columns directly and decide for yourself whether to raise an error. There's also no performance advantage to using TSEQUAL rather than a simple equality comparison. Still, it's not documented in the Books Online, so I'm compelled to include it here. | ```
USE tempdb
CREATE TABLE #testts
(k1 int identity,
rowversion rowversion)

DECLARE @ts1 rowversion, @ts2 rowversion

SELECT @ts1=@@DBTS, @ts2=@ts1

SELECT CASE WHEN TSEQUAL(@ts1, @ts2) THEN
'Equal' ELSE 'Not Equal' END

INSERT #testts DEFAULT VALUES

SET @ts2=@@DBTS

SELECT CASE WHEN TSEQUAL(@ts1, @ts2) THEN
'Equal' ELSE 'Not Equal' END
GO
DROP TABLE #testts
---------
Equal

Server: Msg 532, Level 16, State 2, Line
16
The timestamp (changed to
0x0000000000000093) shows that the row has
been updated by another user.
``` |
| UNCOMPRESS()<br>Uncompresses a string. | ```
SELECT CAST(CASE WHEN ([status] & 2 = 2)
THEN (UNCOMPRESS([ctext])) ELSE [ctext]
END AS nvarchar(4000))
FROM syscomments
WHERE ID=OBJECT_ID('sp_helptext')
``` |
```

## Undocumented Trace Flags

SQL Server trace flags are integer values that you pass to the server to enable special functionality, to provide better diagnostic or system internal info, or to work around problems. You enable trace flags primarily by calling DBCC TRACEON(), but they can also be turned on via the –T server command-line option. Some options only make sense on a serverwide basis, so they're best specified on the server command line. Some only make sense within a particular connection, so they're enabled with DBCC DBCC TRACEON(*flagnum*), where *flagnum* is the flag to be set. DBCC TRACEOFF() is the counterpart to TRACEON(). It turns off specific trace flags for a connection. Separate multiple flags with commas to set/unset them at once.

DBCC TRACESTATUS(*flagnum*) shows whether a flag is enabled. Pass –1 to return a list of all currently enabled flags. Here's a simple DBCC TRACEON() / TRACESTATUS() example:

```
EXEC master..xp_logevent 99999,'CHECKPOINT before setting flag
3502',informational
CHECKPOINT
DBCC TRACEON(3604,3502)
DBCC TRACESTATUS(-1)
EXEC master..xp_logevent 99999,'CHECKPOINT after setting flag
3502',informational
CHECKPOINT
DBCC TRACEOFF(3604,3502)
DBCC TRACESTATUS(-1)
```

(Results)

```
TraceFlag Status
--------- ------
3502      1
3604      1
```

Here's what the error log looks like as a result of these commands (trace flag 3502 enables extra CHECKPOINT log information).

```
2000-07-01 01:10:33.89 spid57   Error: 99999, Severity: 10, State: 1
2000-07-01 01:10:33.89 spid57   CHECKPOINT before setting flag 3502.
2000-07-01 01:10:33.97 spid57   DBCC TRACEON 3604, server process ID (SPID) 57.
2000-07-01 01:10:34.00 spid57   DBCC TRACEON 3502, server process ID (SPID) 57.
2000-07-01 01:10:34.00 spid57   Error: 99999, Severity: 10, State: 1
2000-07-01 01:10:34.00 spid57   CHECKPOINT after setting flag 3502.
```

```
2000-07-01 01:10:34.00 spid57   Ckpt dbid 4 started (100000)
2000-07-01 01:10:34.00 spid57   Ckpt dbid 4 phase 1 ended (100000)
2000-07-01 01:10:34.00 spid57   Ckpt dbid 4 complete
2000-07-01 01:10:34.00 spid57   DBCC TRACEOFF 3604, server process ID (SPID) 57.
2000-07-01 01:10:34.00 spid57   DBCC TRACEOFF 3502, server process ID (SPID) 57.
```

Table 22–3 lists some of the many undocumented SQL Server trace flags. (See the Books Online for a list of documented flags.) This list is not comprehensive; there are many undocumented flags not included here.

**Table 22–3** A few of SQL Server's undocumented trace flags

| Flag | Purpose |
| --- | --- |
| 1717 | Causes new objects being created to be system objects (see the undocumented procedure sp_MS_upd_sysobj_category). |
| 1200 | Displays verbose locking info. |
| 1205 | Complements flag 1204 (deadlock info) by displaying a stack trace when a deadlock occurs. |
| 1206 | Complements flag 1204 by displaying the other locks held by deadlock parties. |
| 1211 | Disables lock escalation. |
| 2509 | Used in conjunction with DBCC CHECKTABLE to return the total count of ghost records in a table. |
| 3502 | Logs extra information to the system error log each time a checkpoint occurs. |
| 3505 | Disables automatic "checkpointing." |
| 3607 | Skips automatic recovery of all databases. |
| 3608 | Skips automatic recovery of all databases except master. |
| 3609 | Skips the creation of tempdb at system start-up. |
| 8501 | Enables tracing of DTC events. |
| 8602 | Disables index hints. |
| 8687 | Disables query parallelism. |
| 8722 | Disables all other types of hints. |
| 8755 | Disables locking hints. |

## Summary

In this chapter we explored a number of undocumented SQL Server features, including undocumented stored procedures, trace flags, DBCC command verbs, and functions. Use these at your own risk. They aren't documented for a reason—chiefly, because Microsoft doesn't want you to use them. If you decide to use them anyway, do so with care and with the expectation that they will likely change in a future version of SQL Server. Also, don't expect any support from Microsoft. From the vendor's perspective, that's the whole idea of not documenting something: You don't have to support it and you can change it as you please. Using the undocumented features of any product—SQL Server or any other—is generally unadvisable. You shouldn't do it unless there's no other way to get the functionality you need. I've covered undocumented features in this book because I want you to understand how SQL Server works behind the scenes. Understanding SQL Server's internal workings is key to writing Transact-SQL that is efficient, robust, extensible, and fast.

# Arrays

*"If you would master the craft of programming do this: never stop learning. Never be satisfied with what you know, always purpose to improve and add to it somehow, in some way. Craft first your mind, then spend the rest of your life letting it craft you."*

—H. W. Kenton

My previous book, *The Guru's Guide to Transact-SQL*, included a chapter on array processing in Transact-SQL that presented a number of ways of working around the fact that Transact-SQL doesn't have built-in array support. These techniques originated from two methods of approximating array support in the language: using tables (with columns simulating array dimensions) and using long varchar columns (with an entire dimension stored in a single column). Although mimicking arrays is better than not having them at all, I took a different approach in this book. I decided to add array support to Transact-SQL myself.

You'll recall from the Preface that I said that the secret to mastering Transact-SQL stored procedure programming was to be found in mastering programming itself, and that one key way of improving one's overall programming skill was to learn multiple programming languages. You'll recall that I mentioned the concept of cross-pollination and the perspective one gains from learning languages with completely different paradigms for creating software.

This chapter is evidence that that philosophy works. That learning multiple programming languages—even those seemingly unrelated to Transact-SQL—will make you a better stored procedure programmer and will open your eyes to techniques and possibilities you might not have otherwise thought of. In this chapter I bring together concepts I've learned from several different languages, including C/C++, Clipper, and, of course, Transact-SQL.

"Clipper?" you ask. C and C++ might seem at least relevant because you know by now that we build extended procedures using them, but Clipper? Yes, Clipper. For those of you who aren't yet sporting your first (or second) gray hairs, Clipper is a compiler for a dBase-style database programming language that had its heyday before Visual Basic came on the scene (and, in case you're not familiar with dBase, it was a programmable database program similar to Microsoft Access or Borland Paradox that was most popular before Access came into its own). Clipper still exists, but it gave up its place as the premier PC database programming language long ago. One of Clipper's niftier features was that it added arrays to the dBase programming language. It did this through functions (dBase UDFs were also a Clipper innovation). It provided functions for creating arrays, searching them, destroying them, and so forth. Behind the scenes, these functions called C code that actually manipulated the arrays. Because C code actually did the slicing and dicing of the arrays, Clipper's implementation was relatively fast, and because it was set up through simple functions, it was easy to use. As you'll see in just a moment, I've taken this same approach in adding array support to Transact-SQL. I've created UDFs that wrap calls to extended stored procedures written in C/C++. These extended procedures handle all the real work of manipulating the arrays. The array processing is fast because it's natively compiled, and it's easy to use because it's accessible through UDF calls.

**WARNING:** Use these routines with care and at your own risk. Failing to deallocate an array will make its memory unavailable to SQL server.

## xp_array.dll

Let's begin by taking a tour through xp_array.dll because it contains the code that does the real array processing. As you'll see in a moment, I've wrapped these procedures in system functions to make them easier to use, but you can still call the procedures directly if you wish. You can find xp_array.dll (and its full source code) on the CD accompanying this book. Although it's compiled with a beta version of Visual Studio 7, it will compile just as easily in Visual Studio 6. I've used nothing from the .NET Frameworks or anything that's Visual Studio specific in it.

Xp_array.dll exports five extended procedures: xp_createarray, xp_setarray, xp_getarray, xp_destroyarray, and xp_listarray. To make these routines available on your SQL Server, copy xp_array.dll to the \BINN folder under your SQL Server instance folder (be sure this is the BINN folder associated with your SQL Server instance and not the one in which the tools binaries are stored—you should see other xp*.dll files here). Once the DLL is copied, run the following script:

```
EXEC sp_addextendedproc 'xp_createarray','xp_array.dll'
EXEC sp_addextendedproc 'xp_setarray','xp_array.dll'
EXEC sp_addextendedproc 'xp_getarray','xp_array.dll'
EXEC sp_addextendedproc 'xp_destroyarray','xp_array.dll'
EXEC sp_addextendedproc 'xp_listarray','xp_array.dll'
```

This will make the extended procedures contained in xp_array.dll available from Transact-SQL. Table 23–1 lists their functions.

**Table 23–1** The extended procedures provided by xp_array.dll

| Procedure | Function |
| --- | --- |
| xp_createarray | Creates an array in memory and returns a handle (as an integer) to it. |
| xp_setarray | Sets an array element. |
| xp_getarray | Gets an array element. |
| xp_destroyarray | Frees the memory associated with an array. |
| xp_listarray | Returns an array as a rowset. |

### xp_createarray

The best way to understand each of the routines in xp_array is to examine its source code. Let's begin with xp_createarray. Here's its source code:

```
RETCODE __declspec(dllexport) xp_createarray(SRV_PROC *srvproc)
{
        int nParams;
        int size;
        char sizestr[30];

        PBYTE*      array      = NULL;

        BYTE  pbType;
        ULONG pcbMaxLen;
        ULONG pcbActualLen;
        BOOL  pfNull;

    nParams = srv_rpcparams(srvproc);

    // Check number of parameters
```

```
if (nParams != 2) {
    // Send error message and return
    srv_sendmsg(srvproc, SRV_MSG_ERROR, XP_ARRAY_ERROR, SRV_INFO,
    (DBTINYINT)0,
    NULL, 0, 0, "Error executing extended stored procedure: Invalid number of
    parameters",
    SRV_NULLTERM);
    // A SRV_DONE_MORE instead of a SRV_DONE_FINAL must complete the
    // result set of an extended stored procedure.
    srv_senddone(srvproc, (SRV_DONE_ERROR | SRV_DONE_MORE), 0, 0);
    return(XP_ERROR);
}
if (!IntParam(1)) {
    srv_sendmsg(srvproc, SRV_MSG_ERROR, XP_ARRAY_ERROR, SRV_INFO,
    (DBTINYINT)0,
    NULL, 0, 0,
    "Error executing extended stored procedure: Invalid Parameter Type",
    SRV_NULLTERM);

    // A SRV_DONE_MORE instead of a SRV_DONE_FINAL must complete the
    // result set of an extended stored procedure.
    srv_senddone(srvproc, (SRV_DONE_ERROR | SRV_DONE_MORE), 0, 0);
    return(XP_ERROR);
}

if (!IntParam(2)) {
    srv_sendmsg(srvproc, SRV_MSG_ERROR, XP_ARRAY_ERROR, SRV_INFO, (DBTINYINT)0,
    NULL, 0, 0,
    "Error executing extended stored procedure: Invalid Parameter Type",
    SRV_NULLTERM);

    // A SRV_DONE_MORE instead of a SRV_DONE_FINAL must complete the
    // result set of an extended stored procedure.
    srv_senddone(srvproc, (SRV_DONE_ERROR | SRV_DONE_MORE), 0, 0);
    return(XP_ERROR);
}

srv_paraminfo(srvproc,2,&pbType, &pcbMaxLen, &pcbActualLen, (BYTE *)&size,
&pfNull);

++size;  // Add one for the length element

/* Step 1 -- Allocate a buffer for the array */
array = (PBYTE*) malloc(size * sizeof(PBYTE));
```

```
/* Step 2 -- Clear the array */
memset(array, 0, size * sizeof(PBYTE));

/* Step 3 -- Set the first element to length of the array */
itoa(size,sizestr,10);
setelement(array,0,sizestr);

/* Step 4 -- Return a pointer to the array in the output param */
srv_paramsetoutput(srvproc, 1, (BYTE *)&array, 4, FALSE);
return XP_NOERROR ;
}
```

Xp_createarray takes two parameters: an integer output parameter, in which it will store the handle (a pointer) to the newly created array, and an integer that specifies the size of the array. It begins by allocating a buffer of the appropriate size by multiplying the number of elements requested by the size of a pointer (4 bytes) because each element will be a pointer to a string when it's allocated (Step 1). Next, it initializes the array with zeros so that it will be able to distinguish between allocated and unallocated elements (Step 2). Third, it sets the first element of the array (element zero) to a string containing the length of the array. In this way, the array is self-contained; it knows how large it is. This will come in handy when it's time to deallocate the array. Fourth, and last, it returns a pointer to the array in the procedure's output parameter.

### xp_setarray

Next up is xp_setarray. It allows us to set an array element to a specific value. Here's its source code:

```
RETCODE __declspec(dllexport) xp_setarray(SRV_PROC *srvproc)
{
    int        nParams;
    DBINT      paramtype;
    int index;
    int                handle;
    TCHAR  szValue[8000+1];

    PBYTE*     array       = NULL;

    BYTE  pbType;
    ULONG  pcbMaxLen;
    ULONG  pcbActualLen;
    BOOL  pfNull;
```

```
    nParams = srv_rpcparams(srvproc);

// Check number of parameters
if (nParams != 3) {
        // Send error message and return
srv_sendmsg(srvproc, SRV_MSG_ERROR, XP_ARRAY_ERROR, SRV_INFO, (DBTINYINT)0,
        NULL, 0, 0, "Error executing extended stored procedure: Invalid
        number of parameters",
        SRV_NULLTERM);

    // A SRV_DONE_MORE instead of a SRV_DONE_FINAL must complete the
    // result set of an extended stored procedure.
    srv_senddone(srvproc, (SRV_DONE_ERROR | SRV_DONE_MORE), 0, 0);
    return(XP_ERROR);
}

if (!IntParam(1)) {
srv_sendmsg(srvproc, SRV_MSG_ERROR, XP_ARRAY_ERROR, SRV_INFO, (DBTINYINT)0,
    NULL, 0, 0,
    "Error executing extended stored procedure: Invalid Parameter Type",
    SRV_NULLTERM);

    // A SRV_DONE_MORE instead of a SRV_DONE_FINAL must complete the
    // result set of an extended stored procedure.
    srv_senddone(srvproc, (SRV_DONE_ERROR | SRV_DONE_MORE), 0, 0);
    return(XP_ERROR);
}

if (!IntParam(2)) {
srv_sendmsg(srvproc, SRV_MSG_ERROR, XP_ARRAY_ERROR, SRV_INFO, (DBTINYINT)0,
    NULL, 0, 0,
    "Error executing extended stored procedure: Invalid Parameter Type",
    SRV_NULLTERM);

    // A SRV_DONE_MORE instead of a SRV_DONE_FINAL must complete the
    // result set of an extended stored procedure.
    srv_senddone(srvproc, (SRV_DONE_ERROR | SRV_DONE_MORE), 0, 0);
    return(XP_ERROR);
}

    paramtype = srv_paramtype(srvproc, 3);
if (paramtype != SRVVARCHAR) {
srv_sendmsg(srvproc, SRV_MSG_ERROR, XP_ARRAY_ERROR, SRV_INFO, (DBTINYINT)0,
NULL, 0, 0,
```

```
"Error executing extended stored procedure: Invalid Parameter Type",
 SRV_NULLTERM);

// A SRV_DONE_MORE instead of a SRV_DONE_FINAL must complete the
// result set of an extended stored procedure.
srv_senddone(srvproc, (SRV_DONE_ERROR | SRV_DONE_MORE), 0, 0);
return(XP_ERROR);
}
srv_paraminfo(srvproc,1,&pbType, &pcbMaxLen, &pcbActualLen, (BYTE *)&handle,
&pfNull);
srv_paraminfo(srvproc,2,&pbType, &pcbMaxLen, &pcbActualLen, (BYTE *)&index,
&pfNull);
srv_paraminfo(srvproc,3,&pbType, &pcbMaxLen, &pcbActualLen, (BYTE *)szValue,
&pfNull);

array=(PBYTE *)handle;

/* Step 1: Check the element index to be sure it's valid */
if (index>(getarraysize(array)-1)) {
   srv_sendmsg(srvproc, SRV_MSG_ERROR, XP_ARRAY_ERROR, SRV_INFO,
   (DBTINYINT)0,
   NULL, 0, 0,
   "Error executing extended stored procedure: Array index out of range",
   SRV_NULLTERM);

   // A SRV_DONE_MORE instead of a SRV_DONE_FINAL must complete the
   // result set of an extended stored procedure.
   srv_senddone(srvproc, (SRV_DONE_ERROR | SRV_DONE_MORE), 0, 0);
   return(XP_ERROR);
 }

   /* Step 2: Null-terminate the value */
   szValue[pcbActualLen]='\0';

   /* Step 3: Set the element value */
   return setelement(array,index,szValue);
}
```

Xp_setarray takes three parameters: the array handle, the element number to set, and a string containing the value to which to set it. After it validates the number of types of parameters, it begins by checking the specified element index to be sure that it's not passed the end of the array. If it's an invalid index, an error message is returned and the procedure exits. Next, xp_setarray null-terminates the value it has received from the user. Because xp_array processes array elements as strings, it's important that they're properly terminated. We find the start of each array element's data by computing its offset in the array buffer, and we find its end by searching for its null termination character.

Last, xp_setarray sets the element via a call to the setelement() internal function and returns the result to the client. Setelement() simply copies the string specified by the user into the array at the specified index.

### xp_getarray

Xp_getarray retrieves a value from an array previously set by xp_setarray. Here's its source code:

```
RETCODE __declspec(dllexport) xp_getarray(SRV_PROC *srvproc)
{
        int         nParams;
        DBINT       paramtype;
        int                index;
        int                handle;
        TCHAR   szValue[8000+1] = "";
        PBYTE*      array      = NULL;
        BYTE   pbType;
        ULONG  pcbMaxLen;
        ULONG  pcbActualLen;
        BOOL   pfNull;


        nParams = srv_rpcparams(srvproc);

    // Check number of parameters
    if (nParams != 3) {
            // Send error message and return
        srv_sendmsg(srvproc, SRV_MSG_ERROR, XP_ARRAY_ERROR, SRV_INFO,
        (DBTINYINT)0,
        NULL, 0, 0, "Error executing extended stored procedure: Invalid number of
        parameters",
        SRV_NULLTERM);

        // A SRV_DONE_MORE instead of a SRV_DONE_FINAL must complete the
        // result set of an extended stored procedure.
        srv_senddone(srvproc, (SRV_DONE_ERROR | SRV_DONE_MORE), 0, 0);
        return(XP_ERROR);
    }
    if (!IntParam(1)) {
        srv_sendmsg(srvproc, SRV_MSG_ERROR, XP_ARRAY_ERROR, SRV_INFO,
        (DBTINYINT)0,
```

```
       NULL, 0, 0,
        "Error executing extended stored procedure: Invalid Parameter Type",
        SRV_NULLTERM);
       // A SRV_DONE_MORE instead of a SRV_DONE_FINAL must complete the
       // result set of an extended stored procedure.
        srv_senddone(srvproc, (SRV_DONE_ERROR | SRV_DONE_MORE), 0, 0);
        return(XP_ERROR);
    }

    if (!IntParam(2)) {
        srv_sendmsg(srvproc, SRV_MSG_ERROR, XP_ARRAY_ERROR, SRV_INFO, (DBTINYINT)0,
        NULL, 0, 0,
        "Error executing extended stored procedure: Invalid Parameter Type",
        SRV_NULLTERM);

        // A SRV_DONE_MORE instead of a SRV_DONE_FINAL must complete the
        // result set of an extended stored procedure.
        srv_senddone(srvproc, (SRV_DONE_ERROR | SRV_DONE_MORE), 0, 0);
        return(XP_ERROR);
    }

    paramtype = srv_paramtype(srvproc, 3);
    if (paramtype != SRVVARCHAR) {
        srv_sendmsg(srvproc, SRV_MSG_ERROR, XP_ARRAY_ERROR, SRV_INFO, (DBTINYINT)0,
        NULL, 0, 0,
        "Error executing extended stored procedure: Invalid Parameter Type",
        SRV_NULLTERM);
        // A SRV_DONE_MORE instead of a SRV_DONE_FINAL must complete the
        // result set of an extended stored procedure.

        srv_senddone(srvproc, (SRV_DONE_ERROR | SRV_DONE_MORE), 0, 0);
        return(XP_ERROR);
    }

    srv_paraminfo(srvproc,1,&pbType, &pcbMaxLen, &pcbActualLen, (BYTE *)&handle,
    &pfNull);
    srv_paraminfo(srvproc,2,&pbType, &pcbMaxLen, &pcbActualLen, (BYTE *)&index,
    &pfNull);
    array=(PBYTE *)handle;

    /* Step 1: Get the value requested by the user */
    if (array[index]!=NULL) {
        strcpy(szValue,(char *)array[index]);
    }
```

```
/* Step 2: Return the value in the output parameter */
srv_paramsetoutput(srvproc, 3, (BYTE *)szValue, strlen(szValue), FALSE);

return XP_NOERROR;
}
```

Xp_getarray takes three parameters: an array handle, the index of the element to get, and an output parameter to receive the element value. Once its parameters are validated, xp_getarray begins by copying the value the user has requested into a character buffer (Step 1). It then copies this buffer into the output parameter (Step 2).

### xp_destroyarray

As its name implies, xp_destroyarray deallocates an array that was previously created with xp_createarray. Here's its source code:

```
RETCODE __declspec(dllexport) xp_destroyarray(SRV_PROC *srvproc)
{
        int        nParams;
        int               index;
        int               handle;
        int               size;

        char msg[255];

        PBYTE*      array       = NULL;

        BYTE   pbType;
        ULONG  pcbMaxLen;
        ULONG  pcbActualLen;
        BOOL   pfNull;

        nParams = srv_rpcparams(srvproc);

    // Check number of parameters
    if (nParams != 1) {
    // Send error message and return
        srv_sendmsg(srvproc, SRV_MSG_ERROR, XP_ARRAY_ERROR, SRV_INFO,
        (DBTINYINT)0,
        NULL, 0, 0, "Error executing extended stored procedure: Invalid
        number of parameters",
        SRV_NULLTERM);
```

```
        // A SRV_DONE_MORE instead of a SRV_DONE_FINAL must complete the
        // result set of an extended stored procedure.
        srv_senddone(srvproc, (SRV_DONE_ERROR | SRV_DONE_MORE), 0, 0);
        return(XP_ERROR);
    }
    if (!IntParam(1)) {
        srv_sendmsg(srvproc, SRV_MSG_ERROR, XP_ARRAY_ERROR, SRV_INFO,
        (DBTINYINT)0,
        NULL, 0, 0,
        "Error executing extended stored procedure: Invalid Parameter Type",
        SRV_NULLTERM);

        // A SRV_DONE_MORE instead of a SRV_DONE_FINAL must complete the
        // result set of an extended stored procedure.
        srv_senddone(srvproc, (SRV_DONE_ERROR | SRV_DONE_MORE), 0, 0);
        return(XP_ERROR);
    }

    srv_paraminfo(srvproc,1,&pbType, &pcbMaxLen, &pcbActualLen, (BYTE
    *)&handle, &pfNull);

    array=(PBYTE *)handle;
    size=getarraysize(array);

    /* Step 1: Free all array elements */
    for (index = 0; index < size; index++)
        if (array[index]!=NULL) free(array[index]);

    /* Step 2: Free the array itself */
    free(array);
    return XP_NOERROR ;
}
```

Xp_destroyarray takes one parameter: the handle of the array that is to be deallocated. This is an integer that must have been returned by an earlier call to xp_createarray. Once it validates its lone parameter, xp_destroyarray begins by freeing all the elements in the array. It knows how many elements exist in the array by examining element 0 (getarraysize() returns the contents of element 0 as an integer). Once all elements have been freed, xp_destroyarray frees the array itself. You'll recall that the array itself is simply a collection of pointers. These pointers are initially null. An array element doesn't point to anything nor is any memory allocated for it until xp_setarray is called to set its value. This keeps the memory use of the array to a minimum while allowing for extremely large arrays.

## xp_listarray

Xp_listarray returns the contents of an array as a rowset. Although it would certainly be possible to call xp_getarray in a loop to retrieve all the elements in an array one at a time, xp_listarray is more efficient because it grabs all the elements at once. Here's its source code:

```
RETCODE __declspec(dllexport) xp_listarray(SRV_PROC *srvproc)
{
        int             nParams;
        int                     index;
        int                     handle;
        int                     size;
        int                     len;

        char* emptystr = "";

        PBYTE*      array       = NULL;
        PBYTE*      ppData          = NULL;

        BYTE   pbType;
        ULONG  pcbMaxLen;
        ULONG  pcbActualLen;
        BOOL   pfNull;

        nParams = srv_rpcparams(srvproc);

    // Check number of parameters
    if (nParams != 1) {
    // Send error message and return
        srv_sendmsg(srvproc, SRV_MSG_ERROR, XP_ARRAY_ERROR, SRV_INFO,
        (DBTINYINT)0,
        NULL, 0, 0, "Error executing extended stored procedure: Invalid number of
        parameters",
        SRV_NULLTERM);
        // A SRV_DONE_MORE instead of a SRV_DONE_FINAL must complete the
        // result set of an extended stored procedure.
        srv_senddone(srvproc, (SRV_DONE_ERROR | SRV_DONE_MORE), 0, 0);
        return(XP_ERROR);
    }
    if (!IntParam(1)) {
```

```
      srv_sendmsg(srvproc, SRV_MSG_ERROR, XP_ARRAY_ERROR, SRV_INFO,
      (DBTINYINT)0,
      NULL, 0, 0,
      "Error executing extended stored procedure: Invalid Parameter Type",
      SRV_NULLTERM);

       // A SRV_DONE_MORE instead of a SRV_DONE_FINAL must complete the
       // result set of an extended stored procedure.
       srv_senddone(srvproc, (SRV_DONE_ERROR | SRV_DONE_MORE), 0, 0);
       return(XP_ERROR);
  }

      srv_paraminfo(srvproc,1,&pbType, &pcbMaxLen, &pcbActualLen, (BYTE
      *)&handle, &pfNull);

      array=(PBYTE *)handle;
      size=getarraysize(array);
      len = 255;

/* Step 1: Set up a result set */
for (index = 1; index < size; index++)
   {
          srv_describe(srvproc,
                1,
                "idx",
                SRV_NULLTERM,
                SRVINT4,                    // Dest data type.
                (DBINT) sizeof(SRVINT4),      // Dest data length.
                SRVINT4,                 // Source data type.
                (DBINT) sizeof(SRVINT4),      // Source data length.
                (PBYTE) &index);
          srv_describe(srvproc,
                2,
                "value",
                SRV_NULLTERM,
                SRVVARCHAR,                      // Dest data type.
                (DBINT) len,       // Dest data length.
                SRVVARCHAR,                      // Source data type.
                (DBINT) len,       // Source data length.
                (PBYTE) NULL);

              /* Step 2: Copy the array data into a row to send to the client */
              if (array[index]!=NULL) srv_setcoldata(srvproc, 2, array[index]);
              else srv_setcoldata(srvproc, 2, emptystr);
```

```
                    /* Step 3: Send the row to the client */
                    if (srv_sendrow(srvproc) != SUCCEED) goto safeexit;
        }
safeexit:
    /* Step 4: Indicate that the result set is complete */
    if (index > 0)
        srv_senddone(srvproc, SRV_DONE_MORE | SRV_DONE_COUNT, (DBUSMALLINT)0,
        index);
    else
        srv_senddone(srvproc, SRV_DONE_MORE, (DBUSMALLINT)0, (DBINT)0);

        return XP_NOERROR ;

}
```

Xp_listarray takes one parameter: the handle of the array to list. It begins by
setting up a result set in which it can return the array (Step 1). This result set
has two columns: **idx** and **value**. The **idx** column will contain the index number of each array element; **value** will contain its string value.

Once the result set is initialized, xp_listarray iterates through the array, setting the result set columns to the appropriate array element values as it goes
(Step 2). Once each result set row has been filled with column values, xp_list-
array returns it to the client via a call to srv_sendrow() (Step 3). Once all rows
are sent, xp_listarray marks the result set as complete and exits. As you'll see in
a moment, even though we can easily set up a table-valued UDF to return an
array as a table, calling xp_listarray is much more efficient and fast.

To see how these work together, run the following script. It creates an
array, sets an element, retrieves the element, lists the array, then destroys it.
Here's the code:

```
DECLARE @hdl int, @siz int set @siz=1000
EXEC master..xp_createarray @hdl OUT, @siz
SELECT @hdl AS ArrayHandle
EXEC master..xp_setarray @hdl,998,'test5'
DECLARE @value varchar(30)
EXEC master..xp_getarray @hdl,998,@value OUT
SELECT @value AS ArrayValue
EXEC master..xp_listarray @hdl
EXEC master..xp_destroyarray @hdl
```

(Results abridged)

```
ArrayHandle
-----------
13910056


ArrayValue
-----------------------------
test5


idx          value
-----------  -----------------------------------------------------------
1
2
3
4
5
6
...
996
997
998          test5
999
1000
```

# Array System Functions

Once the extended procedures have been added to the server, the next thing we need to do is set up system functions to call them. This will make our arrays easier to use and more functional than would be possible with extended procedures only. You'll recall from Chapter 10 that system functions can be created through an undocumented process involving the system_function_schema pseudo-user. We'll create these array functions as system functions to make them available from any database without requiring a database prefix. Here's a script that creates them:

```
USE master
GO
EXEC sp_configure 'allow updates',1
GO
RECONFIGURE WITH OVERRIDE
GO
```

```
DROP FUNCTION system_function_schema.fn_createarray,
system_function_schema.fn_setarray, system_function_schema.fn_getarray,
system_function_schema.fn_destroyarray,
system_function_schema.fn_listarray, system_function_schema.fn_arraylen
GO
CREATE FUNCTION system_function_schema.fn_createarray(@size int)
RETURNS int
AS
BEGIN
  DECLARE @hdl int
  EXEC master..xp_createarray @hdl OUT, @size
  RETURN(@hdl)
END
GO
CREATE FUNCTION system_function_schema.fn_destroyarray(@hdl int)
RETURNS int
AS
BEGIN
  DECLARE @res int
  EXEC @res=master..xp_destroyarray @hdl
  RETURN(@res)
END
GO
CREATE FUNCTION system_function_schema.fn_setarray(@hdl int, @index int,
@value sql_variant)
RETURNS int
AS
BEGIN
  DECLARE @res int, @valuestr varchar(8000)
  SET @valuestr=CAST(@value AS varchar(8000))
  EXEC @res=master..xp_setarray @hdl, @index, @valuestr
  RETURN(@res)
END
GO
CREATE FUNCTION system_function_schema.fn_getarray(@hdl int, @index int)
RETURNS sql_variant
AS
BEGIN
  DECLARE @res int, @valuestr varchar(8000)
  EXEC @res=master..xp_getarray @hdl, @index, @valuestr OUT
  RETURN(@valuestr)
END
GO
CREATE FUNCTION system_function_schema.fn_listarray(@hdl int)
```

```
RETURNS @array TABLE (idx int, value sql_variant)
AS
BEGIN
  DECLARE @i int, @cnt int
  SET @cnt=CAST(fn_getarray(@hdl,0) AS int)
  SET @i=1
  WHILE (@i<@cnt) BEGIN
    INSERT @array VALUES (@i, fn_getarray(@hdl,@i))
    SET @i=@i+1
  END
  RETURN
END
GO
CREATE FUNCTION system_function_schema.fn_arraylen(@hdl int)
RETURNS int
AS
BEGIN
  RETURN(CAST(fn_getarray(@hdl,0) AS int)-1)
END
GO
EXEC sp_configure 'allow updates',0
GO
RECONFIGURE WITH OVERRIDE
GO
```

This script creates six functions. Table 23–2 lists each one and its purpose.

The fn_getarray() and fn_setarray() functions treat array elements as variants, so you can store any data type in an array that can be converted from a variant to a string and vice versa. For example, you can pass a date into fn_setarray() (which will receive it as a variant) and the function will convert it into a

**Table 23–2** The array system functions

| Function | Purpose |
| --- | --- |
| fn_createarray | Creates an array (returns the handle as its function result). |
| fn_setarray | Sets an array element. |
| fn_getarray | Returns an array element as its result. |
| fn_destroyarray | Deallocates an array. |
| fn_listarray | Returns an array as a table. |
| fn_arraylen | Returns the length of an array. |

string before calling xp_setarray. Likewise, you can retrieve a date stored in an array using fn_getarray() and assign it directly to a datetime variable or column. The function handles the conversion from the string element for you.

## The Pièce de Résistance

To grasp how powerful this new array functionality is, let's take it out for a spin. Here's a simple Transact-SQL script that uses our new array functionality to create, manipulate, list, and destroy an array:

```
DECLARE @hdl int, @siz int, @res int
SET @siz=1000

-- Create the array and return its handle and length
SET @hdl=fn_createarray(@siz)
SELECT @hdl, fn_arraylen(@hdl)

-- Set elements 10 and 998

SELECT @res=fn_setarray(@hdl,10,'test10'),
@res=fn_setarray(@hdl,998,'test998')

-- Get element 10
SELECT fn_getarray(@hdl,10)

-- Get element 998
SELECT fn_getarray(@hdl,998)

-- List the array
SELECT * from ::fn_listarray(@hdl)
SET @res=fn_destroyarray(@hdl)
```

(Results abridged)

```
----------- -----------
13910056    1000


-------------------------------------------------------------------
test10


-------------------------------------------------------------------
test998
```

```
idx         value
-------  ------------------------------------------------------------------
2
3
4
5
6
7
8
9
10          test10
11
12
13
14
15
16
...
995
996
997
998          test998
999
1000
(1000 row(s) affected)
```

As you can see, using arrays in Transact-SQL is now as easy as calling a function. And because arrays are accessible via functions, we can easily use them with table values. Here's an example:

```
DECLARE @h int, @res int, @arraybase int

-- Create the array
SELECT @h=fn_createarray(1000), @arraybase=10247

-- Load all the Order dates into it
SELECT @res=fn_setarray(@h,OrderId-@arraybase,OrderDate)
FROM Northwind..orders

-- List an array element
SELECT idx+@arraybase AS OrderId, value AS OrderDate
FROM ::fn_listarray(@h)
WHERE idx=10249-@arraybase
```

```
-- Destroy it
SET @res=fn_destroyarray(@h)
```

In this example we load the **OrderDate** column for all the orders in the Northwind Orders table into an array. We set up @arraybase so that we can use OrderId as the array indexer (Northwind's OrderIds happen to start at 10248, so subtracting 10247 from each one gives us a one-based array). On the machine on which I'm writing this book, the array takes less than half a second to load. Once it's loaded into memory, we then use the fn_listarray() table-valued function to locate a specific order in the array.

## Multidimensional Arrays

Because array elements can store nearly any type of data, they can also store handles to other arrays. This means that you can easily set up multidimensional arrays and that these arrays can be of either the jagged or the smooth variety. Here's an example:

```
DECLARE @yhdl int, @xhdl int, @xsiz int, @ysiz int, @res int,
        @xcnt int, @ycnt int
SELECT @ysiz=20, @xsiz=10

-- Allocate the y dimension
SET @yhdl=fn_createarray(@ysiz)

-- Allocate and fill each row
SET @ycnt=1
WHILE @ycnt<=@ysiz BEGIN
  SET @xhdl=fn_createarray(@xsiz)
  SET @res=fn_setarray(@yhdl,@ycnt,@xhdl)
  SET @xcnt=1
  WHILE @xcnt<=@xsiz BEGIN
    SET @res=fn_setarray(@xhdl,@xcnt,RAND()*100)
    SET @xcnt=@xcnt+1
  END
  SET @ycnt=@ycnt+1
END

-- List each row
SET @ycnt=1
WHILE @ycnt<=@ysiz BEGIN
```

```
       PRINT 'Listing row: '+CAST(@ycnt AS varchar)
       SET @xhdl=CAST(fn_getarray(@yhdl,@ycnt) AS int)
       SELECT * FROM ::fn_listarray(@xhdl)
       SET @ycnt=@ycnt+1
END

-- Get a value using x-,y-coordinates

SELECT fn_getarray(CAST(fn_getarray(@yhdl,16) AS int),9) AS 'Element at
[9,16]'
-- Deallocate each row
SET @ycnt=1
WHILE @ycnt<=@ysiz BEGIN
   SET @xhdl=CAST(fn_getarray(@yhdl,@ycnt) AS int)
   SET @res=fn_destroyarray(@xhdl)
   SET @ycnt=@ycnt+1
END

-- Deallocate the y dimension
SET @res=fn_destroyarray(@yhdl)
```

## (Results)

```
Listing row: 1
idx          value
---------- -----------------------------------------------------------------
28.7541
2            89.3502
3            3.53946
4            23.5332
5            86.0147
6            65.5272
7            55.1878
8            28.106
9            54.9643
10           45.7077

Listing row: 2
idx          value
---------- -------------------------------------------------------------
62.1757
2            88.8092
3            83.9364
4            48.1814
```

```
5           46.8372
6           11.51
7           66.9179
8           51.3207
9           87.2797
10          3.83372


Listing row: 3
idx         value
----------- -------------------------------------------------------------
60.2789
2           4.09385
3           37.9455
4           2.57299
5           52.0562
6           70.8885
7           47.8154
8           54.1449
9           59.3168
10          87.9367


Listing row: 4
idx         value
----------- -------------------------------------------------------------
24.996
2           94.1695
3           99.9406
4           18.491
5           87.2228
6           30.5012
7           21.4947
8           68.7588
9           78.544
10          80.717
...


Listing row: 16
idx         value
----------- -------------------------------------------------------------
72.5644
2           11.6483
3           98.446
4           63.0639
5           64.6387
```

```
6           71.462
7           18.1232
8           69.4337
9           14.1641
10          12.0571

Listing row: 17
idx         value
----------- -------------------------------------------------------------
12.8128
2           49.1211
3           44.5183
4           97.7341
5           79.8344
6           94.7446
7           93.0003
8           63.0217
9           31.3682
10          41.8146

Listing row: 18
idx         value
----------- -------------------------------------------------------------
33.1187
2           23.9623
3           22.8832
4           15.6967
5           88.0725
6           31.4168
7           71.7862
8           99.8463
9           70.8513
10          99.2734

Listing row: 19
idx         value
----------- -------------------------------------------------------------
66.3026
2           26.2505
3           30.7053
4           16.8188
5           25.4275
6           46.9594
7           39.897
```

```
8            36.4633
9            18.7707
10           15.3608


Listing row: 20
idx          value
----------   ----------------------------------------------------------------
57.3852
2            70.897
3            4.85462
4            17.4024
5            28.5141
6            92.8508
7            19.5683
8            50.7395
9            89.062
10           94.2366


Element at [9,16]
------------------------------------------------------------------------------
14.1641
```

In this example, we allocate the y dimension of a two-dimensional array up
front, then enter a loop in which we allocate each row separately. We fill each
row with a series of random floating point values, although we could just as well
have stored practically any series of values, including those from tables, as we've
seen.

We store the array handle from each row allocation as an element in the y
array. This allows us to then loop through the y dimension and list each row. It
also allows us to access an element using x-,y-coordinates. Because SQL Server
doesn't allow us to implicitly cast a sql_variant as an integer, we have to do so
explicitly using CAST(), but this is a minor inconvenience.

It should be obvious by now that you can have as many array dimensions as
you want, and that these dimensions can be either jagged (varying numbers of
elements) or smooth.


# Summary

In this chapter you were introduced to arrays in Transact-SQL. Although Transact-SQL itself doesn't offer support for arrays, we've built the next best thing
using extended procedures and system functions. The end result is functional-

ity that's relatively seamless, efficient, and fast. We were able to add this powerful functionality to Transact-SQL through our knowledge and familiarity with other languages and tools. The array model presented here brings together the strengths of multiple languages: It's based on functionality that originally appeared in Clipper, and it's written in C/C++ and Transact-SQL.

# Essays on Software Engineering

# Creating a Workable Environment

*Undiluted concentration is key to building good software.*
*Interruptions lead to bugs and poor code.*

*—Kim Kokkonen*

My first day at my first programming job was a humbling one. The secretary led me down one passageway after another through the bowels of the building until we wound up in the middle of the computer room, and there wasn't another human in sight. "This is your spot," she said, motioning toward an armless chair at a folding table next to a large chain printer angrily churning out paper and print at that very moment. She noticed the look of bewilderment on my face. Although I hadn't even hoped to have my own office, I'd never guessed that I'd be sharing my space with a noisy, temperamental machine.

Over time, I developed a certain tolerance for the machine-gun rattle-tat-tap of the printer, but I still found it hard to concentrate. We kept our distance from one another, and I went about trying to learn to program by reading books and studying other people's code. Many times, the noise was just too much. I wasn't going crazy from it, but I also wasn't learning as quickly as I wanted and needed to. There were no other offices. I was the low man on the totem pole, and there was little or no chance of finding a place more conducive to deep thought and learning.

The one respite I would sometimes get came after hours. Occasionally, late in the evenings, the printer would stop. Normally, it ran pretty much all the time. On a rare occasion, though, it would run out of things to print and would rest for a bit. I came to cherish those moments. When they came, it almost— *almost*—seemed like I had a real job, something that might have a future. Then, just about the time I'd begun to relax and dig into my studies, the furious, jackhammer-like racket would start all over again, leaving my concentration in shambles.

I often worked late into the evening in those days. One night, as I walked back through the maze of offices that populated the building, I happened upon a door I'd never noticed before. I checked under the door. No light was on, so I opened it slowly. I was surprised at what I found. It was a storeroom, about two meters across and three or four deep. To one side was a set of stairs leading up to an attic area. On the other side were a table, a chair, and a couple of retired computer terminals, their keyboards stacked on top of their CRTs. The entire room was covered in dust. It appeared that no one had been in there in years. I closed the door gently and was heading back toward the salt mine when a thought hit me: *What a great office that would make!* I returned, opened the door, and peered into the storeroom once more. I flipped on the light—a single, bare 60-Watt bulb hanging from a wire in the center of the room. *This place has possibilities,* I thought. *I could concentrate here.*

So, immediately I retrieved my books and printouts and bid my noisy office-mate farewell for the evening. For the next several hours, I sat in the chair in the little storeroom, studying in the sheer ecstasy of silence, euphoric in my discovery.

I repeated my evening visits to the storeroom every weeknight for the next several weeks, each time being careful to return my books to my desk and leave the storeroom just as I'd found it. In time, I managed to piece together a working terminal from the parts I'd found there, then ran a cable through the attic over to the mainframe, and, with a certain youthful audaciousness, plugged it in. Much to my surprise and relief, it worked. Now, I had a computer from which to work. I had my books, a quiet place to work, and a workable, although ancient, terminal. Life was good.

I continued on in my blissful subterfuge until one evening a couple of hours after everyone had left, I heard a knock at the door. Startled, I nearly fell out of my chair as my body tried simultaneously to answer the door and run the other way. Finally, after another knock, the door opened on its own. It was my boss. "What are you doing in here?" he asked, the vein in his forehead bulging. "I'm working," I said sheepishly, "I couldn't concentrate out there." "Where did you get all this stuff?" he asked, motioning toward the terminal I'd built. "It was already in here," I replied, "I just put it together." He stood there for a moment, contemplating what I'd just said, the wheels in his head whirling silently. "I didn't think it would hurt anything," I offered. He looked at me. "We'll have to see about that," he replied, the look of a disappointed father on his face. "For now, you'd just better go home. It's late."

So, I returned my books and materials to my table, my boss looking on incredulously as I lugged one mainframe manual after another back to their homes on the folding table that was my desk. Then I walked out the back door of the office, not knowing whether I had a job anymore.

It was dark outside, and I decided to walk around downtown a bit before going home. Across the street from the office was a row of movie theaters, their marquees lighting up the street like neon candy. I walked up and down each street of the old part of town repeatedly as I contemplated what had just happened at the office. *Did I still have a job? What was really wrong with what I'd done? Should I have just asked for permission in the first place? What would I do now? How will I pay my rent?*

Eventually, I took a seat on the steps of the old bank building next door to the office where I had a clear view of the moviegoers entering and leaving the theaters. I watched them come and go, their cares seemingly suspended for the moment. According to the plaque on the front of the bank, it had been erected in the 1920s. Its Gothic trappings and granite columns harkened back to ages long past, to prosperity and history long since gone. I sat there and pondered my fate while gargoyles and griffons gaped down from the ledges above.

As I thought things over, I came to the conclusion that it was I who'd been wronged, that even to expect me to work in such a teeth-rattling atmosphere had been inconsiderate on the part of the company. I decided that if they fired me for trying to compensate for this unfairness, well, I guess I'd have to find another job. I had loved the peace and quiet I'd found in the storeroom. It was sublime while it lasted—my *sanctum sanctorum*. It wasn't much, but it was enough that I could at least concentrate and do the job for which they were paying me. I decided they could fire me if they wanted, but I had to have a quiet place to work. If they let me go, then I'd just leave. It would be time to find another storeroom.

## Get Rid of Distractions

The moral? Find a quiet place to work. Very few people can concentrate in a noisy atmosphere or in one with frequent interruptions. Programming is cerebral. It requires copious concentration. All phases of software development, particularly design and analysis, require deep thought. See to it that you create an environment that's conducive to this sort of thing. Get alone, wear headphones, do whatever it takes to remove distractions from your work environment, even if it means having to work in a storeroom.

Of course, there are people who have no trouble concentrating in noisy environments. If you're one of them, good for you. The rest of us mere mortals need peace and quiet. It's crucial that your work environment is conducive to, well, work, before you begin going about the actual business of trying to create software. You'll find that you'll make fewer mistakes and enjoy quicker progress when you don't have to deal with 15 different entities simultaneously contending for your time.

## Close the Door

Ideally, your work environment should be a place with a door that you can close to eliminate disturbance. If this isn't possible, at least shoot for your own office. If you work at home, your office should be a room away from the rest of the family, a place where they know you're working. If you work away from home, try to snag your own office, and, failing that, shoot for a quiet corner cube or other place removed from the typical noise and traffic flow in the office. Some people have found that headphones go a long way toward blocking ambient noise. Do whatever it takes to cut down on distractions and interruptions, and focus on your job. I've even been known to unplug my phone when I'm working on something very complex. That's what voice mail is for. Your employer would probably agree that what they pay you to do is more important than most of the phone calls you receive.

Personally, I've found it useful to lay down a few basic ground rules about the home office. When I'm in the office, if the door is shut, I've asked my family to assume that this means that I don't want to be disturbed. If the door is open, they can assume that I'm not doing anything requiring great concentration and can come in whenever they feel like it. I try to leave the door open as often as I can; I only close it when absolutely necessary. It's common for my kids to join me in the office when I'm working with the door open, something I actually look forward to. Truth be told, people usually don't want to interrupt others who are trying to think hard. The trick is in letting them know exactly when that is.

## Internal Distractions

Sometimes distractions aren't external in nature. Sometimes, they can be found within the office itself. One of mine was the one-eyed monster—the television. By choice, I do not have a television in my office. I removed it some years ago. It's too tempting to flip it on when I'm waiting on a compile to finish or a file to transfer. Perhaps you have more willpower than I do, but my recommendation is that you remove everything that might distract you—including the television—from your work environment.

The Internet is also a good source of distraction. It's a wonderful information library and has certainly revolutionized the way people interact with computers and with one another. However, it is also the biggest time sink ever invented. If you find yourself cruising the Web when you should be working, you'll have to find a way to deal with that. Ditto for e-mail interruptions. It might be a good idea to disable the chime your e-mail program plays when a new message arrives. My recommendation is to reward yourself for completing a task by permitting a fixed amount of time afterward to cruise the Web, read e-mail, play computer games, scan newsgroups, chat, and so forth. Don't be your own distraction. A little self-control goes a long way.

Some years ago, Chevy Chase starred in the movie *Funny Farm*, a comedy in which he played a writer who'd moved to a rural town to write his first novel. He and his wife bought a scenic house, on scenic grounds, next to a scenic lake, complete with ducks, squirrels, and a dog that looked like he was straight out of a Disney flick. He purchased a huge desk and an expensive writing chair, positioned them both near a window, and set about to write his novel.

There was just one problem: He couldn't concentrate on his work for watching all the goings-on outside. Frankly, the ducks were more interesting than his typewriter, and he knew it. So, day after day, he squandered away precious hours, never really getting anything done.

I've seen programmers do the same thing. You don't need a huge desk, the latest hardware, or the corner office with a view in order to build software. You need a quiet place where you can work.

## Form Over Function

Sometimes distractions are more subtle than a ringing phone. Sometimes they come in the form of a gorgeous view out your window; sometimes they come in the form of techno-gadgets in the your office, the toys of programmers everywhere. Sometimes they come in the form of an emphasis on form over function. You buy the flat-screen monitor, the fire-breather of a machine, and the $100 mouse, but you never get down to the business of actually working. Do yourself a favor and put aside anything that distracts you from your work.

In his wonderful book, *On Writing*, Stephen King had this to say about one's priorities in the work environment: "It starts with this: put your desk in the corner, and every time you sit down to write, remind yourself why it isn't in the middle of the room. Life isn't a support system for art. It's the other way around."[1] You need balance and you need to remember that all the hardware in the world won't help you if it becomes a distraction for you. The tools of the trade—the quiet place to work, the computer, the books you buy—are a means to an end. You are an engineer because you like to build things. Get rid of things that prevent or sidetrack you from this.

## Silence Is Golden; Communication Divine

Of course, you don't want to seem aloof or unapproachable to your coworkers or family. On the contrary, if people know to call you between certain hours if they want to reach you immediately, they'll usually happily comply. After all, they just want to reach you. Also, because you'll have periods of uninterrupted concentration time, you're more likely to be available and at ease at other times. You'll feel better about your work and the progress you're making, and it will show. There's nothing wrong with trying to budget your time a bit to maximize your productivity, and most reasonable people will support you in it.

## Conclusion

The first step you should take before beginning a development effort is to fortify your work environment. Make sure it's as quiet and free of distractions as possible—both internal and external. Building good software requires uninterrupted concentration. Do what you can to facilitate it.

## Epilogue

The next morning came too soon. "I'll make this short and sweet," my boss began. "You shouldn't have been working in the storeroom." My heart sank. "I stopped by there again this morning and was surprised at what I found. Come with me." He rose from behind his desk and motioned for me to follow. I followed him silently down the familiar hall toward the storeroom like a sheep on its way to slaughter.

---

1. King, Stephen. *On Writing*. New York: Scribner, 2000. Page 101.

He walked up to the storeroom door, paused momentarily, then unlocked the door immediately adjacent to it. He stepped in, flipped on the light and motioned for me to step in myself. Then he said, "This is your new spot. You showed some initiative and ingenuity in setting up your cubbyhole next door. We need those kinds of things around here. You should have come to me if you had a problem. Next time, be sure you do." And with that, he placed the key in my hand and left me standing speechless in the center of my very first private office.

# Evolutionary Development

*The current state of the software industry is as if leading-edge doctors had tested penicillin, found it to be effective, and integrated it into their practices, only to have 75 percent of doctors continue to use leeches and mustard poultices.*

*—Steve McConnell*[1]

In the cool of an early Spring evening, as the sun begins to dip behind the red oaks of northern Virginia, I take a stroll from my hotel in downtown Washington toward the Lincoln Memorial. The quiet of the evening is setting in, and I long to get out into it, away from the bustle and noise of the city.

Before me, the grassy Mall stretches out in a vast, verdant promenade—a clearing in a medieval forest, evincing mystery and inviting discovery. As I walk, I'm flanked on either side by the Smithsonian, its columns and arches rising majestically into the evening sky. I amble past the tour buses and shutterbugs, topping the hill beneath the Washington Monument, and catch a distant glimpse of the Memorial glowing in the gray twilight.

I wander through the tall pines standing sentry beside the water and look out over the Reflecting Pool toward the Memorial, its image cast upon the iridescent stillness like a golden tapestry. As I walk, squirrels scamper to and fro, birds settle in for the evening, and the crickets, frogs, and other musically inclined wildlife launch once more into their *sinfonia nocturnus*, introducing the wondrous night for all the world.

I cross the greenbelt and make my way up the Memorial steps. There, atop his throne, sits Lincoln, forever gazing down upon the silver colonnade before him. The sky is clear—shimmering even—as the orange-blue of early twilight fades to the gray-blue of dusk.

Strangely, the profound sadness with which Lincoln usually greets me is nowhere to be found tonight. Instead, he seems amused. And I marvel too at

---

[1]McConnell, Steve. *After the Gold Rush.* Redmond, WA: Microsoft Press, 1999. Page 150.

the exquisite beauty on display before us—a gleaming radiance from the darkness, as life teems around us and nature's children frolic in the tranquility of nightfall.

Suddenly, from the corner of my eye, I spot a white heron, rousing itself in an awkward fluster. Startled, it flies swiftly left to right across my field of vision, dipping momentarily over the water, then flapping off in ageless, autonomic grace.

As I watch it top the trees, ascend the Monument, and become ever smaller in the distance, it occurs to me that the bird is an engineering marvel—a masterpiece of design. Its wings are light, yet powerful; its body large, yet airworthy. That its cumbersomeness can fly at all is a wonder in and of itself. And yet it does—marvelously, elegantly, effortlessly. The heron, it seems, is a flying contradiction in terms.

As I stand there, it strikes me that this extraordinary creature did not come into existence overnight. It is the product of craftsmanship, of millions of years of evolution gradually honing the bird's design, little by little, until the nimbleness of predation and the miracle of flight found a way to coexist in the same creature. Those herons too heavy for flight—they didn't make it. Those too clumsy to hunt successfully—they were phased out too. The better flyers and the better hunters—the better herons—out-competed their peers, had offspring, and generally prospered. As with all living things, natural selection has gradually shaped and reshaped the heron, continually refining it for time immemorial.

It seems to me that developing software is much like this. It happens gradually. It is a process of steady craftsmanship that may take a very long time to come to fruition. It is an iterative, deliberate, sometimes tedious, process made up of small gains spread out over time in an ongoing cycle of continual improvement. It is a process in which extinction is common and the road is littered with discarded ideas and designs that seemed workable but weren't. It is an undertaking that can produce spectacular accomplishments and magnificent elegance—tributes to the human spirit that tower over all those before, but it is one that requires patience and discipline—a workmanlike dedication. If software is to evolve into something better, the craftsman must make it so through diligence, skill, and sheer resolve. Unlike nature, software cannot craft itself.

The moral? Make changes iteratively, working on small sections of code at a time. When you change your code gradually, it begins to evolve on its own. Over time, the code becomes better and hopefully closer to what your users want. It becomes more fit to survive. The cycle becomes change-test, change-test, change-test. Your code is progressively honed throughout its lifetime, just as in nature species steadily evolve throughout their existence.

## *Kaizen*

*Kaizen* refers to the Japanese business philosophy of making continuous small improvements in one's personal and professional life. It is a key tenet of Japanese business process management and an essential element in Japanese culture. It's viewed by many as the primary reason for the phenomenal progress the Japanese have enjoyed during the last 20 years in the areas of quality assurance and productivity, and has been emulated in the West extensively. It is a philosophy that works, and it's directly applicable to the production of high-quality software.

## The Benefits of Small Changes

Changing code in small chunks has a number of intrinsic benefits. Chief among them is that making small changes reduces the risk of introducing bugs. Bugs are the result of human error, and the smaller the change, the less chance there is for something to get past you. By reducing the chances that an initiative (however small) you've undertaken in your code will fail, you increase the chances that the project will succeed overall. A project is nothing more than a number of related smaller initiatives tied together by a common goal. As Kent Beck says in his book *Extreme Programming Explained*, lowering the risk of project failure by shortening the release cycle (and thereby reducing the number of changes made in a particular release) helps ensure both the survival and the success of the project.[2]

This admonition holds regardless of whether you're cleaning up existing code or adding new features. When adding new features, adding them one at a time ensures that each feature works before adding the next (because you test each feature before moving on), and it also introduces flexibility into the development process. If your user base or management hierarchy decides that Feature X is more important than Feature D, this reshuffling of the priorities shouldn't derail the project if you're still completing Feature C. In the hectic world that is software development today, you must be able to adapt quickly to what your users and management want, and working on small pieces of code at a time helps you do that.

Like a sculpture, the ultimate shape a software creation takes is not entirely knowable in advance. It evolves as the process continues to fruition. Software development consists of a series of tradeoffs between the desirable and the

---

[2]Beck, Kent. *Extreme Programming Explained: Embrace Change*. Reading, MA: Addison-Wesley, 2000. Page 4.

possible, with what is perceived as desirable and what is perceived as possible evolving during the course of the project.

Michelangelo liked to say that his sculptures were present in the quarry stones before human hands ever touched them. His job, he felt, was to find these creations among the fissures and imperfections of the source stones and expose them to the light of day. He would often spend weeks or months studying a stone to determine its possibilities before ever striking it with a chisel. Although his work was immensely creative, a certain amount of forethought and planning went into it. He studied and planned to innovate. The software craftsman does the same thing: He extracts, from the raw materials handed him, software sculptures waiting to be uncovered, creations derived directly from their source materials, imperfections and all. These "imperfections" may consist of changing user requirements, unpredictable resources, and premature assumptions and conclusions regarding what's do-able and what isn't—things that seem to change with each passing day. The craftsman's job is to find a creation that pleases his benefactors in spite of—and, indeed, because of—these unpredictable elements.

## Software

Another intrinsic benefit of making changes in small steps is that it helps keep software malleable—something people tend to like because they think software should be *soft*. It should be easy to change. Making enhancements or fixing bugs in small pieces helps keep the system very granular. This improves the softness of the system and makes it easier to recover from mistakes, add more features, and test existing functionality.

Note that I'm not suggesting that software actually is or should be soft—that it's easy to change. Changing complex software is every bit as difficult as changing complex hardware. It's just that the difficulty manifests itself in different ways. As Steve McConnell says in his book *After the Gold Rush*, "the insidious notion that it's easy to modify the behavior of complex software defies logic."[3] Any complicated creation—be it hardware, software, a complex mathematical formula, or some other sophisticated construction—is inherently difficult to modify significantly because it was likely difficult to build in the first place.

Certain types of software changes are tougher and more pernicious than others. For example, requirements changes late in the development cycle are

[3]McConnell, Steve. *After the Gold Rush*. Redmond, WA: Microsoft Press, 1999. Page 19.

among the most damaging to a software project. In fact, substantial requirements changes late in a project can destabilize the project to such an extent that it can't be finished at all.[4]

A common response to complaints about late requirements changes is that developers should build software as flexibly as possible in order to anticipate future changes. This is easier said than done. Flexible software comes at a price. It takes more time to build than less flexible software. Flexibility is nearly infinitely variable. Saying a piece of software should be flexible could literally mean just about anything. Flexible to what extent? So that it can run on multiple operating systems or different computers, handle alternate currencies, or use a dissimilar user interface metaphor? How far is too far? When does flexibility become wasted effort? And when is software so intransigent that it is no longer, by definition, soft? The only answer here is *experience*. The perceptive craftsman learns through experience how to design the software he builds with the right amount of flexibility—no more and no less.

## Software Entropy

Another key benefit of building or improving software gradually is that it counteracts software entropy. As with physical entropy, software entropy (often referred to as *software rot*) refers to the amount of disorder present in a system. How does software entropy creep into a system? Entropy's favorite pathway into a project is by means of minor flaws that are never addressed. It starts with a kludge that you allow into the code to meet some arbitrary deadline. Next, you find yourself cornered into hacking together a solution to a related problem because you "kludged" the earlier code. Next, you discover that you can't build a new module as you'd like because the hack you were forced into yesterday prevents it. Entropy is contagious, especially in engineering disciplines such as software development. A kludge here and a kludge there, and, before you know it, chaos is knocking at the door.

Working on code in small pieces helps prevent this. You create new features little by little and work at them until they're right. If you later discover that you made a mistake, you stop what you're doing and fix it. Again, working on as small a section of code as possible. Everything is a gradual cycle of improvement, an evolution of the code through minor changes.

In their book *The Pragmatic Programmer*, Andrew Hunt and David Thomas describe software entropy using the analogy of the broken window.

---

[4]Ibid.

They cite a study in which the difference between urban buildings that were regularly vandalized and those that remained more or less intact was directly related to whether the buildings' owners repaired minor vandalism, such as broken windows, when it occurred. Those that didn't fix minor damage to their properties saw the vandalism escalate until there was virtually no building left. Hunt and Thomas[5] contend that leaving minor flaws in your app (for example, poor designs or decisions, bad code, and so on) leads to general disorder in your project that will eventually be its undoing. You should fix flaws in your code when you discover them, just as nature corrects itself and its creations over time.

# Refactoring

No discussion on evolutionary software development would be complete without at least mentioning the practice of *refactoring*—improving the structure of existing software without changing its functionality. Refactoring changes the internal structure of software to make it easier to understand and cheaper to modify without altering its observable behavior.[6]

The term *refactoring* first surfaced in SmallTalk circles, but is now bantered about in nearly every programming discipline and language. Early proponents of refactoring included Ward Cunningham, Kent Beck, Ralph Johnson, Bill Opdyke, Martin Fowler, and many others. To be sure, I suspect many expert developers were refactoring before the term ever existed. It is a natural outgrowth of experience in the trenches. You refactor to save yourself trouble down the road and because you don't like to solve the same problem twice. Seasoned developers knew this before the term *refactoring* existed.

Martin Fowler's seminal work on the subject, *Refactoring: Improving the Design of Existing Code*, adeptly articulates and catalogs what has become its own software engineering discipline. Refactoring is an important skill. As important, in fact, as just about anything else in the programmer's toolbox. Understanding it and learning to ably refactor existing code is as essential as any other talent you will acquire as a developer.

The key to keeping code readable and modifiable is constant refactoring. Expert developers tend to be a bit compulsive about refactoring, and this is a

---

[5]Hunt, Andrew, and David Thomas. *The Programmatic Programmer*. Reading, MA: Addison-Wesley, 1999. Pages 4–5.

[6]Fowler, Martin. *Refactoring: Improving the Design of Existing Code*. Reading, MA: Addison-Wesley, 1999. Page 53.

good thing. Cleaning up messes (especially someone else's) is rarely anyone's favorite job, so programmers who care enough about quality to do so on their own are a special breed indeed.

You can make many changes to software without changing its external behavior, but only those that make it easier to understand or cheaper to modify qualify as refactoring. This means that performance tuning, often cited as a type of refactoring, really isn't, because it amounts to changing the observable behavior of the system.

Note that refactoring isn't blind code modification either. It's not change for the sake of change. To work consistently over the course of a project, refactoring must be done systematically. Otherwise, you risk digging your own grave, making so many disorganized and untested changes that you break the software beyond repair. As I mentioned earlier, the development cycle has to be change-test, change-test, change-test.

The two key components of refactoring are small changes and exhaustive testing.[7] You cannot begin to refactor an application without a solid suite of tests. To do so is to invite disaster. If you can't verify that your change, no matter how small, did not break something, how can you with confidence proceed to the next change? You can't. And that's why you need to construct comprehensive tests before reworking code you may or may not understand well.[8]

Testing is a subject of its own chapter in this book, so I won't go into it much here except to say that all tests should be automated and should check their own results. That is, you shouldn't check your work by hand; you should construct tests in the program code itself. Your code should expose test methods that can be called to quickly check its accuracy. Once you refactor an existing piece of code, testing it should be as easy as clicking a button. Tests that are difficult to run or less than foolproof tend not to get run. If a test is difficult to run, developers are likely to skip it during crunch time. If it's not foolproof, it won't be trusted, and running it will eventually begin to seem like a waste of time.

The single most common type of refactoring is the removal of duplication from a system. All of software engineering boils down to just this: representing each piece of logic required by the user in exactly one place. Hunt and Thomas[9] refer to this as the *DRY (Do not Repeat Yourself) principle*, and it applies across the broad spectrum of computer engineering. Quite often, refactoring concerns itself with eliminating duplication from a system so that each logical ele-

---

[7]Ibid. Pages 12–13.

[8]Beck, Kent. *Extreme Programming Explained: Embrace Change*. Reading, MA: Addison-Wesley, 2000. Page 66.

[9]Hunt, Andrew, and David Thomas. *The Programmatic Programmer*. Reading, MA: Addison-Wesley, 1999. Page 27.

ment is represented once and only once within the system—so that it complies with the DRY principle. This is not unlike database normalization. Think of it as "code normalization."

Duplication creeps into a project in a number of ways. The chief way is through impatience. A developer looks at a problem, sees that it's similar to one he solved yesterday, grabs the code he wrote yesterday, pastes it into a new method, and changes it a little. This saves time now, but will likely cost him later. Sometimes supposed shortcuts aren't shortcuts at all. Sometimes they lead to long delays. Don't take the poisoned apple of easy duplication. And if you come across it in your code, refactor it on sight.

## Selling Management (or Yourself) on Refactoring

One of the toughest things about refactoring is getting people to buy into it. Management tends to frown on changing code that "works" regardless of how dreadfully bad it may be. There is an inherent myopia that seems to afflict all but the most seasoned of coders: "If it ain't broke, don't fix it" is the common response you'll hear when suggesting that a piece of code would benefit greatly from internal improvements. Another is: "Can I sell that to the customer?"—a rhetorical question meant to point out that the customer would not even be aware of any internal refactorings that you, in your compulsive zeal, might wish to implement. The fundamental point that both of these arguments miss is that code that is difficult to understand or difficult to enhance *is* broken and *will* affect the customer indirectly if not directly. How so? What happens the first time the customer wants what should be a very simple change, but one that is needlessly complex because of the poor manner in which the code was constructed? Often, what happens is unacceptable to most users: long delays, buggy releases, reduced functionality, and so forth. Crappy code has a sinister tendency to float to the top at the most inopportune moments, usually during a demo for an important client or in the middle of a weekend-long batch run at month-end. The fact is, code that is difficult to understand is difficult to extend and maintain, and code that's difficult to extend and maintain is difficult code. It's that simple. It *is* broken, whether you realize it or not.

Recently, I had a discussion along these lines with a coder on my development team. A customer had called and complained about a particular portion of one of our products being terribly slow. When we investigated the problem, we tracked it down to some SQL code that this particular developer had written. The code was already in production and had been for years, so he was reluctant to change it. When it became obvious that it had to be fixed, I agreed to take on the task because I was the more experienced SQL developer. I discovered the problem with the SQL fairly quickly, wrote a query that performed much better, then changed the application code to use it. This did two things: one good and one not so good. First, it sped up the query tenfold. The new query ran in a fraction of the time of the old one. This was a good thing. However, the side effect was that the change broke three other pieces of unrelated code. It turns out that there were undocumented, illogical dependencies between methods in this particular class. Three other methods were constructed so that they depended on the SQL in the original method being constructed in a very specific way. Even something as insignificant as inserting a carriage return into the original SQL would have caused them to fail. Recoding the SQL to use my faster approach broke them outright.

On seeing this, it was obvious to me that these methods needed to be refactored—very badly. My cohort wasn't so sure. He began by hacking (I mean this in the pejorative sense of the word) together a solution that allowed the dependent methods to think that the SQL code hadn't changed. When I suggested that what he should really do is refactor the methods so that they didn't have illogical dependencies on one another, he resisted me pretty strongly. "It compiles," he said. "It does what it's supposed to."

And he was right: It did compile, and compilers don't know or care when they compile ugly code. But, as I explained to him, when we change a system, people are usually involved, and people do care. Writing code that a computer can "understand" is not terribly difficult, because the computer never really understands it in the way that humans do. It just slavishly compiles and executes it. It has no sense of what it's actually doing; it's a machine. Conscious beings like us need a little more than that. We need something that's coherent and logical. We need something that makes sense. As Martin Fowler[10] points out, any idiot can write code a computer can read, but it takes a good programmer to write code that humans can read.

After some "discussions" back and forth, I finally wore him down and he refactored the code as we'd discussed. When he finished, he told me he was glad he'd done it, and, whether he knew it or not, he'd just become a better developer for it.

Note that refactoring doesn't have to be something for which you hold up a development effort. Most refactorings are fairly quick to implement. As I've said, the typical refactoring is a small change followed by an automated test. Because changes are small, they're quick to implement, and bugs introduced by them are easy to catch. Refactoring is something you can and should do regularly during the course of your main development work. Kent Beck compares

---

[10]Fowler, Martin. *Refactoring: Improving the Design of Existing Code*. Reading, MA: Addison-Wesley, 1999. Page 15.

this constant alternation between the two tasks to "switching hats."[11] It's something you'll do frequently while programming, so the analogy is a good one.

Even in situations when refactoring is weighty enough to require a temporary suspension of your main development effort, the time you will save over the long run will make it worthwhile. Unless shipping is imminent, refactoring is not something you should put off because you don't have the time.[12] On the contrary, if you feel you don't have the time to refactor, chances are that you need to refactor all the more in order to loosen the schedule a bit through the efficiencies gained by refactoring. Poorly designed code usually takes more code (and therefore more time) to do the same things. Getting rid of it will help you complete the rest of the schedule more efficiently. In other words, you'll run the marathon a lot better if you take the time to get in shape before the race. When dealing with fat, bloated code that has gradually lost its shape over time, what you don't have time for is *not* to refactor.

The bottom line when selling management or other developers on refactoring is that refactoring saves time, often lots of it. It will also save your sanity, and make those who have to work on the code happier in their jobs because very few of us like to work on junk—even our own. If it's difficult to figure out what to change or where to change it, or if making a change breaks unrelated code, there's a good chance that someone on your team will make a mistake and introduce bugs into your app. The way to minimize such things is to constantly and consistently refactor your code. Hopefully you'll have the autonomy and trust from your superiors to do what you feel is necessary to accomplish the tasks you've been given. This is a simple matter of the Powers That Be delegating authority and responsibility together, as they always should be.

Refactoring is also a teaching tool that will directly affect your own coding practices. You'll learn from your mistakes and those of others, and, slowly but surely, get closer to the ideal of writing code that doesn't need to be refactored immediately. You'll develop a certain intuition for putting software together that is a direct by-product of your experiences cleaning up coding messes and revisiting poor designs. Refactoring will never become obsolete, but you will definitely become a better coder the first time around because of it. Surely management and your fellow coders will see some value in this.

You could also try relating horror stories of projects that failed because they were too complex to extend, maintain, or tune to acceptable performance. There are plenty of case studies in the trade rags from which you could draw (perhaps you can even draw from your own experiences). There's nothing like a little fear to bring the naysayers of the world around.

---

[11]Ibid. Page 55.

[12]Ibid. Page 66.

And if all these tactics fail to sway management that refactoring is worth the trouble, refactor anyway, then take Martin Fowler's advice and don't tell them!

## When Not to Refactor

There are situations when refactoring makes less sense than it normally does. One such situation is when refactoring comes at the expense of performance. Contrary to Fowler's otherwise masterful treatment of the subject, I do not believe that refactoring code such that it performs poorly is a good idea, regardless of the frequency with which it is called. In *Refactoring*, Fowler[13] provides an example in which a temporary variable is eliminated by calling a function repeatedly rather than caching its result. So, rather than having a single call to the function, with its result stored in a variable that is then referenced by the remainder of the method, we have multiple calls. Each time the function's result is needed, the function is called. This, despite the fact that the function is deterministic in nature. Its result never changes between calls. Fowler[14] refers to this refactoring as the *Replace Temp with Query* technique.

This is a poor practice for a number of reasons. First, it leads to performance problems that will likely have to be cleaned up later. Although performance tuning is technically not refactoring, this type of development defeats the whole purpose of evolving your code (of which refactoring is only a part), which is to improve it gradually over time. A change is, by definition, not an "improvement" if it changes performance for the worse. Being easy to read and maintain is only part of the story. In Fowler's example, if the function being called takes a significant amount of time to return, you'll have to "unfactor" your refactoring in order to attain reasonable performance. Second, even if the code does not require an inordinate amount of time to execute, or is not called often, it can still negatively affect performance. Big performance problems are often aggregations of little ones. That is, no single call in a chain of execution may be prohibitively expensive, but, taken together, the entire chain can simply take too long to execute. The little foxes spoil the vines. Coding like this will leave you scratching your head for hours, trying to find out where you went wrong and what you can do about it. Nothing will jump off the screen as the obvious culprit of your performance problems. Instead, everyone's to blame and an inefficient style of coding is the real culprit.

---

[13]Ibid. Page 27.

[14]Ibid. Page 120.

A case in point here is screen updating. Often, no single line of code is to blame for subpar screen updates. Instead, the problem is usually one of approach: Individually, many of the lines being executed simply aren't efficiently coded. To fix them, you'll get to do a fair amount of rewriting. It's far better to code with efficiency in mind in the first place, than to have to work and rework code just to get acceptable performance.

Fowler's[15] contention here is that because temporary variables are useful only within the routine that contains them, they lead to overly long and complex routines. This is a good point, but it's far from compelling. The simple answer is to avoid writing such long routines in the first place and to break up inordinately long ones when you find them. The use or nonuse of temporary variables is a separate issue. Fowler[16] also contends that you cannot know before you profile the code what effect Replace Temp with Query will have on performance. I disagree with this as well. If you have some idea of how long a function should take to return, you can have a fair idea of the ramifications on performance of calling the function unnecessarily. It may not be scientific or exact, but you can have an empirical estimate of the performance cost of such an inefficiency, and you can have it without firing up a code profiler.

One concession I would make on the issue is that constructing method functions to return the result of a computation is generally more useful than storing the results of the computation in a variable, especially to other methods. Adding these functions to the interface of the class to make them available to other methods is trivial, and can prove to be quite useful. This said, I still would temper my enthusiasm for this with a good dose of pragmatism. Coding an interface inefficiently because it may be used in the future makes little sense when refactoring is the order of the day anyway.[17] You can always go back and extract a method if the need actually arises. Until then, don't refactor when it costs you tangible application performance and yields little in the way of making the code easier to follow.

## Databases

Another area about which you should think carefully before refactoring is in production databases. When you refactor a database design, you incur the bur-

---

[15]Ibid. Page 26.

[16]Ibid. Page 32.

[17]Beck, Kent. *Extreme Programming Explained: Embrace Change*. Reading, MA: Addison-Wesley, 2000. Page 57.

den of porting data from the old design to the new one. This may be more trouble than it's worth, particularly if the database is already in production. Then again, you may find that it's an absolute necessity. It depends on the situation. If you're going to refactor a database, do so as early in the development process as possible. As with any type of software, the cost of changing a database on which applications are already based rises exponentially over time, the aspirations of Extreme Programming (XP) notwithstanding.

### To Rename or Not to Rename?

Is renaming worth the effort? Some would say it isn't. That names for variables, functions, methods, and classes, once assigned and known by the code's owner, are insignificant in and of themselves. After all, they're symbolic names only, right? Renaming code elements to make them more sensible, so the thinking goes, is a simple case of compulsive behavior on the part of the programmer.

I disagree with this line of thinking. First, code should be self-documenting. It's been my experience that copious comments are usually a sign of poor coding or poor naming conventions in the code itself. They're often intended to obscure or justify bad code. Instead, I prefer meaningful names and minimal comments. Although I may know that Foo is the indexer for my **for** loop today, I may forget it tomorrow. It's far better to adopt a convention for such things so that I won't have to trust my fragile memory to keep from breaking the code, or waste time looking up poorly named code elements to figure out what they do. If a picture is worth a thousand words, a good name is worth at least a couple hundred.

Second, except when it comes at the expense of performance, improving the clarity of code is always a good thing, and renaming code elements with sensible names certainly improves the code's clarity—not just for me, but for anyone who follows me in the code down the line. Renaming to improve clarity is just as valid a refactoring tool as Extract Method and Move Method[18] and is easily done via global find/replace editor commands.

I once heard an old programmer tell the tale of a fellow coder who attempted to ensure his job security by naming all the variables in his lengthy COBOL app using proper names from the Bible. (And you thought Foo was a bad loop indexer. Try Zechariah!) Although it may have protected his job for a time, I'll wager that it did little to endear his colleagues to him, and I'll bet the day came when he needed divine help to remember the names himself. Good names help everyone—you and anyone else who ever works on your code.

---

[18]Fowler, Martin. *Refactoring: Improving the Design of Existing Code.* Reading, MA: Addison-Wesley, 1999. Page 15.

## Can You Refactor Instead of Design?

Another area in which I think refactoring is of questionable value is as an alternative to up-front design. There's a school of thought that says up-front design can be minimized because you can always change the design as you go along through refactoring.[19] The proponents of XP are often portrayed as favoring refactoring over initial design.

This approach is fraught with pitfalls and unresolved issues. First, what happens if the coders happen not to be very good designers? Can refactoring save them? I doubt it. When XPers who've been tasked with designing a complex system turn out to be *extremely* bad designers, the word *extreme* suddenly takes on a whole new meaning. Second, how would one effectively task a large team of coders without a design from which to work? How do we know that the database team needs to build an OLEDB provider that can return market data to the GUI if that particular portion of the app hasn't even been conceived of yet, let alone designed? Should we just make it up as we go?

Third, and most important, refactoring that is used to supplement a lack of initial design is really not refactoring at all because it changes the observable behavior of the application. In this use, refactoring has gone from being a tool to improve the internal design of a system to a tool for improving it externally. It is being used to define new functionality in the app. In this sense, refactoring is merely a thinly veiled excuse to hack—to code with no particular design strategy in mind, in the hope that somehow we'll make it to the finish line without knowing how to get there or where the finish line even is.

## Code Extinction

Naturally, there are times when code simply cannot be evolved, times when it needs to be discarded and started over. In nature, we call this *extinction*, and if you've coded for very long, I'm sure you've seen code that really needed to go the way of the dinosaurs. I once had the misfortune of having to work on a financial software package for a Wall Street-based technology company. The GUI portion of this code was so poorly thrown together that I would find myself looking for ways to get out of even going into the office. It was one of the worst messes I'd ever seen. The original developers thought it was more important to cobble something together quickly in order to impress the nontechnical folk in the company (who didn't know any better), than to improve their education and

---

[19]Ibid. Page 67.

skills as coders, to learn how to use their tools properly before billing people for it, and to build something that developers down the road (themselves included) could venture into without stepping on a landmine. That code needed to go away—very badly.

In such cases, it's often better to start anew. One sure indicator that it's time to discard a project and start from scratch is when the software simply doesn't work. At all. If it's infested with bugs inside and out, gradually reshaping it may not be possible. You can't build a house on a rotten foundation or add onto a building that's infested with termites. Conventional wisdom says you should probably just tear it down and start over. Remember, the refactoring game requires you to preserve the functionality of the system while improving it internally. Preserving functionality is kind of tough when the app isn't functional. You may be better off starting over. Some software is so poorly constructed that there's just no other way.

Even when you decide to rebuild, work on small pieces at a time, gradually evolving your new creation until it has the functionality you need. Strong componentization and encapsulation may allow you to make the refactor-versus-rewrite decision on a module-by-module basis.[20] When you do opt to rewrite, change-test, change-test, change-test. Eventually the new effort will either begin to resemble what you and your users envision, or you'll discard it and start fresh. Of course, you don't want to discard an effort prematurely or reject it because you don't understand it because you haven't made an honest effort to understand it. Too many wasted efforts, and you may find *yourself* on the brink of extinction. Management tends to frown on tossing out work for which it has already paid. The judgment to know "when to hold 'em and when to fold 'em" comes with years of experience. No book, including this one, can tell you exactly when it's time to pull the plug or to press on. That's an exercise best left to the reader.

## Extreme Programming

As with refactoring, no discussion of building software in small pieces would be complete without broaching Extreme Programming (XP), the recent software development methodology espoused by Kent Beck and others. Because short release cycles and iterative development are key tenets of the methodology, it's natural that we should delve into XP a bit here.

---

[20]Ibid. Page 66.

XP is a relatively new approach to software development that attempts to capture, in a formal methodology, the way that many developers already work. It emphasizes flexibility during the development process in lieu of rigid design and analysis. It has been described as a distillation of the way that programmers behave "in the wild," and I suspect that that's probably true. Most programmers probably don't adhere to rigid design methodologies or analysis. This is especially true of hackers—developers without formal training or the desire to follow what training they have. In this sense, XP is the hacker's methodology. It codifies what hackers have been doing for years.

According to the XP methodology, cost, time, quality, and scope are the four key control variables in software projects, and if any three of these change during the project, the fourth can be adjusted to compensate for them. Scope is viewed as the most useful of the four variables. If cost, time, or quality changes during the project, scope can be adjusted to offset them. For example, if the project deadline is suddenly moved up from 12 months to 6 months, the scope of the project can be narrowed commensurately. As long as at least one of the four variables remains in control of the programmers doing the work, the project should be do-able. When all four variables are controlled by entities outside the development team, you typically end up getting bad software late.[21] In this situation, your chances of project success are extremely low.

This said, there's no simple relationship between the four variables. For example, increasing the resources (cost) on a project does not necessarily ensure that you can also increase scope. Some things have sequential, time-based, or otherwise complex relationships that are beyond simple resource management. As the old saying goes, "Nine women can't make a baby in one month."

Quality is a poor control variable because the gains you can make by sacrificing quality are short term at best. Exchanging quality for producing software in less time is a Faustian bargain that has doomed more than one software company. Sacrificing internal quality (defined by programmers) while hoping that it won't affect external quality (defined by customers) is merely wishful thinking. Eventually, it will catch up with you. Either the software will be too expensive to maintain, or it will never be able to reach a competitive level of external quality.[22] Don't do it unless you like laying awake at night or changing jobs.

The scope "safety valve" in XP operates based upon two assumptions: One, because you'll get lots of practice and feedback making estimates, the commit-

---

[21]Beck, Kent. *Extreme Programming Explained: Embrace Change*. Reading, MA: Addison-Wesley, 2000. Page 15.

[22]Ibid. Page 18.

ments you make regarding project scope will be generally accurate. And two, because tasks are prioritized in order of importance to the user, if a task has to be dropped because of a scope adjustment, it will be of lesser importance than the tasks that were not dropped.

XP subscribes to the notion that it's better to do a simple thing today and pay a little more tomorrow to change it than to pay a little more today for functionality that may not be used tomorrow. When such functionality is needed down the road, it can simply be refactored into the system.

Testing is an integral component of XP. In fact, tests determine project completeness: If tests fail to run, the project isn't done. If they do run, the project is complete.

Development is done iteratively, in small pieces in XP. Each time new functionality is added, it is tested via an automated test before proceeding with the next feature. According to the XP methodology, functionality for which no tests exist does not itself exist. The XP development cycle is change-test, change-test, change-test.

All production-level code is done with two developers at one computer—a concept XP refers to as *pair programming*. The two developers review one another's code, solve problems together, and generally function as one entity in getting the work of software development done. Pairs are not permanent fixtures. You may participate in one pair in the morning and another in the afternoon. With good communication and adherence to XP's other values, you are able to be more productive as a member of a pair than you would be individually.

XP embraces the notion of constant integration. Each time a new feature is added, it is integrated into the main build of the application. This helps avoid breaking other parts of the system "at a distance," and helps detect integration bugs early.

XP teams tend to become "intellectual nomads."[23] They have to be prepared to pull up stakes and follow the caravan at a moment's notice. The principle that software design should be more or less static once construction begins is thrown completely out the window. XPers adapt to whatever the customer wants, as long as it's humanly possible.

I think that about sums up what XP is and what its major tenets are. What do I think of XP? Like most software methodologies, there's good and bad in XP. Obviously, it works for Kent Beck and others. However, I don't think it would work for the majority of developers out there, nor do I think all its tenets are even good ideas. Let me explain.

---

[23]Ibid. Page 42.

When I ask myself what's wrong with XP, the first thing that jumps to mind is pair programming. I find the very notion of this a bit loopy. When I code, I need to concentrate. Interruptions, distractions, and most especially someone sitting right next to me, tend to interfere with my ability to concentrate, as they would, I think, most anyone. Coding is about thinking—thinking deeply. You can't do that when someone else is typing 18 inches from you or talking incessantly. Interruptions and distractions lead to shallow designs, poor code, and bugs.

Also, I'd think employers would have a problem with paying two highly trained software engineers to do the work of one (usually, they like it the other way around). The XP camp may respond that pairs are at least twice as productive as a single programmer, and therefore the difference is a wash, but I'd have to doubt this. Like most coders, I think best when I'm at a keyboard typing. I need to visualize what I'm thinking to delve into it deeply. Working through it on my computer is the most expedient way to do this. There's no way I could be as productive with someone else working immediately next to me, and management would have a legitimate complaint that I wasn't getting as much work done because of it.

I'll concede that I've never tried this particular tenet of XP specifically for the purpose of evaluating its fitness as a development technique, so I could be wrong. Moreover, I'd confess that I've solved more than one hairy coding problem by having someone sit at a computer with me and work through the obvious and not-so-obvious elements of it together. I know collaboration of this type can work. What I have a hard time swallowing is that it could work day in and day out, in lieu of the typical one-on-one interaction between the coder and the computer that has been the norm practically since the dawn of computers.

Another key flaw I see in XP is the deemphasis on up-front design. I think this is a mistake. We need to know all we can know up-front. Sure there are things we can't know, things that would be a waste of time even to attempt to know up-front, but jumping into the coding phase without a clue as to what we're to do is a recipe for disaster. It's like leaving on a cross-country trip without a map or a destination: You might come up with a destination along the way, and you might reach it, but you'll surely spend a lot of time lost, and you'll make it very hard for people to follow you or anticipate your arrival.

As a project manager, if an app is going to need a particular business object, I need to know that as soon as possible so that I can task someone with creating it before the other pieces of the app that use it are complete. If we're creating a new transformation service that uses XML to move data, I need to know that soon so I can have someone get to work on some XML style sheets quickly, before the portion of the app that uses them needs them. Scheduling, particularly elements that have dependencies on other elements, requires up-front design and careful planning. If you don't schedule your resources according to your needs, you may not reach your goals. It's that simple.

There's a reason projects have been managed, for time immemorial, by planning them out as much as possible to begin with. It's because the strategy works. Abandoning the tried-and-true in favor of a seat-of-the-pants approach to project management is lunacy, and I have a very hard time believing that it could work consistently.

But the real problem with XP's deemphasis on design isn't the uncertainty of taking a trip without a road map, nor is it the fact that meaningful scheduling depends on detailed design. It is that such a practice encourages programmers to abandon application design altogether. I wouldn't think that overdesign or overplanning is a big problem with most coders. Perhaps this was a problem with an isolated project here or there that the proponents of XP could name, but not with programmers in general. No, the problem with most coders is that they do not analyze, design, or plan enough. In *After the Gold Rush*, Steve McConnell[24] estimates that as much as 75% of the developers building software today do little or no design work before they begin coding. By sanctioning designless programming, XP is encouraging them to continue on in their sinful ways. This can only lead to poorly conceived software and failed projects. It is a world where estimates mean nothing and where design is an afterthought, not the guiding principle that keeps the software on track, a framework on which the system is built.

## Code First, Think Later

In *After the Gold Rush*, McConnell[25] refers to this approach to software creation as "code-and-fix" development. I like to call it "code first, think later" development. Code is created rapidly, but, because the quality is low and the overall strategy is not well thought out, it must be fixed repeatedly after the fact. Often, and certainly by the end of a project, more time is spent fixing code than writing it, with deep-seated bugs tending to snowball right around the time the software ships. Writing code without properly analyzing the problems to be solved courts disaster because it fails to acknowledge the obvious—that writing quality software is hard, and, like most complex undertakings, requires careful analysis and planning to be carried out successfully.

You have to remember that the fact that you're making progress on a project doesn't mean that you're making sufficient progress. If you spend the first

---

[24]McConnell, Steve. *After the Gold Rush*. Redmond, WA: Microsoft Press, 1999. Page 69.

[25]Ibid. Page 11.

10 days of a 90-day project jumping straight into the construction phase, but only move 5 days closer to completion, you've actually lost time. Now you have to pick up the pace just to catch up. The construction of the application tends to be the easy part, the part that goes fastest. Properly analyzing and designing a system is more cerebral, and often requires a significant time investment. If you wait to the last minute to analyze the problem and to design a system to solve it, you'll likely find yourself knee-deep in a swamp full of alligator-sized defects, no closer to having a shippable product than when you started. As McConnell says, "quick movement off the starting line doesn't necessarily translate to quick movement toward the finish line."[26]

And the problems with underanalyzed and underdesigned systems go beyond simple software defects. Sometimes the code isn't buggy; it's just that it doesn't meet the needs of the customer. In other words, the building is square and the roof doesn't leak, but it's the wrong building. This sort of misstep is usually the result of poor planning, a lack of design, or a lack of user involvement with a project. The first two causes are symptoms of code first, think later development—a practice the industry has known to be ineffective for more than 20 years now.

Proponents of code first, think later like to romanticize the notion of programmers eagerly diving into the coding phase on a whim, like so many paratroopers jumping to their commando targets at a moment's notice. Developers who'd rather plan the assault before making it are branded as dawdling technocrats. There's a certain smugness associated with being first and foremost a code warrior, a soldier in the great crusade to liberate the minds of staunchy engineer-types the world over.

But this idea is a fallacy. Omitting the analysis and design phases of software creation leads inevitably to code "thrashing"—an endless cycle of debugging, fixing, and testing from which few projects ever really recover, even those that eventually ship. Coding is fun, but code first, think later relegates much of the time spent "coding" merely to fixing bugs introduced in earlier coding sessions—not the typical code warrior's idea of exhilaration. The cycle is a vicious one and has doomed many a project.

The ironic thing about this style of development is that its participants usually spend as much time planning and designing as those who take a more systematic approach to software creation.[27] It's just that they do so out of sequence and usually when it will do the least amount of good. The cost of changing software increases exponentially over time, so analyzing and designing a problem

---

[26]Ibid. Page 11.

[27]Ibid. Page 13.

upstream—that is, working out the bugs in how you think about the problem—can yield dividends downstream that aren't otherwise attainable.

McConnell compares the code-and-fix approach to software development to fool's gold—it is attractive to unsophisticated organizations because it allows the project to begin showing signs of progress immediately and because it requires little training. The problems with the approach aren't immediately obvious and are repeatedly missed by the very organizations suffering from them. Any old hack can throw together code that compiles and appears to run correctly, especially with today's tools. It takes an engineer to carefully analyze, plan, and conceptualize something as intricate as a complex software system before building it.

## Redemption

These things aside, XP does have several redeeming qualities. First, I think the concept of iterative development and short release cycles is a good one. Making small changes is, as I've said, one of the primary keys to successful projects. Also, I think XPs four values (courage, communication, simplicity, and feedback) are good ones and make sense independent of XP itself. Of course you need courage to build software in this day and age. And as Beck[28] so insightfully points out, courage without the other values (communication, simplicity, and feedback) is merely hacking.

Refactoring belongs in any serious software development methodology, so XP's emphasis on it is a good thing. Testing is similarly important. That XP places such emphasis on testing is a tribute to its proponents' depth of experience. Expert developers know how crucial good testing is. The really great developers get a little jolt of confidence every time they hit the test button. This might seem counterintuitive. Perhaps you'd think that expert developers are so good that they don't need to test their code, but the opposite is true. The more experience and skill you develop as a coder, the more you realize how little you know, how flawed your brain can be at times, and how nice tools are that can test your work for you.

The bottom line is that there are good things and bad things in XP. Because I find some of its tenets impractical, I don't expect it to displace more established development methodologies anytime soon. And I don't believe there will ever be a day when it is more common to see two programmers at a computer than one. Moreover, I do not think that a lack of emphasis on up-front design and analysis can be successful over the long haul with the majority of developers. Yes, I could

---

[28]Beck, Kent. *Extreme Programming Explained: Embrace Change.* Reading, MA: Addison-Wesley, 2000. Page 34.

believe that expert developers could pull it off on occasion, but the average developer needs to design and plan up-front, and XP fails to recognize this.

## Conclusion

Working on code in small pieces is less risky than other means of creating software. Mitigating risk is key to ensuring project success and survival, because you simply don't know what will happen. Gradually evolving your code over time is the most surefire way of accomplishing your project goals without unnecessarily risking the project itself. Whether you're writing new code or improving existing code, doing so a little at a time is the best way to avoid mistakes.

## Epilogue

Walking back from the Memorial, I meandered through the trees and the jogging trails skirting the water. Night had set in, and I was somehow melancholy for the friend I'd seen soar away in such a harried rush. As I broke the tree line and came into the clearing, a joyous sight met my eyes: a white heron—my white heron—in swift grace descending the Monument and heading straight for me. He rose and dipped, in elegant control, his wings catching this waft and that, until he approached the perch from which he'd launched. I watched as he swooped up to light upon the branch, then abruptly changed his mind and headed on out of sight over the Memorial, down toward the fertile waters of the Potomac. As he flew away, I realized that he was doing what he'd always done—before Lincoln, before Washington, before man even. And as I watched him soar so freely, I recalled the words of the French writer and aviator, Antoine de Saint-Exupery, "A designer knows he has arrived at perfection not when there is no longer anything to add, but when there is no longer anything to take away."[29] The heron, in its simple elegance, *was* perfect—a gift from Nature to the world.

---

[29]De Saint-Exupery, Antoine. *Wind, Sand and Stars*. Harvest Books; London, 1967. Page 21.

# The Gestalt of Testing

*And everyone that heareth these sayings of mine, and doeth them not,*
*shall be likened unto a foolish man which built his house upon the*
*sand: and the rain descended, and the floods came, and the winds*
*blew, and beat upon that house; and it fell: and great was the fall of it.*

—*Jesus Christ*[1]

It is early evening and the rain has just stopped. In the middle of a tan cornfield, in the center of a green patch, a white Kansas farmhouse sheds the last drops of a late afternoon shower. A rainbow arcs across the silken canopy and fades into the horizon. The sun resumes it place atop the firmament. A stately oak in front of the house stretches up into the evening sky, yawning at the change of weather, and drinking in the heavenly dew, fresh sunlight streaming through his wet limbs. A windmill turns in the light waft. Distantly, lightning flashes between earth and sky, a silent reprise of the earlier performance.

The house is gabled on either side and circumvented by an open portico that wraps it to the right, beside the driveway. It is a large porch, with broad steps and a painted handrail leading up to the house. On it, aloe plants flank the house's front door, and a wooden swing rocks itself in the breeze. A set of wind chimes, hanging on the right edge of the porch roof, begins to jingle.

The smell of ozone permeates the air. An eerie silence forebodes great danger. The animals and insects remain perfectly still. The wind chimes continue to jangle amongst themselves.

Abruptly, the wind picks up, knocking the swing against the house. Leaves and debris tumble past the house and up against it. The giant tree sways in the onslaught; the house creaks under the strain. The wind chimes jingle furiously.

Then, just as suddenly as it picked up, the wind relents, and nature's assault on the house seems over for now. After a while, a woman inside opens the wooden blinds, and the sun smiles on the little house once more. The wind chimes jingle a simple, ominous lilt, over and over, in singsong repetition.

---

[1] *The Bible.* Kings James version. Matthew 7:25–27.

Without warning, the tempest hits. A tornado nearly as wide as the corn-field descends in the east and churns its way toward the house. The corn is mowed under like dry winter grass; the sky fills with dirt, plants, and rubble.

The great tree is next in line. As the tornado besieges the house, it begins with the great tree—faithful in his post for nigh 50 years—angrily ripping him from the ground and tossing him aside. He lands 100 feet away, on top of the barn.

Next is the farm truck in the driveway. First the contents of the bed are sucked out in an instant and whirled away, then the truck itself is vacuumed up into the giant plume and hurled skyward. It lands upside down on top of the barn, beside the tree, crashing through the roof and coming to rest on the hay bales inside.

The last victim is the house itself. As the vortex moves methodically, step by step across it, searching for weaknesses, the roof begins to lift. The windows suddenly combust inward, shattering inside the house. The bricks on the chimney are stripped away, vanishing instantly in the violent funnel. The house begins to rock on its foundations, moving back and forth, and then all at once—

All at once—

*Nothing.*

As quickly as it appeared, the violent cloud rises back into the darkened sky and dissipates. The old house has survived yet another of nature's tantrums. It will not be the last.

The lesson? Test your work. Things happen. Sometimes really bad things. Sooner or later, they'll happen to your software. The rain will come, the winds will blow, and the earth will shake. Will your software survive? That depends on how well you built and tested it.

Testing is the most commonly underemphasized step in the development process. Inexperienced programmers are natural optimists. Experienced programmers are a little more cynical. They've written enough code to know how easy it is to let something simple get by you and how embarrassing it is when that something shows up in production code.

Testing is a natural shortcut target. If we can get it right the first time, we don't need to test, right? If we were skilled enough to avoid having bugs in the first place, there'd be no need for testing, right? Wrong. This kind of thinking is based on two grave misconceptions: one, that good programmers don't write buggy code, and two, that it's possible to "get it right the first time" with anything but the simplest of software.

First, no matter how skilled a developer you become, you'll accidentally introduce bugs into the code you write as long as you write code. Martin Fowler says plainly: "I'm still human and I still make mistakes."[2] Until someone figures

---

[2]Fowler, Martin. *Refactoring: Improving the Design of Existing Code.* Reading, MA: Addison-Wesley, 1999. Page 7.

out how to embed infallible computers in our fabulous-but-flawed brains, we will continue to make small errors in most everything we do. It is part of our pact with nature: In exchange for emotions, abstract thought, and consciousness, we have traded away machinelike precision.

Second, anything but the simplest of applications is impossible to get exactly right the first time through. Things change. User requirements change. Technical requirements change. Project resources change. Your understanding of the business problem you're attempting to solve changes. These elements all impact your software. Kent Beck claims that the problem isn't change itself, because change is inevitable. The problem, he says, ". . . is the inability to cope with change when it comes."[3] Whatever the case, simple human error and the constant state of flux that seems to characterize every complex software development effort combine to virtually ensure that you won't produce perfect software the first time through. So, even if you somehow manage to build a bug-free application with your initial effort, it will still almost certainly require modification. It won't be right the first time around. Count on it.

Testing is key to project success. It's every bit as important as coding, perhaps even more important, because it provides an opportunity to correct problems not only in a program's code, but also in its analysis and design.

Testing provides a means of accurately gauging progress. The completeness of the project isn't based merely on how much work you've done, but on how well you've done it. In his book *Extreme Programming Explained*, Kent Beck goes so far as to say: ". . . until the tests run, you're not done. Once they all run, you're done."[4]

Testing should be automated when possible. What do I mean by this? Testing should be as easy as compiling your application. You should be able to click a button or type a simple command to test your app completely. How? By using automated testing tools, by building a testing harness into your application, and by having the testing mechanism check its own results. See the following sections for more info.

## Where to Begin

Ah, where to begin. How do you begin to test a body of code? Start by analyzing assumptions. Bugs tend to result from two kinds of errors: errors in logic

---

[3]Beck, Kent. *Extreme Programming Explained: Embrace Change*. Reading, MA: Addison-Wesley, 2000. Page 28.

[4]Ibid. Page 33.

and errors in assumptions. Every time you call a function, you make assumptions about what the function's valid parameters are and the valid contexts in which it may be called. This is especially true when you're calling code you didn't write such as operating system or library routines. Contrary to what may seem obvious, the most challenging aspect of working through a large body of code is not figuring out the logic behind each line of code. The most challenging aspect is understanding the assumptions in place when the code was written. You have to analyze the assumptions being made about and by the code you're testing.

For example, in the interest of performance, it's perfectly valid for a deep subroutine not to thoroughly validate the parameters passed to it based on the assumption that some higher level routine is handling parameter validation. However, if you later exposed the subroutine to the outside world, this assumption would no longer be valid. The best approach here would be not to expose the subroutine itself, but to construct a wrapper routine that handles parameter validation before calling the subroutine.

Errors in assumptions tend to be more elusive than errors in logic. They're sometimes difficult to track down, yet you must do so to test the software thoroughly.

Testing your own code is challenging because it's tough to be objective about your own work. Testing the code of others is challenging in that you must deduce the assumptions and requirements underlying the code without actually having written it. Both types of testing present unique challenges.

Usually, the author of a piece of code is best qualified to detail the assumptions behind it. She should know the thought process that went into writing the code. This thought process gives rise to assumptions about the code, the way in which it will be used, and the environment in which it will run. These assumptions form the basis of formal requirements or preconditions, so knowing them is crucial to knowing the code. When you begin trying to understand code you didn't write, start by talking to its author and gaining an understanding of the assumptions that went into it.

Once you have the assumptions in hand, attempt to simplify them. By simplifying the assumptions underlying a body of code, you gradually narrow the problem space down to just the problem at hand. Sometimes this amounts to redefining the problem to allow greatly simplified solutions; sometimes it means merely focusing on a particular aspect of the problem.

Understand that the author of a piece of code is often the worst person to test it objectively. Of necessity, the person who builds a piece of software spends much of her time thinking about how it should work. A tester, on the other hand, must focus on how the software *does* work. Sometimes familiarity with how the software should work blinds us to ways in which it fails to measure up. Ideally, someone intimately familiar with the assumption and requirement underpinnings of the software, but not its implementation, should be ultimately responsible for testing it. You have to be careful to keep the focus on meeting the requirements, not on implementation details, and you have to be careful not to allow the requirements to be skewed to match the implementation. Your job as the tester is to check the logic of the system as well as the assumptions underlying it.

## The Futility of Testing

"What?!" you ask, "Testing is futile?" Yes, testing is ultimately futile. You cannot possibly test every possible scenario that every feature in an application may face. You can't know every storm to which an application may be subjected in advance. Just when you think everything's been tested and is ready to go, a user finds a way to stress your app in ways you never dreamed.

As a programmer, you typically implement a single solution from a number of possible solutions. As a tester, you have to prove that this solution works when faced with all possible combinations of valid inputs, and fails gracefully for all combinations of invalid inputs. Your job is a futile one indeed. You are attempting to prove a negative—that no bugs exist in the software's handling of valid and invalid inputs.

So, the key to successful testing is in focusing your efforts on the areas in which they'll do the most good. Begin by acknowledging that testing is never really complete, then prioritize the areas that you'd like to test, and the depth to which you'd like to test them. With unlimited time and resources, you'd test the complete breadth of features and the full depth of each feature exhaustively. In the real world, however, there are tradeoffs. You'll test some areas more than others. In a complex application, the degree to which you're able to test the application will definitely vary from area to area. It's far more important, for example, that the app's file-saving feature works, than, say, its About box.

The principle tradeoff here is one of breadth versus depth. Breadth with no depth verifies that at least a semblance of each function is there, but it doesn't really tell you how well it works. Depth with no breadth verifies that a few key areas are working well, but neglects the rest of the app. Successful testing balances these two against one another to ensure that the greatest breadth of functionality is tested to the greatest degree possible given the schedule and resources at hand.

# Types of Tests

There are several different types of tests. In my work, four have proved to be the most valuable: unit tests, functional tests, regression tests, and integration tests. Let's discuss each type separately.

## Unit Tests

Unit tests are written by programmers to ensure that programs work as they're supposed to. What defines what a program is supposed to do? The specifications and design laid out earlier. Unit tests are often built right into the software, with conditional defines either including or excluding them from the compiled executable. Unit tests affirm, module by module, that code correctly implements the functionality the programmer thinks it's supposed to have. Unit tests help identify software bugs.

## Functional Tests

Functional tests are specified by users to ensure that the system as a whole works the way they think it should. Functional tests are more holistic and all encompassing. They are also more final than unit tests. A system can be devoid of bugs and still not pass functional tests. The final word on whether a system performs as it's supposed to rests with its users.

## Regression Tests

Regression tests are tests that compare the results from multiple test runs with one another, usually using automated tools. A regression test ensures that the results from tests today match those from yesterday.

## Integration Tests

Integration tests ensure that the various modules that make up a system play well together. They ensure that changes made in one unit don't break code in another at a distance. Because the XP methodology encourages early and constant integration, the entire development process is itself a type of integration test. Other methodologies relegate integration testing to regular intervals during the development process (say, weekly or monthly, for example), but are careful to isolate problematic modules so that they do not produce bad builds—in other words, builds that cannot be used or tested meaningfully because of fatal flaws in a specific module.

# When to Test

When should you test? Simply put: All the time. Don't wait to test until late in the development cycle unless you like missed deadlines. Doing so is a sure way to completely blow a schedule. And don't regard testing as a separate step in the development cycle. It's not. Instead, test all the time. Test each piece of code as you write it, preferably with an automated test harness that has itself been thoroughly tested.

One of the best times to write tests is prior to coding. When you sit down to begin adding a feature, write its test first. This may seem a little backward, but it isn't. Writing the test first forces you to articulate what the new code is supposed to do before you write it. It's likely that the test may evolve a bit as you write the code, but that's okay. The effort you invest in writing the initial test is still time well spent because it helps you work through the functionality you're trying to add before you add it.

## The Value of Tests When Refactoring

Tests allow you to refactor code with confidence—confidence that if you break the code, you'll know it fairly quickly. You can't safely begin to refactor a section of code unless the code has a full suite of solid tests.[5] To do so is to invite disaster. You could very easily break working code without knowing it. Without complete tests, you could easily change the functionality of your code in subtle ways that are difficult to otherwise detect.

Note that unless your tests of refactored code check the full range of inputs to the original routine, the tests aren't foolproof. One risk of refactoring a routine is that you may inadvertently trim the input domain that the original routine accepted. Only tests that check the full input domain will catch this kind of problem.

# Testing Can Save Time

"How?" you ask. By reducing the amount of time you spend debugging. By building tests into your code, and structuring these tests so that they check themselves, you create a test that is as easy to run as the application itself. When

---

[5]Fowler, Martin. *Refactoring: Improving the Design of Existing Code*. Reading, MA: Addison-Wesley, 1999. Page 89.

tests are easy to run, you'll find yourself running them all the time. Each successful test will give you a little jolt of confidence in your code. You'll also uncover bugs earlier and fix them more easily than you'd be able to without constant testing. All told, you'll spend far less time debugging, and will therefore develop better code more quickly.

It's a common misconception that most of the time spent developing software is spent coding. Actually, more time is spent debugging than coding in the typical project.[6] If you can reduce this through automated, self-checking tests, you can shorten the development cycle dramatically.

How do you build self-checking tests into your code? Every class should have a test method that you can call to check the class. This test should quickly check every functional aspect of the class. Rather than writing the output of the test to the console or to a file, embed the expected output in the test method, then code the method such that it checks its output against the expected results. If the two compare correctly, display a message that says, OK or Tests Successful. If not, display a failure message. This way, you let the computer do what it does best—repetitive, relatively mundane (but critical) tasks.

You can automate the testing of several units at once (and even entire applications) by using automated testing tools. There are several of these available, many with features to test user interfaces as well as the code behind them. Most expose an API that allows an application to identify its built-in test harness, if it has one. These types of tools are often very sophisticated, sporting such advanced features as scripting languages, code analysis, and debugging aids. If you work on large projects, tools like these are a must.

Be careful when writing test methods. Poorly written or incomplete test methods are like a set of rose-colored glasses: They hide potential ugliness and misbehavior in your code.[7] Test methods serve to ensure the solidity of your system, so be sure they're solid themselves.

## Testing in the Extreme

There's a school of thought that says that software functionality that can't be checked via automated tests doesn't exist.[8] I'm afraid I have to disagree with this. There are functional aspects of software design that are difficult if not impossible to test, especially with automated tests. One, in particular, is the

---

[6]McConnell. *After the Gold Rush.* Redmond, WA: Microsoft Press, 1999. Page 11.

[7]Beck, Kent. *Extreme Programming Explained: Embrace Change.* Reading, MA: Addison-Wesley, 2000. Page 47.

[8]Ibid. Page 45.

aspect of extensibility. How do you check extensibility with an automated test? You really can't, and yet you have to design and code for extensibility just as you would any other feature. Another is maintainability. Surely we coders want to write maintainable code, and surely we'd consider code that was too tangled to maintain to be buggy from a design standpoint, yet we might not know this until after the software ships and we begin to try to support it. The code would survive automated tests, but it would still be buggy. My point is this: automated testing presents a baseline by which you can determine basic software health, but it is not the final word. Just as your annual physical exam can miss detecting a number of health problems, automated tests provide only a basic check. They do not ensure program correctness, nor can they even *identify* every feature in a software package. Some elements, such as extensibility and maintainability, are beyond the scope of automated tests but need to be there nonetheless. Testing can't detect everything that might be wrong with software, and therefore can't detect everything that might be right. Software functionality can exist that automated tests could never detect, but that you rely on to extend and maintain the system. This is particularly true of design elements that make the system easier to work on.

Beyond being a tool in your toolbox, testing also brings with it certain responsibilities. Once you take on the onus of writing test methods for your work, you have to write them all and keep them up-to-date. You can't simply write one test method, never update it, and declare your code tested. When you implement a test method, developers who look at your work down the road (including you) have the right to expect the method to do what its name implies: Test its class completely. Anything less is a bug, and hurts more than it helps.

Note that as you gain more experience writing tests, you'll be more able to judge when a test is or isn't necessary. This is rather subjective, and you have to be careful. Once you start looking for tests to eliminate, schedule pressures can coerce you into believing that a critical test isn't really needed. Weed out tests only when you're absolutely sure, and never base these decisions on scheduling concerns. Default to testing too much. If you're going to have a flaw as a developer, this is a good one to have.

# Other Types of Testing

A number of books draw a distinction between testing, code reviews, walkthroughs, and software quality assurance in general. Not this one. From my vantage point, these are all forms of testing. Or, perhaps to say it better, testing is one of many means of ensuring software quality. Whether you're talking about a walkthrough or a code review, the purpose is to identify flaws in the software so that they may be addressed. They are part and parcel of the same activity, and perform the same function in the software development cycle, so, at least in this book, they are grouped under the heading of testing.

That said, these other forms of testing, or other means of ensuring software quality—however you want to refer to them—are crucial to building good software, so we should explore them. Let's begin with general software quality assurance. The very term sounds sterile and is a bit of a mouthful, but it's really what testing is all about. I briefly considered titling this chapter something like "Ensure Software Quality" or "Ensure Software Solidity," but felt these were too formal. Testing is about ensuring software quality. Improving software quality is the reason we test in the first place. We want applications that are as bug free and functional as possible. We want to publish high-quality software, so we test it before giving it to users.

When programmers talk about testing, they're usually talking about unit testing. As I've said, there are many kinds of testing, and unit testing is just one of them. Unit testing is not the only means of ensuring software quality, and, according to Steve McConnell,[9] it's not even the best way. In fact, according to McConnell,[10] testing in general—whether it's unit, functional, or integration testing—is less than 50% effective at finding bugs before a product is shipped.

What does this tell us? If testing can't find all the bugs, what can? The trick isn't to find the bugs, the trick is to avoid them in the first place. The moral here is that you can't test quality into software. You have to design and plan for it. Software quality assurance must be systematic. You must design and consistently follow a standard process to ensure it. With this in mind, let's examine some of the other methods of improving software quality.

## Code Reviews

According to McConnell,[11] code reviews provide a better means of improving software quality than any form of traditional testing. What is a code review? A code review is an examination of a programmer's code by another programmer or team of programmers. Code reviews should be constructive, nonjudgmental affairs that reinforce good practices as much as they discourage bad ones.

Code reviews benefit software quality in many ways. First, they allow less experienced developers to leverage the experience of veteran developers. Lessons that took experienced developers a long time to learn can be quickly

---

[9]McConnell. *Code Complete*. Redmond, WA: Microsoft Press, 1993. Page 571.

[10]Ibid. Page 574.

[11]Ibid. Page 587.

and easily disseminated to other developers through code reviews. The junior developer is able to learn from the veteran through the veteran's comments about her code. So, not only is the quality of today's code improved, the quality of tomorrow's code goes up as well because the junior developer learns better development techniques because of the review.

Code reviews give technical managers a tool for determining project progress and measuring the quality of a developer's work. They allow managers to determine whether the coding is actually being done and whether it is being done correctly. Essentially, code reviews become a tool for assessing quality at the individual developer and coding level. They give the technical manager what he needs to correct quality problems before these problems get out of hand.

Code reviews have a tendency to improve software quality overall in unexpected ways. If you know that your work will be reviewed—that the standard of completeness isn't limited merely to compiling and running the code—you'll probably be much more likely to check and recheck your work. Numerous studies have confirmed this behavior.[12] Also, you'll find that explaining a coding problem is often all you need to solve it. The answer occurs to you midway through the explanation. I've been on the receiving end of this many times, and have observed it numerous times in others. Having to explain a problem to someone else forces you to think about it clearly and analytically, and that's often all you need to solve it.

## Code Reading

You can think of a code reading as a "distributed code review." People take copies of source code, read it, then comment on it regarding style, quality issues, and, of course, defects. Typically, they meet to discuss these issues with the author of the code, but e-mail is very effective for this as well. The value in meeting personally is that the readers can discuss their comments with the author and possibly come to understand why she wrote the code as she did. Also, the author can better understand what issues there might be with her code and why she should address them.

## Inspections

An inspection is a specific type of technical review that focuses on detecting (not fixing) problematic parts of a system. It is not moderated by the author of the software, but by someone trained in moderating inspections. Those participating in an inspection play specific roles and prepare for the inspection by

---

[12]Ibid.. Page 574.

identifying areas of concern in advance. Management should be discouraged from attending inspections. Inspections are supposed to be technical in nature, and management's mere presence can inhibit this.

A key difference between an inspection and a code review is that a report is prepared after an inspection that lists the defects detected by the inspection. The process is much more formal than the typical code review. During a code review, the code's author might take notes regarding suggested changes to his code, and then again, he might not. He might change the code on the spot. It depends on the significance of the change. No coding changes are made during an inspection. The purpose of the exercise is to gather information about flaws in the software and issues that need to be addressed so that they can be dealt with later and can be tracked over time.

The inspection report helps track the defects that need to be corrected as well as identify problem areas in the system. When the inspection is repeated, the previous inspection report will serve as input for the process: Problem areas will be rechecked.

Inspections are common in medium-size and large organizations, but are relatively rare in small ones. They require a team of people and specific training, and resources of this type are often hard to come by in small companies.

The moderator plays a very important role during inspections. The moderator keeps egos from colliding and keeps the meeting focused on technical and business concerns rather than personal ones. She keeps the meeting from becoming a public flogging of the author, while still objectively evaluating the software.

If you're the author of software under inspection, try not to be defensive about your work. This is the worse thing you can do. Listen to the criticisms of it and acknowledge each one. Merely acknowledging a criticism doesn't mean that you agree with it. It means that you recognize that the person bringing the criticism has a concern and that that concern is important enough for you to look into. You should expect a certain number of invalid criticisms and points that seem questionable. Don't worry about it. Later, you can investigate each point privately and decide whether and how to respond to them. When you do respond, don't make it a matter of personal vindication. You were never under personal assault. This is about your work, not you, and as long as you're conducting yourself in a professional matter and doing your job competently, it will likely stay that way.

## Walkthroughs

A walkthrough is a loosely defined technical review. Walkthroughs can be many things. Usually they're a sort of code review/inspection hybrid. Typically, they are conducted by the author of the code under consideration, and focus on determining ways of improving the code's quality. As with code reviews, a walkthrough presents a way for junior-level developers to learn from senior developers, and for junior developers to present fresh alternatives to techniques espoused by the veterans on the team.

Walkthroughs are popular because they can mean just about anything. The meeting might be more formal, with slides and a scripted presentation; or it might be informal, with the author of the software simply talking about what he's done and why. Typically, a walkthrough is not a terribly long meeting (usually less than an hour) and doesn't involve management. It's a flexible type of meeting that can be adapted to a variety of uses depending on the requirements of the parties involved.

## Conclusion

Test your work. Test it often. Test it using built-in tests. Test it using automated tools. Test it using code reviews, inspections, and walkthroughs. Test and retest it. Reward those who find defects in your work by fixing those defects and thanking the finders for their efforts. Don't be defensive when your work comes under inspection. The process is about improving software quality; it's not a personal attack. When software quality improves, everybody wins—not just you and those connected with producing the software but everyone who uses the software too.

The purpose of testing is to mitigate the risk of failure—failure to ship high-quality software that meets customer needs. Testing reduces the risk of failure. Attaining 100% test coverage means you have zero risk of failure. Of course, you never reach zero risk, but you can certainly shoot for it. You can learn to manage the risk of failure down to an acceptable level using the techniques presented in this chapter.

## Epilogue

Once the storm subsides, the truck shifts one last time, falling about six feet farther into the barn and ending up nearly perpendicular to the floor, its bed barely protruding from the roof. As gasoline pours forth from its tanks, a severed electrical line sparks a fire. Soon the entire barn is engulfed in flames, and the great tree, his leaves still moist from the earlier shower, and his days of solemn oversight now behind him, disappears slowly in a makeshift funeral pyre, while the wind chimes jingle across the way.

# References

Bacon, Francis. *The Essays*. London: Penguin Books, 1985.

Beck, Kent. *Extreme Programming Explained: Embrace Change*. Reading, MA: Addison-Wesley, 2000.

Bentley, Jon. *Programming Pearls*. Reading, MA: Addison-Wesley, 1999.

Castro, Liz. *XML for the World Wide Web Visual Quickstart Guide*. Berkeley, CA: Peach Pit Press, 2000.

Chen, Peter. "The Entity Relationship Model—Toward a Unified View of Data." *ACM Transactions on Database Systems*. 1976;1(1):9–36.

Codd, E. M. "A Relational Model of Data for Large Shared Data Banks." *Communications of the ACM*. 1970;13(6):377–387.

Emerson, Ralph Waldo. "Self-Reliance." *Self Reliance and Other Essays*. Mineola, NY: Dover Publications, 1993.

Fowler, Martin. *Refactoring: Improving the Design of Existing Code*. Reading, MA: Addison-Wesley, 1999.

Gamma, Erich et al. *Design Patterns*. Reading, MA, Addison-Wesley, 1995.

Harold, Elliotte Rusty et al. *XML in a Nutshell*. Sebastopol, CA: O'Reilly & Associates Inc., 2000.

Holzner, Steve. *Inside XML*. Indianapolis, IN: New Riders, 2000.

Hunt, Andrew, and David Thomas. *The Programmatic Programmer*. Reading, MA: Addison-Wesley, 1999.

Kay, Michael. *XSLT Programmer's Reference*. City: Birmingham, England: Wrox Press Ltd., 2000.

Kernighan, Brian. *The Practice of Programming*. Reading, MA: Addison-Wesley, 1999.

King, Stephen. *On Writing*. New York: Scribner, 2000.

Knuth, Donald. *The Art of Computer Programming*. Vol. 1. *Fundamental Algorithms*. Reading, MA: Addison-Wesley, 1997.

Knuth, Donald. *The Art of Computer Programming*. Vol. 2. *Seminumerical Algorithms*. Reading, MA: Addison-Wesley, 1998.

McConnell, Steve. *Code Complete.* Redmond, WA: Microsoft Press, 1993.

McConnell, Steve. *After the Gold Rush.* Redmond, WA: Microsoft Press, 1999.

Pagnol, Marcel. *Critique des Critiques.* New York: French and European Publications, Inc., 1949.

Petzold, Charles. *Code.* Redmond, WA: Microsoft Press, 2000.

Ray, Eric et al. *Learning XML.* Sebastopol, CA: O'Reilly & Associates Inc., 2001.

Rogerson, Dale. *Inside COM.* Redmond, WA: Microsoft Press, 1997.

*The Bible.* King James Version.

Tzu, Sun. *The Art of War.* Cambridge, England.: Oxford University Press, 1963.

# Index

Abbreviations, 60
ActiveX, 530
ADDEXTENDEDPROC(), 659
ADDINSTANCE(), 659
Administrative stored procedures. *See* Stored
    procedures, administrative
ADO, 71
Advanced Revelation, 152
*After the Gold Rush* (McConnell), 714, 729–731
AFTER triggers, 215, 229
Aggregations, COM, 535
Allow POST, 385
Allow XPath, 384
ALTER PROCEDURE, 17–18
ALTER TABLE, 16, 23
ALTER TABLE…DISABLE TRIGGER,
    239–240
ALTER TABLE…ENABLE TRIGGER,
    239–240
ANSI, 340
ANSI SQL schema views, 249–265
Arrays
    example, 692–694
    multidimensional, 694–698
    system functions, 689–692
    xp_array.dll, 676–689
*Art of Computer Programming, The* (Knuth),
    191
Associative arrays, 152
Asterisk, used by Query Analyzer, 115
Attribute repository, 166
Attributes, 146
AUDITEVENT(), 660
Auditing, triggers and, 229–233
AUTO, 402, 403–404

_CREATE_STATISTICS, 495
_UPDATE_STATISTICS, 496
Automation. *See* COM automation
Autostart, 26

BCPTABLOCK(), 660
Beck, Kent, 713, 716, 725
BEGIN…END, 42
BEGIN/END, 54–56
Berglund, Anders, 340
Berners-Lee, Tim, 339
Best practices, 106–112
    triggers and, 240–243
BETWEEN, 281–284
Bosak, Jon, 358
Boyce-Codd Normal Form (BCNF), 153
Bray, Tim, 358
BREAK, 42
B-trees, 481–482
BUFFER(), 660
Business process modeling, 130, 131
    data structures, adding, 137–143
    elements in, 132
    external entities, adding, 134–135
    flow objects, adding, 136–137
    notation style, 133
    processes, adding, 135
    stores, adding, 135–136
BYTES(), 661

Caching, 24–26
CALLFULLTEXT(), 661
C and C++, 555
Capitalization, 50–51
Cardinality, 146, 492

CASE tools, 129–131

cdata directive, 412–413

CERN, 339, 340

Chain of Responsibility pattern, 93, 101–102

Chen, Peter, 143

Clipper, 675–676

Clipping, 315–316

CLOSE, 87

COBOL, 152

Code reviews and reading, 742–743

Coding conventions

    comments, 65

    dropping objects, 64–67

    extended properties, 66

    script files, 66

    script recommendations, 64

    script segments, 66–67

    stored procedures and functions, 67–68

    tables and views, 68–71

Column aliases, 57–58

Column headings, HTML, 342–344

Column statistics, 495

COLUMNS_UPDATE(), 216, 217–222

COM

    aggregations, 535

    interfaces, 533–534

    marshaling, 535

    overview of, 529–536

    QueryInterface and IUnknown, 534

    reference counting, 534

COM automation

    sp_checkspelling, 536–539

    sp_exporttable, 539–545

    sp_getSQLregistry, 550–554

    sp_importtable, 545–550

    sp_OA, 536

Command-line parameters, 516–517

Commands

    invalid with triggers, 224

    undocumented DBCC, 658–667

Comments, 65

    disabling, 114

COMPUTE, 71

Computed columns, indexes on, 488

@@CONNECTIONS, 300

Connectivity, 146

Connolly, Dan, 358

Constraints

    defined, 164

    naming, 62–64

    XML Bulk Load and enforcing, 442

CONTINUE, 42

Conveyor pattern, 91–93

CREATE DEFAULT, 18

CREATE FUNCTION, 18

CREATE INDEX, 16

CREATE PROCEDURE, 4, 5

    permissions and limitations, 9

CREATE RULE, 18

CREATE SCHEMA, 18

CREATE STATISTICS, 496

CREATE TABLE, 16, 79

CREATE TRIGGER, 18, 215

CREATE VIEW, 4, 18

Cross join, 184–188

CUBE, 71

Cunningham, Ward, 716

Cursors

    cleaning, 69

    output parameters, 39–40

Data, generating, 183

    cross join, 184–188

    doubling, 191–193

    INSERT...EXEC, 193–194

    Random(), 188–191

    speed of methods, 197

    sp_generate_test_data, 194–196

Data, OPENXML() for inserting, 427–431

Data, retrieving

    AUTO mode, 402, 403–404

    ELEMENTS, 402, 404–406

    EXPLICIT mode, 402, 406–415

    RAW mode, 402–403

    mapping schemas, 415–419

    SELECT...FOR XML, 382, 386–387, 390, 391, 401–402

Database, defined, 163

Database context, setting, 78–79
Database design
 business processes modeling, 131–143
 defining functions, 127–131
 entity-relationship modeling, 130–131,
  143–162
 general, 121–122
 modeling tools, 122–123
 refactoring, 722–724
 relational data modeling, 162–180
 steps/processes, 123–127
Database schemas, generating, 447–448
Data Definition Language. *See* DDL
Data dictionary
 constructing, 165–167
 using, 167–169
Data Modification Language. *See* DML
DBCC ADDEXTENDEDPROC(), 555
DBCC CHECKTABLE, 288–289
DBCC CLEANTABLE, 289
DBCC commands, 16, 658–667
DBCC INDEXDEFRAG, 289, 484, 485–486,
  487
DBCC SHOWCONTIG, 289, 484–485, 486
DBCONTROL(), 662
DBINFO(), 662
dbname, 17
DBRECOVER(), 662
DBREINDEXALL(), 662
DBCC DBTABLE(), 662
DDL (Data Definition Language), 7, 22–24,
  58–59
 generating, 172–179
DEALLOCATE, 87
Debugging, 513–516
 extended procedures, 576–577
 triggers, 516
 UDFs, 516
Declarative referential integrity (DRI), 216
DEFAULT, 37
Default parameter values, 68
Deferred name resolution, 5–8
Defragmenting indexes, 487
DELETEINSTANCE(), 663

Density, 492–493
DES(), 663
Design patterns, 73
 conveyor, 91–93
 executor, 89–91
 intersector, 87–88
 iterator, 84–87
 other types of, 101–102
 prototype, 97–98
 qualifier, 88–89
 restorer, 94–97
 singleton, 98–101
*Design Patterns* (Gamma), 73
DETACHDB(), 663
Developer Edition (DE), 287
Directives, 408–410
 cdata, 412–413
 hide, 412
 id, idref, and idrefs, 413–415
DISTINCT, 510
DLLs, 530–532
 extended stored procedures and, 555–556
DML (Data Modification Language), 7, 22–24
 restrictions, 249
Document Object Model (DOM), 357, 378–379
Document Type Definitions (DTDs), 357, 364–366
Domain, 146
Domain integrity, 146
DONE_IN_PROC, 17
Doubling, 191–193
DROPEXTENDEDPROC(), 663
DROP INDEX, 16
DROP TABLE, 16
dt procs, 105–106
Dynamic Data Exchange (DDE), 529
Dynamic views, 269–271

Edge table format, 426–427
ELEMENTS, 402, 404–406
ENCRYPT(), 668
Encryption, 109–112
Enterprise Edition (EE), 287
Enterprise Manager, 122
 database diagrams in, 179–180

Entity classes, 145
Entity identifiers
　choosing, 158–159
　defined, 147
Entity instance, 145
Entity-relationship modeling (E-R), 130–131
　building, 147–150
　completing, 156–158
　defined, 145
　entity identifiers, 147, 158–159
　finishing, 159–162
　normalization, 147, 150–155
　terms, 145–147
　types of diagrams, 143–144
Environmental issues, 34–37
@@ERROR, 44–45, 68, 203–210
ERRORLOG, 663
Errors
　fatal, 208
　handling, 203–214
　orphaned transactions, 211–212
　reporting, 201–203
　@@ROWCOUNT, 68, 210–212
　SET XACT_ABORT, 212–214
　user, 204–208
　XML Bulk Load, 446
EXEC(), 7, 8, 18, 71
Executing stored procedures, 18–32
Execution, monitoring, 20–26
Execution plans
　automatically loading, 26
　compilation, 20, 22–23
　recompilation of, 24, 26
Executor pattern, 89–91
EXPLICIT mode, 402, 406–415
Extended properties, 66
Extended stored procedures, 32–34
　in C or C++, 555–556
　debugging, 576–577
　differences between stored procedures and,
　　556
　examples, 562–574
　isolating procedures, 577–578
　making, easier to use, 575–576

obtaining, 555
ODS (Open Data Services), 556–562
xp_setpriority, 578–584
Extensible Stylesheet Language Transformation
　(XSLT), 370–378
EXTENTINFO(), 663
Extreme programming (XP), 725–732
*Extreme Programming Explained* (Beck), 713

Façade pattern, 101
@@FETCH_STATUS, 42
Field repository, 166
Fifth normal form (5NF), 154
File extensions recognized by GGSQLBuilder, 118
First normal form (1NF), 151–152
Flags parameter, 425–426
Flow control statements, 42–44
FLUSHPROCINDB(), 664
fn
　_arraylen, 691
　_createarray, 691
　_destroyarray, 691
　_getarray, 691
　_greatest(), 306–307
　_least(), 306–307
　_listarray, 691
　_listextendedproperty(), 66
　_setarray, 691
　_soundex(), 310–315
Formatting source code
　abbreviations and keywords, 60
　BEGIN/END, 54–56
　capitalization, 50–51
　clauses and predicates, alignment of, 53
　column and table aliases, 57–58
　DDL statements, 58–59
　expressions, 53–54
　indentations, 51–56
　names, choosing, 61–64
　owner qualification, 59–60
　parentheses, 56–57
　passing parameters, 60
　space, white, 51–56
　spacing, horizontal, 57

FOR XML, 382, 386–387, 390, 391, 401–402
Fourth normal form (4NF), 154
Fowler, Martin, 74, 716, 719, 721–722
Fragmentation, index, 483–486
Functions, undocumented, 667–670

Gamma, Erich, 73
Gane-Sarson, 133
GETDATE(), 270–271, 300
GET_SID(), 668
GGSQLBuilder, 115–119
Globally unique identifiers (GUIDs), 440
GML (General Markup Language), 340
GoF's Composite pattern, 101
GOTO, 42
GROUP BY, 510

Hash joins, 504, 507–508
hide directive, 412
Histograms, 316–317
HTML (Hypertext Markup Language)
    column headings, 342–344
    limitations of, 357
    origins of, 339–340
    producing, from sp_makewebtask, 344–351
    producing, from Transact-SQL, 340–344
    tables, 340–342
    XML versus, 358–364
HTTP (Hypertext Transfer Protocol), 339
Hunt, Andrew, 715–716, 717
Hyperlinks, 346–348

IBM, 340
id attribute, 437
id directives, 413–415
IDENT_CURRENT(), 222–224
@@IDENTITY, 222, 224
Identity column values, 438–440
    XML Bulk Load and, 443–444
Idioms, 73
    creating objects, 76–78
    looping, 81–82
    nullability, 82–83
    querying meta-data, 75–76

retrieving topmost rows, 83–84
setting database context, 78–79
tables, copying, 79–80
tables, emptying, 79
variable assignment, 80–81
idref and idrefs directives, 413–415
IF...ELSE, 42, 56
IF EXISTS, 76–77
IIS utility, 383
IND(), 664
Indexed views, 286–289
Indexes
    allocation map (IAM), 480–481
    B-trees, 481–482
    covering queries, 483
    defragmenting, 487
    fragmentation, 483–486
    for improving performance, 480–492
    intersection, 483
    locks and, 492
    naming, 61
    prerequisites, 488–491
Indexes (Cont.)
    types of, 481
    on views and computed columns, 487–488
INFORMATION_SCHEMA.
    PARAMETERS, 41
    TABLES, 77
    user-defined function, creating, 257–262
    views, creating, 251–257, 655–656
Inline functions, 291, 295–296
INSERT...EXEC, 19, 193–194
Inspections, 743–744
INSTEAD OF trigger, 101, 215, 226–229
Interfaces, COM, 533–534
Intersector pattern, 87–88
Iterator pattern, 84–87
IUnknown, 534
INVALIDATE_TEXTPTR(), 664

Java, 355
Johnson, Ralph, 716
Joins
    hash, 504, 507–508

Joins *(cont.)*
    merge, 504, 506–507
    nested loop, 504, 506

Kaizen, 713
Keys
    candidate, 164
    duplicate, 442–443
    foreign, 164, 170–171
    primary, 164, 300
Keywords, 11–12, 60
    list of supported VSS, 109
    to sign files, 107–108
Kernighan, Brian, 73
Knuth, Donald, 191

@lastupdated, 345
Law of parsimony, 74
Least Recently Used (LRU) algorithm, 22
Least squares linear regression, 325–328
LOCKOBJECTSCHEMA(), 664
Locks, indexes and, 492
LOG(), 665
Looping, 81–82

Mapping data, updategrams, 433–435
Mapping schemas, 415–419
    annotated, 419
    disabling caching, 385
    updategrams, 434–435
Marshaling, COM, 535
McConnell, Steve, 714, 729–731, 742
Memory, leaking, 577–578
MEMORYSTATUS, 665
Merge joins, 504, 506–507
Merise, 133
Messages, sending ODS, 559–560
Meta-data, retrieving, 75–76
Microsoft
    *See also* COM; .NET; Web releases
    criticism of, 474–476
    SQL7010Stress, 524
    undocumented code, 627, 628
@@MICROSOFTVERSION, 668
Modality, 146

Names, choosing, 61–64
Nested loop joins, 504, 506
@@NESTLEVEL, 42, 46, 239
.NET
    defined, 466–474
    future applications, 465
NEWID(), 300
NOCOUNT ON, 17
Node pages, 481
Nondeterministic functions, 299–300
Normalization, 147, 150–155
NO_TEXTPTR(), 665
NULL, 38, 82–83
    updategrams, 435
    XML Bulk Load and, 444

OBJECT_ID(), 669
OBJECTPROPERTY(), 77–78, 245–246
    for user-defined functions, 300
Objects
    creating, 76–78
    dropping, 64–67
    storing in scripts, 106
ODBC
    calls to interpret result set, 572–573
    connecting from, 567–569
    to execute query, 571–572
    tracing, 524
ODBC CALL, 392–393
ODS (Open Data Services), 556–562
    extended procedure activities, 559
    overview of, 556–557
    processing parameters, 560–561
    returning data, 561–562
    sending messages, 559–560
    start-up code, 557–559
OLE (Object Linking and Embedding), 529
Opdyke, Bill, 716
Open Data Services. *See* ODS
OPENQUERY(), 263–265
OPENROWSET(), 264
OPENXML()
    basic example of, 421–425
    edge table format, 426–427

flags parameter, 425–426
inserting data with, 427–431
role of, 421
Operators, logical and physical, 508–511
@@OPTIONS, 42
ORDER BY, 248–249, 510
OUTPUT, 40
@outputfile, 345
Owner qualification, 19, 59–60

PAGE(), 665
Page chain, 482
Paoli, Jean, 358
Parameterized
user-defined functions, 329–335
views, 268–269
Parameters
coding convention, 68
command-line, 516–517
listing procedure, 41
output, 39–40
passing, 37–38, 60
processing ODS, 560–561
return status codes, 38–39
tips on, 41–42
updategrams, 435–437
Parentheses, 56–57
Partitioned views, 271
basic, 272–274
BETWEEN, 281–284
distributed, 272, 284–285
local, 272
partitioning columns/queries, 275–281
Performance, improving
indexing, 480–492
query optimization, 498–511
statistics, 492–498
Perl, 152
Physical operators, 508–511
PLATFORM(), 669
POST, 385
*Practice of Programming, The* (Kernighan), 73
*Pragmatic Programmer, The* (Hunt and
Thomas), 715–716

PRINT, 71
Procedures, naming, 62
@@PROCID, 42
Profiling, 516–524
Prototype pattern, 97–98
PRTIPAGE(), 666
PSS, 666
PWDCOMPARE(), 669
PWDENCRYPT(), 627, 670

Qualifier pattern, 88–89
@query, 345
Query Analyzer, version control with, 113–115
QueryInterface, 534
Query optimization
cost-based, 500–501
full, 501
identifying plans for, 500
join order and strategy selection, 504–508
operators, logical and physical, 508–511
search arguments, 502–504
selective, 501–502
simplification, 500
statistics loading, 500
sub-, 508
steps for, 498–499

RAISERROR, 44–45, 202–203
RAND(), 300
Random(), 188–191
RANGE_DENSITY, 495–496
RANGE_ROWS, 495–496
RAW mode, 402–403
Recursion, 46–47, 328–329
Refactoring, 716–725
*Refactoring: Improving the Design of Existing
Code* (Fowler), 74, 716, 721
Reference counting, COM, 534
Relational data modeling, 131
data dictionary, constructing, 165–167
data dictionary, using, 167–169
describing model elements, 169–170
diagrams in Enterprise Manager, 179–180
generating DDL, 172–179

Relational data modeling (*cont.*)
  generating foreign keys, 170–171
  loading E-R diagram into, 165
  sizing columns, 169
  terms and concepts, 162–164
  verifying integrity, 171–172
Relationship, 146
Relationship integrity, 146
Remote procedure calls (RPCs), 27
RESOURCE, 666
Restorer pattern, 94–97
@resultstitle, 345–346
RETURN, 38–39, 42
Return values, stored procedure, 67
ROLLBACK, 96–97
ROLLUP, 71
@@ROWCOUNT, 68, 210–212

Scalar functions, 291–292
SCHEMABINDING, 301–304, 489
SCOPE_IDENTITY(), 222–224
ScrambleFloat(), 191
Script(s)
  files, 66
  maintaining separate, 106
  segments, 66–67
  storing objects in, 106
  version control with automated script
    generation, 115–119
Search arguments (SARGs), 502–504
Second normal form (2NF), 152–153
Security issues, 513–515
SELECT...FOR XML, 382, 386–387, 390, 391,
  401–402
SELECT...INTO, 80, 97–98
Selectivity, 493
SET, 80–81
SET ANSI_NULLS, 15–16, 34, 35–37, 249
SET CURSOR_CLOSE_ON_COMMIT, 37
SET IMPLICIT_TRANSACTIONS, 37
SETINSTANCE(), 666
SET QUOTED_IDENTIFIER, 15, 34–37, 249
SET SHOWPLAN_ALL, 4, 18
SET SHOWPLAN_TEXT, 4, 18

SET TEXTSIZE, 37
SET XACT_ABORT, 37, 212–214
SGML (Standard Generalized Markup
  Language), 339–340
Singleton pattern, 98–101
Software development
  entropy/rot, 715–716
  extreme programming, 725–732
  making changes and, 714–716
  refactoring, 716–725
SOUNDEX(), 307–315
Source code formatting. *See* Formatting source
  code
Source code management
  benefits of, 104–105
  best practices, 106–112
  dt procs, 105–106
  version control with automated script
    generation, 115–119
  version control with Query Analyzer, 113–115
sp
  _addextendedproperty, 66, 555
  _autostats, 496–497
  _checknames [@mode], 629
  _checkspelling, 536–539
  _create_backup_job, 617–621
  _createstats, 496
  _delete backuphistory @oldest date, 629
  _diff, 588–590
  _diffdb, 622–625
  _dropextendedproperty, 66
  _enumerrorlogs, 629
  _enumoledbdatasources, 629
  _executesql, 18, 24–26
  _exporttable, 539–545
  _fixindex @dbname, @tabname, @indid,
    629–630
  _generate_script, 590–602
  _generate_test_data, 194–196
  _getSQLregistry, 550–554
  _gettypestring @tabid, @colid, @typestring
    output, 630
  _helptext, 9, 246–247
  _hexstring, 34, 576

_importtable, 545–550

_list_trace, 609–612

_makewebtask, 344–351

sp (*cont.*)

   _MSaddguidcol @sourceOwner, @source_table, 630

   _MSaddguidindex @source_owner, @source_table, 631

   _MSaddlogin_implicit_ntlogin @loginame, 631

   _MSadduser_implicit_ntlogin @ntname, 631

   _MScheck_uid_owns_anything @uid, 631

   _MSdbuseraccess @mode='perm'l'db', @qual=db name mask, 631–632

   _MSdbusepriv @mode='perm'l'serv'l'ver'l' role', 632

   _MSdependencies @objname, @objtype, @flags int, @objlist, 632

   _MSdrop_object [@object_id] [,@object_name] [,@object_owner}, 632–633

   _MSforeachdb @command1 @replacechar = '?' [,@command2] [,@command3] [,@precommand] [,@postcommand], 633–635

   _MSforeachtable @command1 @replacechar = '?' [,@command2] [,@command3] [,@whereand] [,precommand] [,@postcommand], 635–638

   _MSget_oledbinfo @server [,@infotype] [,@login] [,@password], 639

   _MSget_qualified_name @object_id, @qualified_name OUT, 639

   _MSget_type @tabid, @colid, @colname OUT, @type OUT, 639

   _MSguidtostr @guid, @mystr OUT, 639

   _MShelpindex @tablename [,@indexname] [,@flags], 639–640

   _MShelptype [@typename], [,@flags='sdt'l'uddt' INULL], 640–641

   _MSindexspace @tablename [,@index_name}, 641

   _MSis_pk_col @source_table, @colname, @indid, 642

_MSkilldb @dbname, 642

_MSloginmappings @loginname, 642–643

_MS_marksystemobject @objname, 630

_MStable_has_unique_index @tabid, 643

_MStablekeys [tablename] [,@colname] [,@type] [,@keyname] [,@flags], 643–644

_MStablerefs @tablename, @type=N'acutaltables',@direction= N'primary', @reftable, 644

_MStablespace [@name], 644

_MSunc_to_drive @unc+path, @local_server, @local_path OUT, 644

_MSuniquecolname table_name, @base_colname, @unique_colname OUT, 645

_MSuniquename @seed, @start, 645

_MSuniqueobjectname @name_in, @name_out OUT, 645

_MSuniquetempname @name_in, @name_out OUT, 645–646

_MS_upd_sysobj_category @pSeqMode integer, 630

_OA, 536

_object_script_comments, 9–11

_proc_runner, 612–617

_readerroriog [@lognum], 646

_readtextfile, 585–588

_recompile, 26

_remove_tempdb_file @filename, 646

_run_xml_proc, 452–458

_set_local_time [@server_name] [,@adjustment_in_minutes] (for Win9x), 646

_showstatdate, 497–498

_start_trace, 602–607

_stop_trace, 607–609

_tempdbspace, 647

_updatestats, 496

_usage, 11, 12–15

use of prefix, 16–17

_xml_concat, 449–452

Space, white, 51–56

Spacing, horizontal, 57

Sperberg-McQueen, C. M., 358

@@SPID, 42
Spooling, 510–511
SQLAllocHandle(), 567–574
SQLColAttribute(), 572–573
SQLConnect(), 567–574
SQLExecDirect(), 572
SQLISAPI, 382
SQLOLEDB, 382
SQL server, accessing over HTTP, 382–385
SQL7010Stress, 524
SQLVersionControl.VCS_SQL, 105–106
SQLXMLBulkLoad, 445–446
srv
  _bindsession(), 570
  _describe(), 561, 573
  _getbindtoken(), 570
  _paramdata(), 560
  _paraminfo(), 560
  _paramtype(), 560
  _senddone(), 562
  _sendmsg(), 559
  _sendrow(), 561, 573
  _setcoldata(), 561
SRV_PROC, 557–559
STACKDUMP, 667
statblob, 494, 495
Statistics
  column, 495
  listing, 495–496
  performance issues, 493–498
  storage of, 494–495
  terms, 492–493
  updating, 496–497
Stored procedures
  *See also* Extended stored procedures
  advantages of, 4–5
  altering, 17–18
  calling, from views, 262–265
  coding convention, 67–68
  creating, 5–17
  defined, 3–4
  differences between extended stored
     procedures and, 556
  environmental issues, 34–37

executing, 18–32
extended, 32–34
listing, 9
parameters, 37–42
return values, 67
triggers and calling, 235–239
URL queries for executing, 392–393
Stored procedures, administrative
  sp_create_backup_job, 617–621
  sp_diff, 588–590
  sp_diffdb, 622–625
  sp_generate_script, 590–602
  sp_list_trace, 609–612
  sp_proc_runner, 612–617
  sp_readtextfile, 585–588
  sp_stop_trace, 607–609
  sp_start_trace, 602–607
Stress testing, 524–528
Subtypes, 145
Sun Microsystems, 358
Supertypes, 145
Symbols
  dollar ($), 107, 114
  double and single pound signs (#) and (# #),
    27–28
  in URL queries, 388
sysindexes, 480
System functions, 42
  array, 689–692
  creating, 304–307, 656–658
System objects, 30–32
System procedures, 28–30

TAB(), 667
Tables
  aliases, 57–58
  closing, 69
  copying, 79–80
  derived, 267–268
  emptying, 79
  HTML, 340–342
  loading trace files into, 521–522
  locks, 444–445
  naming, 61

retrieving topmost rows, 83–84
system, 69–71
temporary, 68–69
@table_urls, 347–348
Table-valued functions, 291, 292–295
Tags, 11–12
Template queries, 393
   client-side, 399–400
   parameterized, 394–395
   style sheets, 395–398
Templates, 348–351
Temporary procedures, 27–28
Testing
   benefits of, 740–741
   futility of, 737
   stress, 524–528
   time and, 739–740
   types of tests, 738, 741–745
   when to, 739
   where to start, 735–737
Third normal form (3NF), 153
Thomas, David, 715–716, 717
Time series fluctuation, 318–324
Tokens, 114–115
Trace/tracing
   files as XML, 522–523
   grouping data, 523–524
   guidelines, 517–521
   loading, into a table, 521–522
   OBDC, 524
   replaying, 521
   starting, 516
   versus viewing, 516
Trace flags
   4022, 26
   undocumented, 671–672
@@TRANCOUNT, 42
Transactions, XML Bulk Load, 445–446
Trend analysis, 324–325
Triggers
   AFTER, 215, 229
   auditing and, 229–233
   best practices, 240–243
   calling stored procedures, 235–239

debugging, 516
defined, 164, 215
determining what has changed, 216–222
disabling, 239–240
execution, 234–235
INSTEAD OF, 101, 215, 226–229
managing sequential values, 222–224
names for, 61
nested, 239
restrictions, 224–226
as transactions, 234
TRUNCATE TABLE, 16, 79
TSEQUAL(), 670
T-SQL, ad hoc, 71

UDFs (user-defined functions)
   creating INFORMATION_SCHEMA, 257–262
   creating your own system functions, 304–307
   debugging, 516
   inline, 291, 295–296
   limitations, 296–300
   naming, 62
   parameterized, 329–335
   recursion, 328–329
   retrieving information on, 300–304
   scalar, 291–292
   SOUNDEX(), 307–315
   statistical examples, 315–328
   table-valued, 291, 292–295
UML (Unified Modeling Language), 133
UNCOMPRESS(), 670
Undocumented code
   care when using, 627
   DBCC commands, 658–667
   defined, 628
   functions, 667–670
   INFORMATION_SCHEMA views, creating, 251–257, 655–657
   procedures, description of, 628–655
   system functions, creating, 656–658
   trace flags, 671–672
Unicode, 106–107
UNIX, 461–462

UPDATE(), 216–217
updategrams, 431, 432–440
UPDATE STATISTICS, 16, 496
Updating
  statistics, 496–497
  views, 265–266
UPGRADEDB(), 667
@url_query, 347, 348
URLs (uniform resource locators), 339
  content type, 390–391
  executing stored procedures, 392–393
  non-XML results, 391–392
  queries, 385–393
  special characters, 387–388
  style sheets, 388–389
USE, 67, 78–79
User-defined functions. *See* UDFs

Variables
  declaring, 67
  naming, 62
VARYING, 40
Versions
  *See also* Source code management
  controlling with automated script generation,
    115–119
  controlling with Query Analyzer, 113–115
  labels to denote, 107
Views
  accessing, 70
  ANSI SQL schema, 249–265
  calling stored procedures from, 262–265
  defined, 164
  derived tables, 267–268
  dynamic, 269–271
  indexed, 286–289, 487–488
  INFORMATION_SCHEMA user-defined
    function, creating, 257–262
  INFORMATION_SCHEMA views, creating,
    251–257, 655–657
  listing source code for, 246–247
  list of, 250
  OBJECTPROPERTY() meta-data, 245–246
  parameterized, 268–269

  partitioned, 271–285
  restrictions, 247–249
  updateable, 265–266
  WITH CHECK OPTION clause, 266–267
Virtual directories, configuring, 383–385
Visual Basic, 461
Visual Studio Enterprise, 105–106
VSS, 103
  *See also* Source code management
  list of keywords, 109
  project folders recognized by
    GGSQLBuilder, 117
  tool menu entries, 113

WAITFOR, 42
Walkthroughs, 744–745
Ward-Mellor, 133
Web releases, 431–448
  updategrams, 431, 432–440
  XML Bulk Load, 431, 441–448
@whentype, 346
WHILE, 42, 81–82
Windows 3.0 SDK, 460–461
WITH CHECK OPTION clause, 266–267
WITH ENCRYPTION, 17
WITH LOG, 45
WITH NOWAIT, 45
WITH RECOMPILE, 26
WITH SETERROR, 45
Workable environment
  benefits of small changes, 713–714
  creating a, 703–709
Wrapping procedures, 32–34, 575–576

XML
  *See also* OPENXML()
  Document Object Model (DOM), 357,
    378–379
  Document Type Definitions (DTDs), 357,
    364–366
  Extensible Stylesheet Language
    Transformation (XSLT), 370–378
  features, 382
  history of, 358

notational nuances, 361–364
overview of, 356–357
schemas, 367–370
sources of information on, 379
tools, 379–380
trace files as, 522–523
understanding, 353–356
versus HTML, 358–364
XML Bulk Load, 431, 441–448
XMLDATA, 402
XML-Data Reduced (XDR), 416–419
XMLFragment, 442
xp
  _array.dll, 676–689
  _cmdshell, 208
  _createarray, 677–679
  _destroyarray, 684–686
  _dirtree 'rootpath', 647–648
  _dsnifo @systemdsn, 648
  _enumoledb_providers, 648–649
  _enumdsn, 649
  _enumerrorlogs, 649
  _exec, 208, 567, 569, 570–571
  _execresultset 'code query','database', 650
  _fileexist 'filename', 650
  _fixeddrives, 650–651
  _getarray, 682–684
  _getfiledetails 'filename', 651
  _get_MAPI_default_profile, 651

  _get_MAPI_profiles, 651
  _getnetname, 652
  _listarray, 686–689
  _listfile, 562–567
  _logevent, 203
  _oledbinfo @providername, @datasource,
      @location, @providerstring, @catalog,
      @login, @password, @infotype, 652
  _readerrorlog, 588
  _readerrorlog [lognum][filenmae], 652–653
  _regaddmultistr, 654
  _regdeletekey, 654
  _regdeletevalue, 654
  _regenumvalues, 653–654
  _regread, 654
  _regremovemultistring, 654
  _regwrite, 654
  _setarray, 679–682
  _setpriority, 578–584
  _sprintf, 299
  _subdirs, 654
  _test_MAPI_profile 'profile'', 655
  _varbintohexstr, 575–576, 655
XPath, 384
XP (extreme programming), 725–732
XSLT (Extensible Stylesheet Language
      Transformation), 370–378

Yourdon-DeMarco, 133

# Also from Addison-Wesley

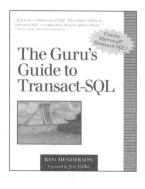

## The Guru's Guide to Transact-SQL

By Ken Henderson

0-201-61576-2
Paperback
592 pages with CD-ROM
© 2000

Comprehensive, written in understandable terms, and full of practical information and examples, *The Guru's Guide to Transact-SQL* is an indispensable reference for anyone working with this database development language.

## Essential SQL Server™ 2000

*An Administration Handbook*

By Buck Woody

0-201-74203-9
Paperback
416 pages
© 2002

This hands-on guide covers the installation, configuration, and administration of SQL Server while providing practical solutions to the daily challenges faced by busy administrators.

## SQL Queries for Mere Mortals

*A Hands-On Guide to Data Manipulation in SQL*

By Michael J. Hernandez and John L. Viescas

0-201-43336-2
Paperback
528 pages
© 2000

*SQL Queries for Mere Mortals* will help new users learn the foundations of SQL queries, and will prove an essential reference guide for intermediate and advanced users.

## The Practical SQL Handbook, Fourth Edition

*Using SQL Variants*

By Judith S. Bowman, Sandra L. Emerson, and
Marcy Darnovsky

0-201-70309-2
Paperback
512 pages with CD-ROM
© 2001

This latest edition of the best-selling implementation
guide to the Structured Query Language teaches SQL
fundamentals while providing practical solutions for
critical business applications.

## Practical SQL

*The Sequel*

By Judith S. Bowman

0-201-61638-6
Paperback
352 pages with CD-ROM
© 2001

For those who are working with SQL systems—or
preparing to do so—this book offers information
organized by use rather than by feature. Readers can
turn to specific business problems and learn how to
solve them with the appropriate SQL features.

# CD ROM Warranty

Addison-Wesley warrants the enclosed disc to be free of defects in materials and faulty workmanship under normal use for a period of ninety days after purchase. If a defect is discovered in the disc during this warranty period, a replacement disc can be obtained at no charge by sending the defective disc, postage prepaid, with proof of purchase to:

Editorial Department
Addison-Wesley Professional
Pearson Technology Group
75 Arlington Street, Suite 300
Boston, MA 02116
Email: AWPro@awl.com

Addison-Wesley and Ken Henderson make no warranty or representation, either expressed or implied, with respect to this software, its quality, performance, merchantability, or fitness for a particular purpose. In no event will Ken Henderson or Addison-Wesley, its distributors, or dealers be liable for direct, indirect, special, incidental, or consequential damages arising out of the use or inability to use the software. The exclusion of implied royalties is not permitted in some states. Therefore, the above exclusion may not apply to you. This warranty provides you with specific legal rights. There may be other rights that you may have that vary from state to state. The contents of this CD-ROM are intended for non-commercial use only.

More information and updates are available at:
http://www.awl.com/cseng/titles/